DSL Engineering

Designing, Implementing and Using
Domain-Specific Languages

Markus Voelter

with

Sebastian Benz
Christian Dietrich
Birgit Engelmann
Mats Helander
Lennart Kats
Eelco Visser
Guido Wachsmuth

(c) 2010 - 2013 Markus Voelter

Feedback, Slides, and other updates at
http://dslbook.org

ISBN-13: 978-1481218580
ISBN-10: 1481218581

Contents

I Introduction 5

1 About this Book 7
- 1.1 Thank You! 7
- 1.2 Versions of this Book 8
- 1.3 Why this Book 9
- 1.4 What you will Learn 10
- 1.5 Who should Read this Book 10
- 1.6 About the Cover 11
- 1.7 Feedback, Bugs and Updates 11
- 1.8 The Structure of the Book 11
- 1.9 How to Read the Book 12
- 1.10 Example Tools 13
- 1.11 Case Studies and Examples 14

2 Introduction to DSLs 23
- 2.1 Very Brief Introduction to the Terminology 23
- 2.2 From General Purpose Languages to DSLs 25
- 2.3 Modeling and Model-Driven Development 29
- 2.4 Modular Languages 32
- 2.5 Benefits of using DSLs 38
- 2.6 Challenges 41
- 2.7 Applications of DSLs 45
- 2.8 Differentiation from other Works and Approaches 48

II DSL Design 51

3 Conceptual Foundations 55
- 3.1 Programs, Languages and Domains 55
- 3.2 Model Purpose 59
- 3.3 The Structure of Programs and Languages 61

    3.4 Parsing versus Projection 65

4 Design Dimensions   67
    4.1 Expressivity 68
    4.2 Coverage 78
    4.3 Semantics and Execution 80
    4.4 Separation of Concerns 100
    4.5 Completeness 109
    4.6 Language Modularity 114
    4.7 Concrete Syntax 130

5 Fundamental Paradigms   139
    5.1 Structure 139
    5.2 Behavior 147
    5.3 Combinations 156

6 Process Issues   159
    6.1 DSL Development 159
    6.2 Using DSLs 166

III   DSL Implementation   171

7 Concrete and Abstract Syntax   175
    7.1 Fundamentals of Free Text Editing and Parsing . 177
    7.2 Fundamentals of Projectional Editing 186
    7.3 Comparing Parsing and Projection 187
    7.4 Characteristics of AST Formalisms 194
    7.5 Xtext Example 198
    7.6 Spoofax Example 205
    7.7 MPS Example 210

8 Scoping and Linking   219
    8.1 Scoping in Spoofax 221
    8.2 Scoping in Xtext 227
    8.3 Scoping in MPS 232

9 Constraints   237
    9.1 Constraints in Xtext 239
    9.2 Constraints in MPS 240
    9.3 Constraints in Spoofax 245

10 Type Systems   251
    10.1 Type Systems Basics 252
    10.2 Type Calculation Strategies 253

10.3 Xtext Example 258
10.4 MPS Example 261
10.5 Spoofax Example 265

11 Transformation and Generation 269
11.1 Overview of the approaches 270
11.2 Xtext Example 272
11.3 MPS Example 279
11.4 Spoofax Example 288

12 Building Interpreters 295
12.1 Building an Interpreter with Xtext 297
12.2 An Interpreter in MPS 304
12.3 An Interpreter in Spoofax 306

13 IDE Services 311
13.1 Code Completion 311
13.2 Syntax Coloring 314
13.3 Go-to-Definition and Find References 319
13.4 Pretty-Printing 321
13.5 Quick Fixes 325
13.6 Refactoring 327
13.7 Labels and Icons 331
13.8 Outline 332
13.9 Code Folding 334
13.10 Tooltips/Hover 335
13.11 Visualizations 337
13.12 Diff and Merge 339

14 Testing DSLs 341
14.1 Syntax Testing 342
14.2 Constraints Testing 344
14.3 Semantics Testing 347
14.4 Formal Verification 354
14.5 Testing Editor Services 361
14.6 Testing for Language Appropriateness 365

15 Debugging DSLs 367
15.1 Debugging the DSL Definition 367
15.2 Debugging DSL Programs 374

16 Modularization, Reuse and Composition 391
16.1 Introduction 391
16.2 MPS Example 392

    16.3 Xtext Example 412
    16.4 Spoofax Example 426

IV DSLs in Software Engineering   437

17 DSLs and Requirements   441
    17.1 What are Requirements? 441
    17.2 Requirements versus Design versus Implementation 443
    17.3 Using DSLs for Requirements Engineering 445
    17.4 Integration with Plain Text Requirements 448

18 DSLs and Software Architecture   453
    18.1 What is Software Architecture? 453
    18.2 Architecture DSLs 455
    18.3 Component Models 466

19 DSLs as Programmer Utility   475
    19.1 The Context 476
    19.2 Jnario Described 477
    19.3 Implementation 480
    19.4 Summary 485

20 DSLs in the Implementation   487
    20.1 Introduction 487
    20.2 Challenges in Embedded Software 489
    20.3 The mbeddr Approach 491
    20.4 Design and Implementation 499
    20.5 Experiences 509
    20.6 Discussion 516

21 DSLs and Product Lines   519
    21.1 Introduction 519
    21.2 Feature Models 520
    21.3 Connecting Feature Models to Artifacts 521
    21.4 From Feature Models to DSLs 526
    21.5 Conceptual Mapping from PLE to DSLs 532

22 DSLs for Business Users   537
    22.1 Intentional Software 537
    22.2 The Project Challenge 538
    22.3 The DSL-Based Solution 539
    22.4 Wrapping Up 556

Part I

Introduction

1
About this Book

This book is about creating domain-specific languages. It covers three main aspects: DSL design, DSL implementation and software engineering with DSLs. The book only looks at external DSLs and focuses mainly on textual syntax. The book emphasizes the use of modern language workbenches. It is not a tutorial for any specific tool, but it provides examples and some level of detail for some of them: Xtext, MPS and Spoofax. The goal of the book is to provide a thorough overview of modern DSL engineering. The book is based on my own experience and opinions, but strives to be objective.

1.1 Thank You!

Before I do anything else, I want to thank my reviewers. This book has profited tremendously from the feedback you sent me. It is a lot of work to read a book like this with sufficient concentration to give meaningful feedback. All of you did that, so thank you very much! Here is the list, in alphabetical order: Alexander Shatalin, Bernd Kolb, Bran Selic, Christa Schwanninger, Dan Ratiu, Domenik Pavletic, Iris Groher, Jean Bezivin, Jos Warmer, Laurence Tratt, Mats Helander, Nora Ludewig, Sebastian Zarnekow and Vaclav Pech.

I also want to thank the contributors to the book. They have added valuable perspectives and insights that I couldn't have delivered myself. In particular:

- Eelco Visser contributed significantly to the DSL design section. In fact, this was the part we started out with when we still had the plan to write the book together. It was initially his idea to have a section on DSL design that is independent of implementation concerns and particular tools.

- Guido Wachsmuth and Lennart Kats contributed all the examples for the Spoofax language workbench and helped a lot with the fundamental discussions on grammars and parsing.

- Mats Helander contributed the Business DSL case study with the Intentional Domain Workbench in Part IV of the book.

- Birgit Engelmann and Sebastian Benz wrote the chapter on utility DSLs that features the JNario language based on Xtext and Xbase.

- Christian Dietrich helped me with the language modularization examples for Xtext and Xbase.

Also, Moritz Eysholdt has contributed a section on his Xpext testing framework. Finally, some parts of this book are based on papers I wrote with other people. I want to thank these people for letting me use the papers in the book: Bernd Kolb, Domenik Pavletic, Daniel Ratiu and Bernhard Schaetz.

A special thank you goes to my girlfriend Nora Ludewig. She didn't just volunteer to provide feedback on the book, she also had to endure all kinds of other discussions around the topic all the time. Thanks Nora!

Alex Chatziparaskewas, Henk Kolk, Magnus Christerson and Klaus Doerfler allowed me to use "their" applications as examples in this book. Thank you very much!

I also want to thank itemis, for whom I have worked as an independent consultant for the last couple of years. The experience I gained there, in particular while working with MPS in the LWES research project, benefitted the book greatly!

Finally, I want to thank my copyeditor Steve Rickaby. I had worked with Steve on my pattern books and I really wanted to work with him again on this one – even though no publisher is involved this time. Luckily he was willing to work with me directly. Thank you, Steve!

1.2 Versions of this Book

This book is available as a print version and as a PDF version. You are currently reading the print version. The PDF can be acquired via `http://dslbook.org`. The PDF is donationware, which means that I expect readers do donate an appropriate amount of money for the book. Since you have already bought the print edition, you are obviously welcome to get the PDF without and additional donation. You can also register the book at the website; if you do, I will keep you up-to-date with new versions.

There is no Kindle version of the book because the layout/figures/code do not translate very well into the Kindle format. However, you can of course read PDFs on a Kindle. I tried using my Nexus 7 tablet to read the book: if you use landscape format, it works reasonably well.

Here is some background on why I didn't go with a real publisher. Unless you are famous or write a book on a mainstream topic, you will make maybe one or two euros for each copy sold if you go through a publisher. So if you don't sell tens or hundreds of thousands of copies, the money you can make out of a book directly is really not relevant, considering the amount of work you put into it. Going through a publisher will also make the book more expensive for the reader, so fewer people will read it. I decided that it is more important to reach as many readers as possible[1].

[1] Publishers may help to get a book advertised, but in a niche community like DSLs I think that word of mouth, blog or Twitter is more useful. So I hope that you the reader will help me spread the word about the book.

1.3 Why this Book

First of all, there is currently no book available that explicitly covers DSLs in the context of modern language workbenches, with an emphasis on textual languages. Based on my experience, I think that this way of developing DSLs is very productive, so I think there is a need for a book that fills this gap. I wanted to make sure the book contains a lot of detail on how to design and build good DSLs, so it can act as a primer for DSL language engineering, for students as well as practitioners. However, I also want the book to clearly show the benefits of DSLs – not by pointing out general truths about the approach, but instead by providing a couple of good examples of where and how DSLs are used successfully. This is why the book is divided into three parts: DSL Design, DSL Implementation and Software Engineering with DSLs.

Even though I had written a book on Model-Driven Software Development (MDSD) before[2], I feel that it is time for a complete rewrite. So if you are among the people who read

Since writing the original MDSD book, I have learned a lot in the meantime, my viewpoints have evolved and the tools that are available today have evolved significantly as well. The latter is a reflection of the fact that the whole MDSD community has evolved: ten years ago, UML was the mainstay for MDSD, and the relationship to DSLs was not clear. Today, DSLs are the basis for most interesting and innovative developments in MDSD.

[2] M. Voelter and T. Stahl. *Model-Driven Software Development: Technology, Engineering, Management.* Wiley, 2006

the previous MDSD book, you really should continue reading. This book is very different, but in many ways a natural evolution of the old one. It may gloss over certain details present in the older book, but it will expand greatly on others.

1.4 What you will Learn

The purpose of this book is to give you a solid overview of the state of the art of today's DSLs. This includes DSL design, DSL implementation and the use of DSLs in software engineering. After reading this book you should have a solid understanding of how to design, build and use DSLs. A few myths (good and bad) about DSLs should also be dispelled in the process.

Part III of the book, on DSL implementation, contains a lot of example code. However, this part is *not* intended as a full tutorial for any of the three tools used in that part. However, you should get a solid understanding of what these tools – and the classes of tools they stand for – can do for you.

1.5 Who should Read this Book

Everybody who has read my original book on Model-Driven Software Development should read this book. This book can be seen as an update to the old one, even though it is a complete rewrite.

On a more serious note, the book is intended for developers and architects who want to implement their own DSLs. I expect solid experience in object oriented programming as well as basic knowledge about functional programming and (classical) modeling. It also helps if readers have come across the terms *grammar* and *parser* before, although I don't expect any significant experience with these techniques.

The MDSD book had a chapter on process and organizational aspects. Except for perhaps ten pages on process-related topics, this book does not address process and organization aspects. There are two reasons for this: one, these topic haven't changed much since the old book, and you can read them there. Second, I feel these aspects were the weakest part of the old book, because it is very hard to discuss process and organizational aspects in a general way, independent of a particular context. Any working software development process will work with DSLs. Any strategy to introduce promising new techniques into an organization applies to introducing DSLs. The few *specific* aspects are covered in the ten pages at the end of the design chapter.

1.6 About the Cover

The cover layout resembles Addison-Wesley's classic cover design. I always found this design one of the most elegant book covers I have seen. The picture of a glider has been chosen to represent the connection to the cover of the original MDSD book, whose English edition also featured a glider[3].

[3] The MDSD book featured a Schleicher ASW-27, a 15m class racing glider. This book features a Schleicher ASH-26E, an 18m class self-launching glider.

1.7 Feedback, Bugs and Updates

Writing a book such as this is a lot of work. At some point I ran out of energy and just went ahead and published it. I am pretty confident that there are no major problems left, but I am sure there are many small bugs and problems in the book, for which I am sorry. If you find any, please let me know at `voelter@acm.org`. There is also a Google+ community for the book; you can find it via the website `dslbook.org`.

One of the advantages of an electronic book is that it is easy to publish new editions frequently. While I will certainly do other things in the near future (remember: I ran out of energy!), I will try to publish an updated and bug-fixed version relatively soon. In general, updates for the book will be available via my twitter account `@markusvoelter` and via the book website `http://dslbook.org`.

1.8 The Structure of the Book

The rest of this first part is a brief introduction to DSLs. It defines terminology, looks at the benefits and challenges of developing and using DSLs, and introduces the notion of modular languages, which play an important role throughout the book. This first part is written in a personal style: it presents DSLs based on my experience, and is not intended to be a scientific treatment.

Part II is about DSL design. It is a systematic exploration of seven design dimensions relevant to DSL design: expressivity, coverage, semantics, separation of concerns, completeness, language modularization and syntax. It also discusses fundamental language paradigms that might be useful in DSLs, and looks at a number of process-related topics. It uses five case studies to illustrate the concepts. It does not deal at all with implementation issues – we address these in part III.

Part III covers DSL implementation issues. It looks at syntax definition, constraints and type systems, scoping, transformation and interpretation, debugging and IDE support. It uses examples implemented with three different tools (Xtext, MPS, Spoofax). Part III is not intended as a tutorial for any one of these, but should provide a solid foundation for understanding the technical challenges when implementing DSLs.

Part IV looks at using DSLs in for various tasks in software engineering, among them requirements engineering, architecture, implementation and, a specifically relevant topic, product line engineering. Part IV consists of a set of fairly independent chapters, each illustrating one of the software engineering challenges.

1.9 How to Read the Book

I had a lot of trouble deciding whether DSL design or DSL implementation should come first. The two parts are relatively independent. As a consequence of the fact that the design part comes first, there are some references back to design issues from within the implementation part. But the two parts can be read in any order, depending on your interests. If you are new to DSLs, I suggest you start with Part III on DSL implementation. You may find Part II, DSL Design too abstract or dense if you don't have hands-on experience with DSLs.

Some of the examples in Part III are quite detailed, because we wanted to make sure we didn't skim relevant details. However, if some parts become too detailed for you, just skip ahead – usually the details are not important for understanding subsequent subsections.

The chapters in Part IV are independent from each other and can be read in any sequence.

Finally, I think you should at least skim the rest of Part I. If you are already versed in DSLs, you may want to skip some sections or skim over them, but it is important to understand where I am coming from to be able to make sense of some of the later chapters.

1.10 Example Tools

You could argue that this whole business about DSLs is nothing new. It has long been possible to build custom languages using parser generators such as lex/yacc, ANTLR or JavaCC. And of course you would be right. Martin Fowler's DSL book[4] emphasizes this aspect.

[4] M. Fowler. *Domain-Specific Languages*. Addison Wesley, 2010

However, I feel that language workbenches, which are tools to efficiently create, integrate and use sets of DSLs in powerful IDEs, make a qualitative difference. DSL developers, as well as the people who use the DSLs, are used to powerful, feature-rich IDEs and tools in general. If you want to establish the use of DSLs and you suggest that your users use `vi` or `notepad.exe`, you won't get very far with most people. Also, the effort of developing (sets of) DSLs and their IDEs has been reduced significantly by the maturation of language workbenches. This is why I focus on DSL engineering with language workbenches, and emphasize IDE development just as much as language development.

This is not a tutorial book on tools. However, I will show you how to work with different tools, but this should be understood more as representative examples of different tooling approaches[5]. I tried to use diverse tools for the examples, but for the most part I stuck to those I happen to know well and that have serious traction in the real world, or the potential to do so: Eclipse Modeling + Xtext, JetBrains MPS, SDF/Stratego/Spoofax, and, to some extent, the Intentional Domain Workbench. All except the last are open source. Here is a brief overview over the tools.

[5] I suggest you read the examples for all tools, so that you appreciate the different approaches to solving a common challenge in language design. If you want to learn about one tool specifically, there are probably better tutorials for each of them.

1.10.1 Eclipse Modeling + Xtext

The Eclipse Modeling project is an ecosystem – frameworks and tools – for modeling, DSLs and all that's needed or useful around it. It would easily merit its own book (or set of books), so I won't cover it extensively. I have restricted myself to Xtext, the framework for building textual DSLs, Xtend, a Java-like language optimized for code generation, as well as EMF/Ecore, the underlying meta meta model used to represent model data. Xtext may not be as advanced as SDF/Stratego or MPS, but the tooling is very mature and has a huge user community. Also, the surrounding ecosystem provides a huge number of add-ons that support the construction of sophisti-

`eclipse.org/Xtext`

cated DSL environments. I will briefly look at some of these
tools, among them graphical editing frameworks.

1.10.2 JetBrains MPS

The Meta Programming System (MPS) is a projectional language workbench, which means that no grammar and parser is involved. Instead, editor gestures change the underlying AST directly, which is projected in a way that looks like text. As a consequence, MPS supports mixed notations (textual, symbolic, tabular, graphical) and a wide range of language composition features. MPS is open source under the Apache 2.0 license, and is developed by JetBrains. It is not as widely used as Xtext, but supports many advanced features.

jetbrains.com/mps

1.10.3 SDF/Stratego/Spoofax

These tools are developed at the University of Delft in Eelco Visser's group. SDF is a formalism for defining parsers for context-free grammars. Stratego is a term rewriting system used for AST transformations and code generation. Spoofax is an Eclipse-based IDE that provides a nice environment for working with SDF and Stratego. It is also not as widely used as Xtext, but it has a number of advanced features for language modularization and composition.

strategoxt.org/Spoofax

1.10.4 Intentional Domain Workbench

A few examples will be based on the Intentional Domain Workbench (IDW). Like MPS, it uses the projectional approach to editing. The IDW has been used to build a couple of very interesting systems that can serve well to illustrate the power of DSLs. The tool is a commercial offering of Intentional Software.

intentsoft.com

Many more tools exist. If you are interested, I suggest you look at the Language Workbench Competition[6], where a number of language workbenches (13 at the time of writing of this book) are illustrated by implementing the same example DSLs. This provides a good way of comparing the various tools.

[6] **languageworkbenches.net**

1.11 Case Studies and Examples

I strove to make this book as accessible and practically relevant as possible, so I provide lots of examples. I decided against a single big, running example because (a) it becomes increasingly complex to follow, and (b) fails to illustrate different approaches to solving the same problem. However, we use a set of case studies to illustrate many issues, especially in Part II, DSL design. These examples are introduced below. These are taken from real-world projects.

1.11.1   Component Architecture

This language is an architecture DSL used to define the software architecture of a complex, distributed, component-based system in the transportation domain[7]. Among other architectural abstractions, the DSL supports the definition of components and interfaces, as well as the definition of systems, which are connected instances of components. The code below shows interfaces and components. An interface is a collection of methods (not shown) or collections of messages. Components then provide and require ports, where each port has a name, an interface and, optionally, a cardinality.

[7] This langauage is also used in the Part IV chapter on DSLs and software architecture: Chapter 18.

```
namespace com.mycomany {
  namespace datacenter {
    component DelayCalculator {
      provides aircraft: IAircraftStatus
      provides console: IManagementConsole
      requires screens[0..n]: IInfoScreen
    }
    component Manager {
      requires backend[1]: IManagementConsole
    }
    interface IInfoScreen {
      message expectedAircraftArrivalUpdate( id: ID, time: Time )
      message flightCancelled( id: ID )
    }
    interface IAircraftStatus ...
    interface IManagementConsole ...
  }
}
```

The next piece of code shows how these components can be instantiated and connected.

```
namespace com.mycomany.test {
  system testSystem {
    instance dc: DelayCalculator
    instance screen1: InfoScreen
    instance screen2: InfoScreen
    connect dc.screens to (screen1.default, screen2.default)
  }
}
```

Code generators generate code that acts as the basis for the implementation of the system, as well as all the code necessary to work with the distributed communication middleware. It is used by software developers and architects and implemented with Eclipse Xtext.

1.11.2   Refrigerator Configuration

This case study describes a set of DSLs for developing cooling algorithms in refrigerators. The customer with whom we have built this language builds hundres of different refrigerators, and coming up with energy-efficient cooling strategies is a big challenge. By using a DSL-based approach, the development and implementation process for the cooling behavior can be streamlined a lot.

Three languages are used. The first describes the logical hardware structure of refrigerators. The second describes cooling algorithms in the refrigerators using a state-based, asynchronous language. Cooling programs refer to hardware features and can access the properties of hardware elements from expressions and commands. The third language is used to test cooling programs. These DSLs are used by thermodynamicists and are implemented with Eclipse Xtext.

The code below shows the hardware structure definition in the refrigerator case study. An appliance represents the refrigerator. It consists mainly of cooling compartments and compressor compartments. A cooling compartment contains various building blocks that are important to the cooling process. A compressor compartment contains the cooling infrastructure itself, e.g. a compressor and a fan.

```
appliance KIR {

  compressor compartment cc {
    static compressor c1
    fan ccfan
  }

  ambient tempsensor at

  cooling compartment RC {
    light rclight
    superCoolingMode
    door rcdoor
    fan rcfan
    evaporator tempsensor rceva
  }
}
```

The code below shows a simple cooling algorithm. Cooling algorithms are state-based programs. States can have entry actions and exit actions. Inside a state we check whether specific conditions are true, then change the status of various hardware building blocks, or change the state. It is also possible to express deferred behavior with the **perform ...after** keyword.

```
program Standardcooling for KIR {
  start:
```

```
    entry { state noCooling }
  state noCooling:
    check ( RC->needsCooling && cc.c1->standstillPeriod > 333 ) {
      state rcCooling
    }
    on isDown ( RC.rcdoor->open ) {
      set RC.rcfan->active = true
      set RC.rclight->active = false
      perform rcFanStopTask after 10 {
        set RC.rcfan->active = false
      }
    }
  state rcCooling:
    ...
}
```

Finally, the following code is a test script to test cooling programs. It essentially stimulates a cooling algorithm by changing hardware properties and then asserting that the algorithm reacts in a certain way.

```
cooling test for Standardcooling {
  prolog {
    set cc.c1->standstillPeriod = 0
  }
  // initially we are not cooling
  assert-currentstate-is noCooling
  // then we say that RC needs cooling, but
  // the standstillPeriod is still too low.
  mock: set RC->needsCooling = true
  step
  assert-currentstate-is noCooling
  // now we increase standstillPeriod and check
  // if it now goes to rcCooling
  mock: set cc.c1->stehzeit = 400
  step
  assert-currentstate-is rcCooling
}
```

1.11.3   mbeddr C

This case study covers a set of extensions to the C programming language tailored to embedded programming[8], developed as part of mbeddr.com[9]. Extensions include state machines, physical quantities, tasks, as well as interfaces and components. Higher-level DSLs are added for specific purposes. An example used in a showcase application is the control of a Lego Mindstorms robot. Plain C code is generated and subsequently compiled with GCC or other target device specific compilers. The DSL is intended to be used by embedded software developers and is implemented with MPS.

[8] This system is also used as the example for implementation-level DSLs in Part IV of the book. It is covered in Chapter 20.
[9] mbeddr.com

```
module DecisionTableExample from cdesignpaper.gswitch imports nothing {

  enum mode { MANUAL; AUTO; FAIL; }

  mode nextMode(mode mode, int8_t speed) {
    return mode, FAIL |             | mode == MANUAL | mode == AUTO | ;
                      | speed < 30  | MANUAL         | AUTO         |
                      | speed > 30  | MANUAL         | MANUAL       |
  } nextMode (function)
}
```

Figure 1.1: A simple C module with an embedded decision table. This is a nice example of MPS' ability to use non-textual notations thanks to its projectional editor (which we describe in detail in Part III).

```
module Units from cdesignpaper.units imports nothing {

  unit kg for int8_t
  unit lb for int8_t
  kg/int8_t addWeights(kg/int8_t w1, kg/int8_t w2) {
    return w1 + w2;
  } addWeights (function)
  void s Error: type lb is not a subtype of kg
    addWeights(10kg, 20lb);
    addWeights(10kg, 20kg);
  } someClientCode (function)
  exported test case simpleUnits {
    kg/int8_t m1 = 10kg;
    lb/int8_t m2 = 10lb;
    assert(0) m1 + 10kg == 20kg;
  } simpleUnits(test case)
}
```

Figure 1.2: This extension to C supports working with physical units (such as `kg` and `lb`). The type system has been extended to include type checks for units. The example also shows the unit testing extension.

```
module Statemachine from cdesignpaper.statemachine imports nothing {

  statemachine Counter {
    in events
      start() <no binding>
      step(int[0..10] size) <no binding>
    out events
      << ... >>
    local variables
      int[0..10] currentVal = 0
      int[0..10] LIMIT = 10
    states ( initial = start )
      state start {
        on start [ ] -> countState {  }
      }
      state countState {
        on step [currentVal + size > LIMIT] -> start {  }
        on step [currentVal + size <= LIMIT]
             -> countState { currentVal = currentVal + size; }
        on start [ ] -> start {  }
      }
  }
}
```

```
var Counter c1;

void aFunction() {
  trigger(c1, start);
  trigger(c1, step(1));
} aFunction (function)
```

Figure 1.3: This extension shows a state machine. Notice how regular C expressions are used in the guard conditions of the transitions. The inset code shows how the state machine can be triggered from regular C code.

1.11.4 *Pension Plans*

This DSL is used to describe families of pension plans for a large insurance company efficiently. The DSL supports mathematical abstractions and notations to allow insurance mathematicians to express their domain knowledge directly (Fig. 1.5), as well as higher-level pension rules and unit tests using a table notation (Fig. 1.4). A complete Java implementation of the calculation engine is generated. It is intended to be used by insurance mathematicians and pension experts. It has been built by Capgemini with the Intentional Domain Workbench.

Figure 1.4: This example shows high-level business rules, together with a tabular notation for unit tests. The prose text is in Dutch, but it is not important to be able to understand it in the context of this book.

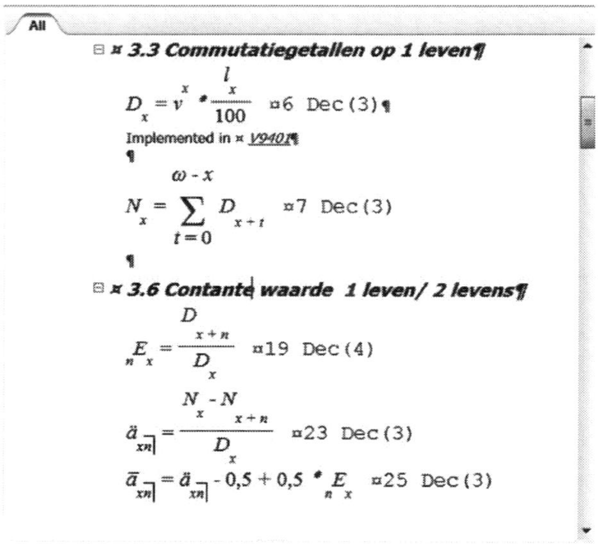

Figure 1.5: Example Code written using the Pension Plans language. Notice the mathematical symbols used to express insurance mathematics.

1.11.5 WebDSL

WebDSL is a language for web programming[10] that integrates languages to address the different concerns of web programming, including persistent data modeling (**entity**), user interface templates (**define**), access control[11], data validation[12], search and more. The language enforces inter-concern consistency checking, providing early detection of failures[13]. The fragments in Fig. 1.6 and Fig. 1.7 show a data model, user interface templates and access control rules for posts in a blogging application. WebDSL is implemented with Spoofax and is used in the researchr digital library[14].

[10] E. Visser. WebDSL: A case study in domain-specific language engineering. In *GTTSE*, pages 291–373, 2007

[11] D. M. Groenewegen and E. Visser. Declarative access control for WebDSL: Combining language integration and separation of concerns. In *ICWE*, pages 175–188, 2008

[12] D. Groenewegen and E. Visser. Integration of data validation and user interface concerns in a dsl for web applications. *SoSyM*, 2011

[13] Z. Hemel, D. M. Groenewegen, L. C. L. Kats, and E. Visser. Static consistency checking of web applications with WebDSL. *JSC*, 46(2):150–182, 2011

```
entity Post {
  key       :: String (id)
  blog      → Blog
  urlTitle  :: String
  title     :: String (searchable)
  content   :: WikiText (searchable)
  public    :: Bool (default=false)
  authors   → Set<User>
  function isAuthor(): Bool {
    return principal() in authors;
  }
  function mayEdit(): Bool {
    return isAuthor();
  }
  function mayView(): Bool {
    return public || mayEdit();
  }
}
```

Figure 1.6: Example Code written in WebDSL. The code shows data structures and utility functions.

```
access control rules
  rule page post(p: Post, title: String) {
    p.mayView()
  }
  rule template newPost(b: Blog) {
    b.isAuthor()
  }
section posts
  define page post(p: Post, title: String) {
    title{ output(p.title) }
    bloglayout(p.blog){
      placeholder view { postView(p) }
      postComments(p)
    }
  }
  define permalink(p: Post) {
    navigate post(p, p.urlTitle) { elements }
  }
```

Figure 1.7: More WebDSL example code. This example shows access control rules as well as a page definition.

2
Introduction to DSLs

Domain-Specific Languages (DSLs) are becoming more and more important in software engineering. Tools are becoming better as well, so DSLs can be developed with relatively little effort. This chapter starts with a definition of important terminology. It then explains the difference between DSLs and general-purpose languages, as well as the relationship between them. I then look at the relationship to model-driven development and develop a vision for modular programming languages which I consider the pinnacle of DSLs. I discuss the benefits of DSLs, some of the challenges for adopting DSLs and describe a few application areas. Finally, I provide some differentiation of the approach discussed in this book to alternative approaches.

2.1 Very Brief Introduction to the Terminology

While we explain many of the important terms in the book as we go along, here are a few essential ones. You should at least roughly understand those right from the beginning.

I use the term *programming language* to refer to general-purpose languages (GPLs) such as Java, C++, Lisp or Haskell. While DSLs could be called programming languages as well (although they are not *general purpose* programming languages) I don't do this in this book: I just call them DSLs.

I use the terms *model*, *program* and *code* interchangeably because I think that any distinction is artificial: code can be written in a GPL or in a DSL. Sometimes DSL code and program code are mixed, so separating the two makes no sense. If the distinction is important, I say "DSL program" or "GPL code". If I use model and program or code in the same sentence, the model usually refers to the more abstract representation. An example would be: "The program generated from the model is …".

If you know about DSLs, you will know that there are two main schools: *internal* and *external* DSLs. In this book I only address external DSLs. See Section 2.8 for details.

I distinguish between the execution engine and the target platform. The *target platform* is what your DSL program has to run on in the end and is assumed to be something we cannot change (significantly) during the DSL development process. The *execution engine* can be changed, and bridges the gap between the DSL and the platform. It may be an interpreter or a generator. An *interpreter* is a program running on the target platform that loads a DSL program and then acts on it. A *generator* (aka compiler) takes the DSL program and transforms it into an artifact (often GPL source code) that can run directly on the target platform.[1]

A language, domain-specific or not, consist of the following main ingredients. The *concrete syntax* defines the notation with which users can express programs. It may be textual, graphical, tabular or a mix of these. The *abstract syntax* is a data structure that can hold the semantically relevant information expressed by a program. It is typically a tree or a graph. It does not contain any details about the notation – for example, in textual languages, it does not contain keywords, symbols or whitespace. The *static semantics* of a language are the set of constraints and/or type system rules to which programs have to conform, in addition to being structurally correct (with regards to the concrete and abstract syntax). *Execution semantics* refers to the meaning of a program once it is executed. It is realized using the *execution engine*. If I use the term *semantics* without any qualification, I refer to the execution semantics, not the static semantics.

Sometimes it is useful to distinguish between what I call *technical* DSLs and *application domain* DSLs[2]. The distinction is not always clear and not always necessary, but generally I consider technical DSLs to be used by programmers and application domain DSLs to be used by non-programmers. This can have significant consequences for the design of the DSL.

There is often a confusion around meta-ness (as in meta

Note that considering programs and models the same thing is only valid when looking at *executable* models, i.e. models whose final purpose is the creation of executable software. Of course, there are models used in systems engineering, for communication among stakeholders in business, or as approximations of physical, real-world systems that cannot be considered programs. However, these are outside the scope of this book.

[1] In an example from enterprise systems, the platform could be JEE and the execution engine could be an enterprise bean that runs an interpreter for a DSL. In embedded software, the platform could be a real-time operating system, and the execution engine could be a code generator that maps a DSL to the APIs provided by the RTOS.

[2] Sometimes also called business DSLs, vertical DSLs or "fachliche DSLs" in German.

model) and abstraction. I think these terms are clearly different and I try to explain my understanding here.

The meta model of a model (or program) is a model that defines (the abstract syntax of) a language used to describe a model. For example, the meta model of UML is a model that defines all those language concepts that make up the UML, such as classifier, association or property. So the prefix *meta* can be understood as *the definition of*. The reverse direction of the relationship is typically called *instance of* or *conforms to*. It also becomes clear that every meta model is a model[3]. A model m can *play the role* of a meta model with regards to a set of other models O, where m defines the language used to express the models in O.

[3] The reverse statement is of course not true.

The notion of *abstraction* is different, even though it also characterizes the relationship between two artifacts (programs or models). An artifact a_1 is more abstract than an artifact a_2 if it leaves out some of the details of a_2, while preserving those characteristics of a_2 that are important for whatever a_1 is used for – the purpose of a_1 informs the the abstractions we use to approximate a_2 with a_1. Note that according to this definition, *abstraction* and *model* are synonyms: a simplification of reality for a given purpose. In this sense, the term *model* can also be understood as characterizing the relationship between two artifacts. a_1 is a model of a_2.

Based on this discussion it should be clear that it does not make sense to say that *the meta model is the model of a model*, a sentence often heard around the modeling community. *model of* and *meta model of* are two quite distinct concepts.

2.2 From General Purpose Languages to DSLs

General Purpose Programming Languages (GPLs) are a means for programmers to instruct computers. All of them are Turing complete, which means that they can be used to implement anything that is computable with a Turing machine. It also means that anything expressible with one Turing complete programming language can also be expressed with any other Turing complete programming language. In that sense, all programming languages are interchangeable.

So why is there more than one? Why don't we program everything in Java or Pascal or Ruby or Python? Why doesn't an embedded systems developer use Ruby, and why doesn't a Web developer use C?

Of course there is the execution strategy. C code is compiled to efficient native code, whereas Ruby is run by a virtual machine (a mix between an interpreter and a compiler). But in principle, you could compile (a subset of) Ruby to native code, and you could interpret C.

The real reason why these languages are used for what they are used for is that the features they offer are optimized for the tasks that are relevant in the respective domains. In C you can directly influence memory layout (which is important when communicating with low-level, memory-mapped devices), you can use pointers (resulting in potentially very efficient data structures) and the preprocessor can be used as a (very limited) way of expressing abstractions with zero runtime overhead. In Ruby, closures can be used to implement "postponed" behavior (very useful for asynchronous web applications); Ruby also provides powerful string manipulation features (to handle input received from a website), and the meta programming facility supports the definition of internal DSLs that are quite suitable for Web applications (the Rails framework is *the* example for that).

So, even within the field of general-purpose programming, there are different languages, each providing different features tailored to the specific tasks at hand. The more specific the tasks get, the more reason there is for specialized languages[4]. Consider relational algebra: relational databases use tables, rows, columns and joins as their core abstractions. A specialized language, SQL, which takes these features into account has been created. Or consider reactive, distributed, concurrent systems: Erlang is specifically made for this environment.

So, if we want to "program" for even more specialized environments, it is obvious that even more specialized languages are useful. A Domain-Specific Language is simply a language that is optimized for a given class of problems, called a *domain*. It is based on abstractions that are closely aligned with the domain for which the language is built[5]. Specialized languages also come with a syntax suitable for expressing these abstractions concisely. In many cases these are textual notations, but tables, symbols (as in mathematics) or graphics can also be useful. Assuming the semantics of these abstractions is well defined, this makes a good starting point for expressing programs for a specialized domain effectively.

■ *Executing the Language*   Engineering a DSL (or any language) is not just about syntax, it also has to be "brought to life" – DSL programs have to be executed somehow. It is im-

[4] We do this is real life as well. I am sure you have heard about Eskimos having many different words for snow, because this is relevant in their "domain". Not sure this is actually true, but it is surely a nice metaphor for tailoring a language to its domain.

[5] SQL has tables, rows and columns, Erlang has lightweight tasks, message passing and pattern matching.

portant to understand the separation of domain contents into DSL, execution engine and platform (see Fig. 2.1):

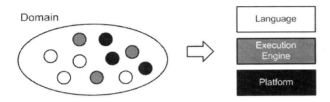

Figure 2.1: Fixed domain concerns (black) end up in the platform, variable concerns end up in the DSL (white). Those concerns that can be derived by rules from the DSL program end up in the execution engine (gray).

- Some concerns are different for each program in the domain (white circles). The DSL provides tailored abstractions to express this variability concisely.

- Some concerns are the same for each program in the domain (black circles). These typically end up in the platform.

- Some concerns can be *derived by fixed rules* from the program written in the DSL (gray circles). While these concerns are not identical in each program in the domain, they are always the same *for a given DSL program structure*. These concerns are handled by the execution engine (or, in some cases, in frameworks or libraries that are part of the platform).

There are two main approaches to building execution engines: *translation* (aka *generation* or *compilation*) and *interpretation*. The former translates a DSL program into a language for which an execution engine on a given target platform already exists. Often, this is GPL source code. In the latter case, you build a new execution engine (on top of your desired target platforms) which loads the program and executes it directly.

If there is a big semantic gap between the language abstractions and the relevant concepts of the target platform (i.e. the platform the interpreter or generated code runs on), execution may become inefficient. For example, if you try to store and query graph data in a relational database, this will be very inefficient, because many joins will be necessary to reassemble the graph from the normalized tabular structure. As another example, consider running Erlang on a system which only provides heavyweight processes: having thousands of processes (as typical Erlang programs require) is not going to be efficient. So, when defining a language for a given domain, you should be aware of the intricacies of the target platform and the interplay between execution and language design[6].

[6] This may sound counterintuitive. Isn't a DSL supposed to abstract away from just these details of execution? Yes, but: it has to be possible to implement a reasonably efficient execution engine. DSL design is a compromise between appropriate domain abstractions and the ability to get to an efficient execution. A good DSL allows the DSL *user* to ignore execution concerns, but allows the DSL *implementor* to implement a reasonable execution engine

■ *Languages versus Libraries and Frameworks*   At this point you should to some extent believe that specific problems can be more efficiently solved by using the right abstractions. But why do we need full-blown languages? Aren't objects, functions, APIs and frameworks good enough? What does creating a *language* add to the picture?

- Languages (and the programs you write with them), are the cleanest form of abstraction – essentially, you add a notation to a conceptual model of the domain. You get rid of all the unnecessary clutter that an API – or anything else embedded in or expressed with a general-purpose language – requires. You can define a notation that expresses the abstractions concisely and makes interacting with programs easy and efficient.

- DSLs sacrifice some of the flexibility to express *any* program (as in GPLs) for productivity and conciseness of *relevant* programs in a particular domain. In that sense, DSLs are limited, or restricted. DSLs may be so restricted that they only allow the creation of correct programs (*correct-by-construction*).

- You can provide non-trivial static analyses and checks, and an IDE that offers services such as code completion, syntax highlighting, error markers, refactoring and debugging. This goes far beyond what can be done with the facilities provided by general-purpose languages.

> In the end, this is what allows DSLs to be used by non-programmers, one of the value propositions of DSLs: they get a clean, custom, productive environment that allows them to work with languages that are closely aligned with the domain in which they work.

■ *Differences between GPLs and DSLs*   I said above that DSLs sacrifice some of the flexibility to express *any* program in favor of productivity and conciseness of *relevant* programs in a particular domain. But beyond that, how are DSLs different from GPLs, and what do they have in common?

The boundary isn't as clear as it could be. Domain-specificity is not black-and-white, but instead gradual: a language is *more* or *less* domain specific. The following table lists a set of language characteristics. While DSLs and GPLs can have characteristics from both the second and the third columns, DSLs are more likely to have characteristics from the third column.

Considering that DSLs pick more characteristics from the third rather than the second column, this makes designing DSLs a more manageable problem than designing general-pur-

	GPLs	DSLs
Domain	large and complex	smaller and well-defined
Language size	large	small
Turing completeness	always	often not
User-defined abstractions	sophisticated	limited
Execution	via intermediate GPL	native
Lifespan	years to decades	months to years (driven by context)
Designed by	guru or committee	a few engineers and domain experts
User community	large, anonymous and widespread	small, accessible and local
Evolution	slow, often standardized	fast-paced
Deprecation/incompatible changes	almost impossible	feasible

Figure 2.2: Domain-specific languages versus programming languages. DSLs tend to pick more characteristics from the third column, GPLs tend to pick more from the second.

pose languages. DSLs are typically just much smaller and simpler[7] than GPLs (although there are some pretty sophisticated DSLs).

There are some who maintain that DSLs are always *declarative* (it is not completely clear what "declarative" means anyway), or that they may never be Turing complete. I disagree. They may well be. However, if your DSL becomes as big and general as, say, Java, you might want to consider just using Java[8]. DSLs often start simple, based on an initially limited understanding of the domain, but then grow more and more sophisticated over time, a phenomenon Hudak notes in his '96 paper[9].

So, then, are Mathematica, SQL, State Charts or HTML actually DSLs? In a technical sense they are. They are clearly optimized for (and limited to) a special domain or problem. However, these are examples of DSLs that pick more characteristics from the GPL column, and therefore aren't necessarily good examples for the kinds of languages we cover in this book.

[7] Small and simple can mean that the language has fewer concepts, that the type system is less sophisticated or that the expressive power is limited.

[8] Alternatively, if your tooling allows it, extending Java with domain-specific concepts.

[9] P. Hudak. Building domain-specific embedded languages. *ACM Comput. Surv.*, 28(4es):196, 1996

Ira Baxter suggests only half-jokingly that as soon as a DSL is really successful, we don't call them DSLs anymore.

2.3 Modeling and Model-Driven Development

There are two ways in which the term *modeling* can be understood: descriptive and prescriptive. A *descriptive* model represents an existing system. It abstracts away some aspects and emphasizes others. It is usually used for discussion, communication and analysis. A *prescriptive* model is one that can be used to (automatically) construct the target system. It must be much more rigorous, formal, complete and consistent. In the context of this chapter, and of the book in general, we always mean prescriptive models when we use the term model[10]. Using models in a prescriptive way is the essence of model-driven (software) development (MDSD).

[10] Some people say that models are always descriptive, and once you become prescriptive, you enter the realm of programming. That's fine with me. As I have said above, I don't distinguish between programming and modeling, just between more or less abstract languages and models.

Defining and using DSLs is a flavor of MDSD: we create formal, tool-processable representations of specific aspects of software systems[11]. We then use interpretation or code generation to transform those representations into executable code expressed in general-purpose programming languages and the associated XML/HTML/whatever files. With today's tools it is technically relatively simple to define arbitrary abstractions that represent some aspect of a software system in a meaningful way[12]. It is also relatively simple to build code generators that generate the executable artifacts (as long as you don't need sophisticated optimizations, which can be challenging). Depending on the particular DSL tool used, it is also possible to define suitable notations that make the abstractions easily understandable by non-programmers (for example opticians or thermodynamics engineers).

[11] One can also do MDSD without DSLs by, for example, generating code from general-purpose modeling languages such as UML.

[12] Designing a *good* language is another matter – Part II, DSL Design, provides some help with this.

However, there are also limitations to the classical MDSD approach. The biggest one is that modeling and programming often do not go together very well: modeling languages, environments and tools are distinct from programming languages, environments and tools. The level of distinctness varies, but in many cases it is big enough to cause integration issues that can make adoption of MDSD challenging.

Let me provide some specific examples. Industry has settled on a limited number of meta meta models, EMF/EMOF being the most widespread. Consequently, it is possible to navigate, query and constrain arbitrary models with a common API. However, programming language IDEs are typically *not* built on top of EMF, but come with their own API for representing and accessing the syntax tree. Thus, interoperability between models and source code is challenging – you cannot treat source code in the same way as models in terms of how you access the AST programmatically.

A similar problem exists regarding IDE support for model-code integrated systems: you cannot mix (DSL) models and (GPL) programs while retaining reasonable IDE support. Again, this is because the technology stacks used by the two are different[13]. These problems often result in an artificial separation of models and code, where code generators either create skeletons into which source code is inserted (directly or via the generation gap pattern), or the arcane practice of pasting C snippets into 300 by 300 pixel sized text boxes in graphical state machine tools (and getting errors reported only when the resulting in-

[13] Of course, an integration can be created, as Xtext/Xtend/Java shows. However, this is a *special* integration with Java. Interoperability with, say, C code, would require a new and different integration infrastructure.

tegrated C code is compiled). So what really is the difference between programming and (prescriptive) modeling today? The table in Fig. 2.3 contains some (general and broad) statements:

	Modeling	Programming
Define your own notation/language	Easy	Sometimes possible to some extent
Syntactically integrate several langs	Possible, depends on tool	Hard
Graphical notations	Possible, depends on tool	Usually only visualizations
Customize generator/compiler	Easy	Sometimes possible based on open compilers
Navigate/query	Easy	Sometimes possible, depends on IDE and APIs
View Support	Typical	Almost Never
Constraints	Easy	Sometimes possible with Findbugs etc.
Sophisticated mature IDE	Sometimes, effort-dependent	Standard
Debugger	Rarely	Almost always
Versioning, diff/merge	Depends on syntax and tools	Standard

Figure 2.3: Comparing modeling and programming

■ *Why the Difference?* So one can and should ask: why is there a difference in the first place? I suspect that the primary reason is history: the two worlds have different origins and have evolved in different directions.

Programming languages have traditionally used textual concrete syntax, i.e. the program is represented as a stream of characters. Modeling languages traditionally have used graphical notations. Of course there are textual domain-specific languages (and mostly failed graphical general-purpose languages), but the use of textual syntax for domain-specific modeling has only recently become more prominent. Programming languages have traditionally stored programs in their textual, concrete syntax form, and used scanners and parsers to transform this character stream into an abstract syntax tree for further processing. Modeling languages have traditionally used editors that directly manipulate the abstract syntax, and used projection to render the concrete syntax in the form of diagrams[14]. This approach makes it easy for modeling tools to define *views*, the ability to show the same model elements in different contexts, often using different notations. This has never really been a priority for programming languages beyond outline views, inheritance trees or call graphs.

Here is one of the underlying premises of this book: there should be no difference[15]! Programming and (prescriptive) modeling should be based on the same conceptual approach and tool suite, enabling meaningful integration[16]. In my experience, most software developers don't want to model. They want to program, but:

[14] This is not something we think about much. To most of us this is obvious. If it were different, we'd have to define grammars that could parse two-dimensional graphical structures. While this is possible, it has never caught on in practice.

[15] This is my personal opinion. While I know enough people who share it, I also know people who disagree.

[16] As we will see in this book, Xtext/Xbase/Xtend and MPS' BaseLanguage and mbeddr C are convincing examples of this idea.

at different levels of abstraction: some things may have to be described in detail, low level, algorithmically (a sorting algorithm); other aspects may be described in more high-level terms (declarative UIs)

from different viewpoints: separate aspects of the system should be described with languages suitable to these aspects (data structures, persitence mapping, process, UI)

with different degrees of domain-specificity: some aspects of systems are generic enough to be described with reusable, generic languages (components, database mapping). Other aspects require their own dedicated, maybe even project-specific DSLs (pension calculation rules).

with suitable notations, so all stakeholders can contribute directly to "their" aspects of the overall system (a tabular notation for testing pension rules)

with suitable degrees of expressiveness: aspects may be described imperatively, with functions, or other Turing complete formalisms (a routing algorithm), and other aspects may be described in a declarative way (UI structures)

always integrated and tool processable, so all aspects *directly* lead to executable code through a number of transformations or other means of execution.

This vision, or goal, leads to the idea of modular languages, as explained in the next section.

2.4 Modular Languages

I distinguish between the size of a language and its scope. Language size simply refers to the number of language concepts in that language. Language scope describes the area of applicability for the language, i.e. the size of the domain. The same domain can be covered with big and small languages. A big language makes use of linguistic abstraction, whereas a small language allows the user to define their own in-language abstractions. We discuss the tradeoffs between big and small languages in detail as part of the chapter on Expressivity (Section 4.1), but here is a short overview, based on examples from GPLs.

Examples of big languages include Cobol (a relatively old language intended for use by business users) or ABAP (SAP's language for programming the R/3 system). Big languages (Fig. 2.4) have a relatively large set of very specific language concepts. Proponents of these languages say that they are easy to learn, since "There's a keyword for everything". Constraint checks, meaningful error messages and IDE support are relatively simple to implement because of the large set of language concepts. However, expressing more sophisticated algorithms can be clumsy, because it is hard to write compact, dense code.

Figure 2.4: A Big Language has many very specific language concepts.

Let us now take a look at small languages (Fig. 2.5). Lisp or Smalltalk are examples of small GPLs. They have few, but very powerful language concepts that are highly orthogonal, and hence, composable. Users can define their own abstractions. Proponents of this kind of language also say that those are easy to learn, because "You only have to learn three concepts". But it requires experience to build more complex systems from these basic building blocks, and code can be challenging to read because of its high density. Tool support is harder to build because much more sophisticated analysis of the code is necessary to reverse engineer its domain semantics.

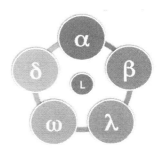

Figure 2.5: A Small Language has few, but powerful, language concepts.

There is a third option: modular languages (Fig. 2.6). They are, in some sense, the synthesis of the previous two. A modular language is made up of a minimal language core, plus a library of language modules that can be imported for use in a given program. The core is typically a small language (in the way defined above) and can be used to solve any problem at a low level, just as in Smalltalk or Lisp. The extensions then add first class support for concepts that are interesting the target domain. Because the extensions are linguistic in nature, interesting analyses can be performed and writing generators (transforming to the minimal core) is relatively straightforward. New, customized language modules can be built and used at any time. A language module is like a framework or library, but it comes with its own syntax, editor, type system and IDE tooling. Once a language module is imported, it behaves as an integral part of the composed language, i.e. it is integrated with other modules by referencing symbols or by being syntactically embedded in code expressed with another module. Integration on the level of the type system, the semantics and the IDE is also provided. An extension module may even be embeddable in *different* core languages[17].

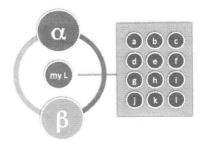

Figure 2.6: A Modular Language: a small core, and a library of reusable language modules.

[17] This may sound like internal DSLs. However, static error checking, static optimizations and IDE support is what differentiates this approach from internal DSLs.

This idea isn't new. Charles Simonyi[18] and Sergey Dmitriev[19] have written about it, so has Guy Steele in the context of Lisp[20]. The idea of modular and extensible languages also relates very much to the notion of language workbenches as defined by Martin Fowler[21]. He defines language workbenches as tools where:

- *Users can freely define languages that are fully integrated with each other.* This is the central idea for language workbenches, but also for modular languages, since you can easily argue that each language module is what Martin Fowler calls a language. "Full integration" can refer to referencing as well as embedding, and includes type systems and semantics.

- *The primary source of information is a persistent abstract representation* and *language users manipulate a DSL through a projectional editor.* This implies that projectional editing must be used[22]. I don't agree. Storing programs in their abstract representation and then using projection to arrive at an editable representation is very useful, and maybe even the best approach to achieve modular languages[23]. However, in the end I don't think this is important, as long as languages are modular. If this is possible with a different approach, such as scannerless parsers[24], that is fine with me.

- *Language designers define a DSL in three main parts: schema, editor(s) and generator(s).* I agree that ideally a language should be defined "meta model first", i.e. you first define a schema (aka the meta model or AST), and then the concrete syntax (editor or grammar), based on the schema: MPS does it this way. However, I think it is also ok to start with the grammar, and have the meta model derived. This is the typical workflow with Xtext, although it can do both. From the language user's point of view, it does not make a big difference in most cases.

- *A language workbench can persist incomplete or contradictory information.* I agree. This is trivial if the models are stored in a concrete textual syntax, but it is not so trivial if a persistent representation based on the abstract syntax is used.

Let me add two additional requirements. For all the languages built with the workbench, tool support must be available: syntax highlighting, code completion, any number of static analyses (including type checking in the case of a statically typed

[18] C. Simonyi, M. Christerson, and S. Clifford. Intentional software. In *OOPSLA*, pages 451–464, 2006

[19] S. Dmitriev. Language oriented programming: The next programming paradigm, 2004

[20] G. L. S. Jr. Growing a language. *lisp*, 12(3):221–236, 1999

[21] M. Fowler. Language workbenches: The killer-app for domain specific languages?, 2005

[22] Projectional editing means that users don't write text that is subsequently parsed. Instead, user interactions with the concrete syntax directly change the underlying abstract syntax. We'll discuss this technology much more extensively in Part III of the book.

[23] In fact, this is what I think personally. But I don't think that this characteristic is essential for language workbenches.

[24] Scannerless parsers do not distinguish between recognizing tokens and parsing the structure of the tokens, thereby avoiding some problems with grammar composability. We'll discuss this further in the book as well

language) and ideally also a debugger[25]. A final requirement is that I want to be able to program complete systems within the language workbench. Since in most interesting systems you will still write parts in a GPL, GPLs must also be available in the environment based on the same language definition/editing/processing infrastructure. Depending on the target domains, this language could be Java, Scala or C#, but it could also be C/C++ for the embedded community. Starting with an existing general-purpose language also makes the adoption of the approach simpler: incremental language extensions can be developed as the need arises.

[25] A central idea of language workbenches is that language definition always includes IDE definition. The two should be integrated.

■ *Concrete Syntax* By default, I expect the concrete syntax of DSLs to be textual. Decades of experience show that textual syntax, together with good tool support, is adequate for large and complex software systems[26]. This becomes even more true if you consider that programmers will have to write less code in a DSL – compared to expressing the same functionality in a GPL – because the abstractions available in the languages will be much more closely aligned with the domain. And programmers can always define an additional language module that fits a domain.

[26] This is not true for all formalisms. Expressing hierarchical state charts textually can be a challenge. However, textual syntax is a good *default* that can be used unless otherwise indicated.

Using text as the default does not mean that it should stop there. There are worthwhile additions. For example, symbolic (as in mathematical) notations and tables should be supported. Finally, graphical editing is useful for certain cases. Examples include data structure relationships, state machine diagrams or data flow systems. The textual and graphical notations must be integrated, though: for example, you will want to embed the expression language module into the state machine diagram to be able to express guard conditions.

The need to *see* graphical notations to gain an overview over complex structures does not necessarily mean that the program has to be *edited* in a graphical form: custom visualizations are important as well. Visualizations are graphical representations of some interesting aspect of the program that is read-only, automatically laid out and supports drill-down back to the program (you can double-click on, say, a state in the diagram, and the text editor selects that particular state in the program text).

■ *Language Libraries* The importance of being able to build your own languages varies depending on the concern at hand. Assume that you work for an insurance company and you want to build a DSL that supports your company's specific way of defining insurance contracts. In this case it is essential that the language is aligned exactly with your business, so you have to define the language yourself[27]. There are other similar examples: building DSLs to describe radio astronomy observations for a given telescope, our case study language to describe cooling algorithms for refrigerators, or a language for describing telecom billing rules (all of these are actual projects I have worked on).

However, for a large range of concerns relating to software engineering or software architecture, the relevant abstractions are well known. They could be made available for reuse (and adaptation) in a library of language modules. Examples include:

- Hierarchical components, ports, component instances and connectors.

- Tabular data structure definition (as in the relational model) or hierarchical data structure definition (as in XML and XML schema), including specifications for persisting that data.

- Definition of rich contracts, including interfaces, pre- and post conditions, protocol state machines and the like.

- Various communication paradigms, such as message passing, synchronous and asynchronous remote procedure calls and service invocations.

- Abstractions for concurrency based on transactional memory or actors.

[27] Examples concepts in the insurance domain include native types for dates, times and time periods, currencies, support for temporal data and the supporting operators, as well as business rules that are "polymorphic" regarding their period of applicability

This sounds like a lot to put into a programming language. But remember: it will not all be in one language. Each of those concerns will be a separate language module that will be used in a program only if needed.

It is certainly not possible to define all these language modules in isolation. Modules have to be designed to work with each other, and a clear dependency structure has to be established. Interfaces on language level support "plugging in" new language constructs. A minimal core language, supporting primitive types, expression, functions and maybe OO, will act as the focal point around which additional language modules are organized.

Many of these architectural concerns interact with frameworks, platforms and middleware. It is crucial that the abstractions in the language remain independent of specific technology solutions. In addition, when interfacing with a specific technology, additional (hopefully declarative) specifications might be necessary: such a technology mapping should be a separate model that references the core program that expresses the application logic. The language modules define a language for specifying persistence, distribution or contract definition. Technology suppliers can support customized generators that map programs to the APIs defined by their technology, taking into account possible additional specifications that configure the mapping[28].

[28] This is a little like service provider interfaces (SPIs) in Java enterprise technology.

```
module CounterExample from counters imports nothing {
  
  var int8_t theI;
  var boolean theB;
  var boolean hasBeenReset;
  var Counter c1;
  
  verifiable
  statemachine Counter {
    in events
      start() <no binding>
      step(int[0..10] size) <no binding>
    out events
      someEvent(int[0..100] x, boolean b) => handle_someEvent
      resetted() => resetted
    local variables
      int[0..100] currentVal = 0
      int[0..100] LIMIT = 10
    states ( initial = initialState )
      state initialState {
        on start [ ] -> countState { send someEvent(100, true && false || true); }
      }
      state countState {
        on step [currentVal + size > LIMIT] -> initialState { send resetted(); }
        on step [currentVal + size <= LIMIT] -> countState { currentVal = currentVal + size; }
        on start [ ] -> initialState {  }
      }
  }
  
  exported test case test1 {
    initsm(c1);
    assert(0) isInState<c1, initialState>;
    test statemachine c1 {
      start -> countState
      step(1) -> countState
      step(2) -> countState
      step(7) -> countState
      step(1) -> initialState
    }
  } test(test case)
}
```

Figure 2.7: A program written in a modularly extendible C (from the mbeddr.com project).

■ *A Vision of Programming*   For me, this is the vision of programming I am working towards. The distinction between modeling and programming vanishes. People can develop code using a language directly suitable to the task at hand and aligned with their role in the overall development project. They can also build their own languages or language extensions, if that makes their work easier. Most of these languages will be relatively small, since they only address one aspect of a system, and typically extend existing languages (Fig. 3.13 shows an example of extensions to C). They are not general-purpose: they are DSLs.

Tools for this implementing this approach exist. Of course they can become even better, for example in the development of debuggers or integration of graphical and textual languages, but we are clearly getting there.

> MPS is one of them, which is why I focus a lot on MPS in this book. Intentional's Domain Workbench is another one. Various Eclipse-based solutions (with Xtext/ Xbase/Xtend at the core) are getting there as well.

2.5 Benefits of using DSLs

Using DSLs can reap a multitude of benefits. There are also some challenges you have to master: I outline these in the next section. Let's look at the upside first.

2.5.1 Productivity

Once you've got a language and its execution engine for a particular aspect of your development task, work becomes much more efficient, simply because you don't have to do the grunt work manually[29]. This is the most obviously useful if you can replace a lot of GPL code with a few lines of DSL code. There are many studies that show that the mere amount of code one has to write (and read!) introduces complexity, independent of what the code expresses, and how. The ability to reduce that amount while retaining the same semantic content is a huge advantage.

> [29] Presumably the amount of DSL code you have to write is much less than what you'd have to write if you used the target platform directly.

You could argue that a good library or framework will do the job as well. True, libraries, frameworks and DSLs all encapsulate knowledge and functionality, making it easily reusable. However, DSLs provide a number of additional benefits, such as a suitable syntax, static error checking or static optimizations and meaningful IDE support.

2.5.2 Quality

Using DSLs can increase the quality of the created product: fewer bugs, better architectural conformance, increased maintainability. This is the result of the removal of (unnecessary) degrees of freedom for programmers, the avoidance of duplication of code (if the DSL is engineered in the right way) and the consistent automation of repetitive work by the execution

> The approach can also yield better performance if the execution engine contains the necessary optimizations. However, implementing these is a lot of work, so most DSLs do not lead to significant gains in performance.

engine[30]. As the next item shows, more meaningful validation and verification can be performed on the level of DSL programs, increasing the quality further.

2.5.3   Validation and Verification

Since DSLs capture their respective concern in a way that is not cluttered with implementation details, DSL programs are more semantically rich than GPL programs. Analyses are much easier to implement, and error messages can use more meaningful wording, since they can use domain concepts. As mentioned above, some DSLs are built *specifically* to enable non-trivial, formal (mathematical) analyses. Manual review and validation also becomes more efficient, because the domain-specific aspects are uncluttered, and domain experts can be involved more directly.

2.5.4   Data Longevity

If done right, models are independent of specific implementation techniques. They are expressed at a level of abstraction that is meaningful to the domain – this is why we can analyze and generate based on these models. This also means that models can be transformed into other representations if the need arises, for example, because you are migrating to a new DSL technology. While the investments in a DSL implementation are specific to a particular tool (and lost if you change it), the models should largely be migratable[31].

2.5.5   A Thinking and Communication Tool

If you have a way of expressing domain concerns in a language that is closely aligned with the domain, your thinking becomes clearer, because the code you write is not cluttered with implementation details. In other words, using DSLs allows you to separate essential from accidental complexity, moving the latter to the execution engine. This also makes team communication simpler.

But not only is using the DSL useful; also, the act of *building* the language can help you improve your understanding of the domain for which you build the DSL. It also helps straighten out differences in the understanding of the domain that arise from different people solving the same problem in different ways. In some senses, a language definition is an "executable analysis model"[32]. I have had several occasions on which customers said, after a three-day DSL prototyping workshop, that

---

[30] This is also known as correct-by-construction: the language only allows the construction of correct programs.

[31] This leads to an interesting definition of legacy code: it is legacy, if you cannot access the domain semantics of a data structure, and hence you cannot automatically migrate it to a different formalism.

Building a language requires formalization and decision making: you can't create a DSL if you don't really know what you're talking about.

[32] Remember the days when "analysts" created "analysis models"?

they had learned a lot about their own domain, and that even if they never used the DSL, this alone would be worth the effort spent on building it. In effect, a DSL is a formalization of the Ubiquitous Language in the sense of Eric Evans' Domain Driven Design[33].

[33] E. Evans. *Domain-driven design: tackling complexity in the heart of software.* Addison-Wesley, 2004

2.5.6 Domain Expert Involvement

DSLs whose domain, abstractions and notations are closely aligned with how domain experts (i.e. non-programmers) express themselves, allow for very good integration between developers and domain experts: domain experts can easily read, and often write program code, since it is not cluttered with implementation details irrelevant to them. And even when domain experts aren't willing to write DSL code, developers can at least pair with them when writing code, or use the DSL code to get domain experts involved in meaningful validation and reviews (Fowler uses the term "business-readable DSLs" in this case). At the very least you can generate visualizations, reports or even interactive simulators that are suitable for use by domain experts.

Of course, the domain (and the people working in it) must be suitable for formalization, but once you start looking, it is amazing how many domains fall into this category. Insurance contracts, hearing aids and refrigerators are just some examples you maybe didn't expect. On the other hand, I once helped build a DSL to express enterprise governance and business policies. This effort failed, because the domain was much too vague and too "stomach driven" for it to be formalizable.

2.5.7 Productive Tooling

In contrast to libraries, frameworks, and internal DSLs (those embedded into a host language and implemented with host language abstractions), external DSLs can come with tools, i.e. IDEs that are aware of the language. This can result in a much improved user experience. Static analyses, code completion, visualizations, debuggers, simulators and all kinds of other niceties can be provided. These features improve the productivity of the users and also make it easier for new team members to become productive[34].

[34] JetBrains once reported the following about their *webr* and *dnq* Java extensions for web applications and database persistence: "Experience shows that the language extensions are easier to learn than J2EE APIs. As an experiment, a student who had no experience in web development was tasked to create a simple accounting application. He was able to produce a web application with sophisticated Javascript UI in about 2 weeks using the *webr* and *dnq* languages."

2.5.8 No Overhead

If you are generating source code from your DSL program (as opposed to interpreting it) you can use domain-specific abstractions without paying any runtime overhead, because the generator, just like a compiler, can remove the abstractions and generate efficient code. And it generates the same low-overhead code, every time, automatically. This is very useful in cases where performance, throughput or resource efficiency is a concern (i.e. in embedded systems, but also in the cloud, where you run many, many processes in server farms; energy consumption is an issue these days).

2.5.9 Platform Independent/Isolation

In some cases, using DSLs can abstract from the underlying technology platform[35]. Using DSLs and an execution engine makes the application logic expressed in the DSL code independent of the target platform[36]. It is absolutely feasible to change the execution engine and the target platform "underneath" a DSL to execute the code on a new platform. Portability is enhanced, as is maintainability, because DSLs support separation of concerns – the concerns expressed in the DSL (e.g. the application logic) is separated from implementation details and target platform specifics.

Often no single one of the advantages would drive you to using a DSL. But in many cases you can benefit in multiple ways, so the sum of the benefits is often worth the (undoubtedly necessary) investment in the approach.

[35] Remember OMG's MDA? They introduced the whole model-driven approach primarily as a means to abstract from platforms (probably a consequence of their historical focus on interoperability). There are cases where interoperability is the primary focus: cross-platform mobile development is an example. However, in my experience, platform independence is often just one driver in many, and it is typically not the most important one.

[36] This is not necessarily true for architecture DSLs and utility DSLs, whose abstractions may be tied relatively closely to the concepts provided by the target platform.

2.6 Challenges

There is no such thing as a free lunch. This is also true for DSLs. Let's look at the price you have to pay to get all the benefits described above.

2.6.1 Effort of Building the DSLs

Before a DSL can be used, it has to be built[37]. If the DSL has to be developed as part of a project, the effort of building it has to be factored into the overall cost-benefit analysis. For technical DSLs[38], there is a huge potential for reuse (e.g. a large class of web or mobile applications can be described with the same DSL), so here the investment is easily justified. On the other hand, application domain-specific DSLs (e.g. pension plan specifications) are often very narrow in focus, so the investment in building them is harder to justify at first glance. But these DSLs are often tied to the core know-how of a business and provide a way to describe this knowledge in a formal, uncluttered, portable and maintainable way. That should be a priority for any business that wants to remain relevant! In both cases, modern tools reduce the effort of building DSLs considerably, making it a feasible approach in more and more projects.

[37] If it has been built already, before a project, then using the DSL is obviously useful.

[38] Technical DSLs are those that address aspects of software engineering such as components, state machines or persistence mappings, not application domain DSLs for a technical domain (such as automotive software or machine control).

There are three factors that make DSL creation cheaper: deep knowledge about a domain, experience of the DSL developer and productivity of the tools. This is why focussing on tools in the context of DSLs is important.

2.6.2 Language Engineering Skills

Building DSLs is not rocket science. But to do it well requires experience and skill: it is likely that your first DSL will not be great. Also, the whole language/compiler thing has a bad reputation that mainly stems from "ancient times" when tools like lex/yacc, ANTLR, C and Java were the only ingredients you could use for language engineering. Modern language workbenches have changed this situation radically, but of course there is still a learning curve. In addition, the definition of good languages – independent of tooling and technicalities – is not made simpler by better tools: how do you find out which abstractions need to go into the languages? How do you create "elegant" languages? The book provides some guidance in Part II, DSL Design, but it nevertheless requires a significant element of experience and practice that can only be build up over time.

2.6.3 Process Issues

Using DSLs usually leads to work split: some people build the languages, others use them. Sometimes the languages have been built already when you start a development project; sometimes they are built as part of the project. In the latter case especially, it is important that you establish some kind of process for how language users interact with language developers and with domain experts[39]. Just like any other situation in which one group of people creates something that another group of people relies on, this can be a challenge[40].

2.6.4 Evolution and Maintenance

A related issue is language evolution and maintenance. Again, just like any other asset you develop for use in multiple contexts, you have to plan ahead (people, cost, time, skills) for the maintenance phase. A language that is not actively maintained and evolved will become outdated over time and will become a liability. During the phase where you introduce DSLs into an organization especially, rapid evolution based on the requirements of users is critical to build trust in the approach[41].

2.6.5 DSL Hell

Once development of DSLs becomes technically easy, there is a danger that developers create new DSLs instead of searching for and learning existing DSLs. This may end up as a large

[39] For some DSLs, the users of the DSL are the same people who build the DSL (often true for utility DSLs). This is great because there is no communication overhead or knowledge gap between the domain expert (you) and the DSL developer (you). It is a good idea to choose such a DSL as your first DSL.

[40] This is not much different for languages than for any other shared artifact (frameworks, libraries, tools in general), but it also isn't any simpler and needs to be addressed.

[41] While this is an important aspect, once again it is no worse for DSLs than it is for any other shared, reused asset.

set of half-baked DSLs, each covering related domains, possibly with overlap, but still incompatible. The same problem can arise with libraries, frameworks or tools. They can all be addressed by governance and effective communication in the team[42].

[42] It also helps if DSLs are incrementally extensible, so an existing language can be extended instead of creating a completely new language.

2.6.6 Investment Prison

The more you invest in reusable artifacts, the more productive you become. However, you may also get locked into a particular way of doing things. Radically changing your business may seem unattractive once you've become very efficient at the current one. It becomes expensive to "move outside the box". To avoid this, keep an open mind and be willing to throw things away and come up with more appropriate solutions.

With the advent of the digital age, we all know of many businesses that went bankrupt because they had stuck to a dying business model. Maybe they just couldn't see that things would change, but maybe it way because they were so efficient at what they were doing, they couldn't invest into new ideas or approaches for fear of canibalizing their mainstream business.

2.6.7 Tool Lock-in

Many of the DSL tools are open source, so you don't get locked into a *vendor*. But you will still get locked into a *tool*. While it is feasible to exchange model data between tools, there is essentially no interoperability between DSL tools themselves, so the investments in DSL implementation are specific to a single tool.

2.6.8 Cultural Challenges

Statements like "Language Engineering is complicated", "Developers want to program, not model", "Domain experts aren't programmers" and "If we model, we use the UML standard" are often-overheard prejudices that hinder the adoption of DSLs. I hope to provide the factual and technical arguments for fighting these in this book. But an element of cultural bias may still remain. You may have to do some selling and convincing that is relatively independent of the actual technical arguments. Problems like this always arise if you want to introduce something new into an organization, especially if it changes significantly what people do, how they do it or how they interact. A lot has been written about introducing new ideas into organizations, and I recommend reading *Fearless Change* by Rising and Manns[43] if you're the person who is driving the introduction of DSLs into your organization.

[43] L. Rising and M. L. Manns. *Fearless Change: Patterns for Introducing New Ideas: Introducing Patterns into Organizations.* Addison-Wesley, 2004

Of course there are other things that can go wrong: your DSL or generator might be buggy, resulting in buggy systems. You might have the DSL developed by external parties, giving away core domain knowhow. The person who built the DSL may leave the company. However, these things are not specific to DSLs: they can happen with anything, so we don't address them as challenges in the context of DSLs specifically.

■ *Is it worth it?* Should you use DSLs? The only realistic answer is: it depends. With this book I aim to give you as much help as possible. The better you understand the topic, the easier it is to make an informed decision. In the end, you have to decide for yourself, or maybe ask for the help of people who have done it before.

Let us look at when you should *not* use DSLs. If you don't understand the domain you want to write a DSL for, or if you don't have the means to learn about it (e.g. access to somebody who knows the domain), you're in trouble. You will identify the wrong abstractions, miss the expectations of your future users and generally have to iterate a lot to get it right, making the development expensive[44]. Another sign of problems is this: if you build your DSL iteratively and over time and the changes requested by the domain experts don't become fewer and smaller, and concern more and more detailed points, then you know you are in trouble, because it seems there is no common understanding about the domain. It is hard to write a DSL for a set of stakeholders who can't agree on what the domain is all about.

Another problem is an unknown target platform. If you don't know how to implement a program in the domain on the target platform manually, you'll have a hard time implementing an execution engine (generator or interpreter). You might want to consider writing (or inspecting) a couple of representative example applications to understand the patterns that should go into the execution engine.

DSLs and their tooling are sophisticated software programs themselves. They need to be designed, tested, deployed and documented. So a certain level of general software development proficiency is a prerequisite. If you are struggling with unit testing, software design or continuous builds, then you should probably master these challenges before you address DSLs. A related topic is the maturity of the development process. The fact that you introduce additional dependencies (in the form of a supplier-consumer relationship between DSL de-

[44] If everyone is aware of this, then you might still want to try to build a language as a means of building the understanding about the domain. But this is risky, and should be handled with care.

velopers and DSL users) into your development team requires that you know how to track issues, handle version management, do testing and quality assurance and document things in a way accessible to the target audience. If your development team lacks this maturity, you might want to consider first introducing those aspects into the team before you start using DSLs in a strategic way – although the occasional utility DSL is the obvious exception.

2.7 Applications of DSLs

So far we have covered some of the basics of DSLs, as well as the benefits and challenges. This section addresses those aspects of software engineering in which DSLs have been used successfully. Part IV of the book provides extensive treatment of most of these.

2.7.1 Utility DSLs

One use of DSLs is simply as utilities for developers. A developer, or a small team of developers, creates a small DSL that automates a specific, usually well-bounded aspect of software development. The overall development process is not based on DSLs, it's a few developers being creative and simplifying their own lives[45].

Examples include the generation of array-based implementations for state machines, any number of interface/contract definitions from which various derived artifacts (classes, WSDL, factories) are generated, or tools that set up project and code skeletons for given frameworks (as exemplified in Rails' and Roo's scaffolding). The Jnario language for behavior-driven development is discussed as an example of a utility DSL in Chapter 19.

[45] Often, these DSL serve as a "nice front end" to an existing library or framework, or automates a particularly annoying or intricate aspect of software development in a given domain.

2.7.2 Architecture DSLs

A larger-scale use of DSLs is to use them to describe the architecture (components, interfaces, messages, dependencies, processes, shared resources) of a (larger) software system or platform. In contrast to using existing architecture modeling languages (such as UML or the various existing architecture description languages (ADLs)), the abstractions in an architecture DSL can be tailored specifically to the abstractions relevant to the particular platform or system architecture. Much more meaningful analyses and generators are possible in this way. From the architecture models expressed in the DSL, code skeletons are generated into which manually written application code is inserted. The generated code usually handles the integration with the runtime infrastructure. Often, these DSLs also capture non-functional constraints such as timing or resource consumption. Architecture DSLs are usually developed during the architecture exploration phase of a project. They can help to ensure that the system architecture is consistently implemented by a potentially large development team.

For example in AUTOSAR[46], the architecture is specified in models, then the complete communication middleware for a distributed component infrastructure is generated. Examples in embedded systems in general abound: I have used this approach for a component architecture in software-defined radio, as well as for factory automation systems, in which the distributed components had to "speak" an intricate protocol whose handlers could be generated from a concise specification. Finally, the approach can also be used well in enterprise systems that are based on a multi-tier, database-based distributed server architecture. Middleware integration, server configuration and build scripts can often be generated from relatively concise models.

[46] AUTOSAR is an architectural standard for automotive software development.

We discuss an example architecture DSL for distributed, component-based systems as one of the case studies in Part II of the book, and also in Chapter 18.

2.7.3 Full Technical DSLs

For some domains, DSLs can be created that don't just embody the architectural structure of the systems, but their complete application logic as well, so that 100% of the code can be generated. DSLs like these often consist of several language modules that play together to describe all aspects of the underlying system. I emphasize the word "technical", since these DSLs are used by developers, in contrast to application domain DSLs.

Examples include DSLs for some types of Web application, DSLs for mobile phone apps, as well as DSLs for developing state-based or dataflow-based embedded systems. As an example of this class of DSLs we discuss mbeddr, a set of extensions to C for embedded software development as an example in Part II and in Chapter 20.

2.7.4 Application Domain DSLs

In this case the DSLs describe the core business logic of an application system independent of its technical implementation. These DSLs are intended to be used by domain experts, usually non-programmers. This leads to more stringent requirements regarding notation, ease of use and tool support. These also typically require more effort in building the language, since a "messy" application domain first has to be understood, structured and possibly "re-taught" to the domain experts[47].

Examples include DSLs for describing pension plans, a DSL for describing the cooling algorithms in refrigerators, a DSL for configuring hearing aids or DSLs for insurance mathematics. We discuss the pension plan example in Part II, and discuss a DSL for defining health monitoring applications in Chapter 22.

[47] In contrast, technical DSLs are often much easier to define, since they are guided very much by existing formal artifacts (architectures, frameworks, middleware infrastructures).

2.7.5 DSLs in Requirements Engineering

A related topic to application domain DSLs is the use of DSLs in the context of requirements engineering. Here, the focus of the languages is not so much on automatic code generation, but rather on a precise and checkable complete description of requirements. Traceability to other artifacts is important. Often, the DSLs need to be embedded or otherwise connected to prose text, to integrate them with "classical" requirements approaches.

Examples include a DSL for helping with the trade analysis for satellite construction, or pseudo-structured natural language DSLs that assume some formal meaning for domain entities and terms such as *should* or *must*[48]. We discuss the connection of DSLs and requirements engineering in Chapter 17.

[48] The latter kind of DSLs, also called *Controlled Natural Language*, is quite different from the kinds of DSLs we cover in this book. I will not cover it any furter.

2.7.6 DSLs used for Analysis

Another category of DSL use is as the basis for analysis, checking and proofs. Of course, checking plays a role in all use cases for DSLs – you want to make sure that the models you release for downstream use are "correct" in a sense that goes beyond what the language syntax already enforces. But in some cases, DSLs are used to express concerns in a formalism that lends itself to formal verification (safety, scheduling, concurrency, resource allocation). While code generation is often a part of it, code generation is not the driver for the use of this type of DSL. This is especially relevant in complex technical systems, or in systems engineering, where we look beyond only software and consider a system as a whole (including mechanical, electric/electronic or fluid-dynamic aspects). Sophisticated mathematical formalisms are used here – I will cover this aspect only briefly in this book, as part of the Semantics chapter (Section 4.1).

2.7.7 DSLs used in Product Line Engineering

At its core, PLE is mainly about expressing, managing and then later binding variability between a set of related products. Depending on the kind of variability, DSLs are a very good way of capturing the variability, and later, in the DSL code, of describing a particular variant. Often, but not always, these DSLs are used more for configuration than for "creatively constructing" a solution to a problem.

Examples include the specification of refrigerator models as the composition of the functional layout of a refrigerator and a cooling algorithm, injected with specific parameter values. We look at the relationship of DSLs and PLE in Chapter 21.

2.8 Differentiation from other Works and Approaches

2.8.1 Internal versus External DSLs

Internal DSLs are DSLs that are embedded into general-purpose languages. Usually, the host languages are dynamically typed and the implementation of the DSL is based on meta programming (Scala is an exception here, since it is a statically typed language with type inference). The difference between an API and an internal DSL is not always clear, and there is a middle ground called a *Fluent API*. Let's look at the three:

- We all know what a regular object-oriented API looks like. We instantiate an object and then call a sequence of methods on the object. Each method call is packaged as a separate statement.

- A fluent API essentially chains method calls. Each method call returns an object on which subsequent calls are possible. This results in more concise code, and, more importantly, by returning suitable intermediate objects from method calls, a sequence of valid subsequent method calls can be enforced (almost like a grammar – this is why it could be considered a DSL). Here is a Java/Easymock example, taken from Wikipedia:

```
Collection coll = EasyMock.createMock(Collection.class);
EasyMock.expect(coll.remove(null)).andThrow(new NullPointerException()).
    atLeastOnce();
```

- Fluent APIs are chained sequences of method calls. The syntax makes this obvious, and there is typically no way to change this syntax, as a consequence of the inflexible syntax rules of the host language. Host languages with more flexible syntax can support internal DSL that look much more like actual, custom languages. Here is a Ruby on Rails example[49], which defines a data structure (and, implicitly, a database table) for a blog post:

[49] taken from **rubyonrails.org**

```
class Post < ActiveRecord::Base
  validates :name,  :presence => true
  validates :title, :presence => true,
                    :length => { :minimum => 5 }
end
```

While I recognize the benefits of fluent APIs and internal DSLs, I think they are fundamentally limited by the fact that an important ingredient is missing: IDE support[50]. In classical internal DSLs, the IDE is not aware of the grammar, constraints or other properties of the embedded DSL beyond what the type system can offer, which isn't much in the case of dynamically typed languages. Since I consider IDE integration an important ingredient to DSL adoption, I decided not to cover internal DSLs in this book[51].

[50] Note that with modern language workbenches, you can also achieve language extension or embedding, resulting in the same (or even a somewhat cleaner) syntax. However, these extensions and embeddings are *real* language extensions (as opposed to meta programs) and do come with support for static constraint checking and IDE support. We cover this extensively in the book.

[51] In addition, I don't have enough real-world experience with internal DSLs to be able to talk about them in a book.

2.8.2 Compiler Construction

Language definition, program validation and transformation or interpretation are obviously closely related to compiler construction – even though I don't make this connection explicit in the book all the time. And many of the techniques that are traditionally associated with compiler construction are applicable to DSLs. However, there are also significant differences. The tools for building DSLs are more powerful and convenient and also include IDE definition[52], a concern not typically associated with compiler construction. Compilers also typically generate machine code, whereas DSLs typically transform to source code in a general-purpose language. Finally, a big part of building compilers is the implementation of optimizations (in the code generator or interpreter), a topic that is not as prominent in the context of DSLs. I recommend reading the "Dragon Book"[53] or Appel's Modern Compiler Construction[54].

[52] There are universities who teach compiler construction based on language workbenches and DSLs.

[53] A. V. Aho, M. S. Lam, R. Sethi, and J. D. Ullman. *Compilers: Principles, Techniques, and Tools (2nd Edition)*. Addison Wesley, August 2006

[54] A. W. Appel. *Modern Compiler Implementation in Java*. Cambridge University Press, 1998

2.8.3 UML

So what about the Unified Modeling Language – UML? I decided not to cover UML in this book. I focus on mostly textual DSLs and related topics. UML does show up peripherally in a couple of places, but if you are interested in UML-based MDSD, then this book is not for you. For completeness, let us briefly put UML into the context of DSLs.

UML is a general-purpose modeling language. Like Java or Ruby, it is not specific to any domain (unless you consider software development in general to be a domain, which renders the whole DSL discussion pointless), so UML itself does not count as a DSL[55]. To change this, UML provides profiles, which are a (limited and cumbersome) way to define variants of UML language concepts and to effectively add new ones. It depends on the tool you choose how well this actually works and how far you can adapt the UML syntax and the modeling tool as part of profile definition. In practice, most people use only a very small part of UML, with the majority of concepts defined via profiles. It is my experience that because of that, it is much more productive, and often less work, to build DSLs with "real" language engineering environments, as opposed to using UML profiles.

So is UML used in MDSD? Sure. People build profiles and use UML-based DSLs, especially in large organizations where the (perceived) need for standardization is para- mount[56].

2.8.4 Graphical versus Textual

This is something of a religious war, akin to the statically-typed versus dynamically-typed languages debate. Of course, there is a use for both flavors of notation, and in many cases, a mix is the best approach. In a number of cases, the distinction is even hard to make: tables or mathematical and chemical notations are both textual and graphical in nature[57].

However, this book does have a bias towards textual notations, for several reasons. I feel that the textual format is more generally useful, that it scales better and that the necessary tools take (far) less effort to build. In the vast majority of cases, starting with textual languages is a good idea – graphical visualizations or editors can be built on top of the meta model later, if a real need has been established. If you want to learn more about graphical DSLs, I suggest you read Kelly and Tolvanen's book *Domain Specific Modeling* [58].

When I wrote my "old" book on MDSD, UML played an important role. At the time, I really did use UML a lot for projects involving models and code generation. Over the years, the importance of UML has diminished significantly (in spite of the OMG's efforts to popularize both UML and MDA), mainly because of the advent of modern language workbenches.

[55] UML can be seen as an integrated *collection* of DSLs that describe various aspects of software systems: class structure, state based behavior, or deployment. However, these DSLs still address the overall domain of *software*.

[56] It is interesting to see that even these sectors increasingly embrace DSLs. I know of several projects in the aerospace/defense sector where UML-based modeling approaches were replaced with very specific and much more productive DSLs. It is also interesting to see how sectors define their own standard languages. While I hesitate to call it a DSL, the automotive industry is in the process of standardizing on AUTOSAR and its modeling languages.

[57] The ideal tool will allow you to use and mix all of them, and we will see in the book how close existing tools come to this ideal.

[58] S. Kelly and J.-P. Tolvanen. *Domain-Specific Modeling: Enabling Full Code Generation*. Wiley-IEEE Computer Society Press, March 2008

Part II

DSL Design

This part of the book has been written together with Eelco Visser of TU Delft. You can reach him at `e.visser@tudelft.nl`.

Throughout this part of the book we refer back to the five case studies introduced in Part I of the book (Section 1.11). We use a the following labels:

Component Architecture: This refers to the component architecture case study described in Section 1.11.1. ◂

Refrigerators: This refers to the refrigerator configuration case study described in Section 1.11.2. ◂

mbeddr C: This refers to the mbeddr.com extensible C case study described in Section 1.11.3. ◂

Pension Plans: This refers to the pension plans case study described in Section 1.11.4. ◂

WebDSL: This refers to the WebDSL case study described in Section 1.11.5. ◂

Note that in this part of the book the examples will only be used to illustrate DSL *design* and the driving design decisions. Part III of the book will then discuss the implementation aspects.

Some aspects of DSL design have been formalized with mathematical formulae. These are intended as an additional means of explaining some of the concepts. Formulae are able to state properties of programs and languages in an unambiguous way. However, I want to emphasize that reading or understanding the formulae is *not* essential for understanding the language design discussion. So if you're not into mathematical formulae, just ignore them.

This part consists of three chapters. In Chapter 3 we introduce important terms and concepts including *domain*, model *purpose* and the structure of programs and languages. In Chapter 4 we discuss a set of seven dimensions that guide the design of DSLs: expressivity, coverage, semantics, separation of concerns, completeness, language modularization and syntax. Finally, in Chapter 5 we look at well-known structural and behavioral paradigms (such as inheritance or state based behaviour) and discuss their applicability to DSLs.

3
Conceptual Foundations

This chapter provides the conceptual foundations for the discussion of the design dimensions. It consists of three sections. The first one, Program, Languages and Domain *defines some of the terminology around DSL design we will use in the rest of this chapter. The second section briefly address the* Purpose *of programs as a way of guiding their design. And the third section briefly introduces parser-based and projectional editing, since some design considerations depend on this rather fundamental difference in DSL implementation.*

3.1 *Programs, Languages and Domains*

Domain-specific languages live in the realm of *programs*, *languages* and *domains*. So we should start by explaining what these things are. We will then use these concepts throughout this part of the book.

As part of this book's treatment of DSLs, we are primarily interested in *computation*, i.e. we are aimed at creating executable software[1]. So let's first consider the relation between programs and languages. Let's define P to be the set of all conceivable programs. A *program p* in P is the *conceptual* representation of some *computation* that runs on a universal computer (Turing machine). A *language l* defines a structure and notation for *expressing* or *encoding* programs from P. Thus, a program p in P may have an expression in L, which we will denote as p_l.

There can be several languages l_1 and l_2 that express the *same* conceptual program p in different way p_{l_1} and p_{l_2} (**fac-**

[1] This is opposed to just communicating among humans or describing complete systems.

torial can be expressed in Java and Lisp, for example). There may even be multiple ways to express the same program in a single language l (in Java, **factorial** can be expressed via recursion or with a loop). A transformation T between languages l_1 and l_2 maps programs from their l_1 encoding to their l_2 encoding, i.e. $T(p_{l_1}) = p_{l_2}$.

It may not be possible to encode all programs from P in a given language l. We denote as P_l the subset of P that can be expressed in l. More importantly, some languages may be *better* at expressing certain programs from P: the program may be shorter, more readable or more analyzable.

> **Pension Plans:** The pension plan language is very good at representing pension calculations, but cannot practically be used to express other software. For example, user defined data structures and loops are not supported. ◂

Notice that this transformation only changes the language used to express the program. The conceptual program does not change. In other words, the transformation preserves the semantics of p_{l_1}. We will come back to this notion as we discuss semantics in more detail in Section 4.3.

Turing-complete languages can by definition express all of P

■ *Domains* What are domains? We have seen one way of defining domains in the previous paragraph. When we said that a language l covers a subset of P, we can simply call this subset the *domain* covered with l. However, this is not a very useful approach, since it equates the scope of a domain trivially with the scope of a language (the subset of P in that domain P_D is equal to the subset of P we can express with a language l P_l). We cannot ask questions like: "Does the language adequately cover the domain?", since it always does, by definition.

There are two more useful approaches. In the *inductive* or *bottom-up* approach we define a domain in terms of existing software used to address a particular class of problems or products. That is, a domain D is identified as a set of programs with common characteristics or similar purpose. Notice how at this point we do *not* imply a special language to express them. They could be expressed in any Turing-complete language. Often such domains do not exist outside the realm of software.

An especially interesting case of the inductive approach is where we define a domain as a subset of programs written in a specific language P_l instead of the more general set P. In this case we can often clearly identify the commonalities among the programs in the domain, in the form of their consistent use of a set of domain-specific patterns or idioms[2]. This makes building a DSL for D relatively simple, because we know exactly what the DSL has to cover, and we know what code to generate from DSL programs.

[2] Some people have argued for a long time that the need to use idioms or patterns in a language is a smell, and should be understood as hints at missing language features: c2.com/cgi/wiki?AreDesignPatternsMissingLanguageFeatures

mbeddr C: The domain of this DSL has been defined bottom-up. Based on idioms commonly employed when using C for embedded software development, linguistic abstractions have been defined that provide a "shorthand" for those idioms. These linguistic abstractions form the basis of the language extensions. ◄

The above examples can be considered relatively general – the domain of embedded software development is relatively broad. In contrast, a domain may also be very specific, as is illustrated by the refridgerator case study.

Refrigerators: The cooling DSL is tailored specifically towards expressing refrigerator cooling programs for a very specific organization. No claim is made for broad applicability of the DSL. However, it perfectly fits into the way cooling algorithms are described and implemented in that particular organization. ◄

The second approach for defining a domain is *deductive* or *top-down*. In this approach, a domain is considered a body of knowledge about the real world, i.e. outside the realm of software. From this perspective, a domain D is a body of knowledge for which we want to provide some form of software support. P_D is the subset of programs in P that implement interesting computations in D. This case is much harder to address using DSLs, because we first have to understand precisely the nature of the domain and identify the interesting programs in that domain.

Pension Plans: The pensions domain has been defined in this way. The customer had been working in the field of old-age pensions for decades and had a detailed understanding of that domain. That knowledge was mainly contained in the heads of pension experts, in pension plan requirements documents, and, to a limited extent, encoded in the source of existing software. ◄

In the context of DSLs, we can ultimately consider a domain D by a set of programs P_D, whether we take the deductive or inductive route. There can be multiple languages in which we can express P_D programs. Possibly, P_D can only be partially expressed in a language l (Figure 3.1).

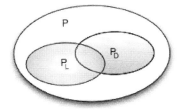

Figure 3.1: The programs relevant to a domain P_D and the programs expressible with a language P_L are both subsets of the set of all programs P. A good DSL has a large overlap with its target domain ($P_L \approx P_D$).

■ *Domain-Specific Languages* We can now understand the notion of a domain-specific language. A *domain-specific language*

l_D for a domain D is a language that is *specialized* for encoding programs from P_D. That is, l_D is more efficient[3] in representing P_D programs than other languages, and thus, is particularly well suited for P_D. It achieves this by using *abstractions* suitable to the domain, and avoiding details that are irrelevant to programs in D (typically because they are similar in all programs and can be added automatically by the execution engine).

It is of course possible to express programs in P_D with a general-purpose language. But this is less efficient – we may have to write much more code, because a GPL is not specialized to that particular domain. Depending on the expressivity of a DSL, we may also be able to use it to describe programs outside of the D domain[4]. However, this is often not efficient at all, because, by specializing a DSL for D, we also restrict its efficiency for expressing programs outside of D. This is not a problem as long as we have scoped D correctly. If the DSL actually just covers a subset of P_D, and we have to express programs in D for which the DSL is *not* efficient, we have a problem.

This leads us to the crucial challenge in DSL design: finding regularity in a non-regular domain and capturing it in a language. Especially in the deductive approach, membership of programs in the domain is determined by a human and is, in some sense, arbitrary. A DSL for the domain hence typically represents an explanation or interpretation of the domain, and often requires trade-offs by under- or over-approximation (Figure 3.2). This is especially true while we develop the DSL: an iterative approach is necessary that evolves the language as our understanding of the domain becomes more and more refined over time. In a DSL l that is adequate for the domain, the sets P_l and P_D are the same.

■ *Domain Hierarchy* In the discussion of DSLs and progressively higher abstraction levels, it is useful to consider domains organized in a hierarchy[5], in which higher domains are a subset (in terms of scope) of the lower domains (Fig. 3.3).

At the bottom we find the most general domain D_0. It is the domain of all possible programs P. Domains D_n, with $n > 0$, represent progressively more specialized domains, where the set of interesting programs is a subset of those in D_{n-1} (abbreviated as D_{-1}). We call D_{+1} a subdomain of D. For example, $D_{1.1}$ could be the domain of embedded software, and

[3] There are several ways of measuring efficiency. The most obvious one is the amount of code a developer has to write to express a problem in the domain: the more concise, the more efficient. We will discuss this in more detail in Section 4.1.

[4] For example, you *can* write any program with some dialects of SQL.

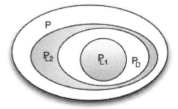

Figure 3.2: Languages L1 and L2 under-approximate and over-approximate domain D.

[5] In reality, domains are not always as neatly hierarchical as we make it seem here. Domains may overlap, for example. Nonetheless, the notion of a hierarchy is very useful for discussing many of the advanced topics in this book. In terms of DSLs, overlap may be addressed by factoring the common aspects into a separate language module that can be used in both the overlapping domains.

$D_{1.2}$ could be the domain of enterprise software. The progressive specialization can be continued ad infinitum, in principle. For example, $D_{2.1.1}$ and $D_{2.1.2}$ are further subdomains of $D_{1.1}$: $D_{2.1.1}$ could be automotive embedded software and $D_{2.1.2}$ could be avionics software[6].

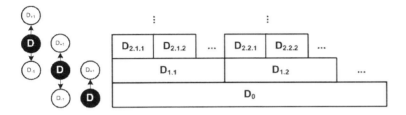

[6] At the top of the hierarchy we find singleton domains that consist of a single program (a non-interesting boundary case).

Figure 3.3: The domain hierarchy. Domains with higher index are called subdomains of domains with a lower index (D_1 is a subdomain of D_0). We use just D to refer to the current domain, and D_{+1} and D_{-1} to refer to the relatively more specific and more general ones.

Languages are typically designed for a particular domain D. Languages for D_0 are called general-purpose languages[7]. Languages for D_n with $n > 0$ become more domain-specific for growing n. Languages for a particular D_n can also be used to express programs in D_{n+1}. However, DSLs for D_{n+1} may add additional abstractions or remove some of the abstractions found in languages for D_n. To get back to the embedded systems domain, a DSL for $D_{1.1}$ could include components, state machines and data types with physical units. A language for $D_{2.1.1}$, automotive software, will retain these extensions, but in addition provide direct support for the AUTOSAR standard and prohibit the use of **void*** to conform to the MISRA-C standard.

[7] We could define D_0 to be those programs expressible with Turing machines, but using GPLs for D_0 is a more useful approach for this book.

> **mbeddr C:** The C base language is defined for D_0. Extensions for tasks, state machines or components can argued to be specific to embedded systems, making those sit in $D_{1.1}$. Progressive specialization is possible; for example, a language for controlling small Lego robots sits on top of state machines and tasks. It could be allocated to $D_{2.1.1}$. ◂

3.2 Model Purpose

We have said earlier that there can be several languages for the same domain. These languages differ regarding the abstractions they make use of. Deciding which abstractions should go into a particular language for D is not always obvious. The basis for the decision is to consider the *model purpose*. Models[8], and hence the languages to express them, are intended for a specific purpose. Examples of model purpose include automatic derivation of a D_{-1} program, formal analysis and model checking, platform-independent specification of functionality or generation of documentation[9]. The same domain concepts can often be abstracted in different ways, for different purposes. When defining a DSL, we have to identify the different purposes required, and then decide whether we can create one DSL that fits all purposes, or create a DSL for each purpose[10].

mbeddr C: The model purpose is the generation of an efficient low-level C implementation of the system, while at the same time providing software developers with meaningful abstractions. Since *efficient* C code has to be generated, certain abstractions, such as dynamically growing lists or runtime polymorphic dispatch, are not supported even though they would be convenient for the user. The state machines in the `statemachines` language have an additional model purpose: model checking, i.e. proving certain properties about the state machines (e.g., proving that a certain state is definitely going to be reached after some event occurs). To make this possible, the action code used in the state machines is limited: it is not possible, for example, to read and write the same variable in the same action. ◀

Refrigerators: The model purpose is the generation of efficient implementation code for various different target platforms (different types of refrigerators use different electronics). A secondary purpose is enabling domain experts to express the algorithms and experiment with them using simulations and tests. The DSL is not expected to be used to visualize the actual refrigerator device for sales or marketing purposes. ◀

Pension Plans: The model purpose of the pension DSL is to enable insurance mathematicians and pension plan developers (who are not programmers) to define complete pension plans, and to allow them to check their own work for correctness using various forms of tests. A secondary purpose is the generation of the complete calculation engine for the computing center and the website. ◀

[8] As we discuss below, we use the terms *program* and *model* as synonyms.

[9] Generation of documentation is typically not the main or sole model purpose, but may be an important secondary one. In general, we consider models that only serve communication among humans to be outside the scope of this book, because they don't have to be formally defined to achieve their purpose.

[10] Defining several DSLs for a single domain is especially useful if different stakeholders want to express different aspects of the domain with languages suitable to their particular aspect. We discuss this in the section on Viewpoints (Section 4.4)

The purpose of a DSL may also change over time. Consequently, this may require changes to the abstractions or notations used in the language. From a technical perspective, this is just like any other case of language evolution (discussed in Chapter 6).

3.3 The Structure of Programs and Languages

The discussion above is relatively theoretical, trying to capture somewhat precisely the inherently imprecise notion of domains. Let us now move into the field of language engineering. Here we can describe the relevant concepts in a much more practical way.

■ *Concrete and Abstract Syntax*   Programs can be represented in their abstract syntax and the concrete syntax forms. The *concrete syntax* is the notation with which the user interacts as he edits a program. It may be textual, symbolic, tabular, graphical or any combination thereof. The *abstract syntax* is a data structure that represents the semantically relevant data expressed by a program (Fig. 3.4 shows an example of both). It does not contain notational details such as keywords, symbols, white space or positions, sizes and coloring in graphical notations. The abstract syntax is used for analysis and downstream processing of programs. A language definition includes the concrete and the abstract syntax, as well as rules for mapping one to the other. *Parser-based* systems map the concrete syntax to the abstract syntax. Users interact with a stream of characters, and a parser derives the abstract syntax by using a grammar and mapping rules. *Projectional* editors go the other way round: user interactions, although performed through the concrete syntax, *directly* change the abstract syntax. The concrete syntax is a mere projection (that looks and feels like text when a textual projection is used). No parsing takes place. Spoofax and Xtext are parser-based tools, MPS is projectional.

While concrete syntax modularization and composition can be a challenge and requires a discussion of textual concrete syntax details, we will illustrate most language design concerns based on the abstract syntax. The abstract syntax of programs are primarily trees of program *elements*. Each element is an instance of a *language concept*, or *concept* for short. A language is essentially a set of concepts (we'll come back to this below). Every element (except the root) is contained by exactly one parent

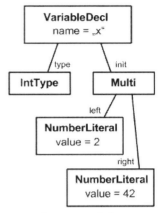

Figure 3.4: Concrete and abstract syntax for a textual variable declaration. Notice how the abstract syntax does not contain the keyword **var** or the symbols : and ;.

The abstract syntax is very similar to a meta model in that it represents only a data structure and ignores notation. The two are also different: the abstract syntax is usually automatically derived from a grammar, whereas a meta model is typically defined *first*, independent of a notation. This means that, while the abstract syntax may be structurally affected by the grammar, the meta model is "clean" and represents purely the structure of the domain. In practice, the latter isn't strictly true either, since editing and tool considerations typically influence a meta model as well. In this book, we consider the two to be synonyms.

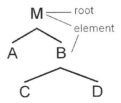

Figure 3.5: A program is a tree of program elements, with a single root element.

element. Syntactic nesting of the concrete syntax corresponds to a parent-child relationship in the abstract syntax. There may also be any number of non-containing cross-references between elements, established either directly during editing (in projectional systems) or by a name resolution (or *linking*) phase that follows parsing and tree construction.

■ *Fragments* A program may be composed from several program *fragments*. A fragment is a standalone tree, a partial program. Conversely, a program is a set of fragments connected by references (discussed below). E_f is the set of program elements in a fragment f.

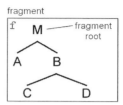

Figure 3.6: A fragment is a program tree that stands for itself and potentially references other fragments.

■ *Languages* A language l consists a set of language concepts C_l and their relationships[11]. We use the term *concept* to refer to all aspects of an element of a language, including concrete syntax, abstract syntax, the associated type system rules and constraints as well as some definition of its semantics. In a fragment, each element e is an instance of a concept c defined in some language l.

[11] In the world of grammars, a concept is essentially a *Nonterminal*. We will discuss the details about grammars in the implementation section of this book

mbeddr C: In C, the statement `int x = 3;` is an instance of the `LocalVariableDeclaration` concept. `int` is an instance of `IntType`, and the `3` is an instance of `NumberLiteral`. ◀

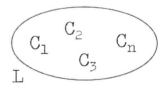

Figure 3.7: A language is a set of concepts.

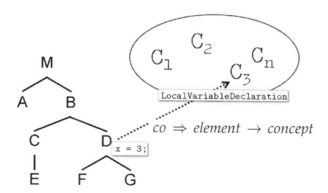

Figure 3.8: The statement `int x = 3;` is an instance of the `LocalVariableDeclaration`. *co* returns the concept for a given element.

■ *Functions* We define the *concept-of* function *co* to return the concept of which a program element is an instance: $co \Rightarrow$ *element* $\rightarrow$ *concept* (see Fig. 3.8). Similarly we define the *language-of* function *lo* to return the language in which a given concept is defined: $lo \Rightarrow concept \rightarrow language$. Finally, we define a *fragment-of* function fo that returns the fragment that contains a given program element: $fo \Rightarrow element \rightarrow fragment$ (Fig. 3.9).

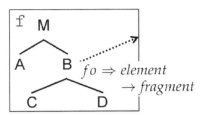

Figure 3.9: fo returns the fragment for a given element.

■ *Relationships* We also define the following sets of relationships between program elements. Cdn_f is the set of parent-child relationships in a fragment f. Each $c \in Cdn$ has the properties *parent* and *child* (see figure Fig. 3.10; Cdn are all the parent-child "lines" in the picture).

mbeddr C: In `int x = 3;` the local variable declaration is the *parent* of the `type` and the `init` expression 3. The concept `Local- VariableDeclaration` defines the containment relationships `type` and `init`, respectively. ◂

$Refs_f$ is the set of non-containing cross-references between program elements in a fragment f. Each reference r in $Refs_f$ has the properties *from* and *to*, which refer to the two ends of the reference relationship (see figure Fig. 3.10).

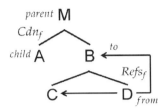

Figure 3.10: fo returns the fragment for a given element.

mbeddr C: For example, in the `x = 10;` assignment, `x` is a reference to a variable of that name, for example, the one declared in the previous example paragraph. The concept `LocalVariableRef` has a non-containing reference relationship `var` that points to the respective variable. ◂

Finally, we define an inheritance relationship that applies the Liskov Substitution Principle (LSP) to language concepts. The LSP states that,

> In a computer program, if S is a subtype of T, then objects of type T may be replaced with objects of type S (i.e., objects of type S may be substitutes for objects of type T) without altering any of the desirable properties of that program (correctness, task performed, etc.)

The LSP is well known in the context of object-oriented programming. In the context of language design it implies that a concept c_{sub} that extends another concept c_{super} can be used in places where an instance of c_{super} is expected. Inh_l is the set of inheritance relationships for a language l. Each $i \in Inh_l$ has the properties *super* and *sub*.

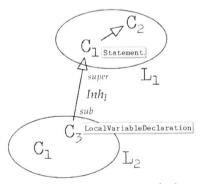

Figure 3.11: Concepts can extend other concepts. The base concept may be defined in a different language.

mbeddr C: The `LocalVariableDeclaration` introduced above extends the concept `Statement`. This way, a local variable declaration can be used wherever a `Statement` is expected, for example, in the body of a function, which is a `StatementList`. ◂

■ *Independence* An important concept is the notion of independence. An *independent language* does not depend on other languages. This means that for all parent/child, reference and inheritance relationships, both ends refer to concepts defined in the same language. Based on our definitions above we can define an independent language l as a language for which the following hold[12]:

$$\forall r \in \mathit{Refs}_l \mid lo(r.to) = lo(r.from) = l \qquad (3.1)$$
$$\forall s \in \mathit{Inh}_l \mid lo(s.super) = lo(s.sub) = l \qquad (3.2)$$
$$\forall c \in \mathit{Cdn}_l \mid lo(c.parent) = lo(c.child) = l \qquad (3.3)$$

[12] Formulae like these are not essential for understanding. You may ignore them if you like.

Independence can also be applied to fragments. An *independent fragment* is one in which all non-containing cross-references Refs_f point to elements within the same fragment:

$$\forall r \in \mathit{Refs}_f \mid fo(r.to) = fo(r.from) = f \qquad (3.4)$$

Notice that an independent language l can be used to construct dependent fragments, as long as the two fragments just contain elements from this single language l. Vice versa, a dependent language can be used to construct independent fragments. In this case we just have to make sure that the non-containing cross references are "empty" in the elements in fragment f.

Refrigerators: The hardware definition language is independent, as are fragments that use this language. In contrast, the cooling algorithm language is dependent. **BuildingBlockRef** declares a reference to the **BuildingBlock** concept defined in the hardware language (Fig. 3.12). Consequently, if a cooling program refers to a hardware setup using an instance of **BuildingBlockRef**, the fragment becomes dependent on the hardware definition fragment that contains the referenced building block. ◀

Hardware:
```
compressor compartment cc {
    static compressor c1
    fan ccfan
}
```

Cooling Algorithm
```
macro kompressorAus {
    set cc.c1->active = false
    perform ccfanabschalttask after 10 {
        set cc.ccfan->active = false
    }
}
```

Figure 3.12: A **BuildingBlockRef** references a hardware element from within a cooling algorithm fragment.

■ *Homogeneity* We distinguish *homogeneous* and *heterogeneous* fragments. A homogeneous fragment is one in which all elements are expressed with the same language (see formula 1.5). This means that for all parent/child relationships (Cdn_f), the elements at both ends of the relationship have to be instances of concepts defined in one language l (1.6):

An independent language can only express homogeneous fragments. However, a homogeneous fragment can be expressed with a dependent language if the dependencies all come via the Refs relationship.

$$\forall e \in E_f \mid lo(co(e)) = l \qquad (3.5)$$
$$\forall c \in \mathit{Cdn}_f \mid lo(co(c.parent)) = lo(co(c.child)) = l \qquad (3.6)$$

mbeddr C: A program written in plain C is homogeneous. All program elements are instances of the C language. Using the state machine language extension allows us to embed state machines in C programs. This makes the respective fragment heterogeneous (see Fig. 3.13). ◂

```
module CounterExample from counterd imports nothing {

  var int8_t theI;
  var boolean theB;
  var boolean hasBeenReset;
  var Counter c1;

  verifiable
  statemachine Counter {
    in events
      start() <no binding>
      step(int[0..10] size) <no binding>
    out events
      someEvent(int[0..100] x, boolean b) => handle_someEvent
      resetted() => resetted
    local variables
      int[0..100] currentVal = 0
      int[0..100] LIMIT = 10
    states ( initial = initialState )
      state initialState {
        on start [ ] -> countState { send someEvent(100, true && false || true); }
      }
      state countState {
        on step [currentVal + size > LIMIT] -> initialState { send resetted(); }
        on step [currentVal + size <= LIMIT] -> countState { currentVal = currentVal + size; }
        on start [ ] -> initialState {  }
      }
  }

  exported test case test1 {
    initsm(c1);
    assert(0) isInState<c1, initialState>;
    test statemachine c1 {
      start -> countState
      step(1) -> countState
      step(2) -> countState
      step(7) -> countState
      step(1) -> initialState
    }
  } test1(test case)
}
```

Figure 3.13: An example of a heterogeneous fragment. This module contains global variables (from the *core* language), a state machine (from the *statemachines* language) and a test case (from the *unittest* language). Note how concepts defined in the *statemachine* language (`trigger`, `isInState` and `test statemachine`) are used inside a `TestCase`.

3.4 Parsing versus Projection

This part of the book is not about implementation techniques. However, the decision of whether to build a DSL using a projectional editor instead of the more traditional parser-based approach can have some consequences for the design of the DSL.

So we have to provide *some* level of detail on the two at this point.

In the parser-based approach, a grammar specifies the sequence of tokens and words that make up a structurally valid program. A parser is generated from this grammar. A parser is a program that recognizes valid programs in their textual form and creates an abstract syntax tree or graph. Analysis tools or generators work with this abstract syntax tree. Users enter programs using the concrete syntax (i.e. character sequences) and programs are also stored in this way. Example tools in this category include Spoofax and Xtext.

Projectional editors (also known as structured editors) work without grammars and parsers. A language is specified by defining the abstract syntax tree, then defining projection rules that render the concrete syntax of the language concepts defined by the abstract syntax. Editing actions *directly* modify the abstract syntax tree. Projection rules then render a textual (or other) representation of the program. Users read and write programs through this projected notation. Programs are stored as abstract syntax trees, usually as XML. As in parser-based systems, backend tools operate on the abstract syntax tree.

Projectional editing is well known from graphical editors; virtually all of them use this approach[13]. However, they can also be used for textual syntax[14]. Example tools in this category include the Intentional Domain Workbench[15] and JetBrains MPS.

In this section, we do not discuss the relative advantages and drawbacks of parser-based versus projectional editors in any detail (although we do discuss the trade-offs in the chapter on language implementation, Section 7). However, we will point out if and when there are different DSL design options depending on which of the two approaches is used.

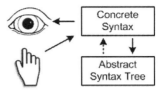

Figure 3.14: In parser-based systems, the user only interacts with the concrete syntax, and the AST is constructed from the information in the text.

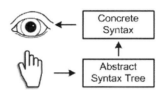

Figure 3.15: In projectional systems, the user sees the concrete syntax, but all editing gestures directly influence the AST. The AST is *not* extracted from the concrete syntax, which means the concrete syntax does not have to be parsable.

[13] You could argue that they are not *purely* projectional because the user can move the shapes around and the position information has to be persistent. Nonetheless, graphical editors are fundamentally projectional.

[14] While in the past projectional text editors have acquired a bad reputation mostly because of bad usability, as of 2011, the tools have become good enough, and computers have become fast enough to make this approach feasible, productive and convenient to use.

[15] www.intentsoft.com

4
Design Dimensions

This chapter has been written in association with Eelco Visser of TU Delft. You can contact him via **e.visser@tudelft.nl**.

> *DSLs are powerful tools for software engineering, because they can be tailor-made for a specific class of problems. However, because of the large degree of freedom in designing DSLs, and because they are supposed to cover the intended domain, consistently, and at the right abstraction level, DSL design is also hard. In this chapter we present a framework for describing and characterizing domain specific languages. We identify seven design dimensions that span the space within which DSLs are designed: expressivity, coverage, semantics, separation of concerns, completeness, language modularization and syntax.*

We illustrate the design alternatives along each of these dimensions with examples from our case studies. The dimensions provide a vocabulary for describing and comparing the design of existing DSLs, and help guide the design of new ones. We also describe drivers, or forces, that lead to using one design alternative over another. This chapter is not a complete methodology. It does not present a recipe that guarantees a great DSL if followed. I don't believe in methodologies, because they pretend precision where there isn't any. Building a DSL is a craft. This means that, while there are certain established approaches and conventions, building a good DSL also requires experience and practice.

4.1 Expressivity

One of the fundamental advantages of DSLs is increased expressivity over more general programming languages. Increased expressivity typically means that programs are shorter, and that the semantics are more readily accessible to processing tools (we will return to this). By making assumptions about the target domain and encapsulating knowledge about the domain in the language and in its execution strategy (and not just in programs), programs expressed using a DSL can be significantly more concise.

> **Refrigerators:** Cooling algorithms expressed with the cooling DSL are approximately five times shorter than the C version that users would have to write instead. ◂

While it is always possible to produce short but incomprehensible programs, in general shorter programs require less effort to read and write than longer programs, and are therefore be more efficient in software engineering. We will thus assume that, all other things being equal, shorter programs are preferable over longer programs.[1] We use the notation $|p_L|$ to indicate the size of program p as encoded in language L.[2] The essence is the assumption that, within one language, more complex programs will require larger encodings. We also assume that p_L is the smallest encoding of p in L, i.e. does not contain dead or convoluted code. We can then qualify the expressivity of a language relative to another language.

> A language L_1 is *more expressive in domain D* than a language L_2 ($L_1 \prec_D L_2$), if for each $p \in P_D \cap P_{L_1} \cap P_{L_2}$, $|p_{L_1}| < |p_{L_2}|$.

A weaker but more realistic version of this statement requires that a language is *mostly* more expressive, but may not be in some obscure special cases: DSLs may optimize for the common case and may require code written in a more general language to cover the corner cases[3].

Compared to GPLs, DSLs (and the programs expressed with them) are more *abstract*: they avoid describing details that are irrelevant to the model purpose. The execution engine then fills in the missing details to make the program executable on a given target platform, based on knowledge about the domain encoded in the execution engine. Good DSLs are also *declarative*: they provide linguistic abstractions for relevant domain

---

[1] The size of a program may not be the only relevant metric to asses the usefulness of a DSL. For example, if the DSL requires only a third of the code to write, but it takes four times as long to write the code per line, then there is no benefit for writing programs. However, often when reading programs, less code is clearly a benefit. So it depends on the ratio between writing and reading code as to whether a DSL's conciseness is important.

[2] We will not concern ourselves with the exact way to measure the size of a program, which can be textual lines of code or nodes in a syntax tree, for example.

[3] We discuss this aspect in the section on completeness (Section 4.5).

concepts that allow processors to "understand" the domain semantics without sophisticated analysis of the code. Linguistic abstraction means that a language contains concepts for the abstractions relevant in the domain. We discuss this in more detail below.

Note that there is a trade-off between expressivity and the scope of the language. We can always invent a language with exactly one symbol Σ that represents exactly one single program. It is extremely expressive! It is trivial to write a code generator for it. However, the language is also useless, because it can only express *one single program*, and we'd have to create a new language if we wanted to express a different program. So in building DSLs we are striving for a language that has maximum expressivity while retaining enough coverage (see next chapter) of the target domain to be useful.

DSLs have the advantage of being more expressive than GPLs in the domain they are built for. But there is also a disadvantage: before being able to write these concise programs, users have to learn the language[4]. This task can be separated into learning the domain itself, and learning the syntax of the language. For people who understand the domain, learning the syntax can be simplified by using good IDEs with code completion and quick fixes, as well as with good, example-based documentation. In many cases, DSL users already understand the domain, or would have to learn the domain even if no DSL were used to express programs in it: learning the domain is independent of the language itself. It is easy to see, however, that, if a domain is supported by well-defined language, this can be a good reference for the domain itself. Learning a domain can be simplified by working with a good DSL[5]. In conclusion, the learning overhead of DSLs is usually not a huge problem in practice.

> **Pension Plans:** The users of the pension DSL are pension experts. Most of them have spent years describing pension plans using prose, tables and (informal) formulas. The DSL provides formal languages to express the same thing in a way that can be processed by tools. ◄

The close alignment between a domain and the DSL can also be exploited during the construction of the DSL. While it is not a good idea to start building a DSL for a domain about which

---

[4] While a GPL also has to be learned, we assume that there is a relatively small number of GPLs and developers already know them. There may be a larger number of DSLs in any given project or organization, and new team members cannot be expected to know them.

[5] This can also be read the other way round: a measure for the quality of a DSL is how long it takes domain experts to learn it.

we don't know much, the process of building the DSL can help deepen the understanding about a domain. The domain has to be scoped, fully explored and systematically structured to be able to build a language.

> **Refrigerators:** Building the cooling DSL has helped the thermodynamicists and software developers to understand the details of the domain, its degrees of freedom and the variability in refrigerator hardware and cooling algorithms in a much more structured and thorough way than before. Also, the architecture of the generated C application that will run on the device became much more well-structured as a consequence of the separation between reusable frameworks, device drivers and generated code. ◄

4.1.1 Expressivity and the Domain Hierarchy

In the section on expressivity above we compare arbitrary languages. An important idea behind domain-specific languages is that progressive specialization of the domain enables progressively more specialized and expressive languages. Programs for domain $D_n \subset D_{n-1}$ expressed in a language $L_{D_{n-1}}$ typically use a set of characteristic idioms and patterns. A language for D_n can provide linguistic abstractions for those idioms or patterns, which makes their expression much more concise and their analysis and translation less complex.

> **mbeddr C:** Embedded C extends the C programming language with concepts for embedded software including state machines, tasks and physical quantities. The state machine construct, for example, has concepts representing states, events, transitions and guards. Much less code is required compared to **switch/case** statements or cross-indexed integer arrays, two typical idioms for state machine implementation in C. ◄

> **WebDSL:** WebDSL entity declarations abstract over the boilerplate code required by the Hibernate[6] framework for annotating Java classes with object-relational mapping annotations. This reduces code size by an order of magnitude [7]. ◄

4.1.2 Linguistic versus In-Language Abstraction

There are two major ways of defining abstractions. Abstractions can be built into the language (in which case they are

[6] www.hibernate.org/

[7] E. Visser. WebDSL: A case study in domain-specific language engineering. In *GTTSE*, pages 291–373, 2007

called *linguistic* abstractions), or they can be expressed by concepts available in the language (*in-language* abstractions). DSLs typically rely heavily on linguistic abstraction, whereas GPLs rely more on in-language abstraction.

■ *Linguistic Abstraction*   A specific domain concept can be modeled with the help of existing abstractions, or one can introduce a *new* abstraction for that concept. If we do the latter, we use *linguistic* abstraction. By making the concepts of D first-class members of a language L_D, i.e. by defining linguistic abstractions for these concepts, they can be uniquely identified in a D program and their structure and semantics is well defined. No semantically relevant[8] idioms or patterns are required to express interesting programs in D. Consider these two examples of loops in a Java-like language:

[8] By "semantically relevant" we mean that the tools needed to achieve the model purpose (analysis, translation) have to treat these cases specially.

```
int[] arr = ...                       int[] arr = ...
for (int i=0; i<arr.size(); i++) {    OrderedList<int> l = ...
    sum += arr[i];                    for (int i=0;  i<arr.size(); i++) {
}                                         l.add( arr[i] );
                                      }
```

The loop in the left-hand example can be parallelized, since the order of summing up the array elements is irrelevant. The right-hand one cannot, since the order of the elements in the **OrderedList** class *is* relevant. A transformation engine that translates and optimizes these programs must perform (sophisticated, and sometimes impossible) program analysis to determine that the left-hand loop example can indeed be parallelized. The following alternative expression of the same behavior uses better linguistic abstractions, because it is clear without analysis that the first loop can be parallelized and the second cannot:

```
for (int i in arr) {        seqfor (int i in arr) {
    sum += i;                   l.add( arr[i] );
}                           }
```

The property of a language L_D of having first-class concepts for abstractions relevant in D is often called *declarativeness*: no sophisticated pattern matching or program flow analysis is necessary to capture the semantics of a program (relative to the purpose) and treat it correspondingly. The decision can simply be based on the language concept used (**for** versus **seqfor**)[9].

[9] Without linguistic abstraction, the processor has to analyze the program to "reverse engineer" the semantics to be able to act on it. With linguistic abstraction, we rely on the language user to use the correct abstraction. We assume that the user is able to do this! The trade-off makes sense in DSLs because we assume that DSL users are familiar with the domain, and we often don't have the budget or experience to build the sophisticated program analyses that could do the semantic reverse engineering.

mbeddr C: State machines are represented with first class concepts. This enables code generation, as well as meaningful validation. For example, it is easy to detect states that are not reached by any transition and report this as an error. Detecting this same problem in a low-level C implementation requires sophisticated analysis on the switch-case statements or indexed arrays that constitute the implementation of the state machine[10]. ◄

mbeddr C: Another good example is optional ports in components. Components (see Fig. 20.6) define required ports that specify the interfaces they *use*. For each component instance, each required port is connected to a provided port of another instance (that has a compatible interface). Required ports may be optional[11], so for a given instance, an optional port may be connected or not. Invoking an operation on an unconnected required port would result in an error, so this has to be prevented. This can be done by enclosing the invocation on a required port in an `if` statement, checking whether the port is connected. However, an `if` statement can contain any arbitrary Boolean expression as its condition (e.g., `if (isConnected(rp) || somethingRandom()) { port.doSomething(); }`). So checking *statically* that the invocation only happens if the port is connected is impossible. A better solution based on linguistic abstraction is to introduce a new language concept that checks for a connected port directly: `with port (rp) { rp.doSomething(); }`. The `with port` statement doesn't use an expression as its argument, but only a reference to an optional required port (Fig. 4.2). In this way the IDE can check that an invocation on a required optional port `rp` is only done inside of a `with port` statement referencing that same port. ◄

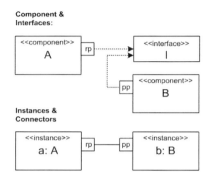

[10] This approach assumes that the generator works correctly – we'll discuss this problem in Section 4.3 on semantics.

Figure 4.1: Example component diagram. The top half defines components, their ports and the relationship of these ports to interfaces. The bottom half shows instances whose ports are connected by a connector.

[11] The terminology may be a little confusing here: *required* means that the component invokes operations on the port (as opposed to providing them for other to invoke); *optional* refers to the fact that, for any given *instance* of that component, the port may be connected or not.

```
exported component EcRobot_Compass_Impl extends nothing {

    provides EcRobot_Compass compass
    requires optional EcRobot_Display display
    requires EcRobot_Util util

    int16_t compass_heading() <- op compass.heading {
      int16_t sum = 0;
      for (int8_t i; in [0..9]) {
        sum += ecrobot_get_compass_sensor(compassPort);
        util.wait(5);
      } for
      Error: access to an optional port has to happen inside a 'with port' statement for that port
        display.showIntAt(res, 3, 0, 0);
      with port (display) { display.showIntAt(res, 3, 0, 0); }
      return res;
    }
}
```

Figure 4.2: The `with port` statement is required to surround an invocation on an optional required port; otherwise, an error is reported in the IDE. If the port is not connected for any given instance, the code inside the `with port` is not executed. It acts like an `if` statement, but since it cannot contain an expression as its condition, the correct use of the `with port` statement can be statically checked.

Linguistic abstraction also means that no details irrelevant to the model purpose are expressed. Once again, this increases conciseness, and avoids the undesired specification of unintended semantics (over-specification). Overspecification is usually bad because it limits the degrees of freedom available to a transformation engine. In the example with the parallelizable loops, the first loop is over-specified: it expresses ordering of the operations, although this is (most probably) not intended by the person who wrote the code.

> **mbeddr C:** State machines can be implemented as switch/case blocks or as arrays indexing into each other. The DSL program does not specify which implementation should be used and the transformation engine is free to chose the more appropriate representation, for example based on desired program size or performance characteristics. Also, `log` statements and `task` declarations can be translated in different ways depending on the target platform. ◄

■ *In-Language Abstraction*   Conciseness can also be achieved by a language that provides facilities to allow users to define new (non-linguistic) abstractions in programs. Well-known GPL concepts for building new abstractions include procedures, classes, or functions and higher-order functions, generics, traits and monads. It is *not* a sign of a bad DSL if it has in-language abstraction mechanisms as long as the abstractions created don't require special treatment by analysis or processing tools – at which point they should be refactored into linguistic abstractions. An example of such special treatment would be if the compiler of the above example language knew that the `OrderedList` library class is actually ordered, and that, consequently, the respective loop cannot be parallelized. Another example of special treatment can be constructed in the context of the optional port example. If we had solved the problem by having a library function `isConnected(port)`, we could enforce a call on an optional port to be surrounded by an `if (isConnected(port))` *without any other expression* in the condition. In this case, the static analyzer would have to treat `isConnected` specially[12]. In-language abstraction can, as the name suggests, provide *abstraction*, but it cannot provide *declarativeness*: a model processor has to "understand" what the user wanted to express by building the in-language abstraction, in order to be able to act on it.

It is worth understanding these to some extent, so that you can make an informed decision which of these – if any – are useful in a DSL.

[12] Treating program elements specially is dangerous because the semantics of `isConnected` or `OrderedList` could be changed by a library developer without changing the static analyzer of code generator in a consistent way.

Refrigerators: The language does not support the construction of new abstractions since its user community consists of non-programmers who are not familiar with defining abstractions. As a consequence, the language had to be modified several times during development, as new requirements came from the end users which had to be integrated directly into the language. ◂

mbeddr C: Since C is extended, C's abstraction mechanisms (functions, **struct**s, **enum**s) are available. Moreover, we added new mechanisms for building abstractions, including interfaces and components. ◂

WebDSL: WebDSL provides *template definitions* to capture partial web pages, including rendering of data from the database and form request handling. User defined templates can be used to build complex user interfaces. ◂

■ *Standard Library*   If a language provides support for in-lang- uage abstraction, these facilities can be used by the *language developer* to provide collections of domain specific abstractions to language users. Instead of adding language features, a standard library is deployed along with the language to all its users. It contains abstractions relevant to the domain, expressed as in-language abstractions. This approach keeps the language itself small, and allows subsequent extensions of the library without changing the language definition and processing tools.

This approach is of course well known from programming languages. All of them come with a standard library, and the language can hardly be used without relying on it. It is effectively a part of the language

Refrigerators: Hardware building blocks have properties. For example, a **fan** can be turned **on** or **off**, and a **compressor** has a speed (**rpm**). The set of properties available for the various building blocks is defined via a standard library and is not part of the language (see code below). The reason why this is *not* a contradiction to what we discussed earlier is this: as a consequence of the structure of the framework used on the target platform, new properties can be added to hardware elements *without* the need to change the generator. They are not treated specially! ◂

```
lib stdlib {
  command compartment::coolOn
  command compartment::coolOff
  property compartment::totalRuntime: int readonly
  property compartment::needsCooling: bool readonly
  property compartment::couldUseCooling: bool readonly
  property compartment::targetTemp: int readonly
  property compartment::currentTemp: int readonly
```

```
    property compartment::isCooling: bool readonly
}
```

Some languages treat certain abstractions defined in the standard library specially. For example, Java's **WeakReference** has special semantics for garbage collection. While an argument can be made that special treatment is acceptable for a standard library (after all, it can be considered an essential companion to the language itself), it is still risky and dangerous. Considering that, in the case of DSLs, we can change the language relatively easily, I would suggest avoiding special treatment even in a standard library and recommend providing linguistic abstractions for these cases.

■ *Comparing Linguistic and In-Language Abstraction*   A language that contains linguistic abstractions for all relevant domain concepts is simple to process; the transformation rules can be tied to the identities of the language concepts. It also makes the language suitable for domain experts, because relevant domain concepts have a direct representation in the language. Code completion can provide specific and meaningful support for "exploring" how a program should be written. However, using linguistic abstractions extensively requires that the relevant abstractions be known in advance, or frequent evolution of the language is necessary. It can also lead to languages that feel large, bloated or inelegant. In-language abstraction is more flexible, because users can build just those abstractions they actually need. However, this requires that users are actually trained to build their own abstractions. This is often true for programmers, but it is typically not true for domain experts.

Using a standard library may be a good compromise, in which one set of users develops the abstractions to be used by another set of developers. This is especially useful if the same language is to be used for several, related, projects or user groups. Each can build their own set of abstractions in the library.

Note that languages that provide good support for in-language abstraction feel different from those that use a lot of linguistic abstraction (compare Scala or Lisp to Cobol or ABAP). Make sure that you don't mix the two styles unnecessarily: the resulting language may be judged as being ugly, especially by programmers.

Modular language extension, as discussed later in Section 4.6.2, provides a middle ground between the two approaches. A language can be flexibly extended, while retaining the advantages of linguistic abstraction.

4.1.3 Language Evolution Support

If a language uses a lot of linguistic abstraction, it is likely, especially during the development of the language, that these abstractions will change. Changing language constructs may break existing models, so special care has to be taken regarding language evolution. This requires any or all of the following: a strict configuration management discipline, versioning information in the models to trigger compatible editors and model processors, keeping track of the language changes as a sequence of change operations that can be "replayed" on existing models, or model migration tools to transform models based on the old language into the new language.

Whether model migration is a challenge or not depends on the tooling. There are tools that make model evolution very smooth, but many environments don't. Consider this when deciding on the tooling you want to use!

It is always a good idea to minimize those changes to a DSL that break existing models[13]. Backward compatibility and deprecation are techniques well worth keeping in mind when working with DSLs. For example, instead of just changing an existing concept in an incompatible way, you may add a new concept in addition to the old one, along with deprecation of the old one and a migration script or wizard. Note that you might be able to instrument your model processor to collect statistics on whether deprecated language features continue to be used. Once no more instances show up in models, you can safely remove the deprecated language feature.

If the DSL is used by a closed, known user community that is accessible to the DSL designers, it will be much easier to evolve the language over time, because users can be reached, making them migrate to newer versions[14]. Alternatively, the set of all models can be migrated to a newer version using a script provided by the language developers. In cases where the set of users, and the DSL programs, are not easily accessible, much more effort must be put into maintaining backward compatibility, and the need for coordinated evolution should be kept minimal[15].

4.1.4 Precision versus Algorithm

We discussed earlier the fact that some DSLs may be Turing complete (and feel more like a programming language), whereas others are purely declarative and maybe just describe facts,

---

In parser-based languages, you can always at the very least open the file in a text editor and run some kind of global search/replace to migrate the program. In a projectional editor, special care has to be taken to enable the same functionality.

[13] This is especially true if you don't have access to all programs to migrate them in one fell swoop: you have to deploy migration scripts with the language, or rely on the users to perform the migration manually.

[14] The instrumentation mentioned above may even report uses of deprecated language features after the official expiration date.

[15] This is the reason why many GPLs can never get rid of deprecated language features.

structures and relationships in a domain. The former may not be usable by domain users (i.e. non-programmers). They are often able to formally and precisely specify facts, structures and relationships about their domain, but they are often not able to define algorithmic behavior.

In this case, a DSL has to be defined that abstracts far enough to hide these algorithmic details. Alternatively, you can create an incomplete language (Section 4.5) and have developers fill in the algorithmic details in GPL code. One way to do this is to provide a set of predefined behaviors (in some kind of library) which are then just parametrized or configured by the users.

> **Pension Plans:** Pension rules are at the boundary between being declarative and algorithmic. The majority of the models define data structures (customers, pension plans, payment schedules). However, there are also mathematical equations and calculation rules. These are algorithmic, but in the pension domain, the domain users are well able to deal with these. ◄

4.1.5 Configuration Languages

Configuration languages are purely declarative. They consist of a well-defined set of configuration parameters and constraints among them. "Writing programs" boils down to setting values for these parameters. In many cases, the parameters are Booleans, in which case a program is basically a selection of a subset of the configuration switches. Feature models constitute a well-known configuration language. We discuss configuration languages in more detail in the chapter on DSLs and Product Line Engineering (Section 21).

4.1.6 Platform Influence

In theory, the design of the abstractions used in a language should be independent of the execution engine and the platform. However, this is not always the case[16]. There are two reasons why the platform may influence the language.

■ *Runtime Efficiency*   In most systems, the resulting system has to execute in a reasonably efficient way. Efficiency can mean performance, scalability, as well as resource consumption (memory, disk space, network bandwidth). Depending on the semantic gap between the platform and the language, building efficient code generators can be a lot of work (we discuss this in

[16] It is obviously not the case for architecture DSLs where you build a language that resembles the architectural abstractions in a platform. But that's not what we're talking about here.

some detail in the section on semantics (Section 4.3)). Instead of building the necessary optimizers, you can also change the language to use abstractions that make global optimizations simpler to build. [17]

[17] While this may be considered "cheating", it may be the only practical way given project constraints.

mbeddr C: The language does not support dynamically growing lists, because it is hard to implement them in an efficient way considering we are targeting embedded software. Dynamic allocation of memory is often not allowed, and even if it were, the necessary copying of existing list data into a new, bigger buffer is too expensive for practical use. The incurred overhead is also *not* obvious to the language user (he just increases list size or adds another element that triggers list growth), making it all the more dangerous. ◀

mbeddr C: Another example includes floating point arithmetic. If the target platform has no floating point unit (FPU), floating point arithmetic is expensive to emulate. We had to build the language in a way that could prevent the use of **float** and **double** types if the target platform had no FPU. ◀

■ *Platform Limitations*   The platform may have limitations regarding the size of data structures, the memory or disk space, or the bandwidth of the network, that limit or otherwise influence language design.

Refrigerators: In the cooling language we had to introduce time units (seconds, minutes, hours) into the DSL after we'd noticed that the time periods relevant for cooling algorithms were so diverse that no single unit could fit all necessary values into the available integer types. If we had used only seconds, the days or months periods would not fit into the available **int**s. Using only hours or days obviously would not let us express the short periods without using fractions of floating point data types. So the language now has the ability to express periods, as in **3s** or **30d**. ◀

4.2 Coverage

A language L always defines a domain D such that $P_D = P_L$. Let's call this domain D_L, i.e. the domain determined by L.

Note that we can achieve full coverage by making L too general. Such a language, may, however, be less expressive, resulting in bigger (unnecessarily big) programs. Indeed this is the reason for designing DSLs in the first place: general purpose languages are too general.

This does not work the other way around: given a (deductively defined) domain D, there is not necessarily a language that *fully covers* that domain unless we revert to a universal language at a D_0 (cf. the hierarchical structure of domains and languages).

> A language L *fully covers* domain D if for each program p relevant to the domain P_D a program p_L can be written in L. In other words, $P_D \subseteq P_L$.

Full coverage is a Boolean predicate: a language either fully covers a domain or it does not. In practice, many languages do not fully cover their respective domain. We would like to indicate the *coverage ratio*. The domain coverage ratio of a language L is the portion of programs in a domain D that it can express. We define $C_D(L)$, *the coverage of domain D by language L*, as:

$$C_D(L) = \frac{number\ of\ P_D\ programs\ expressable\ by\ L}{number\ of\ programs\ in\ domain\ D}$$

At first glance, an ideal DSL will cover all of its domain ($C_D(L)$ is 100%). It requires, however, that the domain is well-defined and we can actually know what full coverage is. Also, over time, it is likely that the domain will evolve and grow, and the language has to be continuously evolved to retain full coverage.

In addition to the evolution-related reason given above, there are two reasons for a DSL *not* to cover all of its *own* domain D. First, the language may be deficient and need to be redesigned. This is especially likely for new and immature DSLs. Scoping the domain for which to build a DSL is an important part of DSL design.

Second, the language may have been defined expressly to cover only a subset of D, typically the subset that is most commonly used. Covering all of D may lead to a language that is too big or complicated for the intended user community because of its support for rarely used corner cases of the domain[18]. In this case, the remaining parts of D may have to be expressed with code written in D_{-1} (see also Section 4.5). This requires coordination between DSL users and D_{-1} users, if this not the same group of people.

WebDSL: WebDSL defines web pages through "page definitions" which have formal parameters. `navigate` statements generate links to such pages. Because of this stylized idiom, the WebDSL compiler can check that internal

---

As the domain evolves, language evolution has to keep pace, requiring responsive DSL developers. This is an important process aspect to keep in mind!

[18] Incremental language extension provides a third option: you can put the common parts into the base language and the support for the corner cases into optionally included language modules.

links are to existing page definitions, with arguments of the right type. The price that the developer pays is that the language does not support free-form URL construction. Thus, the language cannot express all types of URL conventions and does not have full coverage of the domain of web applications. ◂

Refrigerators: After trying to write a couple of algorithms, we had to add a `perform ...after t` statement to run a set of statements after a specified time **t** has elapsed. In the initial language, this had to be done manually with events and timers. Over time we noticed that this is a very typical case, so we added first-class support. ◂

mbeddr C: Coverage of this set of languages is full, although any particular extension to C may only cover a part of the respective domain. However, even if no suitable linguistic abstraction is available for some domain concept, it can be implemented in the D_0 language C, while retaining complete syntactic and semantic integration. Also, additional linguistic abstractions can be easily added because of the extensible nature of the overall approach. ◂

4.3 Semantics and Execution

Semantics can be partitioned into static semantics and execution semantics. Static semantics are implemented by the constraints and type system rules. Execution semantics denote the observable behavior of a program p as it is executed. We look at both aspects in this section; but we refer to execution semantics if we don't explicitly say otherwise.

Using a function OB that defines this observable behavior, we can define the semantics of a program p_{L_D} by mapping it to a program q in a language for D_{-1} that has the same observable behavior:

$$semantics(p_{L_D}) := q_{L_{D-1}} \quad \text{where } OB(p_{L_D}) == OB(q_{L_{D-1}})$$

Equality of the two observable behaviors can be established with a sufficient number of tests, or with model checking and proof (which takes a lot of effort and is hence rarely done). This definition of semantics reflects the hierarchy of domains and works both for languages that describe only structure, as well as for those that include behavioral aspects.

There are also a number of approaches for formally defining semantics independent of operational mappings to target languages. However, they don't play an important role in real-world DSL design, so we don't address them in this book.

The technical implementation of the mapping to D_{-1} can be provided in two different ways: a DSL program can literally be transformed into a program in an L_{D-1}, or an interpreter can be written in L_{D-1} or L_{D_0} to execute the program. Before we spend the rest of this section looking at these two options in detail, we first briefly look at static semantics.

4.3.1 Static Semantics/Validation

Before establishing the execution semantics by transforming or interpreting the program, its static semantics has to be validated. Constraints and type systems are used to this end and we describe their implementation in Part III of the book. Here is a short overview.

■ *Constraints*   Constraints are simply Boolean expressions that check some property of a model. For example, one might verify that the names of a set of attributes of some entity are unique. For a model to be statically correct, all constraints have to evaluate to **true**. Constraint checking should only be performed for a model that is structurally/syntactically correct[19].

> **mbeddr C:** One driver in selecting the linguistic abstractions that go into a DSL is the ability to easily implement meaningful constraints. For example, in the state machine extension it is trivial to find states that have no outgoing transitions (dead end, Fig. 4.3). In a functional language, such a constraint could be written in the way shown in the code below. ◀

```
states
  .select(s|!s.isInstanceOf(StopState))
  .select(s|s.transitions.size == 0)
```

When defining languages and transformations, developers often have a set of constraints in their mind that they consider obvious. They assume that no one would ever use the language in a particular way. However, DSL users may be creative and actually use the language in that way, leading the transformation to crash or create non-compilable code. Make sure that all constraints are actually implemented. This can sometimes be hard. Only extensive (automated) testing can prevent these problems from occurring.

In many cases, a multi-stage transformation is used in which a model expressed in L_3 is transformed into a model expressed in L_2, which is then in turn transformed into a program ex-

---

[19] In projectional systems you cannot build structurally/syntactically incorrect programs in the first place. For parser-based systems, the AST, on which the constraint checks are performed, often is not constructed unless the syntactic structure is correct. This automatically leads to constraint checks being performed only on structurally/syntactically correct models.

Sometimes constraints are used instead of grammar rules. For example, instead of using a 1..*n* multiplicity in the grammar, I often use 0..*n* together with a constraint that checks that there is at least one element. The reason for using this approach is that if the grammar mechanism is used, a possible error message comes from the *parser*. That error message may read something like *expecting SUCH_AND_SUCH, found SOMETHING_ELSE*. This is not very useful to the DSL user. If a more tolerant (0..*n*) grammar is used, the constraint error message can be made to express a real domain constraint (e.g., *at least one SUCH_AND_SUCH is required, because ...*).

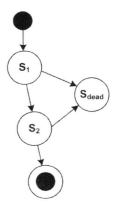

Figure 4.3: An example state machine with a *dead end* state, a state that cannot be left once entered (no outgoing transitions).

pressed in L_1[20]. In this case it is important that *every* valid program in L_3 leads to a valid program in L_2. If the processing of L_2 fails with an error message using abstractions from L_2 (e.g., compiler errors), users of L_3 will not be able to understand them; they may have never seen the programs generated in L_2. Again, automated testing is the way to address this issue.

If many or complex constraints (or type system rules) are executed on a large model, performance may become an issue. Even if the DSL tool is clever about this and only revalidates the constraints for those program elements that changed, it can still be a problem if some kind of whole-model validation is tied to a particular element. To solve this problem, many DSL tools allow users to classify the constraints according to their cost (i.e. performance overhead). Cheap constraints are executed for each changing program element, in real-time, as it changes. Progressively more expensive constraints are checked, for example, as a fragment is saved or only upon explicit request by the user.

[20] Note how this also applies to the classical case in which L_2 is your DSL and L_1 is a GPL which is then compiled.

■ *Type Systems*   Type systems are a special kind of constraint. Consider the example of `var int x = 2 * someFunction( sqrt(2));`. The type system constraint may check that the type of the variable is the same or a supertype of the type of the initialization expression. However, establishing the type of the init expression is non-trivial, since it can be an arbitrarily complex expression. A type system is a formalism or framework for defining the rules to establish the types of arbitrary expressions, as well as type checking constraints. It is a form of constraint checking. We cover the implementation of type systems in Part III of the book (Section 10).

When designing constraints and type systems in a language, a decision has to be made between one of two approaches: (a) declaration of intent and checking for conformance, and (b) deriving characteristics and checking for consistency. Consider the following examples.

mbeddr C: For variables, the type has to be specified explicitly. A type specification expresses the intent that this variable be, for example, of type `int`. Alternatively, a type system could be built to automatically derive the type of the variable declaration based on the type of the `init` expression, an approach known as *type inference*. This would allow the following code: `var x = 2 * someFunction( sqrt(2));`. Since no type is explicitly specified, the type system will infer the type of `x` to be the type calculated for the init expression. ◂

mbeddr C: State machines that are supposed to be verified by the model checker have to be marked as *verified*. In that case, additional constraints kick in that report specific ways of writing actions as invalid, because they cannot be handled by the model checker. An alternative approach could check a state machine for whether these "unverifiable" ways of writing actions are used, and if so, mark the state machine as not verifiable. ◂

Pension Plans: Pension plans can inherit from another plan (called the base plan). If a pension calculation rule overrides a rule in the base plan, then the overriding rule has to be marked as *overrides*. In this way, if the rule in the base plan is removed or renamed, validation of the sub-plan will report an error. An alternative design would simply infer the fact that a rule overrides another one if they have the same name and signature. ◂

Note how in all three cases the constraint checking is done in two steps. First we declare an *intent* (variable is intended to be `int`, this state machine is intended to be verifiable, a rule is intended to override another one). We then *check* whether the program conforms to this intention. The alternative approach would infer the fact from the program (the variable's type is whatever the expression's type evaluates to, state machines are verifiable if the "forbidden" features aren't used, rules override another rule if they have the same name and signature) *without* any explicitly specified intent.

When designing constraints and type systems, a decision has to be made regarding when to use which approach. Here are some trade-offs. The specification/conformance approach requires more code to be written, but results in more meaningful and specific error messages. A message can express that fact that one part of a program does not conform to a specification made by another part of the program[21]. The derivation/consistency approach is less effort to write and can hence be seen to be more convenient, but it requires more effort in constraint checking, and error messages may be harder to understand because of the missing, explicit "hard fact" about the program.

[21] It also reduces the chance that users do something they do not intend by mistake. For example, a user might not *want* to override a method from the base class, but it might happen just because the user uses the same name and parameters.

The specification/conformance approach can also be used to "anchor" the constraint checker, because a fixed fact about the program is explicitly given instead of having to be derived from a (possibly large) part of the program. This decouples models and can increase scalability. Consider the following example. A program contains a function call, and the type checker needs to check the typing for this call. To do so, it has to determine the type of the called function. Assume this function does *not* specify the return type explicitly, instead it is inferred from the returned expressions. These expressions may be calls to other functions, so the process repeats. In the worst case, a whole chain of function calls must be followed in this way to calculate the type of the function initially called by your program. Notice that this requires accessing all the downstream programs, so these all have to be loaded and type checked! In large systems, this can lead to serious performance and scalability issues[22]. If, instead, the type of the called function were given explicitly, no downstream models need to be accessed or loaded.

[22] We have seen such problems in practice with large-scale models.

■ *Multi-Level Constraints* Several sets of constraints can be used to enforce multiple levels of correctness/strictness/compliance for models. The first level typically consists of basic constraints (such as name uniqueness) and typing rules. These are checked for every program. Additional levels are often optional. They are triggered either by a configuration switch or by using the programs for a given purpose. Additional levels always constrain programs *further* relative to more basic levels.

> **mbeddr C:** A nice example of multi-level constraints can be seen in the state machines extension to C. Structural and type system correctness (for C and for state machines) is always checked for every program. However, if a state machine is marked as `verifiable`, then the action code is further restricted via additional constraints. For example, it is not allowed to read and write the same variable during a single state change (i.e. in all of the code in the exit actions of the current state, the transition actions and entry actions of the target state). This is necessary to keep the complexity of the generated model checker input code within limits. ◂

> **mbeddr C:** Another example concerns the use of floating point types. Some target devices may not have floating point units (FPUs), which means that floating point

types (`float`, `double`) cannot be used in programs that should be deployed on such a target device. So, as the user changes the target device in the build configuration, additionawritel constraints are checked that report floating point types as errors if the target has no FPU. ◂

4.3.2   Establishing the Correctness of the Execution Engine

Earlier we defined the meaning of the program p at D_n as the equivalent observable behavior of a program q at D_{n-1}. This essentially *defines* the transformation or interpreter to be correct. However, this is useless in practice. As the language developer, we have a specific behavior in mind, and we want to make sure that the executing DSL program exhibits this behavior. We have to make sure that the execution engine executes the DSL program accordingly.

In classical programming, we write the GPL code based on our understanding of the requirements. We then write unit tests, based on the same understanding, which test that code (Fig. 4.4).

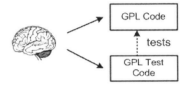

Figure 4.4: Test code tests the application code based on a single understanding of the requirements for the system.

In DSL testing, we write the DSL, the DSL program and the execution engine based on our understanding of the requirements for the system. We can still write unit tests (in the GPL) based on this understanding to check for the correctness of the executing DSL program (Fig. 4.5).

Writing one DSL program and one unit test ensures that this one program executes correctly regarding the test case. Our goal here is, however, to ensure that the transformation is correct *for all programs* we can write with the DSL. This can be achieved by writing many DSL programs and many tests – enough to make sure that every branch of the transformation is covered at least once[23]. As always in testing, we encounter the coverage problem: we have to write enough example programs and tests to cover all aspects of the language and the execution engine. In particular, we have to *first think of the corner cases* to write tests for them[24].

A variant of this approach is to express the test cases in the DSL (after extending the DSL with a way to express tests) and then executing the application code and the test code on the target platform together (Fig. 4.6). This is often more convenient, since the tests can be formulated more concisely on the level of the DSL. As we will see later, this approach is especially useful if we have *several* execution engines: we write the

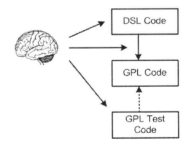

Figure 4.5: Using DSLs, a test written on $D-1$ tests the D program *as well as the transformation* from D to $D-1$.

[23] For the Xpand code generator there is a coverage analysis tool that can be used to make sure that for a given test suite, all branches of the transformation template had been executed at least once.

[24] The coverage problem can be solved in some cases by automatic test case generation and formal verification. We discuss this later in this chapter.

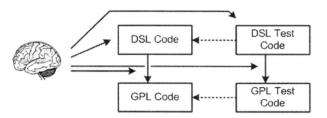

Figure 4.6: Test cases can also be expressed with the DSL and then executed on the target platform together with the application code.

test once and then execute it on all execution engines.

Note that the GPL program may have *additional, unintended* behaviors not prescribed by the DSL. These can often be exploited maliciously and are known as safety or security problems. These will not be found by testing the GPL code based on the requirements, but only by "trying to exploit" the program (known as *penetration testing*).

We will elaborate more on ensuring the correctness of the execution semantics in this chapter, as well as in the Part III chapter on DSL testing (Chapter 14), where we discuss the implementation aspects of DSL and IDE testing.

4.3.3 Transformation

Transformations define the execution semantics of a DSL by mapping it to another language. In the vast majority of cases a transformation for L_D recreates those patterns and idioms in L_{D-1} for which it provides linguistic abstraction. The result may be transformed further, until a level is reached for which a language with an execution infrastructure exists – often D_0. Code generation, the case in which we generate GPL code from a DSL, is thus a special case in which L_{D_0} code is generated.

mbeddr C: The semantics of state machines are defined by their mapping back to C `switch` statements. This is repeated for higher D languages. The semantics of the robot control DSL (Fig. 4.7) is defined by its mapping to state machines and tasks (Fig. 4.8). To explain the semantics to the users, prose documentation is available as well. ◀

Component Architecture: The component architecture DSL describes only structures: interfaces, components and systems. Many constraints about structural integrity are enforced, and a mapping to a distribution middleware is implemented. The formal definition of the semantics are implied by the mapping to the executable code. ◀

```
module impl imports <<imports>> {
  int speed( int val ) {
    return 2 * val;
  }

  robot script stopAndGo
    block main on bump
      accelerate to 2+speed(2) within 3000
      drive on for 2000
      turn left for 200
      decelerate to 0  within 3000
      stop
  }
```

Figure 4.7: The robot control DSL is embedded in C program modules and provides linguistic abstractions for controlling a small Lego car. It can accelerate, decelerate and turn left and right.

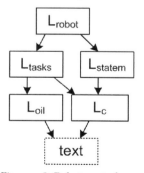

Figure 4.8: Robot control programs are mapped to state machines and tasks. State machines are mapped to C, and tasks are mapped to C as well as to operating system configuration files (the *OIL file*). In the end, everything ends up in text for downstream processing by existing tools.

DSL programs may be mapped to *multiple* languages at the same time. Typically, there is one primary language that is used for execution of the DSL program (C in Fig. 4.9). The other languages may be used to configure the target platform (generated XML files) or provide input for verification tools (NuSMV in Fig. 4.9). In this case, one has to make sure that the semantics of all generated representations is actually the same. We discuss this problem in Section 4.3.7.

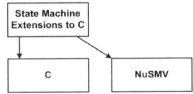

Figure 4.9: From the C state machine extensions, we generate low-level C code (for execution) as well an input file for the NuSMV model checker (for verification).

mbeddr C: The state machines can be transformed to a representation in NuSMV, which is a model checker that can be used to establish properties of state machines by exhaustive search. Examples properties include freedom from deadlocks, assuring liveness and specific safety properties such as "It will never happen that the out events `pedestrian light green` and `car light green` are set at the same time". ◄

■ *Multi-staged Transformation*   There are several reasons why the gap between a language at D and its target platform may not be bridged by a single transformation. Instead, the overall transformation becomes a chain of subsequent transformations, an approach also known as *cascading*.

Multi-staged transformation is a form of modularization, and so the reason for doing it is the same reason we always use for modularization: breaking down a big problem into a set of smaller problems that can be solved independently. In the case of transformations, this "big problem" is a big semantic gap between the DSL and the target language[25]. Modularization breaks down this big semantic gap into several smaller ones, making each of them easier to understand, test and maintain[26].

Another reason for multi-stage transformations is the potential for reuse of each of the stages (Fig. 4.10). Reusing lower D languages and their subsequent transformations also implies reuse of potentially non-trivial analyses or optimizations that can be done at that particular abstraction level[27]. Consider GPL compilers as an example. They can be retargetted relatively easily by exchanging the backends (machine code generation phases) or the frontend (programming language parsers and analyzers). For example, GCC can generate code for many different processor architectures (exchangeable backends), and it can generate backend code for several program-

[25] One could measure this semantic gap between two languages: how many constructs do two languages share, how many "synonyms" exist, how many constructs are the same but have different meanings? In practice, the size of the gap is intuited by the transformation designer.

[26] This approach can only be used if the tools support multi-staged transformation well. This is not true for all DSL tools.

[27] This is one of the reasons why we usually generate GPL source code from DSLs, and not machine code or byte code: we want to reuse existing transformations and optimizations provided by the GPL compiler.

ming languages, among them C, C++ and Ada (exchangeable frontends). The same is possible for DSLs. The same high D models can be executed differently by exchanging the lower D intermediate languages and transformations. Or the same lower D languages and transformations can be used for different higher D languages, by mapping these different languages to the same intermediate language.

mbeddr C: The embedded C language (and some of its higher D extensions) have various translation options, for several different target platforms (Win32 and Osek), an example of backend reuse. All of them are C code, but we generate different idioms in the code and different make files. ◀

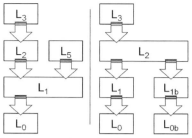

Figure 4.10: *Left:* Backend reuse. Different languages (L_3/L_2 and L_5) are transformed to the same intermediate language L_1, reusing its backend generator to L_0. *Right:* Frontend reuse. L_3 is mapped to L_2, which has two sets of backend generators, reusing the L_3 to L_2 transformation.

Multi-stage transformation can also be a natural consequence of incremental language extension along the domain hierarchy, where we repeatedly build additional higher-level languages on top of lower-level languages. When transforming the higher-level languages, it is natural and obvious to transform them onto the next lower level, and not onto a language at D_0.

mbeddr C: The extensions to C are all transformed back to C idioms during transformation. Higher-level DSLs, for example, a simple DSL for robot control, are reduced to C plus some extensions such as state machines and tasks (Fig. 4.11), reusing the transformations for those abstractions back to C. ◀

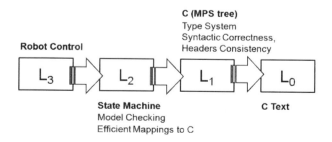

Figure 4.11: Multi-stage transformation in mbeddr. MPS supports multi-stage transformations really well, so managing the interplay of the set of transformations is feasible.

A special case of a multi-staged transformation is a preprocessor to a code generator. Here, a transformation reduces the set of used language concepts in a fragment to a minimal core, and only the minimal core is supported in the code generator. Note how, in this case, the source and target languages of the transformation are the same. However, the target model only uses a *subset* of the concepts defined by the source/target language. A preprocessor simplifies portability of the actual code generator: it becomes simpler, since only the subset of the language has to be mapped to code.

mbeddr C: Consider the case of a state machine to which you want to be able to add an "emergency stop" feature, i.e. a new transition from each existing state to a new STOP state. Instead of handling this case in the code generator, a model transformation script preprocesses the state machine model and adds all the new transitions and the new emergency stop state (Fig. 4.12). Once done, the existing generator is run unchanged. You have effectively modularized the emergency stop concern into a preprocessor transformation. ◂

Component Architecture: The DSL describes hierarchical component architectures (where components are assembled from interconnected instances of other components). Most component runtime platforms don't support such hierarchical components, so you need to "flatten" the structure for execution. Instead of trying to do this in the code generator, you should consider a model transformation step to do it, and then write a simpler generator that works with a flattened, non-hierarchical model. ◂

Multi-stage transformations can be challenging. It becomes harder to understand what is going on in total. Debugging the overall transformation can become hard, and good tool support is needed[28].

■ *Efficiency and Optimization* Transforming from D to D_{-1} allows the use of sophisticated optimizations, potentially resulting in very efficient code. DSL uses domain-specific abstractions and hence includes a lot of domain semantics, so optimizations can take advantage of this and produce very efficient D_{-1} code. However, building such optimizations can be very expensive. It is especially hard to build *global* optimizations that require knowledge about the structure or semantics of large or diverse parts of the overall program. Also, an optimization will always rely on some set of rules that determine when and how to optimize. There will always be corner cases where an experienced developer will be able to write more ef-

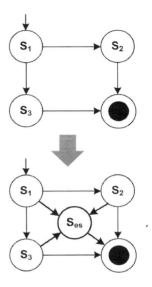

Figure 4.12: A transformation adds an emergency stop feature to a state machine. A new state is added (S_{es}), and a transition from every other state to that new state is added as well. The transition is triggered by the *emergency stop* event (not shown).

[28] MPS addresses this problem by (optionally) keeping all intermediate models around for debugging purposes. The language developer can select a program element in any of the intermediate models and have MPS show a trace from and to where the element was transformed in other (intermediate) models. The trace can also show the transformation code involved in each step.

ficient D_{-1} code manually. However, this requires a competent developer and, usually, a lot of effort *for each specific program*. A tool (i.e. the transformation in this case) will typically address the 90% case well: it will produce reasonably efficient code in the vast majority of cases with very little effort (once the optimizations have been defined). In most cases, this is good enough – in the remaining corner cases, D_{-1} has to be written manually[29].

[29] This argument in favor of tools is used in GPLs for garbage collection and optimizing compilers for higher-level programming languages.

■ *Care about Generated Code* Ideally, generated code is a throwaway artifact, like object files in a C compiler. However, that's not quite true. At least during development and test of the generator you may have to read, understand and debug the generated code. For incomplete DSLs[30], i.e. those in which parts of the resulting program have to be written manually in L_{D-1}, readability and good structure is even more important, because the manually written code has to be integrated with the generated parts of the L_{D-1} program. Hence, generated code should use meaningful abstractions, should be designed well, use good names for identifiers, be documented well, and be indented correctly. In short, generated code should generally adhere to the same standards as manually written code. This also helps to diffuse some of the skepticism against code generation that is still widespread in some organizations. However, there are several exceptions to this rule:

[30] We cover completeness in Section 4.5.

Note that in complete languages (where 100% of the L_{D-1} code is generated), the generated code is never seen by a DSL user. But even in this case, concerns for code quality apply and the code has to be understood and tested during DSL and generator development.

- Sometimes generating really well-structured code makes the generator *much* more complicated. You then have to decide whether you want to live with some less nicely structured generated code, or whether you want to increase generator complexity – a valid trade-off, since the generator also needs to be maintained! A good example is *import* statements when generating Java code. It can be a lot of work to find out exactly which imports are needed in a generated class. In this case it may be better to keep the generator simple and use fully qualified class names throughout the code, and/or to import a few too many classes[31].

[31] Xtend provides special support for this problem based on an `ImportManager`. It makes generating the correct imports relatively simple.

- Using a generator opens up additional options you wouldn't consider when writing code manually (and which are hence considered ugly). An example is generated collection classes. Imagine that your models define entities, and from each entity you generate a Java Bean. In Java version 1.4 and earlier, Java did not have generics, so in order to work with collections of entities you would use the generic `List` class. In the context of generated code you might want to consider generating a specific collection class for each entity, with an API typed to the respective Java Bean. This makes life much more convenient for those people who write Java code that *uses* the generated Beans.

- The third exception to the rule is if the code has to be highly optimized for reasons of performance and code size. While you can still indent your code well and use meaningful names, the *structure* of the code may be convoluted. Note, however, that the code would look the same if it were written by hand in this case.

    mbeddr C: The components extension to C supports components with provided and required ports. A required port declares which interface it is expected to be connected to. The same interface can be provided by different components, implementing the interface differently. Upon translation of the component extension, regular C functions are generated. An outgoing call on a required port has to be routed to the function that has been generated to implement the called interface operation in the target component. Since each component can be instantiated multiple times, and each instance can have its required ports connected to *different* component instances (implementing the same interface) there is no way for the generated code to know which particular function has to be called for an outgoing call on a required port for a given instance. An indirection through function pointers is used instead. Consequently, functions implementing operations in components take an additional `struct` as an argument, which provides those function pointers for each operation of each required port. A call on a required port is therefore a relatively ugly affair based on function pointers. However, to achieve the desired goal, no different, cleaner code approach is possible in C. It is optionally possible to *restrict* a required port to a particular component (Fig. 4.13). In this case, the target function is known statically and no function pointer-based indirection is required. The resulting code is cleaner and more efficient. Programmers trade flexibility for performance. ◂

```
exported component AnotherDriver extends Driver {

  requires ILowLevel lowlevel restricted to LowLevelCode.ll

  field int count = 0

  override int setDriverValue(int addr, int value) {
    lowlevel.doSomeLowlevelStuff();
    count++;
    return 1;
  }
}
```

Figure 4.13: The required port **lowlevel** is not just bound to the **ILowLevel** interface, but restricted to the **ll** port of the **LowLevelCode** component. This way, it is statically known which C function implements the behavior and the generated code can be optimized.

■ *Platform* The complexity can be reduced by splitting the overall transformation into several steps – see above. Another approach is to work with a manually implemented, rich domain specific platform. This typically consists of middleware, frameworks, drivers, libraries and utilities that are taken advantage of by the generated code.

Where the generated code and the platform "meet" depends on the complexity of the generator, requirements regarding code size and performance, the expressiveness of the target language and the potential availability of libraries and frameworks that can be used for the task. In the extreme case, the generator just generates code to populate (or configure) the frameworks (which might already exist, or which you have to grow together with the generator) or provides statically typed facades around otherwise dynamic data structures. Don't go too far towards this end, however: in cases in which you need to consider resource or timing constraints, or when the target platform is predetermined and perhaps limited, code generation is the better approach: trying to make the platform too generic or flexible will increase *its* complexity.

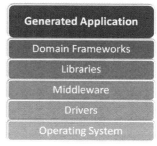

Figure 4.14: Typical layering structure of an application created using DSLs.

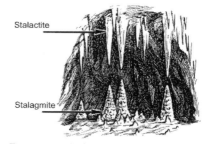

Figure 4.15: Stalagmites and stalactites in limestone caves as a metaphor for a generator and a platform: the stalagmite represents the platform, it grows from up the lower abstraction levels. Stalactites represent the transformations, which grow down from the high abstraction level represented by the DSL.

mbeddr C: For most aspects, we use only a very shallow platform. This is mostly for performance reasons and for the fact that the subset of C that is often used for embedded systems does not provide good means of abstraction. For example, state machines are translated to **switch** statements. If we were to generate Java code in an enterprise system, we might populate a state machine framework instead. In contrast, when we translate the component definitions to the AUTOSAR target environment, a relatively powerful platform is used – namely the AUTOSAR APIs, conventions and generators. ◀

4.3.4 Interpretation

An interpreter is basically a program that acts on the DSL program it receives as an input. How it does that depends on the particular paradigm used (see Section 5.2). For imperative programs it steps through the statements and executes their side effects. In functional programs, the interpreter (recursively) evaluates functions. For declarative programs, some other evaluation strategy, for example based on a solver, may be used. We describe some of the details about how to design and implement interpreters in Section 12.

> **Refrigerators:** The DSL also supports the definition of unit tests for the asynchronous, reactive cooling algorithm. These tests are executed with an in-IDE interpreter. A simulation environment allows the interpreter to be used interactively. Users can "play" with a cooling program, stepping through it in single steps, watching values change. ◂

> **Pension Plans:** The pension DSL supports the in-IDE execution of rule unit tests by an interpreter. In addition, the rules can be debugged. The rule language is functional, so the debugger "expands" the calculation tree, and users can inspect all intermediate results. ◂

For interpretation, the domain hierarchy could be exploited as well: the interpreter for L_D could be implemented in L_{D-1}. However, in practice we see interpreters written in L_{D_0}. They may be extensible, so new interpreter code can be added to deal with the case where higher-level lanuguages add new language concepts.

The abstraction level of an interpreter must be decided. One alternative might ignore for example the use of registers when performing an assignment, avoiding problems resulting from parallelism. Alternatively, the interpreter might model everything, taking into account issues related to parallelism. In other words, an interpreter defines a virtual machine and it is fundamental that this virtual machine has an adequate abstraction level. The users must be aware of exactly what it means for the execution of the program on the target hardware if the program runs on the virtual machine.

4.3.5 Transformation versus Interpretation

When defining the execution semantics for a language, a decision has to be made between transformation (code generation) and interpretation. Here are some criteria to help with this decision.

Code Inspection When using code generation, the resulting code can be inspected to check whether it resembles code that had previously been written manually in the DSL's domain. Writing the transformation rules can be guided by the established patterns and idioms in L_{D-1}. Interpreters are meta programs and as such harder to relate to existing code patterns.

Debugging Debugging generated code is straightforward if the code is well structured (which is up to the transformation) and an execution paradigm is used for which a decent debugging approach exists (not the case for many declarative approaches). Debugging interpreters is harder, because, they are meta programs. For example, setting breakpoints in the DSL program requires conditional breakpoints in the interpreter, which are typically cumbersome to use[32]

Performance and Optimization The code generator can perform optimizations that result in small and tight generated code. The compiler for the generated code may come with its own optimizations which are used automatically if source code is generated and subsequently compiled, simplifying the code generator[33]. Generally, performance is better in generated environments, since interpreters always imply an additional layer of indirection during the execution of the program.

Platform Conformance Generated code can be tailored to any target platform. The code can look exactly as manually written code would look; no support libraries are required. This is important for systems in which the source code (and not the DSL code) is the basis for a contractual obligations or for review and/or certification. Also, if artifacts need to be supplied to the platform that are not directly executable (descriptors, meta data), code generation is more suitable.

Modularization When incrementally building DSLs on top of existing languages, it is natural to use transformations to L_{D-1}[34].

Turnaround Time Turnaround time for interpretation is better than for generation: no generation, compilation and packaging step is required. For target languages with slow compilers especially, large amounts of generated code can be a problem.

[32] This is especially useful during the development of the execution engine. Once the DSL and the engine are finished, users should be able to debug DSL programs on the level of the DSL. However, since building DSL debuggers is not directly supported by most language workbenches, this is a lot of work – and users are required to debug on L_{D-1}.

[33] For example, it is not necessary to optimize away calls to empty functions, **if** statements that always evaluate to **true**, or arithmetic expressions containing only constants.

[34] While it is theoretically possible to also extend interpreters incrementally along a hierarchy of languages, I have not seen this in practice. Interpreters are typically written in a GPL.

Runtime Change In interpreted environments, the DSL program can be changed as the target system runs; the DSL editor can even be integrated into the target system[35].

[35] The term *data-driven* system is often used in this case.

Refrigerators: There were two reasons for implementing the interpreter for the cooling programs. The first was that initially we didn't have a code generator, because the target architecture was not yet defined. To be able to execute cooling programs, we needed an interpreter and simulator. Second, the turn-around time for the domain experts as they experimented with the DSL programs is much reduced compared to generating, compiling and running C code. The (interpreted) simulator also allowed the domain experts to run the programs at a speed they could follow. This proved an important means of understanding and debugging the asynchronous reactive cooling programs. ◄

mbeddr C: This DSL exploits incremental extension to the C programming language (inductive DSL definition). In this case it is natural to use transformation to L_{D-1} as a means of defining the semantics of extensions. Also, since the target domain is embedded software, performance, code size and reuse of the optimizations provided by the C compiler is essential. Interpretation was never an option. ◄

Component Architecture: The driving factor for using generation over interpretation was platform conformance. The reason for the DSL is to automate the generation of target platform artifacts and thereby make working with the platform more efficient. ◄

Pension Plans: Turnaround time was important for the pension contract specification. Also, the domain experts, as they created the pension plans, did not have access to the final execution platform. An in-IDE interpreter was clearly the best choice. ◄

WebDSL: Platform conformance was key here. Web applications have to use the established web standards, and the necessary artifacts have to be generated. An interpreted approach would not work in this scenario. ◄

Combinations between the two approaches are also possible. For example, transformation can create an intermediate representation which is then interpreted. Or an interpreter can generate code on the fly as a means of optimization. While this approach is common in GPLs (e.g., the JVM), we have not seen this approach used for DSLs.

4.3.6 Sufficiency

A program fragment is *sufficient for transformation T* if the fragment itself contains all the data necessary to executed the transformation. While dependent fragments are by definition not sufficient without the transitive closure of fragments they depend on, an independent fragment may be sufficient for one transformation, and insufficient for another.

> **Refrigerators:** The hardware structure is sufficient for a transformation that generates an HTML document that describes the hardware. It is insufficient regarding the C code generator, since the behavior fragment is required as well. ◀

Sufficiency is important where large systems are concerned. An sufficient fragment can be used for code generation without checking out and/or loading other fragments. This supports modular, incremental transformations of only the changed fragments, and hence, potentially significant improvements in performance and scalability.

4.3.7 Synchronizing Multiple Mappings

Ensuring the semantics of the execution engine becomes more challenging if we transform the program to *several different* targets using several different transformations. We have to ensure that the semantics of all resulting programs are identical[36]. In practice, this case often occurs if an interpreter is used in the IDE for "experimenting" with the models, and a code generator creates efficient code for execution in the target environment. To synchronize the semantics in this case, we recommend providing a set of test cases that are expressed on DSL level, and that are executed in all executable representations, expecting them to succeed in all of them. If the coverage of these test cases is high enough to cover all of the observable behavior, then it can be assumed with reasonable certainty that the semantics are indeed the same[37].

> **Pension Plans:** The unit tests in the pension plans DSL are executed by an interpreter in the IDE. However, as Java code is generated from the pension plan specifications, the same unit tests are also executed by the generated Java

[36] At least to the extent we care – we may not care if one of the resulting programs is faster or more scalable. In fact, these differences may be the very reason for having several mappings).

[37] Strictly speaking they are just bug-compatible, i.e. they may all make the same mistakes.

code, expecting the same results as in the interpreted version. ◄

Refrigerators: A similar situation occurs with the cooling DSL where an IDE-interpreter is used for testing and experimenting with the models, and a code generator creates the executable version of the cooling algorithm that actually runs on the microcontroller in the refrigerator. A suite of test cases is used to ensure the same semantics. ◄

4.3.8   Choosing between Several Mappings

Sometimes there are several *alternative* ways in which a program in L_D can be translated to a single L_{D-1}, for example to realize different non-functional requirements (optimizations, target platform, tracing or logging). There are several ways in which one alternative may be selected:

- In analogy to compiler switches, the decision can be controlled by additional external data. Simple parameters passed to the transformation are the simplest case. A more elaborate approach is to have an additional model, called an annotation model, which contains data used by the transformation to decide how to translate the core program. The transformation uses the L_D program and the annotation model as its input. There can be several different annotation models for the same core model that define several different transformations, to be used alternatively. An annotation model is a separate viewpoint (Section 4.4) an can hence be provided by a different stakeholder than the one who maintains the core L_D program.

- Alternatively, L_D can be extended to directly contain additional data to guide the decision. Since the data controlling the transformation is embedded in the core program, this is only useful if the DSL user can actually decide which alternative to choose, and if only one alternative should be chosen for each program. Annotation models provide more flexibility.

- Heuristics, based on patterns, idioms and statistics extracted from the L_D program, can be used to determine the applicable transformation as well. Codifying these rules and heuristics can be hard though, so this approach is rarely used.

As we have suggested above in the case of multiple transformations of the *same* L_D program, here too extensive testing must be used to make sure that all translations exhibit the same semantics (except for the non-functional characteristics that may be expected to be different, since they often are the reason for the different transformations in the first place).

4.3.9 Reduced Expressiveness and Verification

It may be beneficial to limit the expressiveness of a language. Limited expressiveness often results in more sophisticated analyzability. For example, while state machines are not very expressive (compared to fully fledged C), sophisticated formal verification algorithms are available (e.g., model checking using SPIN[38] or NuSMV[39]). The same is true for first-order logic, where satisfiability (SAT) solvers[40] can be used to check programs for consistency. If these kinds of analyses are useful for the model purpose, then limiting the expressiveness to the respective formalism may be a good idea, even if it makes expressing some programs in D more cumbersome[41]. Possibly a DSL should be partitioned into several sub-DSLs, where some of them are verifiable and some are not.

[38] `spinroot.com`

[39] `nusmv.fbk.eu/`

[40] D. G. Mitchell. A sat solver primer. *eatcs*, 85:112–132, 2005

[41] A simple example is to use integers with ranges `int[0..10] x;` instead of general integers. This makes programs harder to write (ranges must be specified every time) but easier to analyze.

> **mbeddr C:** This is the approach used here: model checking is provided for the state machines. No model checking is available for general-purpose C, so behavior that should be verifiable must be isolated into a state machine explicitly. State machines interact with their surrounding C program in a limited and well-defined way to isolate them and make them checkable. Also, state machines marked as **verifiable** cannot use arbitrary C code in its actions. Instead, an action can only change the values of variables local to the state machine and set output events (which are then mapped to external functions or component runnables). The key here is that the state machine is completely self-contained regarding verification: adapting the state machine to its surrounding C program is a separate concern and irrelevant to the model checker. ◀

However, the language may have to be reduced to the point where domain experts are not able to use the language because the connection to the domain is too loose. To remedy this problem, a language with limited expressiveness can be used at D_{-1}. For analysis and verification, the L_D programs are transformed down to the verifiable L_{D-1} language. Verification is performed on L_{D-1}, mapping the results back to L_D. Transforming to a verifiable formalism also works if the formalism is not at D_{-1}, as long as a mapping exists. The problem with this approach is the interpretation of analysis results in the context of the DSL. Domain users may not be able to interpret the results of model checkers or solvers, so they have to be translated back to the DSL. Depending on the semantic gap between the generated model checker input program and the DSL, this can be very hard.

4.3.10 Documentation

Formally, defining semantics happens by mapping the DSL concepts to D_{-1} concepts for which the semantics is known. For DSLs used by developers, and for domains that are defined inductively (bottom-up), this works well. For application domain DSLs, and for domains defined deductively (top-down), this approach is not necessarily good enough, since the D_{-1} concepts has no inherent meaning to the users and/or the domain. An additional way of defining the meaning of the DSL is required. Useful approaches include prose documentation[42] as well as test cases or simulators. This way, domain users can "play" with the DSL and write down their expectations formally in test cases.

[42] We suggest always writing such documentation in tutorial style, or as FAQs. Hardly anyone reads "reference documentation": while it may be complete and correct, it is boring to read and does not guide users through using the DSL.

mbeddr C: The extensible C language comes with a 100-page PDF that shows how to use the MPS-based IDE, illustrates the changes to regular C, provides examples for all C extensions and also discusses how to use the integrated analysis tools. ◂

Refrigerators: This DSL has a separate viewpoint for defining test cases where domain experts can codify their expectations regarding the behavior of cooling programs. An interpreter is available to simulate the programs, observe their progress and stimulate them to see how they react. ◂

Pension Plans: This DSL supports an Excel-like tabular notation for expressing test cases for pension calculation rules (Fig. 4.16). The calculations are functional, and the calculation tree can be extended as a way of debugging the rules. ◂

Name	Documentation	Tags	Valid time	Transaction time	Fixture	Product	Element	Expected value	Actual value
Accrued right at retireme		🏷	2006-12-31	2007-9-24	Jan De Jong	Old Age Pension	Accrued right	761.0402	761.0402
Accrued Right last final pay		🏷	2004-1-1	2007-9-24	Jan De Jong	Old Age Pension	Accrued right	705.0589	705.0589
premium last year		🏷	2006-1-1	2007-9-24	Jan De Jong	Old Age Pension	Premium old age pension	329.0625	329.0625
Accrued right at retireme 2)		🏷	2006-12-31	2007-9-24	Piet Van Dijk	Old Age Pension	Accrued right	740.94	724.7658
		🏷	1985-12-31	2007-9-24	Jan De Jong	Old Age Pension	Accrued Right in service period	73.661	73.661
		🏷	1985-12-31	2007-9-24	Jan De Jong	Old Age Pension	Years of service in service period	3.7534	3.7534
		🏷	1987-12-31	2007-9-24	Jan De Jong	Old Age Pension	Pension base average FP	7750	7750
		🏷	1998-12-31	2007-9-24	Jan De Jong	Old Age Pension	Accrued Right in service period	387.7449	387.7449
		🏷	1998-12-31	2007-9-24	Jan De Jong	Old Age Pension	Years of service in service period	10.8082	10.8082
		🏷	1998-12-31	2007-9-24	Jan De Jong	Old Age Pension	Pension base average FP	8250	8250

4.4 Separation of Concerns

A domain D may be composed from different concerns. Each concern covers a different aspect of the overall domain. When developing a system in a domain, all the concerns in that domain have to be addressed. Separation into concerns is often driven by different aspects of the system being specified by different stakeholders or at different times in the development process. Fig. 4.17 shows $D_{1.1}$ composed from the concerns A, B and C.

Figure 4.16: Test cases in the pension language allow users to specify test data for each input value of a rule. The rules are then evaluated by an interpreter, providing immediate feedback about incorrect rules (table rows are colored red and green – not visible in the printed version).
For embedded software, these could be component and interface definitions (A), component instantiation and connections (B), as well as scheduling and bus allocation (C).

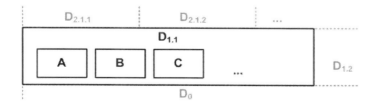

Figure 4.17: A domain may consist of several concerns. A domain is covered either by a DSL that addresses all of these concerns, or by a set of related, concern-specific DSLs.

Two fundamentally different approaches are possible to deal with the set of concerns in a domain. Either a single, integrated language can be designed that addresses all concerns of D in one integrated model. Alternatively, separate concern-specific DSLs can be defined, each addressing one or more of the domain's concerns[43]. A complete program then consists of a set of dependent, concern-specific fragments that relate to each other in a well-defined way. Viewpoints support this separation of domain concerns into separate DSLs. Fig. 4.18 illustrates the two different approaches.

[43] Strictly speaking, this is not quite true: some concerns are typically also addressed by the execution engine. We discuss this below in the section on Cross-Cutting Concerns.

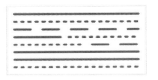 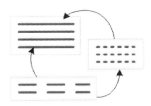

Figure 4.18: *Left:* An integrated DSL, where the various concerns (represented by different line styles) are covered by a single integrated language (and consequently, one model). *Right:* Several viewpoint languages (and model fragments), each covering a single concern. Arrows in Part B highlight dependencies between the viewpoints.

mbeddr C: The tasks language module includes the task implementation as well as task scheduling in one language construct. Scheduling and implementation are two concerns that could have been separated. We opted against this, because both concerns are specified by the same person. The language used for implementation code is `med.core`, whereas the task constructs are defined in the `med.tasks` language. So the languages are modularized, but they are used together in a single heterogeneous fragment. ◄

WebDSL: Web programs consists of multiple concerns including persistent data, user interface and access control. WebDSL provides specific languages for these concerns, but *linguistically integrates* them into a single language[44]. Declarations in the languages can be combined in WebDSL modules. A WebDSL developer can choose how to factor declarations into modules; e.g., all access control rules in one module, or all aspects of some feature together in one module. ◄

[44] Z. Hemel, D. M. Groenewegen, L. C. L. Kats, and E. Visser. Static consistency checking of web applications with WebDSL. *JSC*, 46(2):150–182, 2011

Component Architecture: The specification of interfaces and components is done with one DSL in one viewpoint. A separate viewpoint is used to describe component instantiation and connection. This choice has been made because the same set of interfaces and components will be instantiated and connected *differently* in different usage scenarios, so separate fragments are useful. ◄

4.4.1   Viewpoints for Concern Separation

If viewpoints are used, the concern-specific DSLs, and consequently the viewpoint models, should have well-defined dependencies; cycles should be avoided. If dependencies between viewpoint fragments are kept cycle-free, the independent fragments may be sufficient for certain transformations; this can be a driver for using viewpoints in the first place.

The dependent viewpoint fragment (and the language to express it) have to provide a way of pointing to the referenced element. This usually means that the referenced element has to provide a qualified name that can be used in the reference[45].

Separating out a domain concern into a separate viewpoint fragment can be useful for several reasons. If different concerns of a domain are specified by different stakeholders, then separate viewpoints make sure that each stakeholder has to deal only with the information they care about. The various fragments can be modified, stored and checked in/out separately, maintaining only referential integrity with the referenced fragment[46]. The viewpoint separation has to be aligned with the development process: the order of creation of the fragments must be aligned with the dependency structure.

Another reason for separate viewpoints is a 1:n relationship between the independent and the dependent fragments. If a single core concern may be enhanced by several different additional concerns, then it is crucial to keep the core concern independent of the information in the additional concerns. Viewpoints make this possible.

4.4.2   Viewpoints as Annotation Models

A special case of viewpoint separation is annotation models (already mentioned in Section 4.3.8). An annotation provides additional, often technical or transformation-controlling data for elements in a core program[47]. This is especially useful in a multi-stage transformation (Section 4.3.3), where additional data may have to be specified for the result of the first phase to control the execution of the next phase. Since that intermediate model is generated, it is not possible to add these additional specifications to the intermediate model directly. Externalizing it into an annotation model solves that problem.

Refrigerators: One concern in this DSL specifies the logical hardware structure of refrigerators installations. Another one describes the refrigerator cooling algorithm. Both

---

The IDE should provide navigational support: if an element in viewpoint B points to an element in viewpoint A then it should be possible to follow this reference ("Ctrl-Click"). It should also be possible to query the dependencies in the opposite direction ("Find the persistence mapping for this entity" or "Find all UI forms that access this entity").

[45] In projectional editors one can *technically* use the UUID of the target element for the reference, but for the user, some kind of qualified name is still necessary.

[46] Projectional editors can use a different approach. They can store the information of all concerns in a single model, but then use different projections to address the needs of different stakeholders. This solves the problem of referential integrity. However, this approach does not support separate store and check in/out.

A final (very pragmatic) reason for using viewpoints is when the tooling used does not support embedding of a reusable language because syntactic composition is not supported.

[47] For those who know Eclipse EMF: **genmodel**s are annotation models for **ecore** models.

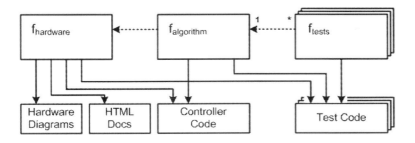

Figure 4.19: The hardware fragment is independent, and sufficient for generation of hardware diagrams and documentation. The algorithms fragment depends on the hardware fragment. The two of them together are sufficient for generating the controller code. Tests depend on the algorithm. There are many test fragments for a single algorithm fragment.

are implemented as separate viewpoints, where the algorithm DSL references the hardware structure DSL. Using this dependency structure, different algorithms can be defined for the same hardware structure. Each of these algorithms resides in its own fragment. While the C code generation requires both behavior and hardware structure fragments, the hardware fragment is sufficient for a transformation that creates a visual representation of the hardware structures (see Fig. 4.19). ◄

Example: For example, if you create a relational data model from an object oriented data model, you might automatically derive database table names from the name of the class in the OO model. If you need to "change" some of those names, use an annotation model that specifies an alternate name. The downstream processor knows that the name in the annotation model overrides the name in the original model[48]. ◄

[48] This is a typical example of where the easiest thing in a projectional editor would be to just place a field for holding an overriding table name under the program element that represents the table. Users can edit that table name in a special projection.

4.4.3 Viewpoint Consistency

If viewpoints are used, constraints have to be defined to check consistency of the viewpoints. A dependent viewpoint fragment contains program elements that reference program elements in another fragment. It is straightforward to check that the target elements of these actually exist, since the reference will break if it does not; in most tools these kinds of checks are available by default.

The other direction is more interesting. Assume two viewpoints: business data structure and persistence mapping. There may be a constraint that says that every **Entity** in the business data viewpoint has to have exactly one **EntityPersis-**

tenceMapping element that points to the respective **Entity**. It is an error if such an **EntityPersistenceMapping** does not exit. Checking this constraint has two problems:

- The first problem may be performance. The *whole world* has to be searched to check if a referencing program element exists somewhere. If the tool supports it, this problem can be solved by automatically maintained reverse indices[49].

- The second problem is more fundamental: it is not clear what constitutes the whole world. The fragment with the persistence mapping for a given **Entity** may reside on a different machine or be under the control of a different user. It may not be accessible to the constraint checker when the user edits the business data fragment. To solve this problem, it is necessary to define explicitly what *the world* is, using some kind of configuration. For example, a C compiler's include path or Java's classpath are ways of defining the scope within which the overall system description must be complete. This does not necessarily have to be done by each developer who, for example, works on the business data. But at the point when the final system is generated or built, such a "world definition" is essential.

[49] This data should also be exploited by the IDE. UI actions should be available to navigate from the referenced element (the **Entity**) to the referencing elements (the **EntityPersistenceMapping**). This is more than a generic Find Usages functionality, since it specifically searches for certain kinds of usages (the **EntityPersistenceMapping** in this example). Further tool support may include creation of such referencing elements based on a policy that determines into which fragment the created element should go.

4.4.4 Cross-Cutting Concerns

In the discussion so far we have considered concerns that can be modularized clearly. Fig. 4.17 emphasizes this: the concern boxes are neatly arranged next to each other. However, there may also be concerns that do *not* fit into the chosen modularization approach. These are typically called *cross-cutting concerns*; see Fig. 4.20.

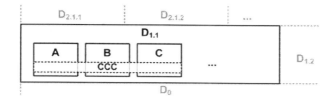

Figure 4.20: Cross-cutting concerns cannot be modularized: they permeate other concerns.

In the context of DSLs we have to separate several classes of cross-cutting concerns:

■ *Handled by Execution Engine*   If we are lucky, a concern that is cross-cutting in the domain can be handled completely by the execution engine. For example the collection of performance data, billing information or audit logs typically does not have to be described in the DSL at all. Since every program in the domain has to address this concern in the same way, the implementation can be handled by the execution engine by inserting the respective code at the relevant locations (in the case of a generator).

> **Component Architecture:** The component architecture DSL supports the collection of performance data. Using mock objects, we started running load tests early on. For a load test, we have to collect the times it takes to execute operations on components. Based on a configuration switch, the generator adds the necessary code to collect the performance data automatically. ◂

■ *Modularized in DSL* Another class of cross-cutting concerns are those that cut across the resulting executable system, but can be modularized on the DSL level. A good example is permissions. Specifying users, roles and permissions to access certain resources in the system can be modularized into a concern, and is typically described in a separate viewpoint. It is then the job of the execution engine to consider the specified permissions in all relevant places in the resulting system.

> **WebDSL:** WebDSL has a means of specifying access control for web pages. The generator injects the necessary code to check these permissions into the client side and server side parts of the resulting web application. ◂

■ *Cross-Cutting in the DSL* The third class is when the concern cross-cuts the programs written in the DSL and can *not* be modularized, as in the previous class. In this case we have to deal with cross-cutting concerns in the same way as we do today in programming languages: we either have to manually insert the code in *all* the relevant places in the DSL program, or we have to resort to aspect weaving on the DSL level[50].

> **Component Architecture:** We implemented a simple weaver that is able to introduce additional ports into existing components. It was used, among other things, to modularize the monitoring concern: if monitoring was enabled, this aspect component would add the `mon` port to all other components, enabling the `MonitoringConsole` to connect to the other components and query monitoring data (see the code below[51]). ◂

[50] Building a (typically relatively limited) aspect weaver on the DSL's level is not a big problem, since we already have access to the AST, and transforming it in a way where we inject additional code based on a DSL-specific pointcut specification is relatively straightforward.

[51] The * specifies that this aspect applies to *all* existing components. Other selectors could be used instead of the * to select only a subset.

```
namespace monitoring feature monitoring {

  component MonitoringConsole ...
  instance monitor: ...
  dynamic connect monitor.devices .. .

  aspect (*) component {
    provides mon: IMonitoring
  }
}
```

4.4.5 Views on Programs

In projectional editors it is also possible to store the data for all viewpoints in the same model tree, while using different projections to show different views onto the model to materialize the various viewpoints. The particular benefit of this approach is that additional concern-specific views can be defined later, after programs have been created. It also avoids the need for defining sophisticated ways of referencing program elements from other viewpoints.

MPS also provides *annotations*, allowing additional model data to be "attached" to any model element, and shown optionally.

Pension Plans: Pension plans can be shown in a graphical notation highlighting the dependency structure (Fig. 4.21). The dependencies can still be edited in this view, but the actual content of the pension plans is not shown. ◀

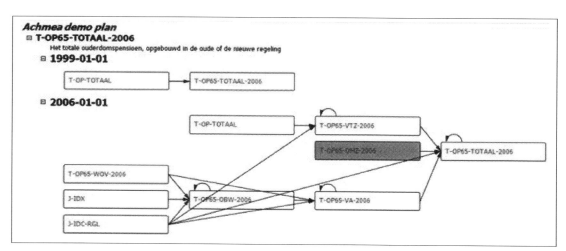

Figure 4.21: Graphical notation for dependencies among rules in a pension plan.

mbeddr C: Annotations are used for storing requirements traces and documentation in the models (Fig. 20.22). The program can be shown and edited with and without requirements traces and documentation text. ◀

```
requirements modules: HighLevelRequirements
module ExampleCode from test.ts.requirements.code imports StrUtil {

  int8_t add(int8_t a, int8_t b) {   trace AddFct
    return a + b;
  } add (function)
  int8_t main(string[ ] args, int8_t argc) {              trace Main
    if ( argc == 2 ) {
      return  add(str2int(args[0]), str2int(args[1]))  trace Add;
    } else {
       return -1;  trace FailOtherwise
    } if

  } main (function)
}
```

Figure 4.22: The shaded annotations are traces into a requirements database. The program can be edited with and without these annotations. The annotations language has no dependency on the languages it annotates.

4.4.6 Viewpoints for Progressive Refinement

There is an additional use case for viewpoint models not related to the concerns of a domain, but to progressive refinement. Consider the development of complex systems, which typically proceeds in phases: it starts with requirements, proceeds to high-level component design and specification of non-functional properties, and finishes with the implementation of the components. In each of these phases, models can be used to represent the system with abstractions that are appropriate for the phase. An appropriate DSL is needed to represent the models in each phase (Fig. 4.23). The references between model elements are called *traces*[52]. Since the same conceptual elements may be represented on different refinement levels (e.g., component design and component implementation), synchronization between the viewpoint models is often required (see the next subsection).

[52] W. Jirapanthong and A. Zisman. Supporting product line development through traceability. In *apsec*, pages 506–514, 2005

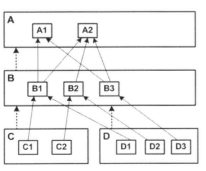

Figure 4.23: Progressive refinement: the boxes represent models expressed with corresponding languages. The dotted arrows express dependencies, whereas the solid arrows represent references between model elements.

4.4.7 Model Synchronization

In the discussion of viewpoints so far we have assumed that there is no overlap between the viewpoints: every piece of information lives in exactly one viewpoint. Relationships between viewpoints are established by references (which means that the Referencing language composition technique can be used; this is discussed in Section 4.6.1). However, sometimes this is not the case, and the same (conceptual) information is represented in two viewpoint models. Obviously there is a constraint that enforces consistency between the viewpoints; the models have to be synchronized[53].

In some cases the rules for establishing consistency between viewpoints can be described formally, and hence the synchronization can be automated, if the DSL tool supports such synchronization[54]. An example occurs in mbeddr C:

mbeddr C: Components implement interfaces. Each component provides an implementation for each method defined in each of the interfaces it implements. If a new method is added to an interface, all components that implement that particular interface must get a new, empty method implementation. This is an example of model synchronization. ◂

In this example the synchronization is trivial, for two reasons: first, there is a clear (unidirectional) dependency between the method implementation and the operation specification in the interface, so the synchronization is also unidirectional. Second, the information represented in both models/places is identical, so it is easy to detect an inconsistency and fix it. However, there are several more complicated cases:

- The dependency might be bidirectional, and changes may be allowed in either model. This means that two transformations have to be written, one for each direction, or a formalism for expressing the transformation has to be used that can be executed in both directions[55]. In multi-user scenarios it is also possible that the two models are changed at the same time, in an inconsistent way. In this case the changes have to be merged, or a clear priority (who will win) has to be established.

- The languages expressing the viewpoints may have been defined independent of each other, with *no dependency*. This probably means that it was discovered only *after the fact* that some parts of the model have to be synchronized. In this case the synchronization must be put into some kind of adapter language. It also means that the synchronization is

[53] Thanks are due to the participants of the MoDELS 2012 workshop on Multi-Paradigm Modeling who, by discussing this issue, reminded me that it is missing from the book.

[54] MPS has a nice way of automatically executing a quick fix for a constraint violation. If the constraint detects an inconsistency between viewpoints, the quick fix can automatically correct the problem. This also solves the *whole world* problem neatly, since every dependent fragment is "corrected" as soon as it is opened in the editor.

[55] The QVT-R transformation language has this capability, for example.

not as clean as if it had been "designed into" the languages (see the next item).

- In the mbeddr example, the information (the signature of the operation) was simply replicated, so the transformation was trivial. However, there may not be a 1:1 correspondence between the information in the two viewpoints. This makes the transformation more complex to write. In the worst case it may mean that the synchronization cannot be formally described and automated.

Sometimes the correspondence between models can only be expressed on an instance level (as in "This functional block corresponds to this software component")[56]. Consequently, developers have to express the correspondence (the trace links mentioned earlier) manually. However, consistency checks (and possibly automatic synchronization) may still be possible, based on the manually expressed trace links.

In my work with DSLs I have only encountered the simplest cases of synchronization, which is why we don't put much emphasis on this topic in the rest of the book. For more details, see the papers by Diskin[57] and Stevens[58].

[56] This often happens in the context of progressive refinement, as discussed in the previous subsection.

[57] Z. Diskin, Y. Xiong, and K. Czarnecki. From state- to delta-based bidirectional model transformations. In *ICMT*, pages 61–76, 2010

[58] P. Stevens. Bidirectional model transformations in qvt: semantic issues and open questions. *SoSyM*, 9(1):7–20, 2010

4.5 Completeness

Completeness[59] refers to the degree to which a language L can express programs that contain all necessary information to execute them. An program expressed in an incomplete DSL requires additional specifications (such as configuration files or code written in a lower-level language) to make it executable.

[59] This has nothing to do with Turing completeness.

Let us introduce a function G ("code generator") that transforms a program p in L_D to a program q in L_{D-1}. For a complete language, p and q have the same semantics, i.e. $OB(p) == OB(G(p)) == OB(q)$ (see Section 4.3). For incomplete languages where $OB(G(p)) \subset OB(p)$ we have to write additional code in L_{D-1} to obtain a program in D_{-1} that has the same semantics as intended by the original program in L_D. In cases in which we use several viewpoints to represent various concerns of D, the set of fragments written for these concerns must be enough for complete D_{-1} generation.

Another way of stating this is that G produces a program in L_{D-1} that is not sufficient for a subsequent transformation (e.g., a compiler), only the manually written L_{D-1} code leads to sufficiency.

mbeddr C: The Embedded C language is complete regarding D_{-1}, or even D_{-m} for higher levels of D, since higher levels are always built as extensions of its D_{-1}. Developers can always fall back to D_{-1} to express what is not expressible directly with L_D. Since the users of this system are developers, falling back to D_{-1} or even D_0 is not a problem. ◂

4.5.1 Compensating for Incompleteness

Integrating the L_{D-1} in the case of an incomplete L_D language can be done in several ways:

- By calling "black box" code written in L_{D-1}. This requires concepts in L_D for calling D_{-1} foreign functions. No syntactic embedding of D_{-1} code is required, beyond the ability to call functions[60].

- By directly embedding L_{D-1} code in the L_D program. This is useful if L_D is an extension of L_{D-1}, or if the tool provides adequate support for embedding the D_{-1} language into L_D programs. Note that L_{D-1} may not be analyzable, so mixing L_{D-1} into L_D code may compromise analyzability of the L_D code.

- By using composition mechanisms of L_{D-1} to "plug in" the manually written code into the generated code without actually modifying the generated files (also known as the Generation Gap[61] pattern). Example techniques for realizing this approach include generating a base class with abstract methods (requiring the user to implement them in a manually written subclass) or with empty callback methods which the user can use to customize in a subclass[62]. You can delegate, implement interfaces, use **#include**, use reflection tricks, AOP or take a look at the well-known design patterns for inspiration. Some languages provide partial classes, where a class definition can be split over a generated file and a manually written file.

- By inserting manually-written L_{D-1} code into the L_{D-1} code generated from the L_D program using protected regions. Protected regions are areas of the code, usually delimited by special comments, whose (manually written) contents are not overwritten during regeneration of the file.

For DSLs used by developers, incompleteness is usually not a problem because they are comfortable with writing the D_{-1} code in a programming language. Specifically, the DSL users are the same people as those who provide the remaining D_{-1} code, so coordination between the two roles is not a problem.

[60] In the simplest case, these functions don't even have arguments, so the syntax to call such a function is essentially just the function name.

Just "pasting text into a text field", an approach used by several graphical modeling tools, is not productive, since no syntactic and semantic integration between the languages is provided. In most cases there is no tool support (syntax highlighting, code completion, error checking)

[61] J. Vlissidis. Generation gap. C++ Report, 1996

[62] For example, in user interfaces, such a method could return a position object for a widget. The default implementation returns **null**, indicating to the framework to use the the generic layout algorithm. If a position is returned, it is used instead of the one computed by the layout algorithm.

We discourage the use of protected regions. You'll run into all kinds of problems: generated code is not a throw-away product any more, you have to check it in leading to funny situations with your version control system. Also, often you will accumulate a "sediment" of code that has been generated from elements that are no longer in the model, leading to compilation errors in the worst case – even though the code is in fact not longer required. If you don't use protected regions, you can delete the whole generated source directory from time to time, cleaning up the sediment.

Component Architecture: This DSL is not complete. Only class skeleton and infrastructure integration code is generated from the models. The component implementation has to be implemented manually in Java using the Generation Gap pattern. The DSL is used by developers, so writing code in a subclass of a generated class is not a problem. ◄

For DSLs used by domain experts, the situation is different. Usually, they are not able to write D_{-1} code, so other people (developers) have to fill in the remaining concerns. Alternatively, developers can develop a predefined set of foreign functions that can be called from within the DSL. In effect, developers provide a standard library (cf. Section 4.1.2) which can be invoked as black boxes from DSL programs.

> This requires elaborate collaboration schemes, because the domain experts have to communicate the remaining concerns via text or verbal communication.

WebDSL: The core of a web application is concerned with persistent data and its presentation. However, web applications need to perform additional duties outside that core, for which useful libraries often exist. WebDSL provides a *native interface* that allows a developer to call into a Java library by declaring types and functions from the library in a WebDSL program. ◄

Note that a DSL that does not *cover* all of D can still be *complete*: not all of the programs imaginable in a domain may be expressed with a DSL, but those programs that can be expressed can be expressed completely, without any manually written code. Also, the code generated from a DSL program may require a framework written in L_{D-1} to run in. That framework represents aspects of D outside the scope of L_D.

Refrigerators: The cooling DSL only supports reactive, state-based systems that make up the core of the cooling algorithm. The drivers used in the lower layers of the system, or the control algorithms controlling the actual compressors in the fridge, cannot be expressed with the DSL. However, these aspects are developed once and can be reused without adaptations, so using DSLs is not sensible. These parts are implemented manually in C. ◄

■ *Controlling D_{-1} Code* Allowing users to manually write D_{-1} code, and especially if it is actually a GPL in D_0, comes with two additional challenges. Consider the following example: the generator generates an abstract class from some model element. The developer is expected to subclass the generated class and implement a couple of abstract methods. The manually written subclass needs to conform to a specific naming convention so that some other generated code can instantiate the manually written subclass. The generator, however, just generates the base class and stops: how can you make sure developers actually do write that subclass, using the correct name[63]?

To address this issue, make sure there is there a way to make those conventions and idioms interactive. One way to do this is to generate checks/constraints *against the code base* and have them evaluated by the IDE, for example using Findbugs[64] or similar code checking tools. If one fails, an error message is reported to the developer. That error message can be worded by the developer of the DSL, helping the developer understand what exactly has to be done to solve the problem with the code.

■ *Semantic Consistency* As part of the definition of a DSL you will implement constraints that validate the DSL program in order to ensure some property of the resulting system (see Section 20.5). For example, you might check dependencies between components in an architecture model to ensure components can be exchanged in the actual system. Of course such a validation is only useful if the manually written code does not introduce dependencies that are not present in the model. In that case the "green light" from the constraint check does not help much.

To ensure that promises made by the models are kept by the (manually written) code, use one of the following two approaches. First, generate code that does not allow violation of model promises. For example, don't expose a factory that allows components to look up and use any other component (creating dependencies), but rather use dependency injection to supply objects for the valid dependencies expressed in the model[65].

Component Architecture: The Java code generator generates component implementation classes that use dependency injection to supply the targets for required ports. This ensures that the implementation class will have access to exactly those interfaces specified in the model. An alternative approach would be to simply hand to the implementation class some kind of factory or registry where a component implementation can look up instances of com-

[63] Of course, if the constructor of the concrete subclass is called from another location of the generated code, and/or if the abstract methods are invoked, you'll get compiler errors. By their nature, they are on the abstraction level of the implementation code, however. It is not always obvious what the developer has to do in terms of the model or domain to get rid of these errors.

[64] findbugs.sourceforge.net/

[65] A better approach is to build a *complete* DSL. The language used to express the behavior (which might otherwise plugged in manually in the generated code) is suitably limited and/or checked to enforce that it does not lead to inconsistencies. This is a nice use case for language extension and embedding.

ponents that provide the interfaces specified by the required ports of the current component. However, this way it would be much harder to make sure that only those dependencies are accessed that are expressed in the model. Using dependency injection *enforces* this constraint in the implementation code. ◄

A second approach uses code checkers (like the Findbugs mentioned above) or architecture analysis tools to validate manually written code. You can easily generate the relevant checking rules for those tools from the models.

4.5.2 Roundtrip Transformation

Roundtrip transformation means that an L_D program can be recovered from a program in L_{D-1} (written from scratch, or changed manually after generation from a previous iteration of the L_D program). This is challenging, because it requires reconstituting the semantics of the L_D program from idioms or patterns used in the L_{D-1} code. This is the general reverse engineering problem and is not generally possible, although progress has been made over recent years (see for example[66]).

Note that for complete languages roundtripping is generally not useful, because the complete program can be written in L_D in the first place. Even if recovery of the semantics is possible it may not be practical: if the DSL provides significant abstraction over the L_{D-1} program, then the generated L_{D-1} program is so complicated that manually changing the D_{-1} code in a consistent and correct way is tedious and error-prone.

Roundtripping has traditionally been used with respect to UML models and generated class skeletons. In that case, the abstractions between the model and the code are similar (both are classes); the tool basically just provides a different concrete syntax (diagrams). This similarity of abstractions in the code and the model made roundtripping possible to some extent. However, it also made the models relatively useless, because they did *not* provide a significant benefit in terms of abstraction over code details. We generally recommend avoiding any attempt to build support for roundtripping.

> **mbeddr C:** This language does not support roundtripping, but since all DSLs are extensions of C, one can always add C code to the programs, alleviating the need for roundtripping in the first place. ◄

[66] D. Beyer, T. A. Henzinger, and G. Theoduloz. Program analysis with dynamic precision adjustment. In *ASE*, pages 29–38, 2008; M. Pistoia, S. Chandra, S. J. Fink, and E. Yahav. A survey of static analysis methods for identifying security vulnerabilities in software systems. *IBMSJ*, 46(2):265–288, 2007; and M. Antkiewicz, T. T. Bartolomei, and K. Czarnecki. Fast extraction of high-quality framework-specific models from application code. *ASE*, 16(1):101–144, 2009

Notice that the problem of "understanding" the semantics of a program written at a too-low abstraction level is the reason for DSLs in the first place: by providing linguistic abstractions for the relevant semantics, no "recovery" is necessary for meaningful analysis and transformation.

Refrigerators: Roundtripping is not required here, since the DSL is complete. The code generators are quite sophisticated, and nobody would want to manually change the generated C code. Since the DSL has proved to provide good coverage, the need to "tweak" the generated code has not come up. ◀

Component Architecture: Roundtripping is not supported. Changes to the interfaces, operation signatures or components have to be performed in the models. This has not been reported as a problem by the users, since both the implementation code and the DSL "look and feel" the same way – they are both Eclipse-based textual editors – and generation of the derived low-level code happens automatically on saving a changed model. The workflow is seamless. ◀

Pension Plans: This is a typical application domain DSL where the users never see the generated Java code. Consequently, the language has to be complete and roundtripping is not useful and would not fit with the development process. ◀

4.6 Language Modularity

Reuse of modularized parts makes software development more efficient, since similar functionality does not have to be developed over and over again. A similar argument can be made for languages. Being able to reuse languages, or parts of languages, in new contexts makes designing DSLs more efficient.

Language composition requires the composition of abstract syntax, concrete syntax, constraints/type systems and the execution semantics[67]. We discuss all of these aspect in this section. However, in the discussion of semantic integration, we consider only the case in which the composed language uses the same (or closely related) behavioral paradigms[68], since otherwise the composition can become very challenging. We mostly focus on imperative programs. We discuss behavioral paradigms in more detail in Section 5.

■ *Composition Techniques* We have identified the following four composition strategies: referencing, extension, reuse and embedding. We distinguish them regarding fragment structure

Language modularization and reuse is often not driven by end user or domain requirements, but rather, by the experience of the language designers and implementers striving for consistency and avoidance of duplicate implementation work.

[67] It requires the composition of the IDE as well. However, with the language workbenches used in this book, this is *mostly* automatic.

[68] The behavioral paradigm is also known as the Model of Computation.

and language dependencies, as illustrated in Fig. 4.24. Fig. 4.25 shows the relationships between fragments and languages in these cases[69].

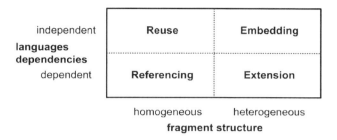

[69] Note how in both cases the language definitions are modular: *invasive* modification of a language definition is not something we consider language modularity!

Figure 4.24: We distinguish the four modularization and composition approaches regarding their consequences for fragment structure and language dependencies.

We consider these two criteria to be relevant for the following reasons. *Language dependencies* capture whether a language has to be designed with knowledge about a particular composition partner in mind in order to be composable with that partner. It is desirable in many scenarios that languages be composable *without* previous knowledge about all possible composition partners. *Fragment Structure* captures whether the two composed languages can be syntactically mixed, or whether separate viewpoints are used. Since modular concrete syntax can be a challenge, this is not always possible, though often desirable.

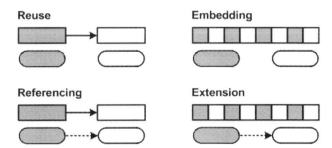

Figure 4.25: The relationships between fragments and languages in the four composition approaches. Boxes represent fragments, rounded boxes are languages. Dotted lines are dependencies, solid lines references/associations. The shading of the boxes represent the two different languages.

■ *DSL Hell?*   Reusing DSL also helps avoid the "DSL Hell" problem we discussed in the introduction. DSL hell refers to the danger that developers create new DSLs all the time, resulting in a large set of half-baked DSLs, each covering related domains, possibly with overlap, but still incompatible. Language modularization and reuse can help to avoid this problem. Language extension allows users to add new language constructs to existing languages. They can reuse all the features of the existing language while still adding their own higher-level abstractions. Language embedding lets language designers embed existing languages into new ones. This is particularly interesting in the case of expression or query languages, which are relevant in many different contexts.

■ *More Detailed Examples* Part III of the book discusses the implementation of these modularization techniques with various tools (Section 16). As part of this discussion we present much more concrete and detailed examples of the various composition techniques. You may want to take a look at those examples while you read this section.

4.6.1 Language Referencing

Language referencing enables *homogeneous* fragments with cross-references among them, using *dependent* languages (Fig. 4.26).

A fragment f_2 depends on f_1. f_2 and f_1 are expressed with different languages l_2 and l_1. The referencing language l_2 depends on the referenced language l_1 because at least one concept in the l_2 references a concept from l_1. We call l_2 the *referencing* language, and l_1 the *referenced* language. While equations (1.2) and (1.3) (see Section 3.3) continue to hold, (1.1) does not. Instead:

$$\forall r \in \textit{Refs}_{l_2} \mid lo(r.from) = l_2 \wedge (lo(r.to) = l_1 \vee lo(r.to) = l_2) \tag{4.1}$$

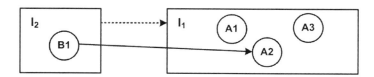

Figure 4.26: Referencing. Language l_2 depends on l_1, because concepts in l_2 reference concepts in l_1. (We use rectangles for languages, circles for language concepts, and UML syntax for the lines: dotted arrows = dependency, normal arrows = associations, hollow-triangle-arrow for inheritance.)

■ *Viewpoints* As we have discussed before in Section 4.4, a domain D can be composed from different concerns. One way of dealing with this is to define separate concern-specific DSLs, each addressing one or more of the domain's concerns. A program then consists of a set of concern-specific fragments, which relate to each other in a well-defined way using language referencing. This approach has the advantage that different stakeholders can modify "their" concern independent of others. It also allows reuse of the independent fragments and languages with different referencing languages. The obvious drawback is that for tightly integrated concerns the separation into separate fragments can be a usability problem.

Referencing implies knowledge about the relationships of the languages as they are designed. Viewpoints are the classical case for this. The dependent languages *cannot* be reused, because of the dependency on the other language.

> **Refrigerators:** As an example, consider the domain of refrigerator configuration. The domain consists of three concerns. The first concern H describes the hardware structure of refrigerator appliances including compartments, compressors, fans, valves and thermometers. The second concern A describes the cooling algorithm using a state-based, asynchronous language. Cooling programs refer to hardware building blocks and access their properties in expressions and commands. The third concern is testing, T. A cooling test can test and simulate cooling programs. The dependencies are as follows: $A \rightarrow H$ and $T \rightarrow A$. Each of these concerns is implemented as a separate language, with references between them. H and A are separated because H is defined by product management, whereas A is defined by thermodynamicists. Also, several algorithms for the same hardware must be supported, which makes separate fragments for H and A useful. T is separate from A because tests are not strictly part of the product definition and may be enhanced after a product has been released. These languages have been built as part of a single project, so the dependencies between them are not a problem. ◂

■ *Progressive Refinement*   Progressive refinement, also introduced earlier (Section 4.4.6), also makes use of language referencing.

4.6.2   Language Extension

Language extension enables *heterogeneous* fragments with *dependent* languages (Fig. 4.27). A language l_2 extending l_1 adds additional language concepts to those of l_1. We call l_2 the *extending* language (or language extension), and l_1 the *base* language. To allow the new concepts to be used in the context provided by l_1, some of them extend concepts in l_1. So, while

l_1 remains independent, l_2 becomes dependent on l_1, since:

$$\exists i \in Inh(l_2) \mid i.sub = l_2 \wedge i.super = l_1 \quad (4.2)$$

Consequently, a fragment f contains language concepts from both l_1 and l_2:

$$\forall e \in E_f \mid lo(e) = l_1 \vee lo(e) = l_2 \quad (4.3)$$

In other words, $C_f \subset (C_{l_1} \cup C_{l_2})$, so f is *heterogeneous*. For heterogeneous fragments (1.3) does not hold anymore, since:

$$\forall c \in Cdn_f \mid (lo(co(c.parent)) = l_1 \vee lo(co(c.parent)) = l_2) \wedge$$
$$(lo(co(c.child)) = l_1 \vee lo(co(c.child)) = l_2) \quad (4.4)$$

Note that copying a language definition and changing it does not constitute a case of language extension, because the extension is not modular, it is invasive. Also, native interfaces that support calling one language from another (like calling C from Perl or Java) is not language extension; rather it is a form of language referencing. The fragments remain homogeneous.

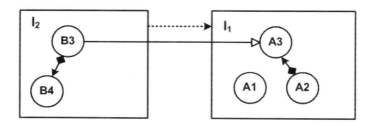

Figure 4.27: Extension: l_2 extends l_1. It provides additional concepts $B3$ and $B4$. $B3$ extends $A3$, so it can be used as a child of $A2$, just like $A3$. This plugs l_2 into the context provided by l_1. Consequently, l_2 depends on l_2.

Language extension fits well with the hierarchical domains introduced in Section 3.1: a language L_B for a domain D may extend a language L_A for D_{-1}. L_B contains concepts specific to D, making analysis and transformation of those concepts possible without pattern matching and semantics recovery. As explained in the introduction, the new concepts are often reified from the idioms and patterns used when using an L_A for D. Language semantics are typically defined by mapping the new abstractions to just these idioms (see Section 4.3) *inline*. This process, also known as *assimilation*, transforms a heterogeneous fragment (expressed in L_D and L_{D+1}) into a homogeneous fragment expressed only with L_D.

Extension is especially useful for bottom-up domains. The common patterns and idioms identified for a domain can be reified directly into linguistic abstractions, and used directly in the language from which they have been embedded. Incomplete languages are not a problem, since users can easily fall back to D_{-1} to implement the rest. Since DSL users see the D_{-1} code all the time anyway, they will be comfortable falling

Language extension is especially interesting if D_0 languages are extended, making a DSL an extension of a general purpose language.

back to D_{-1} in exceptional cases. This makes extensions suitable only for DSLs used by developers. Domain expert DSLs are typically not implemented as extensions.

mbeddr C: As an example, consider embedded programming. The C programming language is typically used as the GPL for D_0 in this case. Extensions for embedded programming include state machines, tasks or data types with physical units. Language extensions for the subdomain of real-time systems may include ways of specifying deterministic scheduling and worst-case execution time. For the avionics subdomain support for remote communication using some of the bus systems used in avionics could be added. ◄

Extension comes in two flavors. One really feels like extension, the other feels more like embedding.

- *Extension Flavor* In the first case we provide (a little, local) additional syntax to an otherwise unchanged language. For example, C may be extended with new data types and literals for complex numbers, as in `complex c = (3+2i);`. The programs still essentially look like C programs, with specific extensions in a few places.

- *Embedding Flavor* The other case is where we create a completely new language, but reuse some of the syntax provided by the base language. For example, we could create a state machine language that reuses C's expression and types in guard conditions. This use case *feels* like embedding (we embed syntax from the base language in our new language), but in the classification according to syntactic integration and dependencies, it is still extension. Embedding would prevent dependencies between the state machine language and C.

> The embedding flavour *is* often suitable for use with DSLs that are used by non-programmers, since the "embedded" subset of the language is often small and simple to understand. Once again, expression languages are the prime example for this.

Language extension is also a very useful way to address the problem of DSLs often starting as simple, but then becoming more complicated over time, because new corners or intricacies in the domain are discovered as users gain more experience in the domain. These corner cases and intricacies can be factored into a separate language module that extends the core DSL. The use of these extensions can then initially be restricted to a few users in order to find out if they are really needed. Different experiments can even be performed at the same time, with different groups of users using different extensions. Even once these extensions have proved useful, "advanced" language features can be restricted in this way to a small group of "advanced" users who handle the hard cases by using the extension.

Incremental extension can help to avoid the feared "customization cliff". The customization cliff is a term introduced by Steve Cook[70]: *once you step outside of what is covered by your DSL, you plunge down a cliff onto the rocks of the low-level platform.* If DSLs are built as incremental extensions of the next lower language, then stepping outside any DSL on level D will only plunge you down to the language for D_{-1}. And presumably you can always create an additional extension that extends your DSL to cover an additional, initially unexpected aspect.

Defining a D language as an extension of a D_{-1} language can also have drawbacks. The language is tightly bound to the D_{-1} language it is extended from. While it is possible for a stand-alone DSL in D to generate implementations for different D_{-1} languages, this is not easily possible for DSLs that are extensions of a D_{-1} language. Also, interaction with the D_{-1} language may make meaningful semantic analysis of complete programs (using L_D and L_{D-1} concepts) hard. This problem can be limited if isolated L_D sections are used in which interaction with L_{D-1} concepts is limited and well-defined. These isolated sections remain analyzable.

[70] `blogs.msdn.com/b/stevecook/archive/2005/12/16/504609.aspx`

■ *Restriction*   Sometimes language extension is also used to *restrict* the set of language constructs available in the subdomain. For example, the real-time extensions for C may restrict the use of dynamic memory allocation, or the extension for safety-critical systems may prevent the use of **void** pointers and certain casts. Although the extending language is in some sense smaller than the extended one, we still consider this a case of language extension, for two reasons. First, the restrictions are often implemented by adding *additional* constraints that report errors if the restricted language constructs are used. Second, a marker concept may be added to the base language. The restriction rules are then enforced for children of these marker concepts (e.g., in a module marked as "safe", one cannot use void pointers and the prohibited casts).

Restriction is often useful for the embedding-flavor of extension. For example, when embedding C expressions into the state machine language, we may want to restrict users from using the pointer-related expressions.

mbeddr C: Modules can be marked as *MISRA-compliant*, which prevents the use of those C constructs that are not allowed in MISRA-C[71]. Prohibited concepts are reported as errors directly in the program. ◀

[71] www.misra.org.uk/Publications/tabid/57/Default.aspx#label-c2

4.6.3 Language Reuse

Language reuse enables *homogenous* fragments with *independent* languages (Fig. 4.28). Given are two independent languages l_2 and l_1 and two fragment f_2 and f_1. f_2 depends on f_1, so that:

$$\exists r \in Refs_{f_2} \mid fo(r.from) = f_2 \wedge \\ (fo(r.to) = f_1 \vee fo(r.to) = f_2) \quad (4.5)$$

Since l_2 is independent, it cannot directly reference concepts in l_1. This makes l_2 reusable with different languages (in contrast to language referencing, where concepts in l_2 reference concepts in l_1). We call l_2 the *context* language and l_1 the *reused* language.

One way of realizing dependent fragments while retaining independent languages is using an adapter language l_A where l_A extends l_2, and:

$$\exists r \in Refs_{l_A} \mid lo(r.from) = l_A \wedge lo(r.to) = l_1 \quad (4.6)$$

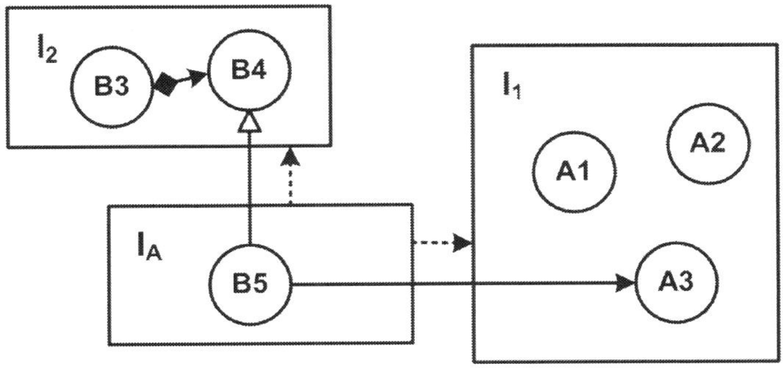

One could argue that in this case reuse is just a clever combination of referencing and extension. While this is true from an implementation perspective, it is worth describing as a separate approach, because it enables the combination of two *independent* languages by adding an adapter *after the fact*, so no pre-planning during the design of l_1 and l_2 is necessary.

Figure 4.28: Reuse: l_1 and l_2 are independent languages. Within an l_2 fragment, we still want to be able to reference concepts in another fragment expressed with l_1. To do this, an adapter language l_A is added that depends on both l_1 and l_2, using inheritance and referencing to adapt l_1 to l_2.

While language referencing supports reuse of the referenced language, language reuse supports the reuse of the *referencing* language as well. This makes sense for DSLs that have the potential to be reused in many domains, with minor adjustments. Examples include role-based access control, relational database mappings and UI specification.

Example: Consider a language for describing user interfaces. It provides language concepts for various widgets, layout definition and disable/enable strategies. It also supports data binding, where data structures are associated with widgets, to enable two-way synchronization between the UI and the data. Using language reuse, the same UI language can be used with *different* data description languages. Referencing would not achieve this goal, because the UI language would have a direct dependency on a particular data description language. Changing the dependency direction to *data* → *ui* doesn't solve the problem either, because this would go against the generally accepted idiom that UI has dependencies to the data, but not vice versa (cf. the MVC pattern). ◀

Generally, the referencing language is built with the knowledge that it will be reused with other languages, so hooks may be provided for adapter languages to plug in.

Example: The UI language thus may define an abstract concept `DataMapping`, which is then extended by various adapter languages. ◀

4.6.4 Language Embedding

Language embedding (Fig. 4.29) enables *heterogeneous* fragments with *independent* languages. It is similar to reuse, in that there are two independent languages l_1 and l_2, but instead of establishing references between two homogeneous fragments, we now embed instances of concepts from l_2 in a fragment f expressed with l_1, so:

$$\forall c \in Cdn_f \mid lo(co(c.parent)) = l_1 \land$$
$$(lo(co(c.child)) = l_1 \lor lo(co(c.child)) = l_2)) \quad (4.7)$$

Unlike language extension, where l_2 depends on l_1 because concepts in l_2 extends concepts in l_1, there is no such dependency in this case. Both languages are independent. We call l_2 the *embedded* language and l_1 the *host* language. Again, an adapter language l_A that extends l_1 can be used to achieve this, where:

$$\exists c \in Cdn_{l_A} \mid lo(c.parent) = l_A \land lo(c.child) = l_1 \quad (4.8)$$

Embedding supports syntactic composition of independently developed languages. As an example, consider a state machine language that can be combined with any number of programming languages such as Java or C. If the state machine language is used together with Java, then the guard conditions used in the transitions should be Java expressions. If it is used with

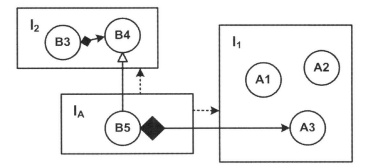

Figure 4.29: Embedding: l_1 and l_2 are independent languages. However, we still want to use them in the same fragment. To enable this, an adapter language l_A is added. It depends on both l_1 and l_2, and uses inheritance and composition to adapt l_1 to l_2 (this is almost the same structure as in the case of reuse; the difference is that $B5$ now *contains* $A3$, instead of just referencing it).

C, then the expressions should be C expressions. The two expression languages, or in fact, any others, must be embeddable in the guard conditions. So the state machine language cannot depend on any particular expression language, and the expression languages of C or Java obviously cannot be designed with knowledge about the state machine language. Both have to remain independent, and have to be embedded using an adapter language.

Another example is embedding a database query language such as Linq or SQL in *different* programming languages (Java, C#, C). Again, the query language may not have a dependency on any programming language (otherwise it would not be embeddable in all of them). The problem could be solved by extension (with embedding flavor), but then the programming language would have to be invasively changed – it now has to have a dependency on the query language. Using embedding, this dependency can be avoided.

When embedding a language, the embedded language must often be extended as well. In the state machine example, new kinds of expressions must be added to support referencing event parameters defined in the host language. In the case of the query language, method arguments and local variables should probably me usable as part of the queries (`... WHERE somecolumn = someMethodArg`). These additional expressions will typically reside in the adapter language as well.

Just as in the embedding-flavored extension case (cf. Section 4.6.2), sometimes the embedded language must also be restricted. If you embed the C expression language in state machine guard conditions, you may want to restrict the user from using pointer types or all the expressions related to pointers in C.

Note that if the state machine language is specifically built to "embed" C expressions, then this is a case of language Extension, since the state machine language depends on the C expression language.

WebDSL: In order to support queries over persistent data, WebDSL embeds the Hibernate Query Language (HQL) such that HQL queries can be used as expressions. Queries can refer to entity declarations in the program and to variables in the scope of the query. ◄

Pension Plans: The pension workbench DSL embeds a spreadsheet language for expressing unit tests for pension plan calculation rules. The spreadsheet language comes with its own simple expression language to be used inside the cells. A new expression has been added to reference pension rule input parameters so that they can be used inside the cells. ◄

■ *Cross-Cutting Embedding, Meta Data*   A special case of embedding is handling meta data. We define meta data as program elements that are not essential to the semantics of the program, and are typically not handled by the primary model processor. Nonetheless this data must relate to program elements, and, at least from a user's perspective, they often need to be embedded in programs. Since most of them are rather generic, embedding is the right composition mechanism: no dependency to any specific language should be necessary, and the meta data should be embeddable in any language. Example meta data includes:

Documentation , which should be attachable to any program element, and in the documentation text, other program elements should be referenceable.

Traces , to capture typed relationships between program elements, or between program elements and requirements or other documentation ("this program element *implements* that requirement").

Presence Conditions in product line engineering, to describe if a program element should be available in the program for a given product configuration ("this procedure is only in the program in the *international* variant of the product").

In projectional editors, this meta data can be stored in the program tree and shown only optionally, if some global configuration switch is `true`. In textual editors, meta data is often stored in separate files, using pointers to refer to the respective model elements. The data may be shown in hovers or views adjacent to the editor itself.

> **mbeddr C:** The system supports various kinds of meta data, including traces to requirements and documentation. They are implemented with MPS' *attribute* mechanism, which is discussed in the part on MPS in Section 16.2.7. As a consequence of how MPS attributes work, these meta data can be applied to program elements defined in any arbitrary language. ◂

4.6.5 Implementation Challenges and Solutions

The previous subsections discussed four strategies for language composition. In this section we describe some of the challenges regarding syntax, type systems and transformations for these four strategies.

■ *Syntax* Referencing and Reuse keeps fragments homogeneous. Mixing of concrete syntax is not required. A reference between fragments is usually simply an identifier and does not have its own internal structure for which a grammar would be required[72]. The name resolution phase can then create the actual cross-reference between abstract syntax objects.

> **Refrigerators:** The algorithm language contains cross-references into the hardware language. Those references are simple, dotted names such as `compartment1.valve`. ◂

> **Example:** In the UI example, the adapter language simply introduces dotted names to refer to fields of data structures. ◂

Extension and embedding requires modular concrete syntax definitions because additional language elements must be mixed with programs written with the base/host language. As we discuss in Part III (mostly in Section 7), combining independently developed languages after the fact can be a problem: depending on the parser technology, the combined grammar may not be parsable with the parser technology at hand. There are parser technologies that do not exhibit this problem, and projectional editors avoid it by definition. However, several widely used language workbenches have problems in this respect.

> **mbeddr C:** State machines are hosted in regular C programs. This works because the C language's `Module` con-

[72] Sometimes the references use qualified names, in which case the strings use dots and colons. However, this is still a trivial token structure, so it is acceptable to define the structure separately in both languages.

struct contains a collection of **IModuleContents**, and the **StateMachine** concept implements the **IModuleContent** concept interface. This state machine language is designed specifically to be embedded into C, so it can access and extend **IModuleContent** (Fig. 4.30). If the state machine language were embeddable in any host language in addition to C, this dependency on **ModuleContent** (from the C base language) would not be allowed. An adapter language would have to be created which adapts a **StateMachine** to **IModuleContent**. ◀

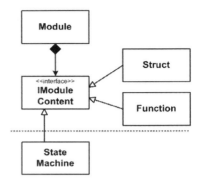

Figure 4.30: The core language (above the dotted line) defines an interface **IModuleContent**. Anything that should be hosted inside a **Module** has to implement this interface, typically from another language. **StateMachines** are an example.

■ *Type Systems* For referencing, the type system rules and constraints of the referencing language typically have to take into account the referenced language. Since the referenced language is known when developing the referencing language, the type system can be implemented with the referenced language in mind as well.

Refrigerators: In the refrigerator example, the algorithm language defines typing rules for hardware elements (from the hardware language), because these types are used to determine which properties can be accessed on the hardware elements (e.g., a compressor has a property **active** that controls whether it is on or off). ◀

In the case of extension, the type systems of the base language must be designed in a way that allows adding new typing rules in language extensions. For example, if the base language defines typing rules for binary operators, and the extension language defines new types, then those typing rules may have to be overridden to allow the use of existing operators with the new types.

mbeddr C: A language extension provides types with physical units (as in **100 kg**). Additional typing rules are needed to override the typing rules for C's basic operators (+, -, *, /, etc.). MPS supports declarative type system specification, so you can just *add* additional typing rules for the case in which one or both of the arguments have a type with a physical unit. ◀

For reuse and embedding, the typing rules that affect the interplay between the two languages reside in the adapter language. The type systems of both languages must be extensible in the way described in the previous paragraph on extension.

Example: In the UI example the adapter language will have to adapt the data types of the fields in the data description to the types the UI widgets expect. For example, a combo box widget can only be bound to fields that have some kind of text or enum data type. Since the specific types are specific to the data description language (which is unknown at the time of creation of the UI language), a mapping must be provided in the adapter language. ◄

■ *Transformation* In this section we use the terms *transformation* and *generation* interchangeably. In general, transformation is used if one tree of program elements is mapped to another tree, while generation describes the case of creating text from program trees. However, for the discussions in this section, this distinction is generally not relevant.

Three cases have to be considered for referencing. The first one (Fig. 4.31) propagates the referencing structure to the target fragments. We call these two transformations *single-sourced*, since each of them only uses a single, homogeneous fragment as input and creates a single, homogeneous fragment as output, typically with references between them. Since the referencing language is created with knowledge about the referenced language, the generator for the referencing language can be written with knowledge about the names of the elements that have to be referenced in the fragment generated from the referenced fragment. If a generator for the referenced language already exists, it can be reused unchanged. The two generators basically share knowledge about the names of generated elements.

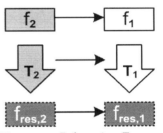

Figure 4.31: Referencing: Two separate, dependent, single-source transformations

Component Architecture: In the types viewpoint, interfaces and components are defined. The types viewpoint is independent, and it is sufficient for the generation of the code necessary for implementing component behavior: Java base classes are generated that act as the component implementations (expected to be extended by manually written subclasses). A second, dependent viewpoint describes component instances and their connections; it depends on the types viewpoint. A third describes the deployment of the instances to execution nodes (servers, essentially). The generator for the deployment viewpoint generates code that actually instantiates the classes that implement components, so it has to know the names of those generated (and hand-written) classes. ◀

The second case (Fig. 4.32) is a multi-sourced transformation that creates one single homogeneous fragment. This typically occurs if the referencing fragment is used to guide the transformation of the referenced fragment, for example by specifying transformation strategies (annotation models). In this case, a new transformation has to be written that takes the referencing fragment into account. The possibly existing generator for the referenced language cannot be reused as is.

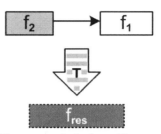

Figure 4.32: A single multi-sourced transformation.

Refrigerators: The refrigerator example uses this case. The code generator that generates the C code that implements the cooling algorithm takes into account the information from the hardware description model. A single fragment is generated from the two input models. The generated code is C-only, so the fragment remains homogeneous. ◀

The third case, an alternative to rewriting the generator, is the use of a preprocessing transformation (Fig. 4.33), that changes the referenced fragment in a way consistent with what the referencing fragment prescribes. The existing transformations for the referenced fragment can then be reused.

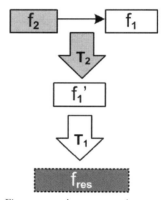

Figure 4.33: A preprocessing transformation that changes the referenced fragment in a way specified by the referencing fragment

As we have discussed above, language extensions are usually created by defining linguistic abstractions for common idioms of a domain D. A generator for the new language concepts can simply recreate those idioms when mapping L_D to L_{D-1}, a process also called assimilation. In other words, transformations for language extensions map a heterogeneous fragment (containing L_{D-1} and L_D code) to a homogeneous fragment that contains only L_{D-1} code (Fig. 4.34). In some cases additional files may be generated, often configuration files. In any case, the subsequent transformations for L_{D-1}, if any, can be reused unchanged.

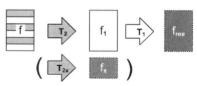

Figure 4.34: Extension: transformation usually happens by assimilation, i.e. generating code in the host language from code expressed in the extension language. Optionally, additional files are generated, often configuration files.

mbeddr C: State machines are generated down to a function that contains a `switch` statement, as well as `enum`s for states and events. Then the existing C-to-text transformations are reused unchanged. In addition, the state machines are also transformed into a dot file that is used to render the state machine graphically via graphviz. ◀

Sometimes a language extension requires rewriting transformations defined by the base language. In this case, the transformation engine must support the *overriding* of transformations by transformations defined in another language.

mbeddr C: In the data-types-with-physical-units example, the language also provides range checking and overflow detection. So if two such quantities are added, the addition is transformed into a call to a special **add** function instead of using the regular plus operator. This function performs overflow checking and addition. MPS supports transformation priorities that can be used to override the existing transformation with a new one. ◂

Language extension introduces the risk of semantic interactions. The transformations associated with several independently developed extensions of the same base language may interact with each other. To avoid the problem, transformations should be built in a way so that they do not "consume scarce resources" such as inheritance links[73].

[73] It would be nice if DSL tools would detect such conflicts statically, or at least supported a way of marking two languages or extensions as *incompatible*. However, none of the tools I know support such features.

Example: Consider the (somewhat artificial) example of two extensions to Java that each define a new statement. When assimilated to pure Java, both new statements require the surrounding Java class to extend a specific but different base class. This won't work, because a Java class can only extend one base class. ◂

Interactions may also be more subtle and affect memory usage or execution performance. Note that this problem is not specific to languages; it can occur whenever several independent extensions of a something can be used together, ad hoc. A more thorough discussion of the problem of semantic interactions is beyond the scope of this book.

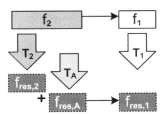

Figure 4.35: Reuse: Reuse of existing transformations for both fragments plus generation of adapter code.

In the reuse scenario, it is likely that both the reused and the context language already come with their own generators. If these generators transform to different, incompatible target languages, no reuse is possible. If they transform to a common target languages (such as Java or C) then the potential for reusing previously existing transformations exists.

There are three cases to consider. The first one, illustrated in Fig. 4.35, describes the case in which there is an existing transformation for the reused fragment and an existing transformation for the context fragment – the latter being written with the knowledge that later extension will be necessary. In this case, the generator for the adapter language may "fill in the holes" left by the reusable generator for the context language.

For example, the generator of the context language may generate a class with abstract methods; the adapter may generate a subclass and implement these abstract methods.

In the second case, Fig. 4.36, the existing generator for the reused fragment has to be enhanced with transformation code specific to the context language. A mechanism for composing transformations is needed.

The third case, Fig. 4.37, leaves composition to the target languages. We generate three different independent, homogeneous fragments, and a some kind of weaver composes them into one final, heterogeneous artifact. Often, the weaving specification is the intermediate result generated from the adapter language. An example implementation could use AspectJ.

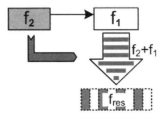

Figure 4.36: Reuse: composing transformations

An embeddable language may not come with its own generator, since, at the time of implementing the embeddable language, one cannot know what to generate – its purpose is to be embedded! In that case, when embedding the language, a suitable generator has to be developed. It will typically either generate host language code (similar to generators in the case of language extension) or directly generate to the same target language that is generated to by the host language.

If the embeddable language comes with a generator that transforms to the same target language as the embedding language, then the generator for the adapter language can coordinate the two, and make sure a single, consistent fragment is generated. Fig. 4.38 illustrates this case.

Just as for language extension, language embedding may also lead to semantic interactions if multiple languages are embedded into the same host language.

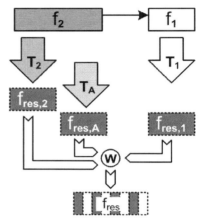

Figure 4.37: Reuse: generating separate artifacts plus a weaving specification.

4.7 Concrete Syntax

A good choice of concrete syntax is important for DSLs to be accepted by the intended user community. Especially (but not exclusively) in business domains, a DSL will only be successful if and when it uses notations that directly fit the domain – there might even be existing, established notations that should be reused. A good notation makes expression of common concerns simple and concise and provides sensible defaults. It is acceptable for less common concerns to require a little more verbosity in the notation.

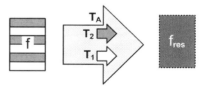

Figure 4.38: In transforming embedded languages, a new transformation has to be written if the embedded language does not come with a transformation for the target language of the host language transformation. Otherwise the adapter language can coordinate the transformations for the host and for the embedded languages.

4.7.1   Design Concerns for Concrete Syntax

In particular the following concerns may be addressed when designing a concrete syntax[74]:

Writability A writable syntax is one that can be written efficiently. This usually means that the syntax is concise, because users have to type less. However, a related aspect is tool support: the degree to which the IDE can provide better editing support[75] (code completion and quick fixes in particular) makes a difference to readability.

Readability A readable syntax means that it can be read effectively. A more concise syntax is not necessarily more readable, because context may be missing[76], in particular for people other than those who have written the code.

Learnability A learnable syntax is useful to novices in particular, because it can be "explored", often exploiting IDE support[77]. For example, the more the language uses concepts that have a direct meaning in the domain, the easier it is for domain users to lean the language.

Effectiveness Effectiveness relates to the degree that a language enables routine users to effectively express typical domain problems *after* they have learned the language.

■ *Tradeoffs*   It is obvious that some of these concerns are in conflict. A very writable language may not be very readable. If a group of stakeholders R uses artifacts developed by another group W (e.g. by referencing some of the program elements), it is important that a readable language is used. A learnable language may feel "annoyingly verbose and cumbersome" to routine users after a while[78]. However, creating an effective syntax and trying to convince users to adopt the language even though it is hard(er) to learn may be a challenge.

For DSLs whose programs have a short lifetime (as in scripting languages) readability is often not very important, because the programs are thrown away once they have performed their particular task.

■ *Multiple Notations*   One way to solve these dilemmas is to provide different concrete syntaxes for the same abstract syntax, and let users choose. For example, beginners can chose a more learnable one, and switch to a more effective one over

---

[74] These concerns do not just depend on the concrete syntax, but also on the abstract syntax and the expressiveness of the language itself (which is discussed in Section 4.1). However, the concrete syntax has a major influence, which is why we discuss it here.)

[75] See the example of the `select` statement in Section 4.7.2.

[76] A good example of this dilemma are the APL or M languages: the syntax is so concise that it is really hard to read.

[77] "Just press Ctrl-Space and the tool will tell you what you can type next."

[78] Note that if a specific DSL is only used irregularly, then users probably never become routine users, and have to relearn the language each time they use it.

time. However, depending on the tooling used, this can be a lot of work.

■ *Multiple Notations* For projectional editors it is relatively easy to define several notations for the same language concept. By changing the projection rules, existing programs can be shown in a different way. In addition, different notations (possibly showing different concerns of the overall program) can be used for different stakeholders.

We have the equivalent of multiple notations for the same language in the real world. English can be spoken, written, transported via morse code or even expressed via sign language. Each of these is optimized for certain contexts and audiences.

> **mbeddr C:** For state machines, the primary syntax is textual. However, a tabular notation is supported as well. The projection can be changed as the program is edited, rendering the same state machine textually or as a table. A graphical notation will be added in the future, as MPS' support for graphical notations improves. ◀

> **Refrigerators:** The refrigerator DSL uses graphical visualizations to render diagrams of the hardware structure, as well as a graphical state charts representing the underlying state machine. ◀

Another option to resolve the learnability vs. effectiveness dilemma is to create an effective syntax and help new users by good documentation, training and/or IDE support (templates, wizards).

■ *Reports and Visualization* A visualization is a graphical representation of a model that cannot be edited. It is created from the core model using some kind of transformation, and highlights a particular aspect of the source program. It is often automatically laid out[79]. The resulting diagram may be static (i.e. an image file is generated) or interactive (where users can show, hide and focus on different parts of the diagram). It may provide drill-down back to the core program (double-clicking on the figure in the image opens the code editor at the respective location)[80].

A report has the same goals (highlighting a particular aspect of the source program, while not being editable) but uses a textual notation.

Visualizations and reports are a good way of resolving a potential conflict if the primary DSL users want to use a writable notation and other stakeholders want a more readable representation. Since reports and visualizations are not the primary

[79] Automatic layout requires a good layout algorithm. The best one is available commercially in yFiles/yEd. Sometimes it is necessary manually adjust the layout of the generated visualization. Doing so of course is problematic because the manual adjustments are lost if the visualization is regenerated. A better approach is to create another model that *specifies properties of the visualization*, such as the subset of model elements that should be in the diagram, semantic coloring or selecting of shapes or layout hints for the algorithm.

[80] Graphviz is one of the most well-known tools for this kind of visualization. Another is Jan Koehnlein's Generic Graph View at `github.com/JanKoehnlein/Generic-Graph-View`.

notation, it is possible to create several different visualizations or reports for the source program, highlighting different aspects of the core program.

mbeddr C: In the mbeddr components extension, we support several notations. The first shows interfaces and the components that provide and require these interfaces. The second shows component instances and the connections between their provided and required ports. Finally, there is a third visualization that applies to all mbeddr models, not just those that use components: it shows the modules, their imports (i.e. module dependencies) as well as the public contents of these modules (functions, structs, components, test cases). ◂

figure 4.39: mbeddr C also supports graphical visualizations of state machines. For every state machine, a dot representation is automatically generated. The image is then rendered by graphviz directly in the IDE. Double-clicking on a state selects the respective program element in the editor.

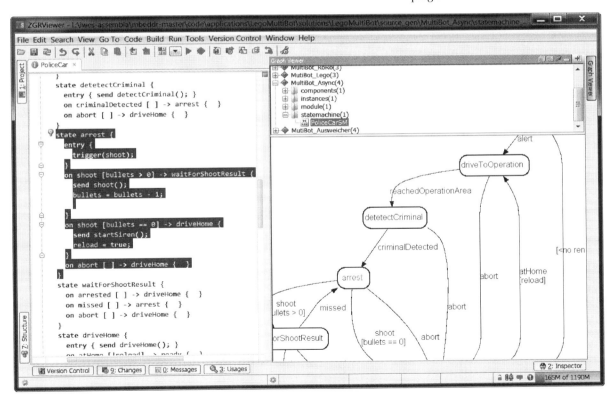

4.7.2 Classes of Concrete Syntax

There are a couple of major classes for DSL concrete syntax[81]: *textual* DSLs use linear textual notations, typically based on ASCII or Unicode characters. They basically look and feel like

[81] Sometimes form-based GUIs or tree views are considered DSLs. I disagree, because this would make any GUI application a DSL.

traditional programming languages. *Graphical* DSLs use graphical shapes. An important subgroup is represented by those that use box-and-line diagrams that look and feel like UML class diagrams or state machines. However, there are more options for graphical notations, such as those illustrated by UML timing diagrams or sequence diagrams. *Symbolic* DSLs are textual DSLs with an extended set of symbols, such as fraction bars, mathematical symbols or subscript and superscript. *Tables and matrices* are a powerful way to represent certain kinds of data and can play an important part for DSLs.

The perfect DSL tool should support free combination and integration of the various classes of concrete syntax, and be able to show (aspects of) the same model in different notations. As a consequence of tool limitations, this is not always possible, however. The requirements for concrete syntax are a major driver in tool selection.

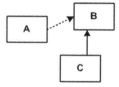

Figure 4.40: Graphical notation for relationships

■ *When to Use Which Form* We do not want to make this section a complete discussion between graphical and textual DSLs – a discussion that is often heavily biased by previous experience, prejudice and tool capabilities. Here are some rules of thumb. Purely textual DSLs integrate well with existing development infrastructures, making their adoption relatively easy. They are well suited for detailed descriptions, anything that is algorithmic or generally resembles (traditional) program source code. A good textual syntax can be very effective (in terms of the design concerns discussed above). Symbolic notations can be considered "better textual", and lend themselves to domains that make heavy use of symbols and special notations; many scientific and mathematical domains come to mind. Tables are very useful for collections of similarly structured data items, or for expressing how two independent dimensions of data relate. Tables emphasize readability over writability. Finally, graphical notations are very good for describing relationships (Fig. 4.40), flow (Fig. 4.41) or timing and causal relationships (Fig. 4.42). They are often considered easier to learn, but may be perceived as less effective by experienced users.

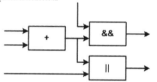

Figure 4.41: Graphical notation for flow

Figure 4.42: Graphical notation for causality and timing

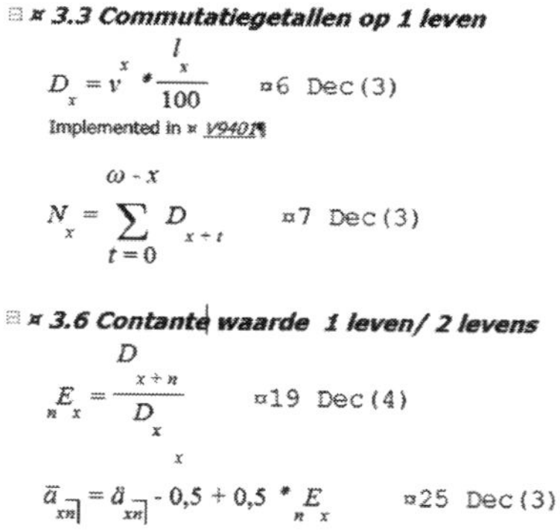

Pension Plans: The pension DSL uses a mathematical notation to express insurance mathematics (Fig. 4.43). A table notation is embedded to express unit tests for the pension plan calculation rules. A graphical projection shows dependencies and specialization relationships between plans. ◂

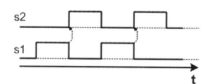

Figure 4.43: Mathematical notations used to express insurance math in the pension workbench.

mbeddr C: The core DSLs use mostly textual notations with some tabular enhancements, for example for decision tables (Fig. 20.4). However, as MPS' capability for handling graphical notations improves, we will represent state machines as diagrams. ◄

```
module DecisionTableExample from cdesignpaper.gswitch imports nothing {

  enum mode { MANUAL; AUTO; FAIL; }

  mode nextMode(mode mode, int8_t speed) {
    return mode, FAIL    |            | mode == MANUAL | mode == AUTO |  ;
                         | speed < 30 | MANUAL         | AUTO         |
                         | speed > 30 | MANUAL         | MANUAL       |
  } nextMode (function)
}
```

Figure 4.44: Decision tables use a tabular notation. It is embedded seamlessly into a C program.

Selection of a concrete syntax is simple for domain user DSLs if there is an established notation in the domain. The challenge then is to replicate this notation as closely as possible with the DSL, while cleaning up possible inconsistencies in the notation (since presumably it had not been used formally before). I like to use the term "strongly typed (Microsoft) Word" in this case[82].

For DSLs targeted at developers, a textual notation is usually a good starting point, since developers are used to working with text, and they are very productive with it. Tree views and some visualizations are often useful for outlines, hierarchies or overviews, but not necessarily for editing. Textual notations also integrate well with existing development infrastructures.

[82] In some cases it is useful to come up with a better notation than the one used historically. This is especially true if the historic notation is Excel.

mbeddr C: C is the baseline for embedded systems, and everybody is familiar with it. A textual notation is useful for many concerns in embedded systems. Note that several languages create visualizations on the fly, for example for module dependencies, component dependencies and component instance wirings. The graphviz tool is used here since it provides decent auto-layout. ◄

There are very few DSLs where a *purely* graphical notation makes sense, because in most cases some textual languages are embedded in the diagrams or tables: state machines embedded expressions in guards and statements in actions (Fig. 20.7); component diagrams use text for specifications of operations in interfaces, maybe using expressions for preconditions; block diagrams use a textual syntax for the implementation/parametrization of the blocks (Fig. 4.45); tables may embed textual notations in the cells (Fig. 4.46). Integrating textual languages into graphical ones is becoming more and more important, and tool support is improving.

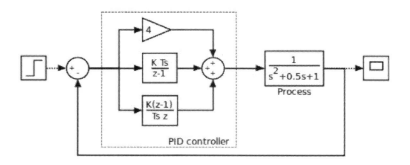

A text box where textual code can be entered without language support should only be used as a last resort. Instead, a textual notation, with additional graphical visualizations should be used.

Figure 4.45: A block diagrams built with the Yakindu modeling tools. A textual DSL is used to implement the behavior in the blocks. While the textual DSL is not technically integrated with the graphical notation (separate viewpoints), semantic integration is provided.

Note that initially domain users prefer a graphical notation, because of the perception that things that are described graphically are simple(r) to comprehend. However, what is most important regarding comprehensibility is the alignment of the domain concepts with the abstractions in the language. A well-designed textual notation can go a long way. Also, textual languages are more productive once the learning curve has been overcome. I have had several cases where domain users started preferring textual notations later in the process.

In my consulting practice, I almost always start with a textual notation and try to stabilize language abstractions. Only then will I engage in a discussion about whether a graphical notation on top of the textual one is necessary. Often it is not, and if it is, we have avoided iterating the implementation of the graphical editor implementation, which, depending on the tooling, can be a lot of work.

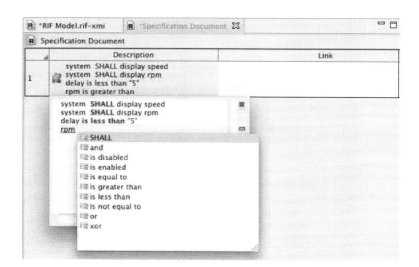

Figure 4.46: The Yakindu Requirements tools integrates a textual DSL for formal requirements specification into a table view. The textual specifications are stored as text in the requirements database; consequently, the entities defined textually cannot be referenced (which is not a problem in this domain).

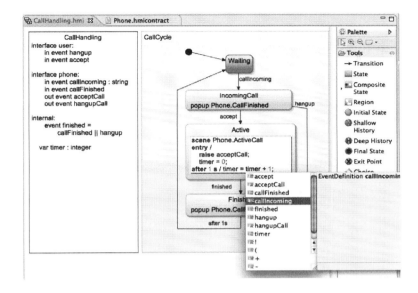

Figure 4.47: The Yakindu State Chart Tools support the use of Xtext DSLs in actions and guard conditions of state machines, mixing textual and graphical notations. The DSL can even be exchanged, to support domain specific action languages, for example for integrating with user interface specifications. In this case, the textual specification are stored as the AST in terms of EMF, not as text.

■ *IDE Supportability* For textual languages, it is important to keep in mind if and how a syntax can be support by the IDE, especially regarding code completion. Consider query languages. An example SQL query looks like this:

```
SELECT field1, field2 FROM aTable WHERE ...
```

When entering this query the IDE cannot provide code completion for the fields after the **SELECT** because at this point the table has not yet been specified. A more suitable syntax, with respect to IDE support, would be:

```
FROM aTable SELECT field1, field2 WHERE ...
```

It is better because now the IDE can provide support code completion for the fields based on the table name that has already been entered when you specify the fields[83].

Another nice example is dot-notation for function calls. Consider a functional language. Typical function call syntax is `f(a, b, c)` or possiby `(f a b c)`. In either case, the function comes first. Now consider a notation where you can (optionally) write the first argument before the dot, i.e. `a.f(b, c)`. This has a significant advantage in terms of IDE support: after the user enters `a.`, code completion can propose all the functions that are available for the type of `a`. This leads to much better explorability of the language compared to the normal function-first syntax: since at the time of writing the function, the user has not yet written the value on which to apply the function, the IDE can provide no support[84].

[83] SQL is a relatively old language and IDE concerns were probably not very important at the time. More modern query languages such as HQL or Linq in fact use the more IDE-friendly syntax.

[84] This example was motivated by Daan Leijen's Koka language which supports the dot-notation for just this reason.

Note that tool supportability in general is not fundamentally different in graphical and textual languages. While IDEs for textual languages can provide code completion, the palette or the context buttons in a graphical DSL play the same role. I often hear that a graphical DSL is more suitable for simulation (because the execution of the program can be animated on the graphical notation). However, this is only true if the graphical notation works well in the first place. A textual program can also be animated; a debugger essentially does just that.

■ *Relationship to Hierarchical Domains*   Domains at low D are most likely best expressed with a textual or symbolic concrete syntax. Obvious examples include programming languages at D_0. Mathematical expressions, which are also very dense and algorithmic, use a symbolic notation. As we progress to higher Ds, the concepts become more and more abstract, and as state machines and block diagrams illustrate, graphical notations become useful. However, these two notations are also a good example of language embedding, since both of them require expressions: state machines in guards and actions (Fig. 20.7), and block diagrams as the implementation of blocks (Fig. 4.45 and Fig. 5.5). Reusable expression languages should be embedded into the graphical notations. If this is not supported by the tool, viewpoints may be an option. One viewpoint could use a graphical notation to define coarse-grained structures, and a second viewpoint use a textual notation to provide "implementation details" for the structures defined by the graphical viewpoint[85].

mbeddr C: As the graphical notation for state machines becomes available, the C expression language that is used in guard conditions for transitions will be usable as labels on the transition arrows. In the table notation for state machines, C expressions can be embedded in the cells as well. ◄

[85] Not every tool can support every (combination of) form of concrete syntax, so this aspect is limited by the tool, or drives tool selection.

5
Fundamental Paradigms

Every DSL is different. It is driven by the domain for which it is built. However, as it turns out, there are also a number of commonalities between DSLs. These can be handled by modularizing and reusing (parts of) DSLs, as discussed in the last section of the previous chapter. In this section we look at common paradigms for describing DSL structure and behavior.

5.1   Structure

Languages have to provide a means of structuring large programs in order to keep them manageable. Such means include modularization and encapsulation, specification vs. implementation, specialization, types and instances, as well as partitioning.

> The language design alternatives described in this section are usually not driven directly by the domain, or the domain experts guiding the design of the language. Rather, they are often brought in by the language designer as a means of managing overall complexity. For this reason they may be hard to "sell" to domain experts.

5.1.1   Modularization and Visibility

DSLs often provide some kind of logical unit structure, such as namespaces or modules. Visibility of symbols may be restricted to the same unit, or to referencing ("importing") units. Symbols may be declared as **public** or **private**, the latter making them invisible to other modules, which guarantees that changes to these symbols cannot affect other modules. Some form of namespaces and visibility is necessary in almost any DSL. Often there are domain concepts that can play the role of the module, possibly oriented towards the structure of the organization in which the DSL is used.

> Most contemporary programming languages use some form of namespaces and visibility restriction as their top-level structure.

>   **mbeddr C:** As a fundamental extension to C, this DSL contains modules with visibility specifications and imports. Functions, state machines, tasks and all other top-level

concepts reside in modules. Header files (which are effectively a poor way of managing symbol visibility) are only used in the generated low-level code and are not relevant to the user of mbeddr C. ◄

Component Architecture: Components and interfaces live in namespaces. Components are implementation units, and are always private. Interfaces and data types may be public or private. Namespaces can import each other, making the public elements of the imported namespace visible to the importing namespace. The OSGi generator creates two different bundles: an interface bundle that contains the public artifacts, and an implementation bundle with the components. In the case of a distributed system, only the interface bundle is deployed on the client. ◄

Pension Plans: Pension plans constitute namespaces. They are grouped into more coarse-grained packages that are aligned with the structure of the pension insurance business. ◄

5.1.2 Partitioning

Partitioning refers to the breaking down of programs into several physical units such as files (typically each model fragment is stored in its own partition). These physical units do not have to correspond to the logical modularization of the models within the partitions. For example, in Java a public class has to live in a file of the same name (logical module == physical partition), whereas in C# there is no relationship between namespace, class names and the physical file and directory structure. A similar relationship exists between partitions and viewpoints, although in most cases, different viewpoints are stored in different partitions.

Note that a reference to an element should not take into account the partition in which the target element lives. Instead, it should only use the logical structure. Consider an element `E` that lives in a namespace `x.y`, stored in a partition `mainmodel`. A reference to that element should be expressed as `x.y.E`, not as `mainmodel.E` or `mainmodel/x.y.E`. This is important, as it allows elements to move freely between partitions without this leading to updates of all references to the element.

Partitioning may have consequences for language design. Consider a textual DSL in which a concept A contains a list of

If a repository-based tool is used, the importance of partitioning is greatly reduced. Although even in that case there may be a set of federated and distributed repositories that can be considered partitions.

instances of concept B. The B instances then have to be physically nested within an instance of A in the concrete syntax. If there are many instances of B in a given model, they cannot be split into several files, so these files may become big and result in performance problems. If such a split must be possible, this has to be designed into the language.

> **Component Architecture:** A variant of this DSL that was used in another project had to be changed to allow a namespace to be spread over several files for reasons of scalability and version-control granularity. In the initial version, namespaces actually *contained* the components and interfaces. In the revised version, components and interfaces were owned by no other element, but model files (partitions) had a namespace declaration at the top, logically putting all the contained interfaces and components into this namespace. Since there was no technical containment relationship between namespaces and their elements, several files could now declare the same namespace. Changing this design decision lead to a significant reimplementation effort, because all kinds of naming and scoping strategies changed. ◄

Other concerns influence the design of a partitioning strategy as well:

Change Impact Which partition changes as a consequence of a particular change of the model (changing an element name might require changes to all references to that element from other partitions).

Link Storage Where are links stored (are they always stored in the model that logically "points to" another one?), and if not, how/where/when to control reference/link storage.

Model Organization Partitions may be used as a way of organizing the overall model. This is particularly important if the tool does not provide a good means of presenting the overall logical structure of models and finding elements by name and type. Organizing files with meaningful names in directory structures is a workable alternative.

Tool Chain Integration Integration with existing, file-based tool chains. Files may be the unit of check in/check out, versioning, branching or permission checking.

It is often useful to ensure that each partition is processable separately to reduce processing times. An alternative approach supports the explicit definition of those partitions that should be processed in a given processor run (or at least a search path, a set of directories, to find the partitions, like an include path in C compilers or the Java classpath). You might even consider a separate build step to combine the results created from the separate processing steps of the various partitions (again like a C compiler, which compiles every file separately into an object file, after which the linker handles overall symbol/reference resolution and binding).

The partitioning scheme may also influence users' team collaboration when editing models. There are two major collaboration models: real-time and commit-based. In real-time collaboration, a user sees his model change in real time as another user changes the same model. Change propagation is immediate. A database-backed repository is often a good choice regarding storage, since the granularity tracked by the repository is the model element. In this case, the partitioning may not be visible to the end user, since they just work "on the repository". This approach is often (at least initially) preferred by non-programmer DSL users.

The other collaboration mode is commit-based, in which a user's changes are only propagated to the repository if he performs a *commit*, and incoming changes are only visible after a user has performed an *update*. While this approach can be used with database-backed repositories, it is most often used with file-based storage. In this case, the partitioning scheme is visible to DSL users, because it is those files they commit or update. This approach tends to be preferred by developers, maybe because well-known versioning tools have used the approach for a long time.

5.1.3 Specification vs. Implementation

Separating specification and implementation supports plugging in different implementations for the same specification and hence provides a way to "decouple the outside from the inside"[1]. This supports the exchange of several implementations behind a single interface. This is often required as a consequence of the development process: one stakeholder defines the specification and a client, whereas another stakeholder provides one or more implementations.

Another driver for using partitions is the scalability of the DSL tool. Beyond a certain file size, the editor may become sluggish.

[1] Interfaces, pure abstract classes, traits or function signatures are a realization of this concept in programming languages.

The separation of specification and implementation can also have positive effects on scalability and performance. If the specification and implementation are separated into different fragments, then, in order to type check a client's access to some provided service, only the fragment that contains the specification has to be loaded/parsed/checked. This is obviously faster than processing complete implementation.

A challenge for this approach is how to ensure that all implementations are consistent with the specification. Traditionally, only the structural/syntactic/signature compatibility is checked. To ensure semantic compatibility, additional means that specify the expected *behavior* are required. This can be achieved with pre- or post-conditions, invariants or protocol state machines.

mbeddr C: This DSL adds interfaces and components to C. Components provide or use one or more interfaces. Different components can be plugged in behind the same interface. To support semantic specifications, the interfaces support pre- and post-conditions as well as protocol state machines. Fig. 5.1 shows an example. Although these specifications are attached to interfaces, they are actually checked (at runtime) for all components that provide the respective interface. ◂

```
exported c/s interface DriveTrain {
  void driveForwardFor(uint8_t speed, uint32_t ms)
    pre(0) speed <= 100
    post(1) currentSpeed() == 0
    protocol init(0) -> init(0)
  void driveContinuouslyForward(uint8_t speed)
    pre(0) speed <= 100
    post(1) currentSpeed() == speed
    protocol init(0) -> new forward(1)
  void accelerateBy(uint8_t delta)
    pre(0) currentSpeed() + delta < 100
    post(1) currentSpeed() == old[currentSpeed()] + delta
    protocol forward -> forward
  query uint8_t currentSpeed()
}
```

Figure 5.1: An interface using semantic specifications. Preconditions check the values of arguments for validity. Postconditions express constraints on the values of **query** operations after the execution of the operation. Notice how the value of the **query** before executing the operation can be referred to (the **old** keyword used in the postcondition for **accelerateBy**). In addition, protocols constrain the valid sequence of operation invocations. For example, the **accelerateBy** operation can only be used if the protocol state machine is already in the **forward** state. The system gets into the **forward** state by invoking the **driveContinuouslyForward** operation.

Refrigerators: Cooling programs can access hardware elements (compressors, fans, valves); those are defined as part of the refrigerator hardware definition. To enable cooling programs to run with different, but similar hardware configurations, the hardware structure can use "trait inheritance", by which a hardware trait defines a set of hardware elements, acting as a kind of interface. Other hardware configurations can inherit these traits. As long as cooling programs are only written against traits, they work with any refrigerator that implements the particular set of traits against which the program is written. ◂

5.1.4 Specialization

Specialization enables one entity to be a more specific variant of another. Typically, the more specific one can be used in all contexts in which the more general one is expected (the Liskov substitution principle[2]). The more general one may be incomplete, requiring the specialized ones to "fill in the holes". Specialization in the context of DSLs can be used for implementing variants or for evolving a program over time.

[2] B. Liskov and J. M. Wing. A behavioral notion of subtyping. *TOPLAS*, 16(6):1811–1841, 1994

In GPLs, we know this approach from class inheritance. "Leaving holes" is realized by abstract methods.

Defining the semantics of inheritance for domain-specific language concepts is not always easy. The various approaches found in programming languages, as well as the fact that some of them lead to problems (multiple inheritance, diamond inheritance, linearization, or code duplication in Java's interface inheritance) shows that this is not a trivial topic. It is a good idea to just copy a suitable approach *completely* from a programming language in which inheritance seems to work well. Even small changes can make the whole approach inconsistent.

Pension Plans: The customer using this DSL had the challenge of creating a huge set of pension plans, implementing changes in relevant law over time, or implementing related plans for different customer groups. Copying complete plans and then making adaptations was not feasible, because this resulted in a maintenance nightmare: a large number of similar but not identical pension plans. Hence the DSL provides a way for pension plans to inherit from one another. Calculation rules can be marked *abstract* (needing to be overwritten in sub-plans), *final* rules are not overwritable. Visibility modifiers control which rules are considered "implementation details". ◄

Refrigerators: A similar approach is used in the cooling DSL. Cooling programs can specialize other cooling programs. Since the programs are fundamentally state-based, we had to define what it means to specialize a cooling program: a subprogram can add additional event handlers and transitions to states. New states can be added, but states defined in the super-program cannot be removed. ◄

5.1.5 Types and Instances

Types and instances supports the definition of structures that can be parametrized upon instantiation. This allows reuse of common parts, and expressing variability via parameters.

In programming languages we know this from classes and objects (where constructor parameters are used for parametrization) or from components (where different instances can be connected differently to other instances).

mbeddr C: Apart from C's **structs** (which are instantiatable data structures) and components (which can be instantiated and connected), state machines can be instantiated as well. Each instance can be in a different state at any given time. ◂

5.1.6   Superposition and Aspects

Superposition refers to the ability to merge several model fragments according to some DSL-specific merge operator. Aspects provide a way of "pointing to" several locations in a program based on a pointcut operator (essentially a query over a program or its execution), adapting the model in ways specified by the aspect. Both approaches support the compositional creation of many different model variants from the same set of model fragments.

This is especially important in the context of product line engineering and is discussed in Section 21.

Component Architecture: This DSL provides a way of advising component definitions from an aspect (Fig. 5.2). An aspect may introduce an additional **provided port mon: IMonitoring** that allows a central monitoring component to query the advised components via the **IMonitoring** interface. ◂

```
component DelayCalculator {
    ...
}
component AircraftModule {
    ...
}
component InfoScreen {
    ...
}
           aspect (*) component {
               provides mon: IMonitoring
           }
                                   component DelayCalculator {
                                       ...
                                       provides mon: IMonitoring
                                   }
                                   component AircraftModule {
                                       ...
                                       provides mon: IMonitoring
                                   }
                                   component InfoScreen {
                                       ...
                                       provides mon: IMmonitoring
                                   }
```

Figure 5.2: The aspect component contributes an additional required port to each of the other components defined in the system.

WebDSL: Entity declarations can be *extended* in separate modules. This makes it possible to declare in one module all data declarations of a particular feature. For example, in the *researchr* application, a **Publication** can be **Tag**ged, which requires an extension of the **Publication** entity. This extension is defined in the **tag** module, together with the definition of the **Tag** entity. This is essentially a use of superposition. ◄

5.1.7   *Versioning*

Often, variability over time of elements in DSL programs has to be tracked. One alternative is to simply version the model files using existing version control systems, or the version control mechanism built into the language workbench. However, this requires users to interact with often complex version control systems and prevents domain-specific adaptations of the version control strategy.

The other alternative is to make versioning and tracking over time a part of the language. For example, model elements may be tagged with version numbers, or specify a revision chain by pointing to a previous revision, enforcing compatibility constraints between those revisions. Instead of declaring explicit versions, business data is often time-dependent, where different revisions of a business rule apply to different periods of time. Support for these approaches can be built directly into the DSL, with various levels of tool support.

mbeddr C: No versioning is defined into the DSL. Users work with MPS' integration with popular version control systems. Since this DSL is intended for use by programmers, working with existing version control systems is not a problem. ◄

Component Architecture: Components can specify a **new version of** reference to another component. In this case, the new version may specify additional provided ports with the same interfaces, or with new versions of these interfaces. The new version may also deprecate required ports. Effectively, this means that the new version of something must be replacement-compatible with the old version (the Liskov substitution principle again). ◄

Pension Plans: In the pension workbench, calculation rules declare applicability periods. This supports the evolution of calculation rules over time, while retaining reproducability for calculations performed at an earlier point in time. Since the Intentional Domain Workbench is a projectional tool, pension plans can be shown with only the version of a rule that is valid for a given point in time. ◄

5.2 Behavior

The behavior expressed with a DSL must of course be aligned with the needs of the domain. However, in many cases, the behavior required for a domain can be derived from well-known behavioral paradigms[3], with slight adaptations or enhancements, or simply by interacting with domain-specific structures or data.

[3] The term *Model of Computation* is also used to refer to behavioral paradigms. I prefer "behavioral paradigm" because the term *model* is obviously heavily overloaded in the DSL/MDSD space already.

Note that there are two kinds of DSLs that don't make use of these kinds of behavior descriptions. Some DSLs really just specify structures. Examples include data definition languages or component description languages (although both of them often use expressions for derived data, data validation or pre- and post-conditions). Other DSLs specify a set of expectations regarding some behavior (declaratively), and the generator creates the algorithmic implementation. For example, a DSL may specify, simply with a tag such as *async*, that the communication between two components shall be asynchronous. The generator then maps this to an implementation that behaves according to this specification.

Component Architecture: The component architecture DSL is an example of a structure-only DSL, since it only describes black box components and their interfaces and relationships. It uses the specification-only approach to specify whether a component port is intended for synchronous or asynchronous communication. ◄

mbeddr C: The component extension provides a similar notion of interfaces, ports and components as in the previous example. However, since here they are directly integrated with C, C expression can be used for pre- and post-conditions of interface operations (see Fig. 5.1). ◄

Using an established behavioral paradigm for a DSL has several advantages[4]. First, it is not necessarily simple to define consistent and correct semantics in the first place. By reusing an existing paradigm, one can learn about advantages and drawbacks from existing experience. Second, a paradigm may already come with existing means for performing interesting

[4] Which is why we discuss these paradigms in this book.

analyses (as in model checking or SMT solving) that can easily be used to analyse DSL programs. Third, there may be existing generators from a behavioral paradigm to an efficient executable for a given platform (state machines are a prime candidate). By generating a model in a formalism for which such a generator exists, we reduce the effort for building an end-to-end generator. If our DSL uses the same behavioral paradigm as the language for which the generator exists, writing the necessary transformation is straightforward (from a semantic point of view).

The last point emphasizes that using an existing paradigm for a DSL (e.g. state-based) does not mean that the concepts have to directly use the abstractions used by that paradigm (just because a program is state-based does not mean that the concept that acts as a state has to be called state, etc.).

. This section describes some of the most well-known behavioral paradigms that can serve as useful starting points for behavior descriptions in DSLs. In addition to describing the paradigm, we also briefly investigate how easily programs using the paradigm can be analyzed, and how complicated it is to build debuggers.

This is only an overview over a few paradigms; many more exist. I refer to the excellent Wikipedia entry on *Programming Paradigms* and to the book

P. V. Roy and S. Haridi. *Concepts, Techniques, and Models of Computer Programming*. MIT Press, 2004

5.2.1 *Imperative*

Imperative programs consist of a sequence of statements, or instructions, that change the state of the program. This state may be local to some kind of module (e.g., a procedure or an object), global (as in global variables) or external (when communicating with peripheral devices). Procedural and object-oriented programming are both imperative, using different means for structuring and (in the case of OO) specialization. Because of aliasing and side effects, imperative programs are expensive to analyse. Debugging imperative programs is straightforward and involves stepping through the instructions and watching the state change.

For many people, often including domain experts, this approach is easy to understand. Hence it is often a good starting point for DSLs.

mbeddr C: Since C is used as a base language, this language is fundamentally imperative. Some of the DSLs on top of it use other paradigms (the state machine extension is state-based, for example). ◀

Refrigerators: The cooling language integrates various paradigms, but contains sequences of statements to implement aspects of the overall cooling behavior. ◀

5.2.2 Functional

Functional programming uses functions as the core abstraction. In purely functional programming, a function's return value only depends on the values of its arguments. Calling the same function several times with the same argument values returns the same result (that value may even be cached!). Functions cannot access global mutable state, no side effects are allowed. These characteristics make functional programs very easy to analyze and optimize. These same characteristics, however, also make purely functional programming relatively useless, because it cannot affect its environment (after all, this would be a side effect). So, functional programming is often only used for parts ("calculation core") of an overall program and integrates with, for example, an imperative part that deals with IO.

Since there is no changing state to observe as the program steps through instructions, debugging can be done by simply showing all intermediate results of all function calls as some kind of tree, basically "inspecting" the state of the calculation. This makes building debuggers relatively simple.

> **Pension Plans:** The calculation core of pension rules is functional. Consequently, a debugger has been implemented that, for a given set of input data, shows the rules as a tree that shows all intermediate results of each function call (Fig. 5.3). No "step through" debugger is necessary. ◂

Pure expressions are an important subset of functional programming (as in `i > 3*2 + 7`). Instead of calling functions, operators are used. However, operators are just infix notations for function calls. Usually the operators are hard wired into the language and it is not possible for users to define their own functional abstractions. The latter is the main differentiator to functional programming in general. It also limits expressivity, since it is not possible to modularize an expression or to reuse expressions by packaging into a user-defined function. Consequently, only relatively simply tasks can be addressed with a pure expression language[5].

> **mbeddr C:** We use expressions in the guard conditions of the state machine extension as well as in pre- and post-conditions for interface operations. In both cases it is not possible to define or call external functions. Of course, (a subset of) C's expression language is reused here. ◂

[5] However, many DSLs do not require anything more sophisticated, especially if powerful domain-specific operators are available. So, while expression languages are limited in some sense, they are still extremely useful and widespread.

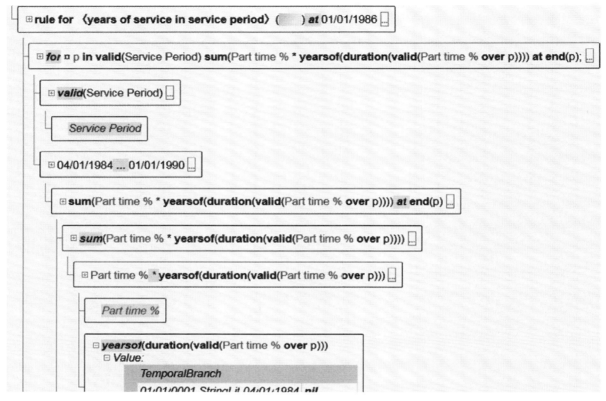

Figure 5.3: Debugging functional programs can be done by showing the state of the calculation, for example as a tree.

5.2.3 *Declarative*

Declarative programming can be considered the opposite of imperative programming (and, to some extent, of functional programming). A declarative program does not specify any control flow; it does not specify a sequence of steps of a calculation. A declarative program only specifies *what* the program should accomplish, not *how*. This is often achieved by specifying a set of properties, equations, relationships or constraints. Some kind of evaluation engine then tries to find solutions. The particular advantage of this approach is that it does not predefine how a solution is found; the evaluation engine has a lot of freedom in doing so, possibly using different approaches in different environments, or evolving the approach over time[6]. This large degree of freedom often makes finding the solution expensive – trial and error, backtracking or exhaustive search may be used[7]. Debugging declarative programs can be hard, since the solution algorithm may be very complex and possibly not even be known to the user of the language.

[6] For example, the strategies for implementing SAT solvers have evolved quite a bit over time. SAT solvers are much more scalable today. However, the formalism for describing the logic formulas that are processed by SAT solvers have not changed.

[7] Users often have to provide hints to the engine to make it run fast enough or scale to programs of relevant size. In practice, declarative programming is often not as "pure" as it is in theory.

Declarative programming has many important subgroups. For *concurrent programs*, a declarative approach allows the efficient execution of a single program on different parallel hardware structures. The compiler or runtime system allocates the program to available computational resources. In *constraint programming*, the programmer specifies constraints between a set of variables. The engine tries to find values for these variables that satisfy all constraints. Solving mathematical equation systems is an example, as is solving sets of Boolean logic formulas. *Logic programming* is another sub-paradigm, in which users specify logic clauses (facts and relations) as well as queries. A theorem prover then tries to solve the queries.

> The Prolog language works in this way.

Component Architecture: This DSL specifies timing and resource characteristics for component and interface operations. Based on this data, one could run an algorithm which allocates the component instances to computing hardware so that the hardware is used as efficiently as possible, while at the same time reducing the amount of network traffic. This is an example of constraint solving used to synthesize a schedule. ◄

mbeddr C: This DSL supports presence conditions for product line engineering. A presence condition is a Boolean expression over a set of configuration features that determines whether the associated piece of code is present for a given combination of feature selections (Fig. 5.4). To verify the structural integrity of programs in the face of varying feature combinations, constraint programming is used (to ensure that there is no configuration of the program in which a reference to a symbol is included, but the referenced symbol is not). A set of Boolean equations is generated from the program and the attached presence conditions, . A solver then makes sure they are consistent by trying to find an example solution that violates the Boolean equations. ◄

Example: The Yakindu DAMOS block diagram editor supports custom block implementation based on the Mscript language (Section 5.5). It supports declarative specification of equations between input and output parameters of a block. A solver computes a closed, sequential solution that efficiently calculates the output of an overall block diagram. ◄

```
[Variability from FM: Deployment ]
[Rendering Mode: product line    ]
module Sensor from test.ex.cc.secondExample imports Driver {

  typedef int8_t replace if {highRes} with double as dataType;
  #define int8_t DATA_SIZE = 100;
  var dataType[DATA_SIZE] data;
  var int8_t idx;

  {logging}
  message list messages {
    INFO startingMeasurement() active: entering main function
    INFO finishingMeasurement() active: exitingMainFunction
  }

  dataType measure() {
    {logging}
    report(0) messages.startingMeasurement() on/if;
    dataType res = 0;
    {!highRes}
    res = readPortInt(1);
    {highRes}
    res = readPortDouble(1);
    {logging}
    report(1) messages.finishingMeasurement() on/if;
    data[idx] = res;
    idx++;
    return res;
  } measure (function)

}
```

Figure 5.4: This module contains variability expressed with presence conditions. The affected program elements are highlighted in a color (shade in the screenshot) that represents the condition. If the feature **highRes** is selected, the code uses a **double** instead of an **int8_t**. The log messages are only included if the **logging** feature is selected. Note that one cannot just depend on single features (such as **logging**) but also on arbitrary expressions such as **logging && highRes**.

Example: Another example for declarative programming is the type system DSL used by MPS itself. Language developers specify a set of type equations containing free type variables, among other things. A unification engine tries to solve the set of equations by assigning actual types to the free type variables so that the set of equations is consistent. We describe this approach in detail in Section 10.4. ◄

5.2.4 Reactive/Event-based/Agent

In this paradigm, behavior is triggered based on received events. Events may be created by another entity or by the environment (through a device driver). Reactions are expressed by the creation of other events. Events may be globally visible or explicitly routed between entities, possibly using filters and/or using priority queues. This approach is often used in embedded systems that have to interact with the real world, where the real

```
synchronous blockType org::eclipse::damos::lib::_discrete::DiscreteDerivative

input u
output y

parameter initialCondition = 0
parameter gain = 1(s) // normalized

behavior {

  stateful func main<initialCondition, gain, fs>(u) -> y {
    check<0, 1(s), 1(1/s)>(real) -> real

    static assert u is real() :
            error "Input value must be numeric"

    static assert initialCondition is real() :
            error "Initial condition must be numeric"

    static assert initialCondition is real() && u is real()
                      => unit(initialCondition) == unit(u) :
            error "Initial condition and input value must have same unit"

    static assert gain is real() :
            error "Gain value must be numeric"

    eq u{-1} = initialCondition
    eq y{n} = fs * gain * (u{n} - u{n-1})
  }

}
```

Figure 5.5: An Mscript block specifies input and output arguments of a block (u and v) as well as configuration parameters (*initialCondition* and *gain*). The assertions specify constraints on the data the block works with. The *eq* statements specify how the output values are calculated from the input values. Stateful behaviors are supported, where the value for the n-th step depends on values from previous steps (e.g., $n-1$).

world produces events as it changes. A variant of this approach queries input signals at intervals controlled by a scheduler and considers changes in input signals as the events.

Refrigerators: The cooling algorithms are reactive programs that control the cooling hardware based on environment events. Such events include the opening of a refrigerator door, the crossing of a temperature threshold, or a timeout that triggers defrosting of a cooling compartment. Events are queued, and the queues are processed in intervals determined by a scheduler. ◄

Debugging is simple if the timing/frequency of input events can be controlled. Visualizing incoming events and the code that is triggered as a reaction is relatively simple. If the timing of input events cannot be controlled, then debugging can be almost impossible, because humans are much too slow to fit "in between" events that may be generated by the environment in rapid succession. For this reason, various kinds of simulators are used to debug the behavior of reactive systems, and sophisticated diagnostics regarding event frequencies or queue filling levels may have to be integrated into the programs as they run in the real environment.

Refrigerators: The cooling language comes with a simulator (Fig. 5.6) based on an interpreter in which the behavior of a cooling algorithm can be debugged. Events are explicitly created by the user, on a timescale that is compatible with the debugging process. ◄

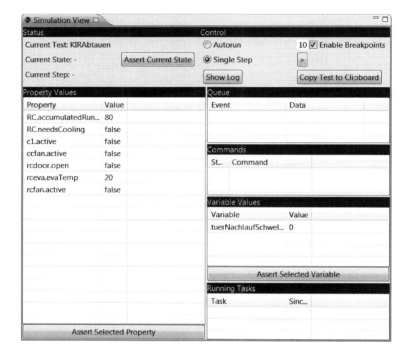

Figure 5.6: The simulator for the cooling language shows the state of the system (commands, event queue, value of hardware properties, variables and tasks). The program can be single-stepped. The user can change the value of variables or hardware properties as a means of interacting with the program.

5.2.5 Dataflow

The dataflow paradigm is centered around variables with dependencies (in terms of calculation rules) among them. As a variable changes, the variables that depend on the changing variable are recalculated. We know this approach mainly from two use cases. One is spreadsheets: cell formulas express dependencies to other cells. As the values in these other cells change, the dependent cells are updated. The other use case is data flow (or block) diagrams (Fig. 5.7), used in embedded software, extraction-transfer-load data processing systems and enterprise messaging/complex event processing. There, the calculations or transformations are encapsulated in the blocks, and the lines represent dependencies – the output of one blocks "flows" into the input slot of another block. There are three different execution modes:

- The first one considers the data values as continuous sig-

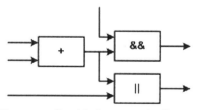

Figure 5.7: Graphical notation for flow.

nals. At the time one of the inputs changes, all dependent values are recalculated. The change triggers the recalculation, and the recalculation ripples through the dependency graph. This is the model used in spreadsheets.

- The second one considers the data values as quantized, unique messages. A new output message is calculated only if a message is available for all inputs. The recalculation synchronizes on the availability of a message at each input, and upon recalculation, these messages are consumed. This approach is often used in ETL and CEP systems.

- The third approach is time-triggered. Once again, the inputs are understood to be continuous signals, and a scheduler determines when a new calculation is performed. The scheduler also makes sure that the calculation "ripples through from left to right" in the correct order. This model is typically used in embedded systems.

Debugging these kinds of systems is relatively straightforward because the calculation is always in a distinct state. Dependencies and data flow, or the currently active block and the available messages, can easily be visualized in a block diagram notation. Note that the calculation rules themselves are considered black boxes here, whose internals may be built from any other paradigm, often functional. Integrating debuggers for the internals of boxes is a more challenging task.

5.2.6 State-based

The state-based paradigm describes a system's behavior in terms of the states the system can be in, the transitions between these states, events that trigger these transitions and actions that are executed as states change. State machines are useful for systematically organizing the behavior of an entity. They can also be used to describe valid sequences of events, messages or procedure calls. State machines can be used in an event-driven mode in which incoming events actually trigger transitions and the associated actions. Alternatively a state machine can be run in a timed mode, in which a scheduler determines when event queues are checked and processed. Except for possible real-time issues, state machines are easy to debug by highlighting the contents of event queues and the current state[8].

[8] Apart from the imperative paradigm and simple expression languages, state machines are probably the paradigm that is most often used in DSLs.

mbeddr C: This language provides an extension that supports directly working with state machines. Events can be passed into a state machine from regular C code, or by mapping incoming messages in components to events in state machines that reside in components. Actions can contain arbitrary C code, unless the state machine is marked as verifiable, in which case actions may only create outgoing events or change state machine-local variables. ◄

Refrigerators: The behavior of cooling programs is fundamentally state-based. A scheduler is used to execute the state machine at regular intervals. Transitions are triggered either by incoming, queued events or by changing property values of hardware building blocks. This language is an example where a behavioral paradigm is used without significant alterations, but working with domain-specific data structures – refrigerator hardware and its properties. ◄

State-based behavior description is also interesting in the context of model checking. The model checker either determines that the state chart conforms to a set of specifications or provides a counter-example that violates the specifications. Specifications express something about sequences of states such as "It is not possible that two traffic lights show green at the same time" or "Whenever a pedestrian presses the **request** button, the pedestrian lights eventually will show green"[9].

In principle, any program can be represented as a state machine and can then be model checked. However, creating state machines from, say, a procedural C program is non-trivial, and the state machines also become very big very quickly. State-based programs *are already* a state machine, and, they are typically not that big either (after all, they have to be understood by the developer who creates and maintains them). Consequently, many realistically-sized state machines can be model checked efficiently.

[9] A good introduction to model checking can be found in the book mentioned below:

Berard, B., Bidoit, M., Finkel, A., Laroussinie, F., Petit, A., Petrucci, L., Schnoebelen, and P. *Systems and Software Verification*. Springer, 2001

5.3 Combinations

The behavioral paradigm also plays a role in the context of language composition. If two to-be-composed languages use different behavioral paradigms, the composition can become really challenging. For example, combining a continuous system (which works with continuous streams of data) with a discrete event-based system requires temporal integration. We won't discuss this topic in detail in this book[10]. However, it is obvious that combining systems that use the same paradigm is much simpler. Alternatively, some paradigms can be integrated relatively easily; for example, it is relatively simple to map a state-based system onto an imperative system.

Many DSLs use combinations of various behavioral and structural paradigms described in this section[11]. Some combinations are very typical:

- A data flow language often uses a functional, imperative or declarative language to describe the calculation rules that express the dependencies between the variables (the contents of the boxes in data flow diagrams or of cells in spreadsheets). Fig. 4.45 shows an example block diagram, and Fig. 5.5 shows an example implementation.

- State machines use expressions as transition guard conditions, as well as typically an imperative language for expressing the actions that are executed as a state is entered or left, or when a transition is executed. An example can be seen in Fig. 20.7.

- Reactive programming, in which "black boxes" react to events, often using data flow or state-based programming to implement the behavior that determines the reactions.

- In purely structural languages, for example those for expressing components and their dependencies, a functional/expression language is often used to express pre- and post-conditions for operations. A state-based language is often used for protocol state machines, which determines the valid order of incoming events or operation calls.

Note that these combinations can be used to make well-established paradigms domain-specific. For example, in the Yakindu State Chart Tools (Fig. 20.7), a custom DSL can be plugged into an existing, reusable state machine language and editor. One concrete example is an action language that references another DSL that describes UI structures. This allows the state machine to be used to orchestrate the behavior of the UI.

Some of the case studies used as examples in this part of the book also use combinations of several paradigms.

Pension Plans: The pension language uses functional abstractions with mathematical symbols for the core actu-

[10] It is still very much a research topic.

[11] Note how this observation leads to the desire to better modularize and reuse some of the above paradigms. Room for research :-)

ary mathematics. A functional language with a plain textual syntax is used for the higher-level pension calculation rules. A spreadsheet/data flow language is used for expressing unit tests for pension rules. Various nesting levels of namespaces are used to organize the rules, the most important of which is the pension plan. A plan contains calculation rules as well as test cases for those rules. Pension plans can specialize other plans as a means of expressing variants. Rules in a sub-plan can override rules in the plan from which the sub-plan inherits. Plans can be declared to be abstract, with abstract rules that have to be implemented in sub-plans. Rules are versioned over time, and the actual calculation formula is part of the version. Thus, a pension plan's behavior can be made to be different for different points in time. ◀

Refrigerators: The cooling behavior description is described as a reactive system. Events are produced by hardware elements[12]. A state machine constitutes the top-level structure. Within it, an imperative language is used. Programs can inherit from another program, overwriting states defined in the base program: new transitions can be added, and the existing transitions can be overridden as a way for an extended program to "plug into" the base program. ◀

[12] Technically it is of course the driver of the hardware element, but in terms of the model the events are associated with the hardware element directly

6
Process Issues

> *Software development with DSLs requires a compatible development process. A lot of what's required is similar to what's required for working with any other reusable artifact such as a framework: a workable process must be established between those who build the reusable artifact and those who use it. Requirements have to flow in one direction, and a finished, stable, tested and documented product has to be delivered in the other direction. Also, using DSLs can be a fundamental change for all involved, especially the domain experts. In this chapter we provide some guidelines for the process.*

6.1   DSL Development

6.1.1   Requirements for the Language

How do you find out what your DSL should express? What are the relevant abstractions and notations? This is a non-trivial issue; in fact it is one of the key issues in developing DSLs. It requires a lot of domain expertise, thought and iteration. The core problem is that you're trying not just to understand one problem, but rather a *class* of problems. Understanding and defining the extent and nature of this class of problems can be a lot of work. There are three typical fundamentally different cases.

The first one conerns technical DSLs where the source for a language is often an existing framework, library, architecture or architectural pattern (the inductive approach). The knowledge often already exists, and building the DSL is mainly about factoring the knowledge into a language: defining a notation, putting it into a formal language, and building generators to generate (parts of) the implementation code. In the process, you often also want to put in place reasonable defaults for some of the framework features, thereby increasing the level of abstraction and making framework use easier.

> **mbeddr C:** This was the approach taken by the extensible C case study. There is a lot of experience in embedded software development, and some of the most pressing challenges are the same throughout the industry. When the DSL was built, we talked to expert embedded software developers to find out what these central challenges were. We also used an inductive approach and looked at existing C code to indentify idioms and patterns. We then defined extensions to C that provided linguistic abstractions for the most important patterns and idioms. ◂

The second case addresses business domain DSLs. There you can often mine the existing (tacit) knowledge of domain experts (deductive approach). In domains like insurance, science or logistics, domain experts are absolutely capable of precisely expressing domain knowledge. They do it all the time, often using Excel or Word. Other domain artifacts can also be exploited in the same way: for example, hardware structures or device features are good candidates for abstractions in the respective domains. So are existing user interfaces: they face users directly, and so are likely to contain core domain abstractions. Other sources are standards for an industry, or training material. Some domains even have an agreed ontology containing concepts relevant to that domain and recognized as such by a community of stakeholders. DSLs can be (partly) derived from such domain ontologies.

> **Pension Plans:** The company for which the pension DSL was built had a lot of experience with pension plans. This experience was mostly in the heads of (soon to be retiring) senior domain experts. They also already had the core of the DSL: a "rules language". The people who defined the pension plans would write rules as Word documents to "formally" describe the pension plan behavior. This was not terribly productive because of the missing tool support, but it meant that the core of the DSL was known. We still had to run a long series of workshops to work out nec-

essary changes to the language, clean up loose ends and discuss modularization and reuse in pension plans. ◀

In the two cases discusses so far, it is pretty clear how the DSL is going to look in terms of core abstractions; discussions will be about details, notation, how to formalize things, viewpoints, partitioning and the like (although all these can be pretty non-trivial too!).

In the remaining third case, however, we are not so lucky. If no domain knowledge is easily available we have to do an actual domain analysis, digging our way through requirements, stakeholder "war stories" and existing applications. People may be knowledgeable, but they might be unable to conceptualize their domain in a structured way – it is then the job of the language designer to provide the structure and consistency that is necessary for defining a language. Co-evolving language and concepts (see below) is a successful technique, especially in this case.

> One of my most successful approaches in this case is to build "straw men": trying to understand something, factor it into some kind of regular structure, and then re-explain that structure back to the stakeholders.

Refrigerators: At the beginning of the project, all cooling algorithms were implemented in C. Specifications were written in Word documents as prose (with tables and some physical formulas). It was not really clear at the beginning what the right abstraction level would be for a DSL suitable for the thermodynamics experts. It took several iterations to settle on the asynchronous, state-based structure described earlier. ◀

For your first DSL, try to catch case one or two. Ideally, start with case one, since the people who build the DLSs – software architects and developers – are often the same as the domain experts.

6.1.2   Iterative Development

Some people use DSLs as an excuse to reintroduce waterfall processes. They spend months and months developing languages, tools and frameworks. Needless to say, this is not a very successful approach. You need to iterate when developing the language.

Start by developing some deep understanding of a small part of the domain for which you build the DSL. Then build a little bit of language, build a little bit of generator and develop a small example model to verify what you just did. Ideally, implement all aspects of the language and processor for each new domain requirement before focusing on new requirements[1].

[1] IDE polishing is probably something you want to postpone a little, and not do as part of every iteration.

Novices to DSLs especially tend to get languages and meta models wrong because they are not used to "thinking meta". You can avoid this pitfall by immediately trying out your new language feature by building an example model and developing a compatible generator to verify that you can actually generate the relevant artifacts.

Refrigerators: To solidify our choices regarding language abstractions, we prototypically implemented several example refrigerators. During this process we found the need for more and more language abstractions. We noticed early on that we needed a way to test the example programs, so we implemented the interpreter and simulator relatively early. In each iteration, we extended the language as well as the interpreter, so the domain experts could experiment with the language even though we did not yet have a C code generator. ◄

It is important that the language approaches some kind of stable state over time (Fig. 6.1). As you iterate, you will encounter the following situation: domain experts express requirements that may sound inconsistent. You add all kinds of exceptions and corner cases to the language. You language grows in size and complexity. After a number of these exceptions and corner cases, ideally the language designer will spot the systematic nature behind them and refactor the language to reflect this deeper understanding of the domain. Language size and complexity is reduced. Over time, the amplitude of these changes in language size and complexity (the error bars in Fig. 6.1) should become smaller, and the language size and complexity should approach a stable level (ss in Fig. 6.1).

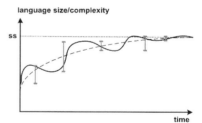

Figure 6.1: Iterating towards a stable language over time. It is a sign of trouble if the language complexity does not approach some kind of stable state over time.

Component Architecture: A nice example of spotting a systematic nature behind a set of special cases was the introduction of data replication as a core abstraction in the architecture DSL (we also discuss this in Section 18). After modeling a number of message-based communication channels, we noticed that the interfaces all had the same set of methods, just for different data structures. When we finally saw the pattern behind it, we created new linguistic abstractions: data replication. ◄

6.1.3 Co-evolve Concepts and Language

In cases in which you perform a real domain analysis, i.e. when you have to find out which concepts the language should contain, make sure you evolve the language in real-time as you discuss the concepts.

Defining a language requires formalization. It requires becoming very clear and unambiguous about the concepts that go into the language. In fact, building the language, because of the need for formalization, helps you become clear about the domain abstractions in the first place. Language construction acts as a catalyst for understanding the domain! I recommend actually building a language in real-time as you analyze your domain.

> **Refrigerators:** This is what we did in the cooling language. Everybody learned a lot about the possible structure of refrigerators and the limited feature combinations (based on limitations imposed by the way in which some of the hardware devices work). ◄

To make this feasible, your DSL tool must be lightweight enough to support language evolution during domain analysis workshops. Turnaround time should be minimal.

> **Refrigerators:** The cooling DSL is built with Xtext. Xtext allows very fast turnaround regarding grammar evolution, and, to a lesser extent, scopes, validation and type systems. We typically evolved the grammar in real-time, during the language design workshops, together with the domain experts. We then spent a day offline finishing scopes, constraints and the type system, as well as the interpreter. ◄

6.1.4 Let People Do What They are Good At

DSLs offer a chance to let everybody do what they are good at. There are several clearly defined roles, or tasks, that need to be done. Let me point out two, specifically.

Experts in a specific target technology can dig deep into the details of how to efficiently implement, configure and operate that technology. They can spend a lot of time testing, digging and tuning. Once they have found out what works best, they can put their knowledge into platforms and execution engines, efficiently spreading the knowledge across the team. For the latter task, they will collaborate with generator experts and language designers – our second example role.

Component Architecture: In building the language, an OSGi expert was involved in building the generation templates. ◀

The language designer works with domain experts to define abstractions, notations and constraints to capture domain knowledge accurately. The language designer also works with the architect and the platform experts in defining code generators or interpreters. Be aware that language designers need to have some kind of predisposition: not everybody is good at "thinking meta", some people are comfortable with concrete work. Make sure you use "meta people" to do the "meta work". And of course, the language designer must be fluent with the DSL tool used in the project.

The flip side is that you have to make sure that you actually have people on your team who are good at language design, know the domain and understand the target platforms, otherwise the benefits promised by using DSLs may not materialize.

6.1.5 Domain Users vs. Domain Experts

When building business DSLs, people from the domain can play two different roles. They can either participate in the domain analysis and the definition of the DSL itself, or they can use the DSL to create domain-specific models or programs.

It is useful to distinguish these two roles explicitly. The first role (language definition) must be filled by a domain *expert*. These are people who have typically been working in the domain for a long time, often in different roles, and who have a deep understanding of the relevant concepts, which they are able to express precisely and maybe even formally. The second group of people are the domain *users*. They are of course familiar with the domain, but they are typically not as experienced as the domain experts.

This distinction is relevant because you want to work with the domain *experts* when defining the language, but you want to build a language that is suitable for use by the domain *users*. If the experts are too far ahead of the users, the users might not be able to "follow", and you will not be able to roll out the language to the actual target audience.

Hence, make sure that when defining the language that you actually cross-check with real domain users whether they are able to work with the language.

Pension Plans: The core domain abstractions were contributed by Herman. Herman was the most senior pension expert in the company. In workshops we worked with a number of other domain users who didn't have as much experience. We used them to validate that our DSL would work for the average future user. Of course they also found actual problems with the language, so they contributed to the evolution of the DSL beyond just acting as guinea pigs. ◄

6.1.6 DSL as a Product

The language, constraints, interpreters and generators are usually developed by one (smaller) group of people and used by another (larger) group of people. To make this work, consider the "language stuff" as a product developed by one group for use by another. Make sure there's a well-defined release schedule, that development happens in short, predefined increments, that requirements and issues are reported and tracked, errors are fixed reasonably quickly, there is ample documentation and that support staff is available to help with problems and the unavoidable learning curve. These things are critical for acceptance!

A specific best practice is to exchange people: from time to time, make application developers part of the language team so that they can appreciate the challenges of "meta", and make people from the language development team participate in actual application development to make sure they understand if and how their work products suit the people who do the actual application development.

mbeddr C: One of our initial proof-of-concept projects didn't really work out very well. So in order to try out our first C extensions and come up with a showcase for an upcoming exhibition, the language developers built the proof-of-concept themselves. As it turned out, this was really helpful. We didn't just find a lot of bugs, we also experienced first-hand some of the usability challenges of the system at the time. It was easy for us to fix, because it was we who experienced the problems in the first place. ◄

6.1.7 Documentation is still necessary

Building the DSLs and execution engines is not enough to make the approach successful. You have to communicate to the users how to use these things in real-world contexts. Specifically, here's what you have to document: the language structure and syntax, how to use the editors and the generators, how and where to write manual code and how to integrate it into generated code, as well as platform/framework decisions (if applicable).

Keep in mind that there are other media than paper. Screencasts, videos that show flip chart discussions, or even a regular podcast that talks about how the tools change are good choices, too. Also keep in mind that hardly anybody reads reference documentation. If you want to be successful, make sure the majority of your documentation consists of example-driven or task-based tutorials.

Component Architecture: The documentation for the component architecture DSL contains a set of example applications. Each of them guides a new user through building an increasingly complex application. It explains installation of the DSL into Eclipse, concepts of the target architecture and how they map to language syntax, use of the editor and generator, as well as how to integrated manually written code into the generated base classes. ◂

6.2 Using DSLs

6.2.1 Reviews

A DSL limits the user's freedom in some respect: they can only express things that are within the limits of DSLs. Specifically, low-level implementation decisions are not under a DSL user's control because they are handled by the execution engine.

However, even with the nicest DSL, users can still make mistakes, the DSL users can still misuse the DSL – the more expressive the DSL, the bigger this risk. So, as part of your development process, make sure you perform regular model reviews. This is critical, especially for the adoption phase, when people are still learning the language and the overall approach.

Reviews are easier on the DSL level than on the code level. Since DSL programs are more concise and support better separation of concerns than their equivalent specification in GPL code, reviews become more efficient.

If you notice recurring mistakes, things that people do in the "wrong" way regularly, you can either add a constraint check that detects the problem automatically, or (maybe even better) consider this as input to your language designers: maybe what the users expect is actually correct, and the language needs to be adapted.

6.2.2 Compatible Organization

Done right, using DSLs requires a lot of cross-project work. In many settings the same language (module) will be used in several projects or contexts. While this is of course a big plus, it also requires that the organization is able to organize, staff, schedule and pay for cross-cutting work. A strictly project-focused organization will have a very hard time finding resources for these kinds of activities. DSLs, beyond the small ad-hoc utility DSL, are very hard to introduce into such environments.

In particular, make sure that the organizational structure, and the way project cost is handled, is compatible with cross-cutting activities. Any given project will not invest in assets that are reusable in other projects if the cost for developing the asset is billed only to the particular project. Assets that are useful for several projects (or the company as a whole) must also paid for by those several projects (or the company in general).

6.2.3 Domain Users Programming?

Technical DSLs are intended for use by programmers. Application domain DSLs are targeted towards domain users, non-programmers who are knowledgeable in the domain covered by the DSL. Can they actually work with DSLs?

In many domains, usually those that have a scientific or mathematical flavor, users can precisely describe domain knowledge. In other domains you might want to aim for a somewhat lesser goal. Instead of expecting domain users and experts to independently specify domain knowledge using a DSL, you might want to pair a developer and a domain expert. The developer can help the domain expert to be precise enough to "feed" the DSL. Because the notation is free of implementation clutter, the domain expert feels much more at home than when staring at GPL source code.

Initially, you might even want to reduce your aspirations to the point where the developer does the DSL coding based on discussions with domain users, then showing them the resulting model and asking confirming or disproving questions about it. Putting knowledge into formal models helps you

> Executing the program, by generating code or running some kind simulator, can also help domain users understand better what has been expressed with the DSL.

point out decisions that need to be made, or language extensions that might be necessary.

If you are not able to teach a business domain DSL to the domain users, it might not necessarily be the domain users' fault. Maybe your language isn't really suitable to the domain. If you encounter this problem, take it as a warning sign and consider changing the language.

6.2.4 DSL Evolution

A DSL that is successfully used will have to be evolved. Just as for any other software artifact, requirements evolve over time and the software has to reflect these changes. In the context of DSLs, the changes can be driven by several different concerns:

Target Platform Changes The target platform may change because of the availability of new technologies that provide better performance, scalability or usability. Ideally, no changes to either the language or the models are necessary: a new execution engine for the changed target platform can be created. In practice it is not always so clean: the DSL may make assumptions about the target platform that are no longer true for the changed or new platform. These may have to be removed from the languages and existing models. Also, the new platform may support different execution options, and the existing models do not contain enough information to make the decision of which option to take. In this case, additional annotation models may become necessary[2].

Domain Changes As the domain evolves, it is likely that the language has to evolve as well[3]. The problem then is: what do you do with existing models? You have two fundamental options: keep the old language and don't change the models, or evolve the existing models to work with the new (version of the) language. The former is often not really practical, especially in the face of several such changes.

The amount of pain in evolving existing models depends a lot on the nature of the change[4]. The most pragmatic approach keeps the new version of the language backward compatible, so that existing models can still be edited and processed. Under this premise, adding new language concepts is never a problem. However, you must never just delete existing concepts or change them in an incompatible way. Instead, these old concepts should be marked as *deprecated*, and the editor will show a corresponding warning in

[2] Despite the caveats discussed in this paragraph, a target platform change is typically relatively simple to handle.

[3] If you use a lot of in-language abstraction or a standard library, you may be lucky and the changes can be realized without changes to the language.

[4] It also depends a lot on the DSL tool. Different tools support model evolution in different ways.

the IDE. The IDE may also provide a quick fix to change the old, deprecated concept to a new (version of the) concept, if such a mapping is straightforward. Otherwise the migration must be done manually. If you have access to *all* models, you may also run a batch transformation during a quiet period to migrate them all at once. Note that, although deprecation has a bad reputation from programming languages from which deprecated concepts are never removed, this is not necessarily comparable to DSLs: if, after a while, people still use the deprecated concepts, you can have the IDE send an email to the language developers, who can then work with the "offending user" to migrate the programs.

Note that for the above approach to work, you have to have a structure process for versioning the languages and tools, otherwise you will quickly end up in version chaos.

DSL Tool Changes The third change is driven by evolution of the DSL tool. Of course, the language definition (and potentially, the existing models) may have to evolve if the DSL tool changes in an incompatible way (which, one could argue, it shouldn't!). This is similar to every other tool, library or framework you may use. People seem particularly afraid of the situation in which they have to switch to a completely new DSL tool because the current one is no longer supported, or a new one is just better. Of course it is very likely that you'll have to completely redo the language definitions: there is no portability in terms of language definitions among DSL tools (not even among those that reside on Eclipse). However, if you had designed your languages well you will probably be able to *automatically transform existing models* into the new tool's data structures[5].

One central pillar of using DSLs is the high degree to which they support separation of concerns and the expression of domain knowledge at a level of abstraction that makes the domain semantics obvious, thus avoiding complex reverse engineering problems. Consequently you can generate all kinds of artifacts from the models. This characteristic also means that it is relatively straightforward to write a generator that creates a representation of the model in a new tool's data structures[6].

[5] It is easy to see that over time the real value is in the *models*, and not so much in the language definitions and IDEs. Rebuilding those is hence not such a big deal, especially if we consider that a new, better tool may require less effort to build the languages.

[6] For example, we have built a generic MPS to EMF exporter. It works for meta models as well as for the models.

6.2.5 Avoiding Uncontrolled Growth and Fragmentation

If you use DSLs successfully, there may be the danger of uncontrolled growth and diversification in languages, with the obvious problems for maintenance, training and interoperability[7]. To avoid this, there is an organizational approach.

The organizational approach requires putting in place governance structures for language development. Maybe developers have to coordinate with a central entity before they are "allowed" to define a new language. Or an open-source like model is used, in which languages are developed in public and the most successful ones will survive and attract contributions. Maybe you want to limit language development to some central "language team"[8]. Larger organizations in which uncontrolled language growth and fragmentation might become a problem are likely to already have established processes for coordinating reusable or cross-cutting work. You should just plug into these processes.

The technical approach (which should be used together with the organizational one) exploits language modularization, extension and composition. If (parts of) languages can be reused, the drive to develop something completely new (that does more or less the same as somebody else's language) is reduced. Of course this requires that language reuse actually works with your tool of choice. It also requires that the potentially reusable languages are robust, stable and documented – otherwise nobody will use them. In a large organization I would assume that a few languages will be strategic: aligned with the needs of the whole organization, well-designed, well tested and documented, implemented by a central group, used by many developers and reusable by design[9]. In addition, small teams may decide to develop their own smaller languages or extensions, reusing the strategic ones. Their focus is much more local, and the development requires much less coordination.

[7] While this may become a problem, this may also become a problem with libraries or framework... the solution is also the same, as we will see.

[8] Please don't overdo this – don't make it a bureaucratic nightmare to develop a language!

[9] The development of these languages should be governed by the organizational approach discussed above.

Part III

DSL Implementation

This part of the book has been written together Lennart Kats and Guido Wachsmuth, who contributed the material on Spoofax, and Christian Dietrich, who helped with the language modularization in Xtext.

In this part we describe language implementation with three language workbenches, which together represent the current state of the art: Spoofax, Xtext and MPS. All of them are Open Source, so you can experiment with them. For more example language implementations using more language workbenches, take a look at the Language Workbench Competition website[10].

[10] **languageworkbenches.net**

This part of the book does not cover a lot of design decisions or motivation for having things like constraints, type systems, transformations or generators. Conceptually these topics are introduced in Part II of the book on DSL design. This part really just looks at the "how", not the "what" or "why".

Each chapter contains examples implemented with all three tools. The ordering of the tools is different from chapter to chapter, based on the characteristics of each tool: if the example for tool A illustrates a point that is also relevant for tool B, then A is discussed before B.

The examples are not intended to serve as a full tutorial for any of these tools, but as an illustration of the concepts and ideas involved with language implementation in general. However, they should give you a solid understanding of the capabilities of each of the tools, and the class of tools they stand for. Also, if a chapter does not explain topic X for tool Y, this does *not* imply that you cannot do X with Y – it just means that Y's approach to X is not significantly different from things that have already been discussed in the chapter.

7
Concrete and Abstract Syntax

> *In this chapter we look at the definition of abstract and concrete syntax, and the mapping between the two in parser-based and projectional systems. We also discuss the advantages and drawbacks of these two approaches. We discuss the characteristics of typical AST definition formalisms. The meat of the chapter is made up of extensive examples for defining language structure and syntax with our three example tools.*

The *concrete syntax* (CS) of a language is what the user interacts with to create programs. It may be textual, graphical, tabular or any combination thereof. In this book we focus mostly on textual concrete syntaxes; examples of other forms are briefly discussed Section 4.7. In this chapter we refer to other forms where appropriate.

The *abstract syntax* (AS) of a language is a data structure that holds the core information in a program, but without any of the notational details contained in the concrete syntax: keywords and symbols, layout (e.g., whitespace), and comments are typically not included in the AS. In parser-based systems the syntactic information that doesn't end up in the AS is often preserved in some "hidden" form so the CS can be reconstructed from the combination of the AS and this hidden information – this bidirectionality simplifies the creation of IDE features such as quick fixes or formatters.

As we have seen in the introduction, the abstract syntax is essentially a tree data structure. Instances that represent actual programs (i.e. sentences in the language) are hence often called an abstract syntax tree or AST. Most formalisms also support cross-references across the tree, in which case the data structure becomes a graph (with a primary containment hierarchy). It is still usually called an AST.

While the CS is the interface of the language to the user, the AS acts as the API to access programs by processing tools: it is used by developers of validators, transformations and code generators. The concrete syntax is not relevant in these cases. To illustrate the relationship between the concrete and abstract syntax, consider the following example program:

```
var x: int;
calc y: int = 1 + 2 * sqrt(x)
```

This program has a hierarchical structure: definitions of **x** and **y** at the top; inside **y** there's a nested expression. This structure is reflected in the corresponding abstract syntax tree. A possible AST is illustrated in Fig. 7.1[1].

[1] We write *possible* because there are typically several ways of structuring the abstract syntax.

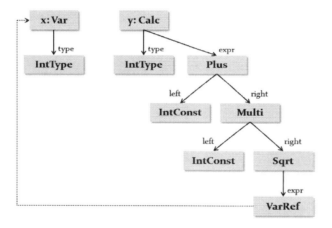

Figure 7.1: Abstract syntax tree for the above program. Boxes represent instances of language concepts, solid lines represent containment, dotted lines represent cross-references.

There are two ways of defining the relationship between the CS and the AS as part of language development:

CS first From a concrete syntax definition, an abstract syntax is derived, either automatically or using hints in the concrete syntax specification[2]. This is the default use for Xtext, where Xtext derives the Ecore meta model from an Xtext grammar.

AS first We first define the AS. We then define the concrete syntax, referring to the AS in the definition of the concrete syntax[3]. For example, in Xtext it is possible to define grammar for an existing meta model.

Once the language is defined, there are again two ways in

[2] This is more convenient, but the resulting AS may not be as clean as if it were defined manually; it may contain idiosyncrasies that result from the automatic derivation from the CS. For example, an Ecore meta model derived from an Xtext grammar will never contain interfaces, because these cannot be expressed with the Xtext grammar language. However, the use of interfaces may result in a meta model that is easier to process (richer typing). In this case it makes sense to use the AS first approach.

[3] This is often done if the AS structure already exists, has to conform to externally imposed constraints or is developed by another party than the language developer.

which the abstract syntax and the concrete syntax can relate as the language is used to create programs[4]:

Parsing In the parser-based approach, the abstract syntax tree is constructed from the concrete syntax of a program; a parser instantiates and populates the AS, based on the information in the program text. In this case, the (formal) definition of the CS is usually called a *grammar*[5]. Xtext and Spoofax use this approach.

Projection In the projectional approach, the abstract syntax tree is built directly by editor actions, and the concrete syntax is rendered from the AST via projection rules. MPS is an example of a tool that uses projectional editing.

Fig. 7.2 shows the typical combinations of these two dimensions. In practice, parser-based systems typically derive the AS from the CS – i.e. CS first. In projectional systems, the CS is usually annotated onto the AS data structures – i.e. AS first.

7.1 Fundamentals of Free Text Editing and Parsing

Most programming environments rely on free text editing, where programmers edit programs at the text/character level to form (key)words and phrases.

A *parser* is used to check the program text (concrete syntax) for syntactic correctness, and create the AST by populating the AS data structures from information extracted from the textual source. Most modern IDEs perform this task in real-time as the user edits the program, and the AST is always kept in sync with the program text. Many IDE features – such as content assist, validation, navigation or refactoring support – are based on this synchronized AST.

A key characteristic of the free text editing approach is its strong separation between the concrete syntax (i.e. text) and the abstract syntax. The concrete syntax is the principal representation, used for both editing and persistence[6]. The abstract syntax is used under the hood by the implementation of the DSL, e.g., for providing an outline view, validation, and for transformations and code generation. The AS can be changed (by changing the mapping from the CS to an AS) without any effect on the CS and existing programs.

Many different approaches exist for implementing parsers. Each may restrict the syntactic freedom of a language, or con-

[4] We will discuss these two approaches in more detail in the next subsection.

[5] Sometimes the parser creates a concrete syntax tree, which is then transformed to an AST – however, we ignore this aspect in the rest of the book, as it is not essential.

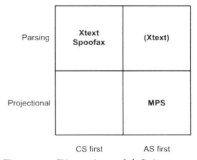

Figure 7.2: Dimensions of defining the concrete and abstract syntax of a language. Xtext is mentioned twice because it supports CS first and AS first, although CS first is the default. Note also that as of now there is no projectional system that uses CS first. However, JetBrains are currently experimenting with such a system.

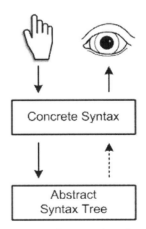

Figure 7.3: In parser-based systems, the user only interacts with the concrete syntax, and the AST is constructed from the information in the text via a parser.

[6] In projectional editing it is the other way round: the CS can be changed easily (by changing the projection rules) while keeping the AS constant.

strain the way in which a particular syntax must be specified. It is important to be aware of these restrictions, since not all languages can be comfortably implemented by every parser implementation approach, or even at all. You may have heard terms like context free, ambiguity, look-ahead, LL, (LA)LR or PEG. These all pertain to a certain class of parser implementation approaches. We provide more details on the various grammar and parser classes further on in this section.

7.1.1 Parser Generation Technology

In traditional compilers and IDEs (such as gcc or the Eclipse JDT), parsers are often written by hand as a big, monolithic program that reads a stream of characters and uses recursion to create a tree structure. However, manually writing a parser requires significant expertise in parsing and a significant development effort. For standardized programming languages that don't change very often, and that have a large user community, this approach makes sense. It can lead to very fast parsers that also provide good error reporting and error recovery (the ability to continue parsing after a syntax error has been found).

In contrast, language workbenches, and most of today's compilers, *generate* a parser from a grammar. A grammar is a syntax specification written in a DSL for formally defining textual concrete syntax. These generated parsers may not provide the same performance or error reporting/recovery as a hand-tailored parser constructed by an expert, but they provide bounded performance guarantees that make them (usually) more than fast enough for modern machines. Also, they generate a *complete* parser for the *complete* grammar – developers may forget corner cases if they write the parser manually. However, the most important argument for using parser generation is that the effort of building a parser is *much* lower than manually writing a custom parser[7]. Finally, it means that the developer who defines a language does not have to be an expert in parsing technology.

■ *Parsing versus Scanning*   Because of the complexity inherent in parsing, parser implementations tend to split the parsing process into a number of phases. In the majority of cases the text input is first separated into a sequence of *tokens* (i.e. keywords, identifiers, literals, comments or whitespace) by a *scanner* (sometimes also called lexer or tokenizer). The *parser* then constructs the actual AST from the token sequence[8]. This

---

[7] The grammar definition is also much more readable and maintainable than the actual parser implementation, either custom-written or generated.

[8] Note that many parser generators allow you to add arbitrary code (called actions) to the grammar, for example to check constraints or interpret the program. We strongly recommend against this: instead, a parser should *only* check for syntactic correctness and build the AST. All other processing should be built on top of the AST. This separation between AST construction and AST processing results in much more maintainable language implementations.

simplifies the implementation compared to directly parsing at the character level. A scanner is usually implemented using direct recognition of keywords and a set of regular expressions to recognize all other valid input as tokens.

Both the scanner and parser can be generated from grammars (see below). A well-known example of a scanner (lexer) generation tool is `lex`[9]. Modern parsing frameworks, such as ANTLR[10], do their own scanner generation.

A separate scanning phase has direct consequences for the overall parser implementation, when the scanner is not aware of the context of its input. An example of a typical problem that arises from this is that keywords can't be used as identifiers even though the use of a keyword frequently wouldn't cause ambiguity in the actual parsing. The Java language is an example of this: it uses a fixed set of keywords, such as `class` and `public`, that cannot be used as identifiers.

A context-unaware scanner is also problematic when grammars are extended or composed. In the case of Java, this was seen with the `assert` and `enum` keywords that were introduced in Java 1.4 and Java 5, respectively. Any programs that used identifiers with those names (such as unit testing APIs) were no longer valid. For composed languages, similar problems arise, as constituent languages have different sets of keywords and can define incompatible regular expressions for lexicals such as identifiers and numbers.

A recent technique to overcome these problems is *context-aware scanning*, in which the lexer relies on the state of the parser to determine how to interpret the next token[11]. With *scannerless parsing*, there is no separate scanner at all. Instead, the parser operates at the character level and statefully processes lexicals and keywords, avoiding the problems of context-unaware scanning illustrated above. Spoofax (or rather, the underlying parser technology SDF) uses scannerless parsing.

■ *Grammars*   Grammars are the formal definition for concrete textual syntax. They consist of *production rules* that define how valid textual input ("sentences") look like[12]. Grammars are the basis for syntax definitions in text-based workbenches such as Spoofax and Xtext[13].

Fundamentally, production rules can be expressed in Backus-Naur Form (BNF)[14], written as $S ::= P_1 \ldots P_n$. This grammar defines a symbol S by a series of pattern expressions $P_1 \ldots P_n$.

[9] `dinosaur.compilertools.net/`

[10] `www.antlr.org/`
Note that the word "parser" now has more than one meaning: it can either refer to the combination of the scanner and the parser, or to the post-scanner parser only. Usually the former meaning is intended (both in this book as well as in general) unless scanning and parsing are discussed specifically.

[11] E. Van Wyk and A. Schwerdfeger. Context-Aware Scanning for Parsing Extensible Languages. In *Intl. Conf. on Generative Programming and Component Engineering, GPCE 2007*. ACM Press, 2007

[12] They can also be used to "produce" valid input by executing them "the other way round", hence the name.

[13] In these systems, the production rules are enriched with information beyond the pure grammatical structure of the language, such as the semantical relation between references and declarations.

[14] `en.wikipedia.org/wiki/Backus-Naur_Form`

Each pattern expression can refer to another symbol or can be a literal such as a keyword or a punctuation symbol. If there are multiple possible patterns for a symbol, these can be written as separate productions (for the same symbol), or the patterns can be separated by the | operator to indicate a choice. An extension of BNF, called Extended BNF (EBNF)[15], adds a number of convenience operators such as ? for an optional pattern, * to indicate zero or more occurrences, and + to indicate one or more occurrences of a pattern expression.

[15] en.wikipedia.org/wiki/Extended_Backus-Naur_Form

The following code is an example of a grammar for a simple arithmetic expression language using BNF notation. Basic expressions are built up of **NUM** number literals and the + and * operators[16].

[16] These are the + and * operators of the defined language, not those mentioned for EBNF above.

```
Exp ::= NUM
      | Exp "+" Exp
      | Exp "*" Exp
```

Note how expression nesting is described using recursion in this grammar: the **Exp** rule calls itself, so sentences like 2 + 3 * 4 are possible. This poses two practical challenges for parser generation systems: first, the precedence and associativity of the operators is not described by this grammar. Second, not all parser generators provide full support for recursion. For example, ANTLR cannot cope with left-recursive rules. We elaborate on these issues in the remainder of the section and in the Spoofax and Xtext examples.

■ *Grammar classes* BNF can describe any grammar that maps textual sentences to trees based only on the input symbols. These are called *context-free grammars* and can be used to parse the majority of modern programming languages[17]. In contrast, *context-sensitive grammars* are those that also depend on the context in which a partial sentence occurs, making them suitable for natural language processing but at the same time, making parsing itself a lot harder, since the parser has to be aware of a lot more than just the syntax.

[17] An exception is SAP's ABAP language, which requires a custom, handwritten parser.

Parser generation was first applied in command-line tools such as **yacc** in the early seventies[18]. As a consequence of relatively slow computers, much attention was paid to the efficiency of the generated parsers. Various algorithms were designed that could parse text in a bounded amount of time and memory. However, these time and space guarantees could only be provided for certain subclasses of the context-free grammars, described by acronyms such as LL(1), LL(*k*), LR(1), and

[18] dinosaur.compilertools.net

so on. A particular parser tool supports a specific class of grammars – e.g., ANTLR supports LL(*k*) and LL(*). In this naming scheme, the first L stands for left-to-right scanning, and the second L in LL and the R in LR stand for leftmost and rightmost derivation. The constant *k* in LL(*k*) and LR(*k*) indicates the maximum number (of tokens or characters) the parser will look ahead to decide which production rule it can recognize. The bigger *k*, the more syntactic forms can be parsed[19]. Typically, grammars for "real" DSLs tend to need only finite lookahead and many parser tools effectively compute the optimal value for *k* automatically. A special case is LL(*), where *k* is unbounded and the parser can look ahead arbitrarily many tokens to make decisions.

Supporting only a subclass of all possible context-free grammars poses restrictions on the languages that are supported by a parser generator. For some languages, it is not possible to write a grammar in a certain subclass, making that particular language unparseable with a tool that only supports that particular class of grammars. For other languages, a natural context-free grammar exists, but it must be written in a different, sometimes awkward or unintuitive way to conform to the subclass. This will be illustrated in the Xtext example, which uses ANTLR as the underlying LL(*k*) parser technology.

Parser generators can detect whether a grammar conforms to a certain subclass, reporting conflicts that relate to the implementation of the parsing algorithm[20]. Language developers can then attempt to manually refactor the grammar to address those errors[21]. As an example, consider a grammar for property or field access, expressions of the form `customer.name` or `"Tim".length`[22]:

```
Exp ::= ID
      | STRING
      | Exp "." ID
```

This grammar uses left-recursion: the left-most symbol of one of the definitions of `Exp` is a call to `Exp`, i.e. it is recursive. Left-recursion is not supported by LL parsers such as ANTLR.

The left-recursion can be removed by *left-factoring* the grammar, i.e. by changing it to a form where all left recursion is eliminated. The essence of left-factoring is that the grammar is rewritten in such a way that all recursive production rules consume at least one token or character before going into the recursion. Left-factoring introduces additional rules that act as intermediaries and often makes repetition explicit using the +

[19] Bigger values of *k* may also reduce parser performance, though.

[20] You may have heard of *shift/reduce* or *reduce/reduce* conflicts for LR parsers, or *first/first* or *first/follow* conflicts and direct or indirect *left recursion* for LL parsers. We will discuss some of these in detail below.

[21] Understanding these errors and then refactoring the grammar to address them can be non-trivial, since it requires an understanding of the particular grammar class and the parsing algorithm.

[22] Note that we use ID to indicate identifier patterns and STRING to indicate string literal patterns in these examples.

and * operators. Our example grammar from above uses recursion for repetition, which can be made explicit as follows:

```
Exp ::= ID
    | STRING
    | Exp ("." ID)+
```

The resulting grammar is still left-recursive, but we can introduce an intermediate rule to eliminate the recursive call to **Exp**:

```
Exp ::= ID
    | STRING
    | FieldPart ("." ID)+

FieldPart ::= ID
        | STRING
```

Unfortunately, this resulting grammar still has overlapping rules (first/first conflicts), as the **ID** and **STRING** symbols both match more than one rule. This conflict can be eliminated by removing the **Exp ::= ID** and **Exp := STRING** rule and making the + (one or more) repetition into a * (zero or more) repetition:

```
Exp       ::= FieldPart ("." ID)*

FieldPart ::= ID
        | STRING
```

This last grammar describes the same language as the original grammar shown above, but conforms to the LL(1) grammar class[23]. In the general case, not all context-free grammars can be mapped to one of the restricted classes. Valid, unambiguous grammars exist that cannot be factored to any of the restricted grammar classes. In practice, this means that some languages cannot be parsed with LL or LR parsers.

■ *General parsers*   Research into parsing algorithms has produced parser generators specific to various grammar classes, but there has also been research in parsers for the full class of context-free grammars. A naive approach to avoid the restrictions of LL or LR parsers may be to add backtracking, so that if any input doesn't match a particular production, the parser can go back and try a different production. Unfortunately, this approach risks exponential execution times or non-termination and usually exhibits poor performance.

There are also general parsing algorithms that can *efficiently* parse the full class. In particular, generalized LR (GLR) parsers[24] and Earley parsers[25] can parse in linear time $O(n)$ in the common case. In the case of ambiguities, the time required can increase, but in the worst case they are bounded by cubic $O(n^3)$ time. In practice, most programming languages have few or no

[23] Unfortunately, it is also much more verbose. Refactoring "clean" context free grammars to make them conform to a particular grammar class usually makes the grammars larger and/or uglier.

[24] en.wikipedia.org/wiki/GLR_parser

[25] en.wikipedia.org/wiki/Earley_parser

ambiguities, ensuring good performance with a GLR parser. Spoofax is an example of a language workbench that uses GLR parsing.

∎ *Ambiguity* Grammars can be *ambiguous*, meaning that at least one valid sentence in the language can be constructed in more than one (non-equivalent) way from the production rules[26], corresponding to multiple possible ASTs. This obviously is a problem for parser implementation, as some decision has to be made on which AST is preferred. Consider again the expression language introduced above.

[26] This also means that this sentence can be parsed in more than one way.

```
Exp ::= NUM
      | Exp "+" Exp
      | Exp "*" Exp
```

This grammar is ambiguous, since for a string **1 * 2 + 3** there are two possible trees (corresponding to different operator precedences).

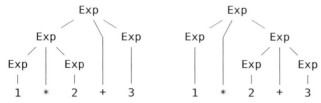

The grammar does not describe which interpretation should be preferred. Parser generators for restricted grammar classes and generalized parsers handle ambiguity differently. We discuss both approaches below.

∎ *Ambiguity with Grammar Classes* LL and LR parsers are deterministic parsers: they can only return one possible tree for a given input. This means they can't handle a grammar that has ambiguities, including our simple expression grammar. Determining whether a grammar is ambiguous is a classic undecidable problem. However, it is possible to detect violations of the LL or LR grammar class restrictions, in the form of conflicts. These conflicts do not always indicate ambiguities (as seen with the field access grammar discussed above), but by resolving all conflicts (if possible) an unambiguous grammar can be obtained.

Resolving grammar conflicts in the presence of associativity, precedence, and other risks of ambiguity requires carefully layering the grammar in such a way that it encodes the desired properties. To encode left-associativity and a lower priority for the + operator, we can rewrite the grammar as follows:

```
Expr ::= Expr "+" Mult
       | Mult
Mult ::= Mult "*" NUM
       | NUM
```

The resulting grammar is a valid LR grammar. Note how it puts the + operator in the highest layer to give it the lowest priority[27], and how it uses left-recursion to encode left-associativity of the operators. The grammar can be left-factored to a corresponding LL grammar as follows[28]:

```
Expr ::= Mult ("+" Mult)*
Mult ::= NUM ("*" NUM)*
```

[27] A + will end up further up in the expression tree than a *. This means that the * has higher precedence, since any interpreter or generator will encounter the * first.

[28] We will see more extensive examples of this approach in the section on Xtext (Section 7.5).

■ *Ambiguity with Generalized Parsers* Generalized parsers accept grammars regardless of recursion or ambiguity. So our expression grammar is readily accepted as a valid grammar. In the case of an ambiguity, the generated parser simply returns *all possible abstract syntax trees*, e.g. a left-associative tree and a right-associative tree for the expression 1 * 2 + 3. The different trees can be manually inspected to determine what ambiguities exist in the grammar, or the desired tree can be programmatically selected. A way of programmatically selecting one alternative is *disambiguation filters*. For example, left-associativity can be indicated on a per-production basis:

```
Exp ::= NUM
      | Exp "+" Exp {left}
      | Exp "*" Exp {left}
```

This indicates that both operators are left-associative (using the {left} annotation from Spoofax). Operator precedence can be indicated with relative priorities or with precedence annotations:

```
Exp ::= Exp "*" Exp {left}
>
Exp ::= Exp "+" Exp {left}
```

The > indicates that the * operator binds stronger than the + operator. This kind of declarative disambiguation is commonly found in GLR parsers, but typically is not available in parsers that support only more limited grammar classes[29].

[29] As even these simple examples show, this style of specifying grammars leads to simpler, more readable grammars. It also makes language specification much simpler, since developers don't have to understand the conflicts/errors mentioned above.

■ *Grammar Evolution and Composition* Grammars evolve as languages change and new features are added. These features can be added by adding single, new productions, or by composing the grammar with an existing grammar. Composition of grammars is an efficient way of reusing grammars and quickly constructing or extending new grammars. As a basic example of grammar composition, consider once again our simple grammar for arithmetic expressions:

```
Expr ::= NUM
       | Expr "*" Expr
       | Expr "+" Expr
```

Once more operators are added and the proper associativities and precedences are specified, such a grammar forms an excellent unit for reuse[30]. As an example, suppose we want to compose this grammar with the grammar for field access expressions[31]:

```
Expr ::= ID
       | STRING
       | Expr "." ID
```

In the ideal case, composing two such grammars should be trivial – just copy them into the same grammar definition file. However, reality is often less than ideal. There are a number of challenges that arise in practice, related to ambiguity and to grammar class restrictions[32].

- Composing arbitrary grammars risks introducing ambiguities that did not exist in either of the two constituent grammars. In the case of the arithmetic expressions and field access grammars, care must specifically be taken to indicate the precedence order of all operators with respect to all others. With a general parser, new priority rules can be added without changing the two imported grammars. When an LL or LR parser is used, it is often necessary to change one or both of the composed grammars to eliminate any conflicts. This is because in a general parser, the precedences are *declarative* (additional preference specification can simply be added at the end), whereas in LL or LR parsers the precedence information is encoded in the grammar structure (and hence invasive changes to this structure may be required).

- We have shown how grammars can be massaged with techniques such as left-factoring in order to conform to a certain grammar class. Likewise, any precedence order or associativity can be encoded by massaging the grammar to take a certain form. Unfortunately, all this massaging makes grammars very resistant to change and composition: after two grammars are composed together, the result is often no

[30] For example, expressions can be used as guard conditions in state machines, for pre- and postconditions in interface definitions, or to specify derived attributes in a data definition language.

[31] Here we consider the case where two grammars use a symbol with the identical name **Expr**. Some grammar definition formalisms support mechanisms such as grammar mixins and renaming operators to work with grammar modules where the symbol names do not match.

[32] See Laurence Tratt's article *Parsing – the solved problem that isn't*. at **tratt.net/laurie/tech_articles/articles/parsing_the_solved_problem_that_isnt**.

longer LL or LR, and another manual factorization step is required.

- Another challenge is in composing scanners. When two grammars that depend on a different lexical syntax are composed, conflicts can arise. For example, consider what happens when we compose the grammar of Java with the grammar of SQL:

```
for (Customer c : SELECT customer FROM accounts WHERE balance < 0) {
    ...
}
```

The SQL grammar reserves keywords such as **SELECT**, even though they are not reserved in Java. Such a language change could break compatibility with existing Java programs which happen to use a variable named **SELECT**. A common programmatic approach to solve this problem is the introduction of easy-to-recognize boundaries, which trigger switches between different parsers. In general, this problem can only be avoided completely by a scannerless parser, which considers the lexical syntax in the context in which it appears; traditional parsers perform a separate scanning stage in which no context is considered.

7.2 Fundamentals of Projectional Editing

In parser-based approaches, users use text editors to enter character sequences that represent programs. A parser then checks the program for syntactic correctness and constructs an AST from the character sequence. The AST contains all the semantic information expressed by the program.

In projectional editors, the process happens the other way round: as a user edits the program, the AST is modified *directly*. A projection engine then creates some representation of the AST with which the user interacts, and which reflects the changes. This approach is well-known from graphical editors in general, and the model-view-controller (MVC) pattern specifically. When users edit a UML diagram, they don't draw pixels onto a canvas, and a "pixel parser" then creates the AST. Rather, the editor creates an instance of `uml.Class` as you drag a class from the palette to the canvas. A projection engine renders the diagram, in this case drawing a rectangle for the class. Projectional editors generalize this approach to work with any notation, including textual.

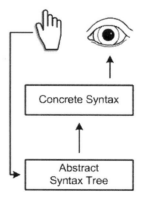

Figure 7.4: In projectional systems, the user sees the concrete syntax, but all editing gestures directly influence the AST. The AST is *not* extracted from the concrete syntax, which means the CS does not have to be parseable.

This explicit instantiation of AST objects happens by picking the respective concept from the code completion menu using a character sequence defined by the respective concept (typically the "leading keyword" of the respective program construct, or the name of a referenced variable). If at any given program location two concepts can be instantiated using *the same character sequence*, then the projectional editor prompts the user to decide[33]. Once a concept is instantiated, it is stored in the AST as a node with a unique ID (UID). References between program elements are pointers to this UID, and the projected syntax that represents the reference can be arbitrary. The AST is actually an abstract syntax graph *from the start* because cross-references are first-class rather than being resolved after parsing[34]. The program is stored using a generic tree persistence mechanism, often XML[35].

Defining a projectional editor, instead of defining a grammar, involves the definition of projection rules that map language concepts to a notation. It also involves the definition of event handlers that modify the AST based on a user's editing gestures. The way to define the projection rules and the event handlers is specific to the particular tool used.

The projectional approach can deal with arbitrary syntactic forms including traditional text, symbols (as in mathematics), tables or graphics. Since no grammar is used, grammar classes are not relevant here. In principle, projectional editing is simpler in principle than parsing, since there is no need to "extract" the program structure from a flat textual source. However, as we will see below, the challenge in projectional editing lies making the editing experience convenient[36]. Modern projectional editors, and in particular MPS, do a good job in meeting this challenge.

7.3 Comparing Parsing and Projection

7.3.1 Editing Experience

In free text editing, any regular text editor will do. However, users expect a powerful IDE that includes support for syntax coloring, code completion, go-to-definition, find references, error annotations, refactoring and the like. Xtext and Spoofax provide IDE support that is essentially similar to what a modern IDE provides for mainstream languages (e.g. Eclipse for Java)[37]. However, you can always go back to any text editor to

[33] As discussed above, this is the situation where many grammar-based systems run into problems from ambiguity.

[34] There is still one single containment hierarchy, so it is really a tree with cross-references.

[35] And yes, the tools provide diff/merge based on the projected syntax, not based on XML.

[36] In particular, editing notations that look like text should be editable with the editing gestures known from text editors.

[37] We assume that you are familiar with modern IDEs, so we do not discuss their features in great detail in this section.

edit the programs.

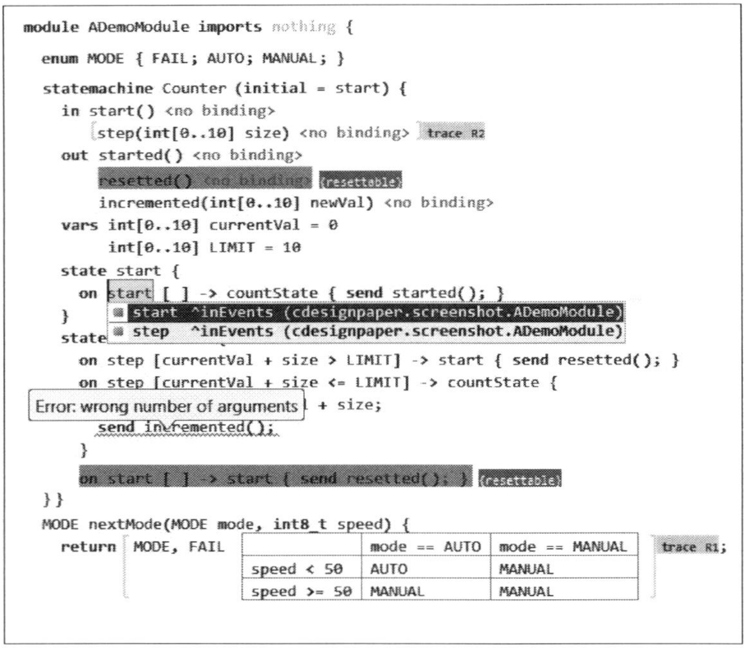

Figure 7.5: An mbeddr example program using five separate but integrated languages. It contains a module with an **enum**, a state machine (**Counter**) and a function (**nextMode**) that contains a decision table. Inside both of them developers can write regular C code. The IDE provides code completion for all language extensions (see the **start**/**stop** suggestions) as well as static error validation (**Error...** hover). The green **trace** annotations are traces to requirements that can be attached to arbitrary program elements. The red parts with the **{resettable}** next to them are presence conditions (in the context of product line engineering): the respective elements are only in a program variant if the configuration feature **resettable** is selected.

In projectional editing, this is different: a normal text editor is obviously not sufficient; a specialized editor has to be supplied to perform the projection (an example is shown in Fig. 7.5). As in free text editing, it has to provide the IDE support features mentioned above. MPS provides those. However, there is another challenge: for textual-looking notations, it is important that the editor tries to make the editing experience as text-like as possible, i.e. the keyboard actions we have become used to from free-text editing should work as far as possible. MPS does a decent job here, using, among others, the following strategies[38]:

- Every language concept that is legal at a given program location is available in the code completion menu. In naive implementations, users have to select the language concept based on its name and instantiate it. This is inconvenient. In MPS, languages can instead define aliases for language concepts, allowing users to "just type" the alias, after which the concept is immediately instantiated[39].

- *Side transforms* make sure that expressions can be entered conveniently. Consider a local variable declaration **int a = 2;**. If this should be changed to **int a = 2 + 3;** the **2** in the

[38] The following list may be hard to relate to if you have never used a projectional editor. However, understanding this section in detail is not essential for the rest of the book.

[39] By making the alias the same as the leading keyword (e.g. **if** for an **IfStatement**), users can "just type" the code.

init expression needs to be replaced by an instance of the binary + operator, with the 2 in the left slot and the 3 in the right. Instead of removing the 2 and manually inserting a +, users can simply type + on the right side of the 2. The system performs the tree restructuring that moves the + to the root of the subtree, puts the 2 in the left slot, and then puts the cursor into the right slot, so the user can enter the second argument. This means that expressions (or anything else) can be entered linearly, as expected. For this to work, operator precedence has to be specified, and the tree has to be constructed taking these precedences into account. Precedence is typically specified by a number associated with each operator, and whenever a side transformation is used to build an expression, the tree is automatically reshuffled to make sure that those operators with a higher precedence number are further down in the tree.

- Delete actions are used to similar effect when elements are deleted. Deleting the **3** in **2 + 3** first keeps the plus, with an empty right slot. Deleting the **+** then removes the **+** and puts the **2** at the root of the subtree.

- Wrappers support instantiation of concepts that are actually children of the concepts allowed at a given location. Consider again a local variable declaration **int a;**. The respective concept could be **LocalVariableDeclaration**, a subconcept of **Statement**, to make it legal in method bodies (for example). However, users simply want to start typing **int**, i.e. selecting the content of the **type** field of the **LocalVariableDeclaration**. A wrapper can be used to support entering **Type**s where **LocalVariableDeclaration**s are expected. Once a **Type** is selected, the wrapper implementation creates a **LocalVariableDeclaration**, puts the **Type** into its **type** field, and moves the cursor into the **name** slot. Summing up, this means that a local variable declaration **int a;** can be entered by starting to type the **int** type, as expected.

- Smart references achieve a similar effect for references (as opposed to children). Consider pressing **Ctrl-Space** after the **+** in **2 + 3**. Assume further, that a couple of local variables are in scope and that these can be used instead of the **3**. These should be available in the code completion menu. However, technically, a **VariableReference** has to be instantiated, whose **variable** slot is then made to point to any of the variables in scope. This is tedious. Smart references trigger special editor behavior: if in a given context a **VariableReference** is allowed, the editor *first* evaluates its scope to find the possible targets, then puts those targets into the code completion menu. If a user selects one, *then* the **VariableReference** is created, and the selected element is put into its **variable** slot. This makes the reference object effectively invisible in terms of the editing experience.

- Smart delimiters are used to simplify inputting list-like data, where elements are separated with a specific separator symbol. An example is argument lists in functions: once a parameter is entered, users can press comma, i.e. the list delimiter, to instantiate the next element.

Except for having to get used to the somewhat different way of editing programs, the strategies mentioned above (plus some others) result in a reasonably good editing experience. Traditionally, projectional editors have *not* used these or similar strategies, and projectional editors have acquired a bit of a bad reputation because of that. In the case of MPS this tool support is available, and hence MPS provides a productive and pleasant working environment.

7.3.2 Language Modularity

As we have seen in Section 4.6, language modularization and composition is an important building block in working with DSLs. Parser-based and projectional editors come with different trade-offs in this respect.

In parser-based systems the extent to which language composition can be supported depends on the supported grammar class. As we have said above, the problem is that the result of combining two or more independently developed grammars into one may become ambiguous, for example, because the same character sequence is defined as two different tokens. The resulting grammar cannot be parsed and has to be disambiguated manually, typically by invasively changing the composite grammar. This of course breaks modularity and hence is not an option. Parsers that do not support the full set of context-free grammars, such as ANTLR, and hence Xtext, have this problem. Parsers that do support the full set of context-free grammars, such as the GLR parser used as part of Spoofax, are better off. While a grammar may become ambiguous in the sense that a program may be parseable in more than one way, this can be resolved by declaratively specifying which alternative should be used. This specification can be made externally, *without* invasively changing either the composed or the component grammars, retaining modularity.

In projectional editors, language modularity and composition is not a problem at all[40]. There is no grammar, no parsing, no grammar classes, and hence no problem with composed grammars becoming ambiguous. Any combination of languages will be syntactically valid. In cases where a composed language would be ambiguous in a GLR-based system, the user has to make a disambiguating decision *as the program is entered*. For example, in MPS, if at a given location two language concepts are available with the same alias, just typing the alias won't bind, and the user has to manually decide by picking one alternative from the code completion menu.

7.3.3 Notational Freedom

Parser-based systems process linear sequences of character symbols. Traditionally, the character symbols were taken from the ASCII character set, resulting in textual programs being made up from "plain text". With the advent of Unicode, a much wider variety of characters is available while still sticking to the linear sequence of characters approach. For example, the Fortress programming language[41] makes use of this: Greek letters and a wide variety of different bracket styles can be used in Fortress programs. However, character layout is always ignored. For example it is not possible to use parsers to handle tabular notations, fraction bars or even graphics[42].

In projectional editing, this limitation does not exist. A projectional editor never has to extract the AST from the concrete syntax; editing gestures directly influence the AST, and the concrete syntax is rendered from the AST. This mechanism is basically like a graphical editor and notations other than text can be used easily. For example, MPS supports tables, fraction bars and "big math" symbols[43]. Since these non-textual notations are handled in the same way as the textual ones (possibly with other input gestures), they can be mixed easily[44]: tables can be embedded into textual source, and textual languages can be used within table cells (see Fig. 7.6).

7.3.4 Language Evolution

If the language changes, existing instance models temporarily become outdated, in the sense that they were developed for the

[40] An example for a composed language is shown in Fig. 7.5. It contains code expressed in C, in a statemachines extension, a decision tables extension and in languages for expressing requirements traces and product line variability.

[41] en.wikipedia.org/wiki/Fortress_(programming_language)

[42] There have been experimental parsers for two-dimensional structures such as tables and even for graphical shapes, but these have never made it beyond the experimental stage. Also, it is possible to approximate tables by using vertical bars and hyphens to some extent. JNario, described in Section 19, uses this approach.

```
component AComp extends nothing {
  provides Decider d

  int8 decide(int8 x, int8 y) ⇐ op d.decide {
    return int8, 0
  }
}
```

	x == 0	x > 0
y == 0	0	1
y > 0	1	2

Figure 7.6: A table embedded in an otherwise textual program

[43] The upcoming version 3.0 of MPS will also support graphical notations.

[44] Of course, the price you pay is the somewhat different style of interacting with the editor, which, as we have said, approximates free text editing quite well, but not perfectly.

old version of the language. If the new language is not backward compatible, these existing models have to be migrated to conform to the updated language.

Since projectional editors store the models as structured data in which each program node points to the language concept it is an instance of, the tools have to take special care that such "incompatible" models can still be opened and then migrated, manually or by a script, to the new version of the language. MPS supports this feature, and it is also possible to distribute migration scripts with (updated) languages to run the migration automatically[45].

[45] It is also possible to define quick fixes that run *automatically*; so whenever a concept is marked as **deprecated**, this quick fix can trigger an automatic migration to a new concept.

Most textual IDEs do not come with explicit support for evolving programs as languages change. However, since a model is essentially a sequence of characters, it can *always* be opened in the editor. The program may not be parseable, but users can always update the program manually, or with global search and replace using regular expressions. More complex migrations may require explicit support via transformations on the AST.

7.3.5 Infrastructure Integration

Today's software development infrastructure is typically text-oriented. Many tools used for diff and merge, or tools like **grep** and regular expressions, are geared towards textual storage. Programs written with parser-based textual DSLs (stored as plain text) integrate automatically and nicely with these tools.

In projectional IDEs, special support needs to be provided for infrastructure integration. Since the CS is not pure text, a generic persistence format is used, typically based on XML. While XML is technically text as well, it is not practical to perform diff, merge and the like on the level of the XML. Therefore, special tools need to be provided for diff and merge. MPS provides integration with the usual version control systems and handles diff and merge in the IDE, using the concrete, projected syntax[46]. Fig. 7.7 shows an example of an MPS diff. However, it clearly is a drawback of projectional editing (and the associated abstract syntax-based storage) that many well-known text utilities don't work[47].

[46] Note that since every program element has a unique ID, *move* can potentially be distinguished from *delete/create*, providing richer semantics for diff and merge.

[47] For example, web-based diffs in github or gerrit are not very helpful when working with MPS.

Also, copy and paste with textual environments may be a challenge. MPS, for example, supports pasting a projected program that has a textual-looking syntax into a text editor. However, for the way back (from a textual environment to the projectional editor), there is no automatic support. However, special support for specific languages can be provided via *paste handlers*. Such a paste handler is available for Java, for example: when a user pastes Java text into a Java program in MPS, a parser is executed that builds the respective MPS tree[48].

[48] While this works reasonably well for Java, it has to be developed specifically for each language used in MPS. If a grammar for the target language is available for a Java-based parser generator, it is relatively simple to provide such an integration.

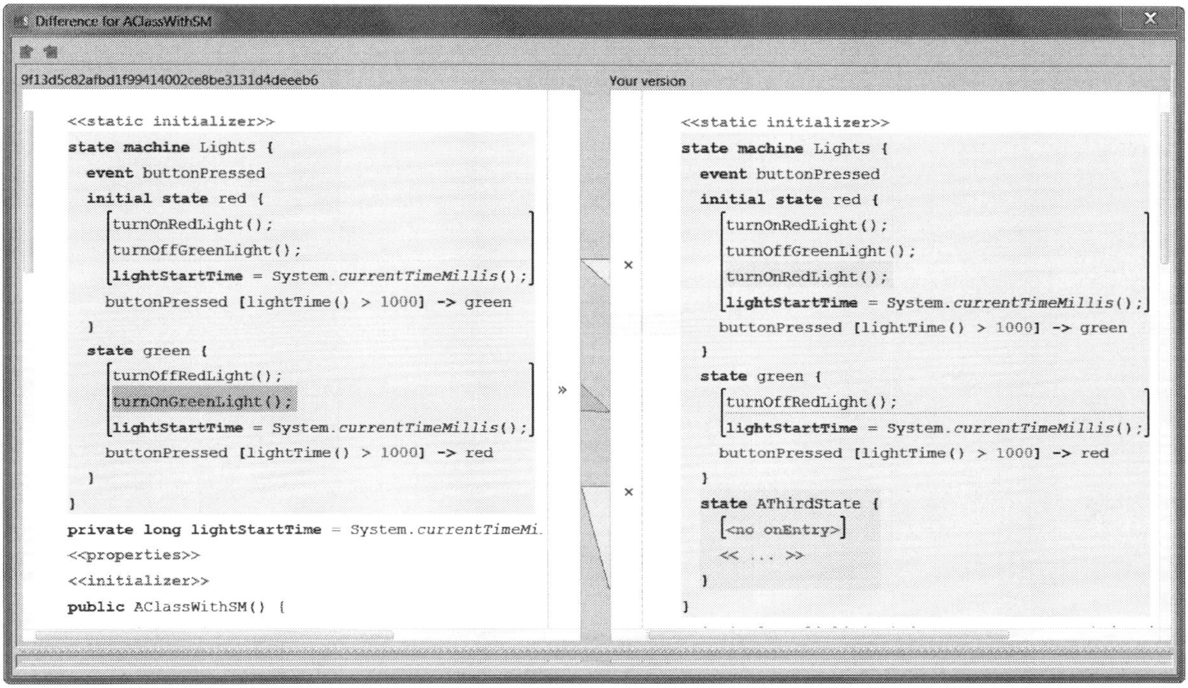

Figure 7.7: The diff/merge tool presents MPS programs in their concrete syntax, i.e. text for textual notations. However, other notations, such as tables, would also be rendered in their native form.

7.3.6 Tool Lock-in

In the worst case, textual programs can be edited with any text editor. Unless you are prepared to edit XML, programs expressed with a projectional editor *always* require that editor to edit programs. As soon as you take IDE support into account though, both approaches lock users into a particular tool. Also, there is essentially no standard for exchanging language definitions between the various language workbenches[49]. So the effort of implementing a language is always lost if the tool must be changed.

[49] There is *some* support for exchanging the abstract syntax based on formalisms such as MOF or Ecore, but most of the effort for implementing a language is in areas other than the abstract syntax.

7.3.7 Other

In parser-based systems, the complete AST has to be reconstructable from the CS. This implies that there can be no information in the tree that is *not* obtained from parsing the text.

This is different in projectional editors. For example, the textual notation could only project a subset of the information in the tree. The same information can be projected with different projections, each possibly tailored to a different stakeholder, and showing a different subset of the overall data. Since the tree uses a generic persistence mechanism, it can hold data that has not been planned for in the original language definition. All kinds of meta data (documentation, presence conditions, requirements traces) can be stored, and projected if required[50].

[50] MPS supports *annotations*, where additional data can be added to model elements of existing languages. The data can be projected inside the original program's projection, all without changing the original language specification.

7.4 Characteristics of AST Formalisms

Most AST formalisms, aka meta meta models[51], are ways to represent trees or graphs. Usually, such an AST formalism is "meta circular" in the sense that it can describe itself.

This section is a brief overview over the three AST formalisms relevant to Xtext, Spoofax and MPS. We will illustrate them in more detail in the respective tool example sections.

[51] *Abstract syntax* and *meta model* are typically considered synonyms, even though they have different histories (the former comes from the parser/grammar community, whereas the latter comes from the modeling community). Consequently, the formalisms for defining ASTs are conceptually similar to meta meta models.

7.4.1 EMF Ecore

The Eclipse Modeling Framework[52] (EMF) is at the core of all Eclipse Modeling tools. It provides a wide variety of services and tools for persisting, editing and processing models and abstract syntax definitions. EMF has grown to be a fairly large ecosystem within the Eclipse community and numerous projects use EMF as their basis.

[52] www.eclipse.org/modeling/emf/

Its core component is Ecore, a variant of the EMOF standard[53]. Ecore acts as EMF's meta meta model. Xtext uses Ecore as the foundation for the AS: from a grammar definition, Xtext derives the AS as an instance of Ecore. Ecore's central concepts are: **EClass** (representing AS elements or language concepts), **EAttribute** (representing primitive properties of **EClass**es), **EReference** (representing associations between **EClass**es) and **EObject** (representing instances of **EClass**es, i.e. AST nodes). **EReferences** can have containment semantics or not and each **EObject** can be contained by at most one **EReference** instance. Fig. 7.8 shows a class diagram of Ecore.

[53] en.wikipedia.org/wiki/Meta-Object_Facility

When working with EMF, the Ecore file plays a central role. From it, all kinds of other aspects are derived; specifically, a generic tree editor and a generated Java API for accessing an AST. It also forms the basis for Xtext's model processing: The Ecore file is derived from the grammar, and the parser, when

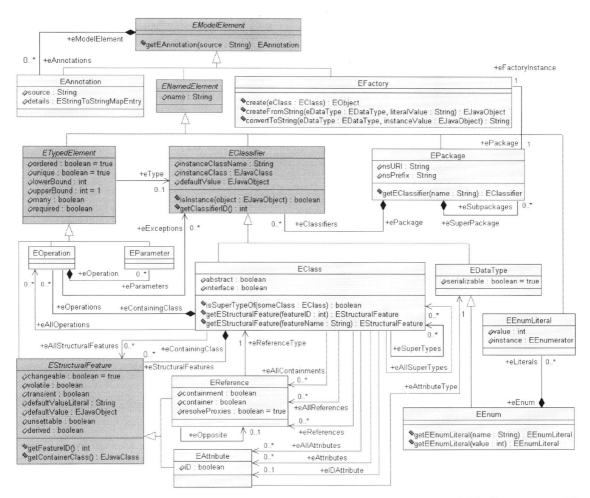

Figure 7.8: The Ecore meta model rendered as a UML diagram.

executed, builds an in-memory tree of **EObject**s representing the AST of the parsed program.

7.4.2 Spoofax' ATerm

Spoofax uses the ATerm format to represent abstract syntax. ATerm provides a generic tree structure representation format that can be serialized textually similar to XML or JSON. Each tree node is called an ATerm, or simply a *term*. Terms consist of the following elements: Strings (**"Mr. White"**), Numbers (**15**), Lists (**[1,2,3]**) and constructor applications (**Order(5, 15, "Mr. White")**) for labeled tree nodes with a fixed number of children.

The structure of valid ATerms is specified by an algebraic *signature*. Signatures are typically generated from the concrete-syntax definition, but can also be specified manually. A signature introduces one or more algebraic *sorts*, i.e. collections of terms. The sorts `String`, `Int`, and `List`[54] are predefined. User-defined sorts are inhabited by declaring term *constructors* and *injections*. A constructor has a name and zero or more subterms. It is declared by stating its name, the list of sorts of its direct subterms, and the sort of the constructed term. Constructor names may be overloaded. Injections are declared as nameless constructors. The following example shows a signature for expressions:

[54] `List` is a parameterized sort, i.e. it takes the sort of the list elements as a parameter.

```
signature

  sorts
    Exp

  constructors
    Plus : Exp * Exp -> Exp
    Times: Exp * Exp -> Exp
         : Int        -> Exp
```

The signature declares sort `Exp` with its constructors `Plus` and `Times`, which both require two expressions as direct subterms. Basic expressions are integers, as declared by the injection rule `: Int -> Exp`.

Compared to XML or JSON, perhaps the most significant distinction is that ATerms rely on the order of subterms rather than on labels. For example, a product may be modeled in JSON as follows:

```
{
  "product": {
    "itemnumber": 5,
    "quantity": 15,
    "customer": "Mr. White"
  }
}
```

Note how this specification includes the actual data describing the particular product (the model), but also a description of each of the elements (the meta model). With XML, a product would be modeled in a similar fashion. An equivalent of the JSON above written in ATerm format would be the following:

```
Order([ItemNumber(5), Quantity(15), Customer("Mr.\ White")])
```

However, this representation contains a lot of redundant information that also exists in the grammar. Instead, such a product can be written as `Order(5, 15, "Mr. White")`. This more concise notation tends to make it slightly more convenient to use in handwritten transformations.

The textual notation of ATerms can be used for exchanging data between tools and as a notation for model transformations or code generation rules. In memory, ATerms can be stored in a tool-specific way (i.e. simple Java objects in the case of Spoofax)[55].

In addition to the basic elements above, ATerms support annotations to add additional information to terms. These are similar to attributes in XML. For example, it is possible to annotate a product number with its product name:

```
Order(5{ProductName("Apples")}, 15, "Mr. White")
```

Spoofax also uses annotations to add information about references to other parts of a model to an abstract syntax tree. While ATerms only form trees, the annotations are used to represent the graph-like references.

[55] The generic structure and serializability of ATerms also allows them to be converted to other data formats. For example, the `aterm2xml` and `xml2aterm` tools can convert between ATerms and XML.

7.4.3 MPS' Structure Definition

In MPS, programs are trees/graphs of *nodes*. A node is an instance of a *concept* which defines the structure, syntax, type system and semantics of its instance nodes[56]. Like `EClass`es[57], concepts are meta circular, i.e. there is a concept that defines the properties of concepts:

```
concept ConceptDeclaration extends AbstractConceptDeclaration
                           implements INamedConcept

  instance can be root: false

  properties:
    helpURL  : string
    rootable : boolean

  children:
    InterfaceConceptReference  implementsInterfaces         0..n
    LinkDeclaration            linkDeclaration              0..n
    PropertyDeclaration        propertyDeclaration          0..n
    ConceptProperty            conceptProperty              0..n
    ConceptLink                conceptLink                  0..n
    ConceptPropertyDeclaration conceptPropertyDeclaration   0..n
    ConceptLinkDeclaration     conceptLinkDeclaration       0..n

  references:
    ConceptDeclaration         extendsConcept               0..1
```

A concept may extend a single other concept and implement any number of interfaces[58]. It can declare references (non-containing) and children (containing). It may also have a number of primitive-type properties as well as a couple of "static" features. In addition, concepts can have behavior methods.

While the MPS structure definition is proprietary to MPS and does not implement any accepted industry standard, it is conceptually very close to Ecore[59].

[56] The term *concept* used in this book, to refer to language constructs including abstract syntax, concrete syntax and semantics, is inspired by MPS' use of the term.

[57] Nodes correspond to `EObject`s in EMF, concepts resemble `EClass`es.

[58] Note that interfaces can provide implementations for the methods they specify – they are hence more like Scala traits or mixins known from AOP and various programming languages.

[59] This is illustrated by the fact the exporters and importers to and from Ecore have been written.

7.5 Xtext Example

Cooling programs[60] represent the behavioral aspect of the refrigerator descriptions. Here is a trivial program that can be used to illustrate some of the features of the language. The program is basically a state machine.

```
cooling program HelloWorld uses stdlib {

    var v: int
    event e

    init { set v = 1 }

    start:
        on e { state s }

    state s:
        entry { set v = 0 }
}
```

[60] This and the other examples in this section refer back to the case studies introduced at the beginning of the book in Section 1.11.

The program declares a variable **v** and an event **e**. When the program starts, the **init** section is executed, setting **v** to **1**. The system then (automatically) transitions into the **start** state. There it waits until it receives the **e** event. It then transitions to the state **s**, where it uses an entry action to set **v** back to **0**. More complex programs include checks of changes of properties of hardware elements (**aCompartment->currentTemp**) and commands to the hardware (**set aCompartment->isCooling = true**), as shown in the next snippet:

```
start:
    check ( aCompartment->currentTemp > maxTemp ) {
        set aCompartment->isCooling = true
        state initialCooling
    }
    check ( aCompartment->currentTemp <= maxTemp ) {
        state normalCooling
    }
state initialCooling:
    check ( aCompartment->currentTemp < maxTemp ) {
        state normalCooling
    }
```

■ *Grammar Basics*   In Xtext, the syntax is specified using an EBNF-like notation, a collection of productions that are typically called *parser rules*. These rules specify the concrete syntax of a program element, as well as its mapping to the AS. From the grammar, Xtext generate the abstract syntax represented in Ecore[61]. Here is the definition of the **CoolingProgram** rule:

```
CoolingProgram:
    "cooling" "program" name=ID "{"
    (events+=CustomEvent |
     variables+=Variable)*
    (initBlock=InitBlock)?
```

It is also possible to first create the Ecore meta model and then define a grammar for it. While this is a bit more work, it is also more flexible, because not all possible Ecore meta models can be described implicitly by a grammar. For example, Ecore interfaces cannot be expressed from the grammar. A middle ground is to have Xtext generate the meta model while the grammar is still in flux and then switch to maintaining the meta model manually when the grammar stabilizes.

[61] The entity that contains the meta classes is actually called an **EPackage**.

```
    (states+=State)*
"}";
```

Rules begin with the name (`CoolingProgram` in the example above), a colon, and then the rule body. The body defines the syntactic structure of the language concept defined by the rule. In our case, we expect the keywords `cooling` and `program`, followed by an `ID`. `ID` is a *terminal rule* that is defined in the parent grammar from which we inherit (not shown). `ID` is defined as an unbounded sequence of lowercase and uppercase characters, digits, and the underscore, although it may not start with a digit. This terminal rule is defined as follows:

```
terminal ID: ('a'..'z'|'A'..'Z'|'_') ('a'..'z'|'A'..'Z'|'_'|'0'..'9')*;
```

In pure grammar languages, one would typically write the following:

```
"cooling" "program" ID "\{ ..."}
```

This expresses the fact that after the two keywords we expect an `ID`. However, Xtext grammars don't just express the concrete syntax – they also determine the mapping to the AS. We have encountered two such mappings so far. The first one is implicit: the name of the rule will be the name of the derived meta class[62]. So we will get a meta class `CoolingProgram`. The second mapping we have encountered is `name=ID`. It specifies that the meta class gets a property `name` that holds the contents of the `ID` from the parsed program text. Since nothing else is specified in the `ID` terminal rule, the type of this property defaults to `EString`, Ecore's version of a string data type.

The rest of the definition of a cooling program is enclosed in curly braces. It contains three elements: first the program contains a collection of events and variables (the * specifies unbounded multiplicity), an optional init block (optionality is specified by the ?) and a list of states. Let us inspect each of these in more detail.

The expression `(states+=State)*` specifies that there can be any number of `State` instances in the program. The `CoolingProgram` meta class gets a property `states`, it is of type `State` (the meta class derived from the `State` rule). Since we use the `+=` operator, the `states` property will be typed to be a *list* of `State`s. In the case of the optional `init` block, the meta class will have an `initBlock` property, typed as `InitBlock` (whose parser rule we don't show here), with a multiplicity of 0..1. Events and variables are more interesting, since the vertical bar

[62] If we start with the meta model and then define the grammar, it is possible to have grammar rule names that are different from meta class names.

operator is used within the parentheses. The asterisk expresses the fact that whatever is inside the parentheses can occur any number of times[63]. Inside the parentheses we expect either a **CustomEvent** *or* a **Variable**, which is expressed with the **|**. Variables are assigned to the **variables** collection, events are assigned to the **events** collection. This notation means that we can mix events and variables in any order. The following alternative notation would first expect all events, and then all variables.

[63] While there are exceptions, the use of a * usually goes hand in hand with the use of a +=.

```
(events+=CustomEvent)*
(variables+=Variable)*
```

The definition of **State** is interesting, since **State** is intended to be an abstract meta class with several subtypes.

```
State:
    BackgroundState | StartState | CustomState;
```

The vertical bar operator is used here to express syntactic alternatives. This is translated to inheritance in the meta model. The definition of **CustomState** is shown in the following code snippet:

```
CustomState:
    "state" name=ID ":"
        (invariants+=Invariant)*
        ("entry" "{"
            (entryStatements+=Statement)*
        "}")?
        ("eachTime" "{"
            (eachTimeStatements+=Statement)*
        "}")?
        (events+=EventHandler | signals+=SignalHandler)*;
```

StartState and **BackgroundState**, the other two subtypes of **State**, share some properties. Consequently, Xtext's AS derivation algorithm pulls them up into the abstract **State** meta class. This way they can be accessed polymorphically. Fig. 7.9 shows the resulting meta model using EMF's tree view.

■ *References*   Let us now look at statements and expressions. **State**s have entry and exit actions which are procedural statements that are executed when a state is entered and left, respectively. The **set v = 1** in the example program above is an example. **Statement** itself is **abstract** and has the various kinds of statements as subtypes/alternatives:

```
Statement:
    Statement | AssignmentStatement | PerformAsyncStatement |
    ChangeStateStatement | AssertStatement;

ChangeStateStatement:
    "state" targetState=[State];
```

```
AssignmentStatement:
    "set" left=Expr "=" right=Expr;
```

The **ChangeStateStatement** is used to transition into another state. It uses the keyword **state** followed by a reference to the target state. Notice how Xtext uses square brackets to express the fact that the **targetState** property points to an *existing* state, as opposed to containing a new one (which would be written as **targetState=State**); i.e. the square brackets express non-containing cross-references.

This is another example of where the Xtext grammar language goes beyond classical grammar languages, where one would write **"state" targetStateName=ID;**. Writing it in this way only specifies that we expect an **ID** after the **state** keyword. The fact that we call it **target- StateName** communicates *to the programmer* that we expect this text string to correspond to the name of a state – a later phase in model processing *resolves* the name to an actual state reference. Typically, the code to resolve the reference has to be written manually, because there is no way for the tool to derive from the grammar automatically the fact that this **ID** is actually a reference to a **State**. In Xtext, the **targetState=[State]** notation makes this explicit, so the resolution of the reference can be automatic. This approach also has the advantage that the resulting meta class types the **targetState** property to **State** (and not just to a string), which makes processing the models much easier.

```
▲ ⓘ platform:/resource/com.bsh.pk.cooling/src-gen/com/bsh/pk/cooling/CoolingLanguage.ecore
   ▲ ■ coolingLanguage
      ▲ 目 Model
         ▷ ⚑ coolingPrograms : CoolingProgram
      ▲ 目 CoolingProgram
         ▷ ▭ name : EString
         ▷ ⚑ events : CustomEvent
         ▷ ⚑ variables : Variable
         ▷ ⇨ initBlock : InitBlock
         ▷ ⚑ states : State
      ▷ 目 Variable -> SymbolDeclaration
      ▷ 目 InitBlock
      ▷ 目 CustomEvent -> SymbolDeclaration
      ▲ 目 State
         ▷ ▭ name : EString
            ⚑ invariants
            ⚑ entryStatements
            ⚑ eachTimeStatements
            ⚑ events
            ⚑ signals
      ▷ 目 BackgroundState -> State
      ▷ 目 StartState -> State
      ▷ 目 CustomState -> State
```

Figure 7.9: Part of the Ecore meta model derived from the Xtext grammar for the cooling program. Grammar rules become **EClass**es, assignments in the grammar rules become **EAttribute**s and **EReference**s. The notation **A -> B** symbolizes that **A** extends **B**.

Note that the cross-reference definition only specifies the target type (**State**) of the cross-reference, but not the concrete syntax of the reference itself. By default, the **ID** terminal is used for the reference syntax, i.e. a simple (identifier-like) text string is expected. However, this can be overridden by specifying the concrete syntax terminal behind a vertical bar in the reference[64]. In the following piece of code, the **targetState** reference uses the **QID** terminal as the reference syntax.

[64] Notice that in this case the vertical bar does not represent an *alternative*, it is merely used as a *separator* between the target type and the terminal used to represent the reference.

```
ChangeStateStatement:
    "state" targetState=[State|QID];

QID: ID ("." ID)*;
```

The other remaining detail is scoping. During the linking phase, where the text of **ID** (or **QID**) is used to find the target node, several objects with the same name might exist, or some target elements might not visible based on visibility rules of the language. To constrain the possible reference targets, scoping functions are used. These will be explained in the next chapter.

■ *Expressions* The **AssignmentStatement** shown earlier is one of the statements that uses expressions. We repeat it here:

```
AssignmentStatement:
    "set" left=Expr "=" right=Expr;
```

The following snippet is a subset of the actual definition of expressions (we have omitted some additional expressions that don't add anything to the description here).

```
Expr:
    ComparisonLevel;

ComparisonLevel returns Expression:
    AdditionLevel ((({Equals.left=current} "==") |
                    ({LogicalAnd.left=current} "&&") |
                    ({Smaller.left=current} "<"))
                                        right=AdditionLevel)?;

AdditionLevel returns Expression:
    MultiplicationLevel ((({Plus.left=current} "+") |
                    ({Minus.left=current} "-")) right=
        MultiplicationLevel)*;

MultiplicationLevel returns Expression:
    PrefixOpLevel ((({Multi.left=current} "*") |
                    ({Div.left=current} "/")) right=PrefixOpLevel)*;

PrefixOpLevel returns Expression:
    ({NotExpression} "!" "(" expr=Expr ")") |
    AtomicLevel;

AtomicLevel returns Expression:
    ({TrueLiteral} "true") |
    ({FalseLiteral} "false") |
    ({ParenExpr} "(" expr=Expr ")") |
    ({NumberLiteral} value=DECIMAL_NUMBER) |
    ({SymbolRef} symbol=[SymbolDeclaration|QID]);
```

To understand the above definition, we first have to explain in more detail how AST construction works in Xtext. Obviously, as the text is parsed, meta classes are instantiated and the AST is assembled. However, instantiation of the respective meta class happens lazily, upon the first assignment to one of its properties. If no assignment is performed at all, no object is created. For example, in the grammar rule `TrueLiteral: "true";` no instance of `TrueLiteral` will ever be created, because there is nothing to assign. In this case, an action can be used to force instantiation: `TrueLiteral: {TrueLiteral} "true";`[65].

Unless otherwise specified, an assignment such as `name=ID` is always interpreted as an assignment on the object that has been created most recently. The `current` keyword can be used to access that object in case it *itself* needs to be assigned to a property of another AST object.

Now we know enough about AST construction to understand how expressions are encoded and parsed. In the expression grammar above, for the rules with the `Level` suffix, no meta classes are created, because (as Xtext is able to find out statically) they are never instantiated. They merely act as a way to encode precedence. To understand this, let's consider how `2 * 3` is parsed:

- The `AssignmentStatement` refers to the `Expr` rule in its `left` and `right` properties, so we "enter" the expression tree at the level of `Expr` (which is the root of the expression hierarchy).

- The `Expr` rule just calls the `ComparisonLevel` rule, which calls `AdditionLevel`, and so on. No objects are created at this point, since no assignment to any property is performed.

- The parser "dives down" until it finds something that matches the first symbol in the parsed text: the `2`. This occurs on `AtomicLevel` when it matches the `DECIMAL_NUMBER` terminal. At this point it creates an instance of the `NumberLiteral` meta class and assigns the number `2` to the `value` property. It also sets the `current` object to point to the just-created `NumberLiteral`, since this is now the AST object created most recently.

- The `AtomicLevel` rule ends, and the stack is unwound. We're back at `PrefixOpLevel`, in the second branch. Since nothing

[65] Notice that the action can instantiate meta classes other than those that are derived from the rule name (we could write `TrueLiteral: {SomeOtherThing} "true";`. While this would not make sense in this case, we'll use this feature later.

else is specified after the call to `AtomicLevel`, we unwind once more.

- We're now back at the `MultiplicationLevel`. The rule is not finished yet and we try to match an * and a /. The match on * succeeds. At this point the *assignment action* on the left side of the * kicks in (`Multi.left=current`). This action creates an instance of `Multi`, and assigns the `current` (the `NumberLiteral` created before) to its `left` property. Then it makes the newly created `Multi` the new `current`. At this point we have a subtree with the * at the root, and the `NumberLiteral` in the `left` property.

- The rule hasn't ended yet. We dive down to `PrefixOpLevel` and `AtomicLevel` once more, matching the 3 in the same way as the 2 before. The `NumberLiteral` for 3 is assigned to the `right` property as we unwind the stack.

- At this point we unwind the stack further, and since no more text is present, no more objects are created. The tree structure has been constructed as expected.

If we'd parsed 4 + 2*3 the + would have matched before the *, because it is "mentioned earlier" in the grammar (it is in a lower-precedence group, the `AdditionLevel`, so it has to end up "higher" in the tree). Once we're at 4 +, we'd go down again to match the 2. As we unwind the stack after matching the 2 we'd match the *, creating a `Multi` again. The `current` at this point would be the 2, so it would be put onto the `left` side of the *, making the * the `current`. Unwinding further, that * would be put onto the `right` side of the +, building the tree just as we'd expect.

Notice how a rule at a given precedence level only always delegates to rules at higher precedence levels. So higher precedence rules always end up further down in the tree. If we want to change this, we can use parentheses (see the `ParenExpr` in the `AtomicLevel`): inside those, we can again embed an `Expr`, i.e. we jump back to the lowest precedence level[66].

Once you understand the basic approach, it is easy to add new expressions with a precedence similar to another one (just add it as an alternative to the respective `Level` rule) or to introduce a new precedence level (just interject a new `Level` rule between two existing ones)[67].

[66] This somewhat convoluted approach to parsing expressions and encoding precedence is a consequence of the LL(*k*) grammar class support by ANTLR, which underlies Xtext. A cleaner approach would be declarative, where precedences are encoded explicitly and the order of the parsing rules in not relevant. Spoofax uses this approach. Xtext also supports syntactic predicates, which are annotations in the grammar that tell the parser which alternative to take in the case of an ambiguity. We don't discuss this any further in the book.

[67] Note that the latter requires an invasive change to the grammar; this prevents the addition of operators with a precedence level *between* existing precedence levels in a sub-language, whose definition cannot invasively change the language it extends.

7.6 Spoofax Example

Mobl's[68] data modeling language provides entities, properties and functions. To illustrate the language, below are two data type definitions related to a shopping list app. It supports lists of items that can be favorited, checked, and so on, and which are associated with some **Store**.

[68] Mobl is a DSL for defining applications for mobile devices. It is based on HTML 5 and is closely related to WebDSL, which has been introduced earlier (Section 1.11).

```
module shopping

entity Item {
  name     : String
  checked  : Bool
  favorite : Bool
  onlist   : Bool
  order    : Num
  store    : Store
}
```

In Mobl, most files start with a module header, which can be followed by a list of entity type definitions. In turn, each entity can have one or more property or function definitions (shown in the next example snippet). Modules group entities. Inside a module, one can only access entities from the same module or from imported modules.

■ *Grammar Basics* In Spoofax, the syntax of languages is described using SDF[69]. SDF is short for Syntax Definition Formalism, and is a modular and flexible syntax definition formalism that is supported by the SGLR[70] parser generator. It can generate efficient, Java-based scannerless and general parsers, allowing Spoofax to support the full class of context-free grammars, grammar composition, and modular syntax definitions. An example of a production written in SDF is:

[69] **www.syntax-definition.org/**

[70] SGLR parsing is a *S*cannerless, *G*eneralized extension of *LR* parsing.

```
"module" ID Entity* -> Start {"Module"}
```

The pattern on the left-hand side of the arrow is matched by the symbol **Start** on the right-hand side[71]. After the right-hand side, SDF productions may specify annotations using curly brackets. Most productions specify a quoted *constructor label* that is used for the abstract syntax. This particular production creates a tree node with the constructor **Module** and two children that represent the **ID** and the list of **Entities** respectively. As discussed earlier, Spoofax represents abstract syntax trees as ATerms. Thus, the tree node will be represented as **Module(..., [...])**. In contrast to Xtext, the children are not named; instead, they are identified via the position in the child collection (the **ID** is first, the **Entity** list is second). Spoofax generates the following signature from the production above:

[71] Note that SDF uses the exact opposite order for productions as the grammars we've discussed so far, switching the left-hand side and right-hand side.

```
signature
  sorts
    Start
  constructors
    Module: ID List(Entity) -> Start
```

The left-hand side of an SDF production is the pattern it matches against. SDF supports symbols, literals and character classes in this pattern. Symbols are references to other productions, such as **ID**. Literals are quoted strings such as **"module"** that must appear in the input literally. Character classes specify a range of characters expected in the input, e.g. **[A-Za-z]** specifies that an alphabetic character is expected. We discuss character classes in more detail below.

The basic elements of SDF productions can be combined using operators. The **A*** operator shown above specifies that zero or more occurrences of **A** are expected. **A+** specifies that one or more are expected. **A?** specifies that zero or one are expected. **{A B}*** specifies that zero or more **A** symbols, separated by **B** symbols, are expected. As an example, **{ID ","}*** is a comma-separated list of identifiers. **{A B}+** specifies one or more **A** symbols separated by **B** symbols.

Fig. 7.10 shows an SDF grammar for a subset of Mobl's entities and functions syntax. The productions in this grammar should have few surprises, but it is interesting to note how SDF groups a grammar in different sections. First, the **context-free start symbols** section indicates the start symbol of the grammar. Then, the **context-free syntax** section lists the context-free syntax productions, forming the main part of the grammar. Terminals are defined in the **lexical syntax** section.

■ *Lexical Syntax*   As Spoofax uses a scannerless parser, all lexical syntax can be customized in the SDF grammar[72]. Most lexical syntax is specified using character classes such as **[0-9]**. Each character class is enclosed in square brackets, and can consist of ranges of characters (**c_1-c_2**), letters and digits (e.g. **x** or **4**), non-alphabetic literal characters (e.g., **_**), and escapes (e.g., **\n**). A complement of a character class can be obtained using the ~ operator, e.g. ~**[A-Za-z]** matches all non-alphabetic characters. For whitespace and comments a special terminal **LAYOUT** can be used.

SDF implicitly inserts **LAYOUT** between all symbols in context-free productions. This behavior is the key distinguishing fea-

[72] It provides default definitions for common lexical syntax elements such as strings, integers, floats, whitespace and comments, which can be reused by importing the module **Commons**.

```
module MoblEntities

context-free start symbols

  Module

context-free syntax

  "module" ID Decl*                        -> Module      {"Module"}
  "import" ID                              -> Decl        {"Import"}
  "entity" ID "{" EntityBodyDecl* "}"      -> Decl        {"Entity"}

  ID ":" Type                              -> EntityBodyDecl {"Property"}
  "function" ID "(" {Param ","}* ")" ":" ID "{" Statement* "}"
                                           -> EntityBodyDecl {"Function"}
  ID ":" Type                              -> Param       {"Param"}
  ID                                       -> Type        {"EntityType"}

  "var" ID "=" Expr ";"                    -> Statement   {"Declare"}
  "return" Exp ";"                         -> Statement   {"Return"}

  Exp "." ID "(" Exp ")"                   -> Exp         {"MethodCall"}
  Exp "." ID                               -> Exp         {"FieldAccess"}
  Exp "+" Exp                              -> Exp         {"Plus"}
  Exp "*" Exp                              -> Exp         {"Mul"}
  ID                                       -> Exp         {"Var"}
  INT                                      -> Exp         {"Int"}

lexical syntax

  [A-Za-z][A-Za-z0-9]*   -> ID
  [0-9]+                 -> INT
  [\ \t\n]               -> LAYOUT
```

Figure 7.10: A basic SDF grammar for a subset of Mobl. The grammar does not yet specify the associativity, priority or name bindings of the language.

ture between context-free and lexical productions: lexical symbols such as identifiers and integer literals cannot be interleaved with layout. The second distinguishing feature is that lexical syntax productions usually do not have a constructor label in the abstract syntax, as they form terminals in the abstract syntax trees (i.e. they don't own any child nodes).

■ *Abstract Syntax*   To produce abstract syntax trees, Spoofax uses the ATerm format, described in Section 7.4.2. SDF combines the specification of concrete and abstract syntax, primarily through the specification of constructor labels. Spoofax allows users to view the abstract syntax of any input file. As an example, the following is the textual representation of an abridged abstract syntax term for the shopping module shown at the beginning of this section:

```
Module(
  "shopping",
  [ Entity(
      "Item",
      [Property("name", EntityType("String")), Property("checked",
      EntityType("Bool")), ...] )
  ]
])
```

Note how this term uses the constructor labels of the syntax above: **Module**, **Entity** and **Property**. The children of each node correspond to the symbols referenced in the production: the **Module** production first referenced **ID** symbol for the module name and then included a list of **Decl** symbols (lists are in square brackets).

In addition to constructor labels, productions that specify parentheses can use the special **bracket** annotation:

```
"(" Exp ")" -> Exp {bracket}
```

The **bracket** annotation specifies that there should not be a separate tree node in the abstract syntax for the production. This means that an expression **1 + (2)** would produce **Plus("1","2")** in the AST, and not **Plus("1",Parens("2"))**.

■ *Precedence and Associativity*   SDF provides special support for specifying the associativity and precedence of operators or other syntactic constructs. As an example, let us consider the production of the **Plus** operator. So far, it has been defined as:

```
Exp "+" Exp -> Exp {"Plus"}
```

Based on this operator, a parser can be generated that can parse an expression such as **1 + 2** to a term **Plus("1", "2")**. However, the production does not specify if an expression **1 + 2 + 3** should be parsed to a term **Plus("1", Plus("2", "3"))** or **Plus(Plus("1", "2"), "3")**. If you try the grammar in Spoofax, it will show *both* interpretations using the special **amb** constructor:

```
amb([
  Plus("1", Plus("2", "3")),
  Plus(Plus("1", "2"), "3")
])
```

The **amb** node indicates an *ambiguity* and it contains all possible interpretations[73]. Ambiguities can be resolved by adding annotations to the grammar that describe the intended interpretation. For the **Plus** operator, we can resolve the ambiguity by specifying that it is left-associative, using the **left** annotation:

```
Exp "+" Exp -> Exp {"Plus", left}
```

[73] Whenever an ambiguity is encountered in a file, it is marked with a warning in the editor.

In a similar fashion, SDF supports the definition of the precedence order of operators. For this, the productions can be placed into the **context-free priorities** section:

```
context-free priorities
```

```
  Exp "*" Exp -> Exp {"Mul", left}
>
  Exp "+" Exp -> Exp {"Plus", left}
```

This example specifies that the **Mul** operator has a higher priority than the **Plus** operator, resolving the ambiguity that arises for an expression such as `1 + 2 * 3`.

■ *Reserved Keywords and Production Preference*   Parsers generated with SDF do not use a scanner, but include processing of lexical syntax in the parser. Since scanners operate without any context information, they will simply recognize any token that corresponds to a keyword in the grammar as a reserved keyword, *irrespective of its location in the program*. In SDF, it is also possible to use keywords that are not reserved, or keywords that are only reserved in a certain context. As an example, the following is a legal entity in Mobl:

```
entity entity {}
```

Since our grammar did not specify that **entity** is a reserved word, it can be used as a normal **ID** identifier. However, there are cases in which it is useful to reserve keywords, for example to prevent ambiguities. Consider what would happen if we added new productions for predefined type literals:

```
"Bool"   -> Type {"BoolType"}
"Num"    -> Type {"NumType"}
"String" -> Type {"StringType"}
```

If we were now to parse a type **String**, it would be ambiguous: it matches the **StringType** production above, but it also matches the **EntityType** production, as **String** is a legal entity identifier[74]. Keywords can be reserved in SDF by using a production that rejects a specific interpretation:

```
"String" -> ID {reject}
```

This expresses that **String** can never be interpreted as an identifier. Alternatively, we can say that we prefer one interpretation over the other:

```
"String" -> Type {"StringType", prefer}
```

This means that this production is to be preferred if there are any other interpretations. However, since these interpretations cannot always be foreseen as grammars are extended, it is considered good practice to use the more specific **reject** approach instead[75].

[74] So it is ambiguous because *at the same location in a program* both interpretations are possible.

[75] This is the situation where a projectional editor like MPS is more flexible, since instead of running into an ambiguity, it would prompt the user to decide which interpretation is correct as he types **String**.

■ *Longest Match*   Most scanners apply a *longest match* policy for scanning tokens[76]. For most languages, this is the expected behavior, but in some cases longest match is not what users expect. SDF instead allows the grammar to specify the intended behavior. In Spoofax, the default is specified in the *Common* syntax module using a `lexical restrictions` section:

```
lexical restrictions
  ID -/- [A-Za-z0-9]
```

[76] This means that if it is possible to include the next character in the current token, the scanner will always do so.

This section restricts the grammar by specifying that any `ID` cannot be directly followed by a character that matches `[A-Za-z0-9]`. Effectively, it enforces a longest match policy for the `ID` symbol. SDF also allows the use of lexical restrictions for keywords. By default it does not enforce longest match, which means it allows the following definition of a Mobl entity:

```
entityMoblEntity {}
```

As there is no longest match, the parser can recognize the `entity` keyword even if it is not followed by a space. To avoid this behavior, we can specify a longest match policy for the `entity` keyword:

```
lexical restrictions
  "entity" -/- [A-Za-z0-9]
```

■ *Name Bindings*   So far we have discussed purely syntax specification in SDF. Spoofax also allows the specification of name binding rules, which specify semantic relations between productions. We discuss how these relations are specified in Chapter 8.

7.7 MPS Example

We start by defining a simple language for state machines, roughly similar to the one used in the state machine extension[77] to mbeddr C. Its core concepts include `StateMachine`, `State`, `Transition` and `Trigger`. The language supports the definition of state machines, as shown in the following piece of code:

[77] In mbeddr, state machines can be embedded into C code, as we will see later.

```
module LineFollowerStatemachine {

  statemachine LineFollower {
    events unblocked()
           blocked()
           bumped()
           initialized()
    states (initial = initializing) {
```

```
    state initializing {
      on initialized [ ] -> running { }
    }
    state paused {
      on unblocked [ ] -> running { }
    }
    state running {
      on blocked [ ] -> paused { }
      on bumped [ ] -> crashed { }
    }
    state crashed {
    }
  }
 }
}
```

■ *Concept Definition* MPS is projectional, so we start with the definition of the AS. The code below shows the definition of the concept **Statemachine**. It contains a collection of **State**s and a collection of **InEvent**s. It also contains a reference to one of the states to mark it as the **initial** state. The **alias** is defined as **statemachine**, so typing this string inside a C module instantiates a state machine (it picks the **Statemachine** concept from the code completion menu). State machines also implement a couple of interfaces: **IIdentifierNamedElement** contributes a property **name**, **IModuleContent** makes the state machine embeddable in C **Module**s[78].

[78] The **Module** owns a collection of **IModuleContents**, just as the state machine contains states and events.

```
concept Statemachine extends BaseConcept
                     implements IModuleContent
                                ILocalVarScopeProvider
                                IIdentifierNamedElement
  children:
    State    states   0..n
    InEvent  inEvents 0..n

  references:
    State    initial  1

  concept properties:
    alias = statemachine
```

A **State** (not shown) contains two **StatementLists** as **entryActions** and **exitActions**. **StatementList** is a concept defined by the com. mbeddr.core.statements language. To make it available visible, our statemachine language extends **com.mbeddr.core.statements**. Finally, a **State** contains a collection of **Transition**s.

```
concept Transition
  children:
    Trigger         trigger 1
    Expression      guard   1
    StatementList   actions 1

  references:
    State           target  1

  concept properties:
    alias = on
```

Transitions contain a **Trigger**, a guard condition, transition actions and a reference to the target state. The trigger is an abstract concept; various specializations are possible: the default implementation is the **EventTrigger**, which references an **Event**[79]. The guard condition is an **Expression**, a concept reused from **com.mbeddr.core.expressions**[80]. The target state is a reference, i.e. we point to an existing state instead of owning a new one. **action** is another **StatementList** that can contain arbitrary C statements used as the transition actions.

[79] It expresses the fact that the referenced event triggers the transition.

[80] A type system rule will be defined later to constrain this expression to be Boolean.

■ *Editor Definition* Editors, i.e. the projection rules, are made of cells. When defining editors, various cell types are arranged so that the resulting syntax has the desired structure. Fig. 7.11 shows the editor definition for the **State** concept. It uses an **indent** collection of cells with various style attributes to arrange the **state** keyword and name, the entry actions, the transitions and the exit actions in a vertical list. Entry and exit actions are shown only if the respective **StatementList** is not empty (a condition is attached to the respective cells, marked by the **?** in front of the cell). An intention[81] is used to add a new statement and hence make the respective list visible.

[81] An intention is what Eclipse calls a Quick Fix – i.e. an entry in a little menu that transforms the program in some way. Intentions are explained in the next section.

```
editor for concept State
  node cell layout:
    [-
    state { name } {
      ?[- entry % entryAction % -]
      (- % transitions % /empty cell: * R/O model access * -)
      ?[- exit ?% exitAction % -]
    }
    -]
```

Fig. 7.12 shows the definition of the editor for a **Transition**. It arranges the keyword **on**, the trigger, the guard condition, target state and the actions in a horizontal list of cells, the guard surrounded by brackets, and an arrow (**->**) in front of the target state. The editor for the **actions StatementList** comes with its own set of curly braces.

Figure 7.11: The definition of the editor for the **State** concept. In MPS, editors are made from cells. In the editor definition you arrange the cells and define their contents; this defines the projection rule that is used when instances of the concept are rendered in the editor.

```
editor for concept Transition
  node cell layout:
    [- on % trigger % [ % guard % ] -> ( % targetState % -> { name } ) % actions % -]
```

Figure 7.12: The editor for transitions. Note how we embed the guard condition expression simply by referring to the **guard** child relationship. We "inherit" the syntax for expressions from the **com.mbeddr.core.expressions** language.

The `%targetState% -> {name}` part expresses the fact that in order to render the target state, the target state's **name** attribute should be shown. We could use any text string to refer to the target state[82].

Note how we use **on** both as the leading keyword for a transition and as the alias. This way, if a user types the **on** alias to instantiate a transition, it feels as if they typed the leading keyword of a transition (as in a regular text editor).

If a language extension defined a new concept **SpecialTransition**, they could use another alias to uniquely identify this concept in the code completion menu. The user decides which alias to type depending on whether they want to instantiate a **Transition** or a **SpecialTransition**. Alternatively, the **SpecialTransition** could use *the same alias* **on**. In this case, if the user types **on**, the code completion menu pops open and the user has to decide which of the two concepts to instantiate[83]. As we have discussed above, this means that there is never an ambiguity that cannot be handled – as long as the user is willing and able to make the decision of which concept should be instantiated. A third option would transform a **Transition** into a **SpecialTransition** on demand, for example if the user executes a specific extension, or types a specific string on the right side of a **Transition**.

■ *Intentions* Intentions are MPS' term for what is otherwise known as a Quick Fix: a little menu can be displayed on a program element that contains a set of actions that change the underlying program element (see Fig. 7.13). The intentions menu is opened via **Alt-Enter**. In MPS, intentions play an important role in the editor. In many languages, certain changes to the program can *only* be made via an intention[84]. Using the intentions menu in a projectional editor is idiomatic. For example, in the previous section we mentioned that we use them to add an entry action to a **State**. Here is the intention code:

```
intention addEntryActions for concept State {
  available in child nodes : true

  description(editorContext, node)->string {
    "Add Entry Action";
  }

  isApplicable(editorContext, node)->boolean {
    node.entryAction.isNull;
  }

  execute(editorContext, node)->void {
    node.entryAction.set new(<default>);
    editorContext.selectWRTFocusPolicy(node.entryAction);
```

[82] We could even use the symbol **X** to render *all* target state references. The reference would still work, because the underlying data structure uses the target's unique ID to establish the reference. It does not matter what we use to represent the target in the model. Using **X** for all references would of course be bad for human readability, but technically it would work.

[83] The code completion menu by default shows from which language a language concept originates, so this is a way to distinguish the two. Alternatively, a short explaining text can be shown for each entry in the code completion menu that helps the user make the decision.

Figure 7.13: The intentions menu for a local variable declaration. It can be opened via **Alt-Enter**. To select an action from the menu, you can just start typing the action label, so this is very keyboard-friendly.

[84] This is mostly because building a just-type-along solution would be a lot of work in a projectional editor in some cases.

```
    }
}
```

An intention is defined for a specific language concept (`State` in the example). It can then be invoked by pressing `Alt-Enter` on any instance of this concept. Optionally it is possible to also make it available in child nodes. For example, if you are in the guard expression of an transition, an intention for `State` with `available in child nodes` set to `true` will be available as well. The intention implementation also specifies an expression used as the title in the menu and an applicability condition. In the example the intention is only applicable if the corresponding state does not yet have any entry action (because in that case you can just type in additional statements). Finally, the `execute` section contains procedural code that performs the respective change on the model. In this case we simply create a new instance of `StatementList` in the `entryAction` child. We also set the cursor into this new `StatementList`[85].

■ *Expressions*   Since we inherit the expression structure and syntax from the C core language, we don't have to define expressions ourselves to be able to use them in guards. It is nonetheless interesting to look at their implementation in the language `com.mbeddr.core.expressions`.

Expressions are arranged into a hierarchy starting with the abstract concept `Expression`. All other kinds of expressions extend `Expression`, directly or indirectly. For example, `PlusExpression` extends `BinaryExpression`, which in turn extends `Expression`. `BinaryExpressions` have `left` and `right` child `Expressions`. This way, arbitrarily complex expressions can be built[86]. The editors are also straightforward – in the case of the + expression, they are a horizontal list of: editor for `left` argument, the + symbol, and the editor for the `right` argument.

As we have explained in the general discussion about projectional editing (Section 7.2), MPS supports linear input of hierarchical expressions using *side transforms*. The code below shows the right side transformation for expressions that transforms an arbitrary expression into a `PlusExpression` by putting the `PlusExpression` "on top" of the current node[87].

```
side transform actions makeArithmeticExpression

  right transformed node: Expression tag: default_

  actions :
    add custom items    (output concept: PlusExpression)
      simple item
```

[85] Notice how we don't have to specify any formatter or serializer for our language. Remember how a projectional editor *always* goes from AS to CS. So after changing the AS procedurally, the respective piece of the tree is simply rerendered to update the representation of the program in the editor. However, we do have to define an editor for each language concept.

[86] Representing expressions as trees is a standard approach that we have seen with the Xtext example already; in that sense, the abstract syntax of mbeddr expressions (and more generally, the way to handle expressions in MPS) is not very interesting.

[87] Using the alias (i.e. the operator symbol) of the respective `BinaryExpression` and the inheritance hierarchy, it is possible to factor all side transformations for all binary operations into one single action implementation, resulting in much less implementation effort.

```
    matching text
      +
    do transform
      (operationContext, scope, model, sourceNode, pattern)->node< > {
        node<PlusExpression> expr = new node<PlusExpression>();
        sourceNode.replace with(expr);
        expr.left = sourceNode;
        expr.right.set new(<default>);
        return expr.right;
      }
```

The fact that you can enter expressions linearly leads to a problem not unlike the one found in grammars regarding operator precedence. If you enter 2 + 3 * 4 by typing these characters sequentially, there are two ways in which the tree could look, depending on whether + or * binds more tightly[88].

To deal with this problem, we proceed as follows: each subconcept of **BinaryExpression** has a numerical value associated with it that expresses its precedence. The higher the number, the higher the precedence (i.e. the lower in the tree). The action code shown above is changed to include a call to a helper function that rearranges the tree according to the precedence values.

[88] Note how this really is a consequence of the linear input method; you could build the tree by first typing the + and then filling in the left and right arguments, in which case it would be clear that the * is lower in the tree and hence binds tighter. However, this is tedious and hence not an option in practice.

```
do transform
  (operationContext, scope, model, sourceNode, pattern)->node< > {
    node<PlusExpression> expr = new node<PlusExpression>();
    sourceNode.replace with(expr);
    expr.left = sourceNode;
    expr.right.set new(<default>);
    // rearranges tree to handle precedence
    PrecedenceHelper.rearrange(expr);
    return expr.right;
  }
```

This method scans through an expression tree and checks for cases in which a binary expression with a higher precedence is an ancestor of a binary expression with a lower precedence value. If it finds one, it rearranges the tree to resolve the problem[89].

[89] Since the problem can only arise as a consequence of the linear input method, it is sufficient to include this rearrangement in the side transformation like the one shown above.

■ *Context Restrictions*   MPS makes strong use of polymorphism. If a language concept defines a child relationship to another concept **C**, then any subtype of **C** can also be used in this child relationship. For example, a function has a **body** which is typed to **StatementList**, which contains a list of **Statement**s. So every subtype of **Statement** can be used inside a function body. In general, this is the desired behavior, but in some cases, it is not. Consider test cases. Here is a simple example:

```
module UnitTestDemo imports nothing {

  test case testMultiply {
    assert (0) times2(21) == 42;
  }
```

```
int8 times2(int8 a) {
  return 2 * a;
}
}
```

Test cases reside in a separate language `com.mbeddr.core.unittest`. The language defines the `TestCase` concept, as well as the `assert` statement. `AssertStatement` extends `Statement`, so by default, an `assert` can be used wherever a `Statement` is expected, once the `com.mbeddr.core.unittest` is used in a program. However, this is not what we want: `assert` statements should be restricted to be used inside a `UnitTest`[90]. To support such a use case, MPS supports a set of constraints. Here is the implementation for `AssertStatement`:

```
concept constraints AssertStatement {
  can be child
    (operationContext, scope, parentNode, link, childConcept)->boolean {
      parentNode.ancestor<TestCase, +>.isNotNull;
    }
}
```

[90] This is, among other reasons, because the transformation of the `assert` statement to C expects code generated from the `UnitTest` to surround it.

This constraint checks that a `TestCase` is among the ancestors of a to-be-inserted `AssertStatement`. The constraint is checked *before* the new `AssertStatement` is inserted and *prevents* insertion if not under a `TestCase`[91].

■ *Tables and Graphics*   The MPS projectional editor associates projection rules with language concepts. A projection rule consists of cells. Each cell represents a primitive rendering element. For example, a `constant` cell contains a constant text that is rendered as-is in the programs. A property cell renders a property (for example, the `name`). Collections cells arrange other cells in some predefined or configurable layout. Among others, MPS has vertical and horizontal collections. To render concepts as a table, a suitable kind of cell is required: MPS provides the `table` cell for this. For example, the editor for the decision table is shown in Fig. 7.14 (and an example table is shown in Fig. 14.7).

However, this is only half of the story. The real definition of the table contents happens via a table model implementation inside the `table` cell. The inspector for the `table` cell contains a function that has to return a `TableModel`, an interface that determines the structure of the table[92]. Here is the code used in the decision table:

[91] This constraint is written from the perspective of the potential child element. For reasons of dependency management, it is also possible to write the constraint from the perspective of the parent or an ancestor. This is useful if a new container concept wants to restrict the use of *existing* child concepts without changing those concepts. For example, the `Lambda` concept, which contains a statement list as well, prohibits the use of `LocalVariableRef`s, in any of its statements.

```
editor for concept DecTab
  node cell layout:
    [- % type % , % def % table -]
```

Figure 7.14: The editor for a decision table contains a horizontal collection of cells. The first one contains the return type of the decision table, the second one contains the default value, and the last one contains the actual table, represented by the `table` cell.

[92] This is similar to the approach used in Java Swing, but it is not exactly the same interface.

```
(node, editorContext)->TableModel {
  return new XYCTableModel(node, link/DecTab : xExpr/,
                                  link/DecTab : yExpr/,
```

```
                       link/DecTab : cExpr/,
                       editorContext);
}
```

The **XYCTableModel** class is a utility class that ships with MPS for tables whose contents are represented by a concept that has three child collections, one for the contents of the row headers, one for the contents of the column headers and one for the remaining cells. We pass in the **node** that represents the table as well as the three child collections (and the **editorcontext**). If none of the existing utility classes is suitable, you have to implement the **TableModel** interface yourself[93]. Here is the definition of the interface:

[93] Later versions of MPS will provide a higher-level approach to defining tables that is more consistent with the approach for editor definition in MPS, and which does not require Java programming for defining a table.

```
public interface TableModel extends <none> {
  int getColumnCount();
  int getRowCount();
  void deleteRow(int rowNumber);
  node<> getValueAt(int row, int column);
  void createElement(int row, int column);
  NodeSubstituteInfo getSubstituteInfo(int row, int column);
  void insertRow(int rowNumber);
  void deleteColumn(int columnNumber);
  void insertColumn(int columnNumber);
  int getMaxColumnWidth(int columnNumber);
}
```

Note how the **getValueAt** method returns a **node<>**. The editor then renders the editor for that node into the respective table cell, supporting nesting of arbitrary other editors into tables.

A similar approach will be used for graphical notations. New kinds of cells (for example, **rectangle** and **line**) may be required[94]. The fundamentally interesting characteristic of projectional editors is that completely different styles of notations can be supported, as long as the necessary primitive cell types are available. The approach to editor definition remains unchanged. Because all the different notations are based on the same paradigm, the combination of different notational styles is straightforward.

[94] At the time of this writing, MPS does not yet support graphical notations; however, it is planned to add them in 2013.

8
Scoping and Linking

> *Linking refers to the resolution of name-based references to the referenced symbols in parser-based languages. In projectional systems this is not necessary, since every reference is stored as a direct pointer to the target element. However, in both cases we have to define which elements are actually visible from a given reference site. This information serves as the basis for code completion and to check existing references for their validity. The set of visible elements for a given reference is called its scope.*

As we discussed in the previous chapter, the abstract syntax in its simplest form is a tree. However, the information represented by the program is semantically almost always a graph; i.e. in addition to the tree's containment hierarchy, it contains non-containment cross-references[1]. The challenge thus is: how to get from the "syntactic tree" to the "semantic graph" – or, how to establish the cross-links. There is a marked difference between the projectional and parser-based approach:

[1] Examples abound and include variable references, procedure calls and target states in transitions of state machines.

- In parser-based systems, the cross-references have to be *resolved*, from the parsed text *after* the AST has been created. An IDE may provide the candidates in a code completion menu, but after selecting a target, the resulting textual representation of the reference must contain all the information to *re-resolve* the reference each time the program is parsed.

- In projectional editors in which every program element has a unique ID, a reference is represented as a pointer to that ID. Once a reference is established, it can always be re-resolved trivially based on the ID. The reference is established directly as the program is edited: the code completion menu shows candidate target elements for a reference in the code completion menu, and selection of one of them creates the reference[2].

[2] The code completion menu shows some human-readable (qualified) name of the target, but the persisted program uses the unique ID once the user makes a selection.

Typically, a language's structure definition specifies which concepts constitute valid target concepts for any given reference (e.g., a **Function**, a **Variable** or a **State**), but this is usually not enough. Language-specific visibility rules determine which *instances* of these concepts are actually permitted as a reference target[3]. The collection of model elements which are valid targets of a particular semantic cross-reference is called the *scope* of that cross-reference. Typically, the scope of a particular cross-reference not only depends on the target concept of the cross-reference, but also on its surroundings, e.g. the namespace within which the element lives, the location inside the larger structure of the site of the cross-reference or something that's essentially non-structural in nature.

[3] For example, only the function and variables *in the local module* or the states *in the same state machine as the transition* may be valid targets.

A scope, the collection of valid targets for a reference, has two uses. First, it can be used to populate the code completion menu in the IDE if the user presses **Ctrl-Space** at the reference site. Second, independent of the IDE, the scope is used for checking the validity of an existing reference: if the reference target is not among the elements in the scope, the reference is invalid.

Scopes can be hierarchical, in which case they are organized as a stack of collections – confusingly, these collections are often called scopes themselves. During resolution of a cross-reference, the lowest or *innermost* collection is searched first. If the reference cannot be resolved to match any of its elements, the parent of the innermost collection is queried, and so forth.

Instead of looking at scopes from the perspective of the reference (and hence calculating a set of candidate target elements), one can also look at scopes from the perspective of visibility. In this case, we (at least conceptually) compute for each location in the program, the set of visible elements. A reference is then restricted to refer to any element from those visible at the particular location. Our notion is more convenient from the cross-reference viewpoint, however, as it centers around resolving particular cross-references one at a time. From an implementation point of view, both perspective are exchangeable.

The hierarchy often mimics the structure of the language itself: e.g., the innermost scope of a reference consists of all the elements present in the immediately-surrounding "block", while the outermost scope is the *global* scope. This provides a mechanism to disambiguate target elements having the same reference syntax (usually the target element's name) by always choosing the element from the innermost scope. This is often called *shadowing*, because the inner elements overshadow the (more) outer elements.

8.1 Scoping in Spoofax

In the previous chapter we described how to specify a grammar for a subset of the Mobl language. This chapter shows how to specify name resolution for this language by means of declarative name binding rules. Spoofax' name binding rules are based on five concepts: namespaces, definitions, references, scopes and imports. We will introduce each of these concepts separately, going from simple to more complicated examples.

8.1.1 Namespaces

To understand naming in Spoofax, the notion of a *namespace* is essential. In Spoofax, a namespace is a collection of names and is not necessarily connected to a specific language concept[4]. Different concepts can contribute names to a single namespace. For example, in Java, classes and interfaces contribute to the same namespace. Namespaces are declared in the **namespace** section of a language definition. For Mobl, we have separate namespaces for modules, entities, properties, functions and local variables.

[4] Some languages such as C# provide namespaces as a language concept to scope the names of declarations such as classes. It is important to distinguish these namespaces as a language concept from Spoofax' namespaces as a language *definition* concept. The two are not related.

```
namespaces Module Entity Property Function Variable
```

8.1.2 Definitions and References

Once we have defined namespaces, we can define name bindings with rules of the form **pattern : clause***, where **pattern** is a term pattern[5], and **clause*** is a list of name binding declarations about the language construct that matches with **pattern**. For example, the following rules declare definition sites for module and entity names. The patterns in these rules match module and entity declarations, binding variables **m** and **e** to module and entity names respectively. These variables are then used in the clauses on the right-hand sides[6].

[5] A term pattern is a term that may contain variables (**x**) and wildcards (_).

[6] In the first rule, the clause specifies any term matched by **Module(m, _)** to define a name **m** in the **Module** namespace. Similarly, the second rule specifies any term matched by **Entity(e, _)** to define a name **e** in the **Entity** namespace.

```
Module(m, _): defines non-unique Module m
Entity(e, _): defines unique Entity e
```

As an example, let us reconsider the example module from the previous chapter:

```
module shopping
entity Item {
  name    : String
  ...
}
```

The parser turns this into an abstract syntax tree, represented as a term:

```
Module(
  "shopping",
  [ Entity(
      "Item",
      [Property("name", EntityType("String")), ...] )
  ]
])
```

The patterns in name binding rules match subterms of this term, indicating definition and use sites. The whole term is a definition site of the module name **shopping**. The first name binding rule specifies this binding. Its pattern matches the term and binds **m** to **"shopping"**. Similarly, the subterm **Entity ("Item", ...)** is a definition site of the entity name **Item**. The pattern of the second name binding rule matches this term and binds **e** to **"Item"**.

While entity declarations are unique definition sites, module declarations are non-unique definition sites. That is, multiple module declarations can share the same name. This allows Mobl users to spread the content of a module over several files, similar to Java packages. Namespaces are by default unique, so the **unique** keyword is only optional and can be omitted. For example, the following rules declare unique definition sites for property and variable names:

```
Property(p, _): defines Property p
Param(p, _)   : defines Variable p
Declare(v, _) : defines Variable v
```

Note how Spoofax distinguishes the name of a namespace from the sort and the constructor of a program element: in the last rule above, the sort of the program element is **Statement**, its constructor is **Declare**, and it lives in the **Variable** namespace. By distinguishing these three things, it becomes easy to add or exclude program elements from a namespace[7].

Use sites which refer to definition sites of names can be declared similarly. For example, the following rule declares use sites of entity names:

```
Type(t): refers to Entity t
```

Use sites might refer to different names from different namespaces. For example, a variable might refer either to a **Variable** or a **Property**. In Spoofax, this can be specified by exclusive resolution options:

```
Var(x):
  refers to Variable x otherwise
  refers to Property x
```

[7] For example, **return** statements are also of the syntactic sort **Statement**, but do not live in any namespace. On the other hand, function parameters also live in the **Variable** namespace, even though (in contrast to variable declarations) they do not belong to the syntactic sort **Statement**.

The **otherwise** keyword signals ordered alternatives: only if the reference cannot be resolved to a variable will Spoofax try to resolve it to a property. As a consequence, variable declarations shadow property definitions. If this is not intended, constraints can be defined to report corresponding errors. We will discuss constraints in Section 9.3 in the next chapter.

8.1.3 Scoping

■ *Simple Scopes*   In Spoofax, *Scopes* restrict the visibility of definition sites[8]. For example, an entity declaration scopes property declarations that are not visible from outside the entity.

[8] Note that Spoofax' use of the word **scope** is different from the general meaning of the word in this chapter.

```
entity Customer {
  name : String // Customer.name
}
entity Product {
  name : String // Product.name
}
```

In this example, both **name** properties live in the **Property** namespace, but we can still distinguish them: if **name** is referenced in a function inside **Customer**, then it references the one in **Customer**, not the one in **Product**.

Scopes can be nested and name resolution typically looks for definition sites from inner to outer scopes. In Mobl, modules scope entities, entities scope properties and functions, and functions scope local variables. This can be specified in Spoofax in terms of **scopes** clauses:

```
Module(m, _):   defines Module m scopes Entity
Entity(e, _):   defines Entity e scopes Property, Function
Function(f, _): defines Function f scopes Variable
```

As these examples illustrate, scopes are often also definition sites. However, this is not a requirement. For example, a block statement[9] has no name, but scopes variables:

```
Block(_): scopes Variable
```

[9] A block statement groups statements syntactically to a single statement. For example, Java provides curly braces to group statements into a block statement.

■ *Definition Sites with Limited Scope*   So far we have seen examples in which definitions are visible in their enclosing scope: entities are visible in the enclosing module, properties and functions are visible in the enclosing entity, and parameters are visible in the enclosing function. However, this does not hold for variables declared inside a function. Their visibility is limited to statements *after* the declaration. Thus, we need to restrict the visibility in the name binding rule for **Declare** to the *subsequent scope*:

```
Declare(v, _): defines Variable v in subsequent scope
```

Similarly, the iterator variable in a **for** loop is only visible in its condition, the update, and the loop's body, but not in the initializing expression. This can be declared as follows:

```
For(v, t, init, cond, update, body):
  defines Variable v in cond, update, body
```

■ *Scoped References*   Typically, use sites refer to names which are declared in its surrounding scopes. But a use site might also refer to definition sites which reside outside its scope. For example, a property name in a property access expression might refer to a property in another entity:

```
entity Customer {
  name : String
}

entity Order {
  customer : Customer
  function getCustomerName(): String {
    return customer.name;
  }
}
```

Here, **name** in **customer.name** refers to the property in entity **Customer**. The following name binding rule is a first attempt to specify this:

```
PropAccess(exp, p): refers to Property p in Entity e
```

But this rule does not specify which entity **e** is the right one. Interaction with the type system[10] is required in this case:

```
PropAccess(exp, p):
  refers to Property p in Entity e
  where exp has type EntityType(e)
```

[10] We will discuss type systems in Section 10.5.

This rule essentially says: give me a property with the name **p** in entity **e**, where **e** is the type of the current expression **exp**.

■ *Imports*   Many languages offer import facilities to include definitions from another scope into the current scope. For example, a Mobl module can import other modules, making entities from the imported modules available in the importing module:

```
module order

import banking

entity Customer {
```

```
  name   : String
  account: BankAccount
}
```

Here, **BankAccount** is not declared in the scope of module **order**. However, module **banking** declares an entity **BankAccount**, which is imported into module **order**. The type of property **account** should refer to this entity. This can be specified by the following name binding rule:

```
Import(m): imports Entity from Module m
```

This rule has two effects. First, **m** is interpreted as a name referring to a module. Second, every entity declared in this module becomes visible in the current scope.

8.1.4 References in Terms

Spoofax uses terms to represent abstract syntax. This enables many interesting features, for example generic tree traversals. But in contrast to object structures as used in MPS and Xtext, terms lack a native concept to represent cross-references. There are two approaches to handle cross-references when working with terms or similar tree structures. First, we can maintain a temporary environment with required information about defined elements during a transformation. This information can then be accessed at use sites. Second, we can maintain similar information in a global environment, which can be shared by various transformations.

Spoofax follows the second approach and stores all definitions and references in an in-memory data structure called the index[11]. By collecting all this summary information about files in a project together, it ensures fast access to global information (in particular, to-be-referenced names). The index is updated automatically when Spoofax model files change (or are deleted) and is persisted as Eclipse exits. All entries in the index have a URI which uniquely identifies the element across a project. These URIs are the basis for name resolution, and, by default, are constructed automatically, based on the name binding rules. As an example, consider the following entity:

```
module storage

entity Store {
  name    : String
  address : Address
}
```

Following the name binding rules discussed so far, there are two scope levels in this fragment: one at the module level and

[11] Spoofax also uses the index to store metadata about definitions, such as type information, as we show in the next chapter.

one at the entity level. We can assign names to these scopes
(**storage** and **Store**) by using the naming rules for modules
and entities. By creating a hierarchy of these names, Spoofax
creates URIs: the URI for **Store** is **Entity://storage.Store**,
and the one for **name** is **Property://storage.Store.name**. URIs
are represented internally as lists of terms that start with the
namespace, followed by a reverse hierarchy of the path names[12].
For the **name** property of the **Store** entity in the **storage** module, this would be:

```
[Property(), "name", "Store", "storage"]
```

[12] The reverse order used in the representation makes it easier to efficiently store and manipulate URIs in memory: every tail of such a list can share the same memory space.

Spoofax annotates each definition and reference with a URI to
connect names with information stored in the index. References are annotated with the same URI as their definition. This
way, information about the definition site is also available at
the reference. We can inspect URIs in Spoofax' analyzed syntax view. This view shows the abstract syntax with all URIs
as annotations[13]. Consider the following example with both
named and anonymous blocks:

[13] To obtain this view, select *Show Analyzed Syntax (selection)* in the *Transform* menu of the Spoofax editor. Spoofax will open a new editor which updates automatically when the content of the original editor changes.

```
module banking

entity BankAccount {
  name   : String
  number : Num

  function toString() : String {
    { // anonymous block
      var result = name + number.toString();
      return result;
    }
  }
}
```

The analyzed abstract syntax for this example is the following:

```
Module(
  "banking"{[Module(),"banking"]},
  [ Entity(
      "BankAccount"{[Entity(),"BankAccount","banking"]},
      [ Property(
          "name"{[Property(),"name","BankAccount","banking"]},
          StringType()
        ),
        Property(
          "number"{[Property(),"number","BankAccount","banking"]},
          NumType()
        ),
        Function(
          "toString"{[Function(),"toString","BankAccount","banking"]},
          [],
          StringType(),
          Block([
            Declare("result"{[Var(),"result",Anon(125),Anon(124),
                    "toString","BankAccount","banking"]},
              Add(
                Var("name"{[Property(),"name","BankAccount","banking"]}),
                MethodCall(..., "toString"{[Unresolved(Function()),
                           "toString", "BankAccount", "banking"]})
              )
```

```
            ),
            Return(
              Var("result"{[Var(),"result",Anon(125),Anon(124),
                "toString","BankAccount","banking"]})
            )
          ])
        )
      ]
    )
  ]
)
```

Any references that cannot be resolved are annotated with a special **Unresolved** constructor. For example, a variable named **nonexistent** could be represented as:

```
Var("nonexistent"{[Unresolved(Var()),"non\-existent",...]})
```

This makes it easy to recognize any unresolved references in constraints[14]: we can simply pattern-match against the **Unresolved** term.

[14] We discuss constraints in Section 9.3.

8.2 Scoping in Xtext

Xtext provides Java APIs for implementing all aspects of languages except the grammar[15]. Language developers typically provide Java classes that implement aspect-specific interfaces and then contribute those to Xtext using dependency injection[16]. For most language aspects, Xtext comes with various default implementations developers can build on. A lot of functionality is provided "out of the box" with minimal configuration, but it's easy to swap specific parts by binding another or a custom class through Guice.

[15] In fact, you can use any JVM-based language for implementing these language aspects, including Xtend.

[16] Xtext's internal configuration is based on dependency injection with Google Guice code.google.com/p/google-guice/

8.2.1 Simple, Local Scopes

To implement scopes, language developers have to contribute a class that implements the **IScopeProvider** interface. It has one method called **getScope** that returns an **IScope** for a given reference. An **IScope** is basically a collection of candidate reference targets, together with the textual representation by which these may be referenced from the current reference site (the same target may be referenced by different text strings from different program locations). The **getScope** method has two arguments: the first one, **context**, is the current program element for which a reference should be scoped; the second one, **reference**, identifies the reference for which the scope that needs to be calculated[17].

[17] The class **EReference** is the Ecore concept that represents references.

```
public interface IScopeProvider {
    IScope getScope(EObject context, EReference reference);
}
```

To make the scoping implementation easier, Xtext provides *declarative scope providers* through the `AbstractDeclarative-ScopeProvider` base class: instead of having to inspect the `reference` and `context` object manually to decide how to compute the scope, the language implementor can express this information via the name of the method (using a naming convention). Two different naming conventions are available:

```
// <X>, <R>: scoping the <R> reference of the <X> concept
public IScope scope_<X>_<R>(<X> ctx, EReference ref );

// <X>: the language concept we are looking for as a reference target
// <Y>: the concept from under which we try to look for the reference
public IScope scope_<X>(<Y> ctx, EReference ref);
```

Let's assume we want to scope the `targetState` reference of the `ChangeStateStatement`. Its definition in the grammar looks like this:

```
ChangeStateStatement:
    "state" targetState=[State];
```

We can use the following two alternative methods:

```
public IScope scope_ChangeStateStatement_targetState
            (ChangeStateStatement ctx, EReference ref ) {
    ...
}

public IScope scope_State(ChangeStateStatement ctx, EReference ref) {
    ...
}
```

The first alternative is specific for the `targetState` reference of the `ChangeStateStatement`. It is invoked by the declarative scope provider only for that particular reference. The second alternative is more generic. It is invoked whenever we are trying to reference a `State` (or any subconcept of `State`) from any reference of a `ChangeStateStatement` and *all its descendants* in the AST. So we could write an even more general alternative, which scopes the visible `State`s from anywhere in a `CoolingProgram`, independent of the actual reference[18].

```
public IScope scope_State(CoolingProgram ctx, EReference ref) {
    ...
}
```

The implementation of the scopes is simple, and relatively similar in all three cases. We write Java code that crawls up the containment hierarchy until we arrive at a `CoolingProgram` (in the last alternative, we already get the `CoolingProgram` as an argument, so we don't need to move up the tree), and then construct an `IScope` that contains the `State`s defined in that `CoolingProgram`. Here is a possible implementation:

[18] It is a good idea to always use the most general variants, unless you specifically want to scope one specific reference. Here is why: depending on the structure of your language, Xtext may have a hard time finding out the current location, and hence the reference that needs to be scoped. In this case, the tighter versions of the scoping method (`scope_ChangeStateStatement_targetState` in the example) might not be called in all the places you expect it to be called. This can be remedied either by changing the syntax (often not possible or not desired), or by using the more general variants of the scoping function `scope_State( CoolingProgram ctx, ... )`.

```
public IScope scope_ChangeStateStatement_targetState
        (ChangeStateStatement ctx, EReference ref ) {
    CoolingProgram owningProgram =
        Utils.ancestor( ctx, CoolingProgram.class );
    return Scopes.scopeFor(owningProgram.getStates());
}
```

The **Scopes** class provides a couple of helper methods to create **IScope** objects from collections of elements. The simple **scopeFor** method will use the **name** of the target element as the text by which it will be referenced[19]. So if a state is called **normalCooling**, then we'd have to write **state normalCooling** in a **ChangeStateStatement** in order to change to that state. The text **normalCooling** acts as the reference – pressing **Ctrl-F3** on that program element will go to the referenced state.

[19] You can pass in code that creates other strings than the name from the target element. This supports the previously mentioned feature of referencing the same program element with different strings from different reference sites.

8.2.2 Nested Scopes

The approach to scoping shown above is suitable for simple cases, such as the **targetState** reference shown above. However, in languages with nested blocks a different approach is recommended. Here is an example of a program expressed in a language with nested blocks:

```
var int x;
var int g;

function add( int x, int y ) {
    int sum = x + y;            // 1
    return sum;
}

function addAll( int es ... ) {
    int sum = 0;
    foreach( e in es ) {
        sum += e;               // 2
    }
    x = sum;                    // 3
}
```

At the program location marked as 1, the local variable **sum**, the arguments **x** and **y** and the global variables **x** and **g** are visible, although the global variable **x** is shadowed by the argument of the same name. At 2, we can see **x**, **g**, **sum** and **es**, but also the iterator variable **e**. At 3, **x** refers to the global, since it is not shadowed by a parameter or local variable of the same name. In general, some program elements introduce blocks (often statement lists surrounded by curly braces). A block can declare new symbols. References from within these blocks can see the symbols defined in that block, as well as all ancestor blocks. Symbols in inner blocks typically hide symbols with the same name in outer blocks[20].

[20] The symbols in outer blocks are either not accessible at all, or a special name has to be used, for example, by prefixing them with some **outer** keyword (for example, **outer.x**).

Xtext's scopes support this scenario. **IScopes** can reference outer scopes. If a symbol is not found in any given scope, that scope delegates to its outer scope (if it has one) and asks it for a symbol of the respective name. Since inner scopes are searched first, this implements shadowing as expected.

Also, scopes are not just collections of elements. Instead, they are maps between a string and an element[21]. The string is used as the reference text. By default, the string is the same as the target element's **name** property. So if a variable is called **x**, it can be referenced by the string **x**. However, this reference string can be changed as part of the scope definition. This can be used to make shadowed variables visible under a different name, such as **outer.x** if it is referenced from location 1. The following is pseudo-code that implements this behavior:

[21] In addition, the text shown in the code completion window can be different from the text that will be used as the reference once an element is selected. In fact, it can be a rich string that includes formatting, and it can contain an icon.

```
// recursive method to build nested scopes
private IScope collect( StatementList ctx ) {
    IScope outer = null
    if ( ctx is within another StatementList parent ) {
        outer = collect(parent)
    }
    IScope scope = new Scope( outer )
    for( all symbols s in ctx ) {
        scope.put( s.name, s )
        if ( outer.hasSymbolNamed( s.name ) ) {
            scope.put( "outer."+s.name, outer.getSymbolByName( s.name ) )
        }
    }
    return scope
}

// entry method, according to naming convention
// in declarative scope provider
public IScope scope_Symbol( StatementList ctx ) {
    return collect( ctx )
}
```

8.2.3 Global Scopes

There is one more aspect of scoping that needs to be discussed. Programs can be separated into several files and references can cross file boundaries. That is, an element in file **A** can reference an element in file **B**. In earlier versions of Xtext file **A** had to explicitly import file **B** to make the elements in **B** available as reference targets[22]. Since Xtext 1.0 both of these problems are solved using the emphindex[23]. The index is a data structure that stores (**String**,**IEObjectDescription**)-pairs. The first argument is the qualified name of the object, and the second one, the **IEObjectDescription**, contains information about a model element, including a URI (a kind of global pointer that also includes the file in which the element is stored) as well as arbitrary additional data provided by the language implementation. By default, all references are checked against this

[22] This resulted in several problems. First, for internal reasons, scalability was limited. Second, as a consequence of the explicit file imports, if the referenced element was moved into another file, the import statements in all referencing files had to be updated.

[23] This is similar to Spoofax' index discussed above.

name in the index, not against the actual object. If the actual object has to be resolved, the URI stored in the index is used. Only then is the respective file loaded[24]. The index is updated whenever a file is changed[25]. This way, if an element is moved to a different file while keeping its qualified name (which is based on the logical program structure) constant, the reference remains valid. Only the URI in the index is updated.

There are two ways to customize what gets stored in the index, and how. The **IQualifiedNameProvider** returns a qualified name for each program element. If it returns **null**, the element is not stored in the index, which means it is not referenceable. The other way is the **IDefaultResourceDescription-Strategy**, which allows language developers to build their own **IEObjectDescription** for program elements. This is important if custom user data has to be stored in the **IEObject-Description** for later use during scoping.

The **IGlobalScopeProvider** is activated if a local scope returns **null** or no applicable methods can be found in the declarative scope provider class (or if they return **null**). By default, the **ImportNamespacesAwareGlobalScopeProvider** is configured[26], which provides the possibility of referencing model elements outside the current file, either through their (fully) qualified name, or through their unqualified name if the respective namespace is imported using an **import** statement[27].

■ *Polymorphic References* In the cooling language, expressions also include references to entities such as configuration parameters, variables and hardware elements (compressors or fans defined in a different model). All of these referenceable elements extend **SymbolDeclaration**. This means that all of them can be referenced by the single **SymbolRef** construct.

```
AtomicLevel returns Expression:
    ...
    ({SymbolRef} symbol=[SymbolDeclaration|QID]);
```

The problem with this situation is that the reference itself does not encode the kind of thing that is referenced[28]. This makes writing code that processes the model cumbersome, since the target of a **SymbolRef** has to be taken into account when deciding how to treat (translate, validate) a symbol reference. A more natural design of the language would use different reference constructs for the different referenceable elements. In this case, the reference itself is specific to the referenced element, making processing much easier[29]:

[24] This is what improved scalability; files are only loaded if a reference target is accessed, not to check a reference for validity.

[25] Even when it has not been saved, so references against dirty editors work as expected.

[26] As with any other Xtext configuration, the specific implementation is configured through a Guice binding.

[27] That **import** statement is different from the one mentioned earlier: it makes the contents of the respective namespace visible; it does not refer to the a particular file.

[28] By looking at the reference alone we only know that we reference some kind of symbol. We don't know whether the reference points to a variable, a configuration parameter or a hardware element.

[29] It would also make writing the scopes and extending the language simpler.

```
AtomicLevel returns Expression:
    ...
    ({VariableRef} var=[Variable]);
    ({ParameterRef} param=[Parameter]);
    ({HardwareBuildingBlockRef} hbb=[HardwareBuildingBlock]);
```

However, this is not possible with Xtext, since the parser cannot distinguish the three cases syntactically. As we can see from the (invalid) grammar above, in all three cases the reference syntax itself is just an **ID**. Only during the linking phase could the system check which kind of element is actually referenced, but this is too late for the parser, which needs an unambiguous grammar. The grammar could be disambiguated by using a different syntax for each element:

```
AtomicLevel returns Expression:
    ...
    ({VariableRef} var=[Variable]);
    ({ParameterRef} "%" param=[Parameter]);
    ({HardwareBuildingBlockRef} "#" hbb=[HardwareBuildingBlock]);
```

While this approach will technically work, it would lead to an awkward syntax and is hence typically not used. The only remaining alternative is to make all referenceable elements extend **SymbolDeclaration** and use a single reference concept, as shown above.

8.3 Scoping in MPS

Making references work in MPS requires several ingredients. First of all, as we have seen earlier, the reference is defined as part of the language structure. Next, an editor is defined that determines how the referenced element is rendered at the referencing site[30]. To determine which instances of the referenced concept are allowed, a scoping function has to be implemented. This simply returns a list of all the elements that are considered valid targets for the reference, as well as an optional text string used to represent the respective element in the code completion menu.

As we explained above (Section 7.2), smart references are an important ingredient to make this work conveniently. They make sure that users can simply type the name (or whatever else is put into the code completion menu by the language developer) of the targeted element; once something is selected, the corresponding reference concept is instantiated, and the selected target is set.

[30] The syntax used to represent the reference is defined by that editor and can be changed at any time, since the actual reference is implemented based on the target element's UID.

■ *Simple Scopes*   As an example, we begin with the scope definition for the target reference of the **Transition** concept. To recap, it is defined as:

```
concept Transition
  // ...
  references:
    State    target   1
```

The scope itself is defined via the search scope constraint below. The system provides an anonymous **search scope** function that has a number of arguments that describe the context including the enclosing node and the referencing node. As the signature shows, the function has to return either an **ISearch-Scope** or simply a sequence of nodes of type **State**. The scope of the target state is the set of states of the state machine that (transitively) contains the transition. To implement this, the expression in the body of this function crawls up the containment hierarchy[31] until it finds a **Statemachine** and then returns its **states**[32].

```
link {target}
  referent set handler:
    <none>
  search scope:
    (referenceNode, linkTarget, enclosingNode, ...)
            ->join(ISearchScope | sequence<node<State>>) {
      enclosingNode.ancestor<Statemachine>.states;
    }
  validator:
    <default>
  presentation :
    <none>
```

In addition to the search scope, language developers can provide code that should be executed if a new reference target is set (**referent set handler**), additional validation (**validator**), as well as customized presentation in the code completion menu (**presentation**)[33].

■ *Nested Scopes*   In a more complex, block-oriented language with nested scopes, a different implementation pattern is recommended[34]:

- All program elements that contribute elements that can be referenced (such as blocks, functions or methods) implement an interface **IScopeProvider**.

- The interface provides **getVisibleElements(concept<> c)**, a method that returns all elements of type **c** that are available in that scope.

[31] Note that for a smart reference, where the reference object is created only *after* selecting the target, the **referenceNode** argument is **null**! This is why we write the scope using the **enclosingNode** argument.

[32] The code used to express scopes can be arbitrarily complex and is implemented in MPS' BaseLanguage, an extended version of Java.

[33] This can be different than the text used to represent the reference once it is established. That text is controlled by the referencing concept's editor.

[34] In this section we describe the approach as we have implemented it for mbeddr C. Since version 2.5, MPS supports this approach out of the box. For example, an interface similar to **IScopeProvider** ships with MPS, and scopes can be inherited from parent nodes.

- The search scope function simply calls this method on the owning **IScopeProvider**, passing in the concept whose instances it wants to see (**State** in the above example).

- The implementation of the method recursively calls the method on its owning **IScopeProvider**, as long as there is one. It also removes elements that are shadowed from the result.

This approach is used in the mbeddr C language, for example for local variables, because those are affected by shadowing from blocks. Here is the code for the **variable** reference of the **LocalVariableReference** concept:

```
link {variable}
  search scope:
    (referenceNode, linkTarget, enclosingNode, ... )
         ->join(ISearchScope | sequence<node<LocalVariableDeclaration>>) {

      // find the statement that contains the future local variable ref
      node<Statement> s = enclosingNode.ancestor<Statement, +>;

      // find the first containing ILocalVariableScopeProvider which is
      // typically next next higher statement that owns a StatementList.
      // An example would be a ForStatement or an IfStatement
      node<ILocalVarScopeProvider> scopeProvider =
            enclosingNode.ancestor<ILocalVarScopeProvider, +>;

      // In case we are not in a Statement or there
      // is no ILocalVarScopeProvider,
      // we return an empty list - no variables visible
      if (s == null || scopeProvider == null) {
        return new nlist<LocalVariableDeclaration>;
      }

      // we now retrieve the position of the current Statement in the
      // context StatementList. This is important because we only want to
      // see those variables that are defined before the reference site
      int pos = s != scopeProvider ? s.index : LocalVarScope.NO_POSITION;

      // finally we query the scopeProvider for the visible local variables
      scopeProvider.getLocalVarScope(s, pos).getVisibleLocalVars();
  }
```

■ *Polymorphic References* We have explained above how references work in principle: they are real pointers to the referenced element, based on the target's unique ID. In the section on Xtext we have seen how from a given location only one kind of reference for any given syntactic form can be implemented. Consider the following example, where we refer to a global variable **a** and an event parameter (**timestamp**) from within the guard condition expression:

```
int a;
int b;

statemachine linefollower {
  in event initialized(int timestamp);
  states (initial=initializing) {
    state initializing {
      on initialized [now() - timestamp > 1000 && a > 3] -> running
```

```
    }
    state running {
    }
  }
}
```

Both references to local variables and to event parameters use the same syntactic form: a text string that represents the name of the respective target element. As we have discussed above, in Xtext, this is implemented with a single reference concept, typically called **SymbolReference**, that can reference to any kind of **Symbol**. **LocalVariableDeclaration** and **EventParameter** would both extend **Symbol**, and scopes would make sure both kinds are visible from within guard expressions[35].

In MPS this is done differently. To solve the example above, one would create a **LocalVariableReference** and an **EventParameterReference**. The former references variables and the latter references event parameters. Both have an editor that renders the name of the referenced element, and each of them has *their own* scope definition[36]. The following is the respective code for the **EventParameterReference** expression:

```
concept EventParameterReference extends Expression

link {parameter}
  search scope:
    (referenceNode, linkTarget, enclosingNode, ...)
        ->join(ISearchScope | sequence<node<EventArg>>) {
      enclosingNode.ancestor<Transition, +>.trigger.event.args;
    }
```

Entering the reference happens by typing the name of the referenced element (cf. the concept of smart references introduced above). In the case in which there are a **LocalVariableDeclaration** and an **EventParameter** of the same name, the user has to make an explicit decision, at the time of entry (the name won't bind, and the code completion menu requires a choice). It is important to understand that, although the names are similar, the tool still knows whether a particular reference refers to a **LocalVariableDeclaration** or to an **EventParameter**, because the reference is encoded using the ID of the target[37].

[35] The problem with this approach is that the reference itself contains no type information about what it references, it is simply a **SymbolReference**. Processing code has to inspect the type of the referenced symbol to find out what a particular **SymbolReference** actually means. It can also be a problem regarding modularity, because every referenceable concept must extend **Symbol**. Referenceable elements contributed by an independently developed language which we may want to embed into the C language will *not* extend **Symbol**, though! We discuss language modularization and composition in Section 16.2.

[36] This retains modularity. Adding new kinds of references to existing expression languages can be done in a modular fashion, since the new reference expression comes with its own, independent scoping rule.

[37] It may not, however, be obvious to the user, so use this approach with caution and/or use different syntax highlighting to distinguish the two. The real benefit of this approach is that if two independent language extensions define such scopes independently, there will not be any ambiguity if these extensions are used together in a single program.

9
Constraints

Constraints are Boolean expressions that must be true for every program expressed with a specific language. Together with type systems, which are discussed in the next chapter, they ensure the static semantics of a language. This chapter introduces the notion of constraints, some considerations regarding languages suitable for expressing constraints, and provides examples with our tools.

As we explained in the DSL Design part of the book, not all programs that conform to the structure (grammar, AS, meta model) of a language are valid. Language definitions include further restrictions that cannot be expressed purely by structure. Such additional restrictions are typically called constraints.

Constraints are Boolean conditions that have to evaluate to `true` in order for the model to be correct ("does `expr` hold?")[1]. An error message is reported if the expression evaluates to `false` ("`expr` does not hold!"). Constraints are typically associated a particular language concept ("for each instance of concept `C`, `expr-with-C` must hold")[2]. There are two major kinds of constraints we can distinguish: well-formedness and type systems. Examples for well-formedness constraints include:

- Uniqueness of names in lists of elements (e.g., functions in a namespace).

- Every non-start state of a state machine has at least one incoming transition.

- A variable is defined before it is used (statement ordering).

Type system rules are different in that they verify the correctness of types in programs, e.g., they make sure you don't as-

[1] Constraints represent the static semantics of a language. The execution semantics are typically represented by transformations, generators or interpreters. We discuss those in Chapter 11.

[2] In addition to just associating a constraint with a language concept, additional applicability conditions or match patterns may be used.

sign a **float** to an **int**. In expression languages particularly, type calculation and checking can become quite complicated, and therefore warrant special support. This is why we distinguish between constraints in general (covered in this chapter) and type systems (which we cover in the next chapter).

Constraints can be implemented with any language or framework that is able to query a model and report errors to the user. To make expressing constraints efficient[3], it is useful if the language has the following characteristics:

- It should be able to effectively navigate and filter the model. Support for path expressions (as in `aClass.operations.arguments.type` as a way to find out the types of all arguments of all operations in a class) is extremely useful.

- Support for higher-order functions is useful, so that one can write generic algorithms and traversal strategies.

- A good collections language, often making use of higher-order functions, is very useful, so it is easily possible to filter collections, create subsets or get the set of distinct values in a list.

- Finally, it is helpful to be able to associate a constraint declaratively with the language concept (or structural pattern) for whose instances it should be executed.

[3] Constraint checking should also be efficient in terms of speed and memory usage, even for large models. To this end, it is useful if the constraint language supports impact analysis, so we can find out efficiently which constraints have to be reevaluated for any given change to a program.

Here is an example constraint written in a pseudo-language:

```
constraint for:
  Class
expression:
  this.operations.arguments.type.filter(ComplexNumber).isNotEmpty &&
  !this.imports.any(i|i.name == "ComplexNumberSupportLib")
message:
  "class "+this.name+" uses complex numbers, "+
     "so the ComplexNumberSupportLib must be imported"
```

Some kinds of constraints require specialized data structures to be built or maintained in sync with the program. Examples include dead code detection, missing returns in some branches of a method's body, or read access to an uninitialized variable. To be able to find these kinds of errors statically, a dataflow graph has to be constructed from the program. It models the various execution paths through a (part of a) program. Once a dataflow graph is constructed, it can be used to check whether there exists a path from program start to a variable read without coming across a write to the same variable. We show an example of the use of a data flow graph in the MPS example (Section 9.2).

9.1 Constraints in Xtext

Just like scopes, constraints are implemented in Java or any other JVM language[4]. Developers add methods to a validator class generated by the Xtext project wizard. In the end, these validations plug into the EMF validation framework[5].

A constraint checking method is a Java method with the following characteristics: it is public, returns **void**, can have an arbitrary name, it has a single argument of the type for which the check should apply, and it has the **@Check** annotation. For example, the following method is a check that is invoked for all instances of **CustomState** (i.e. not for start states and background states). It checks that each such state can actually be reached by verifying that it has incoming transitions (expressed via a **ChangeStateStatement**):

```
@Check(CheckType.NORMAL)
public void checkOrphanEndState( CustomState ctx ) {
    CoolingProgram coopro = Utils.ancestor(ctx, CoolingProgram.class);
    TreeIterator<EObject> all = coopro.eAllContents();
    while ( all.hasNext() ) {
        EObject s = all.next();
        if ( s instanceof ChangeStateStatement ) {
            ChangeStateStatement css = (ChangeStateStatement) s;
            if ( css.getTargetState() == ctx ) return;
        }
    }
    error("no transition ever leads into this state",
      CoolingLanguagePackage.eINSTANCE.getState_Name());
}
```

The method retrieves the cooling program that owns the **ctx** state, then retrieves all of its descendants and iterates over them. If the descendant is a **ChangeStateStatement** and its **targetState** property references the current state, then we return: we have found a transition leading into the current state. If we don't find one of these, we report an error. An error report contains the error message, a severity (**INFO**, **WARNING**, **ERROR**), the element to which it is attached[6], as well as the particular feature[7] of that element that should be highlighted. The **CheckType.NORMAL** in the annotation defines when this check should run:

- **CheckType.NORMAL**: run when the file is saved.

- **CheckType.FAST**: run after each model change (more or less after each keypress).

- **CheckType.EXPENSIVE**: run only if requested explicitly via the context menu.

[4] As mentioned earlier, a language that provides higher-order functional abstractions such as Xtend is very useful for navigating and querying ASTs.

[5] Other EMF **EValidator** implementations can be used in Xtext as well.

[6] The error message in Eclipse will be attached to this program element.

[7] Feature is EMF's term for properties, references and operations of **EClass**es.

Note that neither Xtext nor any of the other tools supports impact analysis by default. Impact analysis is a strategy for finding out whether a particular constraint can potentially be affected by a particular change, and only evaluating the constraint if it can. Impact analysis can improve performance if this analysis is faster than evaluating the constraint itself. For local constraints this is usually not the case. Only for non-local constraints that cover large parts of the model (and possibly require loading additional fragments), is impact analysis important. Xtext uses a pragmatic approach in the sense that these constraints must be marked as **EXPENSIVE** by the user and run only on request (over lunch, during nightly build). As an example, let us get back to the example about orphan states. The implementation of the constraint checks orphan-ness separately for each state. In doing so, it gets all descendants of the cooling program *for each state*. This can be a scalability problem for larger programs. To address this issue, one would write *a single constraint* for the whole cooling program that identifies all orphan states in one or maybe two scans through the program. This constraint could then be marked as **EXPENSIVE** as programs get really big[8].

9.2 Constraints in MPS

9.2.1 Simple Constraints

MPS' approach to constraints is very similar to Xtext's[9]. The main difference is that the constraint is written in BaseLanguage, an extended version of Java that has some of the features that makes constraints more concise. Here is the code for the same *state unreachable* constraint, which we can make use of in the state machines extension to C:

```
checking rule stateUnreachable {
  applicable for concept = State as state
  do {
    if (!state.initial &&
        state.ancestor<Statemachine>.
          descendants<Transition>.
            where({~it => it.target == state; }).isEmpty) {
      error "orphan state - can never be reached" -> state;
    }
  }
}
```

Currently there is no way to control when a constraint is run[10], it is decided based on some MPS-internal algorithm which tracks changes to a model and reevaluates constraints as neces-

[8] In general, local constraints (as shown in the code above) are easier to write than the more optimized global constraints. However, the latter often perform better. Unless it is clear from the start that programs will become big, it is a good idea to first write local, simpler and maybe less efficient constraints, and then use profiling to detect performance bottlenecks later. As usual, premature optimization leads to code that is hard to maintain.

[9] Note that in MPS, constraints are implemented as part of the type system, in *Non-Typesystem Rules*. MPS also has a language aspect called Constraints, but as we have seen before, this is used for scopes and context constraints.

[10] In contrast to Xtext, constraints can also not be marked as **FAST** or **EXPENSIVE**.

sary. However, pressing **F5** in a program or explicitly running the model checker forces all constraints to be reevaluated.

9.2.2 Dataflow

As we have said earlier, dataflow analysis can be used to detect dead code, null access, unnecessary **if**s (because it can be shown statically that the condition is always true or false) or read-before-write errors. The foundation for data flow analysis is the *data flow graph*. This is a data structure that describes the flow of data through a program's code. Consider the following example:

```
int i = 42;
j = i + 1;
someMethod(j);
```

The **42** is "flowing" from the **init** expression in the local variable declaration into the variable **i** and then, after adding **1**, into **j**, and then into **someMethod**. Data flow analysis consists of two tasks: building a data flow graph for a program, and then performing analysis on this data flow graph to detect problems in the program.

MPS comes with predefined data structures for representing data flow graphs, a DSL for defining how the graph can be derived from language concepts (and hence, programs) and a set of default analyses that can be integrated into your language[11]. We will look at all these ingredients in this section.

[11] MPS also comes with a framework for developing custom analyses; however, this is beyond the scope of this book.

■ *Building a Data Flow Graph* Data flow is specified in the *Dataflow* aspect of language definitions. There you can add data flow builders (DFBs) for your language concepts. These are programs expressed in MPS' data flow DSL that build the data flow graph for instances of those concepts in programs. Here is the DFB for **LocalVariableDeclaration**.

```
data flow builder for LocalVariableDeclaration {
  (node)->void {
    if (node.init != null) {
      code for node.init
      write node = node.init
    } else {
      nop
    }
  }
}
```

If the **LocalVariableDecaration** has an **init** expression (it is optional!), then the DFB for the **init** expression has to be executed using the **code for** statement. Then we perform an actual data flow definition: the **write node = node.init** specifies that write access is performed on the current node. The statement also expresses that whatever value was in the **init** expression is now in the node itself. If there is no **init** expression, we still want to mark the **LocalVariableDeclaration** node as visited by the data flow builder using the **nop** statement – the program flow has come across this node[12].

To illustrate a **read** statement, we can take a look at the **LocalVariableRef** expression which read-accesses the variable it references. Its data flow is defined as **read node.var**, where **var** is the name of the reference that points to the referenced variable.

In an **AssignmentStatement**, we first execute the DFB for the **rvalue** and then "flow" the **rvalue** into the **lvalue** – the purpose of an assignment:

```
data flow builder for AssigmentStatement {
  (node)->void {
    code for node.rvalue
    write node.lvalue = node.rvalue
  }
}
```

[12] A subsequent analysis reports all program nodes that have *not* been visited by a DFB as dead code. So even if a node has no further effect on a program's data flow, it has to be marked as visited using **nop**.

For a **StatementList**, we simply mark the list as visited and then execute the DFBs for each statement in the list. We are now ready to inspect the data flow graph for the simple function below. Fig. 9.1 shows the data flow graph.

```
void trivialFunction() {
  int8 i = 10;
  i = i + 1;
}
```

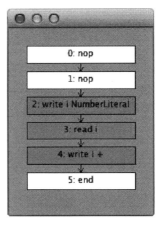

Figure 9.1: An example of a data flow for a simple C function. You can access the data flow graph for a program element (e.g., a C function) by selecting **Language Debug -> Show Data Flow Graph** from the element's context menu. This will render the data flow graph graphically and constitutes a good debugging tool when building your own data flow graphs and analyses.

Most interesting data flow analysis has to do with loops and branching. So specifying the correct DFBs for things like **if**, **switch** and **for** is important. As an example, we look at the DFB for the **IfStatement**. We start with the obligatory **nop** to mark the node as visited. Then we run the DFB for the condition, because that is evaluated in all cases. Then it becomes interesting: depending on whether the condition is true or false, we either run the **thenPart** or we jump to where the **else if** parts begin. Here is the code so far:

```
nop
code for node.condition
ifjump after elseIfBlock // elseIfBlock is a label defined later
code for node.thenPart
{ jump after node }
```

The **ifjump** statement means that we may jump to the specified label (i.e. we then execute the **else if**s). If not (we just "run over" the **ifjump**), then we execute the **thenPart**. If we execute the **thenPart**, we are finished with the whole **IfStatement**

– no **else if**s or **else** parts are relevant, so we jump after the current node (the **IfStatement**) and we're done. However, there is an additional catch: in the **thenPart**, there may be a **return** statement. So we may never actually arrive at the **jump after node** statement. This is why it is enclosed in curly braces: this says that the code in the braces is optional, so if the data flow does not visit it, that's fine (and no *dead code* error is reported).

Let's continue with the **else if**s. We arrive at the label **elseIfBlock** if the condition was **false**, i.e. the above **ifjump** actually happened. We then iterate over the **elseIf**s and execute their DFB. After that, we run the code for the **elsePart**, if there is one. The following code can only be understood if we know that, if we execute one of the **else if**s, then we jump *after the whole* **IfStatement**. This is specified in the DFB for the **ElseIfPart**, which we'll illustrate below. Here is the rest of the code for the **IfStatement**'s DFB:

```
label elseIfBlock
foreach elseIf in node.elseIfs {
  code for elseIf
}
if (node.elsePart != null) {
  code for node.elsePart
}
```

We can now inspect the DFB for the **ElseIfPart**. We first run the DFB for the condition. Then we may jump to after that **else if**, because the condition may be false and we want to try the next **else if**, if there is one. Alternatively, if the condition is true, we run the DFB for the body of the **ElseIfPart**. Then two things can happen: either we jump to after the whole **IfStatement** (after all, we have found an **else if** that is true), or we don't do anything at all anymore because the current **else if** contains a **return** statement. So we have to use the curly braces again for the jump to after the whole **if**. The code is below, and an example data flow graph is shown in figure Fig. 9.2.

```
code for node.condition
ifjump after node
code for node.body
{ jump after node.ancestor<IfStatement> }
```

The DFB for a **for** loop makes use of the fact that loops can be represented using conditional branching. Here is the code:

```
code for node.iterator
label start
code for node.condition
ifjump after node
```

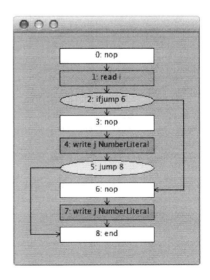

Figure 9.2: A data flow graph for the an if statement if (i > 0) j = 1; else j = 2;

```
code for node.body
code for node.incr
jump after start
```

We first execute the DFB for the `iterator` (which is a subconcept of `LocalVariableDeclaration`, so the DFB shown above works for it as well). Then we define a label `start` so we can jump to this place from further down. We then execute the `condition`. Then we have an `ifjump` to after the whole loop (which covers the case in which the condition is false and the loop ends). In the other case (where the condition is still true) we execute the code for the `body` and the `incr` part of the `for` loop. We then jump to after the `start` label we defined above.

■ *Analyses*   MPS supports a number of data flow analyses out of the box[13]. The following utility class uses the unreachable code analysis:

```
public class DataflowUtil {

  private Program prog;

  public DataflowUtil(node<> root) {
    // build a program object and store it
    prog = DataFlow.buildProgram(root);
  }

  public void checkForUnreachableNodes() {
    // grab all instructions that
    // are unreachable (predefined functionality)
    sequence<Instruction> allUnreachableInstructions =
            ((sequence<Instruction>) prog.getUnreachableInstructions());

    // remove those that may legally be unreachable
    sequence<Instruction> allWithoutMayBeUnreachable =
            allUnreachableInstructions.where({~instruction =>
              !(Boolean.TRUE.equals(instruction.
                    getUserObject("mayBeUnreachable"))); });

    // get the program nodes that correspond
    // to the unreachable instructions
    sequence<node<>> unreachableNodes = allWithoutMayBeUnreachable.
            select({~instruction => ((node<>) instruction.getSource()); });

    // output errors for each of those unreachable nodes
    foreach unreachableNode in unreachableNodes {
      error "unreachable code" -> unreachableNode;
    }
  }
}
```

[13] These analyses operate only on the data flow graph, so the same analyses can be used for any language, once the DFBs for that language map programs to data flow graphs.

The class builds a `Program` object in the constructor. `Program`s are wrappers around the data flow graph and provide access to a set of predefined analyses on the graph. We will make use of one of them here in the `checkForUnreachableNodes` method. This method extracts all unreachable nodes from the graph (see comments in the code above) and reports errors for them. To actually run the check, we call this method from a non-typesystem rule for C functions:

```
checking rule check_DataFlow {
  applicable for concept = Function as fct
  overrides false
  do {
    new DataflowUtil(fct.body).checkForUnreachableNodes();
  }
}
```

9.3 Constraints in Spoofax

Spoofax uses *rewrite rules* to specify all semantic parts of a language definition. In this section, we first provide a primer on rewrite rules. Next we show how they can be used to specify constraints in language definitions[14].

9.3.1 Rewrite Rules

Rewrite rules are functions that operate on terms, transforming one term to another. Rewrite rules in Spoofax are provided as part of the Stratego program transformation language. A basic rewrite rule that transforms a term pattern **term1** to a term pattern **term2** has the following form:

```
rule-name: term1 -> term2
```

Term patterns have the same form as terms: any term is a legal term pattern. In addition to the basic constructors, string literals, integer literals, and so on, they also support variables (e.g., **v** or **name**) and wildcards (indicated by _). As an example, the following rewrite rule rewrites an **Entity** to the list of properties contained in that entity:

```
get-properties:
  Entity(name, properties) -> properties
```

So, for an **Entity("User", [Property("name", String)])**, it binds **"User"** to the variable **name**, and **[Property("name", "String")]** to the variable **properties**. It then returns the collection **properties**. While rewrite rules can be viewed as functions, they have one important difference: they can be defined multiple times for different patterns[15]. In the case of **get-properties**, we could add another definition that works for property access expressions:

```
get-properties:
  PropAccess(expr, property) -> property
```

Rules can have complex patterns. For example, it is possible to write a rule that succeeds only for entities with *only* a **name** property[16]:

[14] Rewrite rules are used for all kinds of other purposes in Spoofax, and we will encounter them again, for example in the chapter on transformation and code generation, Section 11.4. This is why we explain them in some detail here.

[15] This is comparable to polymorphic overloading.

[16] Note how this rule uses a wildcard since it doesn't care about the name of the entity.

```
is-name-only-entity:
  Entity(_, [Property("name", "String")]) -> True()
```

Rewrite rules can be invoked using the syntax `<rule-name> term`[17]. The angle brackets make it easy to distinguish rule invocations from terms, and makes it possible to use invocations in term expressions.

[17] For example, `<get-properties> Entity("Unit", [])` would return an empty list of properties.

Stratego provides a **with** clause that can be used for additional code that should be considered for rewrite rules. The **with** clause is most commonly used for assignments and calls to other rules. As an example, we can write the rule above using a **with**. This rule assigns the value of **get-properties** to a variable **result** and returns that as the result value of the rule:

```
invoke-get-properties:
  Entity(name, properties) -> result
  with
    result := <get-properties> Entity(name, properties)
```

Rules can also have conditions. These can be specified using **where**[18]. These clauses typically use the operators listed in the following table:

[18] If the pattern of a rule does not match, or if its conditions do not succeed, a rule is said to *fail*. As we will see later, whether rules succeed or fail helps guide the execution sequence of sets of languages.

Expression	Description
`<e> t`	Applies **e** to **t**, or fails if **e** is unsuccessful.
`v := t`	Assign a term expression **t** to a variable **v**.
`!t => p`	Match a term **t** against a pattern **p**, or fail.
`not(e)`	Succeeds if **e** does not succeed.
`e1; e2`	Sequence: apply **e1**. If it succeeds, apply **e2**.
`e1 <+ e2`	Choice: apply **e1**, if it fails apply e2 instead.

An example of a rule with a **where** clause is the following:

```
has-properties:
  Entity(name, properties) -> True()
  with
    properties := <get-properties> Entity(name, properties);
  where
    not(!properties => [])
```

This rule only succeeds for entities where the where condition `not(!properties => [])` holds[19]. That is, it succeeds as long as an entity does not have an empty list (indicated by `[]`) of properties. Rewrite rules can have any number of **where** and **with** clauses, and they are evaluated in the order they appear.

[19] `!x => y` matches a term x against a pattern y. It does not mean logical negation.

Like functions or methods in other languages, rewrite rules can have parameters. Stratego distinguishes between parameters that pass other rules and parameters that pass terms, using a vertical bar to separate the two separate lists[20]. The Stratego standard library provides a number of higher-order rules, i.e.

[20] Rules that take both rule and term parameters have a signature of the form `rule(r|t)`, those with only rule parameters use `rule(r)`, and those with only term parameters use `rule(|t)`.

rules that take other rules as their argument. These rules are used for common operations on abstract syntax trees: for example, `map(r)` applies a rule `r` to all elements of a list:

```
get-property-types:
  Entity(_, properties) -> types
  with
    types := <map(get-property-type)> properties

get-property-type:
  Property(_, type) -> type
```

Rules like **map** specify a *traversal* on a certain term structure: they specify how a particular rule should be applied to a term and its subterms. Rules that specify traversals are also called *strategies*[21]. In Spoofax, strategies are used to control traversals in constraints, transformation, and code generation.

[21] This is where the name of the *Stratego* transformation language comes from.

9.3.2 Basic Constraint Rules

Spoofax uses rules with the name `constraint-error` to indicate constraints that trigger errors, `constraint-warning` for warnings, and `constraint-note` for notes. To report an error, warning or information note, these rules have to be overwritten for the relevant term patterns. The following example is created by default by the Spoofax project wizard. It simply reports a note for any module named `example`:

```
constraint-note:
  Module(name, _) -> (name, "This is just an example program.")
  where
    !name => "example"
```

The condition checks if the module `name` matches the string `"example"`. The rule returns (via its right-hand side) a tuple with the tree node where the marker should appear and a string message that should be shown. All constraint rules have this form.

Most constraint rules use string interpolation for error messages. Interpolated strings have the form `$[...]` where variables can be escaped using `[...]`. The following example uses string interpolation to report a warning[22].

```
constraint-warning:
  Entity(theName, _) -> (theName,
    $[Entity [theName] does not have a capitalized name])
  where
    not(<string-starts-with-capital> theName)
```

[22] The rule uses the a standard library rule `string-starts-with-capitals`. These and other library rules are documented on the Spoofax website at www.spoofax.org/.

9.3.3 Index-Based Constraint Rules

Some constraint rules interact with the Spoofax index[23]. One way to do this is to use URI annotations on the abstract syntax.

[23] Notable examples include constraints that forbid references to undefined program elements and duplicate definitions. Newly created Spoofax projects provide default constraint rules for these cases, which can be customized.

These are placed on each reference and definition. For example, a reference to a Mobl variable **v** is represented as `Var("v")`. With an annotation, it reads as follows:

```
Var("v"{[Var(),"v","function","module"]})
```

The annotation is added directly to the name, surrounded with curly braces[24]. Unresolved references are represented by terms such as the following (notice the **Unresolved** term, surrounding the namespace):

```
Var("u"{[Unresolved(Var()),"u","function","module"]})
```

[24] The annotation itself is a URI `Var://module/function/v`, represented as a list consisting of the namespace, the name and the path in reverse order.

In most statically typed languages, references that cannot be statically resolved indicate an error. The following constraint rule reports an error for these cases:

```
constraint-error:
  x -> (x, $[Unable to resolve reference.])
  where
    !x => _{[Unresolved(t) | _]}
```

This rule matches any term **x** in the abstract syntax, and reports an error if it has an **Unresolved** annotation[25]. Note how the pattern `_{[Unresolved(t) | _]}` matches any term (indicated by the wildcard _) that has a list annotation where the head of the list is **Unresolved(t)** and the tail matches _.

[25] For dynamic languages, or languages with optional types, the constraint could be removed or relaxed. In those cases, name resolution may only play a role in providing editor services such as code completion.

In addition to annotations, the Spoofax index provides an API for inspecting naming relations in programs. The following table shows some of the key rules the index provides.

`index-uri`	Gets the URI of a term.
`index-namespace`	Gets the namespace of a term.
`index-lookup`	Returns the first definition of a reference.
`index-lookup-all`	Returns all definitions of a reference.
`index-get-files-of`	Gets all files a definition occurred in.
`index-get-all-in-file`	Gets all definitions for a given file path.
`index-get-current-file`	Gets the path of the current file.

We can use the index API to detect duplicate definitions. In most languages, duplicate definitions are always disallowed. In the case of Mobl, duplicate definitions are not allowed for functions or entities, but they are allowed for variables, just as in JavaScript. The following constraint rules checks for duplicate entity declarations:

```
constraint-error:
  Entity(name, _) -> (name, $[Duplicate definition])
  where
    defs := <index-lookup-all> name;
    <gt> (<length> defs, 1)
```

This rule matches any entity declaration. Then, it fires a helper rule `is-duplicates-allowed`. Next, the constraint rule determines all definition sites of the entity name. If the list has more than one element, the rule reports an error. This is checked by comparing the length of the list with `1` by calling the `gt` ("greater than") rule. More sophisticated constraints and error messages can be specified using a type system, as we show in the next chapter.

10
Type Systems

> *Type systems are a subset of constraints – they implement type calculations and type checks. These can be relatively complex, so special support beyond general-purpose constraint checking is useful. In this chapter we discuss what type systems do in general, we discuss various strategies for computing types, and we provide the usual examples with Xtext, MPS and Spoofax.*

Let us start with a definition of type systems from Wikipedia:

> A type system may be defined as a tractable syntactic framework for classifying phrases according to the kinds of values they compute. A type system associates types with each computed value. By examining the flow of these values, a type system attempts to prove that no type errors can occur. The type system in question determines what constitutes a type error, but a type system generally seeks to guarantee that operations expecting a certain kind of value are not used with values for which that operation makes no sense.

In summary, type systems associate types with program elements and then check whether these types conform to predefined typing rules. We distinguish between dynamic type systems, which perform the type checks as the program executes, and static type systems, where type checks are performed ahead of execution, mostly based on type specifications in the program. This chapter focuses exclusively on static type checks[1].

[1] If a DSL uses dynamic typing, the type checks are performed at runtime based on the actual types of values. Many of the ways of expressing typing rules are similar in this case. However, all the DSLs I have built so far use static typing – the fact you can actually have static type systems is a primary benefit of external DSLs. DSLs with dynamic type systems are probably better implemented as internal DSLs, relying on the dynamic type system of the host language. Internal DSLs are beyond the scope of this book.

10.1 Type Systems Basics

To introduce the basic concepts of type systems, let us go back to the example used at the beginning of the section on syntax. As a reminder here is the example code, and Fig. 10.1 shows the abstract syntax tree.

```
var x: int;
calc y: int = 1 + 2 * sqrt(x)
```

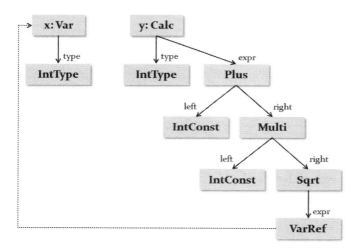

Figure 10.1: Abstract syntax tree for the above program. Boxes represent instances of language concepts, solid lines represent containment, dotted lines represent cross-references.

Using this example, we can illustrate in more detail what type systems have to do:

Declare Fixed Types Some program elements have fixed types. They don't have to be derived or calculated – they are always the same and known in advance. Examples include the integer constants `IntConst` (whose type is `IntType`), the square root concept `sqrt` (whose type is `double`), as well as the type declarations themselves (the type of `IntType` is `IntType`, the type of `DoubleType` is `Double- Type`).

Derive Types For some program elements, the type has to be derived from the types of other elements. For example, the type of a `VarRef` (the variable reference) is the type of the referenced variable. The type of a variable is the type of its declared type. In the example above, the type of `x` and the reference to `x` is `IntType`.

Calculate Common Types Most type systems have some kind of type hierarchy. In the example, `IntType` is a subtype of

DoubleType (so **IntType** can be used wherever **DoubleType** is expected). A type system has to support the specification of such subtype relationships. Also, the type of certain program elements may be calculated from the arguments passed to them; in many cases the resulting type will be the "more general" one based on the subtyping relationship. Examples include the **Plus** and **Multi** concepts: if the left and right arguments are two **IntType**s, the result is an **IntType**. In the case of two **DoubleType**s, the result is a **DoubleType**. If an **IntType** and a **DoubleType** are used, the result is a **DoubleType**, the more general of the two.

Type Checks Finally, a type system has to check for type errors and report them to the user. To this end, a language specifies type constraints or type checks that are checked at editing time by the type system based on the calculated types. In the example, a type error would occur if something with a **DoubleType** were assigned to an **IntType** variable.

The type of a program element is generally not the same as its language concept[2]. Different instances of the same concept can have different types: a + calculates its type as the more general of the two arguments. So the type of each + instance depends on the types of the arguments of that particular instance.

Types are often represented with the same technology as the language concepts. As we will see, in the case of MPS types are just nodes, i.e. instances of concepts. In Xtext, we use **EObjects**, i.e. instances of **EClasses** as types. In Spoofax, any ATerm can be used as a type. In all cases, we can even define the concepts as part of the language. This is useful, because most of the concepts used as types also have to be used in the program text whenever types are explicitly declared (as in **var x: int**).

10.2 Type Calculation Strategies

Conceptually, the core of a type system can be considered to be a function **typeof** that calculates the type for a program element. This function can be implemented in any way suitable; after all, it is just program code. However, in practice, three approaches seem to be used most: recursion, unification and pattern matching. We will explore each of these conceptually, and then provide examples in the tool sections.

[2] For example, the concept (meta class) of the number **1** is **IntConst** and its type is **IntType**. The type of the **sqrt** is **DoubleType** and its concept is **Sqrt**. Only for type declarations themselves the two are (usually) the same: the type of an **IntType** is **IntType**.

10.2.1 Recursion

Recursion is widely used in computer science and we assume that every reader is familiar with it. In the context of type systems, the recursive approach for calculating a type defines a polymorphic function **typeof**, which takes a program element and returns its type, while calling itself[3] to calculate the types of those elements on which its own type depends. Consider the following example grammar (using Xtext notation):

[3] Or, most likely, one of the polymorphic overrides.

```
LocalVarDecl:
    "var" name=ID ":" type=Type ("=" init=Expr)?;
```

The following examples are structurally valid example sentences:

```
var i: int          // 1
var i: int = 42     // 2
var i: int = 33.33  // 3
var i = 42          // 4
```

Let's develop the pseudo-code for **typeof** function the **LocalVarDecl**. A first attempt might look as follows:

```
typeof( LocalVarDecl lvd ) {
    return typeof( lvd.type )
}

typeof( IntType it ) { return it }
typeof( DoubleType dt ) { return dt }
```

Notice how **typeof** for **LocalVarDecl** recursively calls **typeof** for its **type** property. Recursion ends with the **typeof** functions for the types; they return themselves. This implementation successfully calculates the type of the **LocalVarDecl**, but it does not address the type check that makes sure that, if an **init** expression is specified, it has the same type (or a subtype) of the **type** property. This could be achieved as follows:

```
typeof( LocalVarDecl lvd ) {
    if isSpecified( lvd.init ) {
        assert typeof( lvd.init ) isSameOrSubtypeOf typeof( lvd.type )
    }
    return typeof( lvd.type )
}
```

Notice (in the grammar) that the specification of the variable type (in the **type** property) is also optional. So we have created a somewhat more elaborate version of the function:

```
typeof( LocalVarDecl lvd ) {
    if !isSpecified( lvd.type ) && !isSpecified( lvd.init ) 
        raise error
    
    if isSpecified( lvd.type ) && !isSpecified( lvd.init ) 
        return typeof( lvd.type )
    
    if !isSpecified( lvd.type ) && isSpecified( lvd.init ) 
        return typeof( lvd.init )
```

```
    // otherwise...
    assert typeof( lvd.init ) isSameOrSubtypeOf typeof( lvd.type )
    return typeof( lvd.type )
}
```

10.2.2 Unification

Unification is the second well-known approach to type calculation. Let's start with a definition from Wikipedia:

> Unification is an operation ... which produces from ... logic terms a substitution which ... makes the terms equal modulo some equational theory.

While this sounds quite sophisticated, we have all used unification in high-school for solving sets of linear equations. The "equational theory" in this case is algebra. Here is an example:

```
(1) 2 * x == 10
(2) x + x == 10
(3) x + y == 2 * x + 5
```

Substitution refers to assignment of values to **x** and **y**. A solution for this set of equations is **x := 5, y := 10**.

Using unification for type systems means that language developers specify a set of type equations which contain type variables (cf. the **x** and **y**) as well as type values (the numbers in the above example). Some kind of engine is then trying to make all equations **true** by assigning type values to the type variables in the type equations. The interesting property of this approach is that there is no distinction between typing rules and type checks. We simply specify a set of equations that must be **true** for the types to be valid[4]. If an equation cannot be satisfied for any assignment of type values to type variables, a type error is detected. To illustrate this, we return to the **LocalVarDecl** example introduced above.

```
var i: int              // 1
var i: int = 42         // 2
var i: int = 33.33      // 3
var i = 42              // 4
```

The following two type equations constitute the complete type system specification. The **:==:** operator expresses type equation (left side must be the same type as right side), **:<=:** refers to subtype-equation (left side must be same type or subtype of right side, the pointed side of < points to the "smaller", the more specialized type)[5].

```
typeof( LocalVarDecl.type )  :>=:  typeof( LocalVarDecl.init )
typeof( LocalVarDecl )       :==:  typeof( LocalVarDecl.type )
```

[4] Consequently they can be evaluated "in both ways". They can be used for type checking, but they can also be used to compute "missing" types, i.e. support type inference. MPS (which uses this approach) also exploits this declarative nature of typing rules by supporting type-aware code completion (**Ctrl-Shift-Space**), where MPS computes the required type from the current context and then only shows code completion menu entries that fit the context regarding their type (and not just based on the structure).

[5] The operators are taken from MPS, which uses this unification for the type system.

Let us look at the four examples cases. We use capital letters for free type variables. In the first case, the `init` expression is not given, so the first equation is ignored. The second equation can be satisfied by assigning T, the type of the variable declaration, to be `int`. The second equations acts as a type derivation rule and defines the type of the overall `LocalVarDecl` to be `int`.

```
// var i: int
typeof( int ) :>=: typeof( int )     // ignore
typeof( T )   :==: typeof( int )     // T := int
```

In the second case the `type` and the `init` expression are given, and both have types that can be calculated independently of the equations specified for the `LocalVarDecl` (they are fixed). So the first equation has no free type variables, but it is `true` with the type values specified (two `int`s). Notice how in this case the equation acts as a type check: if the equation were not `true` for the two given values, a type error would be reported. The second equation works the same as above, deriving T to be `int`.

```
// var i: int = 42
typeof( int ) :>=: typeof( int )     // true
typeof( T )   :==: typeof( int )     // T := int
```

The third case is similar to the second case; but the first equation, in which all types are specified, is not `true`, so a type error is raised.

```
// var i: int = 33.33
typeof( int ) :>=: typeof( double )  // error!
typeof( T )   :==: typeof( int )     // T := int
```

Case four is interesting because no variable type is explicitly specified; the idea is to use *type inference* to derive the type from the `init` expression. In this case there are two free variables in the equations; substituting both with `int` solves both equations[6].

```
// var i = 42
typeof( U ) :>=: typeof( int )   // U := int
typeof( T ) :==: typeof( U )     // T := int
```

[6] Notice how the unification approach automatically leads to support for type inference!

To further illustrate how unification works, consider the following example, in which we specify the typing rules for array types and array initializers:

```
var i: int[]
var i: int[] = {1, 2, 3}
var i = {1, 2, 3}
```

Compared to the `LocalVarDecl` example above, the additional complication in this case is that we need to make sure that *all* the initialization expressions (inside the curly braces) have the same or compatible types. Here are the typing equations:

```
typevar T
foreach ( e: init.elements )
    typeof(e) :<=: T

typeof( LocalVarDecl.type )  :>=: new ArrayType(T)
typeof( LocalVarDecl )       :==: typeof( LocalVarDecl.type )
```

We introduce an additional type variable T and iterate over all the expression in the array initializer, establishing an equation between each of these elements and T. This results in a set of equations that *each* must be satisfied[7]. The only way to achieve this is for all array initializer members to be of the same (sub-)type. In the examples, this makes T to be **int**. The rest of the equations works as explained above. Notice that if we'd written **var i = {1, 33.33, 3}**, then T := **double**, but the equations would still work because we use the :>=: operator.

[7] This clearly illustrates that the :<=: operator is *not* an assignment, since if it were, only the last of the init.elements would be assigned to T, which clearly makes no sense.

10.2.3 Pattern Matching

In pattern matching we simply list the possible combinations of types in a big table. Cases that are not listed in the table will result in errors. For our **LocalVarDecl** example, such a table could look like this:

typeof(type)	typeof(init)	typeof(LocalVarDecl)
int	int	int
int	-	int
-	int	int
double	double	double
double	-	double
-	double	double
double	int	double

To avoid repeating everything for all valid types, variables could be used. T+ refers to T or subtypes of T.

typeof(type)	typeof(init)	typeof(LocalVarDecl)
T	T	T
T	-	T
-	T	T
T	T+	T

Pattern matching is used for binary operators in MPS and also for matching terms in Spoofax.

10.3 Xtext Example

Up to version 1.0, Xtext provided no support for implementing type systems[8]. In version 2.0 a type system integrated with the JVM's type system is available[9]. It is not as versatile as it could be, since it is limited to JVM-related types and cannot easily be used for languages that have no relationship with the JVM, such as C or C++.

As a consequence of this limitation and the fact that Xtext is widely used, two third-party libraries have been developed: the Xtext Typesystem Framework (developed by the author[10]), and XTypes (developed by Lorenzo Bettini[11]. In the remainder of this section we will look at the Xtext Typesystem Framework[12]).

■ *Xtext Typesystem Framework* The Xtext Typesystem Framework is based on the recursive approach. It provides an interface **ITypesystem** with a method **typeof(EObject)** which returns the type for the program element passed in as an argument. In its simplest form, the interface can be implemented manually with arbitrary Java code. To make sure type errors are reported as part of the Xtext validation, the type system framework has to be integrated into the Xtext validation framework manually:

```
@Inject
private ITypesystem ts;

@Check(CheckType.NORMAL)
public void validateTypes( EObject m ) {
    ts.checkTypesystemConstraints( m, this );
}
```

[8] Beyond implementing everything manually and plugging it into the constraints.
[9] We illustrate it to some extent in the section on language modularity (Section 16.2).

[10] code.google.com/a/eclipselabs.org/p/xtext-typesystem/
[11] xtypes.sourceforge.net/

[12] For a comparison of the various type system implementation approaches for Xtext, see this SLE 2012 paper
  L. Bettini, D. Stoll, and M. Voelter. Approaches and tools for implementing type systems in xtext. In *SLE 2012*, 2012

As we have discussed in Section 10.1, many type systems rely on a limited set of typing strategies[13]. The **DefaultTypesystem** class implements **ITypesystem** and provides support for declaratively specifying these strategies. In the code below, a simplified version of the type system specification for the cooling language, the **initialize** method defines one type (the type of the **IntType** is a clone of itself) and defines one typing constraint (the **expr** property of the **IfStatement** must be a Boolean). Also, for types which cannot be specified declaratively, an operation **type(..)** can be implemented to programmatically define types. The example below shows this for the **NumberLiteral**.

[13] Assigning fixed types, deriving the type of an element from one of its properties, calculating the type as the common type of its two arguments.

```
public class CLTypesystem extends DefaultTypesystem {
    private CoolingLanguagePackage cl = CoolingLanguagePackage.eINSTANCE;
```

```
    @Override
    protected void initialize() {
        useCloneAsType(cl.getIntType());
        ensureFeatureType(cl.getIfStatement(),
            cl.getIfStatement_Expr(), cl.getBoolType());
    }

    public EObject type( NumberLiteral s, TypeCalculationTrace trace ) {
        if ( s.getValue().contains(".")) {
            return create(cl.getDoubleType());
        }
        return create(cl.getIntType());
    }
}
```

In addition to the API used in the code above, the Typesystem Framework also comes with a textual DSL to express typing rules (Fig. 10.2 shows a screenshot). From the textual type system specification, a generator generates the implementation of the Java class that implements the type system using the APIs[14]. The DSL provides the following advantages compared to the specification in Java:

[14] In that sense, the DSL is just a facade on top of a framework; however, it is a nice example of how a DSL can provide added value over a framework or API.

- The notation is much more concise compared to the API.

- Referential integrity and code completion with the target language meta model is provided.

- If the typing rules are incomplete, a static error is shown in the editor, as opposed to getting runtime errors during initialization of the framework (see the warning in Fig. 10.2).

- **Ctrl-Click** on a property jumps to the typing rule that defines the type for that property.

■ *Type System for the Cooling Language* The complete type system for the cooling language is 200 lines of DSL code, and another 100 lines of Java code. We'll take a look at some representative examples. Primitive types usually use a copy of themselves as their type[15]:

[15] It has to be a copy as opposed to the element itself, because the actual program element must not be pulled out of the EMF containment tree.

```
typeof BoolType -> clone
typeof IntType -> clone
typeof DoubleType -> clone
typeof StringType -> clone
```

Alternatively, since all primitive types extend an abstract meta class **PrimitiveType**, this could be shortened to the following, where the + operator specifies that the rule applied for the specified concept and all its subconcepts:

```
typeof PrimitiveType + -> clone
```

```
typeof Multi -> common left right {
    ensureType left :<=: char(NUMERIC)
    ensureType right :<=: char(NUMERIC)
}
typeof Div -> IntType {
    ensureType left :<=: char(NUMERIC)
    ensureType right :<=: char(NUMERIC)
}
typeof NotExpression -> BoolType {
    ensureType expr :<=: BoolType
}

typeof TrueExpr -> BoolType
typeof FalseExpr -> BoolType
typeof ParenExpr -> feature expr
typeof SymbolRef -> feature symbol
typeof Variable -> feature type {
    ensureCompatibility type :<=: init
}
```

Figure 10.2: The Xtext-based editor for the type system specification DSL provided by the Xtext Typesystem Framework. It is a nice example of the benefits of a DSL over an API (on which it is based), since it can statically show inconsistencies in the type system definition, has a more concise syntax and provides customized go-to-definition functionality.

For concepts that have a fixed type that is different from the concept itself (or a clone), the type can be specified explicitly:

```
typeof StringLiteral -> StringType
```

Type systems are most important, and most interesting, in the context of expressions. Since all expressions derive from the abstract **Expr** concept, we can declare that this class is abstract, and hence no typing rule is given[16]:

```
typeof Expr -> abstract
```

The notation provided by the DSL groups typing rules and type checks for a single concept. The following is the typing information for the **Plus** concept. It declares the type of **Plus** to be the common type of the **left** and **right** arguments (the "more general" one) and then adds two constraints that check that the **left** and **right** argument are either **int**s or **double**s[17].

[16] However, the editor reports a warning if there are concrete subclasses of an abstract class for which no type is specified either.

[17] These rules do not support using + for concatenating strings and for concatenating strings with numbers (as in "a" + 1). However, support for this feature can be provided as well by using a coercion rule.

```
typeof Plus -> common left right {
    ensureType left   :<=: IntType, DoubleType
    ensureType right  :<=: IntType, DoubleType
}
```

The typing rules for **Equals** are also interesting. It specifies that the resulting type is **boolean**, that the **left** and **right** arguments must be **COMPARABLE**, and that the left and right arguments be compatible. **COMPARABLE** is a *type characteristic*: this can be considered as collection of types. In this case it is **IntType**, **DoubleType** and **BoolType**. The **:<=>:** operator describes unordered compatibility: the types of the two properties **left** and **right** must either be the same, or **left** must be a subtype or **right**, or vice versa.

```
characteristic COMPARABLE {
    IntType, DoubleType, BoolType
}
typeof Equals -> BoolType {
    ensureType left            :<=: char(COMPARABLE)
    ensureType right           :<=: char(COMPARABLE)
    ensureCompatibility left :<=>: right
}
```

There is also support for *ordered* compatibility, as can be seen from the typing rule for **AssignmentStatement** below. It has no type (it is a statement), but the **left** and **right** argument must exhibit ordered compatibility: they either have to be the same types, or **right** must be a subtype of **left**, *but not vice versa*:

```
typeof AssignmentStatement -> none {
    ensureCompatibility right :<=: left
}
```

The framework uses the generation gap pattern, i.e. from the DSL-based type specification, a generator creates a class **CLTypesystemGenerated** (for the cooling language) that contains all the code that can be derived from the type system specification. Additional specifications that cannot be expressed with the DSL (such as the typing rule for **NumberLiteral** shown earlier, or type coercions) can be implemented in Java[18].

10.4 MPS Example

MPS includes a DSL for type system rule definition. It is based on unification, and pattern matching for binary operators. We discuss each of them.

▪ *Unification* The type of a **LocalVariableReference** is calculated with the following typing rule[19]. It establishes an equa-

[18] The type system DSL is *incomplete*, since some aspects of type systems have to be coded in a lower level language (Java). However, in this case this is appropriate, since it keeps the type system DSL simple and, since the DSL users are programmers, it is not a problem for them to write a few lines of Java code.

[19] Since only the expression within the do {...} block has to be written by the developer, we'll only show that expression in the remaining examples.

tion between the type of the `LocalVariableReference` itself and the variable it references. `typeof` is a built-in operator that returns the type for its argument.

```
rule typeof_LocalVariableReference {
  applicable for concept = LocalVariableReference as lvr
  overrides false

  do {
    typeof( lvr ) :==: typeof( lvr.variable );
  }
}
```

The rules for the Boolean `NotExpression` contains two equations. The first one makes sure that the negated expression is Boolean. The second one types the `NotExpression` itself to be Boolean[20].

```
typeof( notExpr.expression ) :==: new node<BooleanType>();
typeof( notExpr )            :==: <boolean>;
```

A more interesting example is the typing of `struct`s. Consider the following C code:

```
struct Person {
    char* name;
    int age;
}

int addToAge( Person p, int delta ) {
    return p.age + delta;
}
```

At least two program elements have to be typed: the parameter `p` as well as the `p.age` expression. The type of the `FunctionParameter` concept is the type of its `type` property. This is not specific to the fact that the parameter refers to a `struct`.

```
typeof( parameter ) :==: typeof( parameter.type );
```

The language concept that represents the `Person` type in the parameter is a `StructType`. A `StructType` refers to the `StructDeclaration` whose type it represents, and extends `Type`, which acts as the super type for all types in mbeddr C[21].

`p.age` is an instance of a `StructAttributeReference`. It is defined as follows (see Fig. 10.4 as well as the code below). It is an `Expression`, owns another expression property (on the left of the dot), as well as a reference to a `StructAttribute` (`name` or `age` in the example).

```
concept StructAttributeReference extends Expression
                                 implements ILValue
  children:
    Expression context 1

  references:
    StructAttribute attribute 1
```

[20] Just as in Xtext, in MPS types are instances of language concepts, so they can be instantiated like any other concept. MPS supports two ways of doing this. The first one (as shown in the first equation above) uses the BaseLanguage `new` expression. The second one uses a quotation, where a "piece of tree" can be inlined into program code. It uses the concrete syntax of the quoted construct – here: a `BooleanType` – in the quotation.

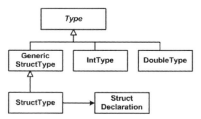

Figure 10.3: Structure diagram of the language concepts involved in typing `struct`s.

[21] This is essentially a use of the Adapter pattern.

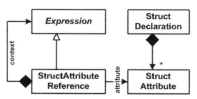

Figure 10.4: Structure diagram of the language concepts involved in references to `struct` attributes.

The typing rule for the **StructAttributeReference** is shown in the code below. The **context**, the expression on which we use the dot operator, has to be a **GenericStructType**, or a subtype thereof (i.e. a **StructType** which points to an actual **StructDeclaration**). Second, the type of the whole expression is the type of the reference **attribute** (e.g., **int** in the case of **p.age**).

```
typeof( structAttrRef.context ) :<=: new node<GenericStructType>();
typeof( structAttrRef )          :==: typeof( structAttrRef.attribute );
```

This example also illustrates the interplay between the type system and other aspects of language definition, specifically scopes. The referenced **StructAttribute** (on the right side of the dot) may only reference a **StructAttribute** that is part of the the **StructDeclaration** that is referenced from the **StructType**. The following scope definition illustrates how we access the type of the expression from the scoping rule:

```
link {attribute}
  search scope:
    (model, scope, referenceNode, linkTarget, enclosingNode)->join(
      ISearchScope | sequence<node< >>) {
      node<> exprType = typeof( referenceNode.expression );
      if (exprType.isInstanceOf(StructType)) {
        return (exprType as StructType).struct.attributes;
      } else {
        return null;
      }
    }
```

■ *Pattern Matching*   As we will discuss in the chapter on language extension and composition, MPS supports incremental extension of existing languages. Extensions may also introduce new types, and, specifically, may allow existing operators to be used with these new types. This is facilitated by MPS' use for pattern matching in the type system, specifically for binary operators such as +, > or ==. As an example, consider the introduction of complex numbers into C. It should be possible to write code like this:

```
complex c1 = (1, 2i);
complex c2 = (3, 5i);
complex c3 = c1 + c2; // results in (4, 7i)
```

The + in **c1 + c2** should be the + defined by the original C language[22]. Reusing the original + requires that the typing rules defined for **PlusExpression** in the original C language will now have to accept complex numbers; the original typing rules must be extended. To enable this, MPS supports *overloaded operations containers*. The following container, taking from the

[22] Alternatively, we could define a new + for complex numbers. While this would work technically (remember there is no parser ambiguity problems), it would mean that users, when entering a +, would have to decide between the original plus and the new plus for complex numbers. This would not be very convenient from a usability perspective. By reusing the original plus we avoid this problem.

mbeddr C core language, defines the type of + and - if both arguments are **int** or **double**.

```
overloaded operations rules binaryOperation

operation concepts: PlusExpression | MinusExpression
left operand type: <int>
right operand type: <int>
operation type: (operation, leftOperandType, rightOperandType)->node<> {
  <int>;
}

operation concepts: PlusExpression | MinusExpression
left operand type: <double>
right operand type: <double>
operation type: (operation, leftOperandType, rightOperandType)->node<> {
  <double>;
}
```

To integrate these definitions with the regular typing rules, the following typing rule must be written[23]. The typing rules tie in with overloaded operation containers via the **operation type** construct:

[23] Note that only one such rule must be written for all binary operations. Everything else will be handled with the overloaded operations containers.

```
rule typeof_BinaryExpression {
  applicable for concept = BinaryExpression as binex
  do {
    node<> optype = operation type( binex , left , right );
    if (optype != null) {
        typeof(binex) :==: optype;
    } else {
        error "operator " + be.concept.name + " cannot be applied to ' +
            left.concept.name + "/" + right.concept.name -> be;
    }
  }
}
```

The important aspect of this approach is that overloaded operation containers are *additive*. Language extensions can simply contribute *additional* containers. For the complex number example, this might look like the following: we declare that as soon as one of the arguments is of type complex, the resulting type will be complex as well.

```
PlusExpression | MinusExpression one operand type: <complex> operation type
    :
(operation, leftOperandType, rightOperandType)->node<> {
  <complex>;
}
```

The type system DSL in MPS covers a large fraction of the type system rules encountered in practice. The type system for BaseLanguage, which is an extension of Java, is implemented in this way, as is the C type system in mbeddr. However, for exceptional cases, procedural BaseLanguage code can be used to implement typing rules as well.

10.5 Spoofax Example

Spoofax' rewrite rules support both the recursive approach and pattern matching in specifying type systems. However, in most projects the recursive approach will be found. Therefore we will focus on it in the remainder of the section.

■ *Typing Rules in Spoofax* For typing rules in Spoofax, the basic idea is to use rewrite rules to rewrite language constructs to their types. For example, the following rule rewrites integer numbers to the numeric type. This is an example of assigning a fixed type to a language element.

```
type-of: Int(value) -> NumType()
```

Similarly, we can rewrite a + expression to the numeric type:

```
type-of: Add(exp1, exp2) -> NumType()
```

However, it is good practice to assign types only to well-typed language constructs. Thus, we should add type checks for the subexpressions:

```
type-of:
  Add(exp1, exp2) -> NumType()
  where
    <type-of> exp1 => NumType();
    <type-of> exp2 => NumType()
```

Spoofax allows for multiple typing rules for the same language construct. This is particular useful for typing overloaded operators, since each case can be handled by a separate typing rule. For example, when the operator + is overloaded to support string concatenation, we can add the following typing rule:

```
type-of:
  Add(exp1, exp2) -> StringType()
  where
    <type-of> exp1 => StringType();
    <type-of> exp2 => StringType()
```

■ *Persistence of Typing Information* Spoofax stores information about the definition sites of names in an in-memory data structure called the index. This typically includes information about types. For example, the type of property and variable references is initially not available at these references, but only at the declaration. But when Spoofax discovers a declaration, it stores its type in the index. Since declaration and references are annotated with the same URI, this information can also be accessed at references. Consider the following name binding rules which also involve type information:

```
Property(p, t): defines Property p of type t
Param(p, t):    defines Variable p of type t
```

These rules match property and parameter declarations, binding their name to **p** and their type to **t**. Spoofax stores this type in the index as an information about the property or parameter name. In the typing rules for variable references and property accesses, we need to retrieve this type information from the index:

```
type-of:
  Var(name) -> <index-lookup-type> name

type-of:
  PropAccess(exp, name) -> <index-lookup-type> name
```

Both rules rewrite references to the type of their definition sites. First, the definition of a reference is looked up in the index. Next, this definition is rewritten to its type. This uses the **index-lookup-type** rule, which implements the actual type lookup in the index.

In the previous example, the type was explicitly declared in property and parameter declarations. But the type of a definition site is not always explicitly declared. For example, variable declarations in Mobl come with an initial expression, but without an explicit type[24].

```
var x = 42;
```

[24] The type is inferred from the initial expression.

The type of **x** is the type of its initial expression **42**, that is, **NumType()**. To make this type of **x** explicit, we need to calculate the type of the initial expression. The following name binding rule makes this connection between name binding and type system:

```
Declare(v, e):
  defines Variable v of type t in subsequent scope
  where e has type t
```

■ *Additional Types* In Spoofax, types are represented as terms. The constructors for these terms are specified in the syntax definition as labels to productions. Without the ability to define additional constructors, type systems are restricted to types which users can explicitly state in programs, for example in variable declarations. But many type systems require additional types which do not originate from the syntax of the language. Typical examples are top and bottom types in type hierarchies[25]. For example, Java's type system has a special type for **null** values at the bottom of its type hierarchy, which

[25] A *top* type is a supertype of every other type; a *bottom* type is a subtype of every other type.

cannot be used as a type in Java programs. Spoofax allows constructors for additional types in signatures to be defined:

```
signature constructors
  FunType: List(Type) * Type -> Type
```

This defines an additional constructor **FunType** for **Type**. In general, a constructor definition is of the form **cons: Arg-1 * ...* Arg-n -> Sort**, where **cons** is the constructor name, **Sort** is the sort this constructor contributes to, and **Arg-1** to **Arg-n** are the sorts of its arguments. In the example, the first subterm should be a list of parameter types (**List(Type)**), while the second subterm should be the return type. We can employ the so-defined function type in the typing rules for function definitions and calls:

```
Function(f, p*, t):
  defines Function f of type FunType(t*, t)
  where p* has type t*
```

```
type-of:
  Call(name, arg*) -> type
  where
    <index-lookup-type> name => FunType(type*, type)
```

■ *Type Constraints* Like any other constraint, type constraints are specified in Spoofax by rewrite rules which rewrite language constructs to errors, warnings or notes. For example, we can define a constraint on additions[26]:

```
constraint-error:
  exp -> (exp, $[Operator + cannot be applied to arguments
              [<pprint> type1], [<pprint> type2].])
  where
    !exp  => Add(exp1, exp2);
    <not(type-of)> exp;
    type1 := <type-of> exp1;
    type2 := <type-of> exp2
```

■ *Type Compatibility* Whether two types are compatible is again defined by rewrite rules. These rules rewrite a pair of types to the second element of the pair, if the first one is compatible with it. In the simplest case, both types are the same:

```
is-compatible-to: (type, type) -> type
```

This rule only succeeds if it gets a tuple with two types that are identical (they both match the same variable **type**). A type might also be compatible with any type with which its supertype is compatible:

```
is-compatible-to:
  (subtype, type) -> type
  where
```

[26] An expression is non-well-typed, or *ill-typed*, if it cannot be rewritten to a type. But reporting an error on all ill-typed expressions will make it hard to discover the root cause of the error, since every expression with an ill-typed subexpression is also ill-typed. That is why we also check the subexpressions of the addition to be well-typed. The types of the subexpressions are then used to construct a meaningful error message.

```
supertype := <supertype> subtype;
<is-compatible-to> (supertype, type)
```

Here, the subtype relation is defined by a rewrite rule, which rewrites a type to its supertype:

```
supertype: IntType() -> FloatType()
```

This approach only works for type systems in which each type has at most one supertype. When a type system allows for multiple supertypes, we have to use lists of supertypes and need to adapt the rule for **is-compatible-to** accordingly:

```
supertypes: IntType() -> [ FloatType() ]

is-compatible-to:
  (subtype, type) -> type
  where
    supertype* := <supertypes> subtype;
    <fetch-elem(is-compatible-to(|type))> supertype*
```

Here, **fetch-elem** tries to find an element in a list of supertypes, which is compatible to **type**. It uses a variant of the rule **is-compatible-to** in order to deal with a list of types. This variant does not rewrite a pair of types, but only the first type. The second type is passed as a parameter to the rewrite rule. It can be defined in terms of the variant for pairs:

```
is-compatible-to(|type2): type1 ->  <is-compatible-to> (type1, type2)
```

The compatibility of types can easily be extended to compatibility of lists of types:

```
is-compatible-to:
  (type1*, type2*) -> type*
  where
    type* := <zip(is-compatible-to)> (type1*, type2*)
```

A list **type1*** of types is compatible with another list **type2*** of types, if each type in **type1*** is compatible with the corresponding type in **type2***. **zip** pairs up the types from both lists, rewrites each of these pairs by applying **is-compatible-to** to them, and collects the results in a new list **type***.

With the extension for lists, we can define a constraint for function calls, which ensures that the types of the actual arguments are compatible with the types of the formal parameters:

```
constraint-error:
  Call(name, arg*) -> (arg*,
      $[Function [name] cannot be applied to arguments
          [<pprint> arg-type*].])
  where
    fun-type  := <index-lookup-type> name ;
    !fun-type => FunType(para-type*, type) ;
    arg-type* := <map(type-of)> arg* ;
    <not(is-compatible-to)> (arg-type*, par-type*)
```

11
Transformation and Generation

> *In the case of both transformation and generation, another artifact is created from a program, often a program in a less abstract language. This is in contrast to interpretation, which executes programs directly without creating intermediate artifacts. Transformation refers to the case in which the created artifact is an AST, and code generation refers to the case in which textual concrete syntax is created. In some systems, for example MPS, the two are unified into a common approach.*

Transformation of models is an essential step in working with DSLs. We typically distinguish between two different cases: if models are transformed into other models, we call this *model transformation*. If models are transformed into text (usually source code, XML or other configuration files), we refer to *code generation*[1]. However, as we will see in the examples below, depending on the approach and tooling used, this distinction is not always easy to make, and the boundary becomes blurred.

A fundamentally different approach to processing models is *interpretation*. While in the case of transformation and generation the model is migrated to artifacts expressed in a different language, in the case of interpretation no such migration happens. Instead, an interpreter traverses an AST and *directly* performs actions depending on the contents of the AST. Strictly speaking, we have already seen examples of interpretation in the sections on constraints and type systems: constraint and type checks can be seen as an interpreter where the actions performed as the tree is traversed are checks of various kinds. However, the term interpretation is typically only used

---

[1] As we discuss in Part I, we do not cover generation of byte code or machine code. This is mainly for the following reason: by generating the source code of a GPL, we can reuse this GPL's compiler or interpreter, including all its optimizations (or platform independence). We'd have to rebuild these optimizations in the DSL's generator. This is a lot of work, and requires skills that are quite different from those most DSL developers (including me) posses.

for cases in which the actions actually *execute* the model. Execution refers to performing the actions that are associated with the language concepts as defined by the execution semantics of the concepts. We discuss interpretation in the next chapter[2].

Note that when developing transformations and code generators, special care must be taken to preserve or record trace information that can be used for error reporting and debugging. In both cases, we have to be able to go back from the generated code to the higher-level abstractions it has been generated from, so we that can report errors in terms of the higher-level abstractions or show the higher-level source code during a debugging session. We discuss this challenge to some extent in Chapter 15.

[2] We elaborate on the trade-offs between transformation and generation versus interpretation in the chapter on language design (Section 4.3.5).

11.1 Overview of the approaches

Classical code generation traverses a program's AST and outputs programming language source code (or other text). In this context, a clear distinction is made between models and source code. Models are represented as an AST expressed with some preferred AS formalism (or meta meta model); an API exists for the transformation to interact with the AST. In contrast, the generated source code is treated as text, i.e. a sequence of characters. The tool of choice for transforming an AST into text are template languages. They support the syntactic mixing of model traversal code and to-be-generated text, separated by some escape character[3]. Since the generated code is treated merely as text, there is no language awareness (and corresponding tool support) for the target language while editing templates. Xtend[4], the language used for code generation in Xtext, is an example of this approach.

[3] Xpand and Xtend use «guillemets».

[4] Xtend is also sometimes referred to as Xtend2, since it has evolved from the old oAW Xtend language. In this chapter we use Xtend to refer to Xtend2. It can be found at www.eclipse.org/xtend/.

Classical model transformation is the other extreme, in that it works with ASTs only and does not consider the concrete syntax of either the source or the target languages. The source AST is transformed using the source language AS API and a suitable traversal language. As the tree is traversed, the API of the target language AS is used to assemble the target model[5]. For this to work smoothly, most specialized transformation languages assume that the source and target models are build with the same AS formalism (e.g., EMF Ecore). Model transformation languages typically provide support for efficiently navigating source models, and for creating instances of AS of

[5] Note that in this chapter we look at transformation in the context of *refinement*, i.e. the target model is less abstract and more detailed than the source model. Model transformations can also be used for other purposes, including the creation of views, refactorings and reverse engineering.

the target language (tree construction). Examples for this approach once again include Xtext's Xtend, as well as QVT Operational[6] and ATL[7]. MPS can also be used in this way. A slightly different approach just establishes relations between the source and target models instead of "imperatively" constructing a target tree as the source is traversed. While this is often less intuitive to write down, the approach has the advantage that it supports transformation in both directions, and also supports model diff[8]. QVT relational[9] is an example of this approach.

In addition to the two classical cases described above, there are also hybrid approaches that blur the boundaries between these two clear-cut extremes. They are based on the support for language modularization and composition, in the sense that the template language and the target language can be composed. As a consequence, the tooling is aware of the syntactic structure and the static semantics of the template language *and* the target language. Both MPS and Spoofax support this approach to various extents.

In MPS, a program is projected and every editing operation directly modifies the AST, while using a typically textual-looking notation as the "user interface". Template code (the code that controls the transformation process) and target-language code (the code you want to generate) can be represented as nested ASTs, each using its own textual syntax. MPS uses a slightly different approach based on a concept called *annotations*. Projectional editors can store arbitrary information in an AST. Specifically, they can store information that does *not* correspond to the language underlying a particular ASTs. MPS code generation templates exploit this approach: template code is fundamentally an instance of the target language. This "example model" is then annotated with template annotations that define how the example model relates to the source model, and which example nodes must be replaced by (further transformed) nodes from the source model. This allows any language to be "templatized" without changing the language definition itself. The MPS example below will elaborate on this approach.

Spoofax, with its Stratego transformation language, uses a similar approach based on parser technology. As we have already seen, the underlying grammar formalism supports flexible composition of grammars. So the template language and the target language can be composed, retaining tool support for

[6] `en.wikipedia.org/wiki/QVT`
[7] `www.eclipse.org/atl/`

[8] It does so by "relating" two instances of the same language and marking both as `readoqnly`; the engine then points out the difference between the two.

both of these languages. Execution of the template directly constructs an AST of the target language, using the concrete syntax of the target language to specify its structure. The Spoofax example will provide details.

11.2 Xtext Example

Since Xtext is based on EMF, generators can be built using any tool that can generate code from EMF models, including Acceleo[10], Jet[11] and of course Xtend. Xtend is a Java-like general-purpose language that removes some of Java's syntactic noise (it has type inference, property access syntax, operator overloading) and adds syntactic sugar (extension methods, multiple-dispatch and closures). Xtend comes with an interpreter and a compiler, the latter generating Java source. Xtend is built with Xtext, so it comes with a powerful Xtext-based editor. One particularly interesting language feature in the context of code generators are Xtend's *template expressions*. Inside these expressions, a complete template language is available (similar to the older Xpand language). Xtend also provides automatic whitespace management[12]. The functional abstractions provided by Xtend (higher-order functions in particular) make it very well suited for navigating and querying models. In the rest of this section we will use Xtend for writing code generators and model transformations.

[10] www.acceleo.org/ pages/home/en

[11] www.eclipse.org/ modeling/m2t/?project=jet

[12] Indentation of template code is traditionally a challenge, because it is not clear whether whitespace in templates is intended to go into the target file, or is just used for indenting the template itself.

11.2.1 Generator

We will now look at generating the C code that implements cooling programs. Fig. 11.1 shows a screenshot of a typical generator. The generator is an Xtend class that implements **IGenerator**, which requires the **doGenerate** method to be implemented. The method is called for each model file that has changed[13] (represented by the **resource** argument), and it has to output the corresponding generated code via the **fsa** (file system access) object[14].

When generating code from models, there are two distinct cases. In the first case, the majority of the generated code is fixed; only some isolated parts of the code depend on the input model. In this case a template language is the right tool, because template control code can be "injected" into code that looks similar to what should be generated. In the other case there are fine-grained structures, such as expressions. Since

[13] This is achieved by a Builder that comes with Xtext. Alternatively, Xtend generators can also be run from the command line, from another Java program or from ant and maven. Also, other strategies can be implemented in the Eclipse IDE itself, based on custom builder participants, buttons or menu entries.

[14] Like any other Xtext language aspect, the generator has to be registered with the runtime module, Xtext's main configuration data structure. Once this is done, the generator is automatically called for each changed resource associated with the respective language.

```
*CoolingLanguageGenerator.xtend
class CoolingLanguageGenerator implements IGenerator {

    @Inject extension StatementExtensions se
    @Inject extension ExpressionExtensions ee
    @Inject extension DataTypeHelper dh

    override void doGenerate(Resource resource, IFileSystemAccess fsa) {
        for( p: (resource.contents.first as CoolingResource).coolingPrograms){
            fsa.generateFile(p.name+"/"+p.name+".c", p.compile)
        }
    }

    def compile(CoolingProgram p){
        '''
        /*
        ================================================================
        Name       : «p.name».c
        Version    :
        Copyright  : Copyright (c) 2011 itemis AG (http://www.itemis.eu). All rights reserved.
        ================================================================
        */

        #include "framework.h"

        void init (void){
            new_state = «p.startState.name»;
            «IF p.initBlock!=null»
                «FOR variable: p.variables.filter(v | v.init != null)»
                    «variable.name» = «variable.init.compileExpr»;
                «ENDFOR»

                «FOR s: p.initBlock.statements»
                    «s.compileStatement»
                «ENDFOR»
            «ENDIF»
        }
```

Figure 11.1: The top-level structure of a generator written in Xtend is a class that implements the **IGenerator** interface, which requires the **doGenerate** method. Inside generator methods, template expressions (delimited with triple single quotes) are typically used. Inside those, guillemets (the small double angle brackets) are used to switch between to-be-generated code (gray background) and template control code. Note also the gray whitespace in the **init** function. Gray whitespace is whitespace that will end up in the generated code. White whitespace is used for indentation of template code; Xtend figures out which is which automatically.

these are basically trees, using template languages for these parts of programs seems unnatural and results in a lot of syntactic noise. A more functional approach is useful. Xtend can deal with both cases elegantly and we will illustrate both cases as part of this example.

We start with the high-level structure of the C code generated for a cooling program. The following piece of code illustrates Xtend's power to navigate a model as well as the template syntax for text generation.

```
def compile(CoolingProgram program) {
    '''
    <<FOR appl:  program.moduleImports.map(mi|mi.module).filter(typeof(
      Appliance))>>
        <<FOR c: appl.contents>>
            #define <<c.name>> <<c.index>>
        <<ENDFOR>>
    <<ENDFOR>>
```

```
    // more ...
    '''
}
```

The `FOR` loop iterates over the `moduleImports` collection of the `program`, follows the `module` reference of each of these, and then selects all `Appliance`s from the resulting collection. The nested loop then iterates over the contents of each `appliance` and generates a `#define`[15]. After the `#define` we generate the name of the respective content element and then its `index`. From within templates, the properties and references of model elements (such as the `name` or the `module` or the `contents`) can simply be accessed using the dot operator. `map` and `filter` are collection methods defined by the Xtend standard library[16]. We also have to generate an `enum` for the states in the cooling program.

```
typedef enum states {
    null_state,
    <<FOR s : program.concreteStates SEPARATOR ",">>
        <<s.name>>
    <<ENDFOR>>
};
```

Here we embed a `FOR` loop inside the `enum` text. Note how we use the `SEPARATOR` keyword to put a comma *between* two subsequent states. In the `FOR` loop we access the `concreteStates` property of the cooling program. However, if you look at the grammar or the meta model, you will see that no `concreteStates` property is defined there. Instead, we call an extension method[17]; since it has no arguments, it looks like property access. The method is defined further down in the `CoolingLanguageGenerator` class and is essentially a shortcut for a complex expression:

```
def concreteStates(CoolingProgram p) {
    p.states.filter(s | !(s instanceof BackgroundState) && !(s instanceof
      ShadowState))
}
```

The following code is part of the generator that generates the code for a state transition. It first generates code to execute the exit actions of the current state, then performs the state change (`current_state = new_state;`) and finally executes the entry actions of the new state (not shown):

```
if (new_state != current_state) {
    <<IF program.concreteStatesWitExitActions.size > 0>>
        // execute exit action for state if necessary
        switch (current_state) {
            <<FOR s: p.concreteStatesWitExitActions>>
                case <<s.name>>:
                    <<FOR st: s.exitStatements>>
```

[15] Notice how the the first two and the last two lines are enclosed in guillemets. Since we are in template expression mode (inside the triple single quotes) the guillemets escape to template control code. The `#define` is *not* in guillemets, so it is generated into the target file.

[16] `map` creates a new collection from an existing collection where, for each element in the existing collection, the expression after the | creates the corresponding value for the new collection. `filter` once again creates a new collection from an existing one where only those elements are included that are an instance of the type passed as an argument to `filter`.

[17] An extension method is an *additional* method for an *existing* class, defined without invasively changing the definition of the class.

```
                <<st.compileStatement>>
            <<ENDFOR>>
                break;
        <<ENDFOR>>
        default:
            break;
    }
    <<ENDIF>>

    // The state change
    current_state = new_state;

    // similar as above, but for entry actions
}
```

The code first uses an **IF** statement to check whether the program has any states with exit actions (by calling the **concreteStatesWitExitActions** extension method). The subsequent **switch** statement is only generated if we have such states. The **switch** switches over the **current_state**, and then adds a **case** for each state with exit actions[18]. Inside the case we iterate over all the **exitStatements** and call **compileStatement** for each of them. **compileStatement** is marked with **dispatch**, which makes it a multimethod: it is polymorphically overloaded based on its argument[19]. For each statement in the cooling language, represented by a subclass of **Statement**, there is an implementation of this method. The next piece of code shows some example implementations.

```
class StatementExtensions {

    def dispatch compileStatement(Statement s){
        // raise error if the overload for the abstract class is called
    }

    def dispatch compileStatement(AssignmentStatement s){
        s.left.compileExpr +" = " + s.right.compileExpr +";"
    }

    def dispatch compileStatement(IfStatement s){
        '''
        if( <<s.expr.compileExpr>> ){
            <<FOR st : s.statements>>
                <<st.compileStatement>>
            <<ENDFOR>>
        }<<IF s.elseStatements.size > 0>> else {
            <<FOR st : s.elseStatements>>
                <<st.compileStatement>>
            <<ENDFOR>>
        }<<ENDIF>>
        '''
    }

    // more ...
}
```

The implementation of the overloaded methods simply returns the text string that represents the C implementation for the respective language construct[20]. Notice how the implementation for the **IfStatement** uses a template string, whereas the one for **AssignmentStatement** uses normal string concatenation.

[18] The **s.name** expression in the **case** is actually a reference to the enum literal generated earlier for the particular state. From the perspective of Xtend, we simply generate text: it is not obvious from the template that the name corresponds to an enum literal. Potential structural or type errors are only revealed upon compilation of the generated code.

[19] Note that Java can only perform a polymorphic dispatch based on the **this** pointer. Xtend can dispatch polymorphically over the arguments of methods marked as **dispatch**.

[20] The two examples shown are simple because the language construct in the DSL closely resembles the C code in the first place.

The `compileStatement` methods are implemented in the class `StatementExtensions`. However, from within the `CoolingLanguageGenerator` they are called using method syntax (`st.compileStatement`). This works because they are injected as extensions using the following statement:

```
@Inject extension StatementExtensions
```

Expressions are handled in the same way as statements. The injected class `ExpressionExtensions` defines a set of overloaded `dispatch` methods for `Expression` and all its subtypes. Since expressions are trees, a `compileExpr` method typically calls `compileExpr` recursively on the children of the expression, if it has any. This is the typical idiom to implement generators for expression languages[21].

```
def dispatch String compileExpr (Equals e){
    e.left.compileExpr + " == " + e.right.compileExpr
}
def dispatch String compileExpr (Greater e){
    e.left.compileExpr + " > " + e.right.compileExpr
}
def dispatch String compileExpr (Plus e){
    e.left.compileExpr + " + " + e.right.compileExpr
}
def dispatch String compileExpr (NotExpression e){
    "!(" + e.expr.compileExpr + ")"
}
def dispatch String compileExpr (TrueExpr e){
    "TRUE"
}
def dispatch String compileExpr (ParenExpr pe){
    "(" + pe.expr.compileExpr + ")"
}
def dispatch compileExpr (NumberLiteral nl){
    nl.value
}
```

[21] Earlier we distinguished between generating a lot of code with only specific parts being model-dependent, and fine-grained tree structures in expressions: this is an example of the latter.

11.2.2 Model-to-Model Transformation

For model-to-model transformations, the same argument can be made as for code generation: since Xtext is based on EMF, any EMF-based model-to-model transformation engine can be used with Xtext models. Examples include ATL, QVT-O, QVT-R and Xtend[22].

Model-to-model transformations are similar to code generators in the sense that they traverse over the model. But instead of producing a text string as the result, they produce another AST. So the general structure of a transformation is similar. In fact, the two can be mixed. Let us go back to the first code example of the generator:

[22] Of course you could use any JVM-based compatible programming language, including Java itself. However, Java is really not very well suited, because of its clumsy support for model navigation and object instantiation. Scala and Groovy are much more interesting in this respect.

```
def compile(CoolingProgram program) {
    val transformedProgram = program.transform
    '''
    <<FOR appl : transformedProgram.modules.map(m|m.module).filter(typeof(
      Appliance))>>
        <<FOR c : appl.contents>>
            #define <<c.name>> <<c.index>>
        <<ENDFOR>>
    <<ENDFOR>>

    // more ...
    '''
}
```

We have added a call to a function **transform** at the beginning of the code generation process. This function creates a new **CoolingProgram** from the original one, and we store it in the **transformedProgram** variable. The code generator then uses the **transformedProgram** as the source from which it generates code. In effect, we have added a "preprocessor" model-to-model transformation to the generator[23].

[23] As discussed in the design section (Section 4.3), this is one of the most common uses of model-to-model transformations.

The **transform** function (see below) enriches the existing model. It creates a new state (**EMERGENCY_STOP**), creates a new event (**emergency_button_pressed**) and then adds a new transition to each existing state that checks whether the new event occurred, and if so, transitions to the new **EMERGENCY_STOP** state. Essentially, this adds emergency stop behavior to any existing state machine. Let's look at the implementation:

```
class Transformation {

  @Inject extension CoolingBuilder
  CoolingLanguageFactory factory = CoolingLanguageFactory::eINSTANCE

  def CoolingProgram transform(CoolingProgram p ) {
    p.states += emergencyState
    p.events += emergencyEvent
    for ( s: p.states.filter(typeof(CustomState)).filter(s|s !=
      emergencyState) ) {
      s.events += s.eventHandler [
          symbolRef [
              emergencyEvent()
          ]
          changeStateStatement(emergencyState())
      ]
    }
    return p;
  }

  def create result: factory.createCustomState emergencyState() {
    result.name = "EMERGENCY_STOP"
  }

  def create result: factory.createCustomEvent emergencyEvent() {
    result.name = "emergency_stop_button_pressed"
  }
}
```

The two **create** methods create new objects, as the **create** prefix suggests[24]. However, simply creating objects could be done with a regular method as well:

[24] The **factory** used in these methods is the way to create model elements in EMF. It is generated as part of the EMF code generator

```
def emergencyState() {
    val result = factory.createCustomState
    result.name = "EMERGENCY_STOP"
    result
}
```

What is different in **create** methods is that they can be called several times, and they still only ever create one object (for each combination of actual argument values). The result of the first invocation is cached, and all subsequent invocations return the object *created during the first invocation*. Such a behavior is very useful in transformations, because it removes the need to keep track of already created objects. For example, in the **transform** method, we have to establish references to the state created by **emergencyState** and the event created by **emergencyEvent**. To do that, we simply call the same **create** extension again. Since it returns the *same* object as during the first call in the first two lines of **transform**, this actually establishes references to those already created objects[25].

We can now look at the implementation of **transform** itself. It starts by adding the **emergencyState** and the **emergencyEvent** to the program[26]. We then iterate over all **CustomState**s except the emergency state we've just created. Notice how we just call the **emergencyState** function again: it returns the same object. We then use a builder to add the following code to each of the existing states.

```
on emergency_button_pressed {
    state EMERGENCY_STOP
}
```

This code could be constructed by procedurally calling the respective factory methods:

```
val eh = factory.createEventHandler
val sr = factory.createSymbolRef
sr.symbol = emergencyEvent
val css = factory.createChangeStateStatement
css.targetState = emergencyState
eh.statements += css
s.events += eh
```

The notation used in the actual implementation is more concise and resembles the tree structure of the code much more closely. It uses the well-known *builder*. Builders are implemented in Xtend with a combination of closures and implicit arguments and a number of functions implemented in the **CoolingBuilder** class[27]. Here is the code:

```
class CoolingBuilder {
    CoolingLanguageFactory factory = CoolingLanguageFactory::eINSTANCE
```

[25] This is a major difference between text generation and model transformation. In text, two textual occurrences of a symbol are the same thing (in some sense, text strings are value objects). In model transformation the identity of elements does matter. It is not the same if we create *one* new state and then reference it, or if we create five new states. So a good transformation language helps keep track of identities. The **create** methods are a very nice way of doing this.

[26] These are the first calls to the respective functions, so the objects are actually created at this point.

[27] Of course, if you add the line count and effort for implementing the builder, then using this alternative over the plain procedural one might not look so interesting. However, if you just create these builder functions once, and then create many different transformations, this approach makes a lot of sense.

```
    def eventHandler( CustomState it, (EventHandler)=>void handler ) {
        val res = factory.createEventHandler
        res
    }

    def symbolRef( EventHandler it, (SymbolRef)=>void symref ) {
        val res = factory.createSymbolRef
        it.events += res
    }

    def symbol( SymbolRef it, CustomEvent event ) {
        it.symbol = event
    }

    def changeStateStatement( EventHandler it, CustomState target ) {
        val res = factory.createChangeStateStatement
        it.statements += res
        res.targetState = target
    }
}
```

This class is imported into the generator with the `@Inject extension` construct, so the methods can be used "just so".

11.3   MPS Example

MPS comes with a `textgen` language for text generation. It is typically just used at the end of the transformation chain where code expressed in GPLs (like Java or C) is generated to text so it can be passed to existing compilers. Fig. 11.2 shows the `textgen` component for mbeddr C's `IfStatement`. MPS' text generation language basically appends text to a buffer. We won't discuss this aspect of MPS any further, since MPS `textgen` is basically a wrapper language around a `StringBuffer`. However, this is perfectly adequate for the task at hand, since it is only used in the last stage of generation where the AST is essentially structurally identical to the generated text[28].

DSLs and language extensions typically use model-to-model transformations to "generate" code expressed in a low-level programming language[29]. Writing transformations in MPS involves two ingredients. Templates define the actual transformation. Mapping configurations define which template to run when and where. Templates are valid sentences of the target language. *Macros* are used to express dependencies on and queries over the input model. For example, when the guard condition (a C expression) should be generated into an `if` statement in the target model, you first write an `if` statement with a dummy condition in the template. The following would work: `if (true) {}`. Then the nodes that should be replaced by the transformation with nodes from the input model are annotated

[28] If you want to generate text that is structurally different, then the textgen language is a bit of a pain to use; in this case, the MPS philosophy recommends that you build a suitable intermediate language (such as for XML, or even for a particular schema).

[29] The distinction between code generators and model-to-model transformations is much less clear in this case. While it is a model-to-model transformation (we map one AST onto another) the transformations look very much like code generators, since the concrete syntax of the target language is used in the "template".

```
text gen component for concept IfStatement {
  (node, context, buffer)->void {
    if (node.condition.isInstanceOf(TrueLiteral)) {
      append ${node.thenPart};
    } else {
      append {if ( } ${node.condition} { ) };
      append ${node.thenPart};
      foreach eip in node.elseIfs {
        append ${eip};
      }
      if (node.elsePart != null) {
        append { else };
        append ${node.elsePart};
      }
    }
  }
}
```

Figure 11.2: The AST-to-text generator for an **if** statement. If first checks if the condition happens to be a **true** literal, in which case the **if** statement is optimized away and only the **thenPart** is output. Otherwise we generate an **if** statement, the condition in parentheses, and then the **thenPart**. We then iterate over all the **elseIfs**; an **elseIf** has its own textgen, and we delegate to that one. We finally output the code for the **else** part.

with macros. In our example, this would look like this: **if (COPY_SRC[true]){}**. Inside the **COPY_SRC** macro you put an expression that describes which elements from the input model should replace the dummy node **true**: we use **node.guard** to replace it with the guard condition of the input node (expected to be of type **Transition** here). When the transformation is executed, the **true** node will be replaced by what the macro expression returns – in this case, the guard of the input transition. We will explain this process in detail below.

■ *Template-based Translation of the State Machine* State machines live inside modules. Just like **struct**s, they can be instantiated. The following code shows an example. Notice the two global variables **c1** and **c2**, which are instances of the same state machine **Counter**.

```
module Statemachine imports nothing {
  statemachine Counter {
    in events
      start()
      step(int[0..10] size)
    out events
      started()
      resetted()
      incremented(int[0..10] newVal)
    local variables
      int[0..10] currentVal = 0
      int[0..10] LIMIT = 10
    states ( initial = start )
      state start {
        on start [ ] -> countState { send started(); }
      }
      state countState {
        on step [currentVal + size > LIMIT] -> start { send resetted(); }
        on step [currentVal + size <= LIMIT] -> countState {
          currentVal = currentVal + size;
          send incremented(currentVal);
```

```
      }
      on start [ ] -> start { send resetted(); }
    }
  }

  Counter c1;
  Counter c2;

  void aFunction() {
    trigger(c1, start);
  }
}
```

State machines are translated to the following lower-level C entities (this high level structure is clearly discernible from the two main templates shown in Fig. 11.3 and Fig. 11.7):

- An **enum** for the states (with a literal for each state).

- An **enum** for the events (with a literal for each event).

- A **struct** declaration that contains an attribute for the current state, as well as attributes for the local variables declared in the state machine.

- And finally, a function that implements the behavior of the state machine using a **switch** statement. The function takes two arguments: one named **instance**, typed with the **struct** mentioned in the previous item, and one named **event** that is typed to the event **enum** mentioned above. The function checks whether the instance's current state can handle the event passed in, evaluates the guard, and if the guard is **true**, executes exit and entry actions and updates the current state.

```
template weave_StatemachineTypesStuffIntoModule
input     Statemachine
content node:
module dummy imports nothing {
  <TF> exported enum $[statemachineInEvents] { $LOOP$[$[anEvent]; ] } TF>
  <TF> exported enum $[statemachineStates]   { $LOOP$[$[aState]; ] } TF>
  <TF> exported struct $[statemachineData] {              TF>
        ->$[statemachineStates] __currentState;
        $LOOP$[$COPY_SRC$[int8_t] $[smLocalVar]; ]
      };
}
```

Figure 11.3: The MPS generator that inserts two **enum** definitions and a **struct** into the module which contains the **StateMachine**.

The MPS transformation engine works in phases. Each phase transforms models expressed in some languages to other models expressed in the same or other languages. Model elements for which no transformation rules are specified are copied from one phase to the next. Reduction rules are used to intercept program elements and transform them as generation progresses through the phases. Fig. 11.4 shows how this affects state machines. A reduction rule is defined that maps state machines to the various elements we mentioned above. Notice how the surrounding module remains unchanged, because no reduction rule is defined for it.

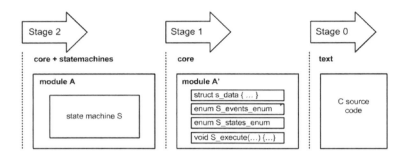

Figure 11.4: State machines are transformed (via a model-to-model transformation, if you will) into two **enum**s, a **struct** and a function. These are then transformed to text via the regular **com.mbeddr.core** textgen.

Let us look in more detail at the template in Fig. 11.3. It reduces a **Statemachine**, the input node, to two **enum**s and a **struct**. We use template fragments (marked with **<TF ... TF>**) to highlight those parts of the template that should actually be used to replace the input node as the transformation executes. The surrounding **module dummy** is scaffolding: it is only needed because **enum**s and **struct**s *must* live in **ImplementationModule**s in any valid instance of the mbeddr C language[30].

We have to create an **enum** literal for each state and each event. To achieve this, we iterate over all states (and events, respectively). This is expressed with the **LOOP** macros in the template in Fig. 11.3. The expression that determines what we iterate over is entered in the Inspector, MPS' equivalent to a properties window; Fig. 11.5 shows the code for iterating over the states[31]. For the literals of the events **enum** we use a similar expression (**node.events;**).

[30] Since the templates are projected example instances of the target language, the template *has to be a valid instance* of any MPS-implemented language.

[31] Note that the only really interesting part of Fig. 11.5 is the body of the anonymous function (**node.states;**), which is why from now on we will only show this part.

```
comment       : <none>
mapping label : <no label>
mapped nodes  : (node, genContext, operationContext)->sequence<node<>> {
                  node.states;
                }
```

Figure 11.5: The inspector is used to provide the implementation details for the macros used in the templates. This one belongs to a **LOOP** macro, so we provide an expression that returns a collection, over which the **LOOP** macro iterates.

The **LOOP** macro iterates over collections and then creates an instance of the concept it is attached to for each iteration. In the case of the two **enum**s, the **LOOP** macro is attached to an

EnumLiteral, so we create an **EnumLiteral** for each event and state we iterate over. However, these various **EnumLiteral**s must all have different names. In fact, the name of each literal should be the name of the state/event for which it is created. We can use a property macro, denoted by the **$** sign, to achieve this. A property macro is used to replace values of properties[32]. In this case we use it to replace the **name** property of the generated **EnumLiteral** with the name of the state/event over which we loop. Here is the implementation expression of the property macro:

[32] The node macros used above (**COPY_SRC**) replace whole nodes, as opposed to primitive *properties* of nodes.

```
node.cEnumLiteralName();
```

In the code above, **cEnumLiteralName** is a behavior method[33]. It concatenates the **name** of the parent **Statemachine** with the string **__state__** and the name of the current state (in order to get a unique name for each state):

[33] Behavior methods are defined as part of the behavior aspect of the concepts, such as **State**.

```
concept behavior State {
  public string cEnumLiteralName() {
    return this.parent : Statemachine.name + "__state__" + this.name;
  }
}
```

The first of the **struct** attributes is also interesting. It is used to store the current state. It has to be typed to the state **enum** that is generated from this particular state machine. The type of the attribute is an **EnumType**; **EnumType**s extend **Type** and reference the **EnumDeclaration** whose type they represent. How can we establish the reference to the correct **EnumDeclaration**? We use a reference macro (**->$**) to retarget the reference. Fig. 11.6 shows the macro's expression.

Figure 11.6: A reference macro has to return either the target node, or the name of the target node. The name is then resolved using the scoping rules for the particular reference concept.

```
comment  : <none>
referent : (node, genContext, operationContext)->join(node<EnumDeclaration> | string) {
             node.cStatesEnumName();
           }
```

Note how a reference macro expects either the target node (here: an **EnumDeclaration**) as the return value, or a **string**. That **string** would be the name of the target element. Our implementation returns the name of the states **enum** generated in the same template. MPS then uses the target language's scoping rules to find and link to the correct target element[34].

Let us now address the second main template, Fig. 11.7, which generates the execute function. The **switch** expression is interesting. It switches over the current state of the cur-

[34] This is not a global name lookup! Since MPS knows the reference is an **EnumLiteralRef** expression, the scope of that concept is used. As long as the name is unique within the scope, this is completely deterministic. Alternatively, the actual node can be identified and returned from the reference macro using mapping labels. However, using names is much more convenient and works also for cross-model references, where mapping labels don't work.

```
template generateSwitchCase
input    Statemachine
content node:
module dummy imports nothing {
  enum events { anEvent; }
  enum states { aState; }
  struct statemachineData {
    states __currentState;
  };
  void statemachineFunction(statemachineData* instance, events event) {
    <TF  switch ( instance->__currentState ) {                                    TF>
        $LOOP$ case ->$[aState]: {
            switch ( event ) {
                $LOOP$ case ->$[anEvent]: {
                    $LOOP$ if ( $COPY_SRC$[true] ) {
                        $COPY_SRCL$[int8_t exitActions;]
                        $COPY_SRCL$[int8_t transActions;]
                        instance->__currentState = ->$[aState];
                        $COPY_SRCL$[int8_t entryActions;]
                        return;
                    } if
                    break;
                }
            } switch
            break;
        }
    } switch

  } statemachineFunction (function)
}
```

rent state machine instance. That instance is represented by the **instance** parameter passed into the function. It has a **__currentState** field. Notice how the function that contains the **switch** statement *in the template* has to have the **instance** argument, and how its type, the **struct**, has to have the **__currentState** attribute *in the template*. If the respective elements were not there in the template, we couldn't write the template code! Since there is a convention that in the *resulting* function the argument will also be called **instance**, and the attribute will also be called **__currentState**, we don't have to use a reference macro to retarget the two.

Inside the **switch** we **LOOP** over all the states of the state machine and generate a **case**, using the state's corresponding **enum** literal. Inside the **case**, we embed another **switch** that switches over the **event** argument. Inside this inner **switch** we iterate over all transitions that are triggered by the event we currently iterate over:

Figure 11.7: The transformation template for generating the **switch**-based implementation of a **StateMachine**. Looking at the template fragment markers (<TF ... TF>) reveals that we only generate the **switch** statement, *not* the function that contains it. The reason is that we need to be able to embed the state machine **switch** into other function-like concepts as well (e.g., operations in components defined in the mbeddr components extension), so we have separated the generation of the function from the generation of the actual state machine behavior. See the text for more details.

```
context state.transitions.where({~it => it.trigger.event == node; });
```

We then generate an **if** statement that checks at runtime whether the guard condition for this transition is **true**. We copy in the guard condition using the **COPY_SRC** macro attached to the **true** dummy node. The **COPY_SRC** macro copies the original node, but it also applies additional reduction rules for this node (and all its descendants), if there are any. For example, in a guard condition it is possible to reference event arguments. The reference to **size** in the **step** transition is an example:

```
statemachine Counter {
  in events
    step(int[0..10] size)
    ...
  states ( initial = start )
    ...
    state countState {
      on step [currentVal + size > LIMIT] -> start { send resetted(); }
    }
}
```

Event arguments are mapped to the resulting C function via a **void*** array. A reference to an event argument (**EventArgRef**) hence has to be reduced to accessing the **n**-th element in the array (where **n** is the index of the event argument in the list of arguments). Fig. 11.8 shows the reduction rule. It accesses the array, casts the element to a pointer to the type of the argument, and then dereferences everything[35].

```
⎡concept      EventArgRef⎤
⎢inheritors   false      ⎥
⎣condition    <always>   ⎦
--> content node:
    module dummy imports nothing {
      void dummy2(void*[ ] arguments) {
        <TF [ (*(($COPY_SRC$[int8_t]*)(arguments[$[1]]))) ] TF>; }
    }
```

[35] The reduction rule creates code that looks like this (for an **int** event attribute): `*((int*)arguments[0])`.

Figure 11.8: The reduction rule for references to event arguments (to be used inside guard conditions of transitions).

Inside the **if** statement, we have to generate the code that has to be executed if a transition fires. We first copy in all the exit actions of the current state. Once again, the **int8 exitActions;** is just an arbitrary dummy statement that will be replaced by the statements in the exit actions (**COPY_SRCL** replaces a node with a *list* of nodes). The respective expression is this:

```
(node, genContext, operationContext)->sequence<node<>> {
  if (node.parent : State.exitAction != null) {
    return node.parent : State.exitAction.statements;
  }
  new sequence<node<>>(empty);
}
```

We then do the same for the transition actions of the current transition, set the **instance->__currentState** to the target state of the transition using a reference macro (**node.targetState.cEnumLiteralName();**), and then we handle the entry actions of the target state. Finally we return, because at most one transition can fire as a consequence of calling the state machine execute function.

As the last example I want to show how the **TriggerSM-Statement** is translated. It injects an event into a state machine:

```
Counter c1;
void aFunction() {
  trigger(c1, start);
}
```

It must be translated to a call to the generated state machine execute function that we have discussed above. For simplicity, we explain a version of the **TriggerSMStatement** that does not include event arguments. Fig. 11.9 shows the template.

```
content node:
module dummy imports nothing {
  enum eventEnum { e1; e2; }
  struct instanceData {
    << ... >>
  };
  void smExecutionFunction(instanceData* instance, eventEnum event) {

  } smExecutionFunction (function)
  var instanceData theStatemachine;
  void someMethod() {
    <TF [ { ->$[smExecutionFunction](&$COPY_SRC$[theStatemachine], ->$[e1]); } ] TF>
  } someMethod (function)
}
```

We use a dummy function **someMethod** so that we can embed a function call, because we have to generate a function call to the execute function generated from the state machine. Only the function call is surrounded with the template fragment markers (and will be generated). The function we call *in the template code* is the **smExecuteFunction**. It has the same signature as the real, generated state machine execute function. We use a reference macro to retarget the **function** reference in the function call. It uses the following expression, which returns the name of the function generated for the state machine referenced in the **statemachine** expression of the trigger statement:

Figure 11.9: The reduction rule for a **trigger** statement. It is transformed to a call to the function that implements the behavior of the state machine that is referenced in the first argument of the **trigger** statement.

```
StatemachineType.machine.cFunctionName();
```

Note how the first argument to the **trigger** statement can be *any* expression (local variable reference, global variable reference, a function call). However, we know (and enforce via the type system) that the expression's type must be a **StatemachineType**, which has a reference to the **Statemachine** whose instance the expression represents. So we can cast the expression's type to **StatemachineType**, access the **machine** reference, and get the name of the execute function generated from that state machine[36].

[36] This is an example of where we use the type system in the code generator, and not just for checking a program for type correctness.

The second argument of the **trigger** statement is a reference to the event we want to trigger. We can use another reference macro to find the **enum** literal generated for this event. The macro code is straight forward:

```
node.event.cEnumLiteralName();
```

■ *Procedural Transformation of a Test Case*   Instead of using the template-based approach shown above, transformations can also be written manually against the MPS API. To do this, a **mapping script** is called from the mapping configuration (instead of the mapping configuration containing rules). Such a mapping script can contain arbitrary BaseLanguage code that operates on the output model of the transformation[37].

[37] This is essentially similar to the implementation code for intentions or refactorings (Section 13.6); those also modify a model using the MPS Node API.

As part of the mbeddr project, we have built a Builder extension to BaseLanguage. In the example below, we will build the following code:

```
module SomeModule imports nothing {

  exported test case testCase1 { }

  exported int32 main(int32 argc, string*[] argv) {
    return test testCase1;
  }
}
```

The code below builds the code above. Notice how by default we work with concepts directly (as when we mention **StatementList** or **ExecuteTestExpression**). However, we can also embed expression in the builder using the **#(..)** expression. Nodes created by the builder can be named (as in **tc:TestCase**) so they can be used as a reference target later (**testcase -> tc**).

```
node<ImplementationModule> immo = build ImplementationModule
  name = #(aNamePassedInFromAUserDialog)
  contents += tc:TestCase
```

```
        name = "testCase1"
        type = VoidType
        contents += #(MainFunctionHelper.createMainFunction())
            body = StatementList statements += ReturnStatement
                    expression = ExecuteTestExpression
                                    tests += TestCaseRef
                                            testcase -> tc
```

Builders in MPS are a first-class extension to BaseLanguage, which means that the IDE can provide support. For example, if a concept has a mandatory child (e.g. the **body** in a **Function**), the IDE will report an error if no node is put into this child slot. Code completion can be provided as well[38].

[38] Users do not have to build the helper functions we have seen for Xtext/Xtend above. On the other hand, the MPS builder extension is specific to building MPS node trees, whereas the approach taken by Xtext/Xtend is generic, as long as users define the helper functions.

11.4 Spoofax Example

In Spoofax, model-to-model transformations and code generation are both specified by rewrite rules[39]. This allows for the seamless integration of model-to-model transformation steps into the code generation process; the clear distinction between model-to-model transformation and code generation vanishes[40]. We look at the various approaches supported by Spoofax in this chapter.

[39] Rewrite rules were introduced in Section 9.3.1.

[40] Similar to MPS, it is also possible to express model-to-model transformations using the concrete syntax of the target language, even though this requires a bit more setup and care.

■ *Code Generation by String Interpolation*   Pure code generation from abstract syntax trees to text can be realized by rewriting to strings. The following simple rules rewrite types to their corresponding representation in Java. For entity types, we use their name as the Java representation:

```
to-java: NumType()       -> "int"
to-java: BoolType()      -> "boolean"
to-java: StringType()    -> "String"
to-java: EntType(name)   -> name
```

Typically, more complex rules are recursive and use string interpolation[41] to construct strings from fixed and variable parts. For example, the following two rewrite rules generate Java code for entities and their properties:

[41] We used string interpolation already before to compose error messages in Section 9.3.

```
to-java:
    Entity(x, ps) ->
    $[ class [x] {
            [ps']
        }
    ]
    with
      ps' := <map(to-java)> ps
to-java:
    Property(x, t) ->
    $[ private [t'] [x];

        public [t'] get_[x] {
            return [x];
```

```
        }
        public void set_[x] ([t'] [x]) {
            this.[x] = [x];
        }
    ]
  with
    t' := <to-java> t
```

String interpolation takes place inside `$[...]` brackets and allows us to combine fixed text with variables that are bound to strings. Variables can be inserted using brackets `[...]` without a dollar sign[42]. Instead of variables, we can also directly use the results from other rewrite rules that yield strings or lists of strings:

[42] You can also use any other kind of bracket: `{...}`, `<...>`, and `(...)` are allowed as well.

```
to-java:
  Entity(x, ps) ->
  $[ class [x] {
       [<map(to-java)> ps]
     }
  ]
```

Indentation is important, both for the readability of rewrite rules and of the generated code: the indentation leading up to the `$[...]` brackets is removed, but any other indentation beyond the bracket level is preserved in the generated output. In this way we can indent the generated code, as well as our rewrite rules. Applying **to-java** to the initial **shopping** entity will yield the following Java code:

```
class Item {

    private String name;

    public String get_name {
        return name;
    }

    public void set_name (String name) {
        this.name = name;
    }

    private boolean checked;

    public boolean get_checked {
        return checked;
    }

    public void set_checked (boolean checked) {
        this.checked = checked;
    }

    private Num order;

    public Num get_order {
        return order;
    }

    public void set_order (Num order) {
        this.order = order;
    }
}
```

When we prefer camelcase in method names, we need to slightly change our code generation rules, replacing **get_[x]** and **set_[x]** by **get[<to-upper-first>x]** and **set[<to-upper-first>x]**. We also need to specify the following rewrite rule:

```
to-upper-first: s -> s'
  where
    [first|chars] := <explode-string> s ;
    upper         := <to-upper> first ;
    s'            := <implode-string> [upper|chars]
```

explode-string turns a string into a list of characters, **to-upper** upper-cases the first character, and **implode-string** turns the characters back into a string[43].

[43] All these strategies are part of Stratego's standard library, documented at **releases.strategoxt.org/docs/api/libstratego-lib/stable/docs/**.

■ *Editor Integration* To integrate the code generation into our editor, we first have to define the following rewrite rule:

```
generate-java:
  (selected, position, ast, path, project-path) -> (filename, result)
  with
    filename := <guarantee-extension(|"java")> path;
    result   := <to-java> ast
```

While we are free to choose the name of this rule[44], the patterns on the left- and right-hand side need to follow Spoofax' convention for editor integration. On the left-hand side, it matches the current **selection** in the editor, its **position** in the abstract syntax tree, the abstract syntax tree itself (**ast**), the **path** of the source file in the editor[45], and the path of the project this file belongs to. As the right-hand side shows, the rule produces the name of the generated file and its content as a string. The file name is derived from the source file's path, while the file content is generated from the abstract syntax tree.

[44] The rule is subsequently registered as a builder to make it known to Spoofax; see below.

[45] By default, generation happens on a per-file basis. We can also just generate code for the current selection: to do so, we can replace the last line by **result := <to-java> selected**.

Once we have defined this rule, we can register it as a **builder** in **editor/Lang-Builders.esv**. Here, we add the following rule:

```
builder: "Generate Java code (selection)" = generate-java (openeditor) (
    realtime)
```

This defines a label for our transformation, which is added to the editor's *Transform* menu. Additional options, such as **(openeditor)** and **(realtime)**, can be used to customize the behaviour of the transformation. The following table illustrates the available options.

Option	Description
`(openeditor)`	Opens the generated file in an editor.
`(realtime)`	Re-generates the file as the source is edited.
`(meta)`	Excludes the transformation from the deployed plugin.
`(cursor)`	Transforms always the tree node at the cursor.

■ *Code Generation by Model Transformation* Rewrite rules with string interpolation support a template-based approach to code generation. Thus, they share two typical problems of template languages. First, they are not *syntax safe*, that is, they do not guarantee the syntactical correctness of the generated code: we might accidentally generate Java code which can not be parsed by a Java compiler. Such errors can only be detected by testing the code generator. Second, they inhibit subsequent transformation steps. For example, we might want to optimize the generated Java code, generate Java bytecode from it, and finally optimize the generate Java Bytecode. At each step, we would first need to parse the generated code from the previous step before we can apply the actual transformation.

Both problems can be avoided by generating abstract syntax trees instead of concrete syntax, i.e. by using model-to-model transformations instead of code (text) generation. This can be achieved by constructing terms on the right-hand side of rewrite rules:

```
to-java: NumType()    -> IntBaseType()
to-java: BoolType()   -> BooleanBaseType()
to-java: StringType() -> ClassType("java.lang.String")
to-java: EntType(t)   -> ClassType(t)

to-java:
  Entity(x, ps) -> Class([], x, ps')
    ps' := <mapconcat(to-java)> ps

to-java:
  Property(x, t) -> [field, getter, setter]
  with
    t'     := <to-java> t ;
    field  := Field([Private()], t', x) ;
    getter := Method([Public()], t', $[get_[x]], [],
              [Return(VarRef(x))]) ;
    setter := Method([Public()], Void(), $[set_[x]],
              [Param(t', x)], [assign]) ;
    assign := Assign(FieldRef(This(), x), VarRef(x))
```

When we generate ASTs instead of concrete syntax, we can easily compose transformation steps into a transformation chain by using the output of transformation n as the input for transformation $n + 1$. But this chain will still result in abstract syntax trees. To turn them back into text, it has to be pretty-printed (or serialized). Spoofax generates a language-specific rewrite rule **pp-\<LangName\>-string** which rewrites an abstract syntax tree into a string according to a pretty-printer definition[46].

■ *Concrete Object Syntax* Both template-based and term-based approaches to code generation have distinctive benefits. While template-based generation with string interpolation allows for concrete syntax in code generation rules, AST generation guarantees syntactical correctness of the generated code and enables transformation chains. To combine the benefits of both approaches, Spoofax can parse user-defined concrete syntax quotations at compile-time, checking their syntax and replacing them with equivalent abstract syntax fragments[47].

For example, a Java return statement can be expressed as `|[ return |[x]|; ]|`, rather than the abstract syntax form `Return(VarRef(x))`. Here, `|[...]|` surrounds Java syntax. It quotes Java fragments inside Stratego code. Furthermore, `|[x]|` refers to a Stratego variable `x`, matching the expression in the return statement. In this case, `|[...]|` is an antiquote, switching back to Stratego syntax in a Java fragment.

To enable this functionality, we have to customize Stratego, Spoofax' transformation language. This requires four steps. First, we need to combine Stratego's syntax definition with the syntax definitions of the source and target languages. There, it is important to keep the sorts of the languages disjunct. This can be achieved by renaming sorts in an imported module, which we do in the following example for the **Java** and the **Stratego** module:

```
module Stratego-Mobl-Java
imports Mobl
imports Java     [ ID   => JavaId ]
imports Stratego [ Id   => StrategoId
                   Var  => StrategoVar
                   Term => StrategoTerm ]
```

Second, we need to define quotations, which will enclose concrete syntax fragments of the target language in Stratego rewrite rules[48]. We add a syntax rule for every sort of concrete syntax fragments that we want to use in our rewrite rules:

```
exports context-free syntax

  "|[" Module         "]|"  -> StrategoTerm {"ToTerm"}
  "|[" Import         "]|"  -> StrategoTerm {"ToTerm"}
  "|[" Entity         "]|"  -> StrategoTerm {"ToTerm"}
  "|[" EntityBodyDecl "]|"  -> StrategoTerm {"ToTerm"}

  "|[" JClass   "]|"  -> StrategoTerm {"ToTerm"}
  "|[" JField   "]|"  -> StrategoTerm {"ToTerm"}
  "|[" JMethod  "]|"  -> StrategoTerm {"ToTerm"}
  "|[" JFeature* "]|" -> StrategoTerm {"ToTerm"}
```

[46] We will discuss these pretty-printer definitions and how they can be customized in Section 13.4

[47] This feature is not as easy to use as it seems from this description: you need to think ahead about what you want to be able to quote, what to unquote, what character sequences to use for that and how to avoid ambiguities. You need a good conceptual understanding of the mapping between concrete and abstract syntax. A partial solution for the problems is an approach called interactive disambiguation, and is discussed in

L. C. L. Kats, K. T. Kalleberg, and E. Visser. Interactive disambiguation of meta programs with concrete object syntax. In *SLE 2012*

[48] These define the `|[ ... ]|` escapes mentioned above.

With these rules, we allow quoted Mobl and Java fragments wherever an ordinary Stratego term is allowed. The first four rules concern Mobl, our example source language[49]. As quotes, we use |[...]|. The second set of rules work similarly for Java, our example target language. All syntax rules extend **Term** from the Stratego grammar, which we renamed to **StrategoTerm** during import. We use **ToTerm** as a constructor label. This allows Stratego to recognize places where we use concrete object syntax inside Stratego code. It will then lift the subtrees at these places into Stratego code. For example, the abstract syntax of |[return |[x]|;]| would be **ToTerm(Return(...))**. Stratego lifts this to **NoAnnoList(Op("Return", [...]))**, which is the abstract syntax tree for the term **Return(x)**.

[49] We like to use concrete syntax for modules (**Module**), import declarations (**Import**), entities (**Entity**), and properties and functions of entities (**EntityBodyDecl**).

Third, we need to define antiquotations, which will enclose Stratego code in target language concrete syntax fragments. Here, we add a syntax rule for every sort where we want to inject Stratego code into concrete syntax fragments:

```
exports context-free syntax
  "|[" StrategoTerm "]|" -> JavaId     {"FromTerm"}
```

This rule allows antiquoted Stratego terms to be used wherever a Java identifier can be used[50]. We use **FromTerm** as a constructor in the abstract syntax tree. Like **ToTerm**, Stratego uses this to recognize places where we switch between concrete object syntax and Stratego code. For example, the abstract syntax of |[return |[x]|;]| would be

[50] We renamed **Id** from the Java grammar to **JavaID** during import.

```
ToTerm(Return(FromTerm(Var("x"))))
```

Stratego lifts this to the following, which is the abstract syntax tree for the term **Return(x)**:

```
NoAnnoList(Op("Return", [Var("x")]))
```

Finally, we need to create a `<filename>.meta` file for every transformation file `<filename>.str` with concrete syntax fragments. In this file, we tell Spoofax to use our customized Stratego syntax definition:

```
Meta([ Syntax("Stratego-Mobl-Java") ])
```

Now, we can use concrete syntax fragments in our rewrite rules[51]:

[51] Since Spoofax replaces concrete syntax fragments with equivalent abstract syntax fragments, indentation in the fragments is lost. But the generated code will still be indented by the pretty-printer.

```
  to-java:
    |[ entity |[x]| { |[ps]| } ]| ->
    |[ class |[x]| { |[<mapconcat(to-java)> ps]| } ]|
to-java:
```

```
|[ |[x]| : |[t]| ]| ->
|[ private |[t']| |[x]|;

   public |[t']| |[x]| { return |[x]|; }

   public void |[x]| (|[t']| |[x]|) { this.|[x]| = |[x]|; } ]|
with
  t' := <to-java> t
```

Using concrete object syntax in Stratego code combines the benefits of string interpolation and code generation by model transformation. With string interpolation, we can use the syntax of the target language in code generation rules, which makes them easy to write. However, it is also easy to make syntactic errors, which are only detected when the generated code is compiled. With code generation by model transformation, we can check if the generated abstract syntax tree corresponds to the grammar of the target language. Actually we can check each transformation rule and detect errors early. With concrete object syntax, we can now use the syntax of the target language in code generation. This syntax is checked by the parser which is derived from the combined grammars of the target language and Stratego.

This comes at the price of adding quotations and antiquotation rules manually. These rules might be generated from a declarative, more concise embedding definition in the future. However, we cannot expect full automation here, since choices for the syntactic sorts involved in the embedding and of quotation and antiquotation symbols require an understanding of Stratego, the target language, and the transformation we want to write. These choices have to be made carefully in order to avoid ambiguities[52].

In general, there is room for more improvements of the embedding of the target language into Stratego. When the target language comes with a Spoofax editor, we want to get editor services like code completion, hover help, and content folding in the embedded editor as well. Until now, only syntax highlighting has been supported, using the Stratego coloring rules. Keywords of the target language will be highlighted like Stratego keywords and embedded code fragments will be given a gray background color.

[52] This is the core difference to MPS' projectional editor in this respect. In MPS, generator macros can be attached to any program element expressed in any language. There is no need to define quotations and antiquotations for each combination.

12
Building Interpreters

Interpreters are programs that execute DSL programs by directly traversing the DSL program and performing the semantic actions associated with the respective program elements. The chapter contains examples for interpreters with Xtext, MPS and Spoofax.

Interpreters are programs that read a model, traverse the AST and perform actions corresponding to the execution semantics of the language constructs whose instances appear in the AST[1]. How an interpreter implementation looks like depends a lot on the programming language used for implementing it. Also, the complexity of the interpreter directly reflects the complexity of the language it processes in terms of size, structure and semantics[2]. The following list explains some typical ingredients that go into building interpreters for functional and procedural languages. It assumes a programming language that can polymorphically invoke functions or methods.

■ *Expressions*   For program elements that can be evaluated to values, i.e., expressions, there is typically a function **eval** that is defined for the various expression concepts in the language, i.e. it is polymorphically overridden for subconcepts of **Expression**. Since nested expressions are almost always represented as nested trees in the AST, the **eval** function calls itself with the program elements it owns, and then performs some semantic action on the result[3]. Consider an expression **3 * 2 + 5**. Since the **+** is at the root of the AST, **eval(Plus)** would be called (by some outside entity). It is implemented to add the values obtained by evaluating its arguments. So it

[1] They may also produce text (in which case such an interpreter is typically called a generator), and/or inspect the structure and check constraints (in which case they are called a validator). In this section we focus on interpreters that directly execute the program.

[2] For example, building an interpreter for a pure expression language with a functional programming language is almost trivial. In contrast, the interpreters for languages that support parallelism can be much more challenging.

[3] The expression generator we saw in the previous chapter exhibited the same structure: the **eval** template for some kind of expression calls the **eval** templates for its children.

calls **eval(Multi)** and **eval(5)**. Evaluating a number literal is trivial, since it simply returns the number itself. **eval(Multi)** would call **eval(3)** and **eval(2)**, multiplying their results and returning the result of the multiplication as its own result, allowing plus to finish its calculation.

■ *Statements* Program elements that don't produce a value only make sense in programming languages that have side effects. In other words, execution of such a language concept produces some effect either on global data in the program (reassignable variables, object state) or on the environment of the program (sending network data or rendering a UI). Such program elements are typically called **Statements**. Statements are either arranged in a list (typically called a statement list) or arranged recursively nested as a tree (an **if** statement has a **then** and an **else** part which are themselves statements or statement lists). To execute those, there is typically a function **execute** that is overloaded for all of the different statement types[4]. Note that statements often contain expressions and more statement lists (as in **if (a > 3) { print a; a=0; } else { a=1;}**), so an implementation of **execute** may call **eval** and perform some action based on the result (such as deciding whether to execute the **then**-part of the **else**-part of the **if** statement). Executing the **then**-part and the **else**-part boils down to calling **execute** on the respective statement lists.

■ *Environments* Languages that support assignment to variables (or modify any other global state) require an environment during execution to remember the values for the variables at each point during program execution[5]. The interpreter must keep some kind of global hash table, known as the *environment*, to keep track of symbols and their values, so it can look them up when evaluating a reference to that symbol. Many (though not all) languages that support assignable variables allow reassignment to the same variable (as we do in **a = a + 1;**). In this case, the environment must be updateable. Notice that in **a = a + 1** both mentions of **a** are references to the same variable, and both **a** and **a+1** are expressions. However, only **a** (and not **a + 1**) can be assigned to: writing **a + 1 = 10 * a;** would be invalid. The notion of an **lvalue** is introduced to describe this. lvalues can be used "on the left side" of an assignment. Variable references are typically lvalues (if they don't point to a **const** variable). Complex expressions usually are not[6].

Technically, **eval** could be implemented as a method of the AST classes in an object-oriented language. However, this is typically not done, since the interpreter should be kept separate from the AST classes, for example, because there may be several interpreters, or because the interpreter is developed by other people than the AST.

[4] It is also overloaded for **StatementList** which iterates over all statements and calls **execute** for each one.

[5] Consider **int a = 1; a = a + 1;**. In this example, the **a** in **a + 1** is a variable reference. When evaluating this reference, the system must "remember" that it has assigned **1** to that variable in the previous statement.

[6] Unless they evaluate to something that is in turn an lvalue. An example of this is would be ***(someFunc(arg1, arg2)) = 12;**, in C, assuming that **someFunc** returns a pointer to an integer.

■ *Call Stacks*   The ability to call other entities (functions, procedures, methods) introduces further complexity, especially regarding parameter and return value passing, and the values of local variables. Assume the following function:

```
int add(int a, int b) {
    return a + b;
}
```

When this function is called via `add(2, 3)` the actual arguments 2 and 3 have to be bound to the formal arguments a and b. An environment must be established for the execution of add that keeps track of these assignments[7]. Now consider the following recursive function:

```
int fac(int i) {
    return i == 0 ? 1 : fac(i - 1);
}
```

In this case, each recursive call to `fac` requires that a new environment is created, with its own binding for the formal variables. However, the original environment must be "remembered" because it is needed to complete the execution of the outer `fac` after a recursively called `fac` returns. This is achieved using a stack of environments. A new environment is pushed onto the stack as a function is called (recursively), and the stack is popped, returning to the previous environment, as a called function returns. The return value, which is often expressed using some kind of `return` statement, is usually placed into the inner environment using a special symbol or name (such as __ret__). It can then be picked up from there as the inner environment is popped.

[7] If functions can also access global state (i.e. symbols that are not explicitly passed in via arguments), then this environment must delegate to the global environment in case a referenced symbol cannot be found in the local environment.

12.1 Building an Interpreter with Xtext

This example describes an interpreter for the cooling language[8]. It is used to allow DSL users to "play" with the cooling programs before or instead of generating C code. The interpreter can execute test cases (and report success or failure) as well as simulate the program interactively. Since no code generation and no real target hardware is involved, the turn-around time is much shorter and the required infrastructure is trivial – only the IDE is needed to run the interpreter. The execution engine, as the interpreter is called here, has to handle the following language aspects:

The example discussed in this section is built using the Xtext interpreter framework that ships with the Xtext typesystem framework discussed earlier: code.google.com/a/eclipselabs.org/p/xtext-typesystem/

[8] The interpreter in this section is built with Java because this is how we did it in the actual project. Instead, since the interpreter just operates on the EMF API, it can be written with any JVM language. In particular, Xtend would be well suited because of support for functional programming and more generally more concise syntax, especially regarding working with EMF abstract syntax trees.

- The DSL supports expressions and statements, for example in the entry and exit actions of states. These have to be supported in the way described above.

- The top-level structure of a cooling program is a state machine. So the interpreter has to deal with states, events and transitions.

- The language supports deferred execution (i.e. perform a set of statements at a later time), so the interpreter has to keep track of deferred parts of the program.

- The language supports writing tests for cooling programs, including mock behavior for hardware elements. A set of constructs exists to express this mock behavior (specifically, ramps to change temperatures over time). These background tasks must be handled by the interpreter as well.

■ *Expressions and Statements* We start our description of the execution engine inside out, by looking at the interpreter for expressions and statements first. As mentioned above, for interpreting expressions, there is typically an overloaded **eval** operation, that contains the implementation of expression evaluation for each subtype of a generic **Expression** concept. However, Java doesn't have polymorphically overloaded member methods[9]. We compensate this by generating a dispatcher that calls a *different* method for each subtype of **Expression**[10]. The generation of this dispatcher is integrated with Xtext via a workflow fragment, i.e. the dispatcher is generated during the overall Xtext code generation process. The fragment is configured with the abstract meta classes for expressions and statements. The following code shows the fragment configuration:

```
fragment = de.itemis.interpreter.generator.InterpreterGenerator {
    expressionRootClassName = "Expression"
    statementRootClassName = "Statement"
}
```

This fragment generates an abstract class that acts as the basis for the interpreter for the particular set of statements and expressions. As the following piece of code shows, the expression evaluator class contains an **eval** method that uses **instanceof** checks to dispatch to a method specific to the subclass, thereby emulating polymorphically overloaded methods[11]. The specific methods throw an exception and are expected to be overridden by a manually written subclass that contains the actual interpreter logic for the particular language concepts[12]:

[9] Java only supports polymorphic dispatch on the **this** pointer, but not on method arguments.

[10] If the interpreter had been built with Xtend instead, we would not have had to generate the dispatcher for the **StatementExecutor** or the **ExpressionEvaluator**, since Xtend provides polymorphic dispatch on method arguments. However, the fundamental logic and structure of the interpreter would have been similar.

[11] A similar class is generated for the statements. Instead of **eval**, the method is called **execute** and it does not return a value. In every other respect the **StatementExecutor** is similar to the **ExpressionEvaluator**.

[12] The class also uses a logging framework (based on the **LogEntry** class) that can be used to create a tree-shaped trace of expression evaluation, which, short of building an actual debugger, is very useful for debugging and understanding the execution of the interpreter.

```
public abstract class AbstractCoolingLanguageExpressionEvaluator
                      extends AbstractExpressionEvaluator {

  public AbstractCoolingLanguageExpressionEvaluator(ExecutionContext ctx) {
    super(ctx);
  }

  public Object eval( EObject expr, LogEntry parentLog )
                throws InterpreterException {
    LogEntry localLog = parentLog.child(LogEntry.Kind.eval, expr,
                   "evaluating "+expr.eClass().getName());
    if ( expr instanceof Equals )
      return evalEquals( (Equals)expr, localLog );
    if ( expr instanceof Unequals )
      return evalUnequals( (Unequals)expr, localLog );
    if ( expr instanceof Greater )
      return evalGreater( (Greater)expr, localLog );
    // the others...
  }

  protected Object evalEquals( Equals expr, LogEntry log )
                               throws InterpreterException {
    throw new MethodNotImplementedException(expr,
           "evalEquals not implemented");
  }

  protected Object evalUnequals( Unequals expr, LogEntry log )
                                 throws InterpreterException {
    throw new MethodNotImplementedException(expr,
           "evalUnequals not implemented");
  }

  // the others...
}
```

Before we dive into the details of the interpreter code below, it is worth mentioning that the "global data" held by the execution engine is stored and passed around using an instance of **EngineExecutionContext**. For example, it contains the environment that keeps track of symbol values, and it also has access to the type system implementation class for the language. The **ExecutionContext** is available through the **eec()** method in the **StatementExecutor** and **ExpressionEvaluator**.

Let us now look at some example method implementations. The following code shows the implementation of **evalNumberLiteral**, which evaluates number literals such as 2 or 2.3 or -10.2. To recap, the following grammar is used for defining number literals:

```
Atomic returns Expression:
    ...
    ({NumberLiteral} value=DECIMAL_NUMBER);

terminal DECIMAL_NUMBER:
    ("-")? ('0'..'9')* ('.' ('0'..'9')+)?;
```

With this in mind, the implementation of **evalNumberLiteral** should be easily understandable. We first retrieve the actual value from the **NumberLiteral** object, and we find the type of the number literal using the **typeof** function in the type system[13]. Based on this distinction, `evalNumberLiteral` returns either a Java `Double` or `Integer` as the value of the `NumberLiteral`. In addition, it creates log entries that document these decisions.

```
protected Object evalNumberLiteral(NumberLiteral expr, LogEntry log) {
    String v = ((NumberLiteral) expr).getValue();
    EObject type = eec().typesystem.typeof(expr,
                    new TypeCalculationTrace());
    if (type instanceof DoubleType) {
        log.child(Kind.debug, expr, "value is a double, " + v);
        return Double.valueOf(v);
    } else if (type instanceof IntType) {
        log.child(Kind.debug, expr, "value is a int, " + v);
        return Integer.valueOf(v);
    }
    return null;
}
```

[13] The type system basically inspects whether the value contains a dot or not and returns either a `DoubleType` or `IntType`.

The evaluator for `NumberLiteral` was simple because number literals are leaves in the AST and have no children, and no recursive invocations of `eval` are required. This is different for the `LogicalAnd`, which has two children in the `left` and `right` properties. The following code shows the implementation of `evalLogicalAnd`.

```
protected Object evalLogicalAnd(LogicalAnd expr, LogEntry log) {
    boolean leftVal = ((Boolean)evalCheckNullLog( expr.getLeft(), log ))
                    .booleanValue();
    if ( !leftVal ) return false;
    boolean rightVal = ((Boolean)evalCheckNullLog( expr.getRight(), log ))
                    .booleanValue();
    return rightVal;
}
```

The first statement calls the evaluator, for the `left` property. If `leftVal` is `false` we return without evaluating the right argument[14]. If it is true we evaluate the right argument[15]. The value of the `LogicalAnd` is then the value of `rightVal`.

So far, we haven't used the environment, since we haven't worked with variables and their (changing) values. Let's now look at how variable assignment is handled. We first look at the `AssignmentStatement`, which is implemented in the `StatementExecutor`:

```
protected void executeAssignmentStatement( AssignmentStatement s,
                                           LogEntry log) {
    Object l = s.getLeft();
    Object r = evalCheckNullLog(s.getRight(), log);
    SymbolRef sr = (SymbolRef) l;
    SymbolDeclaration symbol = sr.getSymbol();
    eec().environment.put(symbol, r);
    log.child(Kind.debug, s, "setting " + symbol.getName() + " to " + r);
}
```

[14] Most programming languages never evaluate the right argument of a logical and if the left one is false and the overall expression can never become true.

[15] The argument evaluation uses a utility method called `evalCheckNullLog` which automatically creates a log entry for this recursive call and stops the interpreter if the value passed in is `null` (which would mean the AST is somehow broken).

The first two lines get the `left` argument as well as the value of the `right` argument. Note how only the right value is evaluated: the left argument is a symbol reference (ensured through a constraint, since only **SymbolRef**s are lvalues in this language). We then retrieve the symbol referenced by the symbol reference and create a mapping from the symbol to the value in the environment, effectively "assigning" the value to the symbol during the execution of the interpreter.

The implementation of the **ExpressionEvaluator** for a symbol reference (if it is used not as an lvalue) is shown in the following code. We use the same environment to look up the value for the symbol. We then check whether the value is **null** (i.e. nothing has been assigned to the symbol as yet). In this case we return the default value for the respective type and log a warning[16], otherwise we return the value.

```
protected Object evalSymbolRef(SymbolRef expr, LogEntry log) {
    SymbolDeclaration s = expr.getSymbol();
    Object val = eec().environment.get(s);
    if (val == null) {
        EObject type = eec().typesystem.typeof(expr,
                            new TypeCalculationTrace());
        Object neutral = intDoubleNeutralValue(type);
        log.child(Kind.debug, expr,
            "looking up value; nothing found, using neutral value: " +
            neutral);
        return neutral;
    } else {
        log.child(Kind.debug, expr, "looking up value: " + val);
        return val;
    }
}
```

[16] This is specialized functionality in the cooling language; in most other languages, we would probably just return **null**, since nothing seems to have been assigned to the symbol yet.

The cooling language does not support function calls, so we demonstrate function calls with a similar language that supports them. In that language, function calls are expressed as symbol references that have argument lists. Constraints make sure that argument lists are only used if the referenced symbol is actually a **FunctionDeclaration**[17]. Here is the grammar.

```
FunctionDeclaration returns Symbol:
    {FunctionDeclaration} "function" type=Type name=ID "("
        (params+=Parameter ("," params+=Parameter)* )? ")" "{"
        (statements+=Statement)*
    "}";

Atomic returns Expression:
    ...
    {SymbolRef} symbol=[Symbol|QID]
        ("(" (actuals+=Expr)? ("," actuals+=Expr)* ")")?;
```

[17] This is a consequence of the symbol reference problem discussed in Section 8.2

The following is the code for the evaluation function for the symbol reference. It must distinguish between references to variables and to functions[18].

```
protected Object evalSymbolRef(SymbolRef expr, LogEntry log) {
    Symbol symbol = expr.getSymbol();
    if ( symbol instanceof VarDecl ) {
        return log( symbol, eec().environment.getCheckNull(symbol, log) );
    }
    if ( symbol instanceof FunctionDeclaration ) {
        FunctionDeclaration fd = (FunctionDeclaration) symbol;
```

[18] This is once again a consequence of the fact that all references to any symbol are handled via the **SymbolRef** class. We discussed this in Section 7.5.

```
            return callAndReturnWithPositionalArgs("calling "+fd.getName(),
                    fd.getParams(), expr.getActuals(), fd.getElements(),
                    RETURN_SYMBOL, log);
        }
        throw new InterpreterException(expr,
            "interpreter failed; cannot resolve symbol reference "
            +expr.eClass().getName())); }
```

The code for handling the **FunctionDeclaration** uses a predefined utility method **callAndReturnWithPositionalArgs**[19]. It accepts as arguments the list of formal arguments of the called function, the list of actual arguments (expressions) passed in at the call site, the list of statements in the function body, a symbol that should be used for the return value in the environment, as well as the obligatory log. The utility method is implemented as follows:

[19] It is part of the interpreter framework used in this example.

```
protected Object callAndReturnWithPositionalArgs(String name,
        EList<? extends EObject> formals, EList<? extends EObject> actuals,
        EList<? extends EObject> bodyStatements) {
    eec().environment.push(name);
    for( int i=0; i<actuals.size(); i++ ) {
        EObject actual = actuals.get(i);
        EObject formal = formals.get(i);
        eec().environment.put(formal, evalCheckNullLog(actual, log));
    }
    eec().getExecutor().execute( bodyStatements, log );
    Object res = eec().environment.get(RETURN_SYMBOL);
    eec().environment.pop();
    return res;
}
```

Remember that each invocation of a function has to get its own environment to handle the local variables for the particular invocation. We can see this in the first line of the implementation above: we first create a new environment and push it onto the call stack. Then the implementation iterates over the actual arguments, evaluates each of them and "assigns" them to the formals by creating an association between the formal argument symbol and the actual argument value in the new environment. It then uses the **StatementExecutor** to execute all the statements in the body of the function. Notice that as the executed function deals with its own variables and function calls, it uses the *new* environment created, pushed onto the stack and populated by this method. When the execution of the body has finished, we retrieve the return value from the environment. The **return** statement in the function has put it there under a name we have prescribed, the **RETURN_SYMBOL**, so we know how to find it in the environment. Finally, we pop the environment, restoring the caller's state of the world and return the return value as the resulting value of the function call expression.

■ *States, Events and the Main program*   Changing a state[20] from within a cooling program is done by executing a **ChangeStateStatement**, which simply references the state that should be entered. Here is the interpreter code in **StatementExecutor**:

```
protected void executeChangeStateStatement(ChangeStateStatement s,
                                           LogEntry l) {
    engine.enterState(s.getTargetState(), log);
}

public void enterState(State targetState, LogEntry logger )
      throws TestFailedException, InterpreterException,
             TestStoppedException {
    logger.child( Kind.info, targetState,
                  "entering state "+targetState.getName());
    context.currentState = targetState;
    executor.execute(ss.getEntryStatements(), logger);
    throw new NewStateEntered();
}
```

[20] State as in state machine, not as in program state.

executeChangeStateStatement calls back to an engine method that handles the state change[21]. The method sets the current state to the target state passed into the method (the current state is kept track of in the execution context). It then executes the set of entry statements of the new state. After this it throws an exception **NewStateEntered**, which stops the current execution step. The overall engine is step driven, i.e. an external "timer" triggers distinct execution steps of the engine. A state change always terminates the current step. The main method **step()** triggered by the external timer can be considered the main program of the interpreter. It looks like this:

[21] Since this is a more global operation than executing statements, it is handled by the engine class itself, and not by the **StatementExecutor**.

```
public int step(LogEntry logger) {
    try {
        context.currentStep++;
        executor.execute(getCurrentState().getEachTimeStatements(),
                         stepLogger);
        executeAsyncStuff(logger);
        if ( !context.eventQueue.isEmpty() ) {
            CustomEvent event = context.eventQueue.remove(0);
            LogEntry evLog = logger.child(Kind.info, null,
                "processing event from queue: "+event.getName());
            processEventFromQueue( event, evLog );
            return context.currentStep;
        }
        processSignalHandlers(stepLogger);
    } catch ( NewStateEntered ignore ) {}
    return context.currentStep;
}
```

It first increments a counter that keeps track of how many steps have been executed since the interpreter has been started. It then executes the **each time** statements of the current state. This is a statement list defined by a state that needs to be re-executed in each step while the system is in the respective state. It then executes asynchronous tasks. We'll explain those below. Next it checks if an event is in the event queue. If so, it removes the first event from the queue and executes it. After processing an event the step is always terminated. Lastly, if there was no event to be processed, we process signal handlers (the **check** statements in the cooling programs).

Processing events checks whether the current state declares an event handler that can deal with the currently processed event. If so, it executes the statement list associated with this event handler.

```
private void processEventFromQueue(CustomEvent event, LogEntry logger) {
    for ( EventHandler eh: getCurrentState().getEventHandlers() ) {
        if ( reactsOn( eh, event ) ) {
            executor.execute(eh.getStatements(), logger);
        }
    }
}
```

The DSL also supports executing code asynchronously, i.e. after a specified number of steps (representing logical program time). The grammar looks as follows:

```
PerformAsyncStatement:
    "perform" "after" time=Expr "{"
        (statements+=Statement)*
    "}";
```

The following method interprets the **PerformAsyncStatement**s:

```
protected void executePerformAsyncStatement(PerformAsyncStatement s,
            LogEntry log) throws InterpreterException {
    int inSteps = ((Integer)evalCheckNullLog(s.getTime(), log)).intValue();
    eec().asyncElements.add(new AsyncPerform(eec().currentStep + inSteps,
        "perform async", s, s.getStatements()));
}
```

It registers the statement list associated with the **PerformAsyncStatement** in the list of async elements in the execution context. The call to **executeAsyncStuff** at the beginning of the **step** method described above checks whether the time has come and executes those statements:

```
private void executeAsyncStuff(LogEntry logger) {
    List<AsyncElement> stuffToRun = new ArrayList<AsyncElement>();
    for (AsyncElement e: context.asyncElements) {
        if ( e.executeNow(context.currentStep) ) {
            stuffToRun.add(e);
        }
    }
    for (AsyncElement e : stuffToRun) {
        context.asyncElements.remove(e);
        e.execute(context, logger.child(Kind.info, null, "Async "+e));
    }
}
```

12.2 An Interpreter in MPS

Building an interpreter in MPS is essentially similar to building an interpreter in Xtext and EMF. All concepts would apply in the same way[22]. However, since MPS' BaseLanguage is itself built with MPS, it can be extended. So instead of using a generator to generate the dispatcher that calls the **eval** methods for the expression classes, suitable modular language extensions can be defined in the first place.

[22] Instead of **EObjects** you would work with the **node<>** types that are available on MPS to access ASTs.

■ *A Dispatch Expression*   For example, BaseLanguage could be extended with support for polymorphic dispatch (similar to what Xtend does with **dispatch** methods). An alternative solution involves a dispatch expression, a kind of "pimped switch". Fig. 12.1 shows an example.

Figure 12.1: An extension to MPS' BaseLanguage that makes writing interpreters simpler. The **dispatch** statement has the neat feature that, on the right side of the **->**, the **$** reference to the **ex** expression is already downcast to the type mentioned on the left of the **->**.

```
public static Double eval(node<Expression> ex, final node<FunctionUnitTest> test) {
  ErrorMarkers.remove(ex);
  return dispatch <Double> (ex)                                                          ;
          MulExpression           -> eval($.leftExpression, test) * eval($.rightExpression, test)
          DivExpressionFraction   -> eval($.numerator, test) / eval($.denominator, test)
          IntegerConstant         -> new Double($.value)
          FloatingPointConstant   -> Double.valueOf($.value)
          Exp                     -> Math.pow(eval($.base, test), eval($.exp, test))
          SymbolReference         -> getValue($, test)
          default: 0.0
}
```

The dispatch expression tests whether the argument **ex** is an instance of the type referenced in the cases. If so, the code on the right side of the arrow is executed. Notice the special expression **$** used on the right side of the arrow. It refers to the argument **ex**, but it is already downcast to the type on the left of the case's arrow. This way, writing annoying downcasts for each property access can be avoided.

Note that this extension is modular in the sense that the definition of BaseLanguage was not changed. Instead, an additional language module was defined that *extends* BaseLanguage. This module can be used as part of the program that contains the interpreter, making the **dispatch** statement available there[23]. Also, the **$** expression is restricted to only be usable on the right side of the **->**, allowing the overall base language namespace to be kept clean[24].

[23] We discuss language modularization and composition in Section 4.6.

[24] Xbase/Xtend comes with a similar "pimped" **switch** statement directly. It supports switching over integer and enum literals (as Java's **switch** does), but it also supports switching over types plus arbitrary Boolean guard conditions. This makes it very suitable for building interpreters, since, as we have seen, an interpreter typically dispatches its behavior based on the metaclass of the node it processes, plus optionally some of its context or children (which can be expressed with a guard condition in Xtend's **switch**.)

■ *Showing Results in the Editor*   Since MPS is a projectional editor, it can show things in the editor that are read-only. For example, the result of an interpreter run can be integrated directly into the editor. In Fig. 12.2, the bottom table contains test cases for the **calculate** rule. Users enter a number for `squareMeters`, `numberOfRooms` and the expected result, and in the last column, the editor shows the actual result of the computation (colored red or green depending on whether the actual result matches the expected result).

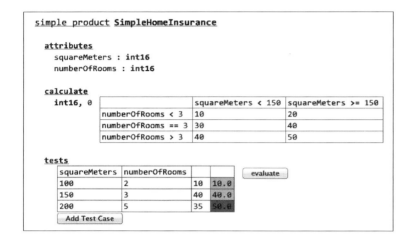

Figure 12.2: This screenshot shows an mbeddr-based demo application in which users can specify insurance rules. The system includes an interpreter that executes the test cases directly in the IDE.

The interpreter is integrated via the **evaluate** button[25]. Its action listener triggers the computation:

[25] In MPS, an editor can embed Swing components, and these Swing components can react to their own events and modify the model in arbitrary ways.

```
component provider: (editorContext, node)->JComponent {
  JButton evalButton = new JButton("evaluate");
  final node<ProductTestSuite> suite = node;
  evalButton.addActionListener(new ActionListener() {
    public void actionPerformed(ActionEvent p0) {
      command {
        foreach tc in suite.cases {
          float result = new RateCalculator(tc).calculate(
              suite.ancestor<ProductType, +>.rateCalculation);
          tc.actualResult.value = result + "";
        }
      }
    }
  });
  return evalButton;
}
```

The coloring of the cells (and making them read-only) is done via query-based formatting:

```
style {
  editable : false
  background-color : (node, editorContext)->Color {
                     node.ancestor<TestCase>.isOK()
                       ? Color.GREEN : Color.RED;
                   }
}
```

12.3 An Interpreter in Spoofax

So far we have seen procedural/functional interpreters in which the program's execution state is separate from the program itself. As the interpreter runs, it updates the execution state. Another approach to writing interpreters is state-based interpreters, where the execution of the interpreter is expressed as a set of transformations between program states. State-based interpreters can be specified with rewrite rules in Spoofax, realizing transitions between execution states. This requires:

- A representation of *states*. The simplest way to represent states are terms, but we can also define a new DSL for representing the states in concrete syntax.

- An *initialization transformation* from a program in the DSL to the initial state of the interpreter.

- A *step transformation* from an actual state of the interpreter to the next state of the interpreter.

In the remainder of the section, we develop an interpreter for a subset of Mobl. We start with a simple interpreter for expressions, which we then extend to handle statements.

12.3.1 An Interpreter for Expressions

If we want to evaluate simple arithmetic expressions without variables, the expression itself is the state of the interpreter[26]. Thus, no extra term signatures are needed and the initialization transformation is given by identity. For the step transformation, we can define rewrite rules for the different expression kinds:

```
eval: Add(Int(x), Int(y)) -> Int(z) where z := <add> (x, y)
eval: Mul(Int(x), Int(y)) -> Int(z) where z := <mul> (x, y)

eval: Not(True())  -> False()
eval: Not(False()) -> True()

eval: And(True(), True())   -> True()
eval: And(True(), False())  -> False()
eval: And(False(), True())  -> False()
eval: And(False(), False()) -> False()

eval: LazyAnd(True(), True()) -> True()
eval: LazyAnd(False(), _)     -> False()
eval: LazyAnd(_, False(), _)  -> False()
```

[26] Remember how in the design chapter we discussed building debuggers for purely functional languages, and in particular, expression languages. We argued that a debugger is trivial, because there is no real "flow" of the program; instead, the expression can be debugged by simply showing the values of all intermediate expressions in a tree-like for. We exploit the same "flowless" nature of pure expression languages when building this interpreter.

We can orchestrate these rules in two different styles. First, we can define an interpreter which performs only a single evaluation step by applying one rule in each step:

```
eval-one: exp -> <oncebu(eval)> exp
```

Here, **oncebu** tries to apply **eval** at one position in the tree, starting from the leaves (the **bu** in **oncebu** stands for bottom-up). We could also use **oncetd**, traversing the tree top-down.

However, evaluations are likely to happen at the bottom of the tree, which is why **oncebu** is the better choice. The result of **eval-one** will be a slightly simpler expression, which might need further evaluation. Alternatively, we can directly apply as many rules as possible, trying to evaluate the whole expression:

```
eval-all: exp -> <bottomup(try(eval))> exp
```

Here, **bottomup** tries to apply **eval** at every node, starting at the leaves. The result of **eval-all** will be the final result of the expression.

12.3.2 An Interpreter for Statements

If we want to evaluate statements, we need states which capture the value of variables and the list of statements which needs to be evaluated. We can define these states with a signature for terms:

```
signature constructors
    : ID * IntValue  -> VarValue
    : ID * BoolValue -> VarValue
State: List(VarValue) * List(Statement) -> State
```

The first two rules define binary tuples which combine a variable name (**ID**) and a value (either **IntValue** or **BoolValue**). The last rule defines a binary constructor **State**, which combines a list of variable values with a list of statements[27]. We first have to adapt the evaluation of expressions to handle variable references in expressions.

```
eval(|varvals): exp -> <eval> exp
eval(|varvals): VarRef(var) -> <lookup> (var, varvals)

eval-one(|s): exp -> <oncebu(eval(|s))> exp
eval-all(|s): exp -> <bottomup(try(eval(|s)))> exp
```

The first two rules take the actual list of variable values of the interpreter (**varvals**) as a parameter. The first rule integrates the existing evaluation rules, which do not need any state information. The second rule looks up the current value **val** of the variable **var** in the list of variable values. The last two rules define small-step and big-step interpreters of expressions, just as before.

We can now define evaluation rules for statements. These rules rewrite the current state into a new state:

```
eval:
  (varvals, [Declare(var, exp)|stmts]) -> (varvals', stmts)
  where
```

[27] This will represent the program as it evolves over time. Starting with a statement list, the program state over time can be represented as a collection of variable values and a remaining list of yet to be interpreted statements. This is what **State** represents.

```
      val      := <eval-all(|varvals)> exp;
      varvals' := <update> ((var, val), varvals)
eval:
  (varvals, [Assign(VarRef(var), exp)|stmts]) -> (varvals', stmts)
  where
    val      := <eval-all(|varvals)> exp;
    varvals' := <update> ((var, val), varvals)
eval:
  (varval, [Block(stmts1)|stmts2]) -> (varvals, <conc> (stmts1, stmts2))
```

The first rule handles variable declarations. On the left-hand side, it matches the current list of variable values **varvals**, the declaration statement **Declare(var, exp)**, and the list of remaining statements **stmts**. It evaluates the expression to a value and updates the list of variable values. The new state (on the right-hand side of the signature) consists of the updated variable values and the list of remaining statements[28]. The second rule handling assignments is quite similar. The third rule handles block statements, by concatenating the statements from a block with the remaining statements. The following rule handle an **if** statement:

[28] Note how on the left side of the rule the **[head|tail]** notation is used for the statements, where **stmts** is the tail. By "returning" **stmts** on the right, we automatically remove the first element from the list (it was the head).

```
eval:
  (varvals, [If(exp, thenStmt, elseStmt)|stmts]) -> (varvals, [stmt|stmts])
  where
    val := <eval-all(|varvals)> exp;
    if !val => True() then
      stmt := thenStmt
    else
      !val => False();
      stmt := elseStmt
    end
```

First, it evaluates the condition. Depending on the result, it chooses the next statement to evaluate. When the result is **True()**, the statement from the **thenStmt** branch is chosen. Otherwise the result has to be **False()** and the statement from the **elseStmt** branch is chosen. If the result is neither **True()** nor **False()**, the rule will fail. This ensures that the rule only works when the condition can be evaluated to a Boolean value. The following rule handles **while** loops:

```
eval:
  (varvals, [While(exp, body)|stmts]) -> (varvals, stmts')
  where
    val := <eval-all(|varvals)> exp;
    if !val => True() then
      stmts' := [body, While(exp, body)|stmts]
    else
      !val => False();
      stmts' := stmts
    end
```

Again, the condition is evaluated first. If it evaluates to **True()**, the list of statements is updated to the body of the loop, the **while** loop again, followed by the remaining statements. If it evaluates to **False()**, only the remaining statements need to be evaluated.

The **eval** rules already define a small-step interpreter, going from one evaluation state to the next. We can define a big-step interpreter by adding a driver, which repeats the evaluation until it reaches a final state:

```
eval-all: state -> <repeat(eval)> state
```

12.3.3 More Advanced Interpreters

We can extend the interpreter to handle function calls and objects in a similar way as we did for statements. First, we always have to think about the states of the extended interpreter. Functions will require a call stack, objects will require a heap. Next, we need to consider how the old rules can deal with the new states. Adjustments might be needed. For example, when we support objects, the heap needs to be passed to expressions. Expressions which create objects will change the heap, so we cannot only pass it, but have to propagate the changes back to the caller.

12.3.4 IDE Integration

We can integrate interpreters as builders into the IDE. For big-step interpreters, we can simply calculate the overall execution result and show it to the user. For small-step interpreters, we can use the initialization transformation in the builder. This will create an initial state for the interpreter. When we define a concrete syntax for these states, they can be shown in an editor. The transition transformation can then be integrated as a refactoring on states, changing the current state to the next one. In this way, the user can control the execution, undo steps, or even modify the current state.

13
IDE Services

In this chapter we discuss various services provided by the IDE. This includes code completion, syntax coloring, pretty-printing, go-to-definition and find references, refactoring, outline views, folding, diff and merge, tooltips and visualization. In contrast to the other chapters, this one is not organized by tool, but rather by IDE service. We then provide examples for each service with one or more of the tools. Note that debugging debugging is discussed in Chapter 15.

In this chapter we illustrate typical services provided by the IDE that are *not* automatically derived from the language definition itself and for which additional configuration or programming is required. Note that we are not going to show every service with every example tool[1].

[1] If we don't show how X works in some tool, this does *not* mean that you cannot do X with this particular tool.

13.1 Code Completion

Code completion is perhaps the most essential service provided by an IDE. We already saw that code completion is implicitly influenced by scopes: if you press **Ctrl-Space** at the location of a reference, the IDE will show you the valid targets of this reference (as defined in the scope) in the code completion menu. Selecting one establishes the reference.

■ *Customizing Code Completion for a Reference in Xtext* Consider the cooling DSL. Cooling programs can reference symbols. Symbols can be hardware building blocks, local variables or configuration parameters. It would be useful in the code completion menu to show what kind of symbol a particular symbol is (Fig. 13.1).

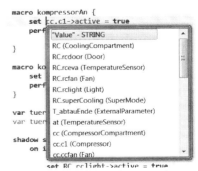

Figure 13.1: Code completion in the cooling language is customized to specify what kind of symbol a particular reference target is (the kind is shown in paranthesis after the name).

To customize code completion, you have to implement a method in the **ProposalProvider** for your language. The method name has to correspond to a rule/property whose code completion menu you want to customize[2]. In this example, we want to customize the **symbol** property of the **Atomic** expression:

```
Atomic returns Expression:
    ...
    ({SymbolRef} symbol=[appliances::SymbolDeclaration|QID]);
```

[2] This also works for containment references or primitive properties and not just for references (which are affected by scopes).

The method takes various arguments; the first one, **model**, represents the program element for which the **symbol** property should be completed.

```
public class CoolingLanguageProposalProvider
            extends AbstractCoolingLanguageProposalProvider {

  @Override
  public void completeAtomic_Symbol(EObject model, Assignment assignment,
                        ContentAssistContext context,
                        ICompletionProposalAcceptor acceptor) {
    ...
  }
}
```

Let us now look at the actual implementation of the method[3]. In line three we get the scope for the particular reference so we can iterate over all the elements and change their appearance in the code completion menu. To be able to get the scope, we need the **EReference** for the particular reference. The first two lines in this method are used to this end.

[3] For this particular example above, where we only change the string representation of the targets computed by the scope (as opposed to changing the actual contents of the code completion menu), we could have overridden the **getStyledDisplayString** method instead. Its task is to provide the textual representation for contents of the scope.

```
CrossReference crossReference = ((CrossReference)assignment.getTerminal());
EReference ref = GrammarUtil.getReference(crossReference);
IScope scope = getScopeProvider().getScope(model, ref);
Iterable<IEObjectDescription> candidates = scope.getAllElements();
for (IEObjectDescription od: candidates) {
    String ccText = od.getName()+" ("+od.getEClass().getName()+")";
    String ccInsert = od.getName().toString();
    acceptor.accept(createCompletionProposal(ccInsert,
              ccText, null, context));
}
```

Once we have the scope, we can iterate over all its contents (i.e. the target elements)[4]. Inside the loop we then use the name of the target object plus the name of the **EClass** to construct the string to be shown in the code completion menu (**ccText**)[5]. The last line then calls the **accept** method on the **ICompletionProposalAcceptor** to finally create a proposal. Note how we also pass in **ccInsert**, which is the text to be inserted into the program if the particular code completion menu item is selected.

[4] Note how the scope does not directly contain the target **EObjects**, but rather **IEObjectDescription**s. This is because the code completion is resolved against the index, a data structure maintained by Xtext that contains all referenceable elements. This approach has the advantage that the target resource, i.e. the file that contains the target element, does not have to be loaded just to be able to reference into it.

[5] Note that we could use a rich string to add some nice formatting to the string.

■ *An Example with MPS* The contents of the code completion menu for references can be customized in MPS as well. It is instructive to look at this in addition to Xtext for two reasons. The first one is brevity. Consider the following code, where we customize the code completion menu for function calls:

```
link {function}
  ...
  presentation :
    (parameterNode, visible, smartReference, inEditor, ...)->string {
        parameterNode.signatureInfo();
    }
```

To customize the contents of the code completion menu, you have to provide the expression that calculates the text in the **presentation** section of the scope provider[6]. In this example we call a method that calculates a string that represents the complete signature of the function.

[6] Styled/Rich strings are not supported here.

The second reason why this is interesting in MPS is that we don't have to specify the text that should be inserted if an element is selected from the code completion menu: the reference is established based on the UUID of the target node, and the editor of the referencing node determines the presentation of this reference[7].

[7] In the example of the function call, it projects the name of the called function (plus the actual arguments).

■ *Code Completion for Simple Properties* In Xtext, code completion can be provided for any property of a rule, not just for references (i.e. also for children or for primitive properties such as strings or numbers). The mechanism to do that is the same as the one shown above. Instead of using the scope (only references have scopes) one could use a statically populated list of strings as the set of proposals, or one could query a database to get a list of candidate values[8].

In MPS, the mechanism is different. Since this is a pure editor customization and has nothing to do with scopes, this behavior is customized in the editor definition. Consider a **LocalVariableDeclaration** (as in **int x = 0;**) where we want to customize the suggested name of the variable. So if you press **Ctrl-Space** in the name field of the variable, we want to suggest one or more reasonable names for the variable. Fig. 13.2 shows the necessary code.

[8] Note that if we use this approach to provide code completion for primitive properties this does not affect the constraint check (in contrast to references, where a scope affects the code completion menu and the constraint checks). Users can always type something that is *not* in the code completion menu. A separate constraint check may have to be written.

An editor cell may have a cell menu (the menu you see when you press **Ctrl-Space**). It consists of several parts. Each part contributes a set of menu entries. In the example in Fig. 13.2, we add a cell menu part of type **property values**, in which we simply return a list of values (one, in the example; we use the name of the type of the local variable, prefixed by an **a**).

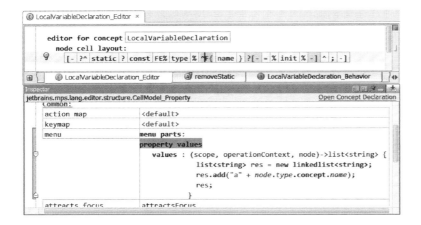

Figure 13.2: A cell menu for the **name** property of a **LocalVariableDeclaration**. In the editor definition (top window) we select the cell that renders the **name**. In the inspector we can then define additional properties for the selected cell. In this case we contribute an additional cell menu that provides the suggested names.

■ *Editor Templates* Templates are more complex syntactic structures that can be selected from the code completion menu. For example, the code completion menu may contain an **if-then-else** entry, which, if you select it, gets expanded into the following code in the program:

```
if ( expr ) {
} else {
}
```

Xtext provides templates for this purpose. These can be defined either as part of the language, or by the user in the IDE. Fig. 13.3 shows the **if-then-else** example as defined in the IDE.

In MPS there are several ways to address this. One is simply an intention (explained in more detail in Section 7.7). It will not be activated via **Ctrl-Space**, but rather via **Alt-Enter**. In every other respect it is identical: the intention can insert arbitrary code into the program. Alternatively we can use a cell menu (already mentioned above). Fig. 13.4 shows the code for a cell menu that also creates the **if-then-else** structure illustrated above.

13.2 Syntax Coloring

There are two cases for syntax coloring: syntactic highlighting and semantic highlighting. Syntactic highlighting is used to color keywords, for example. These keywords are readily

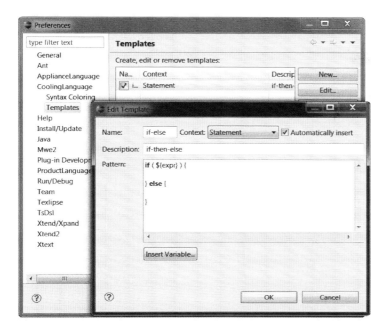

Figure 13.3: Template definitions contain a name (the text shown in the code completion menu), a description, as well as the context and the pattern. The context refers to a grammar rule. The template will show up in the code completion menu at all locations where that grammar rule would be valid as well. The pattern is the actual text that will be inserted into the editor if the template is selected. It can contain *variables*. Once inserted, the user can use **TAB** to step through the variables and replace them with text. In the example, we define the condition expression as a variable.

```
menu parts:
replace node (custom node concept)
    replace with : Statement
generic item
    matching text : if-then-else
    handler       : (node, model, scope, operationContext)->void {
                      node.replace with(<if (true) {
                        <no statements>
                      } else {
                        <no statements>
                      }>);
                    }
```

Figure 13.4: A cell menu to insert the if/then/else statement. Note how we contribute *two* menu parts. The first one inserts the default code completion contents for **Statement**. The second one provides an if/then/else statement under the menu text **if-then-else**. Notice how we can use a quotation (concrete syntax expression) in the cell menu code. Because of MPS's support for language composition, the editor even provides code completion etc. *for the contents of the quotation* in the editor for the cell menu.

available from the grammar. No customization is necessary beyond configuring the actual color. Semantic coloring colors code fragments based on some query over the AST structure. For example, in a state machine, if a state is unreachable (no incoming transitions) the state may be colored in gray instead of black.

■ *An Example with MPS*   Let us first look at syntax coloring in MPS, starting with purely syntactic highlighting. Fig. 13.5 shows a collage of several ingredients: at the top we see the editor for **GlobalVariableDeclaration**. **GlobalVariableDeclaration** implements the interface **IModuleContent**. **IModuleContent**s can be exported (which means they can be seen by

```
editor for concept GlobalVariableDeclaration
  node cell layout:
    [/
      # preventNameManglingFlag #
      [- # externFlag # # exportedFlag # var % type % { name } ; -]
    /]
                                    editor component exportedFlag
                                    applicable concept:
                                      IModuleContent
                                    component cell layout:
                                      ?^ exported
    Style:
    <no base style> {
      text-foreground-color : darkGreen
      font-style : bold
    }
```

Figure 13.5: In MPS, syntax coloring is achieved by associating one or more style properties with the elements at hand. In this case we assign a **darkGreen** text foreground color as well as a **bold** font style.

modules importing the current one), so we define an editor component (a reusable editor fragment) for **IModuleContent** that renders the **exported** flag. This editor component is embedded into the editor of **GlobalVariableDeclaration**, and is also embedded into the editor of all other concepts that implement **IModuleCon- tent**. The editor component simply defines a keyword **exported** that is rendered in dark green and in bold font. This can be achieved by specifying the respective style properties for the editor cell[9].

[9] Groups of style definitions can also be modularized into style sheets and reused for several cells.

Semantic highlighting works essentially the same way. Instead of using a constant (**darkGreen**) for the color, we embed a query expression. The code in Fig. 13.6 renders the **state** keyword of a **State** in a *Statemachine* gray if that particular state has no incoming transitions.

```
Style:
<no base style> {
  text-foreground-color :
      (node, editorContext)->Color {
        boolean hasIncoming = node.ancestor<Statemachine>.
          descendants<Transition>.any({~it =>
            it.targetState == node; });
        if (hasIncoming) {
          return Color.black;
        } else {
          return Color.gray;
        }
      }
}
```

Figure 13.6: A style query that renders the associated cell in gray if the **state** (to which the cell belongs) has no incoming transitions. We first find out if the state has incoming transitions by finding the **Statemachine** ancestor of the state, finding all the **Transitions** in the subtree under the **Statemachine**, and then checking if one exists whose **targetState** is the current state (**node**). We then use the result of this query to color the cell appropriately.

■ *An Example with Xtext*   Xtext uses a two-phase approach. First, you have to define the styles you want to apply to parts of the text. This is done in the highlighting configuration of the particular language:

```
public class CLHighlightingConfiguration extends
      DefaultHighlightingConfiguration {

  public static final String VAR = "var";

  @Override
  public void configure(IHighlightingConfigurationAcceptor acceptor) {
    super.configure(acceptor);
    acceptor.acceptDefaultHighlighting(VAR, "variables", varTextStyle());
  }

  private TextStyle varTextStyle() {
    TextStyle t = defaultTextStyle().copy();
    t.setColor(new RGB(100,100,200));
    t.setStyle(SWT.ITALIC | SWT.BOLD );
    return t;
  }
}
```

The `varTextStyle` method creates a `TextStyle` object. The method `configure` then registers this style with the framework using a unique identifier (the constant `VAR`). The reason for registering it with the framework is that the styles can be changed by the user in the running application using the preferences dialog (Fig. 13.7).

We now have to associate the style with program syntax[10]. The semantic highlighting calculator for the target language is used to this end[11]. It requires the `provideHighlightingFor` method to be implemented. To highlight references to variables (not the variables themselves!) with the style defined above works the following way:

```
public void provideHighlightingFor(XtextResource resource,
                       IHighlightedPositionAcceptor acceptor) {
  EObject root = resource.getContents().get(0);
  TreeIterator<EObject> eAllContents = root.eAllContents();
  while (eAllContents.hasNext()) {
    EObject ref = (EObject) eAllContents.next();
    if ( ref instanceof SymbolRef ) {
        SymbolDeclaration sym = ((SymbolRef) o).getSymbol();
        if ( sym instanceof Variable ) {
           ICompositeNode n = NodeModelUtils.findActualNodeFor(ref);
           acceptor.addPosition(n.getOffset(),
                        n.getLength(),
                        CLHighlightingConfiguration.VAR);
        }
     }
   }
}
```

The method gets passed in an `XtextResource`, which represents a model file. From it we get the root element and iterate over all its contents. If we find a `SymbolRef`, we continue with coloring. Notice that in the cooling language we reference *any*

Figure 13.7: Preferences dialog that allows users to change the styles registered with the framework for a highlighting configuration.

[10] A particularly nice feature of Xtext syntax coloring is that styles are combined if more than one style applies to a given program element.

[11] Even though it is called *semantic* highlighting calculator, it is used for syntactic and semantic highlighting. It simply associates concrete syntax nodes with styles; it does not matter how it establishes the association (statically or based on the structure of the AST).

symbol (variable, event, hardware element) with a `SymbolRef`, so we now have to check whether we reference a `Variable` or not[12]. If we have successfully identified a reference to a variable, we now have to move from the abstract syntax tree (on which we have worked all the time so far) to the concrete syntax tree, so we can identify particular tokens that shall be colored[13]. We use a utility method to find the `ICompositeNode` that represents the `SymbolRef` in the concrete syntax tree. Finally we use the `acceptor` to perform the actual highlighting using the position of the text string in the text. We pass in the `VAR` style defined before[14].

■ *An Example with Spoofax* Spoofax supports syntax coloring on the lexical and the syntactic level. At the lexical level, tokens such as keywords, identifiers, or integers are colored. This is the most common use case of syntax coloring. At the syntactic level, we can color larger code fragments, for example to highlight embeddings. In Spoofax, syntax coloring is specified declaratively as part of the editor specification. For the lexical level, Spoofax predefines the token classes `keyword`, `identifier`, `string`, `number`, `var`, `operator` and `layout`. For each of these, we can specify a color (either by name or by RGB values) and optionally a font style (**bold**, *italic*, or both). Spoofax generates the following default specification:

[12] This is the place where we could perform any other structural or semantic analysis (such as the check for no incoming transitions) as well.

[13] The concrete syntax tree in Xtext is a complete representation of the parse result, including keywords, symbols and whitespace.

[14] Notice how we color the *complete* reference. Since it is only one text string anyway, this is just as well. If we had more structured concrete syntax (as in `state someState {}`), and we only wanted to highlight parts of it (e.g., the `state` keyword), we'd have to do some further analysis on the `ICompositeNode` to find out the actual concrete syntax node for the keyword.

```
module MoblLang-Colorer.generated

colorer Default, token-based highlighting

  keyword    : 127 0 85 bold
  identifier : default
  string     : blue
  number     : darkgreen
  var        : 255 0 100 italic
  operator   : 0 0 128
  layout     : 63 127 95 italic

colorer System colors

  darkgreen = 0 128 0
  green     = 0 255 0
  darkblue  = 0 0 128
  blue      = 0 0 255
  ...
  default   = _
```

The generated specification can be customized on the lexical level, but also extended on the syntactic level. These extensions are based on syntactic sorts and constructor names. For example, the following specification will color numeric types in declarations in dark green:

```
module DSLbook-Colorer
imports DSLbook-Colorer.generated
colorer
  Type.NumType: darkgreen
```

Here **Type** is a sort from the syntax definition, while **NumType** is the constructor for the integer type. There are other rules for **Type** in the Mobl grammar, for example for the string type. When we want other types also to be colored dark green, we can either add more rules to the colorer specification, or replace the current definition with **Type._**, where _ acts as a wildcard and all types will be colored dark green, independent of their constructor. Similarly, we can use a wildcard for sorts. For example, **_.NumType** will include all nodes with a constructor **NumType**, independent of their syntactic sort.

In the current example, predefined types like **int** and entity types are all colored dark green, but only the predefined types will appear in bold face. This is because Spoofax combines specified colors and fonts. The rule on the syntactic level specifies only a color, but no font. Since the predefined types are keywords, they will get the font from the keyword specification, which is bold. In contrast, entity types are identifiers, which will get the default font from the identifier specification.

13.3 *Go-to-Definition and Find References*

Following a reference (go to definition, **Ctrl-Click**) as well as finding references to a given program element works automatically without any customization in any of the language workbenches. However, one might want to change the default behavior, for example because the underlying program element is not a reference at all (but you still want to go somewhere when **Ctrl-Click**ing on it).

■ *Customizing the Target with Xtext*   Let us first look at how to change the target of the go-to-definition functionality. Strictly speaking, we don't change go-to-definition at all. We just define a new hyperlinking functionality. Go-to-Definition is just the default hyperlinking behavior[15]. As a consequence:

- You can define hyperlinking for elements that are *not* references in terms of the grammar (a hyperlink can be provided for any program element).

[15] Hyperlinking gets its name from the fact that, as you mouse over an element while keeping the **Ctrl** key depressed, you see the respective element in blue and underlined. You can then click on it to follow the hyperlink

- You can have several hyperlinks for the same element. If you **Ctrl-Hover** on it, a little menu opens up and you can select the target you are interested in.

To add hyperlinks to a language concept, Xtext provides the **IHyperlinkHelper** interface, which can be implemented by language developers to customize hyperlinking behavior. It requires one method, **createHyperlinksTo**, to be implemented[16]. A typical implementation looks as follows:

[16] Typically, language developers will inherit from one of the existing base classes, such as the **TypeAwareHyperlinkHelper**.

```
public void createHyperlinksTo(XtextResource from, Region region,
                    EObject to, IHyperlinkAcceptor acceptor) {
  if ( to instanceof TheEConceptIAmInterestedIn ) {
    EObject target = // find the target of the hyperlink
    super.createHyperlinksTo(from, region, target, acceptor);
  } else {
    super.createHyperlinksTo(from, region, to, acceptor);
  }
}
```

■ *Customized Finders in MPS*   In many cases, there are different kinds of references to any given element. For example, for an **Interface** in the mbeddr C components extension, references to that interface can either be sub-interfaces (**ISomething extends IAnother**) or components, which can either *provide* an interface (so other components can call the interface's operation), or they can *require* an interface, in which case the component itself calls operations defined by the interface. When finding references, we may want to distinguish between these different cases.

MPS provides *finders* to achieve this. Fig. 13.8 shows the resulting Find Usages dialog for an **Interface** after we have implemented two custom finders in the language: one for components providing the interface, and one for components requiring the interface.

Figure 13.8: The Find Usages dialog for **Interfaces**. The two additional Finders in the top left box are contributed by the language.

Implementing finders is simple, since, as usual, MPS provides a DSL for specifying them. The following code shows the implementation.

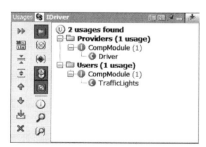

```
finder findProviders for concept Interface
  description: Providers

  find(node, scope)->void {
    nlist<> refs = execute NodeUsages ( node , <same scope> );
    foreach r in refs.select(it|it.isInstanceOf(ProvidedPort)) {
      add result r.parent ;
    }
  }

  getCategory(node)->string {
    "Providers";
  }
```

Figure 13.9: The result dialog of running Find Usages with our customized finders. Note the **Providers** and **Users** categories; these correspond to the strings returned from **getCategory** in the two finders.

We specify a name for the finder (`findProviders`) as well as the type to which it applies (references to which it will find: **Interface** in the example). We then have to implement the **find** method. Notice how in the first line of the implementation we delegate to an existing finder, **Node Usages**, which finds *all* references. We then check whether the referencing element is a **ProvidedPort**, and if so, we add the parent of the port, i.e. a **Component**, to the result[17]. Finally, `getCategory` returns a string that is use to structure the result. Fig. 13.9 shows an example result.

[17] Note how we make use of extensions to the MPS BaseLanguage to concisely specify finders: **execute** and **add result** are only available in the finder specification language.

■ *Customizing the Target with Spoofax* Spoofax provides a default hyperlinking mechanism from references to declarations. Alternative hyperlinking functionality can be implemented in rewrite rules. The names of these rules need to be specified in the editor specification. For example, the following specification tells Spoofax to use a custom rewrite rule to hyperlink **this** expressions to the surrounding class:

```
references
  reference Exp.This : resolve-this
```

On the left-hand side of the colon the **reference** rule specifies a syntactic sort and a constructor, for which the hyperlinking should be customized[18]. On the right-hand side of the colon, the rule names a rewrite rule which implements the hyperlinking:

[18] As in colorer specifications, we can use _ as a wildcard for syntactic sorts and constructors.

```
resolve-this:
    (link, position, ast, path, project-path) -> target
    where
      Entity(t)  := <type-of> link ;
      target     := <index-lookup> t
```

This rule determines the type of a *this* expression and links it to the declaration of this type[19].

13.4 Pretty-Printing

Pretty-printing refers to the reverse activity from parsing[20]. A parser transforms a character sequence into an abstract syntax tree. A pretty printer (re-)creates the text string from the AST. As the term *pretty* printing suggests, the resulting text should be *pretty*, i.e. whitespace must be managed properly.

So when and where is a formatter useful? There is the obvious use case: users somehow mess up formatting, and they want to press **Ctrl-Shift-F** to clean it up. However, there is

[19] Like all rewrite rules implementing hyperlinking functionality, the rule needs to follow a Spoofax-defined signature: on the left-hand side, it matches a tuple consisting of the **link**, the **position** of this node in the abstract syntax tree, the tree itself (**ast**), the **path** of the current file, and the path of the current Eclipse project (**project-path**). On the right-hand side, it returns the target of the hyperlink.

[20] This is also known as *serialization* or *formatting*.

more essential reason. If the AST is modified by a transformation, the updated text has to be rendered correctly. An AST is modified, for example, as part of a quick fix (see the next paragraph) or by a graphical editor that operates in parallel to a text editor on the same AST.

■ *Pretty-Printing in MPS*   In MPS, pretty-printing is a non-issue. The editor always pretty-prints as part of the projection[21]. However, version 3.0 of MPS will support the definition of several different editors for a single concept. They may be fundamentally different (e.g., providing a textual and a graphical syntax for state machines) or just provide different "layouts" for a single notation (different positions of the opening curly brace, for example). More generally, there is no reason why a projectional editor may not provide a certain degree of freedom regarding layout. Users may be able to press **ENTER** to start a new line in a long expression, or press **TAB** to indent a statement[22]. However, MPS does currently not support this.

[21] On the flip side, MPS users do not have the option of changing the layout or formatting of a program, since the projection rules implement the one true way of formatting. Of course, this can be considered a plus or a minus, depending on the context.

[22] Note that such layout information must be stored with the program, or possibly in a separate layout model. This is especially true if the notation is graphical, which will always allow some degree of custom layout and positioning of shapes

■ *Pretty-Printing in Spoofax*   Spoofax generates a language-specific rewrite rule **pp-<LanguageName>-string** which rewrites an abstract syntax tree into a string according to a pretty-printer definition (expressed in the Box language). Spoofax generates a default pretty-printer definition from the syntax definition of a language. For example, Spoofax generates the following pretty-printer definition for Mobl:

```
[
  Module                  -- KW["module"] _1 _2,
  Module.2:iter-star      -- _1,
  Import                  -- KW["import"] _1,
  Entity                  -- KW["entity"] _1 KW["{"] _2 KW["}"],
  Entity.2:iter-star      -- _1,
  Property                -- _1 KW[":"] _2,
  Function                -- KW["function"] _1 KW["("] _2 KW[")"]
                             KW[":"] _3 KW["{"] _4 KW["}"],
  Function.2:iter-star-sep -- _1 KW[","],
  Function.4:iter-star    -- _1,
  Param                   -- _1 KW[":"] _2,
  EntType                 -- _1,
  NumType                 -- KW["int"],
  BoolType                -- KW["boolean"],
  StringType              -- KW["string"],
  Declare                 -- KW["var"] _1 KW["="] _2 KW[";"],
  Assign                  -- _1 KW["="] _2 KW[";"],
  Return                  -- KW["return"] _1 KW[";"],
  Call                    -- _1 KW["."] _2 KW["("] _3 KW[")"],
  PropAccess              -- _1 KW["."] _2,
  Plus                    -- _1 KW["+"] _2,
  Mul                     -- _1 KW["*"] _2,
  Var                     -- _1,
  Int                     -- _1
]
```

In the Box language, rules consist of constructors (i.e. AS elements or language concepts) on the left-hand side of a rule and a sequence of *boxes* and numbers on the right-hand side. The basic box construct is a simple string, representing a string in the output. Furthermore, two kinds of box operators can be applied to sub-boxes: layout operators specify the layout of sub-boxes in the surrounding box, and font operators specify which font should be used. In the example, all strings are embedded in `KW[...]` boxes. `KW` is a font operator, classifying the sub-boxes as keywords of the language[23].

[23] Since font operators are only meaningful when pretty-printing to HTML or LaTeX, we do not dive into the details here.

Numbers on the right-hand side can be used to combine boxes from the subtrees: a number n refers to the boxes from the n-th subtree. When the syntax definition contains nested constructs, additional rules are generated for pretty-printing the corresponding subtrees. On the left-hand side, these rules have *selectors*, which consist of a constructor, a number selecting a particular subtree, and the type of the nesting. The following table shows all nesting constructs in syntax definitions and their corresponding types in pretty-printing rules.

Construct	Selector Type
optionals `S?`	`opt`
non-empty lists `S+`	`iter`
possibly empty lists `S*`	`iter-star`
separated lists `S1 S2+`	`iter-sep`
possibly empty separated lists `S1 S2*`	`iter-star-sep`
alternatives `S1	S2`	`alt`
sequences `(S1 S2)`	`seq`

Additionally, user-defined pretty-printing rules can be defined as well. Spoofax first applies the user-defined rules to turn an abstract syntax tree into a hybrid tree which is only partially pretty-printed. It then applies the default rules to pretty-print the remaining parts. For example, we could define our own pretty-printing rule for Mobl modules:

```
Module              -- V vs=1 is=4 [ H [KW["module"] _1] _2]
```

This rule lets Spoofax pretty-print the term `Module("shopping", [Entity(...), Entity(...)])` as

```
module shopping
    entity ...
    entity ...
```

The **V** box operator places sub-boxes vertically. In the example, it places the entities underneath the `module shopping` line. The desired vertical separation between the sub-boxes can be specified by the spacing option **vs**. Its default value is **0**; that is, no blank lines are added between the boxes. In the example, a blank line is enforced by **vs=1**. For indenting boxes in a vertical combination, the spacing option **is** can be specified. All boxes except the first will be indented accordingly. In the example, the `module shopping` line is unindented, while the entities are indented by 4 spaces. The **H** box operator lays out sub-boxes horizontally. In the example, it is used to lay out the `module` keyword and its name in the same line. The desired horizontal separation between the sub-boxes can be specified by the spacing option **hs**. Its default value is **1**; that is, a single space is added between the boxes.

■ *Pretty-Printing in Xtext*   In Xtext, the use of whitespace can be specified in a language's `Formatter`. Formatters use a Java API to specify whitespace policies for a grammar. Consider an example from the cooling language. Assume we enter the following code:

```
state Hello  : entry { if true { } }
```

If we run the formatter (e.g., by pressing **Ctrl-Shift-F** in the IDE), we want the resulting text to be formatted like this:

```
state Hello:
    entry {
        if true { }
    }
```

The following formatter code implements this.

```
protected void configureFormatting(FormattingConfig c) {
  CoolingLanguageGrammarAccess f =
      (CoolingLanguageGrammarAccess) getGrammarAccess();

  c.setNoSpace().before(
          f.getCustomStateAccess().getColonKeyword_3());
  c.setIndentationIncrement().after(
          f.getCustomStateAccess().getColonKeyword_3());
  c.setLinewrap().before(
          f.getCustomStateAccess().getEntryKeyword_5_0());

  c.setLinewrap().after(
          f.getCustomStateAccess().getLeftCurlyBracketKeyword_5_1());
  c.setIndentationIncrement().after(
          f.getCustomStateAccess().getLeftCurlyBracketKeyword_5_1());

  c.setLinewrap().before(
          f.getCustomStateAccess().getRightCurlyBracketKeyword_5_3());
  c.setIndentationDecrement().before(
          f.getCustomStateAccess().getRightCurlyBracketKeyword_5_3());
}
```

In the first line we get the `CoolingLanguageGrammarAccess` object, an API to refer to the grammar of the language itself. This API is the basis for an internal Java DSL for expressing formatting rules. Let's look at the first block of three lines. In the first line we express that there should be no space before the colon in the `CustomState` rule. Line two states that we want to have indentation after the colon. The third line specifies that the `entry` keyword should be on a new line. The next two blocks of two lines manage the indentation of the entry action code. In the first block we express a line wrap and incremented indentation after the opening curly brace. The second block expresses a wrap before the closing curly brace, as well as a decrement in the indentation level[24].

13.5 Quick Fixes

A quick fix is a semi-automatic fix for a constraint violation. It is semi-automatic in the sense that it is made available to the user in a menu, and after selecting the respective quick fix from the menu, the code that implements the quick fix rectifies the problem that caused the constraint violation[25].

■ *Quick Fixes in Xtext*   Xtext supports quick fixes for constraint violations. Quick fixes can either be implemented on the concrete syntax (i.e. via text replacement) or on the abstract syntax (i.e. via a model modification and subsequent serialization). As an example, consider the following constraint defined in the cooling language's `CoolingLanguageJavaValidator`:

```
public static final String VARIABLE_LOWER_CASE = "VARIABLE_LOWER_CASE";

@Check
public void checkVariable( Variable v ) {
    if ( !Character.isLowerCase( v.getName().charAt(0) ) ) {
        warning("Variable name should start with a lower case letter",
            al.getSymbolDeclaration_Name(), VARIABLE_LOWER_CASE );
    }
}
```

Based on our discussion of constraint checks (Section 9.1), this code should be fairly self-explanatory. What is interesting is the third argument to the `warning` method: we pass in a constant to uniquely identify the problem. The quick fix will be tied to this constant. The following code is the quick fix, implemented in the `CoolingLanguageQuickfixProvider`[26]. Notice how in the `@Fix` annotation we refer to the same constant that was used in the constraint check.

[24] As you can see, specifying the formatting for a complete grammar can require a lot of code! In my opinion, there are two approaches to improve this: one is reasonable defaults or global configurations. Curly braces, for example, are typically formatted the same way. Second, a more efficient way of specifying the formatting should be provided. Annotations in the grammar, or a DSL for specifying the formatting (such as the Box language used by Spoofax) should go a long way.

[25] Notice that a quick fix only makes sense for problems that have one or more "obvious" fixes. This is not true for all problems.

[26] This code resides in the UI part of the language, since, in contrast to the constraint check, it is relevant only in the editor.

```
@Fix(CoolingLanguageJavaValidator.VARIABLE_LOWER_CASE)
public void capitalizeName(final Issue issue,
                           IssueResolutionAcceptor acceptor) {
  acceptor.accept(issue, "Decapitalize name",
                         "Decapitalize the name.",
                         "upcase.png",
    new IModification() {
      public void apply(IModificationContext context)
                    throws BadLocationException {
        IXtextDocument xtextDocument = context.getXtextDocument();
        String firstLetter = xtextDocument.get(issue.getOffset(), 1);
        xtextDocument.replace(
            issue.getOffset(), 1, firstLetter.toLowerCase());
      }
    });
}
```

Quick fix methods accept the **Issue** that caused the problem as well as an **IssueResolutionAcceptor** that is used to register the fixes so they can be shown in the quick fix menu. The core of the fix is the anonymous instance of **IModification** that, when executed after it has been selected by the user, fixes the problem. In our example, we grab the document that contains the problem and use a text replacement API to replace the first letter of the offending variable with its lower case version.

Working on the concrete syntax level is ok for simple problems like this one. More complex problems should be solved on the abstract syntax though[27]. For these cases, one can use an instance of **ISemanticModification** instead:

[27] Imagine a problem that requires changes to the model in several places. Often it is easy to navigate to these places via the abstract syntax (following references, climbing up the tree), but finding the respective locations on the concrete syntax would be cumbersome and brittle.

```
@Fix(CoolingLanguageJavaValidator.VARIABLE_LOWER_CASE)
public void fixName(final Issue issue, IssueResolutionAcceptor acceptor) {
  acceptor.accept(issue, "Decapitalize name",
                         "Decapitalize the name",
                         "upcase.png",
    new ISemanticModification() {
      public void apply(EObject element, IModificationContext context) {
        ((Variable) element).setName(
            Strings.toFirstLower(issue.getData()[0]));
      }
    });
}
```

A quick fix using an **ISemanticModification** basically works the same way; however, inside the **apply** method we now use the EMF Java API to fix the problem[28].

■ *Quick Fixes in MPS*   Quick fixes in MPS work essentially the same way as in Xtext. Of course there are only quick fixes that act on the abstract syntax – the concrete syntax is projected in any case. Here is a constraint that checks that the name of an element that implements **INameAllUpperCase** actually consists of only upper case letters:

[28] Notice that after the problem is solved, the changed AST is serialized back into text. Depending on the scope of the change, a formatter has to be implemented for the language to make sure the resulting serialized text looks nice.

```
checking rule check_INameAllUpperCase {
  applicable for concept = INameAllUpperCase as a
```

```
  do {
    if (!(a.name.equals(a.name.toUpperCase()))) {
      warning "name should be all upper case" -> a;
    }
  }
}
```

The quick fix below upper-cases the name if necessary. The quick fix is associated with the constraint check by simply referencing the fix from the error message. Quick fixes are executed by selecting them from the intentions menu (**Alt-Enter**)[29].

[29] As discussed in Section 7.7, MPS also has intentions. These are essentially quick fixes that are not associated with an error. Instead, they can be invoked on any instance of the concept for which the intention is declared.

```
quick fix fixAllUpperCase

arguments:
  node<IIdentifierNamedConcept> node

description(node)->string {
  "Fix name";
}

execute(node)->void {
    node.name = node.name.toUpperCase();
}
```

■ *Model Synchronization via Quick Fixes*   A particularly interesting feature of MPS' quick fixes is that they can be executed *automatically* in the editor. This can be used for synchronizing different parts of a model: a constraint check detects an inconsistency in the model, and the automatically executed quick fix resolves the inconsistency.

Here is an example where this makes sense. Consider the interfaces and components extension to C. An interface declares a couple of operations, each with their own unique signature. A component that **provides** the interface has to provide implementations for each of the operations, and the implementations must have the same signature as the operation it implements. A constraint checks the consistency between interfaces and implementing components. An automatically executed quick fix adds missing (empty) operation implementations and synchronizes their signatures with the signatures of the operations in the interface.

13.6   Refactoring

Refactoring addresses changing the program structure without changing its behavior. It is typically used to "clean up" the program structure after it has gotten messy over time. While DSLs and their programs tend to be simpler than GPL programs, refactorings are still useful.

■ *Renaming in Xtext* One of the most essential refactorings is renaming a program element[30]. Xtext comes with rename refactoring out of the box, every language supports rename refactoring automatically[31]. The only thing the user has to remember is to not just type a new name, but instead invoke the Rename refactoring, for example via `Ctrl-Alt-R`.

■ *Renaming in Spoofax* Like code generators, refactorings need to be specified in the editor specification and implemented with rewrite rules. For example, the following specification specifies a refactoring for renaming entities:

```
refactorings
  refactoring Decl.Entity : "Rename Entity" = rename-entity (cursor)
    shortcut : "org.eclipse.jdt.ui.edit.text.java.rename.element"
    input
      identifier : "new name" = ""
```

[30] The reason why it is a refactoring (and not just typing a new name) is because all references to this element have to be updated. In textual languages, such references are by name, and if the name of the target element changes, so has the text of the reference.

[31] In fact, it works *across* languages and even integrates with tools that are not implemented with Xtext, such as the JDT or XMI-persisted EMF models such as GMF diagrams.

The specification starts with a syntactic sort and a constructor, on which the refactoring should be available, followed by a label for the refactoring in the context menu, the implementing rewrite rule, and two options. In the example, Spoofax is instructed to use the current `cursor` position to determine the node on which the refactoring should be applied. The specification further defines a `shortcut` for the refactoring, which should be the same key binding as the one used in the JDT for renaming. Finally, it defines an interactive `input` dialog, with a label `"new name"` and an empty default input. The refactoring itself is implemented in a rewrite rule:

Note that in a projectional editor such as MPS, renaming is not even a refactoring. A reference is established with the UUID of the target element. Renaming it does not lead to any structural change. And since the editor for the *referencing* element defines how to render the reference, it will just display the updated name if it changes.

```
rename-entity:
    (newname, Entity(name, elems), position, ast, path, project-path)
              -> ([(ast, new-ast)], errors, [], [])
    with
      new-ast := <topdown(try(rename-entity-local(|name, newname)))> ast;
      [Entity(), oldname|path] := <index-uri> name;
      if <index-lookup> [Entity(), newname|path] then
        errors := [(name, $[Entity of name [newname] already exists.])]
      else
        errors := []
      end
  rename-entity-local(|old-name, new-name):
    Entity(old-name, elems) -> Entity(new-name, elems)
  rename-entity-local(|old-name, new-name):
    EntType(old-name) -> EntType(new-name)
```

As we have seen already for other editor services, rewrite rules for refactorings have to adhere to a specific interface (i.e. signature). On the left-hand side, the example rule matches a tuple consisting of the input from the refactoring dialog (**newname**), the node on which the refactoring is applied, its **position** in the abstract syntax tree, the tree itself (**ast**), and the paths of the current file and the project. On the right-hand side, it yields a tuple consisting of a list of changes in the abstract syntax tree and lists of fatal errors, normal errors and warnings.

For simplicity, the example rule changes the whole abstract syntax tree into a new one and provides only duplicate definition errors. To do so, the new abstract syntax tree is retrieved by traversing the old one in a **topdown** fashion, **try**ing to apply rewrite rules **rename-entity-local**[32]. These rules take the old and new entity name as parameters. They ensure that declarations and references to entities are renamed. The first rule rewrites entity declarations, while the second one rewrites types of the form **EntType(name)**, where **name** refers to an entity.

[32] **try(s)** tries to apply a strategy **s** to a term. Thereby, it never fails. If **s** succeeds, it will return the result of **s**. Otherwise, it will return the original term.

An error is detected if an entity with the new name already exists. Therefore, we match the annotated URI of the old name, change it to the new name, and look it up. If we find an entity, the renamed entity would clash with the one just found.

■ *Introduce Local Variable in MPS*   A very typical refactoring for a procedural language such as C is to introduce a new local variable. Consider the following code:

```
int8 someFunction(int8 v) {
  int8 y = somethingElse(v * FACTOR);
  if ( v * FACTOR > 20 ) {
    return 1;
  } else {
    return 0;
  }
}
```

As you can see, the first two lines contain the same expression (**v * FACTOR**) twice. A nicer version of this code might look like this:

```
int8 someFunction(int8 v) {
  int8 product = v * FACTOR;
  int8 y = somethingElse(product);
  if ( product > 20 ) {
    return 1;
  } else {
    return 0;
  }
}
```

The *Introduce Local Variable* refactoring performs this change. MPS provides a DSL for refactorings, based on which the implementation is about 20 lines of code. We'll go through it in steps[33]. We start with the declaration of the refactoring itself.

[33] In the meantime, the MPS refactoring API has changed to better separate UI aspects (keystrokes, choosers) and the refactoring itself. This is important to support integration of refactorings with IntelliJ IDEA and, in the future, Eclipse. However, I decided to keep the old style, since it is a little more concise and easier to follow in the context of this example.

```
refactoring introduceLocalVariable ( "Introduce Local Variable" )

keystroke: <ctrl+alt>+<V>
target: node<Expression>
allow multiple: false

isApplicableToNode(node)->boolean {
    node.ancestor<Statement>.isNotNull;
}
```

The code above specifies the name of the refactoring (**intro-duceLocalVariable**), the label used in the refactoring menu, the keystroke to execute it directly (**Ctrl-Alt-V**) as well as the target, i.e. the language concept on which the refactoring can be executed. In our case, we want to refactor **Expression**s, but only if these expressions are used in a **Statement**[34]. We find out about that by checking whether the **Expression** has a **Statement** among its ancestors in the tree. Next, we define a parameter for the refactoring:

[34] We cannot refactor an expression if it is used, for example, as the **init** expression for a global constant.

```
parameters:
  varName chooser: type: string
                   title: Name of the new Variable
init(refactoringContext)->boolean {
  return ask for varName;
}
```

The parameter represents the name of the newly introduced variable. In the refactoring's **init** block we ask the user for this parameter[35]. We are now ready to implement the refactoring algorithm itself in the **refactor** block. We first declare two local variables that represent the expression on which we invoked the refactoring (we get it from the **refactoringContext**[36]) and the **Statement** under which this expression is located. Finally, we get the **index** of the **Statement**[37].

[35] The **ask for** expression returns **false** if the user selects **Cancel** in the dialog that prompts the user for the name. The execution of the refactoring stops in this case.

[36] If the refactoring was declared to **allow multiple**, we can use **refactoringContext.nodes** to access all of the selected nodes.

```
node<Expression> targetExpr = refactoringContext.node;
node<Statement> targetStmt = targetExpr.ancestor<Statement>;
int index = targetStmt.index;
```

[37] **.index** returns the index of an element in the collection that owns the element. It is available on any node.

Next, we iterate over all **siblings** of the statement in which the expression lives. As we do that, we look for all expressions that are structurally similar to the one we're executing the refactoring on (using **MatchingUtil.matchNodes**). We remember a matching expression if it occurs in a statement that is *after* the one that contains our target expression.

```
nlist<Expression> matchingExpressions = new nlist<Expression>;
sequence<node<>> siblings =
    targetStmt.siblings.union(new singleton<node<Statement>>(stmt));
foreach s in siblings {
  if (s.index >= index) {
    foreach e in s.descendants<Expression> {
      if (MatchingUtil.matchNodes(targetExpr, e) {
        matchingExpressions.add(e);
} } } }
```

The next step is to actually introduce the new local variable. We create a new **LocalVariableDeclaration** using the API. We set the **name** to the one we've asked the user for (**varName**), we set its type to a copy of the type calculated by the type system for the target expression, and we initialize the variable with a copy of the target expression itself. We then add this new variable to the list of statements, just *before* the one which contains our target expression. We use the **add prev-sibling** built-in function for that.

```
node<LocalVariableDeclaration> lvd = new node<LocalVariableDeclaration>();
lvd.name = varName;
lvd.type = targetExpr.type.copy;
lvd.init = targetExpr.copy;
targetStmt.add prev-sibling(lvd);
```

There is one more step we have to do. We have to replace all the occurrences of our target expression with a reference to the newly introduced local variable. We had collected the **matchingExpressions** above, so we can now iterate over this collection[38]:

```
foreach e in matchingExpressions {
  node<LocalVarRef> ref = new node<LocalVarRef>();
  ref.var = lvd;
  e.replace with(ref);
}
```

[38] Note how the actual replacement is done with the **replace with** built-in function. It comes in very handy, since we don't have to manually find out in which property or collection the expression lives in order to replace it.

All in all, building refactorings is straightforward with MPS' refactoring support. The implementation effort is reduced to essentially the algorithmic complexity of the refactoring itself. Depending on the refactoring, this can be non-trivial.

13.7 Labels and Icons

Labels and icons for language concepts are used in several places, among them the outline view and the code completion menu.

■ *Labels and Icons in Xtext* Labels and icons are defined in the language's **LabelProvider**, which is generated by Xtext for each language by default. To define the label text, you simply override the **text** method for your element, which returns either a **String** or a **StyledString** (which includes formatting information). For the icon, override the **image** method. Here are a couple of examples from the cooling language[39]:

```
public class CoolingLanguageLabelProvider
            extends DefaultEObjectLabelProvider {

    String text(CoolingProgram prg) {
```

[39] Notice how the label and the image are defined via methods, you can change the text and the icon dynamically, based on some property of the model.

```
        return "program "+prg.getName();
    }
    String image(CoolingProgram prg) {
        return "program.png";
    }
    String text(Variable v) {
        return v.getName()+": "+v.getType();
    }
    String image(Variable v) {
        return "variable.png";
    }
}
```

■ *Labels and Icons in MPS*   Labels are defined by overriding the `getPresentation` behavior method on the respective concept. This allows the label to also be adjusted dynamically. The icon can be selected in the inspector (see Fig. 13.10) if we select a language concept. The icon is fixed and cannot be changed dynamically.

Figure 13.10: Assigning an icon to a language concept.

13.8   Outline

The outline provides an overview over the contents of some part of the overall model, typically a file. By default, it usually shows more or less the AST, down to a specific level (the implementations of functions or methods are typically not shown). The contents of the outline view must be user-definable; at the very least, we have to define where to stop the tree. Also, the tree structure may be completely different from the nesting structure of the AST: the elements may have to be grouped based on their concept (first show all variables, then all functions) or they may have to be sorted alphabetically.

■ *Customizing the Structure in Xtext*   Xtext provides an `OutlineTreeProvider` for your language that can be used to customize the outline view structure (labels and icons are taken from the `LabelProvider` discussed above). As an example, let us customize the outline view for cooling programs to look the one shown in Fig. 13.11.

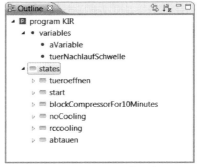

Figure 13.11: A customized outline view for cooling programs in Xtext

The tree view organizes the contents of a file by first showing all programs and then all tests. To do this, we provide a suitable implementation of `_createChildren`:

```
protected void _createChildren(DocumentRootNode parentNode, Model m) {
    for (EObject prg : m.getCoolingPrograms()) {
        createNode(parentNode, prg);
    }
    for (EObject t : m.getTests()) {
```

```
            createNode(parentNode, t);
        }
    }
```

Inside the method, we first grab all the **CoolingProgram**s from the root element **Model** and create a node for them using the **createNote** API, which takes the parent (in terms of the outline view) and the program element for which should be represented by the new outline node[40]. We then do the same for tests.

[40] The text and icon for the outline node is taken from the label provider discussed in the previous section.

Inside a program, we want to show variables and states in separate sections, i.e. under separate intermediate nodes (see Fig. 13.11). Here is how this works:

```
protected void _createChildren(IOutlineNode parentNode, CoolingProgram p) {
    TextOnlyOutlineNode vNode = new TextOnlyOutlineNode(parentNode,
                                    imageHelper.getImage("variable.png"),
                                    "variables");
    for (EObject v: p.getVariables()) {
        createNode(vNode, v);
    }
    TextOnlyOutlineNode sNode = new TextOnlyOutlineNode(parentNode,
                        imageHelper.getImage("state.png"), "states");
    for (EObject s: p.getStates()) {
        createNode(sNode, s);
    }
}
```

We introduce intermediate nodes that do not represent a program element; they are used purely for structuring the tree. The **TextOnlyOutlineNode** is a class we created; it simply extends the class **AbstractOutlineNode** provided by Xtext.

```
public class TextOnlyOutlineNode extends AbstractOutlineNode {
    protected TextOnlyOutlineNode(IOutlineNode parent,
                                Image image, Object text) {
        super(parent, image, text, false);
    }
}
```

Xtext provides alphabetical sorting for outlines by default. There is also support for styling the outline (i.e. using styled labels as opposed to simple text) as well as for filtering the tree.

■ *The Outline in Spoofax* With Spoofax, outlines can be specified declaratively in the editor specification. Abstract syntax tree nodes, which should appear in the outline, are selected based on their syntactic sort and constructor names. For example, the following outline specification will include all entity declarations[41]:

[41] As in the specification of other editor services, we can use _ as a wildcard for sorts and constructors. For example, **Decl._** will include imports and entities in the outline. Similarly, **_.Property** will include all nodes with a constructor **Property**, independent of their syntactic sort.

```
module MoblLang-Outliner

imports MoblLang-Outliner.generated

outliner Entity Outliner
```

```
Decl.Entity
```

Spoofax analyses the syntax definition and tries to come up with a reasonable default outline specification. We can then either extend the generated specification with our own rules, or create a new one from scratch.

■ *The Outline in MPS*   MPS does not have a customizable outline view. It shows the AST of the complete program as part of the project explorer, but the structure cannot be customized. However, it is of course possible to add arbitrary additional views (called *tools* in MPS) to MPS. The MPS tutorial at **bit.ly/xU78ys** shows how to implement your own outline view.

13.9   Code Folding

Code folding refers to the small minuses in the gutter of an editor that let you collapse code regions (see Fig. 13.12). The editor shows an ellipsis (...) for the folded parts of the code. Clicking on the + or on the ellipsis restores the full code.

Figure 13.12: Code folding in Xtext. If you hover over the folded code, a pop-up shows the hidden code.

[42] Xtext also automatically provides hovers for the folded contents that show the text that is "folded away".

■ *Folding in Xtext*   Xtext automatically provides folding for all language concepts that stretch over more than one line[42]. To turn off this default behavior, you have to implement your own subclass of **DefaultFoldingRegionProvider** and overwrite the method **isHandled** in a suitable way. For example, to *not* provide folding for **CustomState**s, you could do the following:

```
public class CLFoldingRegionProvider extends DefaultFoldingRegionProvider {
    @Override
    protected boolean isHandled(EObject eObject) {
        if ( eObject instanceof CustomState ) {
            return false;
        }
        return super.isHandled(eObject);
    }
}
```

■ *Folding in Spoofax*   Spoofax allows to specify folding declaratively in the editor specification. Very similar to the specification of outlines, folding is specified in terms of syntactic sort and constructor names:

```
module Mobl-Folding

folding
  Module._
  Decl.Entity
  _.Function
```

As for outlines, Spoofax analyses the syntax definition and tries to come up with a reasonable default specification. We can then either extend the generated specification with our own rules, disable particular specifications by adding a **(disabled)** annotation, or discard it completely. A **(folded)** annotation tells Spoofax to fold a node by default in a newly opened editor, which is typically seen for import sections.

■ *Folding in MPS*   In MPS, folding can be activated for any collection. For example, in a state machine, each state contains a vertical list of transitions. To enable folding for this collection, we set the **uses folding** property for the collection to **true**[43]. Once we've set the property to **true**, we have to provide a cell that is rendered if the user requests the code to be folded. This allows the text shown as an ellipses to be customized beyond just showing three dots. As Fig. 13.13 shows, we use a **read only model access** cell, which allows us to access the underlying model and return an arbitrary string. In the example, we output the number of "hidden" transitions.

[43] It can also be set to **query**, in which case code can be written that determines at runtime whether folding should be enabled or not. For example, folding could be enabled if there are more than three transitions in the state.

Figure 13.13: After **uses folding** has been set to **true** for the **transitions** collection of a **State**, we have to specify a **folded cell** which is shown in case the collection is folded. In this case we use an **R/O model access** as the folded cell which can return a (read-only) string that is projected if the collection is folded.

```
?[- entry % entryAction % -]
(- % transitions % /empty cell: * R/O model access * /folded cell: * R/O model access * -)
?[- exit ?% exitAction % -]

                                    Value:
                                    (editorContext, node)->string {
                                        "(" + node.transitions.size + " transitions ...)";
                                    }
```

MPS provides a second mechanism that can be used to the same effect. Since MPS is a projectional editor, some parts of the editor may be projected conditionally. Fig. 13.14 shows a list/tree of requirements. After pressing **Ctrl-Shift-D** on a requirement, the editor shows the requirements details (Fig. 13.15). This effect of "expanding editors" is implemented by making the detail part optional in the sense that the projection rule only shows it conditionally. Fig. 13.16 shows the editor definition.

13.10   Tooltips/Hover

A tooltip, or hover, is a small, typically yellow window that is shown if the user hovers the mouse over a program element. A hover may show the documentation of the target element, or, when hovering over a reference, some information about the referenced element.

```
functional Main: Program has to run
   functional Arg2: Argument Count
      functional FailOtherwise: Otherwise
functional Add: The program should return
   functional AddFct: Adding should be a
```

Figure 13.14: A list/tree of requirements in mbeddr.

```
functional Main: Program has to run
   functional Arg2: Argument Count must
      Additional Constraints
         none
      Additional Specifications
         none
      Description
      Some details about this requirement.
      Several lines.

      [Close]
   functional FailOtherwise: Otherwise it
functional Add: The program should return the
   functional AddFct: Adding should be a
```

Figure 13.15: Optionally, the requirement details can be shown inline.

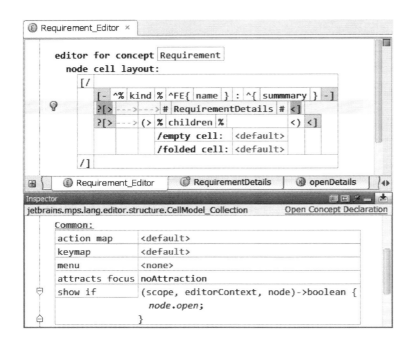

Figure 13.16: The part of the editor that includes the details pane is only projected if the **open** property is true. This property is toggled using `Ctrl-Shift-D`.

■ *Xtext* In Xtext, hovers/tooltips can be customized to various extents. The simplest customization retains the default hover structure (a one-line summary plus a more extensive documentation) and just changes the respective texts.

To change the one-line summary, you override the `getFirstLine` method in `DefaultEObjectHoverProvider` and return a custom string. The program element for which the hover should be created is represented by the `EObject` passed into the method. To customize the documentation, you override `getDocumentation` in `IEObjectDocumentationProvider`[44].

[44] Just as in any other case of Xtext framework configuration, you have to register the two classes in the UI module.

■ *Spoofax* Spoofax supports tooltips directly. Tooltips are provided by rewrite rules, which need to be defined as hovers in the editor specification:

```
hover _: editor-hovering
```

This line tells Spoofax to use a rewrite rule `editor-hovering` to retrieve tooltips for all kinds of abstract syntax tree nodes[45]. When we want to define different rewrite rules for particular constructors, we need to provide a **hover** specification for each constructor, replacing _ by _.`<Constructor>`.

The specified rewrite rules have to follow the typical editor interface on their left-hand side and need to yield strings on

[45] Note the use of the wildcard to express "all kinds of AST nodes".

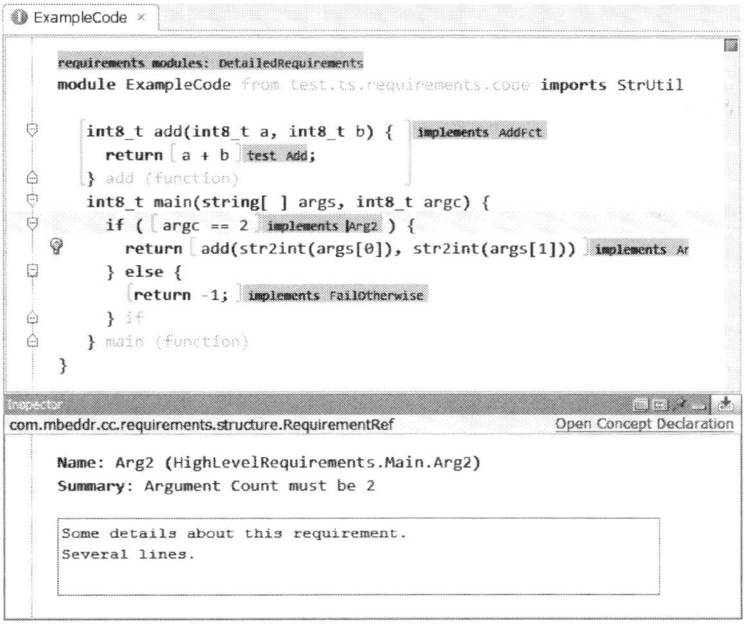

Figure 13.17: If a user selects a reference to a requirement in a requirements trace (**Arg2** in the example), the inspector shows information about the referenced requirement.

their right-hand sides. The strings are then used as tooltips. For example, the following rewrite rule will provide type information for any typeable node:

```
editor-hovering:
    (target, position, ast, path, project-path) ->
        <type-of; pp-MoblLang-string> target
```

■ *MPS* MPS does not support tooltips at this time. However, there is an acceptable workaround: any additional information for a program element can be shown in the inspector. For example, if users click on a reference to a requirement in program code, the inspector shows information about the referenced requirement (see Fig. 13.17).

Looking at the editor definition for a **RequirementRef**, you can see that the actual editor (top in Fig. 13.18) shows only the name of the referenced element. The bottom part, the **inspected cell layout**, projects the details about the referenced element.

13.11 Visualizations

To provide an overview over the structure of programs, read-only graphical representations are useful. Note that these are

```
editor for concept RequirementRef
  node cell layout:
    ( % req % -> { name } )

  inspected cell layout:
    [/
      [- Name: ( % req % -> { name } ) ( * R/O access * ) -]
      [- Summary: ( % req % -> { summmary } ) -]
      <constant>
      $swing component$
    /]
```

Figure 13.18: The editor definition for the **RequirementRef** projects details about the referenced element in the inspector. Notice the use of the **$swing component$** as a means to embed the Swing **JTextArea** that shows the prose description of the requirement. The code behind the **$swing component$** also populates the text area and writes back the changed text to the AST.

not necessarily a workaround for not having graphical editors: visualizations can provide real added value.

■ *MPS* In MPS we have integrated ZGRViewer[46], a Java-based renderer for GraphViz[47] dot files. Fig. 13.19 shows an example.

[46] **zvtm.sourceforge.net/zgrviewer.html**

[47] **www.graphviz.org/**

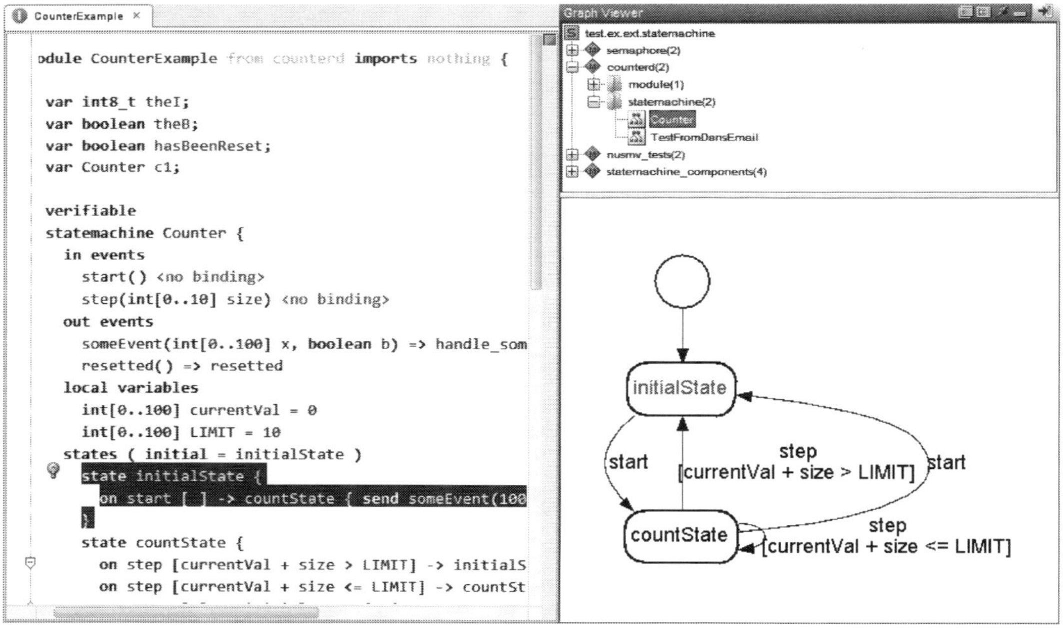

Figure 13.19: Clicking on a node in the Graph Viewer opens the respective program element in the MPS editor.

As part of the transformations, we map the model to another model expressed in a graph description language. This model is then generated into a **dot** file. The graph viewer scans the output directory for **dot** files and shows them in the tree view at the top. Double-clicking on a graph node in the tree opens a rendered **dot** file in the graph view.

■ *Xtext*   In Xtext, Jan Koehnlein's Generic Graph View[48] can be used to render diagrams of Xtext models in real-time – the Generic Graph View is an interpreter, so changes in the model lead to updates in the graph immediately.

The mapping from the model to the graph is expressed with an Xtext-based mapping DSL that extends Xbase (Xtext's reusable expression language), which means you can use Xbase expressions to traverse and query the model you want to visualize (in Fig. 13.20 an example would be the **this.eSuperTypes()** expression). In addition, a separate styling DSL supports the definition of shapes, colors and line styles. Double-clicking a node in the graph opens the corresponding program element in the Xtext editor.

13.12 Diff and Merge

Highlighting the differences between versions of a program and allowing the resolution of conflicts is important in the context of version control integration. For tools like Xtext or Spoofax that store models as plain text this is a non-issue: existing diff/merge tools can be used, be they in the IDE or on the command line.

For projectional editors such as MPS, the story is more complicated. Since they store the programs based on the abstract syntax (e.g., using XML), diff and merge have to be performed on the concrete projected syntax. MPS provides this feature (see Fig. 7.7 for an example). MPS also annotates the editor with gutter annotations that highlight whether a part of the program has changed relative to the last checkout.

[48] **github.com/JanKoehnlein/Generic-Graph-View**

```
diagram EClassHierarchy type EClass {
  node EClassNode for this {
    label Name for this
    edge SuperType for each
           this.getESuperTypes() {
      => call EClassNode for this
    }
  }
}
```

```
stylesheet EClassHierarchy
  for EClassHierarchy

style EClassNode.SuperType {
  var arrow = new PolygonDecoration()
  arrow.setScale(10,10)
  arrow.backgroundColor = color(#ffffff)
  arrow.lineWidth = 2
  this.targetDecoration = arrow
}
style EClassNode.Name {
  font = font("Helvetica", 13,
    if (element.abstract) 3 else 1)
}
```

Figure 13.20: A model-to-graph mapping and a style definition expressed with the Generic Graph Viewer DSLs by Jan Koehnlein.

14
Testing DSLs

All the aspects of DSL implementation we have discussed so far need to be tested to keep them stable. In this chapter we address testing of the language syntax, the constraints and the semantics, as well as some of the editor services, based on examples with Xtext, MPS and Spoofax. We conclude the chapter with a brief look at "testing" a language for appropriateness relative to the domain.

DSL testing is a multi-faceted problem, since it needs to address all the aspects of the DSL implementation we have discussed so far. In particular, this includes the syntax, the constraints and type system, as well as the execution semantics (i.e. transformations or interpreters). Here are some examples:

- Can the syntax cover all required sentences? Is the concrete syntax "correct"?

- Do the scopes work correctly?

- Do the constraints work? Are all "wrong" programs actually detected, and is the right error message attached to the right program element?

- are the semantics correct? Do transformations, generators and interpreters work correctly?

- Can all programs relevant to the users actually be expressed? Does the language cover the complete domain?

An important ingredient to testing is that test execution can be automated via scripts, so they can be run as part of automatic builds. All the test strategies shown below can be executed from `ant` scripts. However, we don't describe in detail how this works for each of the tools.

14.1 Syntax Testing

Testing the syntax is simple in principle. Developers simply try to write a large set of relevant programs and see if they can be expressed with the language. If not, the concrete syntax is incomplete. We may also want to try to write "wrong" programs and check that the errors are detected, and that meaningful error messages are reported.

■ *An Example with Xtext* The following piece of code is the fundamental code that needs to be written in Xtext to test a DSL program using the Xtext testing utilities[1]. It is a JUnit 4 test case (with special support for the Xtext infrastructure[2]), so it can be run as part of Eclipse's JUnit integration.

```
@RunWith(XtextRunner.class)
@InjectWith(CoolingLanguageInjectorProvider.class)
public class InterpreterTests extends XtextTest {

    @Test
    public void testET0() throws Exception {
        testFileNoSerializer("interpreter/engine0.cool", "
                tests.appl", "stdparams.cool" );
    }

}
```

[1] code.google.com/a/eclipselabs .org/p/xtext-utils/wiki/ , Unit_Testing; more testing utilities for Xtext can be found in the `org.eclipse.xtext.junit4` package.

[2] It is tested with Xtext 2.x.

The single test method loads the `interpreter/engine0.cool` program, as well as two more files which contain elements referenced from `engine0.cool`. The `testFileNoSerializer` method loads the file, parses it and checks constraints. If either parsing or constraint checking fails, the test fails[3].

On a more fine-grained level it is often useful to test partial sentences instead of complete sentences or programs. The following piece of Xtext example code tests the `CustomState` parser rule:

```
@Test
public void testStateParserRule() throws Exception {
    testParserRule("state s:",
                "CustomState" );
    testParserRule("state s: entry { do fach1->anOperation }",
                "CustomState" );
    testParserRule("state s: entry { do fach1->anOperation }",
                "State" );
}
```

[3] There is also a `testFile` method which, after loading and parsing the file, reserializes the AST to the text file, writes it back, and loads it again, thus comparing the two ASTs. This way, the (potentially adapted) formatter is tested. Note that for testing the formatting, a text comparison is the only way to go, even though we argue against text comparison in general.

The first line asserts that the string `state s:` can be parsed with the `CustomState` parser rule. The second line passes in a more complex state, one with a command in an entry action. Line three tries the same text with the `State` rule, which itself calls the `CustomState`[4].

[4] These tests really just test the parser. No linking or constraints checks are performed. This is why we can "call" `anOperation` on the `fach1` object, although `anOperation` is not defined as a callable operation anywhere.

■ *An Example with Spoofax* Spoofax supports writing tests for language definitions using a testing language. Consider the following test suite:

```
module example
language MoblEntities

test empty module [[module foo]] parse succeeds
test missing layout (module name) [[modulefoo]] parse fails
```

The first two lines specify the name of the test suite and the language under test. The remaining lines specify positive and negative test cases concerning the language's syntax. Each test case consists of a name, the to-be-tested code fragment in double square brackets, and a specification that determines what kind of test should be performed (**parsing**) and what the expected outcome is (**succeeds** or **fails**). We can also specify the expected abstract syntax based on the ATerm textual notation:

```
test empty module (AST) [[module foo]] parse to Module("foo", [])
```

Instead of specifying a complete abstract syntax tree, we can only specify the interesting parts in a pattern. For example, if we only want to verify that the definition list of an empty module is indeed empty, we can use _ as a wildcard for the module name:

```
test empty module (AST) [[module foo]] parse to Module(_, [])
```

Abstract syntax patterns are particularly useful for testing operator precedence and associativity:

```
test multiply and add [[1 + 2 * 3]] parse to Add(_, Mul(_, _))
test add and multiply [[1 * 2 + 3]] parse to Add(Mul(_, _), _)
test add and add [[1 + 2 + 3]] parse to Add(Add(_, _), _)
```

Alternatively, we can specify an equivalent concrete syntax fragment instead of an abstract syntax pattern:

```
test multiply and add [[1 + 2 * 3]] parse to [[1 + (2 * 3)]]
test add and multiply [[1 * 2 + 3]] parse to [[(1 * 2) + 3]]
test add and add [[1 + 2 + 3]] parse to [[(1 + 2) + 3]]
```

A test suite can be run from the *Transform* menu. This will open the *Spoofax Test Runner View*, which provides information about failing and succeeding test cases in a test suite. Fig. 14.1 shows an example. Additionally, we can also get instant feedback while editing a test suite. Tests can also be evaluated outside the IDE, for example as part of a continuous integration setup.

■ *Syntax Testing with MPS* Syntax testing in the strict sense is not useful or necessary with MPS, since it is not possible to "write text that does not parse". Invalid programs cannot even

Figure 14.1: Spoofax Test Runner View showing success and failure of test cases in a test suite.

be entered. However, it is useful to write a set of programs which the language developer considers relevant. While it is not possible to write syntactically invalid programs, the following scenario is possible (and useful to test): a user writes a program with the language in version 1. The language evolves to version 2, making that program invalid. In this case, the program contains unbound language concepts or "holes". By running the model checker (interactively or via **ant**), such problems can be detected. Fig. 14.2 shows an example.

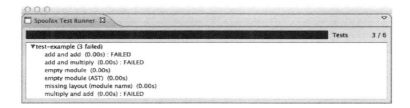

Figure 14.2: *Top:* an interface expressed in the mbeddr C components extension. *Bottom:* The same interface after we have removed the **parameters** collection in an **Operation**. The error reports that the model contains child nodes in a child collection that does not exist.

14.2 Constraints Testing

Testing of constraints is essential, especially for languages with complex constraints, such as those implied by type systems. The goal of constraints testing is to ensure that the correct error messages are annotated to the correct program elements, if those program elements have a constraint or type error.

■ *An Example with Xtext*   A special API is necessary to be able to verify that a program which makes a particular constraint fail actually annotates the corresponding error message to the respective program element. This way, tests can then be written which assert that a given program has a specific set of error annotations.

The unit testing utilities mentioned above also support testing constraints. The utilities come with an internal Java DSL that supports checking for the presence of error annotations after parsing and constraint-checking a model file.

```
@Test
public void testTypesOfParams() throws Exception {
    testFileNoSerializer("typesystem/tst1.cool", "tests.appl", "stdparams.
      cool");
    assertConstraints( issues.sizeIs(3) );                                    // 1
    assertConstraints( issues.forElement(Variable.class, "v1").              // 2
      theOneAndOnlyContains("incompatible type") );                          // 2
    assertConstraints( issues.under(Variable.class, "w1").                   // 3
      errorsOnly().sizeIs(2).oneOfThemContains("incompatible type") ); // 3
}
```

We first load the model file that contains constraint errors (in this case, type system errors). Then we assert the total number of errors in the file to be three (line 1)[5]. Next, in line 2, we check that the instance of **Variable** named **v1** has exactly one error annotation, and that it has the text "incompatible type" in the error message. Finally, in line 3 we assert that there are exactly two errors anywhere under (i.e. in the subtree below) a **Variable** named **w1**, and one of these contains "incompatible type" in the error message. Using the fluent API style shown by these examples, it is easy to express errors and their locations in the program. If a test fails, a meaningful error message is output that supports localizing (potential) problems in the test. The following is the error reported if no error message is found that contains the substring *incompatible type*:

[5] This makes sure that the file does not contain *additional* errors beyond those asserted in the rest of the test case.

```
junit.framework.AssertionFailedError: <no id> failed
  - failed oneOfThemContains: none of the issues
    contains substring 'incompatible type'
  at junit.framework.Assert.fail(Assert.java:47)
  at junit.framework.Assert.assertTrue(Assert.java:20)
  ...
```

A test may also fail earlier in the chain of filter expressions if, for example, there is no **Variable** named **v1** in the program. More output is provided in this case:

```
junit.framework.AssertionFailedError: <no id> failed
  - no elements of type
    com.bsh.pk.cooling.coolingLanguage.Variable named 'v1' found
  - failed oneOfThemContains: none of the issues
    contains substring 'incompatible type'
  at junit.framework.Assert.fail(Assert.java:47)
  ...
```

Scopes can be tested in the same way: we can write example programs where references point to valid targets (i.e. those in scope) and invalid targets (i.e. not in scope). Valid references may not have errors, invalid references must have errors[6].

[6] The absence or presence of these errors can be tested in the same way as the constraint checking tests discussed above.

■ *An Example with MPS* MPS comes with the **NodesTestCase** for testing constraints and type system rules (Fig. 14.3). It supports special annotations to express assertions on types and errors, directly in the program. For example, the third line of the nodes section in Fig. 14.3 reads **var double d3 = d** without annotations. This is a valid variable declaration in mbeddr C. After this has been written down, annotations can be added. They are rendered in green (gray in the hardcopy version of the book). Line three asserts that the type of the variable **d** is **double**, i.e. it tests that variable references assume the type of the referenced variable. In line four we assign a **double** to an

int, which is illegal according to the typing rules. The error is detected, hence the red underline. We use another annotation to assert the presence of the error.

```
Test case testSubtyping
nodes
  ( [ <check types module TestSubtyping imports nothing { > ] )
                <dnode   double d = 10;>
                double d2 = <dref  d>;
                double d3 = <node d has type double>;
                int8 i = <node d has error>;
              }
test methods
  test testReference {
    assert dref.var == dnode;
  }
```

Figure 14.3: Using MPS **NodesTestCase**, assertions about types and the presence of errors can be directly annotated on programs written in any language.

In addition to using these annotations to check types and typing errors, developers can also write more detailed test cases about the structure or the types of programs. In the example we assert that the **var** reference of the node referred to as **dref** points to the node labeled as **dnode**. Note how labels (green, underlined) are used to add names to program elements so they can be referred to from test expressions. This approach can be used to test scopes. If two variables with the same name are defined (e.g., because one of them is defined in an outer block, and we assume that the inner variable shadows the outer variable of the same name), we can use this mechanism to check that a reference actually points to the inner variable. Fig. 14.4 shows an example.

■ *An Example with Spoofax*   In Spoofax' testing language, we can write test cases which specify the number of errors and warnings in a code fragment:

```
test duplicate entities [[
  module foo
  entity X {}
  entity X {}
]] 1 error

test lower case entity name [[
  module foo
  entity x {}
]] 1 warning
```

Additionally, we can specify parts of the error or warning messages using regular expressions:

```
test duplicate entities [[
  module foo
```

```
Test case testShadowing
nodes
  ( [ module dummy imports nothing { ] )

    void aFunction() {
      <outerX  int8_t x = 0;>
      if ( true ) {
        <innerX   int8_t x = 0;>
        <xRef  x>++;
      } if
    } aFunction (function)
  ]}

test methods
  test testShadowing {
    assert xRef.var == innerX;
  }
```

Figure 14.4: Labels and test methods can be used to check that scoping works. In this example, we check shadowing of variables.

```
  entity X {}
  entity X {}
]] 1 error /duplicate/
```

Here, **/duplicate/** is a regular expression that matches error messages like "Duplicate definition of X". As in Xtext and MPS, we can test scopes by means of correct and incorrect references. Alternatively, we can specify the source and target of a link in a test case:

```
test property reference [[
  module foo
  entity X {
    [[p]]: int
    function f(q: int) {
      r: int = 0;
      return [[p]];
    }
  }
]] resolve #2 to #1

test parameter reference [[
  module foo
  entity X {
    p: int
    function f([[p]]: int) {
      r: int = 0;
      return [[p]];
    }
  }
]] resolve #2 to #1

test variable reference [[
  module foo
  entity X {
    p: int
    function f(q: int) {
      [[p]]: int = 0;
      return [[p]];
    }
  }
]] resolve #2 to #1
```

These cases use double square brackets to select parts of the program and specify the expected reference resolving in terms of these selections.

14.3 Semantics Testing

Fundamentally, testing the execution semantics of a program involves writing assertions against the *execution* of a program[7]. In the simplest case this can be done the following way:

- Write a DSL program, based on an understanding what the program is expected to do.

- Generate the program into its executable representation.

[7] While this sounds fancy, this is close to what we do in unit testing "normal" programs. We write a system in a programming language X, and then write more code in X that states assertions about what the system does.

- *Manually* write unit tests (in the target language) that assert the generated program's behavior based on the understanding of what the DSL program should do.

Notice how we do *not* test the structure or syntax of the generated artifact. Instead we test its meaning, which is exactly what we *want* to test. An important variation of this approach is the following: instead of writing the unit tests manually in the target language, we can also write the tests in the DSL, assuming the DSL has syntax to express such tests[8]. Writing the test cases on DSL level results in more concise and readable tests.[9]

The same approach can be used to test execution semantics based on an interpreter, although it may be a little more difficult to manually write the test cases in the target language; the interpreter must provide a means to "inspect" its execution so that we can check whether it is correct. If the tests are written in the DSL and the interpreter executes them along with the core program, the approach works well.

Strictly speaking, the approach discussed here tests the semantics of a *specific* program. As always in testing, we have to write many of these tests to make sure we have covered all[10] of the possible executions paths through a generator or interpreter. If we do that, the set of tests implicitly tests the generator or interpreter – which is the goal we want to achieve in semantics testing.

If we have several execution backends, such as an interpreter *and* a compiler, it must be ensured that both have the same semantics. This can be achieved by writing the tests in the DSL and then executing them in *both* backends. By executing enough tests, we can get a high degree of confidence that the semantics of the backends are aligned.

■ *Testing an Interpreter with Xtext* The cooling language provides a way of expressing test cases for the cooling programs within the cooling language itself[11]. These tests are executed with an interpreter inside the IDE, and they can also be executed on the level of the C program, by generating the program *and* the test cases to C[12]. The following code shows one of the simplest possible cooling programs, as well as a test case for that program:

```
cooling program EngineProgram0 for Einzonengeraet uses stdlib {
    var v: int
    event e1
```

[8] Many DSLs are explicitly extended to support writing tests.

[9] Testing DSL programs by running tests expressed in the same language runs the risk of doubly-negating errors. If the generators for the tests and the core program are wrong in a "consistent" way, errors in either one may not be found. However, this problem can be alleviated by running a large enough number of tests and/or by having the generators for the core system and for the test cases written by different (groups of) people.

[10] There may actually be an infinite number of possible execution paths, so we have to limit ourselves to a reasonable set of tests.

[11] Strictly speaking, tests are a separate viewpoint to keep them out of the actual programs.

[12] Note that this approach is not restricted to testing interpreters or generators – it can also be used to test whether a program written in the DSL works correctly. This is in fact why the interpreter and the test sublanguage have been built in the first place: DSL users should be able to test the programs written in the DSL.

```
    init { set v = 1 }

    start:
        entry { set v = v * 2 }
        on e1 { state s2 }
    state s2:
        entry { set v = 0 }
}

test EngineTest0 for EngineProgram0 {
    assert-currentstate-is ^start     // 1
    assert-value v is 2               // 2
    step                              // 3
    event e1                          // 4
    step                              // 5
    assert-currentstate-is s2         // 6
    assert-value v is 0               // 7
}
```

The test first asserts that, when the program starts, it is in the **start** state (line 1 in the comments in the test script). We then assert that **v** is **2**. The only reasonable way in which **v** can become **2** is that the code in the **init** block, as well as the code in the entry action of the **start** start, have been executed[13]. We then perform one step in the execution of the program in line 3. At this point nothing should happen, since no event was triggered. Then we trigger the event **e1** (line 4) and perform another **step** (line 5). After this step, the program must transition to the state **s2**, whose entry action sets **v** back to 0. We assert both of these in lines 6 and 7.

[13] Note that this arrangement even checks that the **init** block is executed before the entry action of the start state, since otherwise **v** would be **0**!

These tests can be run interactively from the IDE, in which case assertion failures are annotated as error marks on the program, or from within JUnit. The following piece of code shows how to run the tests from JUnit.

```
@RunWith(XtextRunner.class)
@InjectWith(CoolingLanguageInjectorProvider.class)
public class InterpreterTests extends PKInterpreterTestCase {

    @Test
    public void testET0() throws Exception {
        testFileNoSerializer("interpreter/engine0.cool",
            "tests.appl", "stdparams.cool" );
        runAllTestsInFile( (Model) getModelRoot());
    }
}
```

The code above is basically a JUnit test that inherits from a base class that helps with loading models and running the interpreter. We call the **runAllTestsInFile** method, passing in the model's root element. **runAllTestsInFile** is defined by the **PKInterpreterTestCase** base class, which in turn inherits from **XtextTest**, which we have seen before. The method iterates over all tests in the model and executes them by creating and running a **TestExecutionEngine**[14].

[14] The **TestExecutionEngine** is a wrapper around the interpreter for cooling programs that we have discussed before.

```
protected void runAllTestsInFile(Model m) {
    CLTypesystem ts = new CLTypesystem();
    EList<CoolingTest> tests = m.getTests();
    for (CoolingTest test : tests) {
        TestExecutionEngine e = new TestExecutionEngine(test, ts);
        final LogEntry logger = LogEntry.root("test execution");
        LogEntry.setMostRecentRoot(logger);
        e.runTest(logger);
    }
}
```

The cooling programs are generated to C for execution in the refrigerator. To make sure the generated C code has the same semantics as the interpreter, we simply generate C code from the test cases as well. In this way the same tests are executed against the generated C code. By ensuring that all of them work in the interpreter and the generator, we ensure that both behave in the same way.

■ *Testing a Generator with MPS*   The following is a test case expressed using the testing extension of mbeddr C. It contributes **test case**s to modules[15]. **testMultiply** is the actual test case. It calls the to-be-tested function **times2** several times with different arguments and then uses an **assert** statement to check for the expected value.

[15] Instead of using a separate viewpoint for expressing test cases, these are inlined into the same program in this case. However, the *language* for expressing test cases is a modular extension to C, to keep the core C clean.

```
module UnitTestDemo {

  int32 main(int32 argc, int8*[ ] argv) {
    return test testMultiply;
  }

  test case testMultiply {
    assert (0) times2(21) == 42;
    assert (1) times2(0) == 0;
    assert (2) times2(-10) == -20;
  }

  int8 times2(int8 a) {
    return 2 * a;
  }
}
```

Note that, while this unit testing extension can be used to test any C program, we use it a lot to test the generator. Consider the following example:

```
assert (0) 4 * 3 + 2 == 14;
```

One problem we had initially in mbeddr C was to make sure that the expression tree that was created while manually entering expressions like **4 * 3 + 2** is built correctly in terms of operator precedence. If the tree was built incorrectly, the generated code could end up as **4 * (3 + 2)**, resulting in 20. So we've used tests like these to implicitly test quite intricate aspects of our language implementation[16].

[16] This is also the reason why the unit test extension was the first extension we built for C: we needed it to test many other aspects of the language.

We have built much more elaborate support for testing various other extensions. It is illustrative to take a look at two of them. The next piece of code shows a test for a state machine:

```
exported test case test1 {
  initsm(c1);
  assert (0) isInState<c1, initialState>;
  test statemachine c1 {
    start  -> countState
    step(1) -> countState
    step(2) -> countState
    step(7) -> countState
    step(1) -> initialState
  }
}
```

c1 is an instance of a state machine. After initializing it, we assert that it is in the **initialState**. We then use a special **test statemachine** statement, which consists of event/state pairs: after triggering the event (on the left side of the **->**) we expect the state machine to go into the state specified on the right side of the **->**. We could have achieved the same goal by using sequences of **trigger** and **assert** statements, but the syntax used here is much more concise.

The second example concerns mocking. A mock is a part of a program that can be used in place of the real one. It simulates some kind of environment of the unit under test, and it can also verify that some other part of the system under test behaves as expected[17]. We use this with the components extension. The following is a test case that checks if the **client** uses the **PersistenceProvider** interface correctly. Let's start by taking a look at the interface:

[17] See Wikipedia for a more elaborate explanation of mocks: **en.wikipedia.org/wiki/ Mock_object**

```
interface PersistenceProvider {
  boolean isReady()
  void store(DataPacket* data)
  void flush()
}
```

The interface is expected to be used in the following way: clients first have to call **isReady**, and only if that method returns **true** are they supposed to call **store**, and then after any number of calls to **store**, they have to call **flush**. Let us assume now we want to check if a certain client component uses the interface correctly[18]. Assuming the component provides an operation **run** that uses the persistence provider, we could write the following test:

[18] Our components language actually also supports protocol state machines which support the declarative specification of valid call sequences.

```
exported test case runTest {
  client.run();
  // somehow check is behaved correctly
}
```

To check whether the client behaves correctly, we can use a mock. Our mock specifies the *incoming* method calls it expects to see during the test. We have provided a mocking extension to components to support the declarative specification of such expectations. Here is the mock:

```
exported mock component PersistenceMock {
  ports:
    provides PersistenceProvider pp
  expectations:
    total no. of calls: 4
    sequence {
      0: pp.isReady return false;
      1: pp.isReady return true;
      2: pp.store {
          0: parameter data: data != null
        }
      3: pp.flush
    }
}
```

The mock provides the **PersistenceProvider** interface, so any other component that **requires** this interface can use this component as the implementation. But instead of actually implementing the operations prescribed by **PersistenceProvider**, we specify the sequence of invocations we expect to see. We expect a total number of 4 invocations. The first one is expected to be to **isReady**. We return **false**, expecting the client to try again later. If it does, we return **true** and expect the client to continue with persisting data. We can now validate the mock as part of the test case:

```
exported test case runTest {
  client.run();
  validate mock persistenceMock
}
```

If the **persistenceMock** saw behavior different from the one specified above, the **validate mock** statement will fail, and with it the whole test[19].

One particular challenge with this approach to semantics testing is that, if an assertion fails, you get some kind of **assertion XYZ failed at ABC** output from the running test case. To understand and fix the problem, you will have to navigate back to the **assert** statement in the DSL program. If you have many failed assertions, or just generally a lot of test program output, this can be tedious and error-prone. For example, the following piece of code shows the output from executing an mbeddr **test case** on the command line:

[19] The generator for mock components translates the expectations into implementations of the interface methods that track and record invocations. The **validate mock** statement works with this recorded data to determine whether the expectations were met.

```
./TestHelperTest
$$runningTest: running test () @TestHelperTest:test_testCase1
    :0#767515563077315487
```

```
$$FAILED: ***FAILED*** (testID=0) @TestHelperTest:f:0#9125142491355884683
$$FAILED: ***FAILED*** (testID=1) @TestHelperTest:f:1#9125142491355901742
```

We have built a tool in mbeddr that simplifies finding the message source. You can paste arbitrary text that contains error messages into a text area (such as the example above) on the left in Fig. 14.5. Pressing the **Analyze** button will find the nodes that created a particular message[20]. You can then click on the node to select it in the editor.

[20] This process is based on the unique node ID; this is the long number that follows the # in the message text.

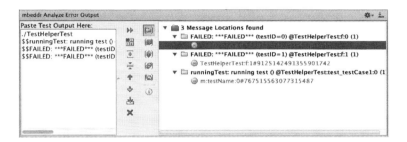

Figure 14.5: The mbeddr error output analyzer parses test output and supports navigating to the source of error messages in the MPS program.

■ *Testing Interpreters and Generators with Spoofax* Spoofax' testing language also supports testing transformations. We use it to test interpreters, assuming that the interpreter is implemented as a transformation from programs to program results. For example, the following tests address a transformation **eval-all**, which interprets expressions:

```
test evaluate addition [[1+2]] run eval-all to [[3]]
test evaluate multiplication [[3*4]] run eval-all to [[12]]
test complex evaluation [[1+2*(3+4)]] run eval-all to [[15]]
```

To test generators, we can rely on Spoofax' testing support for builders. For example, the following tests use a builder **generate-and-execute**, which generates code from expressions, runs the code, and returns the result of the run as a string:

```
test generate addition [[1+2]] build generate-and-execute to "3"
test generate multiplication [[3*4]] run generate-and-execute to "12"
test generate evaluation 1 [[1+2*(3+4)]] run generate-and-execute to "15"
```

■ *Structural Testing* What we suggested in the previous subsection tests the execution semantics of programs written in DSLs, and, if we have enough of these tests, the correctness of the transformation, generator or interpreter. However, there is a significant limitation to this approach: it only works if the DSL actually specifies behavior! If the DSL only specifies structures and cannot be executed, the approach does not work. In this case you have to perform a structural test. In principle, this is simple: you write an example model, you generate it[21], and then you inspect the resulting model or test for the expected structures. Depending on the target formalism, you can use regular expressions, XPath expressions or OCL-like expressions to automate the inspection[22].

Structural testing can also be useful to test model-to-model transformations[23]. Consider the example in Section 11.2.2. There, we inserted additional states and transitions into whatever input state machine our transformation processed. Testing this via execution invariably tests the model-to-model transformation as well as the generator (or interpreter). If we wanted to test the model-to-model transformation in isolation, we have to use structural testing, because the result of that transformation itself is not yet executable. The following piece of Xtend code could be used to check that, for a specific input program, the transformation works correctly:

[21] I have never seen an interpreter to process languages that only specify structures

[22] Note that you really should only use this if you cannot use semantics testing based on execution. Inspecting the generated C code for syntactic correctness, based on the input program, would be much more work. And if we evolve the generator to generate better (faster, smaller, more robust) code, tests based on the execution semantics will still work, while those that test the structure may fail because line numbers or variable names change.

[23] If a program is transformed to an executable representation in several steps, then the approach discussed above tests *all transformations in total*, so it is more like an integration test, and not a unit test. Depending on the complexity and the reuse potential of the transformation steps, it may make sense to test each transformation in isolation.

```
// run transformation
val tp = p.transform

// test result structurally
val states = tp.states.filter(typeof(CustomState))
assert( states.filter(s|s.name.equals("EMERGENCY_STOP")).size == 1 )

val emergencyState = states.findFirst(s|s.name.equals("EMERGENCY_STOP"))
states.findFirst(s|s.name.equals("noCooling")).eAllContents.
    filter(typeof(ChangeStateStatement)).
        exists(css|css.targetState == emergencyState)
```

This program first runs the transformation, and then finds all **CustomState**s (those that are not start or stop states). We then assert that in those states there is exactly one with the name **EMERGENCY_STOP**, because we assume that the transformation has added this state. We then check that in the (one and only) **noCooling** state there's at least one **ChangeStateState- ment** whose target state is the **emergencyState** we had retrieved above[24].

[24] Notice that we don't write an algorithmic check that closely resembles the transformation itself. Rather, we test a specific model for the presence of specific structures. For example, we explicitly look for a state called **noCooling** and check that this one has the correct **ChangeStateStatement**.

14.4 Formal Verification

Formal verification can be used in addition to semantics testing in some cases. The fundamental difference between testing and verification is this: in testing, each test case specifies *one* particular execution scenario. To get reasonable coverage of the whole model or transformation, you have to write and execute a lot of tests. This can be a lot of work, and, more importantly, you may not think about certain (exceptional) scenarios, and hence you may not test them. Bugs may go unnoticed.

Verification checks *the whole program* at once. Various non-trivial algorithms are used to do that[25], and understanding these algorithms in detail is beyond the scope of this book. Also, formal verification has inherent limitations (e.g., the halting problem) that can only be solved by testing. So testing and verification each have sweet spots: neither can fully replace the other. However, it is very useful to know that verification approaches exist, especially since, over the last couple of years, they have become scalable enough to address real-world problems. In this section we look at two examples from mbeddr: model checking and SMT solving.

■ *Model Checking State Machines*   Model Checking is a verification technique for state machines. Here is how it works in principle[26]:

- Some functionality is expressed as a state machine.

- You then specify *properties* about the behavior of the state machine. Properties are expressions that have to be true for every execution of the state machine[27].

- You then run the model checker with the state machine and the properties as input.

- The output of the model checker either confirms that your properties hold, or it shows a counter example[28].

Conceptually, the model checker performs an exhaustive search during the verification process. Obviously, the more complex your state machine is, the more possibilities the checker has to address – a problem known as *state space explosion*. With finite memory, this limits scalability, because at some point you will out of memory, or the verification will run for an unacceptably long time. In reality the model checker does *not* perform an exhaustive search; clever algorithms have been devised that are semantically equivalent to an exhaustive search, but don't actually perform one[29]. This makes model checking scalable and fast enough for real-world problems, although there is still a limit in terms of input model complexity[30].

The interesting aspect of model checking is that the properties you specify are not just simple Boolean expressions such as *each state must have at least one outgoing transition, unless it is*

[25] These include model checking, SAT solving, SMT solving or abstract execution.

[26] In this section we can only scratch the surface; to learn more about model checking, we recommend
Berard, B., Bidoit, M., Finkel, A., Laroussinie, F., Petit, A., Petrucci, L., Schnoebelen, and P. *Systems and Software Verification.* Springer, 2001

[27] For example, such a property could state that whenever you go to state **X**, you will have been in state **Y** directly beforehand.

[28] It may also run out of memory, in which case you have to reformulate or modularize your program and try again.

[29] For example, *bounded* model checking searches for counterexamples only for a bounded set of execution steps. If no counterexample is found within the bounds, the model checker assumes (rightly on not) that the property holds.

[30] Sometimes input models have to be reformulated in a way that makes them better suited for model checking. All in all, model checking is not a trivial technique. However, if and when it is better integrated with the development tools (as we show here), it could be used in many places where today it isn't even considered.

a stop state. Such a check can be performed statically, as part of the constraint checks. The properties addressed by model checkers are more elaborate and are often typically expressed in (various flavors of) temporal logic[31]. Here are some examples, expressed in plain English:

- *It is always true that after we have been in state X we will eventually be reaching state Y*. This is a *Fairness* property. It ensures that the state machine does not get stuck in some state forever. For example, **state Y** may be the green light for pedestrians, and **state X** could be the green light for cars.

- *Wherever we are in the state machine, it is always possible to get into state X*. This is a *Liveliness* property. An example could be a system that you must always be able to turn off.

- *It is not ever possible to get into state X without having gone through state Y before*. This is a *Safety* property. Imagine a state machine where entering state **X** turns the pedestrian lights green and entering state **X** turns the car lights red.

The important property of these temporal logic specifications is that quantifiers such as *always*, *whenever* and *there exists* are available. Using these, one can specify global truths about the *execution* of a system – rather than about its structure[32].

Model checking does come with its challenges. The input language for specifying state machines as well as specifying the properties is not necessarily easy to work with. Interpreting the results of the model checker can be a challenge. And for some of the tools, the usability is really bad[33].

To make model checking more user friendly, the mbeddr C language provides a nice syntax for state machines, then generates the corresponding representation in the input language of the model checker[34]. The results of running the model checker are also reinterpreted in the context of the higher-level state machine. Tool integration is provided as well: users can select the context menu on a state machine and invoke the model checker. The model checker input is generated, the model checker is executed, and the replies are rendered in a nice table in MPS. Finally, we have abstracted the property specification language by providing support for the most important idioms[35]; these can be specified relatively easily (for example **never <expr>** or **always eventually reachable <state>**). Also, a number of properties are automatically checked for each state machine.

[31] There are various formalisms for temporal logic, including LTL, CTL and CTL+. Each of those have particular characteristics and limitations, but they are beyond the scope of this book.

[32] If a state machine has no guard conditions, some of these properties can be reduced to problems that can be solved by "just looking", i.e. by inspecting the structure of the state machine. For example, if the only transition entering some state **X** originates from some state **Y**, then it is clear that we always come through **X** before entering **Y**. However, in the presence of several transitions and guard conditions (which may take into account all kinds of other things, such as the values of variables or event arguments), these verifications become much more complex and cannot be solved by "just looking".

[33] The SPIN/Promela model checker comes to mind here!

[34] We use the NuSMV model checker: **nusmv.fbk.eu/**.

[35] Taken from the well-known properties patterns collection at **patterns.projects.cis.ksu.edu/**

Let's look at an example. The following code shows a state machine that represents a counter. We can send the **step** event into the state machine, and as a consequence, it increments the **currentVal** counter by the **size** parameter passed with the event. If the **currentVal** becomes greater than **LIMIT**, the counter wraps around. We can also use the **start** event to reset the counter to **0**.

```
verifiable statemachine Counter {
  in events
    start()
    step(int[0..10] size)
  local variables
    int[0..100] currentVal = 0
    int[0..100] LIMIT = 10
  states ( initial = initialState )
    state initialState {
      on start [ ] -> countState {  }
    }
    state countState {
      on step [currentVal + size > LIMIT] -> initialState { }
      on step [currentVal + size <= LIMIT] -> countState {
        currentVal = currentVal + size;
      }
      on start [ ] -> initialState {  }
    }
}
```

Since this state machine is marked as **verifiable**, we can run the model checker from the context menu[36]. Fig. 14.6 shows the result of running the model checker.

Here is a subset of the properties it has checked successfully (it performs these checks for all states/transitions by default):

```
State 'initialState' can be reached                         SUCCESS
Variable 'currentVal' is always between its defined bounds  SUCCESS
State 'countState' has deterministic transitions            SUCCESS
Transition 0 of state 'initialState' is not dead            SUCCESS
```

The first one reports that NuSMV has successfully proven that the **initialState** can be reached somehow. The second one reports that the variable **currentVal** stays within its bounds (notice how **currentVal** is a bounded integer). Line three reports that in **countState** it never happens that more than one transition is ready to fire at any time. Finally, it reports that no transitions are dead, i.e. each of them is actually used at some point.

Let's provoke an error. We change the two transitions in **countState** to the following:

```
on step [currentVal + size >= LIMIT] -> initialState { }
on step [currentVal + size <= LIMIT] -> countState {
   currentVal = currentVal + size;
}
```

[36] Marking a state machine as **verifiable** also enforces a few restrictions on the state machine (for example, each state machine local variable may only be assigned once during a transition). State machines restricted in this way are easier to model check.

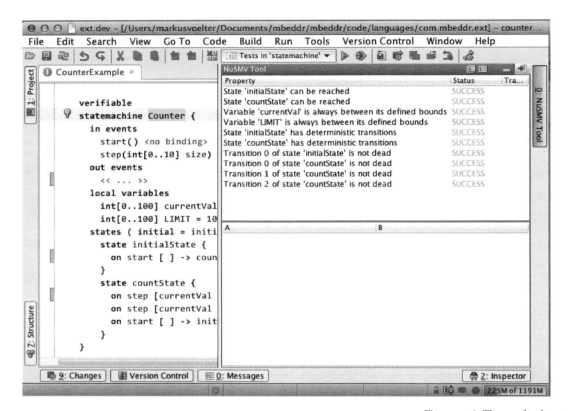

Figure 14.6: The result of running the model checker on a **verifiable** state machine is directly shown in the IDE, listing each property in a table. If a property fails, the lower part of the result view shows an example execution of the state machine (states and local variable values) that leads to the property being violated.

We have changed the > to a >= in the first transition[37]. Running the model checker again, we get, among others, the following messages:

```
State 'countState' contains nondeterministic transitions    FAIL    4
```

This means that there is a case in which the two transitions are non-deterministic, i.e. both are possible based on the guard, and it is not clear which one should be fired. The **4** at the end means that the execution trace to this problem contains four steps. Clicking on the failed property check reveals the problematic execution trace:

[37] You perhaps don't even recognize the difference – which is exactly why you would want to use a formal verification!

```
State initialState
  LIMIT                10
  currentVal            0
State initialState
  in_event: start start()
  LIMIT                10
  currentVal            0
State countState
  in_event: step   step(10)
  LIMIT                10
  currentVal            0
State initialState
  LIMIT                10
  currentVal           10
```

This is one (of potentially many) execution traces of this state machine that leads to the non-determinism: `currentVal` is 10, and because of the `>=`, both transitions could fire.

In addition to these default properties, it is also possible to specify custom properties. Here are two examples, expressed using the property patterns mentioned earlier:

```
verification conditions
  never LIMIT != 10
  always eventually reachable initialState
```

The first one expresses that we want the model checker to prove that a specific Boolean condition will never be true. In our example, we check that the `LIMIT` really is a constant and is never (accidentally) changed. The second one specifies that wherever we are in the execution of the state machine, it is still possible (after an arbitrary number of steps) to reach the `initialState`. Both properties hold for the example state machine.

■ *SAT/SMT Solving* SAT solving, which is short for satisfiability solving, concerns the satisfiability of sets of Boolean equations. Users specify a set of Boolean equations and the solver tries to assign truth values to the free variables so as to satisfy all specified equations. SAT solving is an NP-complete problem, so there is no analytic approach: exhaustive search (implemented, of course, in much cleverer ways) is the way to address these problems. SMT solving (Satisfiability Modulo Theories) is an extension of SAT solving that allows other constructs in addition to logical operators – the most frequently used being linear arithmetic, arrays or bit-vectors.

As an example, SMT solving can be used to verify mbeddr's decision tables. A decision table has a set of Boolean conditions as row headers, a set of Boolean conditions in the column headers, as well as arbitrary values in the content cells. A decision table essentially represents nested `if` statements: the result value of the table is that content cell whose row and column header are `true`. Fig. 14.7 shows an example.
SMT solving can be used to check whether all cases are handled. It can detect whether combinations of the relevant variables exist for which no combination of row header and column header expressions match; in this case, the decision table would not return any value.

SAT and SMT solvers have some of the same challenges as model checkers regarding scalability: a low-level and limited input language and the challenge of interpreting and under-

```
module DecisionTableExample imports nothing {

  enum mode { MANUAL; AUTO; FAIL; }

  mode nextMode(mode mode, int8 speed) {
    return mode, FAIL  |          | mode == MANUAL | mode == AUTO |;
                       | speed < 30 | MANUAL       | AUTO         |
                       | speed > 30 | MANUAL       | MANUAL       |
  }

}
```

Figure 14.7: An example decision table in mbeddr C. SMT solving is used to check it for consistency and completeness.

standing the output of a solver. Hence we use the same approach to solve the problem: from higher-level models (such as the decision table) we generate the input to the solver, run it, and then report the result in the context of the high-level language.

■ *Model Checking and Transformations* A problem with model verification approaches in general is that they verify only the model. They can detect inconsistencies or property violations as a consequence of flaws in the program expressed with a DSL. However, even if we find no flaws in the model on the DSL level, the generator or interpreter used to execute the program may still introduce problems. In other words, the behavior of the actual running system may be different from the (proven correct) behavior expressed in the model. There are three ways to address this:

- You can test your generator manually using the strategies suggested in this chapter. Once you trust the generator based on a sufficiently large set of tests, you then only have to verify the models, since you know they will be translated correctly.

- Some tools, for example the UPAAL model checker[38], can also generate test cases[39]. These are stimuli to the model, together with the expected reactions. You can generate those into your target language and then run them in your target language. This is essentially an automated version of the first approach.

- Finally, you can verify the generated code. For example, there are model checkers for C. You can then verify that the properties that hold on the DSL level also hold on the level

[38] www.uppaal.com/

[39] One can generate test cases by using the model checking technology: just specify that some property is false, and the model checker will provide a counterexample that illustrates the execution of the state machine up to the point where the property is true.

of the generated code. This approach runs into scalability issues relatively quickly, since the state space of a C program is much larger than the state space of a well-crafted state machine[40]. However, you can use this approach to verify the generated code based on a sufficient set of relatively small test cases, making sure that these cover all aspects of the generator. Once you've built trust in the generator in this way, you can resort to verifying just the DSL models (which scales better).

[40] Remember that we use formalisms such as state machines instead of low-level code specifically to allow more meaningful validation.

14.5 Testing Editor Services

Testing IDE services such as code completion (beyond scopes), quick fixes, refactorings or outline structure has some of the challenges of UI testing in general. There are three ways of approaching this:

- The language workbench may provide specific APIs to hook into UI aspects to facilitate writing tests for those.
- You can use generic UI testing tools[41] to simulate typing and clicking in the editor, and checking the resulting behavior.
- Finally, you can isolate the algorithmic aspects of the IDE behavior (e.g., in refactorings or quick fixes) into separate modules (classes) and then unit test those with the techniques discussed in the rest of this chapter, independent of the actual UI.

[41] Such as Eclipse Jubula: `www.eclipse.org/jubula/`

In practice, I try to use the third alternative as much as possible: for non-trivial IDE functionality in quick fixes and refactorings, I isolate the behavior and write unit tests. For simple things I don't do any automated tests. For the actual UI, I typically don't do any automated tests at all, for three reasons: (1) it is simply too cumbersome and not worth the trouble; (2) as we use the editor to try things out, we implicitly test the UI; and (3), language workbenches are frameworks which, if you get the functionality right (via unit tests), provide generic UIs that can be expected to work.

In the remainder of this subsection we show examples of the case in which the language workbench provides specific APIs to test the IDE aspects of languages.

■ *An Example with MPS*   In a parser-based system, you can always type anything. So even if the IDE functionality (particularly regarding code completion) is broken, you can still *type* the desired code. Also, the editing experience of typing code is always the same, fundamentally: you type linear sequences of characters. In a projectional editor, this is not the case: you can only enter things that are available in the code completion menu, and the editing experience itself relies on the editor implementation[42]. Hence it is important to be able to test editor behavior.

MPS supports this with a special DSL for editor testing (see Fig. 14.8). Note how MPS' language composition facilities allow embedding the subject DSL into the DSL for describing the editor test case.

[42] For example, you can only type **1 + 2** linearly (e.g. first the **1**, then the **+**) if the respective right transformation for number literals is implemented.

Figure 14.8: This test tests whether code completion works correctly. We start with an "empty" variable declaration in the **before** slot. It is marked with **cell**, a special annotation used in UI tests to mark the editor cell that has the focus for the subsequent scripted behavior. In the **result** slot, we describe the state of the editor *after* the script code has been executed. The script code then simulates typing the word **myVariable**, pressing **TAB**, pressing **CTRL-SPACE**, typing **boo** (as a prefix of **boolean**) and pressing **ENTER**.

■ *An Example with Xtext/Xpect* Xpect is a framework for integration testing of Xtext DSLs developed by Moritz Eysholdt[43]. It can be used for testing various language aspects, among them, for example, code completion[44]. It does so by embedding test expectations as comments inside the program to be tested. Here is an example based on a Hello World grammar (literally):

[43] https://github.com/meysholdt/Xpect

[44] Xtext itself comes with a set of helpers for IDE service testing such as content assist or builder tests. They run with, and often even without, an SWT display (e.g., headless).

```
Model:
  greetings+=Greeting*;

Greeting:
  'Hello' name=ID '!';
```

The following piece of code shows an example program that includes Xpect statements that test whether code completion works as expected:

```
// XPECT_TEST org.example.MyJUnitContentAssistTest END_TEST

// XPECT contentAssist at |Hel --> Hello
Hello Peter!

// XPECT contentAssist at |! --> !
Hello Heiko!
```

The Xpect processor processes all comments that start with **XPECT**. In this case, we test the content assist (e.g., code completion) functionality. Let us look at the details:

- The `contentAssist` refers to the kind of test to be executed (details on this below).

- `at` is a keyword for improved readability and has no semantic impact.

- `|Hel` and `|!` instruct the test to search for occurrences of `Hel` and `!` somewhere in the code after the **XPECT** statement. The pipe `|` marks the assumed cursor position relative to `Hel` and `!` where the content assist should be triggered.

- The part after `->` marks the expectation of the test. In the first test, content assist is expected to suggest the keyword `Hello`, and in the second test the exclamation point is expected.

Xpext is in fact a generic infrastructure for integration tests. As you can see from the example above, the test references a JUnit test class[45]: `org.example.MyJUnitContentAssistTest`. The term `contentAssist` is actually the name of a test method inside that class. Everything from an Xpect comment after the **XPECT** keyword is passed as parameters into the test method. The test method can do whatever it wants as long as it produces a string as the output. This string is then compared with the expectation, the text behind the `->`. While `contentAssist` is predefined in Xpect-provided unit test base classes, you can define your own methods. Since the actual testing is based on string comparison, the system is easily extensible. The following language aspects can be tested with Xpect[46]:

- The AST created from a DSL document.
- Messages and locations of error and warning markers.
- Names returned by scopes.
- Proposal items suggest by content assist features (as the example above shows).

[45] Xpect implements a custom JUnit runner which allows you to execute Xpect tests as JUnit test; integration into IDEs such as Eclipse and CI environments is ensured.

[46] The general idea behind Xpect is the separation of test data, test expectations and test setup from implementation details. The test data consists of DSL documents written in the language that you want to test. The test expectations are anything you might want the test to verify and which can be expressed as a string. The setup may declare other DSL documents that the test depends on, including Eclipse project setups. Since all these details are hidden, the DSL *user* can potentially understand or even write the test cases, not just the DSL developer.

- Textual diffs that were created by applying refactorings or quick fixes.

- Textual output of a code generator (but use with caution, since generated text may be too fragile).

Results from interpreters or execution of generated code.
By embedding test expectations into the subject programs, Xpect implicitly solves the navigation problem[47] by allowing you to use the | to select offsets inside a DSL document. Xpect also makes it easy to locate the offending expectation if case a test fails: since all expectations are represented as strings, if a test fails, the Eclipse JUnit view provides a comparison dialog that shows all differences between the actual test result and the test expectation. Xpect also makes it easy to specify even large test data scenarios, possibly consisting of multiple languages and multiple Eclipse projects. Finally, since Xpect code is embedded into the DSL code to be tested, you can use your DLS's Xtext editor to edit your test data. In plain JUnit tests you would have to embed snippets of your DSL documents into Java string literals, which won't provide any tool support for your language at all[48].

[47] If you want to test language properties such as content assist or scoping, you will have to navigate/point/refer to to a model element after you have created the test data. This leads to boilerplate code in Java-based tests.

■ *An Example with Spoofax* Spoofax' testing language supports testing editor services such as reference resolution and content completion. For reference resolution, we mark a definition and a use site in a test case with [[...]]. We can refer to these markers by numbers #1 and #2, specifying which marked element should refer to the other marked element. For example, the following test cases mark the name of an entity **A** in its declaration and in the type of a property:

[48] Notice, however, that when editing the program to be tested, there is no tool support for the Xpect syntax and the expectations. The reason is that Xtext does not support language embedding: there is no way to easily define a composed language from the subject DSL and Xpect. While this limitation is not a problem for Xpect itself (after all, its syntax is extremely simple), it may be a problem for expectations with a more complex syntactic structure. Of course, a specialized editor could be developed (based on the default Xtext editor) that provides code completion for the Xpect code in the DSL program comments. But that would require hand-coding and would be quite a bit of work.

```
test entity type reference (1) [[
  module foo

  entity [[A]] {}

  entity B {
    a: [[A]]
  }
]] resolve #2 to #1

test entity type reference (2) [[
  module foo

  entity B {
    a: [[A]]
  }

  entity [[A]] {}
]] resolve #1 to #2
```

The first test case addresses a backward reference, where the second marked name should resolve to the first marked name. The second test case addresses forward reference, where the first marked name should resolve to the second marked name.

For content completion, we mark only one occurrence, and specify one of the expected completions:

```
test entity type reference (1) [[
  module foo

  entity SomeEntity {}

  entity A {
    a: [[S]]
  }
]] complete to "String"
test entity type reference (2) [[
  module foo

  entity SomeEntity {}

  entity A {
    a: [[S]]
  }
]] complete to "SomeEntity"
```

Refactorings are tested in a similar fashion. The selected part of the code is indicated with square brackets, and the name of the refactoring is specified in the test:

```
test Rename refactoring [[
  entity [[Customer]] {

  }
  entity Contract {
    client : Customer
  }
]] refactor rename("Client") to [[
  entity Client {

  }
  entity Contract {
    client : Client
  }
]]
```

14.6 Testing for Language Appropriateness

A DSL is only useful if it can express what it is supposed to express. A bit more formally, one can say that the coverage of the DSL relative to the target domain should be 100%. In practice, this questions is much more faceted, though:

- Do we actually understand completely the domain the DSL is intended to cover?

- Can the DSL cover this domain completely? What does "completely" even mean? Is it ok to have parts of the system written in L_{D-1}, or do we have to express everything with the DSL?

- Even if the DSL covers the domain completely: are the abstractions chosen appropriate for the model purpose?

- Do the users of the DSL like the notation? Can the users work efficiently with the notation?

It is not possible to answer these questions with automated tess. Manual reviews and validation relative to the (explicit or tacit) requirements for the DSL have to be performed. Getting these aspects right is the main reason why DSLs should be developed incrementally and iteratively.

15
Debugging DSLs

Debugging is relevant in two ways in the context of DSLs and language workbenches. First, the DSL developer may want to debug the definition of a DSL, including constraints, scopes or transformations and interpreters. Second, programs written in the DSL may have to be debuggable by the end user. We address both aspects in this chapter.

15.1   Debugging the DSL Definition

Debugging the definition of the DSL boils down to a language workbench providing a debugger for the languages used for language definition. In the section we look at understanding and debugging the structure and concrete syntax, the definition of scopes, constraints and type systems, as well as debugging interpreters and transformations.

15.1.1   Understanding and Debugging the Language Structure

In parser-based systems, the transformation from text to the AST performed by the parser is itself a non-trivial process and has a potential for errors. Debugging the parsing process can be important.

∎ *Xtext*   Xtext uses ANTLR[1] under the hood. In other words, an ANTLR grammar is generated from the Xtext grammar which performs the actual parsing[2]. So understanding and debugging the Xtext parsing process means understanding and debugging the ANTLR parsing process.

[1] `antlr.org`

[2] It contains actions that construct the AST based on the mapping expressed in the Xtext grammar.

There are two ways to do this. First, since ANTLR generates a Java-based parser, you can debug the execution of ANTLR (as part of Xtext) itself[3]. Second, you can have Xtext generate a debug grammar, which contains no action code (so it does not populate the AST). However, it can be used to debug the parsing process with ANTLRWorks[4]. ANTLRWorks comes with an interactive debugger for ANTLR grammars.

[3] For obvious reasons, this is tedious and really just a last resort.

[4] www.antlr.org/works

■ *MPS* In MPS there is no transformation from text to the AST since it is a projectional editor. However, there are still means of helping to better understand the structure of an existing program. For example, any program element can be inspected in the *Explorer*. Fig. 15.1 shows the explorer contents for a trivial C function:

```
int8 add(int8 x, int8 y) {
  return x + y;
}
```

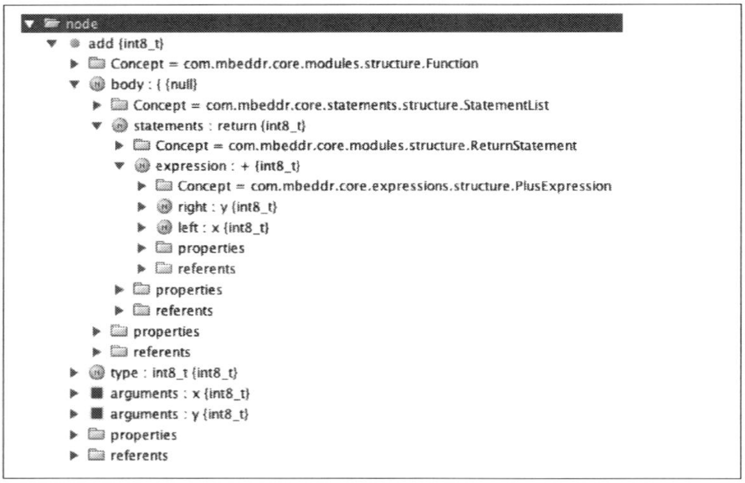

Figure 15.1: The MPS explorer shows the structure of a program as a tree. The explorer also shows the concept for each program element as well as the type, if an element has one.

MPS provides similar support for understanding the projection rules. For any program node MPS can show the cell structure as a tree. The tree contains detailed information about the cell hierarchy, the program element associated with each cell, and the properties of the cell (height, width, etc.).

15.1.2 Debugging Scopes, Constraints and Type Systems

Depending on the level of sophistication of a particular language, a lot of non-trivial behavior can be contained in the code that determines scopes, checks constraints or computes types. In fact, in many languages, these are the most sophisticated aspects of language definition. Consequently, there is a need for debugging those.

■ *Xtext*   In Xtext all aspects of a language except the grammar and the abstract syntax are defined via Java[5] programs using Xtext APIs. This includes scopes, constraints, type system rules and all IDE aspects. Consequently, all these aspects can be debugged by using a Java debugger. To do this, you can simply launch the Eclipse Application that contains the language and editor in debug mode and set breakpoints at the relevant locations[6].

[5] You may also use other JVM languages such as Xtend. If such a language has a debugger, then you can obviously also use that debugger for debugging Xtext DSL implementations.

[6] It is easy to criticize Xtext for the fact that it does not use DSLs for defining DSLs. However, in the context of debugging this is good, because no special debuggers are necessary.

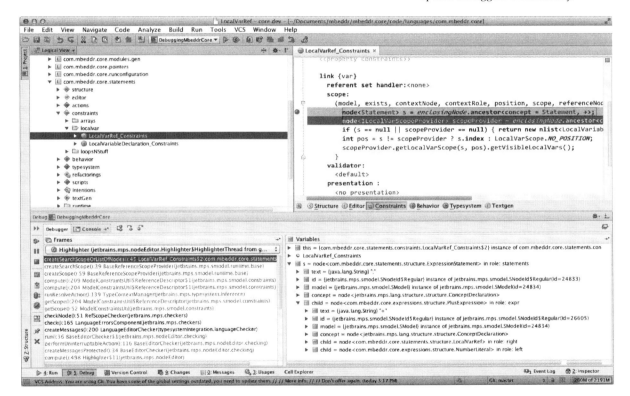

■ *MPS*   MPS comes with a similar facility, in the sense that a second instance of MPS can be run "inside" the current one. This inner instance can be debugged from the outer one. This approach can be used for all those aspects of MPS-defined languages that are defined in terms of the BaseLanguage, MPS' version of Java. For example, scopes can be debugged this way: in Fig. 15.2 we debug the scope for a **LocalVariableRef**.

Figure 15.2: The debugger that can debug MPS while it "executes" a language is aware of all the relevant extensions to BaseLanguage. For example, in this screenshot we debug a scope constraint. Notice how in the **Variables** view program nodes (such as the **Statement**s) are shown on the abstraction level of the node, not in terms of its underlying Java data structure representation.

A related feature of MPS is the ability to analyze exception stack traces. To implement a language, MPS generates Java code from language definitions and then executes this Java code. If an exception occurs in language implementation code it produces a Java stack trace. This stack trace can be pasted into a dialog in MPS. MPS then produces a version of the stack trace in which the code locations in the stack trace (which are relative to the generated Java) have been translated to locations in the DSL definition (expressed in Base Language). The locations can be clicked directly, opening the MPS editor at the respective location.

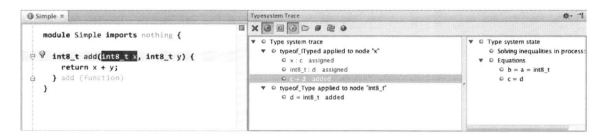

Relative to the type system, MPS comes with two dedicated debug facilities (beyond debugging a new instance of MPS inside MPS mentioned above). First, pressing **Ctrl-Shift-T** on any program element will open a dialog that shows the type of the element. If the element has a type system error, the dialog also lets the user navigate to the rule that reported the error. The second facility is much more sophisticated. For any program node, MPS can show the *type system trace* (Fig. 15.3 shows a simple example). Remember how the MPS type system relies on a solver to solve the type system equations associated with program elements (specified by the language developer for the respective concepts). This means that each program has an associated set of type system equations, which contain explicitly specified types as well as type variables. The solver tries to find type values for these variables such that all type system equations become true. The type system trace essentially visualizes the state of the solver, including the values it assigns to type variables, as well as which type system rules are applied to which program element[7].

Figure 15.3: This example shows the solver state for the **Argument x**. It first applies the rule **typeof_ITyped** (**Argument** implements **ITyped**), which expresses that the type of the element (type variable **c** is the same as the element's **type** property (type variable **d**). It then applies the **typeofype** rule to the argument's type itself. This rule expresses the fact that the type of a **Type** is a clone of itself. Consequently, the type variable **d** can be set to **int8**. In consequence this means that the type variable **c** (which represents the type of the **Argument**) is also **int8**. Note that this is a trivial example. Type system traces can become quite involved and are not always easy to understand.

[7] In the design part we discussed how declarative languages may come with a debugger that fits the particular declarative paradigm used by a particular declarative language (Section 5). The type system trace is an example of this idea.

15.1.3   Debugging Interpreters and Transformations

Debugging an interpreter is simple: since an interpreter is just a program written in some programming language that processes and acts on the DSL program, debugging the interpreter simply uses the debugger for the language in which the interpreter is written (assuming there is one)[8].

Debugging transformations and generators is typically not quite as trivial, for two reasons. First, transformations and generators are typically written in DSLs optimized for this task. So a specialized debugger is required. Second, if multi-step transformations are used, the intermediate models may have to be accessible, and it should be possible to trace a particular element through the multi-step transformation.

■ *Xtext*   Xtext can be used together with any EMF-compatible code generator or transformation engine. However, since Xtext ships with Xtend, we look at debugging Xtend transformations. Model-to-model transformations and code generators in Xtend look very similar: both use Xtend to navigate over and query the model, based on the AST. The difference is that, as a side effect, model-to-model transformations create new model elements and code generators create strings, typically using rich strings (aka template expressions).

Any Xtend program can be debugged using Eclipse "out of the box". In fact, you can debug an Xtend program either on the Xtend level or on the level of the generated Java source[9]. Since interpreters and generators are just regular Xtend programs, they can be debugged in this way as well. Fig. 15.4 shows an example of debugging a template expressions.

Xtend is a fundamentally an object-oriented language, so the step-through metaphor for debuggers works. If Xtend is used for code generation or transformation, debugging boils down to stepping through the code that builds the target model[10].

■ *MPS*   In MPS, working with several chained transformations is normal, so MPS provides support for debugging the transformation process. This support includes two ingredients. The first one is showing the mapping partitioning. For any given model, MPS automatically computes the order in which transformations are executed, based on the relative priorities specified for the generators involved. The mapping partitioning reports the overall transformation schedule to the user.

[8] While it is technically simple to debug an interpreter, it is not necessarily simple to follow what's going on, because the interpreter is a meta program. We discuss this in Section 4.3.

[9] Xtend generates Java source code that is subsequently compiled.

[10] I emphasize this because the next example uses a different approach.

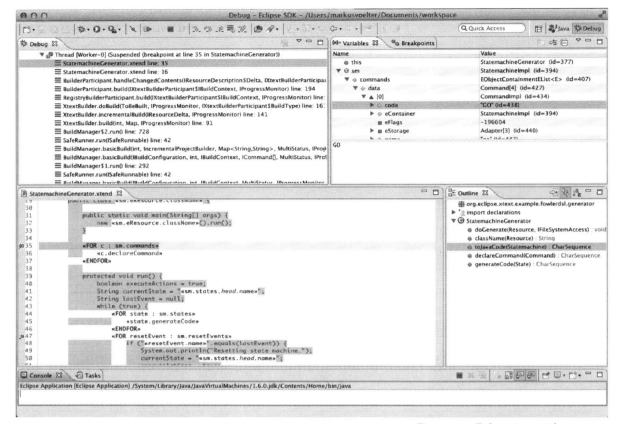

Figure 15.4: Debugging a code generator written in Xtend. The debugger can even step through the template expressions. The Variables view shows the EMF representation (i.e. the implementation) of program elements.

This is useful in understanding which transformations are executed in which order, and in particular, to debug transformation priorities. Let us investigate a simple example C program that contains a message definition and a **report** statement. The **report** statement is transformed to **printf** statements:

```
module Simple imports nothing {

  message list messages {
    INFO aMessage() active: something happened
  }

  exported int32 main(int32 argc, int8*[] argv) {
    report (0) messages.aMessage();
    return 0;
  }
}
```

Below is the mapping configuration for this program:

```
[ 1 ]
com.mbeddr.core.modules.gen.generator.template.main.removeCommentedCode
[ 2 ]
com.mbeddr.core.util.generator.template.main.reportingPrintf
[ 3 ]
com.mbeddr.core.buildconfig.generator.template.main.desktop
com.mbeddr.core.modules.gen.generator.template.main.main
```

This particular model is generated in three phases. The first one removes commented code to make sure it does not show up in the resulting C text file. The second phase runs the generator that transforms `report` statements into `printf`s. Finally, the `desktop` generator generates a `make` file from the build configuration, and the last step generates the C text from the C tree[11].

[11] It is called **desktop** because it generates the code for a desktop computer. It can be exchanged to generate code or make files for arbitrary embedded devices and compilers.

By default, MPS runs all generators until everything is either discarded or transformed into text. While intermediate models exist, they are not shown to the user. For debugging purposes though, these intermediate, transient models can be retained for inspection. Each of the phases is represented by one or more transient models. As an example, here is the program after the `report` statement has been transformed:

```
module Simple imports nothing {

  exported int32 main(int32 argc, int8*[] argv) {
    printf("$$ aMessage: something happened ");
    printf("@ Simple:main:0#240337946125104144 \n ");
    return 0;
  }
}
```

MPS also supports tracing an element through the intermediate models. Fig. 15.5 shows an example. Users can select a program element in the source, target or an intermediate model and trace it to the respective other ends of the transformation.

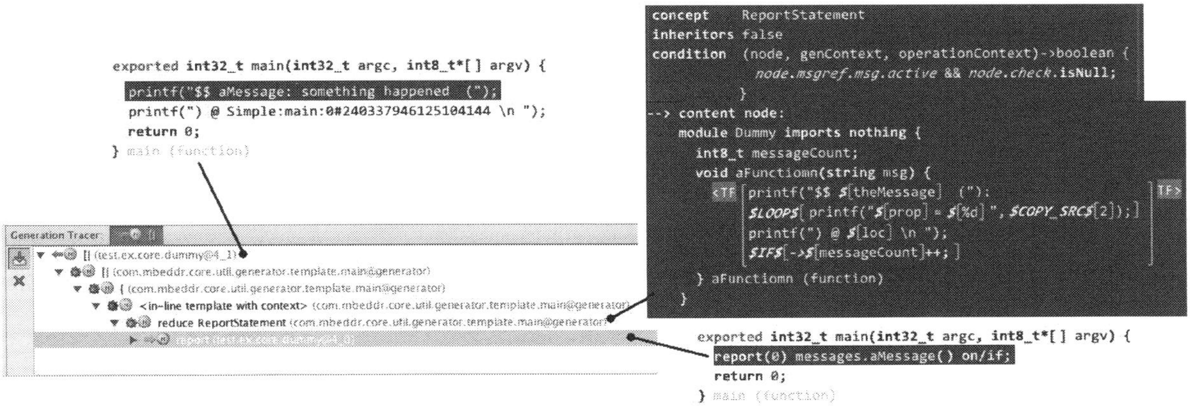

Figure 15.5: The generation trace functionality in MPS allows users to trace how a particular program element is transformed through a chain of transformations. The generation tracer also shows the transformation rules involved in the transformation.

Note how this approach to debugging transformations is very different from the Xtend example above: instead of stepping through the transformation code[12], MPS provides a *static* representation of the transformation in terms of the intermediate models and the element traces through them.

[12] As part of the general Debug-MPS-in-MPS functionality, MPS transformations can also be debugged in a more imperative fashion. This is useful, for example, to debug more complex logic used inside transformation templates.

15.2 Debugging DSL Programs

To find errors in DSL programs, we can either debug them on the level of the DSL program or in its L_{D-1} representation (i.e. in the generated code or the interpreter). Debugging on L_{D-1} is useful if you want to find problems in the execution engine, or, to some extent, if the language users are programmers and they have an intimate understanding of the L_{D-1} representation of the program. However, for many DSLs it is necessary to debug on the level of the DSL program, either because the users are not familiar with the L_{D-1} representation[13], or because the L_{D-1} is so low-level and complex that is bears no obvious resemblance to the DSL program.

[13] This is true particularly for DSLs targeted at domain experts.

The way to build debuggers for DSLs of course depends on the DSL itself. For example, for DSLs that only describe structures, debugging does not make much sense in the first place. For DSLs that describe behavior, the debugging approach depends on the behavioral paradigm used in the DSL. We have discussed this in Section 5. In this section we focus mostly on the imperative paradigm[14].

[14] An example for the functional paradigm was provided in Section 5.3, and the type system tracer described above is an example of a debugger for a declarative language.

Building a debugger poses two challenges. The first one is the debugger UI: creating all the buttons and views for controlling the debugger and for showing variables and treads. The second challenge concerns the control of and data exchange with the program to be debugged. The first challenge is relatively simple to solve, since many IDE frameworks (including Eclipse and MPS) already come with debugger frameworks.

The second challenge can be a bit more tricky. If the DSL is executed by an interpreter, the situation is simple: the interpreter can be run and controlled directly from the debugger. It is easy to implement single-stepping and variable watches, for example, since the interpreter can directly provide the respective interfaces[15]. On the other hand, if the DSL program is transformed into code that is executed in some other environment outside of our control, it may even be impossible to build a debugger, because there is no way to influence and inspect the running program. Alternatively, it may be necessary to build a variant of the code generator which generates a *debug version* of the program that contains specialized code to interact with the debugger. For example, values of variables may be stored in a special data structure inspectable by the debugger, and at each program location where the program may have to stop (in single-step mode or as a consequence of a breakpoint)

[15] This is especially true if the interpreter is written in the same language as the IDE: no language integration issues have to be addressed in this case.

code is inserted that explicitly suspends the execution of the program, for example by **sleep**ing the current thread. However, such an approach is often limited and ugly – in the end, an execution infrastructure must provide debug support to enable robust debugging.

15.2.1   Print Statements – a Poor Man's Debugger

As the above discussion suggests, building full-blown debuggers may be a lot of work. It is worth exploring whether a simpler approach is good enough. The simplest such approach is to extend the DSL with language concepts that simply print interesting aspects of the executing program to the console or a log file. For example, the values of variables may be output this way.

The mbeddr **report** statement is an example of this approach. A **report** statement takes a message text plus a set of variables. It then outputs the message and the values of these variables. The target of the report statement can be changed. By default, it reports to the console. However, since certain target devices may not have any console[16], alternative transformations can be defined for **report** statements, that, for example, could output the data to an error memory or a serial line. A particularly interesting feature of **report** statements is that the transformation that handles them knows where in the program the **report** statement is located and can add this information to the output[17].

An approach based on print *statements* is sometimes clumsy, because it requires factoring out the expression to be printed[18], and it only works for an imperative language in the first place. For languages that make use of sophisticated expressions, a different approach is recommended. Consider the following example:

```
Collection[Type] argTypes = aClass.operations.arguments.type;
```

If you wanted to print the list of operations and arguments, you would have to change the program to something like this:

```
print("operations: " + aClass.operations);
print("arguments: " + aClass.operations.arguments);
Collection[Type] argTypes = aClass.operations.arguments.type;
```

A much simpler alternative uses *inlined* reporting expressions:

```
Collection[Type] argTypes = aClass.operations.print("operations:")
                            .arguments.print("arguments:").type;
```

[16] mbeddr addresses embedded software development, and small microcontrollers may not have a console.

[17] The go-to-error-location functionality discussed in Fig. 14.5 is based on this approach.

[18] It also requires changing the actual program. In fact, any debug approach that requires any kind of change to the program to be debugged (or the compiled machine code), requires that it is known in advance if a particular program is supposed to be debugged. While this is a significant limitation, it is true for almost all compiled languages ("compile with debug options"), and hence accepted.

To make this convenient to use, the `print` function has to return the object it is called on (the one before the dot), and it must be typed accordingly if a language with static type checking is used[19].

[19] The original openArchitectureWare Xtend did it this way.

15.2.2 Automatic Program Tracing

As languages and programs become more complex, an automated tracing of program execution may be useful. In this approach, all execution steps in a program are automatically traced and logged into a tree-like data structure. The refrigerator cooling language uses this approach. Here is an example program:

```
cooling program HelloWorld {
    var temp: int
    start:
        entry { state s1 }
    state s1:
        check temp < 10 { state s2 }
    state s2:
}
```

Upon startup, it enters the `start` state and immediately transitions to state `s1`. It remains in `s1` until the variable `temp` becomes less than 10. It then transitions to `s2`. Below is a test for this program that verifies this behavior:

```
test HelloWorldTest for HelloWorld {
    prolog {
        set temp = 30
    }
    step
    assert-currentstate-is s1
    step
    mock: set temp = 5
    step
    assert-currentstate-is s2
}
```

Fig. 15.6 shows the execution trace. It shows the execution of each statement and the evaluation of each expression. The log viewer is a tree table, so the various execution steps can be selectively expanded and collapsed. Users can double-click on an entry to select the respective program element in the source node. By adding special comments to the source, the log can be structured further[20].

The execution engine for the programs is an interpreter, which makes it particularly simple to collect the trace data[21]. All interpreter methods that execute statements or evaluate expressions take a `LogEntry` object as an additional argument. The methods then add children to the current `LogEntry` that describe whatever the method did, and then pass the child to

[20] Obviously, the approach does not scale for big programs. However, by isolating problems into smaller, representative programs, it does provide a degree of usefulness.

[21] If, instead of an interpreter, a code generator were used, the same approach could essentially be used. Instead of embedding the tracing code in the interpreter, the code generator would generate code that would build the respective trace data structure in the executing program. Upon termination, the data structure could be dumped to an XML file and subsequently loaded by the IDE for inspection.

any other interpreter methods it calls. As an example, here is the implementation of the **AssignmentStatement**:

```
protected void executeAssignmentStatement(AssignmentStatement s,
                                          LogEntry log) {
    LogEntry c = log.child(Kind.info, context,
                    "executing AssignmentStatement" );
    Object l = s.getLeft();
    Object r = eval(s.getRight(), c);
    eec().environment.put(symbol, r);
    c.child(Kind.debug, context,
            "setting " + symbol.getName() + " to " + r);
}
```

15.2.3 *Simulation as an Approximation for Debugging*

The interpreter for the cooling programs mentioned above is of course not the final execution engine – C code is generated that is executed on the actual target refrigerator hardware. However, as we discussed in Section 4.3.7, we can make sure the generated code and the interpreter are semantically identical by running a sufficient (large) number of tests. If we do this, we can use the interpreter to test the programs for logical errors.

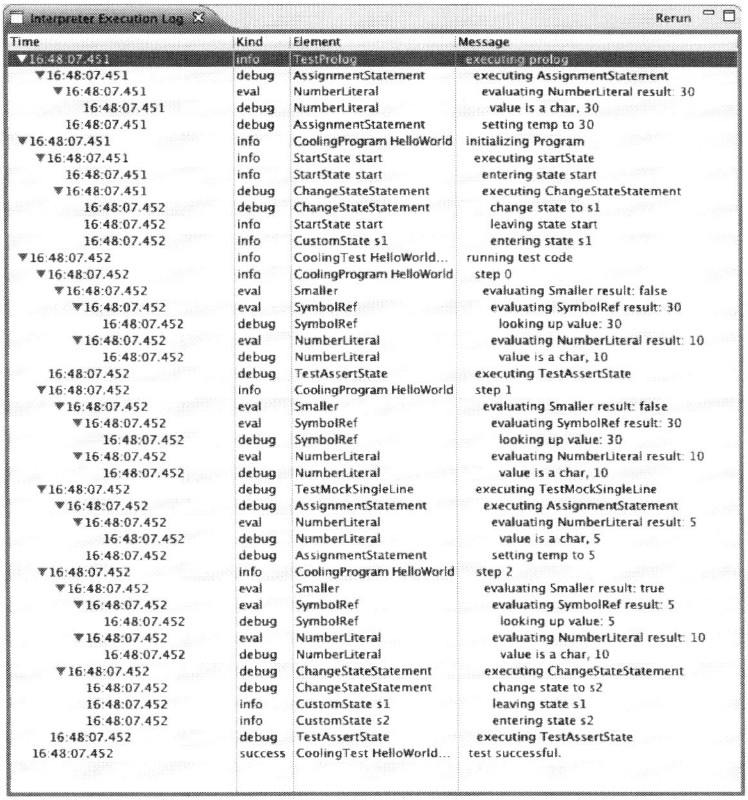

Time	Kind	Element	Message
▼16:48:07.451	info	TestProlog	executing prolog
▼16:48:07.451	debug	AssignmentStatement	executing AssignmentStatement
▼16:48:07.451	eval	NumberLiteral	evaluating NumberLiteral result: 30
16:48:07.451	debug	NumberLiteral	value is a char, 30
16:48:07.451	debug	AssignmentStatement	setting temp to 30
▼16:48:07.451	info	CoolingProgram HelloWorld	initializing Program
▼16:48:07.451	info	StartState start	executing startState
16:48:07.451	info	StartState start	entering state start
▼16:48:07.451	debug	ChangeStateStatement	executing ChangeStateStatement
16:48:07.452	debug	ChangeStateStatement	change state to s1
16:48:07.452	info	StartState start	leaving state start
16:48:07.452	info	CustomState s1	entering state s1
▼16:48:07.452	info	CoolingTest HelloWorld...	running test code
▼16:48:07.452	info	CoolingProgram HelloWorld	step 0
▼16:48:07.452	eval	Smaller	evaluating Smaller result: false
▼16:48:07.452	eval	SymbolRef	evaluating SymbolRef result: 30
16:48:07.452	debug	SymbolRef	looking up value: 30
▼16:48:07.452	eval	NumberLiteral	evaluating NumberLiteral result: 10
16:48:07.452	debug	NumberLiteral	value is a char, 10
16:48:07.452	debug	TestAssertState	executing TestAssertState
▼16:48:07.452	info	CoolingProgram HelloWorld	step 1
▼16:48:07.452	eval	Smaller	evaluating Smaller result: false
▼16:48:07.452	eval	SymbolRef	evaluating SymbolRef result: 30
16:48:07.452	debug	SymbolRef	looking up value: 30
▼16:48:07.452	eval	NumberLiteral	evaluating NumberLiteral result: 10
16:48:07.452	debug	NumberLiteral	value is a char, 10
▼16:48:07.452	debug	TestMockSingleLine	executing TestMockSingleLine
▼16:48:07.452	debug	AssignmentStatement	executing AssignmentStatement
▼16:48:07.452	eval	NumberLiteral	evaluating NumberLiteral result: 5
16:48:07.452	debug	NumberLiteral	value is a char, 5
16:48:07.452	debug	AssignmentStatement	setting temp to 5
▼16:48:07.452	info	CoolingProgram HelloWorld	step 2
▼16:48:07.452	eval	Smaller	evaluating Smaller result: true
▼16:48:07.452	eval	SymbolRef	evaluating SymbolRef result: 5
16:48:07.452	debug	SymbolRef	looking up value: 5
▼16:48:07.452	eval	NumberLiteral	evaluating NumberLiteral result: 10
16:48:07.452	debug	NumberLiteral	value is a char, 10
▼16:48:07.452	debug	ChangeStateStatement	executing ChangeStateStatement
16:48:07.452	debug	ChangeStateStatement	change state to s2
16:48:07.452	info	CustomState s1	leaving state s1
16:48:07.452	info	CustomState s2	entering state s2
16:48:07.452	debug	TestAssertState	executing TestAssertState
16:48:07.452	success	CoolingTest HelloWorld...	test successful.

Figure 15.6: The log viewer represents a program's execution as a tree. The first column contains a timestamp and the tree nesting structure. The second column contains the kind (severity) of the log message. A filter can be used to show only messages above a certain severity. The third column shows the language concept with which the trace step is associated (double-clicking on a row selects this element in the editor). Finally, the last column contains the information about the semantic action that was performed in the respective step.

The interpreter can also be used interactively, in which case it acts as a simulator for the executing program. It shows all variables in the program, the events in the queue, the running tasks, as well as the values of properties of hardware elements and the current state. It also provides a button to single-step the program, to run it continuously, or to run it until it hits a breakpoint. In other words, although the simulator does not use the familiar[22] UI of a debugger, it actually is a debugger[23]!

If you already have the interpreter[24], expanding it into a simulator/debugger is relatively simple. Essentially only three things have to be done:

- First, the execution of the program must be controllable from the outside. This involves setting breakpoints, single-stepping through the program and stopping execution if a breakpoint is hit. In our example case, we do not single-step through statements, but only through steps[25]. Breakpoints are essentially Boolean flags associated with program elements: if the execution processes a statement that has the **breakpoint** flat set to **true**, execution stops.

- Second, we have implemented an Observer infrastructure for all parts of the program state that should be represented in the simulator UI. Whenever one of them changes (as a side effect of executing a statement in the program), an event is fired. The UI registers as an observer and updates the UI in accordance with the event.

- Third, values from the program state must be changeable from the outside. As a value in the UI (such as the temperature of a cooling compartment) is changed by the user, the value is updated in the state of the interpreter as well.

15.2.4 Automatic Debugging for Xbase-based DSLs

DSLs that use Xbase, Xtext's reusable expression language, get debugging mostly[26] for free. This is because of the tight integration of Xbase with the JVM. We describe this integration in more detail in Section 16.3; here is the essence.

A DSL that uses Xbase typically defines its own structural and high-level behavioral aspects, but uses Xbase for the fine-grained, expression-level and statement-level[27] behavior. For example, in a state machine DSL, states, events and transitions would be concepts defined by the DSL, but the guard conditions and the action code would reuse Xbase expressions.

[22] ... familiar to programmers, but not to the target audience!

[23] As we have said above, the fact that it runs in the interpreter instead of the generated code is not a problem if we ensure the two are semantically identical. Of course we cannot find bugs in the implementation (i.e. in the generator) in this way. But to detect those, debugging on the level of the generated C code is more useful anyway.

[24] We discuss how to build one in Section 12.

[25] Remember that the language is time-triggered anyway, so execution is basically a sequence of steps triggered by a timer. In the simulator/debugger, the timer is replaced with the user pressing the **Next Step** button for single stepping.

[26] "Mostly" because in a few cases you have to add trace information manually in transformations.

[27] Technically, Xtend doesn't have statements, and things like **if** or **switch** are expressions.

When mapping this DSL to Java[28], the following approach is used: the structural and high-level behavioral aspects are mapped to Java, but *not* by generating Java text, but by mapping the DSL AST to a Java AST[29]. For the reused Xbase aspects (the finer-grained behavior) a Java generator (called the Xbase compiler) already exists, which we simply call from our generator.

Essentially, we do not create a code generator, but a model-to-model transformation from the DSL AST to the Java AST. As part of this transformation (performed by the *JVMModel inferrer*), trace links between the DSL code and the Java code are established. In other words, the relationship between the Java code and the DSL code is well known. This relationship is exploited in the debugging process. Xbase-based DSLs use the Java debugger for debugging. In addition to showing the generated Java code, the debugger can also show the DSL code, based on the trace information collected by the JVMModel inferrer. In the same way, if a user sets a breakpoint in the DSL code, the trace information is used to determine where to set the breakpoint in the generated Java code.

15.2.5 Debuggers for an Extensible Language

This section describes in some detail the architecture of an extensible debugger for an extensible language[30]. We illustrate the approach with an implementation based on mbeddr, an extensible version of C implemented with the MPS. We also show the debuggers for non-trivial extensions of C.

■ *Requirements for the Debugger* Debuggers for imperative languages support at least the following features: *breakpoints* suspend execution on arbitrary statements; *single-step execution* steps over statements, and into and out of functions or other callables; and *watches* show values of variables, arguments or other aspects of the program state. *Stack frames* visualize the call hierarchy of functions or other callables.

When debugging a program that contains extensions, breakpoints, stepping, watches and call stacks, these elements *at the extension-level* differ from their counterparts *at the base-level*. The debugger has to perform the mapping from the base-level to the extension-level (Fig. 15.7). We distinguish between the *tree* representation of a program in MPS and the generated *text* that is used by the C compiler and the debugger backend. A program in the tree representation can be separated into parts

[28] Xbase-based DSLs *must* be mapped to Java to benefit from Xbase in the way discussed in this section. If you generate code other than Java, Xbase cannot be used sensibly.

[29] The Java AST serves as a hub for all Xbase languages including Xtend, your own DSL or Xcore. All those work nicely together. The JVM level serves as an interoperability layer.

[30] Extensible languages were defined and discussed in Section 4.6. We show in detail in Section 16.2 how this works with MPS.

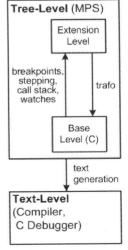

Figure 15.7: An extension-aware debugger maps the debug behavior from the base-level to the extension-level (an extension may also be mapped onto other extensions; we ignore this aspect in this section).

expressed in the base language (C in this case) and parts expressed using extensions. We refer to the latter the *extension-level* or *DSL-level* (see Fig. 15.7). An extensible tree-level debugger for mbeddr that supports debugging on the base-level and extension-level, addresses the following requirements:

Modularity Language extensions in mbeddr are modular, so debugger extensions must be modular as well. No changes to the base language must be necessary to enable debugging for a language extension.

Framework Genericity In addition, new language extensions must not require changes *to the core debugger infrastructure* (not just the base language).

Simple Debugger Definition Creating language extensions is an integral part of using mbeddr. Hence, the development of a debugger for an extension should be simple and not require too much knowledge about the inner workings of the framework, or even the C debugger backend.

Limited Overhead As a consequence of embedded software development, we have to limit the additional, debugger-specific code generated into the binary. This would increase the size of the binary, potentially making debugging on a small target device infeasible.

Debugger Backend Independence Embedded software projects use different C debuggers, depending on the target device. This prevents modifying the C debugger itself: changes would have to be re-implemented for every C debugger used.

■ *An Example Extension* We start out by developing a simple extension to the mbeddr C language[31]. The **foreach** statement can be used to conveniently iterate over C arrays. Users have to specify the array as well as its size. Inside the **foreach** body, **it** acts as a reference to the current iteration's array element[32].

```
int8 s = 0;
int8[] a = {1, 2, 3};
foreach (a sized 3) {
    s += it;
}
```

The code generated from this piece of extended C looks as follows. The **foreach** statement is expanded into a regular **for** statement and an additional variable **__it**:

[31] We assume that you know the basics of MPS language development, for example from reading the earlier implementation chapters in this book.

[32] Note that for the sake of the example, we don't consider nested **foreach** statements, so we don't have to deal with unique names for various (generated) variables.

```
int8 s = 0;
int8[] a = {1, 2, 3};
for (int __c = 0; __c < 3; __c++) {
    int8 __it = a[__c];
    s += __it;
}
```

To make the **foreach** extension modular, it lives in a separate language module named **ForeachLanguage**. The new language extends C, since we will refer to concepts defined in C (see Fig. 15.8).

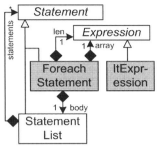

Figure 15.8: UML class diagram showing the structure of the **ForeachLanguage**. Concepts from the C base language are in white boxes, new concepts are gray.

■ *Developing the Language Extension*   In the new language, we define the **ForeachStatement**. To make it usable wherever C expects **Statement**s (i.e. in functions), it extends C's **Statement**. As Fig. 15.8 shows, **ForeachStatement**s have three children: an **Expression** that represents the array, an **Expression** for the array length, and a **StatementList** for the body. **Expression** and **StatementList** are both defined in C.

The editor is shown in Fig. 15.9. It consists of a horizontal list of cells: the **foreach** keyword, the opening parenthesis, the embedded editor of the **array** child, the **sized** keyword, the embedded editor of the **len** expression, the closing parenthesis and the editor of the **body**.

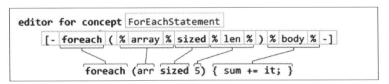

Figure 15.9: The editor definition of the **foreach** statement and its relationship to an example instance.

As shown in the code snippet below, the **array** must be of type **ArrayType**, and the type of **len** must be **int64** or any of its shorter subtypes.

```
rule typeof_ForeachStatement for ForeachStatement as fes do {
    typeof( fes.len ) :<=: <int64>;
    if (!(fes.array.type.isInstanceOf(ArrayType))) {
      error "array required" -> fes.array;
    }
}
```

As shown above, the generator translates a **ForeachStatement** to a regular **for** statement that iterates over the elements with a counter variable **__c** (Fig. 15.10). Inside the **for** body, we create a variable **__it** that refers to the array element at position **__c**. We then copy in the other statements from the body of the **foreach**.

The **ItExpression** extends C's **Expression** to make it usable where expressions are expected. The editor consists of a single cell with the keyword `it`. A constraint enforces the **ItExpression** to be used only inside the body of a **foreach**:

```
concept constraints ItExpression {
  can be child
    (context, scope, parentNode, link, childConcept)->boolean {
      parentNode.ancestor<ForeachStatement, +>.isNotNull &&
      parentNode.ancestor<StatementList, +>.isNotNull;
    }
}
```

The type of `it` must be the base type of the `array` (e.g. `int` in the case of `int[]`), as shown in the code below:

```
node<Type> basetype = typeof(it.ancestor<ForeachStatement>.array)
                           :ArrayType.baseType;
typeof(it) :==: basetype.copy;
```

The **foreach** generator already generated a local variable __it into the body of the **for** loop. We can thus translate an **ItExpression** into a **LocalVariableReference** that refers to __it.

```
concept     ForEachStatement
inheritors  false
condition   <always>
-->
void dummy() {
  int8[ ] x;
  <TF  for ($COPY_SRC$[int64] __c = 0; __c < $COPY_SRC$[10]; __c++) { TF>
         $COPY_SRC$[int8_t] __it = $COPY_SRC$[x][__c];
         $COPY_SRCL$[int8_t x;]
       }
}
```

Figure 15.10: The **foreach** generator template. A **ForeachStatement** is replaced by the code that is framed <TF .. TF> when the template is executed; the **dummy** function around it just provides context. The **COPY_SRC** and **COPY_SRCL** macros contain expressions (not shown) that determine with what the nodes in square brackets (e.g., **10**, **int8 x;**) are replaced during a transformation.

■ *Developing the Debug Behavior* The specification of the debugger extension for **foreach** resides completely in the **ForeachLanguage**; this keeps the debugger definition for the extension local to the extension language.

To set a breakpoint on a concept, it must implement the **IBreakpointSupport** marker interface. **Statement** already implements this interface, so **ForEachStatement** implicitly implements this interface as well.

Stepping behavior is implemented via **ISteppable**. The **ForeachStatement** implements this interface indirectly via **Statement**, but we have to overwrite the methods that define the step over and step into behavior. Assume the debugger is suspended on a **foreach** and the user invokes *step over*. If the array is empty or we have finished iterating over it, a step over ends up on the statement that follows *after the whole* **foreach** statement. Otherwise we end up on the first line of the **foreach** body (`sum += it;`)[33].

[33] This is the first line of the mbeddr program, *not* the first line of the generated base program (which would be `int8 __it = arr[__c];`).

The debugger cannot guess which alternative will occur, since it would need to know the state of the program and to evaluate the expressions in the (generated) **for**. Instead we set breakpoints *on each of the possible next statements* and then resume execution until we hit one of them. The implementations of the **ISteppable** methods specify strategies for setting breakpoints on these possible next statements. The **contributeStepOverStrategies** method collects strategies for the *step over* case:

```
void contributeStepOverStrategies(list<IDebugStrategy> res) {
  ancestor
  statement list: this.body
}
```

The method is implemented using a domain-specific language for debugger specification, which is part of the mbeddr debugger framework[34]. It is an extension of MPS' BaseLanguage, a Java-based language used for expressing behavior in MPS. The **ancestor** statement delegates to the **foreach**'s ancestor; this will lead to a breakpoint on the subsequent statement. The second line leads to a breakpoint on the first statement of the **body** statement list.

Since the **array** and **len** expressions can be arbitrarily complex and may contain invocations of callables (such as function calls), we have to specify the *step into* behavior as well. This requires the debugger to inspect the expression trees in **array** and **len** and find any expression that can be stepped into. Such expressions implement **IStepIntoable**. If so, the debugger has to step into each of those, in turn. Otherwise the debugger falls back to *step over*. An additional method configures the expression trees which the debugger must inspect:

```
void contributeStepIntoStrategies(list<IDebugStrategy> res) {
  subtree: this.array
  subtree: this.len
}
```

By default, the Watch window contains all C symbols (global and local variables, arguments) as supplied by the native C debugger[35]. To customize watches, a concept has to implement **IWatchProvider**. Here is the code for **foreach**, also expressed in the debugger definition DSL:

```
void contributeWatchables(list<UnmappedVariable> unmapped,
                         list<IWatchable> mapped) {
  hide "__c"
  map "__it" to "it"
    type: this.array.type : ArrayType.baseType
    category: WatchableCategories.LOCAL_VARIABLES
    context: this
}
```

[34] This simplifies the implementation of debuggers significantly. It is another example of where using DSLs for defining DSLs is a good idea.

[35] In the case of the **foreach**, this means that **it** is not available, but __**it** and __**c** are. This is exactly the wrong way around: the watch window should show **it**, but not __**it** and __**c**.

The first line hides __c. The rest **map**s a base-level C variable to a watchable. It finds a C variable named __it (inserted by the **foreach** generator) and creates a watch variable named **it**. At the same time, it hides the base-level variable __it. The type of **it** is the base type of the array over which we iterate. We assign the **it** watchable to the local variables section and associate the **foreach** node with it (double-clicking on the **it** in the Watch window will highlight the **foreach** in the code).

Stepping into the **foreach** body does not affect the call stack, since the concept represents no callable (for details, see the next paragraph). So we do not have to implement any stack frame related functionality.

■ *Debugger Framework Architecture*   The central idea of the debugger architecture is this: from the C code in MPS and its extensions (tree level) we generate C text (text level). This text is the basis for the debugging process by a native C debugger. We then use trace data to find out how the generated text maps back to the tree level in MPS.

At the core of the execution architecture is the **Mapper**. It is driven by the **Debugger UI** (and through it, the user) and controls the C debugger via the **Debug Wrapper**. It uses the **Program Structure** and the **Trace Data**. The **Mapper** also uses a language's debug specification, discuss in the next subsection. Fig. 20.6 shows the components and their interfaces.

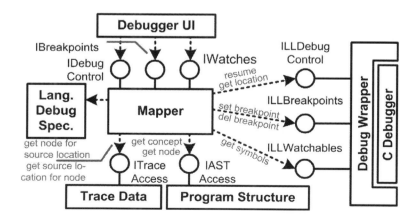

Figure 15.11: The **Mapper** is the central component of the debugger execution architecture. It is used by the **Debugger UI** and, in turn, uses the **Debug Wrapper**, the **Program Structure** and the **Trace Data**.

The **IDebugControl** interface is used by the **Debugger UI** to control the **Mapper**. For example, it provides a **resume** operation. **IBreakpoints** allows the UI to set breakpoints on program nodes. `IWatches` lets the UI retrieve the data items for the Watch window. The `Debug Wrapper` essentially provides the same interfaces, but on the level of C (prefixed with `LL`, for "low level"). In addition, `ILLDebugControl` lets the `Mapper` find out about the program location of the `C Debugger` when it is suspended at a breakpoint. `IASTAccess` lets the `Mapper` access program nodes. Finally, `ITraceAccess` lets the `Mapper` find out the program node (tree level) that corresponds to a specific line in the generated C source text (text level), and vice versa.

To illustrate the interactions of these components, we describe a *step over*. After the request has been handed over from the UI to the `Mapper` via `IDebugControl`, the `Mapper` performs the following steps:

- Asks the current node's concept for its *step over* strategies; these define all possible locations where the debugger could end up after the *step over*.
- Queries `TraceData` for the corresponding lines in the generated C text for those program locations.
- Uses the debugger's `ILLBreakpoints` to set breakpoints on those lines in the C text.
- Uses `ILLDebugControl` to resume program execution. It will stop at any of the breakpoints just created.
- Uses `ILLDebugControl` to get the C call stack.
- Queries `TraceData` to find out, for each C stack frame, the corresponding nodes in the tree-level program.
- Collects all relevant `IStackFrameContributor`s (see the next section). The `Mapper` uses these to construct the tree-level call stack.
- Gets the currently visible symbols and their values via `ILL-Watchables`.
- Queries the nodes for all `WatchableProvider`s and use them to create a set of watchables.

At this point, execution returns to the `Debugger UI`, which then gets the current location and watchables from the `Mapper` to highlight the statement on which the debugger is suspended and populate the Watch window.

In our implementation, the `Debugger UI`, `Program Repository` and `Trace Data` are provided by MPS. In particular, MPS builds a trace from the program nodes (tree level) in MPS to the generated text-level source. The `Debug Wrapper` is part of mbeddr and relies on the Eclipse CDT Debug Bridge[36], which provides a Java API to **gdb**[37] and other C debuggers.

[36] www.eclipse.org/cdt
[37] www.gnu.org/software/gdb/documentation/

■ *Debugger Specification* The debugger specification resides in the respective language module. As we have seen in the `foreach` example, the specification relies on a set of interfaces and a number of predefined strategies, as well as the debugger specification DSL.

The interface `IBreakpointSupport` is used to mark language concepts on which breakpoints can be set. C's `Statement` implements this interface. Since all statements inherit from `Statement` we can set breakpoints on all statements by default.

When the user sets a breakpoint on a program node, the mapper uses `ITraceAccess` to find the corresponding line in the generated C text. A statement defined by an extension may be expanded to several base-level statements, so `ITraceAccess` actually returns a range of lines, the breakpoint is set on the first one.

Stack frames represent the nesting of invoked callables at runtime[38]. We create stack frames for a language concept if it has callable semantics. The only callables in C are functions, but in mbeddr, test cases, state machine transitions and component methods are callables as well. Callable semantics on extension level do not necessarily imply a function call on the base level. There are cases in which an extension-level callable is *not* mapped to a function and where a non-callable *is* mapped to a function. Consequently, the C call stack may differ from the extension call stack shown to the user. Concepts with callable semantics on the extension level or base level implement `IStackFrameContributor`. The interface provides operations that determine whether a stack frame has to be created in the debugger UI and what the name of the stack frame should be.

[38] A *callable* is a language concept that contains statements and can be called from multiple call sites.

Stepping behavior is configured via the `IStackFrameContributor`, `ISteppable`, `ISteppableContext`, `IStepIntoable` and `IDebugStrategy` interfaces. Fig. 15.12 shows an overview.

The methods defined by these interfaces return *strategies* that determine where the debugger may have to stop next if the user selects a stepping operation (remember that the debugger framework sets breakpoints to implement stepping). New strategies can be added without changing the generic execution aspect of the framework.

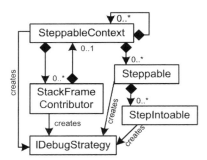

Figure 15.12: The structure of language concepts implementing the stepping-related interfaces. The boxes represent language concepts implementing the interfaces discussed in the text. Those concepts define the containments, so this figure represents a typical setup.

Stepping relies on **ISteppable** contributing *step over* and *step into* strategies. Many **ISteppable**s are embedded in an **ISteppableContext** (e.g., **Statement**s in **StatementList**s). Strategies may delegate to the containing **ISteppableContext** to determine where to stop next (the **ancestor** strategy in the **foreach** example).

For *step into* behavior, an **ISteppable** specifies those subtrees in which instances of **IStepIntoable** may be located (the **array** and **len** expressions in the **foreach** case). The debugger searches these subtrees at debug-time and collects all instances of **IStepIntoable**. An **IStepIntoable** represents a callable invocation (e.g., a **FunctionCall**), and the returned strategies suspend the debugger within the callable.

Step out behavior is provided by implementors of **IStackFrameContributor** (mentioned earlier). Since a callable can be called from many program locations, the call site for a particular invocation cannot be determined by inspecting the program structure; a call stack is needed. We use the ordered list of **IStackFrameContributor**s, from which the tree-level call stack is derived, to realize the *step out* behavior. By "going back" (or "out") in the stack, the call site for the current invocation is determined. For *step out*, the debugger locates the enclosing **IStackFrameContributor** and asks it for its *step out* strategies.

Strategies implement **IDebugStrategy** and are responsible for setting breakpoints to implement a particular stepping behavior. Language extensions can either implement their own strategies or use predefined ones. These include setting a breakpoint on a particular node, searching for **IStepIntoables** in expression subtrees (step into), or delegating to the outer stack frame (step out).

To support *watches*, language concepts implement **IWatchProvider** if they directly contribute one or more items into the Watch window. An **IWatchProviderContext** contains zero or more watch providers. Typically these are concepts that own statement lists, such as **Function**s or **IfStatement**s. If the debugger is suspended on any particular statement, we can find all visible watches by iterating through all ancestor **IWatchProviderContext**s and asking them for their **IWatchProvider**s. Fig. 15.13 shows the typical structure of the concepts.

An **IWatchProvider** implements the **contributeWatchables** operation. It has access to the C variables available in the native

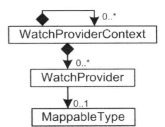

Figure 15.13: Typical structure of language concepts implementing the watches-related interfaces

C debugger. Based on those, it creates a set of watchables. The method may hide a base-level C variable (because it is irrelevant to the extension-level), promote C variable to a watchable or create additional Watchables based on the values of C variables. The representation of a watchable often depends on the variable's type *as expressed in the extension program*. This type may be different from the one in the C program. For example, we represent values of type **Boolean** with *true* and *false*, even though they are represented as **int**s in C. As the watchable is created, we specify the type that should be used. Types that should be used in this way must implement **IMappableType**. Its method **mapVariable** is responsible for computing a type-appropriate representation of a value.

■ *More Examples* To illustrate mbeddr's approach to extensible debuggers further, we have implemented the debugging behavior for mbeddr C and all default extensions. We discuss some interesting cases in this section.

We encounter many cases where we cannot know statically which piece of code will be executed when *stepping into* a callable. Consider polymorphic calls on interfaces.

The mbeddr components extension provides interfaces with operations, as well as components that **provide** and **use** these interfaces. The component methods that implement interface operations are generated to base-level C functions. The same interface can be implemented by *different* components, each implementation ending up in a *different* C function. A client component only specifies the *interface* it uses, not the component. Hence we cannot know statically which C function will be called if an operation is invoked on the interface. However, we do know statically all components that implement the interface, so we know *all possible C functions* that may be invoked. A strategy implemented specifically for this case sets breakpoints on the first line *of each of these functions* to make sure we stop in the first line of any of them if the user *steps into* a method invocation[39].

In many cases a single statement on the extension level is mapped to several statements or whole blocks on the base level. *Stepping over* the single extension-level statement must step over the whole block or list of statements in terms of C. An example is the **assert** statement used in test cases. It is mapped to an **if** statement. The debugger has to step over

[39] We encounter a similar challenge in state machines: as an event is fired into a state machine, we do not know which transition will be triggered. Consequently we set breakpoints in all transitions (translated to **case** branches in a **switch** statement) of the state machine.

the complete **if** statement, independent of whether the condition in the **if** evaluates to **true** or **false**. Note that we get this behavior free[40]: the **assert** statement sets a breakpoint on the base-level counterpart of the *next tree-level statement*. It is irrelevant how many lines of C text further down this is.

Extensions may provide custom data types that are mapped to one or more data types or structures in the generated C. The debugger has to reconstruct the representation in terms of the extension from the base level data. For example, the state of a component is represented by a **struct** that has a member for each of the component fields. Component operations are mapped to C functions. In addition to the formal arguments declared for the respective operation, the generated C function also takes this **struct** as an argument. However, to support the polymorphic invocations discussed earlier, the type of this argument is **void***. Inside the operation, the **void*** is cast down to allow access to the component-specific members. The debugger performs the same downcast to be able to show watchables for all component fields.

■ *Discussion*   To evaluate the suitability of our solution for our purposes, we revisit the requirements described earlier.

Modularity   Our solution requires no changes to the base language or its debugger implementation to specify the debugger for an extension. Also, independently developed extensions retain their independence if they contain debugger specifications[41].

Framework Genericity   The extension-dependent aspects of the debugger behavior are extensible. In particular, stepping behavior is factored into strategies, and new strategies can be implemented by a language extension. Also, the representation of watch values can be customized by making the respective type implement **IMappableType** in a suitable way.

Simple Debugger Definition   This challenge is solved by the debugger definition DSL. It supports the definition of stepping behavior and watches in a declarative way, without concerning the user with implementation details of the framework or the debugger backend.

Limited Overhead   Our solution generates no debugger specific code at all (except the debug symbols added by compiling the C code with debug options). Instead we rely on trace

[40] Remember that we never actually step over statements, we always set breakpoints at the next possible code locations where the debugger may have to stop next.

[41] In particular, MPS' capability of incrementally including language extensions in a program *without defining a composite language first* is preserved in the face of debugger specifications.

data to map the extension level to base level and ultimately to text. This is a trade-off: first, the language workbench must be able to provide trace information. Second, the generated C text cannot be modified by a text processor before it is compiled and debugged, since this would invalidate the trace data[42]. Our approach has another advantage: we do not have to change existing transformations to generate debugger-specific code. This keeps the transformations independent of the debugger.

Debugger Backend Independence We use the Eclipse CDT Debug Bridge to wrap the particular C debugger, so we can use any compatible debugger without changing our infrastructure. Our approach requires no changes to the native C debugger itself, but since we use breakpoints for stepping, the debugger must be able to handle a reasonable number of breakpoints[43]. The debugger also has to provide an API for setting and deleting breakpoints, for querying the currently visible symbols and their values, as well as for querying the code location where the debugger suspended.

[42] The C preprocessor works, it is handled correctly by the compiler and debugger.

[43] Most C debuggers support this, so this is not a serious limitation.

15.2.6 What's Missing?

The support from language workbenches for building debuggers for the DSLs defined with the language workbench is not where it should be. In the face of extensible languages or language composition especially, the construction of debuggers is still a lot of work. The example discussed in Section 15.2.5 above is *not* part of MPS in general, but instead a framework that has been built specifically for mbeddr – although we believe that the architecture can be reused more generally.

Also, ideally, programs should be debuggable at any abstraction level: if a multi-step transformation is used, then users should be able to debug the program at any intermediate step. Debug support for for Xbase-based DSLs is a good example of this, but it is only one translation step, and it is a solution that is specifically constructed for Xbase and Java, and not a generic framework.

So there is a lot of room for innovation in this space.

16
Modularization, Reuse and Composition

Language modularization, extension and composition is an important ingredient in the efficient use of DSLs, just as reuse in general is important to software development. We discuss the need for modularization, extension and composition in the context of DSL design in Section 4.6, where we introduce the four classes of modularization, extension and composition. In this chapter, we look at the implementation approaches taken by our example tools.

16.1 Introduction

When modularizing and composing languages, the following challenges have to be addressed:

- The concrete and the abstract syntaxes of the languages have to be combined. Depending on the kind of composition, this requires the embedding of one syntax into another. This, in turn, requires modular grammars, or more generally, ways of specifying concrete syntax that avoids ambiguities.

- The static semantics, i.e. the constraints and the type system, have to be integrated. For example, in the case of language extension, new types have to be "made valid" for existing operators.

- The execution semantics have to be combined as well. In practice, this may mean mixing the code generated from the composed languages, or composing the generators or interpreters.

- Finally, the IDE services that provides code completion, syntax coloring, static checks and other relevant services have to be extended and composed as well.

In this chapter we show how each of those is addressed with the respective tools. We don't discuss the general problems any further, since those have been discussed in Part II of the book on DSL design.

16.2 MPS Example

With MPS two of these challenges outlined above – composability of concrete syntax and modular IDEs – are solved to a large degree. Modular type systems are reasonably well supported. Semantic interactions are hard to solve in general, but can be handled reasonably in many relevant cases, as we show in this section as well. However, as we will see, in many cases languages have to be designed *explicitly for reuse* to make them reusable. After-the-fact reuse, without consideration during the design of the reusable language, is possible only in limited cases. However, this is true for reuse in software generally.

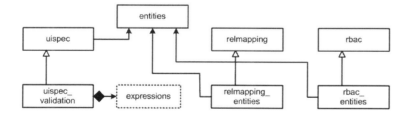

Figure 16.1: **entities** is the central language. **uispec** defines UI forms for the entities. **uispec_validation** adds validation rules, and composes a reusable expressions language. **relmapping** provides a reusable database mapping language, **relmapping_entities** adapts it to the entities language. **rbac** is a reusable language for specifying permissions; **rbac_entities** adapts this language to the **entities** language.

We describe language modularization, extension and composition with MPS based on a set of examples[1]. At the center of this section is a simple **entities** language – the usual entity-with-property-and-references "Hello World" example. We then build additional languages to illustrate extension and composition. Fig. 16.1 illustrates these additional languages. The **uispec** (user interface specification) language illustrates *referencing* with **entities**. **relmapping** (relational database mapping) is an example of *reuse* with separated generated code. **rbac** (role-based access control) illustrates reuse with intermixed generated code. **uispec_validation** demonstrates *extension* (of the **uispec** language) and *embedding* with regard to the expressions language.

[1] These are new examples that have not yet been used before in the book. This is to keep them simple; showcasing these things, for example, with mbeddr would add a lot of additional context and complexity that is not necessary to illustrate the essential techniques.

16.2.1 Implementing the Entities Language

Below is some example code expressed in the **entities** language. *Modules* are root nodes. They live as top-level elements in models[2].

[2] Referring back to the terminology introduced in Section 3.3, root nodes (and their descendants) are considered *fragments*, while the models are partitions. Technically, they are XML files.

```
module company {
  entity Employee {
    id : int
    name : string
    role : string
    worksAt : Department
    freelancer : boolean
  }
  entity Department {
    id : int
    description : string
  }
}
```

■ *Structure and Syntax*   Fig. 16.2 shows a class diagram of the structure of the **entities** language. Each box represents a language concept.

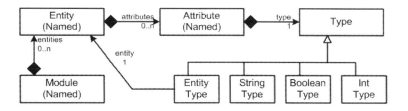

Figure 16.2: The abstract syntax of the entities language. Entities have attributes, which have types and names. **EntityType** extends **Type** and references **Entity**. This "adapts" entities to types (cf. the Adapter pattern).

The following code shows the definition of the **Entity** concept[3]. **Entity** implements the **INamedConcept** interface to inherit a **name** property. It declares a list of children of type **Attribute** in the **attributes** collection. Fig. 16.3 shows the definition of the editor for **Entity**.

[3] This is not the complete definition, concepts can have more characteristics. This is simplified to show the essentials.

```
concept Entity extends BaseConcept implements INamedConcept
  can be root: true
  children:
    Attribute    attributes    0..n
```

■ *Type System*   For the **entities** language, we specify two simple typing rules. The first one specifies that the type of the primitives (**int**, **string**) is a clone of themselves:

```
rule typeof_Type {
  applicable for concept = Type as t
  overrides false
  do {
    typeof(type) :==: type.copy;
  }
}
```

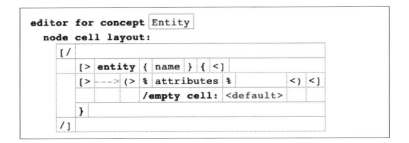

Figure 16.3: The editor for **Entity**. The outermost cell is a vertical list ([/ .. /]). In the first line, we use a horizontal list that contains the "keyword" **entity**, the value of the **name** property and an opening curly brace. In the second line we use indentation and a vertical arrangements of the contents of the **attributes** collection. Finally, the third line contains the closing curly brace.

The only other typing rule is an equation that defines the type of the attribute as a whole to be the type of the attribute's **type** property, defined as

```
typeof(attribute) :==: typeof(attribute.type);
```

■ *Generator*   From **entities** models we generate Java Beans expressed in MPS' BaseLanguage. For the **entities** language, we need a *root mapping rule*[4] and *reduction rules*[5]. The root mapping rule is used to generate a Java class from an **Entity**. The reduction rule transforms the various types (**int**, **string**, etc.) to their Java counterparts. Fig. 16.4 shows a part of the mapping configuration for the **entities** language.

[4] Root mapping rules are used to create new top-level artifacts from existing top-level artifacts (mapping a fragment to another fragment).

[5] Reduction rules are in-place transformations. Whenever the transformation engine encounters an instance of the specified source concept somewhere in a program tree, it replaces that source node with the result of the associated template.

Figure 16.4: The mapping configuration for the **entities** language. The root mapping rule for **Entity** specifies that instances of **Entity** should be transformed with the **map_Entity** template. The reduction rules use inline templates. For example, the **IntType** is replaced with the Java **int** and the **EntityRefType** is reduced to a reference to the class generated from the target entity. The **->$** is a reference macro. It contains code (not shown) that "rewires" the reference to **Double** to a reference to the class generated from the referenced **Entity**.

Fig. 16.5 shows the **map_Entity** template. It generates a Java class. Inside the class, we generate a field for each entity attribute. To do this we first create a prototype field in the class (**private int aField;**). Then we use macros to "transform" this prototype into an instance for each **Entity** attribute. We first attach a **LOOP** macro to the whole field. Based on its expression `node.attributes;`, we iterate over the attributes in the current entity. We then use a `COPY_SRC` macro to transform the type. `COPY_SRC` copies the input node (the inspector specifies the current attribute's type as the input here) and applies reduction rules. So instances of the types defined as part of the `entities` language are transformed into a Java type using the reduction rules defined in the mapping configuration above. Finally we use a property macro (the `$` sign) to change the `name` property of the field we generate from the dummy value `aField` to the name of the attribute we currently transform (once again via an expression in the inspector).

```
root template
input Entity

public class $[map_Entity] {
  $LOOP$[private $COPY_SRC$[int] $[aField]; ]
  $LOOP$[public void $[setter]($COPY_SRC$[int] n ) {
      <<placeholder>> pre-set : $[attr]
      this.aField = n;
   }
  ]

  $LOOP$[public $COPY_SRC$[int] $[getter]() {
      return aField;
   }
  ]
}
```

Figure 16.5: The template for creating a Java class from an `Entity`. The running text explains the details. The «`placeholder`» is a special concept used later.

16.2.2 Referencing

We define a language `uispec` for defining user interface forms based on the `entities`. Below is an example model. Note how the form is another, separate fragment. It is a *dependent* fragment, since it references elements from another fragment (expressed in the `entities` language). Both fragments are *homogeneous*, since they consist of sentences expressed in a single language.

```
form CompanyStructure
  uses Department
  uses Employee
  field Name: textfield(30) -> Employee.name
  field Role: combobox(Boss, TeamMember) -> Employee.role
  field Freelancer: checkbox -> Employee.freelancer
  field Office: textfield(20) -> Department.description
```

■ *Structure and Syntax* The **uispec** language extends[6] the **entities** language. This means that concepts from the **entities** language can be used in the definition of language concepts in the **uispec** language. Fig. 16.6 shows the abstract syntax as a UML diagram.

[6] MPS uses the term "extension" whenever the definition of one language uses or refers to concepts defined in another language. This is not necessarily an example of language extension as defined in this book.

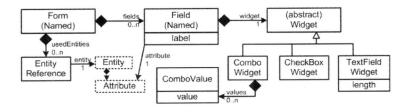

Figure 16.6: The abstract syntax of the **uispec** language. Dotted lines represent classes from another language (here: the **entities** language). A **Form** contains **EntityReference**s that connect to an **entities** model. A form also contains **Field**s, each referencing an **Attribute** from an **Entity** and containing a **Widget**.

A **Form** owns a number of **EntityReferences**, which in turn reference the **Entity** concept. Also, **Field**s refer to the attribute that is intended to be edited via the field. Below is the definition of the **Field** concept. It owns a **Widget** and refers to an **Attribute**.

```
concept Field extends BaseConcept implements <none>
  properties:
    label  : string
  children:
    Widget      widget      1
  references:
    Attribute   attribute   1
```

■ *Type System* The language enforces limitations over which widget can be used with which attribute type[7]. The necessary typing rule is defined in the **uispec** language and references types from the **entities** language[8]. The following is the code for the type check.

[7] A **checkbox** widget requires a Boolean type, a **ComboWidget** requires a **string** type.

[8] This is valid, since in referencing, the referencing language has a dependency on the referenced language.

```
checking rule checkTypes {
  applicable for concept = Field as field
  overrides false
  do {
    if (field.widget.isInstanceOf(CheckBoxWidget)
        && !(field.attribute.type.isInstanceOf(BooleanType))) {
      error "only use checkbox with booleans" -> field.widget;
    }
    if (field.widget.isInstanceOf(ComboWidget)
        && !(field.attribute.type.isInstanceOf(StringType))) {
      error "cannot use combobox with strings" -> field.widget;
    }
  }
}
```

■ *Generation* The defining characteristic of language referencing is that the two languages only *reference* each other, and the instance fragments are dependent, but *homogeneous*. No syntactic integration is necessary in this case. In this example, the generated code exhibits the same separation. From the **Form** definition, we generate a Java class that uses Java Swing to build the UI form. It *uses* the beans generated from the entities: the classes are instantiated, and the getters and setters are called[9]. The generators are separate, but they are *dependent* because they share information. Specifically, the **uispec** generator knows about the names of the generated entity classes, as well as the names of the setters and getters. This dependency is implemented by defining a couple of behavior methods on the **Attribute** concept that are called from both generators:

[9] To get values from the bean when the form is populated and to set the values into the bean if they have been changed in the form.

```
concept behavior Attribute {
  public string qname() {
    this.parent:Entity.name + "." + this.name;
  }
  public string setterName() {
    "set" + this.name.toFirstUpper();
  }
  public string getterName() {
    "get" + this.name.toFirstUpper();
  }
}
```

The original **entities** fragment is still *sufficient* for the transformation that generates the Java Bean. The **uispec** fragment is not sufficient for generating the UI; it needs the **entities** fragment. This is not surprising, since *dependent* fragments can never be sufficient for a transformation: the transitive closure of all dependencies has to be made available.

16.2.3 Extension

We extend the MPS base language with block expressions and placeholders. These concepts make writing generators that generate base language code much simpler. Fig. 16.7 shows an example.

Figure 16.7: Block expressions (in blue, gray in print) are basically anonymous inline methods. Upon transformation, a method is generated that contains the block content, and the block expression is replaced with a call to this method. Block expressions are used mostly when implementing generators; this screenshot shows a generator that uses a block expressions.

```
$LOOP$[->$[o].->$[split]({$COPY_SRC$[String] newValue = $SWITCH$ [null]; name: $[aName]);
        yield newValue;
```

■ *Structure and Syntax*   A block expression is a block that can be used where an **Expression** is expected[10]. The block can contain any number of statements; **yield** can be used to "return" values from within the block[11]. An optional name property of a block expression is used as the name of the generated method. The generator of the block expression in Fig. 16.7 transforms it into this structure:

[10] M. Bravenboer, R. Vermaas, J. J. Vinju, and E. Visser. Generalized type-based disambiguation of meta programs with concrete object syntax. In *GPCE*, pages 157–172, 2005

[11] So, in some sense, a block expression is an "inlined method", or a closure that is defined and called directly.

```
// the argument to setName is what was the block expression,
// it is replaced by a method call to the generated method
aEmployee.setName(retrieve_name(aEmployee, widget0));

...

// this is the method generated from the block expression
public String retrieve_name(Employee aEmployee, JComponent widget0) {
  String newValue = ((JTextField) widget0).getText();
  return newValue;
}
```

The **jetbrains.mps.baselanguage.exprblocks** language extends Ba- seLanguage. To make a block expression valid where BaseLanguage expects an **Expression**, **BlockExpression** extends **Expression**[12].

```
concept BlockExpression extends Expression implements INamedConcept
  children:
    StatementList body 1
```

[12] Consequently, fragments that use the **exprblocks** language can now use **BlockExpression**s in addition to the concepts provided by the BaseLanguage. The fragments become *heterogeneous*, because languages are syntactically mixed.

■ *Type System* The type of the **yield** statement is the type of the expression that is yielded, specified by this equation[13]:

```
typeof(yield) :==: typeof(yield.result);
```

[13] The type of **yield 1;** would be **int**.

Since the **BlockExpression** is used as an **Expression**, it has to have a type as well. However, its type is not explicitly specified, so it has to be calculated as the common supertype of the types of all **yield**s. The following typing rule computes this type. We use the **:>=:** operator to express that the result type must be the same or a supertype of the right argument.

```
typevar resultType ;
for (node<BlockExpressionYield> y :
     blockExpr.descendants<BlockExpressionYield>) {
  resultType :>=: typeof(y.result);
}
typeof(blockExpr) :==: resultType;
```

Figure 16.8: We use a weaving rule to create an additional method for a **BlockExpression**. A weaving rule processes an input element (**BlockExpression**) by creating another node in a different place. The context function defines this other place. In this case, it simply gets the class in which we have defined the block expression.

```
[concept      BlockExpression]
[inheritors   false          ]
[condition    <always>       ]
-->
[ weave_BlockExpression
  context : (node, genContext, operationContext)->node< > {
              node<ClassConcept> cls = node.ancestor<ClassConcept, +>;
              genContext.get copied output for (cls);
            }
]
```

■ *Generator* The generator for **BlockExpression**s reduces the new concept to pure BaseLanguage: it performs assimilation. It transforms a *heterogeneous* fragment (using BaseLanguage and **exprblocks**) to a *homogeneous* fragment (using only BaseLanguage). The first step is the creation of the additional method for the block expression. Fig. 16.8 shows the definition of the weaving rule; Fig. 16.9 shows the template used in that weaving rule.

The template shown in Fig. 16.9 shows the creation of the method. It assigns a mapping label[14] to the created method. The mapping label creates a mapping between the **BlockExpression** and the created method. We will use this label to refer to this generated method when we generate the method call that replaces the **BlockExpression** (shown in Fig. 16.10).

[14] In earlier MPS examples, we had used name-based resolution of references. We use a mapping label here to show how this works.

```
<TF b2M  public $COPY_SRC$[string] $[amethod]($LOOP$v2P[ $COPY_SRC$[int] $[a]]) { TF> ]])
           $COPY_SRCL$[return "hallo"; ]
         }
```

A second concept introduced by the **exprblocks** language is the **PlaceholderStatement**. This extends **Statement** so that it can be used inside method bodies. It also has a name. It is used to mark locations at which subsequent generators can add additional code. These subsequent generators will use a reduction rule to replace the placeholder with whatever they want to put at this location. It is a means of building extensible generators. Both **BlockExpression** and **PlaceholderStatement** will be used in subsequent examples of in this chapter.

Figure 16.9: The generator creates a method from the **BlockExpression**. It uses COPY_SRC macros to replace the **string** type with the computed return type of the block expression, inserts a computed name, adds a parameter for each referenced variable outside the block, and inserts all the statements from the block expression into the body of the method (using the COPY_SRCL macro that iterates over all of the statements in the **ExpressionBlock**). The **blockExprToMethod** mapping label is used later in the method call.

```
public void caller() {
   int j = 0;
   <TF [ ->$[callee]($LOOP$[$COPY_SRC$[j]]) ] TF>;
}
```

A particularly interesting feature of MPS is the ability to use several extensions of the same base language in a given program *without defining a combining language*. For example, a user could decide to use the block expression language defined above together with the **dispatch** extension discussed in Section 12.2. This is a consequence of MPS' projectional nature[15]. Let us consider the potential cases for ambiguity:

Figure 16.10: Here we generate the call to the previously generated method. We use the mapping label **blockExprToMethod** (not shown; happens inside the ->$ macro) to refer to the correct method. We pass in the environment variables as actual arguments.

[15] These same benefits are also exploited in the case of embedding multiple independent languages. Note that there are also potential semantic issues, that are independent of parsing vs. projection.

Same Concept Name The used languages may define concepts with the same name as the host language. This will not lead to ambiguity because concepts have a unique ID as well. A program element will use this ID to refer to the concept whose instance it represents.

Same Concrete Syntax The projection of a concept is not relevant to the functioning of the editor. The program would still be unambiguous to MPS even if *all elements had the same notation*. Of course, it would be confusing to the users.

Same Alias If two concepts that are valid at the same location use the same alias, then, as the user types the alias, it is not clear which of the two concepts should be instantiated. This problem is solved by MPS opening the code completion window and requiring the user to explicitly select which alternative to choose. Once the user has made the decision, the unique ID is used to create an unambiguous program tree.

16.2.4   Reuse with Separated Generated Code

Language reuse covers the case in which a language that has been developed independently of the context in which it should be reused. The respective fragments remain *homogeneous*. In this section, we cover two alternative cases: the first case (in this subsection) addresses a persistence mapping language. The generated code is separate from the code generated from the entities language. The second case (discussed in the next subsection) describes a language for role-based access control. The generated code has to be "woven into" the **entities** code to check permissions when setters are called.

■ *Structure and Syntax*   **relmapping** is a reusable language for mapping arbitrary data to relational tables. The **relmapping** language supports the definition of relational table structures, but leaves the actual mapping to the source data unspecified. As you adapt the language to a specific reuse context, you have to specify this mapping. The following code shows the reusable part: a database is defined that contains tables with columns. Columns have (database-specific) data types.

```
database CompanyDB
  table Departments
    number id
    char descr
  table People
    number id
```

```
  char name
  char role
  char isFreelancer
```

Fig. 16.11 shows the structure of the relmapping language. The abstract concept `ColumnMapper` serves as a hook: if we reuse this language in a different context, we extend this hook in a context-specific way.

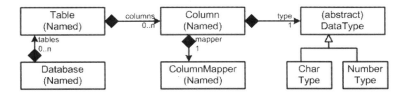

Figure 16.11: A `Database` contains `Tables` which contain `Columns`. A column has a name and a type. A column also has a `ColumnMapper`. This is an abstract concept that determines where the column gets its data from. It is a hook intended to be specialized in sublanguages that are context-specific.

The `relmapping_entities` language extends `relmapping` and adapts it for reuse with the `entities` language[16]. To this end, it provides a subconcept of `ColumnMapper`, the `AttributeCol-Mapper`, which references an `Attribute` from the `entities` language as a means of expressing the mapping from the attribute to the column. The column mapper is projected on the right of the field definition, resulting in the following (heterogeneous) code fragment[17]:

[16] Such a language could be called an Adapter language, in reference to the Adapter pattern from the GoF book.

[17] This "mixed syntax" is fairly trivial, since the `AttributeColMapper` just references an attribute with a qualified name (`Entity.attribute`). However, arbitrary additional syntax could be added, and we could use arbitrary concepts from the `entities` language mixed into the `relmapping` fragment.

```
database CompanyDB
  table Departments
    number id <- Department.id
    char descr <- Department.description
  table People
    number id <- Employee.id
    char name <- Employee.name
    char role <- Employee.role
    char isFreelancer <- Employee.freelancer
```

■ *Type System*   The type of a column is the type of its `type` property. In addition, the type of the column must also conform to the type of the column mapper, so the concrete `Column-Mapper` subtype must provide a type mapping as well. This "typing hook" is implemented as an abstract behavior method `typeMappedToDB` on the `ColumnMapper`[18]. With this in mind, the typing rules of the `relmapping` language look as follows:

[18] It is acceptable from a dependency perspective to have this typing hook, since `relmapping` is designed to be reusable.

```
typeof(column) :==: typeof(column.type);
typeof(column.type) :==: typeof(column.mapper);
typeof(columnMapper) :==: columnMapper.typeMappedToDB();
```

The `AttributeColMapping` concept from the `relmapping_entities` implements this method by mapping `int`s to `number`s and everything else to `char`s.

```
public node<> typeMappedToDB() overrides ColumnMapper.typeMappedToDB {
  node<> attrType = this.attribute.type.type;
  if (attrType.isInstanceOf(IntType)) { return new node<NumberType>(); }
  return new node<CharType>();
}
```

■ *Generator* The generated code is also separated into a reusable part (a class generated by the **relmapping** language's generator) and a context-specific subclass of that class, generated by the **relmapping_entities** language. The generic base class contains code for creating the tables and for storing data in those tables. It contains abstract methods that are used to access the data to be stored in the columns[19].

```
public abstract class CompanyDBBaseAdapter {

  private void createTableDepartments() {
    // SQL to create the Departments table
  }

  private void createTablePeople() {
    // SQL to create the People table
  }

  public void storeDepartments(Object applicationData) {
    Insert i = new Insert("Departments");
    i.add( "id", getValueForDepartments_id(applicationData));
    i.add( "descr", getValueForDepartments_descr(applicationData));
    i.execute();
  }

  public void storePeople(Object applicationData) {
    // like above
  }

  public abstract String getValueForDepartments_id(Object applicationData);

  public abstract String getValueForDepartments_descr(
                         Object applicationData);

  // abstract getValue methods for the People table
}
```

[19] So the dependency structure of the generated fragments, as well as the dependencies of the respective generators, resembles the dependency structure of the languages: the generated fragments are dependent, and the generators are dependent as well (they share the name, and implicitly, the knowledge about the structure of the class generated by the reusable relmapping generator). A **relmapping** fragment (without the concrete column mappers) is sufficient for generating the generic base class.

The subclass, generated by the generator in the **relmapping_entities** language, implements the abstract methods defined by the generic superclass. The interface, represented by the **applicationData** object, has to be kept generic so that any kind of user data can be passed in[20].

```
public class CompanyDBAdapter extends CompanyDBBaseAdapter {
  public String getValueForDepartments_id(Object applicationData) {
    Object[] arr = (Object[]) applicationData;
    Department o = (Department) arr[0];
    String val = o.getId() + "";
    return val;
  }
  public String getValueForDepartments_descr(Object applicationData) {
    Object[] arr = (Object[]) applicationData;
    Department o = (Department) arr[0];
    String val = o.getDescription() + "";
    return val;
  }
}
```

[20] Note how this class references the Beans generated from the **entities**: the generator for **entities** and the generator for **relmapping_ entities** are dependent, the information shared between the two generators is the names of the classes generated from the entities. The code generated from the **relmapping** language is *designed* to be extended by code generated from a sublanguage (the abstract **getValue** methods). This is acceptable, since the **relmapping** language itself is designed to be extended to adapt it to a new reuse context.

16.2.5 Reuse with Interwoven generated code

rbac is a language for specifying role-based access control, to specify access permissions for entities defined with the **entities** language[21]. Here is some example code:

```
RBAC

users:
  user mv : Markus Voelter
  user ag : Andreas Graf
  user ke : Kurt Ebert

roles:
  role admin : ke
  role consulting : ag, mv

permissions:
  admin, W : Department
  consulting, R : Employee.name
```

[21] Like the example in the previous subsection, the models expressed in the two languages are separate and homogeneous. However, the code generated from the **rbac** specification has to be mixed with the code generated from the **entities**.

■ *Structure and Syntax* The structure of **rbac** is shown in Fig. 16.12. Like **relmapping**, it provides a hook, in this case, **Resource**, to adapt it to context languages: the sublanguage **rbac_entities** provides two subconcepts of **Resource**, namely **AttributeResource** to reference to an attribute, and **EntityResource** to refer to an **Entity**, to define permissions for entities and their attributes.

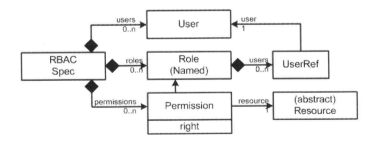

Figure 16.12: Language structure of the **rbac** language. An **RBACSpec** contains **Users**, **Roles** and **Permissions**. Users can be members in several roles. A permission assigns a right to a **Resource**.

■ *Type System* No type system rules apply here.

■ *Generator* What distinguishes this case from the **relmapping** case is that the code generated from the **rbac_entities** language is *not* separated from the code generated from **entities**. Instead, inside the setters of the Java beans, a permission check is required.

```
public void setName(String newValue) {
  // check permissions (from rbac_entities)
  if (!new RbacSpecEntities().currentUserHasWritePermission(
                          "Employee.name")) {
    throw new RuntimeException("no permission");
  }
  this.name = newValue;
}
```

The generated fragment is homogeneous (all Java code), but it is *multi-sourced*, since several generators contribute to the same fragment. To implement this, several approaches are possible:

- We could use AspectJ[22]. This would allow us to generate separate Java artifacts (all single-sourced) and then use the aspect weaver to "mix" them. However, we don't want to introduce the complexity of yet another tool, AspectJ, here, so we will not use this approach.

  [22] www.eclipse.org/aspectj/

- An interceptor[23] framework could be added to the generated Java Beans, with the generated code contributing specific interceptors (effectively building a custom AOP solution). We will not use this approach either, since it would require the addition of a whole interceptor framework to the **entities** implementation. This seems like overkill.

  [23] en.wikipedia.org/wiki/Interceptor_pattern

- We could "inject" additional code generation templates to the existing **entities** generator from the **rbac_entities** generator. This would make the generators *woven*, as opposed to just dependent. Assuming that this would work in MPS, it would be the most elegant solution – but it does not.

- We could define a hook in the generated Java Beans code and then have the **rbac_entities** generator contribute code to this hook. This is the approach we will use. The generators remain dependent, they have to agree on the way the hook works.

Notice that only the AspectJ solution can work without any preplanning from the perspective of the **entities** language, because it avoids mixing the generated code artifacts (it is handled "magically" by AspectJ). All other solutions require the original **entities** generator to "expect" certain extensions.

In our case, we have modified the original generator in the **entities** language to contain a **PlaceholderStatement** (see Fig. 16.13). In every setter, the placeholder acts as a hook at which subsequent generators can add statements. So while we have to pre-plan *that* we want to extend the generator at this location, we don't have to predefine *how*.

```
$LOOP$ public void $[setter]($COPY_SRC$[int] newValue) {
           <<placeholder>> pre-set : $[attr]
           this.aField = newValue;
       }
```

Figure 16.13: This generator fragment creates a setter method for each attribute of an entity. The **LOOP** iterates over all attributes. The **$** macro computes the name of the method, and the **COPY_SRC** macro on the argument type computes the type. The placeholder marks the location where the permission check will be inserted by a subsequent generator.

The **rbac_entities** generator contains a reduction rule for **PlaceholderStatement**s. So when it encounters a placeholder (put there by the **entities** generator) it removes it and inserts the code that checks for the permission (Fig. 16.14). To make this work, we have to make sure that this generator runs *after* the **entities** generator (since the **entities** generator has to create the placeholder first) but *before* the BaseLanguage generator (which transforms BaseLanguage code into Java text for compilation). We use generator priorities to achieve this[24].

[24] Generator priorities express a partial ordering (run before, run after, etc.) between pairs of generators. Upon generation, MPS computes an overall schedule that determines which generators run in which order.

```
concept      PlaceholderStatement
inheritors   false
condition    (node, genContext, operationContext)->boolean {
                 node.name.equals("pre-set");
             }
   -->
content node:
public void dummy() {
   <TF [ {{ // transparent block                                         TF>
        // check permissions (from rbac_entities)
        if (new ->$[RbacSpecEntities]().currentUserHasWritePermission("$[res]
           ")) { throw new RuntimeException("no permission"); }
      }}
}
```

Figure 16.14: This reduction rule replaces **PlaceholderStatement**s with a permission check. Using the condition, we only match those placeholders whose identifier is **pre-set** (notice how we have defined this identifier in Fig. 16.13). The inserted code queries another generated class that contains the actual permission check. A runtime exception is thrown if the check fails.

16.2.6 Embedding

■ *Structure and Syntax* **uispec_validation** extends **uispec**: it is a sublanguage of the **uispec** language. It supports writing code such as the following in the UI form specifications:

```
form CompanyStructure
  uses Department
  uses Employee

  field Name: textfield(30) -> Employee.name validate lengthOf(Employee.
     name) < 30
  field Role: combobox(Boss, TeamMember) -> Employee.role
  field Freelancer: checkbox -> Employee.freelancer
       validate if (isSet(Employee.worksAt)) Employee.freelancer == false
     else
                  Employee.freelancer == true
  field Office: textfield(20) -> Department.description
```

Writing the expressions is supported by embedding an **expressions** language. Fig. 16.15 shows the structure. To be able to use the expressions, the user has to use a **ValidatedField** instead of a **Field**. **ValidatedField** is also defined in **uispec_validation**, and is a subconcept of **Field**.

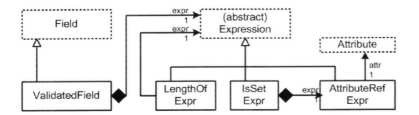

Figure 16.15: The icsnuispec_validation language defines a subtype of **uispec.Field** that contains an **Expression** from an embeddable expression language. The language also defines a couple of additional expressions, specifically the **AttributeRefExpr**, which can be used to refer to attributes of entities.

To support the migration of existing models that use **Field** instances, we provide an intention: the user can press **Alt-Enter** on a **Field** and select **Make Validated Field**. This transforms an existing **Field** into a **ValidatedField**, so that validation expressions can be entered[25]. The core of the intention is the following script, which performs the actual transformation:

```
execute(editorContext, node)->void {
    node<ValidatedField> vf = new node<ValidatedField>();
    vf.widget = node.widget;
    vf.attribute = node.attribute;
    vf.label = node.label;
    node.replace with(vf);
}
```

[25] Alternatively it could be arranged (with 5 lines of code) that users could simply type **validate** on the right of a field definition to trigger the transformation code below.

The **uispec_validation** language extends the **uispec** language. We also extend the existing, embeddable **expressions** language, so we can use **Expressions** in the definition of our language[26]. **ValidatedField** has a property **expr** that contains the validation expression.

As a consequence of polymorphism, we can use any existing subconcept of **Expression** in validations. So without doing anything else, we could write **20 + 40 > 10**, since integer literals and the **+** and **>** operators are defined as part of the composed **expressions** language. However, to write anything useful, we have to be able to reference entity attributes from within expressions[27]. To achieve this, we create the **AttributeRefExpr**, as shown in Fig. 16.15. We also create **LengthOf** and **IsSetExpression** as further examples of how to adapt an embedded language to its new context – i.e. the **uispec** and **entities** languages.

The **AttributeRefExpr** references an **Attribute** from the **entities** language; however, it may only reference those attributes of those entities that are used in the form in which we define the validation expression. The following is the code for the search scope:

[26] Embedding requires that both composed languages (**uispec** and **expressions**) remain independent. The **uispec_validation** language acts as an adapter. In contrast to the reuse examples, this adapter also adapts the concrete syntax.

[27] We argued in the design part that, in order to make an embedded language useful with its host language, it has to be extended: the following is an example of this.

```
(model, scope, referenceNode, linkTarget, enclosingNode)
                    ->join(ISearchScope | sequence<node< >>) {
  nlist<Attribute> res = new nlist<Attribute>;
  node<Form> form = enclosingNode.ancestor<Form, +>;
  if ( form != null ) {
    for (node<EntityReference> er : form.usedEntities) {
      res.addAll(er.entity.attributes);
    }
  }
  res;
}
```

Notice that the actual syntactic embedding of the **expressions** language in the **uispec_validation** language is no problem at all as a consequence of how projectional editors work. We simply define **Expression** to be a child of the **ValidatedField**.

■ *Type System* The general challenge here is that primitive types such as **int** and **string** are defined in the **entities** language *and* in the embeddable **expressions** language. Although they have the same names, they are not the same types. So the two sets of types must be mapped. Here are a couple of examples. The type of the **IsSetExpression** is by definition **expressions.BooleanType**. The type of the **LengthOf**, which takes an **AttrRefExpression** as its argument, is **expressions.IntType**. The type of an attribute reference is the type of the attribute's **type** property:

```
typeof(attrRef) :==: typeof(attrRef.attr.type);
```

However, consider the following code:

```
field Freelancer: checkbox -> Employee.freelancer
  validate if (isSet(Employee.worksAt)) Employee.freelancer == false
           else Employee.freelancer == true
```

This code states that if the **worksAt** attribute of an employee is set, then its **freelancer** attribute must be **false** else it must be **true** (freelancers don't **workAt** anything). It uses the == operator from the **expressions** language. However, that operator expects two arguments with **expressions.BooleanType**, but the type of the **Employee. freelancer** is **entities.BooleanType**[28]. In effect, we have to override the typing rules for the expressions language's == operator. Here is how we do it.

In the **expressions** language, we define *overloaded operation rules*. We specify the resulting type for an **EqualsExpression** depending on its argument types. Here is the code in the **expressions** language that defines the resulting type to be **boolean** if the two arguments are **Equallable**[29]:

```
operation concepts: EqualsExpression
  left operand type: new node<Equallable>()
```

[28] It is probably a good idea to use the same set of primitive types (and expressions) for all languages to avoid mappings like these. This could be achieved by requiring all languages to use a common base language (similar to Xbase). However, if the to-be-composed languages are developed by independent people, then it is hard to enforce a common base language. So the ability to have such mappings is useful.

[29] In addition to this code, we have to specify that **expressions.BooleanType** is a subtype of **Equallable**, so this rule applies if we use equals with two **expressions.BooleanType** arguments.

```
    right operand type: new node<Equallable>()
operation type:
  (operation, leftOperandType, rightOperandType)->node< > {
    <boolean>;
  }
```

We have to tie this overloaded operation specification into a regular type inference rule:

```
rule typeof_BinaryExpression {
  applicable for BinaryExpression as binex
  do {
    node<> opType = operation type( binex , left , right );
    if (opType != null) {
      typeof(binex) :==: opType;
    } else {
      error "operator " + binex.concept.name +
          " cannot apply to these argument types " +
          left.concept.name + "/" + right.concept.name
        -> binex; }
  }
}
```

To override these typing rules to work with **entities.Boolean-Type**, we simply provider another overloaded operation specification in the **uispec_validation** language:

```
operation concepts: EqualsExpression
  one operand type: <boolean> // the entities.BooleanType!
operation type:
  (op, leftOperandType, rightOperandType)->node< > {
    <boolean>;  // the expressions.BooleanType
  }
```

■ *Generator* The generator has to create BaseLanguage code, which is then subsequently transformed into Java text. To deal with the transformation of the expressions language, we can do one of two things:

- Either we can use the **expressions** language's existing to-text generator and wrap the expressions in some kind of **TextHolderStatement**[30].
- Alternatively, we can write a (reusable) transformation from expressions code to BaseLanguage code; these rules would get used as part of the transformation of **uispec** and **uispec_validation** code to BaseLanguage.

Since many DSLs will probably transform code to BaseLanguage, it is worth the effort to write a reusable generator from **expressions** to BaseLanguage[31]. So we choose this second alternative. The generated Java code is multi-sourced, since it is generated by two independent code generators.

Expression constructs from the reusable **expressions** language and those of BaseLanguage are almost identical, so this

[30] Remember that we cannot simply embed text in BaseLanguage, since that would not work structurally: no concept in BaseLanguage expects "text" as children: a wrapper is necessary.

[31] In fact, it would be useful if a simple language with types and expression came with MPS. This language could either be used as part of BaseLanguage as well (so no transformation would be needed) or the transformation to BaseLanguage could ship with MPS as well.

generator is trivial. We create a new language project **expressions.blgen** and add reduction rules[32]. Fig. 16.16 shows some of these reduction rules.

[32] In MPS all "meta stuff" is called a language. So even though **expressions.blgen** only contains a generator it is still a *language* in MPS terminology.

```
[concept      MultiExpression]  -->  <T $COPY_SRC$[1] * $COPY_SRC$[2] T>
[inheritors   false            ]
[condition    <always>         ]

[concept      PlusExpression ]  -->  <T $COPY_SRC$[1] + $COPY_SRC$[2] T>
[inheritors   false           ]
[condition    <always>        ]

[concept      FalseLiteral ]  -->  <T false T>
[inheritors   false         ]
[condition    <always>      ]

[concept      BooleanType ]  -->  <T boolean T>
[inheritors   false        ]
[condition    <always>     ]

[concept      IfExpression ]  -->  <T $COPY_SRC$[true]
[inheritors   false         ]             ? $COPY_SRC$[true] : $COPY_SRC$[true] T>
[condition    <always>      ]
```

In addition, we also need reduction rules for the new expressions that we have added specifically in the **uispec_validation** language (**AttrRefExpression**, **isSetExpression**, **LengthOf**). These transformations are defined in **uispec_validation**, since this language is *not* reusable – it is specifically designed to integrate the **uispec** and the **expressions** languages. As an example, Fig. 16.17 shows the rule for handling the **AttrRefExpression**. The validation code itself is "injected" into the UI form via the same placeholder reduction as in the case of the language **rbac_entities**.

Figure 16.16: A number of reduction rules that map the reusable **expressions** language to BaseLanguage (Java). Since the languages are very similar, the mapping is trivial. For example, a **PlusExpression** is mapped to a + in Java, the **left** and **right** arguments are reduced recursively through the **COPY_SRC** macro.

```
reduction rules:
[concept      AttributeRefExpr]  -->  content node:
[inheritors   false            ]      public void dummy() {
[condition    <always>         ]          Object anObj = null;
                                          <TF [ ->$[anObj].->$[toString]() ] TF>;
                                      }
```

Figure 16.17: References to entity attributes are mapped to a call to their getter method. The template fragment (inside the <TF..TF>) uses two reference macros (->$) to "rewire" the object reference to the Java bean instance, and the **toString** method call to a call to the getter.

Language extension can also be used to prevent the use of specific base language concepts in the sublanguage, possibly in certain contexts. As an example, we restrict the use of some operators provided by the reusable expression language inside validation rules in **uispec_validation**. This can be achieved by implementing a `can be ancestor` constraint on **Validated-Field**.

```
can be ancestor:
  (operationContext, scope, node, childConcept)->boolean {
    return !(childConcept == concept/GreaterEqualsExpression/ ||
             childConcept == concept/LessEqualsExpression/);
  }
```

16.2.7 Annotations

In a projectional editor, the CS of a program is projected from the AST. A projectional system always goes from AS to CS, never from CS to AS (as parsers do). This means that the CS does not have to contain all the data necessary to build the AST (which is necessary in the case of parsers). This has two consequences:

- A projection may be *partial*, in the sense that the AS contains data that is not shown in the CS. The information may, for example, only be changeable via intentions (discussed in Section 7.7), or the projection rule may project some parts of the program only in some cases, controlled by some kind of configuration data.

- It is also possible to project *additional* CS that is not part of the CS definition of the original language. Since the CS is never used as the information source, such additional syntax does not confuse the tool (in a parser-based tool the grammar would have to be changed to take into account this additional syntax to avoid derailing the parser).

In this section we discuss the second alternative, since it constitutes a form of language composition: the additional CS is composed with the original CS defined for the language. The mechanism MPS uses for this is called *annotations*. We have seen annotations when we discussed templates[33]: an annotation is something that can be attached to arbitrary program elements and can be shown together with the CS of the annotated element. In this section we use this approach to implement an alternative approach for the entity-to-database mapping. Using this approach, we can store the mapping from entity attributes to database columns directly in the **Entity**, resulting in the following code:

[33] The generator macros **$**, **->$** or **COPY_SRC** are implemented via the annotation mechanism.

```
module company
  entity Employee {
    id : int -> People.id
    name : string -> People.name
```

```
    role : string -> People.role
    worksAt : Department -> People.departmentID
    freelancer : boolean -> People.isFreelancer
  }

  entity Department {
    id : int -> Departments.id
    description : string -> Departments.descr
  }
```

This is a heterogeneous fragment, consisting of code from the **entities** language, as well as the annotation code (e.g., **-> People.id**). From a CS perspective, the column mapping is "embedded" in the **Entity**. In the AST the mapping information is also actually stored in the **entities** model. However, the definition of the **entities** language does not know that this additional information is stored and projected "inside" entities. No modification to the **entities** language is necessary.

■ *Structure and Syntax* We define an additional language **relmapping_annotations** that extends the **entities** language as well as the **relmapping** language. In this language we define the following concept:

```
concept AttrToColMapping extends NodeAnnotation
  references:
    Column column 1
  properties:
    role = colMapping
  concept links:
    annotated = Attribute
```

AttrToColMapping concept extends **NodeAnnotation**, a concept predefined by MPS[34]. Concepts that extend the concept **NodeAnnotation** have to provide a **role** property and an **annotated** concept link. Structurally, an annotation is a child of the node it annotates. So the **Attribute** has a new child of type **AttrToColMapping**, and the reference that contains the child is called **@colMapping** – the value of the **role** property prefixed by an **@**. The **annotated** concept link points to the concept *to which this annotation can be added*. **AttrToColMapping**s can be annotated to instances of **Attribute**.

[34] In fact, this concept is called **NodeAttribute** in MPS. For historical reasons there a somewhat confused terminology around "attribute" and "annotation". We'll stick with the term "annotation" in this chapter.

Figure 16.18: The editor for the **AttrToColMapping** embeds the editor of the concept it is annotated to (using the **attributed node** cell). It then projects the reference to the referenced column. This gives the editor of the annotation control of if and how the editor annotated element is projected.

```
editor for concept AttrToColMapping
  node cell layout:
    [- [> attributed node <] -> ( % column % -> * R/O model access * ) -]
```

While structurally the annotation is a child of the annotated node, in the CS the relationship is reversed: the editor for **AttrToColMapping** wraps the editor for **Attribute**, as Fig. 16.18 shows.

Since the annotation is not part of the original language, it cannot just be typed in: it must be attached to nodes via an intention. The annotation simply adds a new instance of `AttrToCol- Mapping` to the `@colMapping` property of an `Attribute`, so we don't show the code here.

∎ *Type System*   The same typing rules are necessary as in the `relmapping_entities` language described previously. They reside in `relmapping_annotations`.

∎ *Generator*   The generator is also broadly similar to the previous example with `relmapping_entities`. It takes the `entities` model as the input, and then uses the column mappings in the annotations to create the entity-to-database mapping.

The annotations introduced above were typed to be specific to certain target concepts (`Attribute` in this case). A particularly interesting use of annotations includes those that can be annotated to *any* language concept (formally targeting `BaseConcept`). In this case, there is no dependency between the language that contains the annotation and the language that is annotated. This is very useful for "meta data", as well as anything that can be processed generically.

16.3 Xtext Example

In this section we look at an example roughly similar to the one for MPS discussed in the previous section. We start out with a DSL for entities. Here is an example program:

```
module company {
    entity Employee {
        id : int
        name : string
        role : string
        worksAt : Department
        freelancer : boolean
    }
    entity Department {
        id : int
        description : string
    }
}
```

This section of the book has been written together with Christian Dietrich. Contact him via `christian.dietrich@itemis.de`.

The grammar is straightforward and should be clear if you have read the implementation part of this book so far.

```
grammar org.xtext.example.lmrc.entity.EntityDsl
      with org.eclipse.xtext.common.Terminals

generate entityDsl "http://www.xtext.org/example/lmrc/entity/EntityDsl"
```

```
Module:
    "module" name=ID "{"
        entities+=Entity*
    "}";

Entity:
    "entity" name=ID "{"
        attributes+=Attribute*
    "}";

Attribute:
    name=ID ":" type=AbstractType;

Named: Module|Entity|Attribute;

AbstractType:
    BooleanType|IntType|StringType|EntityReference;

BooleanType: {BooleanType} "boolean";

IntType: {IntType} "int";

StringType: {StringType} "string";

EntityReference: ref=[Entity|FQN];

FQN: ID ("." ID)*;
```

16.3.1 Referencing

Referencing describes the case in which programs written in one DSL reference (by name) program elements written in another DSL[35]. The example we use is the UI specification language, in which a **Form** defined in the UI model refers to **Entities** from the language defined above, and **Field**s in a form refers to entity **Attribute**. Here is some example code:

[35] Both programs reside in different fragments and no syntactic composition is required.

```
form CompanyStructure
  uses Department   // reference to Department Entity
  uses Employee     // reference to Employee Entity

  field Name: textfield(30)                    -> Employee.worksAt
  field Role: combobox(Boss, TeamMember)       -> Employee.role
  field Freelancer: checkbox                   -> Employee.freelancer
  field Office: textfield(20)                  -> Department.description
```

■ *Structure* Referencing concepts defined in another language relies on importing the target meta model and then defining references to concepts defined in this meta model[36]. Here is the header of the grammar of the **uispec** language:

```
grammar org.xtext.example.lmrc.uispec.UispecDsl
    with org.eclipse.xtext.common.Terminals

import "http://www.xtext.org/example/lmrc/entity/EntityDsl" as entity

generate uispecDsl "http://www.xtext.org/example/lmrc/uispec/UispecDsl"
```

Importing a meta model means that the respective *meta classes* can now be used. Note that the meta model import does not make the *grammar rules* visible, so the meta classes can only be

[36] Note that the references to entities and fields do not technically reference into an entity source file. Instead, these references refer to the EMF objects in the AST that has been parsed from the source file. So, a similar approach can be used to reference to other **EObject**s. It does not matter whether these are created via Xtext or not. This is reflected by the fact that the grammar of the **uispec** language does not refer to the *grammar* of the **entity** language, but to the derived meta model.

used in references and as base types (as we will see later). In the case of referencing, we use them in references:

```
EntityReference:
  "uses" entity=[entity::Entity|FQN];

Field:
  "field" label=ID ":" widget=Widget
          "->" attribute=[entity::Attribute|FQN];
```

To make this work, no change is required in the **entities** language[37]. However, the workflow generating the **uispec** language has to be changed. The **genmodel** file for the meta model has to be registered in the **StandaloneSetup**[38].

```
bean = StandaloneSetup {
    ...
    registerGenModelFile = "platform:/resource/org.xtext.example.lmrc.
        entity/src-gen/org/xtext/example/lmrc/entity/EntityDsl.genmodel"
}
```

We have to do one more customization to make the language work smoothly. The only **Attribute**s that should be visible are those from the entities referenced in the current **Form**'s **uses** clauses, and they should be referenced with a qualified name (**Employee.role** instead of just **role**). Scoping has to be customized to achieve this:

```
public IScope scope_Field_attribute(Field context, EReference ref) {
  Form form = EcoreUtil2.getContainerOfType(context, Form.class);
  List<Attribute> visibleAttributes = new ArrayList<Attribute>();
  for (EntityReference useClause : form.getUsedEntities()) {
    visibleAttributes.addAll(useClause.getEntity().getAttributes());
  }
  Function<Attribute, QualifiedName> nameComputation =
    new Function<Attribute, QualifiedName>() {
      @Override
      public QualifiedName apply(Attribute a) {
        return QualifiedName.create(((Entity)a.eContainer()).
                    getName(), a.getName());
      }
    };
  return Scopes.scopeFor(visibleAttributes, nameComputation , IScope.
    NULLSCOPE);
}
```

This scoping function performs two tasks: first, it finds all the **Attribute**s of all **used** entities. We collect them into a list **visibleAttributes**. The second part of the scoping function defines a **Function** object[39] that represents a function from **Attribute** to **QualifiedName**. In the implementation method **apply** we create a qualified name made from two parts: the entity name and the attribute name (the dot between the two is default behavior for the **QualifiedName** class). When we create the scope itself in the last line we pass in the list of attributes, as well as the function object. Xtext's scoping framework uses the function object to determine the name by which each of the attributes is referenceable from this particular context.

[37] This is true as long as the referenced elements are in the index. The index is used by Xtext to resolve references against elements that reside in a different model file. By default, all elements that have a **name** attribute are in the index. **Entity** and **Attribute** have names, so this works automatically.

[38] This is necessary so that the EMF code generator, when generating the meta classes for the **uispec** language, knows where the generated Java classes for the **entities** languages are located. This is an EMF technicality and we won't discuss it in any further detail.

[39] Note how we have to use the ugly function object notation, because Java does not provide support for closures or lambdas at this point! Alternatively you could do this with Xtend, which does support closures.

■ *Type System* As we discussed in Section 20.2, dealing with type systems in the referencing case is not particularly challenging, since the type system of the referencing language can be built with knowledge of the type system of the referenced language.

■ *Generators* The same is true for generators. Typically they just share knowledge about the naming of generated code elements.

16.3.2 Reuse

Referencing concerns the case in which the referencing language is built with knowledge about the referenced language, so it can have direct dependencies. In the example above, the **uispec** language uses **Entity** and **Attribute** from the **entities** language. It directly imports the meta model, so it has a direct dependency. In the case of reuse, such a direct dependency is not allowed. Our goal is to combine two *independent* languages. To illustrate this case, we again use the same example as in the MPS section.

■ *Structure* We first introduce a **db** language, a trivial DSL for defining relational table structures. These can optionally be mapped to a data source, but the language makes no assumption about how this data source looks (and which language is used to define it). Consequently, the grammar has no dependency on any other, and imports no other meta model:

```
grammar org.xtext.example.lmrc.db.DbDsl with org.eclipse.xtext.common.
    Terminals

generate dbDsl "http://www.xtext.org/example/lmrc/db/DbDsl"

Root:
      Database;

Database:
    "database" name=ID
    tables+=Table*;

Table:
    "table" name=ID
    columns+=Column*    ;

Column:
    type=AbstractDataType name=ID (mapper=AbstractColumnMapper)?;

AbstractColumnMapper:
    {AbstractColumnMapper}"not mapped";

AbstractDataType: CharType | NumberType;

CharType: {CharType}"char";

NumberType: {NumberType}"number";
```

Just as in the MPS example, the `Column` rule has an optional `mapper` property of type `AbstractColumnMapper`. Since it is not possible to explicitly mark rules as generating abstract meta classes, we simply define the syntax to be **not mapped**[40]. This language has been designed *for* reuse, because it has this hook `AbstractColumnMapper`, which can be customized later. But the language is still independent. In the next step, we want to be able to reference `Attribute`s from the `entities` language:

[40] Since the `mapper` property in `Column` is optional, you don't ever have to type this.

```
database CompanyDB

table Departments
  number id      <- Department.id
  char descr     <- Department.description

table People
  number id          <- Employee.id
  char name          <- Employee.name
  char role          <- Employee.role
  char isFreelancer  <- Employee.freelancer
```

To make this possible, we create a new language **db2entity** that *extends* the **db** language and *references* the **entities** language[41]. This is reflected by the header of the **db2entity** language (notice the **with** clause):

[41] Notice that we only extend `DbDsl`. The `entities` meta model is just *referenced*. This is because Xtext can only extend one base grammar. For this reason we cannot embed language concepts from the `entities` language in a `db2entity` program, we can only *reference* them. However, for this particular example, this is sufficient.

```
grammar org.xtext.example.lmrc.db2entity.Db2EntityDsl
        with org.xtext.example.lmrc.db.DbDsl

import "http://www.xtext.org/example/lmrc/db/DbDsl" as db
import "http://www.xtext.org/example/lmrc/entity/EntityDsl" as entity

generate db2EntityDsl
        "http://www.xtext.org/example/lmrc/db2entity/Db2EntityDsl"
```

We now have to overwrite the `AbstractColumnMapper` rule defined in the **db** language:

```
AbstractColumnMapper returns db::AbstractColumnMapper:
    {EntityColumnMapper} "<-" entity=[entity::Attribute|FQN];
```

We create a rule that has the same name as the rule in the super-grammar. So when the new grammar calls the `AbstractColumnMapper` rule, our new definition is used. Inside, we define the new syntax we would like to use, and as part of it, we reference an `Attribute` from the imported `entity` meta model. We then use the `{EntityColumnMapper}` action to force instantiation of an `EntityColumnMapper` object: this also implicitly leads to the creation of an `EntityColumnMapper` class in the generated `db2entity` meta model. Since our new rule **returns** an `db::AbstractColumnMapper`, this new meta class extends `AbstractColumnMapper` from the **db** meta model – which is exactly what we need[42].

[42] There are two more things we have to do to make it work. First, we have to register the two `genmodel` files in the `db2entity`'s `StandaloneSetup` bean in the workflow file. Second, we have to address the fact that in Xtext, the first rule in a grammar file is the entry rule for the grammar, i.e. the parser starts consuming a model file using this rule. In our `db2entity` grammar, the first rule is `AbstractColumnMapper`, so this won't work. We simply copy the first rule (`Root`) from the **db** language.

■ *Type System*   The primary task of the type system in this example would be mapping the primitive types used in the **entities** language to those used in the **db** language to make sure we only map those fields to a particular column that are type-compatible. Just as the column mapper itself, this code lives in the adapter language. It is essentially just a constraint that checks for type compatibility.

■ *Generator*   Let us assume there is a generator that generates Java Beans from the **entities**. Further, we assume that there is a generator that generates all the persistence management code from **DbDsl** programs, except the part of the code that fetches the data from whatever the data source is – essentially we leave the same "hole" as we do with the **AbstractColumnMapper** in the grammar. And just in the same way as we define the **EntityColumnMapper** in the adapter language, we have to adapt the executing code. We can use two strategies.

The first one uses the composition techniques of the target language, i.e. Java. The generated code of the **DbDsl** could for example generate an abstract class that has an abstract method **getColumnData** for each of the table columns. The generator for the adapter language would generate a concrete subclass that implements these methods to grab the data from entities[43]. This way the modularity (**entities**, **db**, **db2entity**) is propagated into the generated artifacts as well. No *generator* composition is required[44].

However, consider a situation in which we have to generate inlined code, for reasons of efficiency, e.g., in some kind of embedded system. In this case the **DbDsl** generator would have to be built in an extensible way. Assuming we use Xtend for generation, this can be done easily by using dependency injection[45]. Here is how you would do that:

- In the generator that generates persistence code from a **DbDsl** program, the code that generates the inlined "get data for column" code delegates to a class that is dependency-injected[46]. The Xtend class we delegate to would be an abstract class that has one abstract method **generateGetDataCodeFor(Column c)**.

```
class GetDataGenerator {
    def void generateGetDataCodeFor(Column c)
}

class DbDslGenerator implements IGenerator {
```

[43] This is how we did it in the MPS example.

[44] In a Java/Enterprise world this would most likely be the way we'd do it in practice. The next alternative is a bit constructed.

[45] Sometimes people complain about the fact that Xtend is a general purpose language, and not some dedicated code generation language. However, the fact that one can use abstract classes, abstract methods and dependency injection is a nice example of how and why a general purpose language (with some dedicated support for templating) is useful for building generators.

[46] This is a nice illustration of building a generator that is *intended to be extended* in some way.

```
    @Inject GetDataGenerator gdg
    
    def someGenerationMethod(Column c) {
        // ...
        String getDataCode = gdg.generateGetDataCodeFor(c)
        // then embed getDataCode somewhere in the
        // template that generates the DbDsl code
    }
}
```

- The generator for the adapter language would contain a subclass of this abstract class that implements the **generateGetDataCodeFor** generator method in a way suitable to the **entities** language.

- The adapter language would also set up Google Guice dependency injection in such a way as to use this a singleton instance of this subclass when instances of the abstract class are expected.

16.3.3 Extension

We have already seen the mechanics of extension in the previous example, since, as a way of building the reuse infrastructure, we have extended the **db** language. In this section we look at extension in more detail. Extension is defined as syntactic integration with explicit dependencies. However, as we discussed in Section 4.6.2 there are two use cases that feel different:

1. In one case we provide (small scale, local, fine grained) additional syntax to an otherwise unchanged language[47].

2. The other case is where we create a completely new language, but reuse some of the syntax provided by the base language. This use case *feels* like embedding (we embed syntax from the base language in our new language), but with regard to the classification according to syntactic integration and dependencies, it is still extension. Embedding would prevent explicit dependencies. In this section we look at extension with an embedding flavor.

To illustrate an extension-with-embedding flavor, we will show how to embed Xbase expressions in a custom DSL. Xbase is a reusable expression language that provides primitive types, various unary and binary operators, functions and closures. As we will see, it is very tightly integrated with Java[48]. As an example, we essentially create another entity language; thanks to Xbase, we will be able to write:

[47] The **db2entity** language shown above is an example of this. The **db2entity** programs look essentially like programs written in the **db** base language, but in one (or few) particular place, something is different. In the example, the syntax for referencing attributes is such a small scale change.

[48] This is a mixed blessing. As long as you stay in a JVM world (use Java types, generate Java code), many things are very simple. However, as soon as you go outside of the JVM world, a lot of things become quite complex, and it is questionable whether using Xbase makes sense in this case at all.

```
entity Person {
    lastname : String
    firstname : String
    String fullName(String from) {
        return "Hello " + firstname + " " + lastname + " from " + from
    }
}
```

Below is the essential part of the grammar. Note how it extends the Xbase grammar (the **with** clause) and how it uses various elements from Xbase throughout the code (those whose names start with an **X**).

```
grammar org.xtext.example.lmrc.entityexpr.EntityWithExprDsl
        with org.eclipse.xtext.xbase.Xbase

generate entityWithExprDsl
         "http://www.xtext.org/example/lmrc/entityexpr/EntityWithExprDsl"
Module:
    "module" name=ID "{"
        entities+=Entity*
    "}";
Entity:
    "entity" name=ID "{"
        attributes+=Attribute* operations+=Operation*
    "}";
Attribute:
    name=ID ":" type=JvmTypeReference;
Operation:
    type=JvmTypeReference name=ID "(" (parameters+=FullJvmFormalParameter
        (',' parameters+=FullJvmFormalParameter)*)? ")"
            body=XBlockExpression;
```

Let's look at some of the details. First, the **type** properties of the **Attribute** and the **Operation** are not defined by our grammar; instead we use a **JvmTypeReference**. This makes all Java types legal at this location[49]. We use an **XBlockExpression** as the body of **Operation**, which essentially allows us to use the full Xbase language inside the body of the **Operation**. To make the **parameters** visible, we use the **FullJvmFormalParameter** rule[50].

In addition to using Xbase language concepts in the definition of our grammar, we also tie the semantics of our language to Java and the JVM. To do this, the **JvmModelInferrer**, shown below, maps a model expressed with this language to a structurally equivalent Java "model". By doing this, we get a number of benefits "for free", including scoping, typing and a code generator. Let us look at this crucial step in some detail.

```
class EntityWithExprDslJvmModelInferrer extends AbstractModelInferrer {

    @Inject extension IQualifiedNameProvider
    @Inject extension JvmTypesBuilder

    def dispatch void infer(Entity entity,
```

[49] Limiting this to the primitive types (or some other subset of the JVM types) requires a scoping rule.

[50] Above we wrote that Xbase is tightly integrated with the JVM and Java. The use of **FullJvmFormalParameter** and **JvmTypeReference** is a sign of this. However, the next piece of code makes this even clearer.

```
                        IAcceptor<JvmDeclaredType> acceptor,
                        boolean isPrelinkingPhase) {
        ...
    }
}
```

This Xtend class extends **AbstractModelInferrer** and implements its **infer** method to create structurally equivalent Java code as an EMF tree, and registers it with the **acceptor**. The method is marked as **dispatch**, so it can be polymorphically overwritten for various language concepts. We override it for the **Entity** concept. We have also injected the **IQualifiedNameProvider** and **JvmTypesBuilder**. The latter provides a builder API for creating all kinds of JVM objects, such as fields, setters, classes or operations. The next piece of code makes use of such a builder:

```
acceptor.accept(
    entity.toClass( entity.fullyQualifiedName ) [
        documentation = entity.documentation ...
    ]
)
```

At the top level, we map the **Entity** to a **Class**. **toClass** is one of the builder methods defined in the **JvmTypesBuilder**. The class we create should have the same name as the **entity**; the name of the class is passed into the constructor. The second argument, written conveniently behind the parentheses, is a closure. Inside the closure, we set the documentation of the created class to be the documentation of the **entity**[51]. Next we create a field, a getter and a setter for each of the attributes of the **Entity** and add them to the **Class' members** collection:

```
attr : entity.attributes ) {
    members += attr.toField(attr.name, attr.type) members +=
    attr.toGetter(attr.name, attr.type) members += attr.toSetter(attr.name,
    attr.type)
}
```

[51] Inside a closure, there is a variable **it** that refers to the target element (the class in this case). It is possible to omit the **it**, so when we write **documentation = ...** this actually means **it.documentation = ...**.

toField, **toGetter** and **toSetter** are all builders contributed by the **JvmTypesBuilder**. To better understand what they do, here is the implementation of **toSetter**[52].

```
public JvmOperation toSetter(EObject sourceElement, final String name,
                             JvmTypeReference typeRef) {
  JvmOperation res = TypesFactory.eINSTANCE.createJvmOperation();
  res.setVisibility(JvmVisibility.PUBLIC);
  res.setSimpleName("set" + nullSaveName(Strings.toFirstUpper(name)));
  res.getParameters().add(toParameter(sourceElement, nullSaveName(name),
                          cloneWithProxies(typeRef)));
  if (name != null) {
    setBody(res, new Functions.Function1<ImportManager, CharSequence>() {
      public CharSequence apply(ImportManager p) {
        return "this." + name + " = " + name + ";";
      }
    });
  }
}
```

[52] Note that the first argument supplied by the object in front of the dot, i.e. the **Attribute**, is passed in as the first argument, **sourceElement**.

```
    return associate(sourceElement, res);
}
```

The method first creates a **JvmOperation** and sets the visibility and the name. It then creates a parameter that uses the **typeRef** passed in as the third argument as its type. As you can see, all of this happens via model-to-model transformation. This is important, because these created objects are used implicitly in scoping and typing. The body, however, is created textually; it is not needed for scoping or typing: it is used only in code generation[53]. The last line is important: it associates the source element (the **Attribute** in our case) with the created element (the setter **Operation** we just created). As a consequence of this association, the Xbase scoping and typing framework can work its magic of providing support for our DSL without any further customization!

Let's now continue our look at the implementation of the **Jvm- ModelInferrer** for the **Entity**. The last step before our detour was that we created fields, setters and getters for all attributes of our **Entity**. We have to deal with the operations of our **Entity** next.

[53] Since that is a to-text transformation anyway, it is good enough to represent the body of the setter as text already at this level.

```
for ( op : entity.operations ) {
    members += op.toMethod(op.name, op.type) [
        for (p : op.parameters) {
            parameters += p.toParameter(p.name, p.parameterType)
        }
        body = op.body
    ]
}
```

This code should be easy to understand. We create a method for each **Operation** using the respective builder method, pass in the name and type, create a parameter for each of the parameters of our source operation and then assign the body of the created method to be the body of the operation in our DSL program. The last step is particularly important. Notice that we don't clone the body, we assign the object *directly*. Looking into the **setBody** method (the assignment is actually mapped to a setter in Xtend), we see the following:

```
void setBody(JvmExecutable logicalContainer, XExpression expr) {
    if (expr == null) return; associator.associateLogicalContainer(expr,
    logicalContainer);
}
```

The **associateLogicalContainer** method is what makes the automatic support for scoping and typing happen[54]:

[54] This approach of mapping a DSL to Java "code" via this model transformation works nicely as long as it maps to Java code in a simple way. In the above case of entities, the mapping is trivial and obvious. If the semantic gap becomes bigger, the **JvmTypeInferrer** becomes more complicated. However, what is really nice is this: within the type inferrer, you can of course use Xtend's template syntax to create implementation code. So it is easy to mix model transformation (for those parts of a mapping that are relevant to scoping and type calculation) and then use traditional to-text transformation using Xtend's powerful template syntax for the detailed implementation aspects.

- Because the operation is the container of the expression, the expression's type and the operation's type must be compatible

- Because the expression(s) live inside the operation, the parameters of the operation, as well as the current class's fields, setters and getters are in scope automatically.

■ *Generator* The JVM mapping shown above already constitutes the full semantic mapping to Java. We map entities to Java classes and fields to members and getters/setters. We do not have to do anything else to get a generator: we can reuse the existing Xbase-to-Java code generator.

If we build a language that cannot easily be mapped to a JVM model, we can still reuse the Xbase expression compiler, by injecting the `JvmModelGenerator` and then delegating to it at the respective granularity. You can also change or extend the behavior of the default `JvmModelGenerator` by overriding its `_internalDoGenerate(EObject, IFileSystemAccess)` method for your particular language concept[55].

[55] Notice that you also have to make sure via Guice that your subclass is used, and not the default `JvmModelGenerator`.

■ *Extending Xbase* In the above example we embedded the (otherwise unchanged) Xbase language into a simple DSL. Let's now look at how to extend Xbase itself by adding new literals and new operators. We start by defining a literal for dates:

```
XDateLiteral:
    'date' ':' year=INT '-' month=INT '-' day=INT;
```

These new literals should be literals in terms of Xbase, so we have to make them subtypes of `XLiteral`. Notice how we override the `XLiteral` rule defined in Xbase. We have to repeat its original contents; there is no way to "add" to the literals[56].

[56] Similarly, if you want to remove concepts, you have to overwrite the rule with the concept to be removed missing from the enumeration.

```
XLiteral returns xbase::XExpression:
    XClosure |
    XBooleanLiteral |
    XIntLiteral |
    XNullLiteral |
    XStringLiteral |
    XTypeLiteral |
    XDateLiteral;
```

We use the same approach to add an additional operator that uses the === symbol[57]:

[57] The triple equals represents identity.

```
OpEquality:
    '==' | '!=' | '===';
```

The === operator does not yet exist in Xtend, so we have to specify the name of the method that should be called if the operator is used in a program[58]. The second line of the method **initializeMapping** maps the new operator to a method named **operator_identity**:

[58] Xtend supports operator overloading by mapping operators to methods that can be overridden.

```
public class DomainModelOperatorMapping extends OperatorMapping {

    public static final QualifiedName IDENTITY = create("===");

    @Override
    protected void initializeMapping() {
        super.initializeMapping();
        map.put(IDENTITY, create("operator_identity"));
    }
}
```

We implement this method in a new class that we call **Object-Extensions2**[59]:

[59] The existing class **ObjectExtensions** contains the implementations for the existing == and != operators, hence the name.

```
public class ObjectExtensions2 {
    public static boolean operator_identity(Object a, Object b) {
        return a == b;
    }
}
```

Through the **operator_identity** operation, we have expressed all the semantics: the Xbase generator will generate a call to that operation in the generated Java code[60]. We have also implicitly specified the typing rules: through the mapping to the **operator_identity** operation, the type system uses the types specified in this operation. The type of === is **boolean**, and there are no restrictions on the two arguments; they are typed as **java.lang.Object**[61].

[60] Alternatively, as a performance improvement, you could use the **@Inline** annotation to inline the function in the generated code.

[61] If customizations are required, these could be done by overriding the **_expectedType** operation in **XbaseTypeProvider**.

We also want to override the existing minus operator for the new date literals to calculate the time between two dates. We don't have to specify the mapping to a method name, since the mapping for minus is already defined in Xbase. However, we have to provide an overloaded implementation of the **operator_minus** method for dates:

```
public class DateExtensions {
    public static long operator_minus(Date a, Date b) {
        long resInMilliSeconds = a.getTime() - b.getTime();
        return millisecondsToDays( resInMilliSeconds );
    }
}
```

To make Xtend aware of these new classes, we have to register them. To do so, we extend the **ExtensionClassNameProvider**. It associates the classes that contain the operator implementation methods with the types to which these methods apply:

```
public class DomainModelExtensionClassNameProvider extends
    ExtensionClassNameProvider {
```

```
    @Override
    protected Multimap<Class<?>, Class<?>> simpleComputeExtensionClasses()
      {
        Multimap<Class<?>, Class<?>> result = 
              super.simpleComputeExtensionClasses();
        result.put(Object.class, ObjectExtensions2.class);
        result.put(Date.class, DateExtensions.class);
        return result;
      }
}
```

We now have to extend the type system: it has to be able to derive the types for date literals. We create a type provider that extends the default **XbaseTypeProvider**[62]:

```
@Singleton
public class DomainModelTypeProvider extends XbaseTypeProvider {

  @Override
  protected JvmTypeReference type(XExpression expression,
                    JvmTypeReference rawExpectation, boolean rawType) {
    if (expression instanceof XDateLiteral) {
      return _type((XDateLiteral) expression, rawExpectation, rawType);
    }
    return super.type(expression, rawExpectation, rawType);
  }

  protected JvmTypeReference _type(XDateLiteral literal,
                    JvmTypeReference rawExpectation, boolean rawType) {
    return getTypeReferences().getTypeForName(Date.class, literal);
  }
}
```

Finally we have to extend the Xbase compiler so that it can handle date literals:

```
public class DomainModelCompiler extends XbaseCompiler {
  protected void _toJavaExpression(XDateLiteral expr, IAppendable b) {
    b.append("new java.text.SimpleDateFormat(\"yyyy-MM-dd\").parse(\"" +
         expr.getYear() + "-" + expr.getMonth() + "-" +
         expr.getDay() + "\")");
  }
}
```

■ *Active Annotations*   Xtext's Xtend language comes with Active Annotations. They use the same syntax as regular Java annotations[63]. However, they can influence the translation process from Xtend to Java[64]. Each annotation is essentially associated with a model-to-model transformation that creates the necessary Java code. This allows the execution semantics of the respective Xtend class to be influenced.

At the time of this writing, the most impressive active annotation (prototype) I have seen involves GWT programming[65]. They implement the following two annotations:

Services From a simple Xtend class that contains the server-side implementation methods, the annotation generates the necessary remote interface and the other boilerplate that enables the remote communication infrastructure.

[62] Don't forget to register this class with Guice, just like all the other DSL-specific subclasses of framework classes.

[63] Java annotations are markers you can attach to various program elements such as classes, fields, methods or arguments. For example, the **@Override** annotation declares that a method overrides a similar method in the superclass. Another example is **@NotNull** on an argument, which expresses the fact that that argument may not be **null**. Annotations may also capture metadata: the **@Author(name = .., date = ..)** annotation expresses who wrote a class. Annotations may be standardized (e.g. **@Override**) or may be implemented by users. In the standard case the annotations are typically processed by the compiler (e.g., checking that there actually is a method with the same signature in the superclass or modifying the generated bytecode to report an error if a **NotNull** argument is **null** at runtime). Custom annotations are processed in some way by some external tool (e.g. by checking certain properties of the code, or by modifying the class bytecode via some bytecode processor).

[64] This feature is actually introduced in version 2.4; at the time of this writing, only prototypes are available, so some details about what I describe here may be different in the final release. This is also why we don't show source code here.

[65] This has been built by Sven Efftinge and Oliver Zeigermann. The slides that describe the system are here: **slidesha.re/Shb3S0**. The code is at github: **github.com/DJCordhose/todomvc-xtend-gwt**.

UI Forms In GWT, a UI form is defined by an XML file that defines the structure, as well as by a Java class that implements the behavior. The behavior includes the event handlers for the UI elements defined in the XML file. To this end, the class has to have fields that correspond (in name and type) to the UI elements defined in the XML. By using an annotation, this duplication can be avoided: the annotation implementation inspects the associated XML and automatically introduces the necessary fields.

Active annotations will provide a number of additional features. First, they can implement custom validations and quick fixes for the IDE. Second, they can change the scope and the type system, with the IDE being aware of that[66]. Third, you can pass JVM types or expressions into annotations:

```
@Pre( b != 0 ) def divide(int a, int b) {
   return a / b
}
```

It is possible to define whether the expression is passed in as an AST (`b != 0`), or whether the result of the evaluation of the expression is passed in (`true` or `false`).

While the syntactic limitations of annotations limit the kinds of language extensions that can be built in this way, the current prototypes show that nonetheless some quite interesting language extensions are possible[67].

16.3.4 Embedding

Embedding is not supported by Xtext. The reason is that, as we can see from Section 4.6.4, the adapter language would have to inherit from *two* base languages. However, Xtext only supports extending one base grammar.

We have shown above how to embed Xbase expressions into a custom DSL. However, as we have discussed, this is an example of extension with embedding flavor: we create a *new* DSL into which we embed the existing Xbase expressions. So we only have to extend from *one* base language – Xbase. An example of embedding would be to take an existing, independent SQL language and embed it into the `entity` DSL created above. This is not possible.

The same is true for the combination (in the same program) of several independently developed extensions to the same base language. In that case, too, the composite grammar would have to inherit from several base languages[68].

---

[66] The transformation defined by the active annotation that maps the annotated Xtend construct to Java code is run not just during code generation, but also during editing (like any other JVM model inferrer). Since scoping and the type system of Xtend is based on the inferred JVM model, the annotation transformation can affect these as well.

[67] This is due in particular to the fact that the IDE is aware of the transformation (influencing typing and and code completion) as a consequence of the real-time transformation with a `JVMModelInferrer`.

[68] While this sounds like a rather academic problem to have, the mbeddr case study referred to throughout this book shows where and how the combination of independent language extensions is useful in practice. mbeddr could not have been built with Xtext for this reason.

16.4 Spoofax Example

In this section we look at an example roughly similar to that for MPS and Xtext discussed in the previous sections. We start with Mobl's data modeling language, which we have already seen in previous chapters.

To understand some of the discussions later, we first have to understand how Spoofax organizes languages. In Spoofax, language definitions are typically modularized (they declare their **module** at the top of a file). For example, Mobl's syntax definition comes with a module for entities, which imports modules for statements and expressions:

```
module MoblEntities

imports
  MoblStatements
  MoblExpressions
```

All syntax definition modules reside in the **syntax** directory of a Spoofax project. Typically, subdirectories are used to organize the modules of different sublanguages. For example, we can have subdirectories **entity** for Mobl's entity definition language, **screen** for Mobl's screen definition language, and **common** for definitions shared by both languages:

```
module entity/MoblEntities

imports
  entities/MoblStatements
  entities/MoblExpressions
```

```
module screen/MoblScreens

imports
  common/Lexical
```

```
module common/MoblExpressions

imports
  common/Lexical
```

As the example shows, the directory structure is reflected in module names. You can read them as relative paths from the **syntax** directory to the module.

Similarly to syntax definitions, rewrite rules for program analysis, editor services, program transformation, and code generation are organized in modules, which are imported from Mobl's main module. The various modules for program analysis, editor services and program transformation are organized in subdirectories:

```
module mobl
imports
  analysis/names
  analysis/types
  analysis/checks
  editor/complete
  editor/hover
  editor/refactor
  trans/desugar
  trans/normalize
  generate
```

16.4.1   Referencing

We will illustrate references to elements written in another DSL with Mobl's screen definition language. The following code uses Mobl sublanguage for data definition. It defines an entity **Task** with some properties[69].

[69] The example should look familiar - we have discussed the language in several examples throughout the book already.

```
entity Task {
  name        : String
  description : String
  done        : Bool
  date        : DateTime
}
```

The next piece of code shows a screen definition written in Mobl's screen definition language. It defines a root screen for a list of tasks, using the **name** of a **Task** as a label for **list** elements.

```
screen root() {
  header("Tasks")
  group {
    list(t in Task.all()) {
      item { label(t.name) }
    }
  }
}
```

There are two references to the data model: **Task** refers to an **Entity**, and **name** refers to a property of that **Entity**. In general, a **Screen** defined in the UI model refers to **Entities** from Mobl's entity language, and **Fields** in a screen refer to **Properties** in an entity.

■ *Structure*   When referencing elements of another language, both languages typically share a definition of identifiers. For example, the screen definition language imports the same lexical module as does the data modeling language, via the expression module:

```
module entity/MoblEntities
imports
  ...
  entity/MoblExpressions
```

```
module entity/MoblExpressions
imports
  ...
  common/Lexical
```

```
module screen/MoblScreens
imports common/Lexical
exports context-free syntax
  "list" ID "in" Collection "{" Item* "}" -> List       {"ScreenList"}
  ID "." "all" "(" ")"                    -> Collection {"Collection"}
  "item" "{" ItemPart* "}"                -> Item       {"Item"}
  "label" "(" ID "." ID ")"               -> ItemPart   {"LabelPart"}
```

However, Spoofax also supports the use of different, typically overlapping identifier definitions[70]. In this case, the referencing language needs to import the identifier definition of the referenced language.

[70] This requires scannerless parsing, since a scanner cannot handle overlapping lexical definitions.

■ *Name Binding* Independent of the identifiers used in both languages, the reference has to be resolved. Definition sites are already defined by the referenced language. The corresponding references must be defined in the referencing language by using the namespaces from the referenced language. The previous syntax definition fragment of the screen definition language specifies lists and items in these lists. The following fragment shows the corresponding name binding specifications:

```
module screen/names

imports entity/names

namespaces Item

rules

  ScreenList(i, coll, i*):
    defines Item i of type t
    where coll has type t

  Collection(e):
    refers to Entity e

  LabelPart(i, p):
    refers to Item i
    refers to Property p in Entity e
      where i has type e
```

Here, the screen definition language declares its own namespace **Item** for items, which are declared in the list head, introducing a variable for the current item of a collection. For example, the screen definition we have seen earlier defines an item **t**[71]. When we describe the collection, we can refer to entities. The corresponding namespace **Entity** is defined in the data modeling language. The screen definition language uses

[71] It is the **t** in the **list** element that references a **Task**.

the same namespace, to resolve the references into the referred language[72].

■ *Type System* Similar to the name resolution, the type system of the referencing language needs to be defined with the knowledge of the type system of the referenced language.

```
constraint-error:
  LabelPart(item, property) -> (property, "Label has to be a string.")
  where
    type := <index-type-of> property
    not (!type => !StringType())
```

To be able to check whether a label is a **string**, this constraint has to determine the type of the property used as a label.

■ *Generators* Generators of the referencing language also need to be defined with the knowledge of the generators of the referenced language. Typically, they just share knowledge about the naming and typing of generated code elements.

```
to-java:
  LabelPart(item, property) ->
  |[ new Label([java-item].[java-prop]);
  ]| where
    label    := <fresh-java-var-name> "label";
    java-item := <to-java-var> item;
    java-prop := <to-java-getter> property
```

This rule generates Java code for a **LabelPart**. The generated code should create a new label with a text which should be determined from a **property** of an **item**. To generate the property access, the rule relies on the same scheme as rules from the generator of the entity definition part, by making calls to rules from this generator[73].

16.4.2   Reuse

As discussed in the previous sections, referencing concerns the case in which the referencing language is built with knowledge about the referenced language, so that it can have direct dependencies[74]. In the case of reuse, such direct dependency is not allowed: our goal is to combine two *independent* languages.

■ *Structure* To illustrate this case, we again use the same example as in the MPS section. We first introduce a trivial DSL for defining relational table structures. These can optionally be mapped to a data source, but the language makes no assumption about what this data source looks like (and which language is used to define it). Consequently, the grammar has no dependency on any other one:

[72] Similarly, the screen definition language uses the namespace **Property** from the data modeling language, to refer to properties of entities.

[73] It first generates the Java variable name from **item**. Second, it generates a getter call from **property**. Finally, it composes these fragments with its own Java code.

[74] In the example above, the screen definition language uses the namespaces and types from the entity language directly.

```
module DBTables

  "database" ID Table*      -> Database   {"DB"}
  "table" ID Column*        -> Table      {"DBTable"}
  DataType ID ColumnMapper  -> Column     {"DBColumn"}
                            -> ColumnMapper {"DBMissingMapper"}

  "char"                    -> DataType   {"DBCharType"}
  "number"                  -> DataType   {"DBNumberType"}
```

Again, the **Column** rule has an optional **ColumnMapper** which works as the hook for reuse. The reusable language only provides a rule for a missing column mapper[75]. In the next step, we want to be able to reference properties from Mobl's data modeling language from a table definition:

[75] Rules for a concrete mapper can be added later in a sublanguage.

```
database TaskDB

table Tasks

  char name         <- Task.name
  char description  <- Task.description
```

To do this, we define an adapter module, which imports the reusable table module and the data modeling language. So far, **ColumnMapper** is only an abstract concept, without a useful definition. The adapter module now defines a rule for **ColumnMapper**, which defines the concrete syntax of an actual mapper that can reference properties from the data modeling language:

```
module MoblDBAdapter

imports
  DBTables
  MoblEntities

context-free syntax
  "<-" ID "." ID -> ColumnMapper {"PropertyMapper"}
```

There is only one rule in this module, which defines a concrete mapper. On the right-hand side, it uses the same sort as the rule in the table module (**ColumnMapper**). On the left-hand side, it refers to a property (second ID) in an entity (first ID).

■ *NameBinding* The actual reference to entity and property names from the imported data modeling language needs to be specified in the name binding module of the adapter:

```
module adapter/names

imports entity/names

rules

  PropertyMapper(e, p):
    refers to Entity e
    refers to Property p in Entity e
```

■ *Type System* In our example, the types of the database language needs to be connected to the primitive types used in Mobl[76]. Constraints ensure we only map those fields to a particular column that are type-compatible:

[76] More generally, the type system needs to connect types from the abstract but reusable language to types from the language which actually reuses it.

```
module reuse/dbtables/analysis/types
rules
  constraint-error:
    DBColumn(type, _, mapper) -> (mapper, "Incompatible type")
    where
      type' := <type-of> mapper ;
      <not(compatible-types)> (type, type')

  compatible-types: _ -> <fail>
```

The code above is defined in the generic implementation of the database language. It assumes that a mapper has a type and checks if this type is compatible with the declared column type. It defines a default rule for type compatibility, which always fails. The connection to the type system of the entity language can now be made in an adapter module:

```
module analysis/types/adapter
imports
  module analysis/types
  module reuse/dbtables/analysis/types
rules
  type-of: PropertyMapper(e, p) -> <index-type-of> p

  compatible-types: (DBCharType(), StringType()) -> <id>
  compatible-types: (DBNumberType(), NumType())   -> <id>
```

The first rule defines the type of a `PropertyMapper` to be the type of the property. Then, two rules define type compatibility for Mobl's `String` type with the `char` type in the table language, and Mobl's `Num` type with table language's `number` type.

■ *Generator* As in the Xtext example, we can use two strategies to reuse a generator for the database language. The first strategy relies on composition techniques of the target language, if that language provides such composition facilities[77]. The second strategy we discussed in the Xtext example addressed the generation of inlined code, which requires an extendable generator of the reusable language. With rewrite rules, this can be easily achieved in Spoofax. The reusable generator calls a dedicated rule for generating the inlined code, but defines only a failing implementation of this rule:

[77] As in the MPS example, the code generator of the database language generates an abstract Java class for fetching data, while Mobl's original code generator generates Java classes from entities. We can then define an additional generator, which generates a concrete subclass that fetches data from entities.

```
rules
  db-to-java: Column(t, n, mapper) ->
      [Field([PRIVATE], t', n),
       Method([PROTECTED], BoolType, n', params, stmts)]
```

```
where
  n'    := <to-fetch-method-name> n ;
  param := <to-fetch-method-parameters> mapper ;
  stmts := <to-fetch-statements(|n)> mapper

to-fetch-method-parameters: _ -> <fail>
to-fetch-statements(|n)    : _ -> <fail>
```

This rule generates code for columns. It generates a private field and a protected method to fetch the content. This method needs a name, parameters and an implementation. We assume that the method name is provided by the generic generator. For the other parts (in particular, the implementation of the methods), the generic generator only provides failing placeholder rules. These have to be implemented in a concrete reuse setting by the adapter language generator:

```
module generate/java/adapter

imports
  generate/java
  reuse/table/generate

rules
 to-fetch-method-parameters:
   PropertyMapper(entity, property) -> [Param(type, "entity")]
   where
     type := <entity-to-java-type> entity

 to-fetch-statements(|field-name):
   PropertyMapper(entity, property) ->
        [Assign(VarRef(field-name), MethodCall(VarRef("entity"), m, [])),
         Return(True())]
   where
     m := <property-to-getter-name> property
```

This adapter code generates a single parameter for the fetch method. It is named **entity** and its type is provided by a rule from the entity language generator. The rule maps entity names to Java types. For the implementation body, the second rule generates an assignment and a return statement. The assignment calls the getter method for the property. Again, the name of this getter method is provided by the entity language generator.

16.4.3 Extension

Because of Spoofax' module system and rule-based nature, language extension feels like ordinary language development. When we want to add a new feature for a language, we simply create new modules for syntax, name binding, type system and code generation rules. These modules import the existing modules as needed. In the syntax definition, we can extend a syntactic sort with new definition rules. In the type system, we add additional **type-of** rules for the new language constructs and

Since, in the case of extension, the extending language has a dependency on, and is developed with, knowledge of the base language, it can be designed in a way that will not lead to parsing ambiguities. However, the composition of different, independent extensions of the same base language might lead to ambiguities. These ambiguities will only occur between the extensions. The base language will stay unambiguous, since each module is only imported once.

define constraints for well-typedness. Finally, we add new generator rules, which can handle the new language constructs.

16.4.4 Restriction

In the easiest case, restriction can be handled on the level of syntax rules. SDF's import directives allow not only for renaming of sorts, but also for replacing complete syntax rules. To remove a rule completely, we can replace it with a dummy rule for a sort, which is not used anywhere. The following example restricts Mobl to a version without property access expressions[78]:

```
module MoblWithoutPropertyAccess
imports Mobl[Exp "." ID -> Exp => -> UnusedDummySort]
```

16.4.5 Embedding

Embedding can be easily achieved in Spoofax. In general, the procedure is very similar to reuse. We will discuss the embedding of HQL[79] into Mobl as an example here[80].

■ *Structure* Embedding requires an additional syntax definition module which imports the main modules of the host and guest language and defines additional syntax rules that realize the embedding. In target language embedding into Stratego, this was achieved with quotations and antiquotations. The following module is an initial attempt to embed HQL into Mobl:

```
module Mobl-HQL

imports
   Mobl
   Hql

context-free syntax

  QueryRule           -> Exp {cons("HqlQuery")}
  DeleteStatement ";" -> Statement {cons("HqlStatement")}

  "~" Exp             -> Expression {cons("DslExp")}
```

The module imports syntax definitions of host and guest languages. It embeds HQL queries as Mobl expressions and HQL's delete statement as a Mobl statement without any quotations. Furthermore, it allows us to use quoted Mobl expressions inside HQL queries, using the tilde as a quotation symbol.

There are two issues in this module. First, we might accidentally merge sorts with the same name in host and guest language[81]. Since both languages are developed independently, we cannot assume mutually exclusive names in their syntax

[78] In more complex cases, only parts of a syntax rule need to be restricted. For example, we might restrict Mobl's screen definition language to support only unparameterized screen definitions.

[79] HQL is a declarative query language for entities stored in a relational database. It resembles SQL in syntax.

[80] We have discussed embedding already in Section 11.4, where we embedded the target language into the Stratego transformation language.

[81] Sort names like **Expression**, **Exp** or **Statement** are quite likely to be used in several languages

definitions. One way to avoid name clashes is to rename sorts manually during import:

```
module Mobl-HQL

imports
  Mobl
  Hql [ QueryRule       => HqlQueryRule
        DeleteStatement => HqlDeleteStatement
        Expression      => HqlExpression
        ...
      ]
```

This can be quite cumbersome, since we have to rename all sorts, not only the embedded ones. Alternatively, we can rely on Spoofax to generate a renamed version of a language definition. This *Mix* is a parameterized syntax definition, where Spoofax replaces each sort by a parameterized sort[82]:

[82] This is a bit like generics in programming languages such as Java.

```
module HqlMix[Context]

imports
  Hql [ QueryRule       => QueryRule[[Context]]
        DeleteStatement => DeleteStatement[[Context]]
        Expression      => Expression[[Context]]
        ...
      ]
```

The parameter allows us to distinguish sorts from the host and the target language. We can then import this module with an actual parameter and use the parameterized sorts in the embedding:

```
module Mobl-HQL

imports Mobl HqlMix[HQL]

context-free syntax

  QueryRule[[HQL]]             -> Exp {cons("HqlQuery")}
  DeleteStatement[[HQL]] ";"   -> Statement {cons("HqlStatement")}

  "~" Exp                      -> Expression[[HQL]] {cons("MoblExp")}
```

The second issue is ambiguity: we have to integrate HQL queries into the precedence rules for Mobl expressions. To do this, we do not have to repeat all rules: preceding and succeeding rules are sufficient[83]:

[83] This is necessary because precedence is specified relative to other rules using the > operator introduced earlier.

```
context-free priorities

    Assignment                       -> Exp
  > QueryRule[[HQL]]                 -> Exp
  > "if" "(" Exp ")" Exp "else" Exp  -> Exp
```

■ *Name Binding*   The name bindings of host and embedded language are never connected. For example, only Mobl expressions can refer to Mobl variables. If an HQL query relies on a Mobl variable, it accesses it as an embedded Mobl expression.

■ *Type System* The type system needs to connect the types from the host and guest languages. This can be achieved by adding typing rules for embedded and antiquoted constructs. For example, we need to connect the HQL type of a query to a Mobl type of the embedding expression:

```
module mobl-hql/types

imports
  mobl/types
  hql/types

type-of:
  HqlQuery(query) -> mobl-type
  where
    hql-type  := <type-of> query
    mobl-type := <hql-to-mobl-type> hql-type

type-of:
  MoblExp(exp) -> hql-type
  where
    mobl-type := <type-of> exp
    hql-type  := <mobl-to-hql-type> mobl-type

hql-to-mobl-type: JDBC_Integer() -> NumType()
hql-to-mobl-type: JDBC_Float()   -> NumType()
hql-to-mobl-type: JDBC_Bit()     -> BoolType()

mobl-to-hql-type: NumType()      -> JDBC_Float()
mobl-to-hql-type: BoolType()     -> JDBC_Bit()
```

The first rule determines the type of an embedded HQL query and maps it to a corresponding Mobl type. The second rule determines the type of an antiquoted Mobl expression and maps it to an corresponding HQL type. The remaining rules exemplify actual mappings between HQL and Mobl types[84].

[84] Additional constraints could check for incompatible types which cannot be mapped into the host or guest language.

■ *Generator* There are two strategies for code generation for embedded languages. If the guest language provides a suitable code generator, we can combine it with the code generator of the host language. First, we need rules which generate code for embedded constructs. These rules have to extend the host generator by delegating to the guest generator. Next, we need rules which generate code for antiquoted constructs. These rules have to extend the guest generator by delegating to the host generator.

Another strategy is to define a model-to-model transformation which desugars (or "assimilates") embedded constructs to constructs of the host language. This transformation is then applied first, before the host generator is applied to generate code. The embedding of a target language into Stratego is an example of this approach. The embedded target language will be represented by abstract syntax trees for code generation fragments. These trees need to be desugared into Strat-

ego pattern matching constructs. For example, the embedded
`|[return |[x]|; ]|` will yield the following abstract syntax
tree:

```
ToJava(
  Return(
    FromJava(
      Var("x")
    )
  )
)
```

In ordinary Stratego without an embedded target language,
we would have written the pattern **Return(x)** instead. The
corresponding abstract syntax tree looks like this:

```
NoAnnoList(
  App(
    Op("Result"),
    [Var("x")]
  )
)
```

The desugar transformation now needs to transform the first
abstract syntax tree into the second one:

```
desugar-all: x -> <bottomup(try(desugar-embedded))> x

desugar-embedded: ToJava(e) -> <ast-to-pattern> e

ast-to-pattern:
  ast -> pattern
  where
    if !ast => FromJava(e) then
      pattern := e
    else
      c       := <constructor> ast ;
      args    := <arguments> ast ;
      ps      := <map(ast-to-pattern)> args ;
      pattern := NoAnnoList(App(Op(c), ps))
```

The first rule drives the desugaring of the overall tree. It tries
to apply **desugar-embedded** in a bottom-up traversal. The only
rule for desugaring embedded target language code matches
the embedded code and applies **ast-to-pattern** to it. If this
is applied to an antiquote, the contained subnode is already
a regular Stratego pattern. Otherwise, the node has to be an
abstract syntax tree of the target language. It is deconstructed
into its constructor and subtrees, which are desugared into patterns as well. The resulting patterns and the constructor are
then used to construct the overall pattern.

Part IV

DSLs in Software Engineering

This part of the book looks at how DSLs can be used in various aspects of software engineering. In particular, we look at requirements engineering, software architecture, developer utilities, implementation, product line engineering and business DSLs. Some of the chapters also serve as case studies for interesting, non-trivial DSLs.

Note that this part has many contributory authors, so there may be slight variations in style.

17
DSLs and Requirements

This chapter looks at the role of DSLs in requirements engineering. In particular it explores the use of DSLs to specify requirements formally, at ways of representing requirements as models and at traceability between implementation artifacts and requirements.

17.1 What are Requirements?

Wikipedia defines a requirements as follows:

> A requirement is a singular documented need of what a particular product or service should be or perform.

Wiktionary says:

> [A requirement] specifies a verifiable constraint on an implementation that it shall undeniably meet or (a) be deemed unacceptable, or (b) result in implementation failure, or (c) result in system failure.

In my own words I would probably define a requirement as

> ...a statement about what a system should do, and with what quality attributes, without presupposing a specific implementation.

Requirements are supposed to tell the programmers what the system they are about to implement should do[1]. Requirements are a means of communicating from humans (people who know what the system should do) to other humans (those that have to implement it). Of course, as well all know, there are a number of challenges with this:

[1] However, a requirement typically does not prescribe *how* a developer has to implement some functionality: architecture, design, the use of patterns and idioms and the choice of a suitable implementation technology and language are up to the developer.

- Those who implement the requirements may have a different background than those who write them, making misunderstandings between the two groups likely.

- Those who write the requirements may not actually really know what they want the system to do, at least initially. Requirements change over the course of a project, particularly as people start to "play" with early versions of the system[2].

- Usually requirements are written in plain English (or whatever language you prefer). Writing things down precisely and completely in a non-formal language is next to impossible[3].

[2] As we all know, only when we actually play or experiment with something do we really understand all the details, uncover corner cases and appreciate the complexity in the system.

[3] Writing *any* large prose document consistently and free from bugs is hard. I am sure you will find problems in this book :-)

Traditional requirements documents are a means to communicate from people to people. However, in the end this is not really true. In an ideal world, the requirements (in the brain of the person who writes them down) should be communicated directly to the computer, without the intermediate programmer, to avoid the misunderstandings mentioned above. If we look at the problem in this way, requirements now become formal, computer-understandable.

Wikipedia has a nice list of characteristics that requirements should posses. Here is a slightly adapted version of this list:

Complete The requirement is fully stated in one place with no missing information. This makes the requirement easy to consume, because readers do not have to build the complete picture from scattered information.

Consistent The requirement does not contradict any other requirement and is fully consistent with all authoritative external documentation[4].

Cohesive & Atomic The requirement is atomic, i.e., it does not contain conjunctions[5]. This ensures that traceability from implementation artifacts back to the requirements is relatively simple.

Current The requirement has not been made obsolete by the passage of time. Outdated requirements should be removed or marked as outdated.

Feasible The requirement can be implemented within the constraints of the project[6].

Unambiguous The requirement is concisely stated without recourse to technical jargon, acronyms (unless defined else-

[4] This is extremely hard to achieve with prose, because there is no "compiler" that finds inconsistencies.

[5] For example "The postal code field must validate American and Canadian postal codes" should be written as two separate requirements: (1) "The postal code field must validate American postal codes" and (2) "The postal code field must validate Canadian postal codes".

[6] Of course, as the person who writes the requirements, you may not be able to judge, since you may not know the project constraints, the effort to implement the requirement, or whether the implementation technology is able to address the requirement. This is one reason why interaction with the implementers is critical.

where in the requirements document), or other esoteric verbiage. It expresses objective facts, not subjective opinions. It is subject to one and only one interpretation. Vague subjects, adjectives, prepositions, verbs and subjective phrases are avoided. Negative statements and compound statements are prohibited[7].

Mandatory The requirement represents a stakeholder-defined characteristic the absence of which will result in a deficiency that cannot be ameliorated. An optional requirement is a contradiction in terms[8].

Verifiable The implementation of the requirement can be determined through one of four possible methods: inspection, demonstration, test or analysis. Otherwise it is hard to tell if a system actually fulfills a requirement or not[9].

If requirements are written as pure prose, then making sure all these characteristics are met boils down mostly to a manual review process. Of course, this is tedious and error-prone, and requirements end up in the sorry state we all know.

To get one step better, you can use controlled natural language[10] in which words like *must*, *may* or *should* have a well defined meaning and are used consciously. Using tables and – to some extent – state machines, is also a good way to make some of the data less ambiguous; these formalisms also help to verify requirements for consistency and completeness. To manage large sets of requirements, tools should be used to support unique identification and naming of requirements, as well as the expression of relationships and hierarchies among requirements[11]. However, the requirements themselves are still expressed as plain text, so the fundamental problems mentioned above are not improved significantly.

In this chapter we will give you some ideas and examples on how this situation can be improved with DSLs[12].

17.2 Requirements versus Design versus Implementation

Traditionally, we try to establish a clear line between requirements, architecture and design, and implementation. For example, a requirement may state that the system be 99.99% reliable. The design may use hot-standby and fail-over to continue service if a component breaks. The implementation would then

[7] All of these things are intended to make the prose as precise as possible to avoid misunderstandings. However, we all know how hard this is to achieve with prose.

[8] Although requirements may have priorities that define how important a requirement is relative to others. The implementation process should implement high-priority requirements first, if possible.

[9] Ideally, all requirements can be tested in an automatic way, in the sense that acceptance tests can be specified, and these can be re-executed over and over again.

[10] en.wikipedia.org/wiki/Controlled_natural_language

[11] Example tools include DOORS, Requisite Pro, the Eclipse Requirements Framework (RMF), and itemis' Yakindu.

[12] Note that I don't suggest in this chapter that *all* requirements should be captured with DSLs. Instead, DSLs can be one important ingredient for a well thought out requirements management approach.

select a specific standby/fail-over technology to realize the design. We make this distinction because we want to establish different roles in the software engineering process. For example, product management writes the requirements, a systems architect comes up with the architecture and design, and then a programmer writes the actual code and chooses the technologies[13]. Different organizations may even be involved, leading to a separation between requirements and architecture that is driven by organizational constraints[14]: the OEM writes the requirements, a systems integrator does the architecture, and some outsourcing company does the coding. In such a scenario it is important to draw precise boundaries between the activities. However, in some sense the boundaries are arbitrary. Consequently, the distinction between requirements and architecture are arbitrary as well: we could just as well state the following:

Requirement The system shall be 99.99% reliable by using hot-standby and fail-over to continue service if something breaks.

Architecture/Design We use two application servers running on two machines, using the XYZ messaging middleware as a replication engine for the hot-standby. We use a watchdog for detecting if the primary machine breaks, so we can fail over to the second one.

Implementation ...all the code that is necessary to implement the design above.

From software development we know that it is very hard to get requirements right. In the real world, you have to elaborate on the requirements incrementally[15]. In systems engineering this approach is also very well established. For example, when satellites are built, the scientists come up with initial scientific requirements, for example, regarding the resolution a satellite-based radar antenna looking at the earth should have. Let's look at some of the consequences:

- A given resolution requires a specific size of the antenna, and a specific amount of energy being sent out. (Actually, the two influence each other as well).

- A bigger antenna results in a heavier satellite, and more radar energy requires more solar panel area – increasing the size and weight even further.

[13] A different approach may have the architect selecting the implementation technology and the programmer doing the design work as well.

[14] In effect, everything the OEM does is called requirements (by definition!), what the integrator does is called architecture, and what the outsourcer does is called implementation.

[15] You write some requirements, then you write a prototype and check if the requirements make sense, then you refine the requirements, write a (maybe more detailed) prototype, and so on.

- At some point, the size and weight of the satellite cannot be further increased, because a given launch vehicle reaches its limits – a different launch vehicle might be required.

- A bigger launch vehicle will be much more expensive, or you might have to change the launch provider. For example, you might have to use a Soyuz instead of an Ariane.

- A Soyus launched at Baikonur cannot reach the same orbits as an Ariane launched from Courou, because of the higher latitude. As a consequence, the satellite might be "further away" from the area you want to inspect with your radar, neglecting the advantages gained by the bigger antenna[16].

...and this has just looked at size and weight! Similar problems exist with heat management, pointing accuracy or propulsion. As you can see, a change in any particular requirement can lead to non-trivial consequences you will only detect if you think about the *implementation* of the requirement. A strictly sequential approach (first write all the requirements, then think about the implementation) will not work. So what do the systems engineers do? They come up with a model of the satellite. Using mathematical formulas, they describe how the different properties discussed above relate. These might be approximations or based on past experience – after all, the real physics can be quite complex. They then run a *trade-off analysis*. In other words, they change the input values until a workable compromise is reached. Usually this is a manual process, but sometimes parts of it can be automated.

This example illustrates three things. First, requirements elicitation is incremental. Second, models can be a big help to precisely specify requirements and then "play" with them. And third, the boundary between requirements and design is blurred, and the two influence each other. Fig. 17.1 shows a multi-step approach to requirements definition, intertwined with incrementally more refined designs.

17.3   Using DSLs for Requirements Engineering

So here is the approach for using DSLs we suggest: identify a couple of core areas of the system to be built that lend themselves to specification with a formal language[17]. Then develop one or more DSLs to express these areas and use them to describe the system. The rest of the system – i.e., the areas for

[16] Actually, they now launch Soyuz vehicles from Courou as well, for just that reason.

[17] The trade-off between antenna resolution and size/weight mentioned above is such an area.

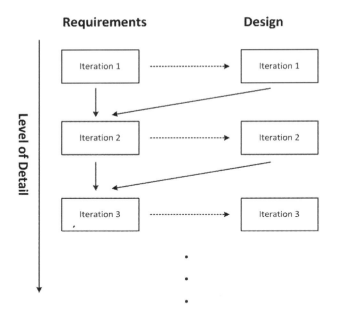

Figure 17.1: Requirements and Design influence each other and are thus best done iteratively, and in parallel.

which a DSL-based description makes no sense – is described textually, with the usual tools[18].

Once a suitable DSL has been found and implemented, those people who have the requirements in mind can *directly* express them – the lossy human-to-human communication is no longer a problem. Various constraint checks, tests and simulations can be used to allow the requirements owners to "play" with the requirements models to see if they really express what they had in mind.

[18] We will discuss the integration between the textual requirements and the DSL-based requirements below.

Of course there is one significant caveat: we first have to build this DSL. So how do we go about that? We could have somebody write prose requirements and hand them over to the DSL developer ... back to square one!

There is a much better approach, though. Since today's language workbenches support extremely rapid prototyping, you can actually build the DSLs interactively with the requirements owner. Since you are not capturing the specific requirements, but rather try to define how specific requirements are described, you essentially perform a domain analysis: you try to understand the degrees of freedom in the domain to be able to represent the domain with the DSL[19]. Here is the process I have use successfully many times:

1. Have the requirements owner explain some particular aspect of the domain.

[19] This is similar to what has been done with "analysis models" (back in the day ...). However, instead of drawing UML analysis diagrams, you capture the domain into a language definition, which makes it executable, in the sense that you can always turn around and have the requirements owner try to express specific requirements with the DSL you're building, verifying the suitability of the DSL.

2. Try to understand that aspect and change your DSL so it can express that aspect.
3. Make the requirements owner try to express a couple of specific, but representative, requirements with the DSL.
4. Most likely you will run into problems, some things cannot be expressed with the DSL. If so, go back to 1 and reiterate. A complete iteration should take no more than 60 minutes.
5. After half a day, stop working with the requirements owner and clean up/refactor the DSL.
6. Start another of the language design sessions with the requirements owner and iterate – over time, you should get closer to *the* DSL for the domain.

Once the DSL is finished, the requirements owners will be able to express domain requirements without involvement of the software developers.

This approach to requirements engineering is very close to regular DSL usage. We identify an aspect of the domain that lends itself to formalization, iteratively build a language, and then let the domain experts – who are the requirements owners for many of the business requirements – express the system directly. The *classical* requirements document is gone[20].

Using DSLs to specify (some parts of the) requirements formally helps achieve some of the desirable characteristics for requirements discussed above. The following lists only those characteristics for which DSLs make a difference.

Consistent Consistency is enforced by the language. If the DSL is crafted correctly, no inconsistent requirements can be expressed.

Feasible Specific requirements are checked for feasibility by being expressible with the DSL: they are within the scope of what the DSL – hence, the domain for which we write the requirements – is intended.

Unambiguous A description of requirements – or application functionality in general – with a DSL always unambiguous, provided the DSL has well-defined semantics.

Verifiable Constraints, tests, verification or simulation can be used to verify the requirements regarding various properties. Inspection and review is simplified, because DSL programs are less verbose than implementation code, and clearer than prose.

[20] In many ways the refrigerator and pension plan examples from Part II of this book are examples of this approach, and so is the Health domain example discussed in Chapter 22.

17.4 Integration with Plain Text Requirements

You will probably not be able to describe all the requirements of a system using the approach described above. There will always be aspects that cannot be formalized, or that are so specific that the effort for building a DSL does not pay off. You therefore have to find some way of integrating plain text requirements with DSL code. Here are some approaches to how this can be done.

17.4.1 Embedding DSL Code in a Requirements Tool

One approach is to mix prose requirements with formalized, DSL-based requirements. We show examples with Xtext and MPS.

■ *Xtext Example* Eclipse-based tooling for requirements engineering is being developed as part of the VERDE[21] and ProR[22] research projects. This includes Eclipse RMF[23], a "classical" requirements engineering tool, in which textual requirements are classified, structured and put into relationships with each other[24]. The requirements structure is represented as an EMF model, to make integration with other model-based artifacts simple. In addition to plain text, requirements can have parameters with well-defined types. The types of these parameters can be primitive (string, int), but they can also be any other Ecore meta class, so any additional model structure can be embedded into a requirement. Integration with Xtext is available, which provides textual concrete syntax for these data structures. In other words, it is possible to enrich prose requirements specifications with additional formal specifications expressed in arbitrary DSLs. Fig. 17.2 shows a screenshot.

[21] www.itea-verde.org/
[22] www.pror.org/
[23] eclipse.org/RMF

[24] The tool actually implements the OMG's ReqIF standard.

■ *MPS Example* We have built a similar solution for MPS in the mbeddr project. The solution supports collecting trees of requirements, where each requirement has an ID, a kind and a short summary. Fig. 17.3 shows an example. In addition, the one-line summary can be expanded to reveal additional details (Fig. 17.4). There users can enter a detailed prose description, as well as additional constraints among requirements (**requires also, conflicts with**.) In the **Additional Specifications** section, users can enter arbitrary DSL programs: since MPS supports language modularization and composition (Section 16.2), embedding arbitrary languages with

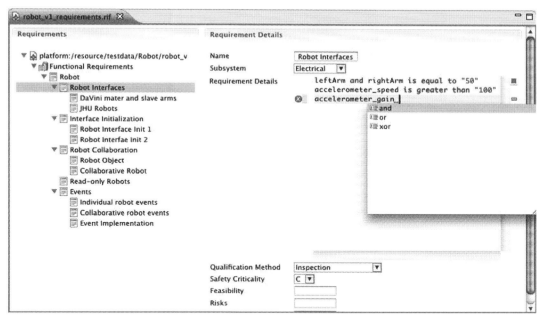

Figure 17.2: An Xtext DSL embedded in a requirements engineering tool based on the Eclipse Requirements Modeling Framework (RMF).

arbitrary syntax into the requirements language is trivial and works out of the box. It is also possible to associate a specific additional specification with a particular requirements kind. This means that if a requirement has a particular kind, the additional data associated with that kind must be present in the `Additional Specifications` section[25].

[25] For example, a requirement kind `timing` may require an instance of `TimingSpecification` in the `Additional Specifications` section.

17.4.2 Requirements Traceability

Requirements traceability establishes links, or traces, between implementation (or design or test) artifacts and requirements. This allows each (part of) an artifact to be traced back to the requirements that drive the artifact[26]. Once such pointers are available, various analyses become possible. For example, it is easy to find out whether each requirement has been implemented (or tested), and we know which implementation artifacts may have to change if a requirement changes.

[26] Traces are typically typed (as in `implements`, `tests` or `refines`), so various different relationships can be established.

Requirements traceability has two challenges. The first one is social, the second one is technical. The social problem is that, while traces are easy to analyze once they are available, they still have to be established manually. This requires discipline by the people, typically developers, whose job it is to establish the traces.

The technical problem addresses how to actually establish the pointers technically. In a world in which requirements –

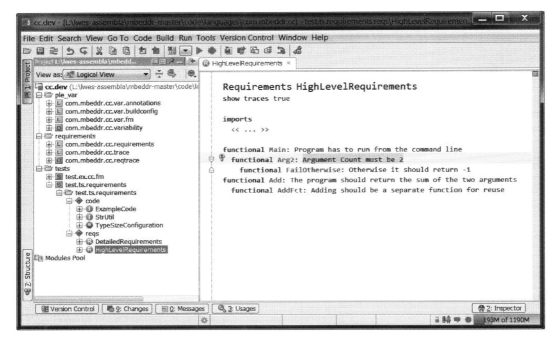

Figure 17.3: The requirements language supports creating trees of requirements. Each requirement has an ID, a kind and short text. In addition, a detailed description and constraints among requirements can be added (Fig. 17.4).

as well as design, implementation and test artifacts – are all model-based, establishing these pointers becomes trivial. In mixed environments with many different tools built on many different foundations, it can become arbitrarily complicated. Again, we show tooling examples for Xtext and MPS.

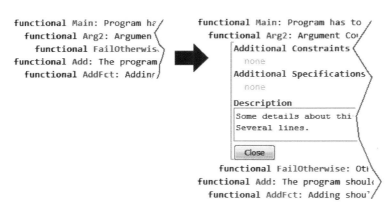

Figure 17.4: The detail view of the requirements language. In the **Additional Specifications** section users can enter arbitrary programs written in arbitrary DSLs. Constraints can be used to make sure that specific additional specifications are *always* added to requirements of a particular kind.

■ *Xtext Example* The VERDE project mentioned above also develops a traceability framework for Eclipse. Various trace kinds can be defined, which can subsequently be used to establish links between arbitrary EMF-based models[27]. The trace-

[27] In addition to generic EMF-based tracing, tool adapters can be plugged in to support for trace links from/into a number of specific tools or formats such as plain text files, non-EMF UML tools or AUTOSAR models.

ability links are kept external to the actual models, so no modifications to existing meta models or languages are required[28].

■ *MPS Example* As part of mbeddr, we have implemented a generic tracing framework base on MPS' language annotations (discussed in Section 16.2.7). Arbitrary models – independent of the language used to create them[29] – can be annotated with traceability links, as shown in the left part of figure 17.5.

A context menu action adds a new trace to any model element: **Ctrl-Space** allows the selection of one or more requirements at which to point. Each trace has a **kind**. The traced requirements are color coded to reflect their trace status (Fig. 17.5, top right). Finally, the **Find Usages** functionality of MPS has been customized to show traces directly (Fig. 17.5, bottom right).

[28] This is also the reason why non-EMF artifacts can be integrated, even though they require a specific tool adapter.

[29] Of course this only works for arbitrary *MPS-based* languages.

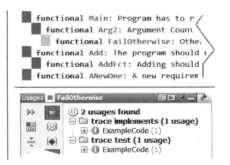

Figure 17.5: *Left:* A C function with an attached requirement trace. Traces can be attached to arbitrary program nodes, supporting tracing at arbitrary levels of detail. *Right, top:* The requirements can be color coded to reflect whether they are traced at all (gray), implemented (blue) and tested (green). Untraced requirements are red. *Right, bottom:* The Find Usages dialog shows the different kinds of traces as separate categories. Programs can also be shown without the traces using conditional projection. We discuss this mechanism in the section on product line variability (Section 7.7).

18
DSLs and Software Architecture

In this chapter we explore the relationship between DSLs and software architecture. In particular we establish the notion of an Architecture DSL (or ADSL), which is a DSL specifically created for a specific architecture. We first discuss ADSLs based on an extensive example, then discuss the conceptual details. The chapter also looks at embedding business logic DSLs, as well as at the role software components can play in the context of DSLs.

18.1   What is Software Architecture?

■ *Definitions*   Software architecture has many definitions, from various groups of people. Here are a few. Wikipedia defines software architecture in the following way:

> The software architecture of a program or computing system is the structure or structures of the system, which comprise software elements, the externally visible properties of those elements, and the relationships between them.

This is a classic definition that emphasizes the (coarse grained) structure of a software system (as opposed to the behavior), observable by analyzing an existing system[1]. A definition by Boehm builds on this:

> A software system architecture comprises a collection of software and system components, connections, and constraints, a collection of system stakeholders' need statements as well as a rationale which demonstrates that the components, connections, and constraints define a system that, if implemented, would satisfy the collection of system stakeholders' need statements.

[1] As you may suspect from my emphasis here, I disagree. Architecture is not limited to structure, and it is not limited to coarse-grained things. I will get back to this later.

In addition to the structure, this definition also emphasizes the relevance of the stakeholders and their needs, and ties the structure of the system to what the system is required to do. Hayes-Roth introduce another aspect:

> The architecture of a complex software system is its style and method of design and construction.

Instead of looking at the structures, they emphasize that there are different architectural styles and they emphasize the "method of design and construction"[2]. Eoin Woods takes it one step further:

> Software architecture is the set of design decisions which, if made incorrectly, may cause your project to be cancelled.

[2] This can be interpreted as emphasizing the process of how something is built, and not just the structures of the built artifact once it is finished.

He emphasizes the design decisions that lead to a given system. So he doesn't look at the system as a set of structures, but rather considers the architecture as a process – the design decisions – that leads to a given system. While I don't disagree with any of these definitions – they all emphasize different aspects of the architecture of a software system – I would like to propose another one:

> Software architecture is everything that needs to be consistent throughout a software system.

[3] A locking protocol for accessing a shared resource is possibly a detail, but it is important to implement it consistently to avoid deadlocks and other concurrency faults.

This definition is useful because it includes structures *and* behavior; it doesn't say anything about coarse-grained versus detailed[3] and it implies that there needs to be some kind of process or method to achieve the consistency. As we will see, DSLs can help with achieving this consistency.

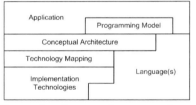

Figure 18.1: Conceptual structure of a software architecture.

■ *Terminology*   Fig. 18.1 looks at software architecture in more detail. At the center of the diagram you can see the *conceptual architecture*. This defines architectural concepts from which concrete systems are built (we will come back to this in the next section). Examples could include: *task, message, queue, component, port*, or *replicated data structure*. Note that these concepts are independent of specific implementation technologies: it is the *technology mapping* that defines how the architecture concepts are implemented based on specific technologies[4]. The *programming model* is the way in which the architectural concepts are implemented in a given programming language[5]. Applications are implemented by instantiating the architectural

[4] Separating the two has the advantage that the conceptual discussions are not diluted by what specific technologies may or may not be able to do, and how. The decision of what technology to map to is then driven by non-functional concerns, i.e. whether and how a given technology can provide the required quality of service.

[5] Ideally, the programming model should not change as long as the architectural concepts remain stable – even if the technology mapping or the implementation technologies change.

concepts, and implementing them based on the programming model.

■ *The Importance of Concepts*   I want to reemphasize the importance of the conceptual architecture. When asking people about the architecture of systems, one often gets answers like: "It's a Web service architecture", or "It's an XML architecture" or "It's a JEE architecture". Obviously, all this conveys is that a certain technology is used. When talking about architectures per se, we should talk about architectural *concepts* and how they relate to each other. Only as a second step should a mapping to one or more technologies be discussed. Here are some of these fundamental architectural concepts:

Modularize Break big things down into smaller things, so they can be understood (and potentially reused) more easily. Examples: procedures, classes, components, services, user stories.

Encapsulate Hide the innards of a module so that they can be changed without affecting clients. Examples: private members, facade pattern, components, layers/rings/levels.

Contracts Describe the external interface of a module clearly. Examples: interfaces, pre- and post-conditions, protocol state machines, message exchange patterns, published APIs.

Decoupling Reduce dependencies in time, data structure or contention. Examples: message queues, eventual consistency, compensating transactions.

Isolate crosscuts Encapsulate handling of cross-cutting concerns. Examples: aspect orientation, interceptors, application servers, exception handling.

As we will see in the following section, architecture DSLs can specify architectures unambiguously while emphasizing these fundamentals, instead of technologies.

18.2   Architecture DSLs

An Architecture DSL (ADSL) is a language that expresses a system's architecture directly. "Directly" means that the language's abstract syntax contains constructs for all the ingredients of the conceptual architecture. The language can hence be used to describe a system on the architectural level without using low-level implementation code, but still in an unambiguous way[6]. Code generation is used to generate representations of the application architecture in the implementation language(s), automating the technology mapping[7]. Finally, the programming model is defined with regards to the generated code plus possibly additional frameworks[8].

I do not advocate the definition of a generic, reusable language such as the various ADLs, or UML (see below). Based on our experience, the approach works best if you define the ADSL in real time as you understand, define and evolve the conceptual architecture of a system[9]. The process of defining the language actually helps the architecture/development team to better understand, clarify and refine the architectural abstractions, as the language serves as a (formalized) ubiquitous language that lets you reason about and discuss the architecture.

18.2.1 An Example ADSL

This section contains an example of an Architecture DSL taken from a real system in the domain of airport management systems[10].

■ *Background* The customer decided they wanted to build a new airport management system. Airlines use systems like these to track and publish information about whether airplanes have landed at airports, whether they are late, and to track the technical status of the aircraft[11]. The system also populates the online-tracking system on the Web and information monitors at airports. This system is in many ways a typical distributed system: there is a central data center to do some of the heavy number crunching, but there are additional machines distributed over relatively large areas. Consequently you cannot simply shut down the whole system, which leads to a requirement to be able to work with different versions of parts of the system at the same time. Different parts of the system will be built with different technologies: Java, C++, C#. This is not an untypical requirement for large distributed systems either. Often you use Java technology for the backend, and .NET technology for a Windows front end. The customer had decided that the backbone of the system would be a messaging infrastructure, and they were evaluating different messaging tools for performance and throughput.

---

[6] Meaning: it is more useful than Powerpoint architecture, even though that is also high level and technology independent :-).

[7] Of course, the decisions about the mapping have to be made manually. But once they are made (and generators are implemented), the mapping can be executed automatically for instances of the architecture.

[8] Architecture DSLs are typically *incomplete*. Only the architecturally relevant structures and behaviors are expressed with the DSL. The application logic is implemented in a GPL.

[9] In other words, like any DSL it should be closely aligned with the domain it is supposed to represent. In this case, the domain is the architecture of system, platform or product line.

[10] I was helping that customer build an architecture DSL for their architecture. They hired me because they needed to get a grip on their architecture independent of specific technologies, since the system was supposed to last for 20 years.

[11] The actual system dealt with a different transportation domain, not aircraft. I had to anonymize the example a bit. However, the rest of the story happened exactly as it appears here.

While my customer knew many of the requirements and had made specific decisions about some architectural aspects, they didn't have a well-defined conceptual architecture. It showed: when the team were discussing their system, they stumbled into disagreements about architectural concepts all the time because they had no *language* for the architecture. Also, they didn't have a good idea of how to maintain the architecture over the 20 years of expected lifetime in the face of changing technologies.

■ *Getting Started*   To solve this issue, an architecture DSL was developed. We started with the notion of a component. At that point the notion of components is defined relatively loosely, simply as the smallest architecturally relevant building block, a piece of encapsulated application functionality[12]. We also assume that components can be instantiated, making components the architectural equivalent to classes in object-oriented programming. To enable components to interact with each other, we also introduce the notion of interfaces, as well as ports, which are named communication endpoints typed with an interface. Ports have a direction[13] (**provides**, **requires**) as well as a cardinality. Based on this initial version of the ADSL, we could write the following example code[14]:

```
component DelayCalculator {
  provides aircraft: IAircraftStatus
  provides managementConsole: IManagementConsole
  requires screens[0..n]: IInfoScreen
}
component Manager {
  requires backend[1]: IManagementConsole
}
component InfoScreen {
  provides default: IInfoScreen
}
component AircraftModule {
  requires calculator[1]: IAircraftStatus
}
```

[12] In many cases it is a good idea to start with the notion of a component, although components may turn out to look different in different systems. Since components are so important, we discuss them in Section 18.3.

[13] It is important not to just state which interfaces a component *provides*, but also which interfaces it *requires*, because we want to be able to understand (and later analyze with a tool) component dependencies. This is important for any system, but is especially important for the versioning requirement.

[14] The following is an example instance that makes use of the architecture DSL. In this section we discuss the ADSL based on an example and don't discuss the implementation in Xtext. The DSL is not very challenging in terms of Xtext.

We then looked at instantiation. There are many aircraft, each running an **AircraftModule**, and there are even more **InfoScreen**s. So we need to express instances of components[15]. We also introduce connectors to define actual communication paths between components (and their ports).

```
instance dc: DelayCalculator
instance screen1: InfoScreen
instance screen2: InfoScreen
connect dc.screens to (screen1.default, screen2.default)
```

[15] Note that these are logical instances. Decisions about pooling and redundant physical instances had not been made yet.

■ *Organizing the System*   At some point it became clear that in order to not get lost in all the components, instances and connectors, we need to introduce some kind of namespace. It became equally clear that we'd need to distribute things to different files:

```
namespace com.mycompany {

  namespace datacenter {

    component DelayCalculator {
      provides aircraft: IAircraftStatus
      provides managementConsole: IManagementConsole
      requires screens[0..n]: IInfoScreen
    }

    component Manager {
      requires backend[1]: IManagementConsole
    }

  }

  namespace mobile {

    component InfoScreen {
      provides default: IInfoScreen
    }

    component AircraftModule {
      requires calculator[1]: IAircraftStatus
    }

  }
}
```

It is also a good idea to keep component and interface definitions (essentially type definitions) separate from system definitions (connected instances), so we introduced the concept of compositions, which make a group of instances and connectors identifiable by a name:

```
namespace com.mycompany.test {

  composition testSystem {
    instance dc: DelayCalculator
    instance screen1: InfoScreen
    instance screen2: InfoScreen
    connect dc.screens to (screen1.default, screen2.default)
  }
}
```

■ *Dynamic Connectors*   Of course in a real system, the **DelayCalculator** would have to dynamically discover all the available **InfoScreen**s at runtime. There is not much point in manually describing those connections. So, we specify a query that is executed at runtime against some kind of naming/trader/lookup/registry infrastructure[16]. It is re-executed every 60 seconds to find the **InfoScreen**s that have just come on line.

[16] Note how the specific realization depends on the technology. In the model, we just express the fact that we have to be able to run the queries specified in the model. We will map this to an implementation later.

```
namespace com.mycompany.production {

  instance dc: DelayCalculator

  // InfoScreen instances are created and started in other configurations
  dynamic connect dc.screens query {
    type = IInfoScreen
    status = active
  }
}
```

A similar approach can be used to address load balancing or fault tolerance. A static connector can point to a primary as well as a backup instance. Or a dynamic query can be re-executed when the currently used instance becomes unavailable. To support registration of instances with the naming or registry service, we add additional syntax to their definition. A registered instance automatically registers itself with the registry, using its name (qualified through the namespace) and all provided interfaces. Additional parameters can be specified, and the following example registers a primary and a backup instance for the **DelayCalculator**:

```
namespace com.mycompany.datacenter {

  registered instance dc1: DelayCalculator {
    registration parameters {role = primary}
  }

  registered instance dc2: DelayCalculator {
    registration parameters {role = backup}
  }
}
```

■ *Interfaces*   So far we hadn't really defined what an interface is. We knew that we'd like to build the system based on a messaging infrastructure. Here's our first idea: an interface is a collection of messages, where each message has a name and a list of typed parameters[17]. After discussing this notion of interfaces for a while, we noticed that it was too simplistic. We needed to be able to define the direction of a message: does it flow in or out of the port? More generally, which kinds of message interaction patterns are there? We identified several; here are examples of **oneway** and **request-reply**[18]:

```
interface IAircraftStatus {

  oneway message reportPosition(aircraft: ID, pos: Position )

  request-reply message reportProblem {
    request (aircraft: ID, problem: Problem, comment: String)
    reply (repairProcedure: ID)
  }
}
```

[17] This also requires the ability to define data structures, but in the interests of brevity we won't show that.

[18] A *oneway* message has no result. It is sent by the client infrastructure to a receiver with best effort. The client does not know if the message ever arrives. A *request-reply* message is exactly what it seems: the client sends a message and expects a reply. Note that at this point we do not specify whether we expect the request as a callback, by polling a Future object, or whether the client blocks until the reply arrives.

We talked a long time about various message interaction patterns. After a while it turned out that one of the core use cases for messages was to push updates of various data structures out to various interested parties. For example, if a flight was delayed because of a technical problem with an aircraft, then this information had to be pushed out to all the **InfoScreen**s in the system. We prototyped several of the messages necessary for "broadcasting" complete updates, incremental updates and removal of data items. And then it hit us: we were working with the wrong abstraction!

■ *Data Replication*   While messaging is a suitable *transport* abstraction for these things, architecturally we're really talking about replicated data structures. It basically works the same way for all of those structures:

- You define a data structure (such as **FlightInfo**).

- The system then keeps track of a collection of such data structures.

- This collection is updated by a few components and typically read by many other components.

- The update strategies from publisher to receiver always include full update of all items in the collection, incremental updates of just one or a few items, and removal of items.

Once we understood that in addition to messaging, there's this additional core abstraction in the system, we added this to our Architecture DSL and were able to write something like the following. We define data structures and replicated items. Components can then publish or consume those replicated data structures. We state that the publisher publishes the replicated data whenever something changes in the local data structure. However, the **InfoScreen** only needs an update every 60 seconds (as well as a full load of data when it is started up).

```
struct FlightInfo {
  from: Airport
  to: Airport
  scheduled: Time
  expected: Time
}

replicated singleton flights {
  flights: FlightInfo[]
}

component DelayCalculator {
  publishes flights { publication = onchange }
```

```
}
component InfoScreen {
  consumes flights { update 60 }
}
```

This is much more concise compared to a description based on messages. We can automatically derive the kinds of messages needed for full update, incremental update and removal, and create these messages in the model using a model transformation. The description reflects much more clearly the actual architectural intent: it expresses better what we want to do (replicate data) compared to a lower-level description of how we want to do it (sending around update messages)[19].

■ *Interface Semantics*   While replication is a core concept for data, there is of course still a need for messages, not just as an implementation detail, but also as a way to express architectural intent[20]. It is useful to add more semantics to an interface, for example to define valid sequencing of messages. A well-known way to do that is to use protocol state machines. Here is an example. It expresses the fact that you can only report positions and problems once an aircraft is registered. In other words, the first thing an aircraft has to do is register itself.

```
interface IAircraftStatus {

  oneway message registerAircraft(aircraft: ID )

  oneway message unregisterAircraft(aircraft: ID )

  oneway message reportPosition(aircraft: ID, pos: Position )

  request-reply message reportProblem {
    request (aircraft: ID, problem: Problem, comment: String)
    reply (repairProcedure: ID)
  }

  protocol initial = new {
    state new {
      registerAircraft => registered
    }
    state registered {
      unregisterAircraft => new
      reportPosition
      reportProblem
    }
  }
}
```

Initially, the protocol state machine is in the **new** state where the only valid message is **registerAircraft**. If this is received, we transition into the **registered** state. In **registered**, you can either **unregisterAircraft** and go back to **new**, or receive a **reportProblem** or **reportPosition** message, in which case you will remain in the **registered** state.

[19] Once again, this shows the advantage of a DSL that is closely aligned with its domain, and that can be evolved together with the understanding of the domain. With a fixed language, we most likely would have had to shoehorn the data replication abstractions into messaging, somehow. And by doing so, we would have lost the opportunity to generate meaningful code based on the actual architectural intent.

[20] Not all communication is actually data replication.

■ *Versioning*   We mentioned above that the system is distributed geographically. This means it is not feasible to update all the software for all parts of the systems (e.g., all **InfoScreen**s or all **AircraftModule**s) at the same time. As a consequence, there might be several versions of the same component running in the system. To make this feasible, many non-trivial things need to be put in place in the runtime system. But the basic requirement is this: you have to be able to mark versions of components, and you have to be able to check them for compatibility with older versions. The following piece of code expresses the fact that the **DelayCalculatorV2** is a new implementation of **DelayCalculator**. **newImplOf** means that no externally visible aspects change, which is why no ports and other externally exposed details of the component are declared[21].

```
component DelayCalculator {
  publishes flights { publication = onchange }
}
newImplOf component DelayCalculator: DelayCalculatorV2
```

[21] For all intents and purposes, it's the same thing – just maybe a couple of bugs are fixed.

To evolve the externally visible signature of a component, one can write this:

```
component DelayCalculator {
  publishes flights { publication = onchange }
}
newVersionOf component DelayCalculator: DelayCalculatorV3 {
  publishes flights { publication = onchange }
  provides somethingElse: ISomething
}
```

The keyword **newVersionOf** allows us to add additional provided ports (such as the **somethingElse** port) and to remove required ports[22].

This wraps up our case study[23]. In the next subsection we recap the approach and provide additional guidance.

[22] You cannot add additional required ports or remove any of the provided ports, since that would destroy the "plug-in compatibility". Constraints make sure that these rules are enforced on the model level.

18.2.2 Architecture DSL Concepts

■ *What we did in a Nutshell*   Using the approach shown here, we were able to quickly get a grip of the overall architecture of the system. All of the above was actually done in the first day of the workshop. We defined the grammar, some important constraints, and a basic editor (without many bells and whistles). We were able to separate what we wanted the system to do from how it would achieve it: all the technology discussions were now merely an implementation detail of the conceptual

[23] While writing this chapter, I contacted the customer, and we talked about the approach in hindsight. As it turns out, they are still happily using the approach as the foundation of their system. They generate several hundred thousand lines of code from the models, and they have to migrate to a new version of Xtext real soon now :-)

descriptions given here[24]. We also achieved a clear and unambiguous definition of what the different architectural concepts mean. The generally nebulous concept of *component* has a formal, well-defined meaning in the context of this system.

The approach discussed in this chapter therefore recommends the definition of a formal language for your project's or system's conceptual architecture. You develop the language as the understanding of your architecture grows. The language therefore always resembles the complete understanding about your architecture in a clear and unambiguous way.

■ *Component Implementation*   By default, architecture DSLs are incomplete; component implementation code is written manually against the generated API, using well-known composition techniques such as inheritance, delegation or partial classes.

However, there are other alternatives for component implementation that do not use a GPL, but instead use formalisms that are specific to certain classes of behavior: state machines, business rules or workflows. You can also define and use a domain-specific language for certain classes of functionality in a specific business domain. If such an approach is used, then the code generator for the application domain DSL has to act as the "implementor" of the components (or whatever other architectural abstractions are defined in the architecture DSL). The code generated from the business logic DSL must fit into the code skeletons generated from the architecture DSL. The code composition techniques discussed for incomplete DSLs in Section 4.5.1 can be used here[25].

■ *Standards, ADLs and UML*   Describing architecture with formal languages is not a new idea. Various communities recommend using Architecture Description Languages (ADLs) or the Unified Modeling Language (UML). However, all of those approaches advocate using existing, *generic* languages for specifying architecture, although some of them, including UML, can be customized to some degree[26].

Unfortunately, efforts like that completely miss the point. We have not experienced much benefit in shoehorning an architecture description into the (typically very limited, as well as too generic) constructs provided by predefined languages – one of the core activities of the approach explained is this chapter is the process of actually building *your own language* to capture your system's specific conceptual architecture.

[24] I don't want to give the impression that technology decisions are unimportant. However, they should be an explicit second step, and not mixed with the concepts. This is particularly important in light of the fact that the system should live for more than 20 years, during which technologies will change more than once.

[25] Be aware that the discussion in this section is only really relevant for application-specific behavior, not for all implementation code. Huge amounts of implementation code are related to the technical infrastructure (e.g., remoting, persistence, workflow) of an application. This can be derived from the architectural models, and generated automatically.

[26] I am not going to elaborate on the reasons why I think profiles are usually not a good alternative to a DSL. It should become clear from the example above and the book in general why I think this is true.

■ *Visualization*   In this project, as well as in many other ones, we have used textual DSLs. We have argued in this book why textual DSLs are superior in many cases, and these arguments apply here as well. However, we did use visualization to show the relationships between the building blocks, and to communicate the architecture to stakeholders who were not willing to dive into the textual models. Figure 18.2 shows an example, created with Graphviz.

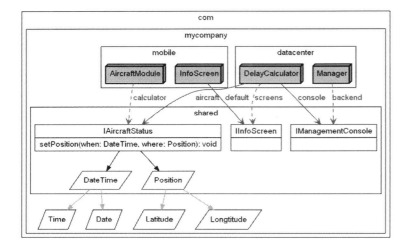

Figure 18.2: This shows the relationship between the ingredients of the example system described above. It contains namespace, components, interfaces and data structures, as well as the **provides** and **requires** relationships between components and interfaces.

■ *Code Generation*   Now that we have a formal model of the conceptual architecture (the language) and also a formal description of system(s) we are building – i.e., the models defined using the language – we can exploit this by generating code[27]:

- We generate an API against which the implementation is coded. That API can be non-trivial, taking into account the various messaging paradigms, replicated state, etc. The generated API allows developers to code the implementation in a way that does not depend on any technological decisions: the generated API hides those from the component implementation code. We call this generated API, and the set of idioms to use it, the *programming model*.

- Remember that we expect some kind of component container or middleware platform to run the components, so we also generate the code that is necessary to run the components (including their technology-neutral implementation)

[27] It should have become clear from the chapter that the primary benefit of developing the architecture DSL (and using it) is just that: understanding concepts by removing any ambiguity and defining them formally. It helps you understand your system and get rid of unwanted technology interference. But of course, exploiting these assets further by generating code is useful.

on the implementation technology of choice. We call this layer of code the *technology mapping* code (or *glue code*). It typically also contains the configuration files for the various platforms involved[28].

It is of course completely feasible to generate APIs for several target languages (supporting component implementation in various languages) and/or generating glue code for several target platforms (supporting the execution of the same component on different middleware platforms). This nicely supports potential multi-platform requirements[29].

Another important point is that you typically generate in several phases: a first phase uses type definitions (components, data structures, interfaces) to generate the API code so you can write the component implementation code. A second phase generates the glue code and the system configuration code. Consequently, it is often sensible to separate type definitions from system definitions into several different viewpoints[30]: these are used at different times in the overall process, and also often created, modified and processed by different people.

In summary, the generated code supports an efficient and technology independent implementation and hides much of the underlying technological complexity, making development more efficient and less error-prone.

■ *What Needs to be Documented?* I advertise the above approach as a way to formally describe a system's conceptual and application architecture. So, this means it serves as some kind of documentation, right? Right, but it does not mean that you don't have to document anything else. The following things still need to be documented[31]:

Rationales/Architectural Decisions The DSLs describe *what* your architecture looks like, but it does not explain *why* it looks the way it does. You still need to document the rationales for architectural and technological decisions. Note that the grammar of your architecture DSL is a really good baseline for such a documentation. Each of the constructs is the result of architectural decisions. So, if you explain for each grammar element why it is there (and why other alternatives have not been chosen) you are well on your way to documenting the important architectural decisions. A similar approach can be used for the application architecture, i.e. the programs written with the DSL.

---

[28] As a side effect, the generators capture best practices in working with the technologies you've decided to use.

[29] Even if you don't have explicit requirements to support several platforms, it may still be useful to be able to do so. For one, it makes future migration to a new platform simpler. Or a second platform may simply be a unit test environment running on a local PC, without the expensive distribution infrastructure of the real system.

[30] Viewpoints were discussed in Section 4.4.

[31] There are probably more aspects of an architecture that might be worth documenting, but the following two are the most important ones when working with Architecture DSLs.

User Guides A language grammar can serve as a well-defined and formal way of capturing an architecture, but it is not a good teaching tool. So you need to create tutorials for your users (i.e., the application programmers) that explain how to use the architecture and the DSL. This includes what and how to model (using your DSL) and also how to generate code and how to use the programming model (how to fill in the implementation code into the generated skeletons).

18.3 Component Models

As I have hinted at already, I think that component-based software architectures are extremely useful. There are many (more or less formal) definitions of what a components is. They range from a building block of software systems, through something with explicitly defined context dependencies, to something that contains business logic and is run inside a container.

Our understanding (notice we are not saying we have a real definition) is that a component is the smallest architectural building block. When defining a system's architecture, you typically don't look inside components. Components have to specify all their architecturally relevant properties declaratively (using meta data, or models). As a consequence, components become analyzable and composable by tools. Typically they run inside a container that serves as a framework to act on the runtime-relevant parts of the meta data. The component boundary is the level at which the container can provide technical services such as as logging, monitoring or fail-over. The component also provides well-defined APIs to its implementation to address cross-cutting architectural concerns such as locking[32].

I don't have any specific requirements for what meta data a component actually contains (and hence, which properties are described). The concrete notion of components has to be defined for each (system/platform/product line) architecture separately: this is exactly what we do with the language approach introduced above.

Based on my experience, it is almost always useful to start by modeling the component structure of the system to be built. To do that, we start by defining what a component actually is – that is, by defining a meta model for component-based development. Independent of the project's domain, these meta

[32] A long time ago I coauthored the book *Server Component Patterns*. While the EJB-based technology examples are no longer relevant, many of the patterns identified and discussed in the book still are. The book was not written with a MDD/DSL background, but the patterns fit very well with such an approach.

models are quite similar, with a set of specific variation points. We show parts of these meta models here to give you a head start when defining your own component architecture.

18.3.1 Three Typical Viewpoints

It is useful to look at a component-based system from several viewpoints (Section 4.4). Three viewpoints form the backbone of the description.

■ *The Type Viewpoint* The Type viewpoint describes component types, interfaces and data structures[33]. A component provides a number of interfaces and references a number of required interfaces (often through ports, as in the example above). An interface owns a number of operations, each with a return type, parameters and exceptions. Fig. 18.3 shows this.

[33] Referring back to the terminology introduced in Section 3.3, this viewpoint is *independent*. It is also *sufficient* for generating all the code that is needed for developers to implement the application logic.

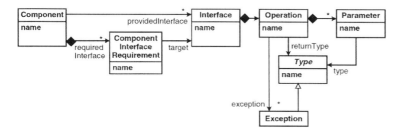

Figure 18.3: The types viewpoint describes interfaces, data types and components. These are referred to as types because they can be instantiated (in the composition viewpoint) to make up the actual application.

To describe the data structures with which the components work (the meta model is shown in Fig. 18.4), we start out with the abstract concept **Type**. We use primitive types as well as complex types. A **ComplexType** has a number of named and typed attributes. There are two kinds of complex types. Data transfer objects are simple (C-style) **struct**s that are used to exchange data among components. Entities have a unique ID and can be persisted (this is not visible from the meta model). Entities can reference each other and can thus build more complex data graphs. Each reference specifies whether it is navigable in only one or in both directions. A reference also specifies the cardinalities of the entities at the respective ends, and whether the reference has containment semantics.

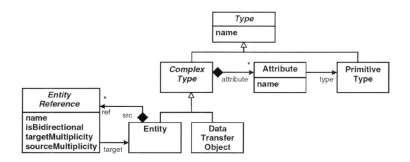

Figure 18.4: The structure of data types of course depends a lot on the application. A good starting point for data definitions is the well-known entity relationship model, which is essentially represented by this meta model.

■ *The Composition Viewpoint* The Composition viewpoint, illustrated in Fig. 18.5, describes component instances and how they are connected[34]. Using the *Type* and *Composition* viewpoints, we can define logical models of applications. A **Configuration** consists of a number of **ComponentInstance**s, each referencing their type (from the *Type* viewpoint). An instance has a number of wires (or connectors): a **Wire** can be seen as an instance of a **ComponentInterfaceRequirement**. Note the constraints defined in the meta model:

- For each **ComponentInterfaceRequirement** defined in the instance's type, we need to supply a wire.

- The type of the component instance at the target end of a wire needs to provide the interface to which the wire's component interface requirement points.

[34] The Composition viewpoint is *dependent*: it depends on the *Type* viewpoint. It is also sufficient for generating stub implementation of the system for unit testing and for doing dependency analyses and other checks for completeness and consistency.

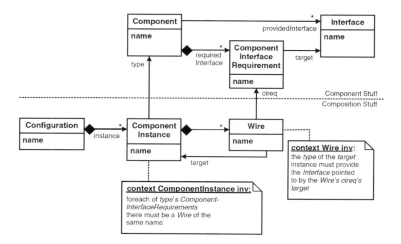

Figure 18.5: The *Composition* viewpoint describes the composition of a logical system from the component types defined in the *Types* viewpoint.

■ *The System Viewpoint* The system viewpoint describes the system infrastructure onto which the logical system defined with the two previous viewpoints is deployed (Fig. 18.6), as well as the mapping of the Composition viewpoint onto this execution infrastructure[35].

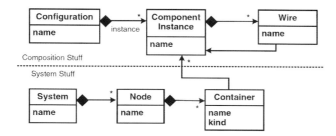

[35] In some cases it may make sense to separate the infrastructure definition from the mapping to the Composition viewpoint (for example, if the infrastructure is configured by some operations department).

Figure 18.6: The *System* viewpoint maps the logical system defined in the *Composition* viewpoint to a specific hardware and systems software configuration.

A system consists of a number of nodes, each one hosting containers. A container hosts a number of component instances. Note that a container also defines its kind – representing technologies such as OSGi, JEE, Eclipse or Spring. Based on this data, together with the data in the Composition viewpoint, you can generate the necessary "glue" code to run the components in that kind of container, including container and remote communication configuration code, as well as scripts to package and deploy the artifacts for each container.

You may have observed that the dependencies among the viewpoints are well-structured. Since you want to be able to define several compositions using the same components and interfaces, and since you want to be able to run the same compositions on several infrastructures, dependencies are only legal in the directions shown in figure 18.7.

Figure 18.7: Viewpoint dependencies are set up so that the same components (*Type* viewpoint) can be assembled into several logical applications (*Composition* viewpoint), and each of those can be mapped to several execution infrastructures (*System* viewpoint).

18.3.2 Aspect Models

The three viewpoints described above are a good starting point for modeling and building component-based systems. However, in many cases these three models are not enough. Additional aspects of the system have to be described using specific aspect models that are arranged "around" the three core viewpoint models. The following aspects are typically handled in separate aspect models:

- Persistence
- Authorization and Authentication (for enterprise systems)
- Forms, layout, page flow (for Web applications)
- Timing, scheduling and other quality of service aspects (especially in embedded systems)
- Packaging and deployment
- Diagnostics and monitoring

The idea of aspect models is that the information is not added to the three core viewpoints, but rather is described using a separate model with a suitable concrete syntax. Again, the meta model dependencies are important: the aspects may depend on the core viewpoint models and maybe even on one another, but the core viewpoints must not depend on any of the aspect models. Figure 18.8 illustrates a simplified persistence aspect meta model.

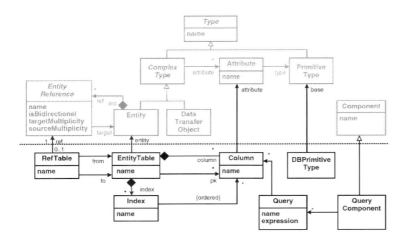

Figure 18.8: An example meta model for a persistence aspect. It maps data defined in the *Type* viewpoint to tables and columns.

18.3.3 Variations

The meta models described above cannot be used in exactly this way in every project. Also, in many cases the notion of what constitutes a *Component* needs to be adapted or extended. As a consequence, there are many variations of these meta models. In this section we discuss a few of them[36].

[36] Consider them as an inspiration for your own case. In the end, the actual system architecture drives these meta models.

■ *Messaging*   Instead of operations and their typical call/block semantics, you may want to use messages, together with the well-known message interaction patterns. The example system in this chapter used messaging.

■ *No Interfaces*   Operations could be added directly to the components. As a consequence, of course, you cannot reuse the interface's "contracts" separately, independently of the supplier or consumer components. You cannot implement interface polymorphism.

■ *Component Kinds*   Often you'll need different kinds of components, such as domain components, data access components, process components or business rules components. Depending on this component classification, you can define the valid dependency structures between components (e.g., a domain component may access a data access component, but not the other way round)[37].

■ *Layers*   Another way of managing dependencies is to mark each component with a layer tag, such as domain, service, GUI or facade, and define constraints on how components in these layers may depend on each other.

■ *Configuration Parameters*   A component might have a number of configuration parameters – comparable to command line arguments in console programs – that help configure the behavior of components. The parameters and their types are defined in the type model, and values for the parameters can be specified later, for example in the models for the Composition or the System viewpoints.

■ *Component Characteristics*   You may want to express whether a components is stateless or stateful, whether they are thread-safe or not, and what their lifecycle should look like (for example, whether they are passive or active, whether they want to be notified of lifecycle events such as activation, and so on).

■ *Asynchronicity*   Even if you use operations (and not messaging), it is not always enough to use simple synchronous communication. Instead, one of the various asynchronous communication paradigms, such as those described in the Remoting Patterns book[38], might be applicable. Because using these

[37] You will typically also use different ways of implementing component functionality, depending on the component kind.

[38] M. Voelter, M. Kircher, and U. Zdun. *Remoting Patterns.* Wiley, 2004

paradigms affects the APIs of the components, the pattern to be used has to be marked up in the model for the *Type* viewpoint, as shown in Fig. 18.9. It is not enough to define it in the Composition viewpoint[39].

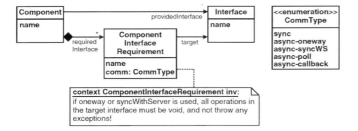

Figure 18.9: A `ComponentInterfaceRequirement` may describe which communication paradigm should be applied.

[39] If your application uses messaging interfaces instead of the RPC-style interfaces discussed in this section, then an API can be designed that remains independent of the communication paradigm.

■ *Events* In addition to the communication through interfaces, you might need (asynchronous) events using a static or dynamic publisher/subscriber infrastructure[40].

[40] The "direction of flow" of these events is typically the opposite of the dependencies discussed above: this allows them to be used for notifications or callbacks.

■ *Dynamic Connection* The Composition viewpoint connects component instances statically. This is not always feasible. If dynamic wiring is necessary, the best way is to embed the information that determines which instance to connect to at runtime into the static wiring model. So, instead of specifying in the model that instance **A** must be wired to instance **B**, the model only specifies that **A** needs to connect to a component with the following properties: it needs to provide a specific interface, and for example offer a certain reliability. At runtime, the wire is "deferenced" to a suitable instance using an instance repository[41].

[41] We have seen this in the example system described above.

■ *Hierarchical Components* Hierarchical components, as illustrated in figure 18.10, are a very powerful tool. Here a component is structured internally as a composition of other component instances. This allows a recursive and hierarchical decomposition of a system to be supported. Ports define how components may be connected: a port has an optional protocol definition that allows for port compatibility checks that go beyond simple interface equality. While this approach is powerful, it is also non-trivial, since it blurs the formerly clear distinction between Type and Composition viewpoints.

■ *Structuring* Finally, it is often necessary to provide additional means of structuring complex systems. The terms *busi-*

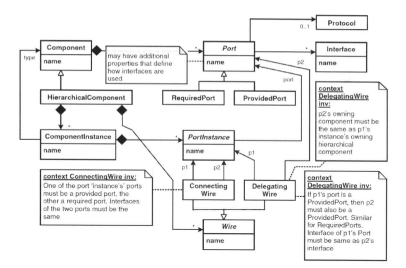

Figure 18.10: Hierarchical components support the recursive hierarchical decomposition of systems. In particular, a `HierarchicalComponent` consists internally of connected instances of other components.

ness component or *subsystem* are often used. Such a higher-level structure consists of a set of components (and related artifacts such as interfaces and data types). Optionally, constraints define which kinds of components may be contained in a specific kind of higher-level structure. For example, you might want to define a business component to always consist of exactly one facade component and any number of domain components.

19
DSLs as Programmer Utility

This chapter was written by Birgit Engelmann and Sebastian Benz. You can reach them via `birgit.engelmann@gmail.com` and `sebastian.benz@gmail.com`.

> *In this chapter we look at an example of a DSL that is used as a developer utility. This means that the DSL is not necessarily used to implement the core application itself, but plays an important role as part of the development process. The example discussed in this chapter is Jnario, an Xtext-based DSL for behavior-driven development and unit testing.*

Tests play an important role in software development[1]: they ensure that an application behaves as expected. However, the benefit of tests goes beyond checking whether a system's output corresponds to the input. They provide valuable feedback about the quality your application's design. For example, if a class is hard to test, this can be an indication of too many dependencies or responsibilities, which in turn hinders future maintainability. Furthermore, tests are effective means for developers to elaborate, together with the stakeholders, how the desired features should work. If done right, tests created in such a way can be used as executable specifications of the application's behavior.

In particular, when tests are used in this latter way, using a general-purpose programming language for writing tests is not

[1] We have covered testing DSLs and the programs written with DSLs earlier in Chapter 14. This DSL is used to specify and test application code.

very suitable, because it is hard for non-developers to read, understand and perhaps even write the specified behavior[2]. It is desirable to describe an application's behavior using a textual format that can be understood by business users, developers and testers. At the same time, it should be possible to make these specifications executable in order to use them to check automatically whether the application fulfills its expected behavior.

[2] Even when stakeholders are *not* involved in the specification and testing of the system, this is still a domain that warrants its own DSL.

19.1 The Context

The core idea of Jnario is to describe features of your application using scenarios. For each scenario, preconditions, events and expected outcomes are described textually with *Given*, *When* and *Then* steps. Here is an example acceptance specification for adding values with a calculator. It is written using Cucumber[3], a popular Java-based tool for behavior-driven development.

[3] `cukes.info`

```
Feature: Basic Arithmetic

Scenario: Addition
  Given a just turned on calculator
  When I enter "50"
  And I enter "70"
  And press add
  Then the result should be "120"
```

This format was introduced six years ago by Dan North[4], and since then has been widely adopted by practitioners. There are tools for most programming languages to turn these scenarios into executable specifications. This is accomplished by mapping each step to corresponding execution logic. For example, in Java/Cucumber you need to declare a separate class with a method for each step:

[4] `dannorth.net/introducing-bdd/`

```
public class CalculatorStepdefs {
  private Calculator calc;

  @Given("^a calculator$")
  public void a_calculator() {
    calc = new Calculator();
  }

  ...
}
```

The method's annotation contains a regular expression matching the text in the **Given** part of a scenario. The method's body contains the actual implementation of the step. The tool then executes a scenario by instantiating the class and executing each step with the associated method. The problem with this approach is that the overhead of adding new steps is quite high, since for every new step, a new implementing method has to be created as well.

19.2 Jnario Described

To make it simpler to define executable scenarios for Java applications, we decided to create Jnario[5]. In Jnario you can directly add the necessary code below your steps. In our example we create a calculator, pass in the parameters defined in the steps (via the implicit variable *args*) and check the calculated result:

[5] www.jnario.org

```
...
Feature: Basic Arithmetic

Scenario: Addition
    Calculator calculator
  Given a just turned on calculator
    calculator = new Calculator()
  When I enter "50"
    calculator.enter(args.first)
  And I enter "70"
   And press add
    calculator.add
  Then the result should be "120"
    result => args.first
```

This reduces the effort of writing scenarios by not needing to maintain separate step definitions. It is still possible to reuse existing step definitions in scenarios. The editor even provides code completion showing all existing steps. In our example, the step **And I enter "70"** reuses the code of the step **Given I enter "50"** with a different parameter value. A step is resolved by removing all keywords and parameter values from its descriptions and then matching the normalized description to the description of steps with an implementation.

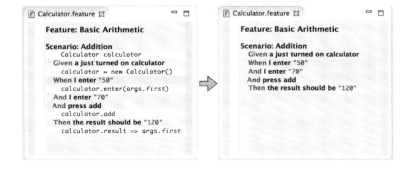

Figure 19.1: Hiding the step implementation in the Editor.

You might think now that mixing code and text in your specs makes everything pretty unreadable. Actually, this is not a problem, as you can hide the code in the editor to improve the readability, as shown in Fig. 19.1. This is accomplished using the code folding feature of Eclipse for hiding the step implementations. When editing a step in an editor, its implementation will automatically be shown[6].

Feature definitions in Jnario compile to plain Java JUnit tests, which can be directly executed from within Eclipse. Figure 19.2 shows the execution result of the Calculator feature in Eclipse.

[6] Mixing prose scenario descriptions and the implementation code is also *not* violating the separation of concerns. This is because we do not mix scenarios and application code. The scenario implementation code really is part of the scenario, so mixing the code with the prose makes sense.

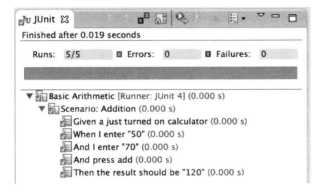

Figure 19.2: Executing Jnario features from within Eclipse.

Scenarios are good for writing high-level acceptance specifications, but writing scenarios for data structures or algorithms quickly becomes tedious. This is why Jnario provides another language for writing unit specifications. This languages removes all the boilerplate from normal JUnit tests, helping you to focus on what is important: specifying facts about your implementation. A fact can be as simple as a single expression asserting a simple behavior:

```
package demo

import java.util.Stack

describe Stack{
  fact new Stack().size => 0
}
```

We use => to describe the expected result of an expression. More complex facts can have an additional description:

```
describe Stack{
  fact "size increases when adding elements" {
    val stack = new Stack<String>
    stack.add("something")
    stack.size => 1
  }
}
```

Objects can behave differently in different contexts. For example, calling **pop** on a non-empty stack decreases its size. However, if the stack is empty, **pop** results in an exception. In Jnario we can explicitly specify such contexts using the **context** keyword:

```
describe "A Stack" {
  val stack = new Stack<String>
  context "empty" {
    fact stack.size => 0
    fact stack.pop throws Exception
  }
  context "with one element" {
    before stack.add("element")
    fact stack.size => 1
    fact "pop decreases size" {
      stack.pop stack.size => 0
    }
  }
}
```

You can execute unit specifications as normal JUnit tests. Note that Jnario uses the description as test name or, if not present, the actual expression being executed. If you look at the executed tests in Fig. 19.3, you can see that your specifications effectively document the behavior of your code.

Figure 19.3: Executing Jnario unit specs from within Eclipse.

Jnario is not just another testing framework. It is actually two domain-specific languages specifically made for writing executable specifications. The main advantage of using a DSL for writing tests is that it becomes possible to adapt the syntax to the skills of the intended users. In our case this means that specifications written in Jnario can be understood by users without a programming background.

Another advantage of using a DSL for writing tests is the possibility of adding features that are not available in a general purpose programming language, but are really helpful when writing tests. If you think about current testing frameworks, they usually "stretch" the syntax of the underlying programming language to be able to write expressive tests. Compare that to a programming language in which the syntax is specifically designed for the purpose of writing tests. For example, a common scenario is to test a class with different sets of input parameters. Writing such tests in Jnario is really easy, as it has a special table syntax:

```
describe "Adding numbers" {
  def additions {
    |  a  |  b  | sum |
    |  1  |  2  |  3  |
    |  4  |  5  |  9  |
    | 10  | 11  | 20  |
    | 21  | 21  | 42  |
  }
  fact additions.forEach[a + b => sum]
}
```

Tables in Jnario are type safe: the type of a column will be automatically inferred to the common supertype of all cells in a column. You can easily iterate over each row in a table and write assertions by accessing the column values as variables. If you execute the example specification, it will fail with the following error:

```
java.lang.AssertionError: examples failed

       |  a  |  b  | sum |
       |  1  |  2  |  3  |
       |  4  |  5  |  9  |
       | 10  | 11  | 20  | X    (1)
       | 21  | 21  | 42  |

(1) Expected a + b => sum but
    a + b is 21 a is 10 b is 11 sum is 20
```

This demonstrates another advantage of Jnario: it tries to give you as much information as possible about which assertion failed, and why. A failed assertion prints the values of all evaluated sub-expressions. This means you don't need to debug your tests any further in order to find the exact reason why an assertion failed.

These are just some examples that demonstrate the advantages of test-centric domain-specific language. Having full control over the syntax of the language and its translation into Java code allows us to add features that are helpful when writing tests, but which would never make sense in a general purpose language[7].

[7] They would also be very hard to implement with a GPL and its associated tooling!

19.3 Implementation

Both Jnario languages – the Feature and Spec languages – are developed with Xtext. Xtext is used for a number of reasons.

Eclipse Integration Jnario targets Java developers, which makes Eclipse the best tooling choice, since it is currently the mostly used Java IDE.

Standalone Support Although Xtext provides tight Eclipse integration, all language features, such as parser and compiler, are not restricted to Eclipse. This is important, as it should be possible to compile Jnario specifications with maven or from the command line.

Resuable Expression Language Implementing a DSL with a custom expression language requires a lot of effort. Xtext provides Xbase, a statically-typed expression language based on Java, which can be integrated into DSLs with relatively little effort. This eliminates the need to implement a custom expression language and ensures compatibility with existing Java code[8].

19.3.1 Language Definition

Xtext's Xbase provides a reusable expression language that can be embedded into DSLs. The Xtend language, which also ships with Xtext, is a general-purpose programming language for the JVM. Xtend enriches Xbase with additional concepts, such as classes, fields and methods. In Jnario we needed similar concepts, which is why we decided to base the Jnario languages on Xtend. Additionally, reusing Xtend had the advantage that we could reuse a lot of the existing tooling for Jnario.

In Jnario we introduced new expressions, for example more expressive assertions, which can be used in both languages. In order to avoid reimplementing these in the feature and the specs language, we created a base language with all common features used by Jnario. The resulting language hierarchy is shown in Fig. 19.4. This example demonstrates that by, carefully modularizing language features, it possible in Xtext to effectively reuse languages together with their tooling in different contexts. Referring back to the design part of the book, these are all examples of language extension.

As we mentioned earlier, Jnario has assertions with improved error messages. An example is the assert statement, which consists of the **assert** keyword followed by an expression evaluating to a Boolean:

```
assert x != null
```

Adding a new expression to the Xtext base language works by overriding the corresponding grammar rules. In our example, we added the new assertion expression as a primary expression[9]:

[8] As we mentioned earlier in this book, Xbase supports extension methods, type inference, lambda expressions and other useful extensions of Java. It compiles to Java source code, and is 100% compatible with the Java type system.

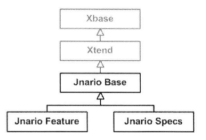

Figure 19.4: Jnario language hierarchy. Xbase and Xtend ship with Xtext, and Xtend reuses the Xbase expression language by extending Xbase, and embedding its expressions into concepts like classes, fields or operations. Since *Jnario Feature* and *Jnario Specs* both use a set of common Xtend extensions, an intermediate language *Jnario Base* was developed that contains these common concepts. *Jnario Feature* and *Jnario Specs* then both extend *Jnario Base* and add their own specific language concepts.

[9] As we discussed in the chapter on modularity with Xtext (Chapter 16.3), this requires repeating the original rule **XPrimaryExpression** and specifying its new contents. In this case, we add **Assertion** to the list of alternatives.

```
XPrimaryExpression returns xbase::XExpression:
  XConstructorCall |
  XBlockExpression |
  ...
  Assertion;
```

The **Assertion** expression itself is defined as a separate rule. Notice how it again embeds concepts from Xbase, namely **XExpression**:

```
Assertion returns xbase::XExpression:
  'assert' expression=XExpression;
```

Tables are another example for an extension of Xtend. Defining the grammar for a table in Xtext is pretty straightforward[10]. A table has a list of columns and rows. Each column in the cells in a row are separated by '|':

```
Table:
  'def' name=ID '{'
    ('|' (columns+=Column)*
      (rows += Row)*)?
  '}';
Column:
  name=ValidID '|';
Row:
  '|' {Row} (cells+=XExpression '|')*;
```

[10] Note that the grammar does not actually specify that the rows and columns are laid out in the two-dimensional structure we associate with tables. However, this is not really a problem since users will naturally use that notation. Also, a formatter could be implemented to format the table correctly. In addition, an editor template could be defined to create an example table that is formatted in a meaningful way.

Cells in the table can contain arbitrary expressions. We reused the typing infrastructure provided by Xtext to calculate the type of each column in the table: a column's type is the common supertype of all expressions in the respective column. Here is the essential part of the code:

```
@Inject extension ITypeProvider
@Inject extension TypeConformanceComputer

def getType(ExampleColumn column){
    val cellTypes = column.cells.map[type]
    return cellTypes.commonSuperType
}
```

In the next section we will have a look at how we map these custom concepts to the generated Java classes.

19.3.2 Code Generation

Jnario specifications are compiled to plain Java JUnit4 tests. Xtext provides a framework for mapping DSL concepts to corresponding JVM concepts. An example mapping for the feature language is shown in Fig. 19.5.

Scenarios and Backgrounds[11] are mapped to Java classes, in which each step is mapped to a JUnit test method. The additional **@Test** annotations required by JUnit are added during the mapping process. The expressions can be completely transformed by the existing Xtend compiler. However, in order to

[11] Backgrounds contain steps being executed before each scenario. They are usually used to set up preconditions required by all scenarios.

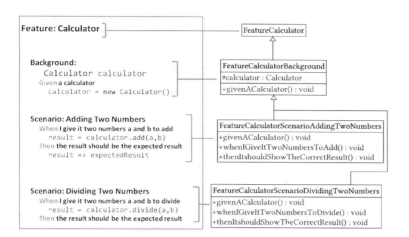

Figure 19.5: Generation from Jnario Feature DSL (left column) to Java classes with JUnit tests (right column).

support custom expressions such as **assert**, the Xtend compiler needs to be extended. Consider the following example:

```
val x = "hello"
val y = "world"
assert x + y == "hello world"
```

The execution of these statements will result in the following error message:

```
java.lang.AssertionError: Expected x + y == "hello world" but
    x + y is "helloworld"
    x is "hello"
    y is "world"
```

Note that the error message contains the original failing expression `x + y == "hello world"` rendered as text, together with the value of all subexpressions. Creating such error messages is not possible in plain Java, as the underlying AST cannot be accessed. However, in a DSL like Jnario we can include this information when generating the Java code from our specifications[12]. To do so, we subclass the XtendCompiler and add a custom generator for our assertion expression:

```
@Override
public void doInternalToJavaStatement(XExpression obj,
    ITreeAppendable appendable, boolean isReferenced) {
  if (obj instanceof Assertion) {
    toJavaStatement((Assertion) obj, appendable, isReferenced);
  } else {
    super.doInternalToJavaStatement(obj, appendable, isReferenced);
  }
}
```

[12] This "transformation-time reflection" is a natural consequence of the fact that a generator can inspect a program's structure (and has access to the AST) during the transformation. We came across this effect earlier when we noted mbeddr outputs the source/location of a **report**ed message together with the message.

The custom generator translates an assertion into the corresponding Java code:

```
private void toJavaStatement(Assertion assertion, ITreeAppendable b) {
  XExpression expr = assertion.getExpr();
  toJavaStatement(expr, b, true);
```

```
    b.newLine();
    b.append("org.junit.Assert.assertTrue(");
    b.append("Expected ");
    b.append(serialize(expr));
    b.append(" but ");
    appendSubExpressionValues(expr, b);
    b.append(", ");
    toJavaExpression(expr, b);
    b.append(");");
}
```

We first get the actual expression of the assertion, which is then compiled by invoking `toJavaStatement(expr,...)`. The Xtend compiler automatically creates a temporary variable for each subexpression[13]. The value of these variables will be used later to generate the error message. The assertion itself is mapped to the JUnit method `Assert.assertTrue(message, result)`. The key to showing the expression in a textual form as part of the error message is that the message is built by serializing the expression as it is written in the Jnario file together with the values of the subexpressions taken from previously created temporary variables. Finally, execution result expression is compiled by invoking `toJavaExpression(expr, ...)`.

[13] This is why the method is called `toJavaStatement` and not `toJavaExpression`.

19.3.3 Tooling

For Jnario, good tooling is essential, since the hurdles of learning a new language should be as low as possible, and being able to work efficiently is a major goal of Jnario.

The Feature language aims at being readable both for software developers and for domain experts who have no programming background. The best way to support both groups is to provide two views on a Jnario Feature file. The editor uses specialized folding to show or hide the implementation code of the scenarios and features[14]. Specialized folding means we used the existing folding component from Xtext and extended it to disable the normal folding functionality. We then introduced a button to trigger the folding of the implementation logic. In addition, syntax highlighting comes in handy when referring to existing steps. We used different colors to show whether a step is implemented (i.e. has its own code associated with it), not implemented (i.e. needs to be implemented before the specification can be run), or is a reference to an existing step (in which case the existing step's implementation code is automatically reused).

[14] This means that domain experts only see (and edit) the prose description of scenarios; they don't have to care about the implementation code, and it therefore feels like working with a text editor.

To improve productivity further, editor features such as quick fixes for importing necessary libraries or for creating new class files were added. Auto completion for steps in features is supported, since you can reuse other steps by referencing them, even if they are not implemented. Another important productivity feature is the debug support of Xtext, which lets you step through your DSL file instead of using the generated code[15].

19.3.4 Testing

Testing is an important part of developing a DSL. This of course applies to Jnario as well. However, Jnario is a special case, since it itself is a language for writing tests. This gave us the chance to bootstrap the implementation of Jnario[16]. The advantage of bootstrapping is that bugs or missing features quickly become apparent just from using the language to build test for the language (we ate our own dog food). Here is an example in which we test Jnario's **throws** expression:

```
Scenario: Testing exceptions with Jnario
  Given a unit spec
  '''
    describe "expecting exceptions in Jnario"{
      fact new Stack().pop throws EmptyStackException
    }
  '''
  Then it should execute successfully
```

When we execute this scenario, the given unit specification will first be parsed and compiled into Java source code[17]. The Java source code will then be compiled into a Java class file using the normal Java compiler. The generated class is then loaded via the Java classloader and executed with JUnit. This process is greatly simplified by the testing infrastructure provided by Xtext, which provides APIs for compiling and classloading DSL artifacts. The advantage of this approach is that the whole compiler chain is tested, and tests are relatively stable, as they are independent of changes in the internal implementation.

19.4 Summary

This chapter introduced Jnario, a DSL for testing, which was developed based on Xtext. Jnario is a good example for a DSL that is targeted towards developers with the goal of easing the development process. It is also a good example of an Xtext-based language that makes use of Xtext's reusable expression language Xbase. Jnario is currently used in various domains, for example to specify and test the behavior of automotive control units, web applications and Eclipse-based applications.

---

[15] This facility did not have to be adapted for Jnario; it worked out of the box. We discussed to some extent how Xtext DSL debugging works in Section 15.2.

[16] This means that all tests for Jnario are written in Jnario.

[17] Note that in this approach, the Jnario code inside the triple single quotes is treated as a string and no IDE support for the Jnario language is available. This is in contrast to some of the tests described for Spoofax in Section 14.1.

20
DSLs in the Implementation

In this chapter we discuss the use of DSLs in the context of software implementation, based on an extensive case study in embedded software development: the mbeddr system that has been discussed in the book before. mbeddr supports extension of C with constructs useful for embedded software. In this chapter we show how language extension can address the challenges of embedded software development, and report on our experience in building these extensions.

This section of the book is based on a paper written together with Daniel Ratiu, Bernd Kolb and Bernhard Schaetz for the SPLASH/Wavefront 2012 conference.

20.1 Introduction

In this section we discuss the use of DSLs in the context of implementation. There it is crucial that the DSLs are tightly integrated with the application code that is typically written in a GPL. Language embedding and extension (Section 4.6) are obviously useful approaches. In this chapter we discuss the mbeddr system[1] which supports domain-specific extensions to C[2].

The amount of software embedded in devices is growing and the development of embedded software is challenging. In addition to functional requirements, strict operational requirements have to be fulfilled as well. These include reliability (a device may not be accessible for maintenance after deployment), safety (a system may endanger life or property if it fails), efficiency (the resources available to the system may be limited)

[1] `mbeddr.com`

[2] mbeddr is built with MPS, so you should make sure that you have read and understood the MPS-based implementation examples in Part III of the book.

or real-time constraints (a system may have to run on a strict schedule prescribed by the system's environment). Addressing these challenges requires any of the following: abstraction techniques should not lead to excessive runtime overhead; programs should be easily analyzable for faults before deployment; and various kinds of annotations, for example for describing and type checking physical units, must be integrated into the code. Process issues such as requirements traceability have to be addressed, and developers face a high degree of variability, since embedded systems are often developed in the context of product lines[3].

Current approaches for embedded software development can be divided roughly into programming and modeling. The *programming* approach mostly relies on C, sometimes C++, and Ada in rare cases[4]. However, because of C's limited support for defining custom abstractions, this can lead to software that is hard to understand, maintain and extend. Furthermore, C's ability to work with very low-level abstractions, such as pointers, makes C code very expensive to analyze statically[5]. The alternative approach uses *modeling* tools with automatic code generation. The modeling tools provide predefined, higher-level abstractions such as state machines or data flow component diagrams[6]. Example tools include ASCET-SD[7] or Simulink[8]. Using higher-level abstractions leads to more concise programs and simplified fault detection using static analysis and model checking (for example using the Simulink Design Verifier[9]). Increasingly, DSLs are used for embedded software, and studies show that DSLs substantially increase productivity in embedded software development. However, most real-world systems cannot be described completely and adequately with a single modeling tool or DSL, and the integration effort between manually written C code and perhaps several modeling tools and DSLs becomes significant.

A promising solution to this dilemma lies in much tighter integration between low-level C code and higher-level abstractions specific to embedded software. We achieve this with an extensible C programming language. The advantages of C can be maintained: existing *legacy* code can be easily integrated, reused, and evolved, and the need for *efficient* code is immediately addressed by relying on C's low-level programming concepts. At the same time, domain-specific extensions such as state machines, components or data types with physical units

[3] We discuss product lines and DSLs specifically in Chapter 21.

[4] Ada is used mainly in safety-critical systems, and traditionally in avionics, space and defense. This has historic reasons, but is also driven by the fact that some Ada compilers are certified to very high levels of reliability.

[5] C is very good for developing low-level aspects of software systems. It is not so good for large-scale software engineering.

[6] A big problem with the vast majority of the tools in this space is that they cannot be extended in meaningful ways; they are hard to adapt to a particular domain, platform or system context.

[7] `www.etas.com/`

can be made available as C extensions. This improves *productivity* via more concise programs, it helps improve *quality* in a constructive way by avoiding low-level implementation errors up front, and leads to system implementations that are more amenable to *analysis*. By directly embedding the extensions into C, the mismatch and integration challenge between domain-specific models and general-purpose code can be removed. An industry-strength implementation of this approach must also include IDE support for C and the extensions: syntax highlighting, code completion, error checking, refactoring and debugging.

The LW-ES research project, run by itemis AG, fortiss GmbH, BMW Car IT and Sick AG explores the benefits of language engineering in the context of embedded software development with the mbeddr system[10].

[10] The code is open source and available via **mbeddr.com**.

20.2 Challenges in Embedded Software

In this section we discuss a set of challenges we address with the mbeddr approach. We label the challenges C_n so we can refer to them from Section 20.3.2, where we show how they are addressed by mbeddr[11].

[11] While these are certainly not *all* the challenges embedded software developers face, based on our experience with embedded software and feedback from various domains (automotive, sensors, automation) and organizations (small, medium and large companies), these are among the most important ones.

■ C_1: *Abstraction without Runtime Cost* Domain-specific concepts provide more abstract descriptions of the system under development. Examples include data flow blocks, state machines, or data types with physical units. On one hand, adequate abstractions have a higher expressive power that leads to programs that are shorter and easier to understand and maintain. On the other hand, by restricting the freedom of programmers, domain-specific abstractions also enable constructive quality assurance. For embedded systems, where runtime efficiency is a prime concern, abstraction mechanisms are needed that can be resolved before or during compilation, and not at runtime.

■ C_2: *C considered Unsafe* While C is efficient and flexible, several of C's features are often considered unsafe[12]. Consequently, the unsafe features of C are prohibited in many organizations. Standards for automotive software development such as MISRA limit C to a safer language subset. However, most C IDEs are not aware of these and other, organization-specific restrictions, so they are enforced with separate checkers that

[12] For example, unconstrained casting via **void** pointers, using **int**s as Booleans, or the weak typing implied by **union**s can result in runtime errors that are hard to track down.

are often not well integrated with the IDE. This makes it hard for developers to comply with these restrictions efficiently.

■ C_3: *Program Annotations*   For reasons such as safety or efficiency, embedded systems often require additional data to be associated with program elements. Examples include physical units, coordinate systems, data encodings or value ranges for variables. These annotations are typically used by specific, often custom-built analysis or generation tools. Since C programs can only capture such data informally as comments or **pragma**s, the C type system and IDE cannot check their correct use in C programs. They may also be stored separately (for example, in XML files) and linked back to the program using names or other weak links[13].

[13] Even with tool support that checks the consistency of these links and helps navigate between code and this additional data, the separation of core functionality and the additional data leads to unnecessary complexity and maintainability problems.

■ C_4: *Static Checks and Verification*   Embedded systems often have to fulfill strict safety requirements. Industry standards for safety such as ISO-26262, DO-178B or IEC-61508 demand that for high safety certification levels various forms of static analyses are performed on the software. These range from simple type checks to sophisticated property checks, for example by model checking. Since C is a very flexible and relatively weakly-typed language, the more sophisticated analyses are very expensive. Using suitable domain-specific abstractions (for example, state machines) leads to programs that can be analyzed much more easily.

■ C_5: *Process Support*   There are at least two cross-cutting and process-related concerns relevant to embedded software development. First, many certification standards (such as those mentioned above) require that code be explicitly linked to requirements such that full traceability is available. Today, requirements are often managed in external tools, and maintaining traceability to the code is a burden to the developers and often done in an ad hoc way, for example via comments. Second, many embedded systems are developed as part of product lines with many distinct product variants, where each variant consists of a subset of the (parts of) artifacts that comprise the product line. This variability is usually captured in constraints expressed over program parts such as statements, functions or states. Most existing tools come with their own variation mechanism, if variability is supported at all. Integration between program parts, the constraints and the variant configuration (for example via feature models) is often done through weak links, and with little awareness of the semantics of the underlying language[14]. As a consequence, variant management is a huge source of accidental complexity.

[14] For example, the C preprocessor, which is often used for this task, performs simple text replacement or removal controlled by the conditions in `#ifdef`s.

An additional concern is tool integration. The diverse requirements and limitations of C discussed so far often lead to the use of a wide variety of tools in a single development project. Most commercial off-the-shelf (COTS) tools are not open enough to facilitate seamless and semantically meaningful integration with other tools, leading to significant accidental tool integration complexity. COTS tools often also do not support meaningful language extension, severely limiting the ability to define and use custom domain-specific abstractions.

20.3 The mbeddr Approach

Language engineering provides a holistic approach to solving these challenges. In this section we illustrate how mbeddr addresses the challenges with an extensible version of the C programming language, growing a stack of languages extensions (see Fig. 20.2, and Section 4.6.2 for a discussion of language extension). The following section explores which ways W_m of extending C are necessary to address the challenges C_n. Section 20.3.2 then shows examples that address each of the challenges and ways of extending C.

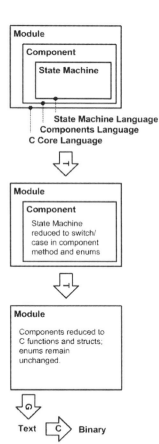

The semantics of an extension are typically defined by a transformation back to the base language. For example, in an extension that provides state machines, these may be transformed to a `switch/case`-based implementation in C. Extensions can be stacked (Fig. 20.2), where a higher-level extension extends (and transforms back to) a lower-level extension instead of C. At the bottom of this stack resides plain C in text form, and a suitable compiler. Fig. 20.1 shows an example in which a module containing a component that contains a state machine is transformed to C, and then compiled.

Figure 20.1: Higher-level abstractions such as state machines or components are reduced incrementally to their lower-level equivalent, reusing the transformations built for lower-level extensions.

As we have seen in Section 16.2, MPS supports *modular* language extension, as well as the use of independently developed language extensions in the same system. For example, in mbeddr a user can include an extension that provides state machines and an extension that provides physical units *in the same program* without first defining a combined language statemachine-with-units. This is very useful, because it addresses real-world constraints: a set of organizations, such as the departments in a large company, will probably not agree on a *single* set of extensions to C, since they typically work in slightly different areas. Also, a language that contains *all* relevant abstractions would become big and unwieldy. Modular language extension solves these problems.

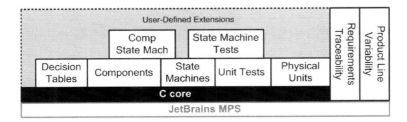

Figure 20.2: Based on MPS, mbeddr comes with an implementation of the C programming language. On top of C, mbeddr defines a set of default extensions (white boxes) stacked on top of each other. Users can use them in their programs, but they don't have to. Support for requirements traceability and product line variability is cross-cutting. Users build their own extensions on top of C or on top of the default extensions. (Component/state machine integration and state machine tests are not discussed in this chapter.)

20.3.1 Ways of Extending C

In this section we discuss in which particular ways C needs to be extensible to address the challenges discussed above[15].

[15] Section 20.3.2 shows examples for each of these.

■ W_1: *Top-Level Constructs*   Top level constructs (on the level of functions or **struct** declarations) are necessary. This enables the integration of test cases or new programming paradigms relevant in particular domains, such as state machines, or interfaces and components.

■ W_2: *Statements*   New statements, such as **assert** or **fail** statements in test cases, must be supported[16]. Statements may have to be restricted to a specific context; for example, **assert** or **fail** statements must *only* be used in test cases and not in any other statement list.

[16] If statements introduce new blocks, then variable visibility and shadowing must be handled correctly, just as in regular C.

■ W_3: *Expressions*   New kinds of expressions must be supported. An example is a decision table expression that represents a two-level decision tree as a two-dimensional table (Fig. 20.4).

■ W_4: *Types and Literals*   New types, e.g., for matrices, complex numbers or quantities with physical units, must be supported. This also requires the definition of new operators, and overriding the typing rules for existing ones. New literals may also be required: for example, physical units could be attached to number literals (as in **10kg**).

■ W_5: *Transformation*   Alternative transformations for existing language concepts must be possible. For example, in a module marked as `safe`, the expression `x + y` may have to be translated into an invocation of `addWithBoundsCheck(x, y)`, an `inline` function that performs bounds-checking, besides the addition.

■ W_6: *Meta Data Decoration*   It should be possible to add meta data, such as trace links to requirements or product line variability constraints, to arbitrary program nodes, without changing the concept of the node.

■ W_7: *Restriction*   It should be possible to define contexts that restrict the use of specific language concepts[17]. For example, the use of pointer arithmetic should be prohibited in modules marked as *safe*, or the use of real numbers should be prohibited in state machines that are intended to be model checked (model checkers do not support real numbers).

[17] Like any other extension, such contexts must be definable *after* the original language has been implemented, without invasive change.

20.3.2   Extensions Addressing the Challenges

In this section we present example extensions that illustrate how we address the challenges discussed in Section 20.2. We show at least one example for each challenge[18]. The table below shows an overview of the challenges, the examples in this section, and the ways of extension each example makes use of[19].

[18] How such extensions are built will be discussed in Section 20.4.

[19] This is not the full set of extensions available in mbeddr. The mbeddr user guide contains the full description.

Challenge	Example Extensions
C_1 (Low-Overhead Abstraction)	State machines (W_1, W_2)
	Components (W_1)
	Decision Tables (W_3)
C_2 (Safer C)	Cleaned up C (W_7)
	Safe Modules (W_5, W_7)
C_3 (Annotations)	Physical Units (W_4)
C_4 (Static Checks, Verification)	Unit Tests (W_1, W_2)
	State Machines (W_1, W_2)
	Safe Modules (W_2, W_5, W_7)
C_5 (Process Support)	Requirements Traceability (W_6)
	Product Line Variability (W_6)

■ *A Cleaned-Up C*   (addresses C_2, uses W_7) To make C extensible, we first had to implement C in MPS. This entails the definition of the language structure, syntax and type system[20]. In the process we changed some aspects of C. Some of these changes are the first step in providing a safer C (challenge C_2). Others changes were implemented, because it is more convenient to the user, or because it simplified the implementation of the language in MPS. Out of eight changes in total, four are for reasons of improved robustness and analyzability, two are for end-user convenience and three are to simplify the implementation in MPS. We discuss some of them below, and the table below shows a summary.

[20] A generator to C text is also required, so that the code can be fed into an existing compiler. However, since this generator merely renders the tree as text, with no structural differences, this generator is trivial: we do not discuss it any further.

Difference	Reason
No Preprocessor	Robustness
Native Booleans (and a cast operator for legacy interop)	Robustness
enums are not ints (special operators for next/previous	Robustness
C99 Integral Types Required	Robustness
Modules instead of Headers	End-User Convenience
hex<..>, oct<..>, bin<..> instead of 0x.. and 0..	Simplified Implementation
Type annotation on type (int[] a instead of int a[])	Simplified Implementation
Cleaned up syntax for function types and function pointers	End-User Convenience, Simplified Implementation

mbeddr C provides *modules* (Fig. 20.3). A module contains the top-level C constructs (such as **struct**s, functions or global variables). These module contents can be exported. Modules can *import* other modules, in which case they can access the exported contents of the imported modules. While header files are generated, we do not expose them to the user: modules provide a more convenient means of controlling modularizing programs and limiting which elements are visible globally.

mbeddr C does not support the *preprocessor*. Empirical studies[21] show that it is often used to emulate missing features of C in ad hoc way, leading to problems regarding maintenance and analyzability. Instead, mbeddr C provides first-class support for the most important use cases of the preprocessor. Examples include the modules mentioned above (replacing **#include**), as well as the support for variability discussed below (replacing **#ifdef**s). Instead of defining macros, users can create first-

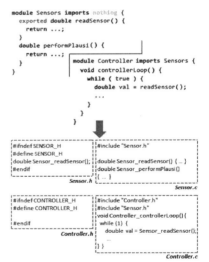

Figure 20.3: Modules are the top-level container in mbeddr C. They can import other modules, whose exported contents they can then use. Exported contents are put into the header files generated from modules.

[21] M. D. Ernst, G. J. Badros, and D. Notkin. An empirical analysis of c preprocessor use. *IEEE Trans. Softw. Eng.*, 28, December 2002

class language extensions, including type checks and IDE support. Removing the preprocessor and providing specific support for its important use cases goes a long way in creating more maintainable and more analyzable programs. The same is true for introducing a separate **boolean** type and not interpreting integers as Booleans by default (an explicit cast operator is available).

Type decorations, such as array brackets or the pointer asterisk, must be specified on the type, not on the identifier (**int[] a;** instead of **int a[];**). This has been done for reasons of consistency and to simplify the implementation in MPS: it is the property of a type to be an array type or a pointer type, not the property of an identifier. Identifiers are just names.

■ *Decision Tables* (addressing C_1, uses W_3) Decision tables are a new kind of expression, i.e. they can be evaluated. An example is shown in Fig. 20.4. A decision table represents nested **if** statements. It is evaluated to the value of the first cell whose column and row headers are **true** (the evaluation order is left to right, top to bottom). A default value (**FAIL**) is specified to handle the case in which none of the column/row header combinations is **true**. Since the compiler and IDE have to compute a type for expressions, the decision table specifies the type of its result values explicitly (**int8**).

■ *Unit Tests* (addresses C_4, uses W_1, W_2) Unit tests are new top-level constructs (Fig. 20.5) introduced in a separate *unittest* language that extends the C core. They are like **void** functions without arguments. The *unittest* language also introduces **assert** and **fail** statements, which can only be used inside test cases. Testing embedded software can be a challenge, and the *unittest* extension is an initial step towards providing comprehensive support for testing.

■ *Components* (addresses C_1, uses W_1) are new top-level constructs that support modularization, encapsulation and the separation between specification and implementation (Fig. 20.6). In contrast to modules, a component uses interfaces and ports to declare the contract it obeys. Interfaces define operation signatures and optional pre- and post-conditions (not shown in the example). Provided ports declare the interfaces offered by a component; required ports specify the interfaces a component expects to use. Different components can implement the same

```
enum mode { MANUAL; AUTO; FAIL; }
mode nextMode(mode mode, int8_t speed) {
    return mode, FAIL
```

	mode == MANUAL	mode == AUTO
speed < 30	MANUAL	AUTO
speed > 30	MANUAL	MANUAL

```
}
```

```
typedef enum __MODE{MANUAL, AUTO, FAIL } _MODE;
_MODE nextMode(_MODE mode, int8_t speed) {
  if (current == MANUAL) {
    if (speed <= 30) {return MANUAL;}
    if (speed >= 30 && speed < 50) {return MANUAL;}
  }
  if (current == AUTO) { ... }
  return FAIL;
}
```

Figure 20.4: A decision table evaluates to the value in the cell for which the row and column headers are **true**, a default value otherwise (**FAIL** in the example). By default, a decision table is translated to nested **if**s in a separate function. The figure shows the translation for the common case where a decision table is used in a **return**. This case is optimized to not use the indirection of an extra function.

```
module UnitTestDemo imports Sensors {
  exported test case sensorReadTest {
    assert(0) readSensor() > 0;
    assert(1) readSensor() < 1000;
  }
}
```

```
#include "Sensor.h"
int8_t UnitTestDemo_test_sensorReadTest() {
  int8_t __failures = 0;
  printf("test  @UnitTestDemo:test_sensorReadTest:0\n");
  if ( !(Sensor_readSensor() > 0) ) {
    __failures++;
    printf("FAIL @UnitTestDemo:test_sensorReadTest:1\n");
    printf("  testID = %d\n",0);
  }
  if ( !(Sensor_readSensor() < 1000) ) { ... }
  return __failures;
}
```

Figure 20.5: The *unittest* language introduces test cases as well as **assert** and **fail** statements which can only be used inside of a test case. Test cases are transformed to functions, and the **assert** statements become **if** statements with a negated condition. The generated code also counts the number of failures so that it can be reported to the user via a binary's exit value.

interface differently. Components can be instantiated (also in contrast to modules), and each instance's required ports have to be connected to compatible provided ports provided by other component instances. Polymorphic invocations (different components "behind" the same interface) are supported.

```
module SensorComp imports Sensors , LoggingService {
  exported c/s interface SensorAccess {
    double readValue()
  }
  exported component SimpleSensor {
    provides SensorAccess sensor

    double read() ← op sensor.readValue {
      return readSensor();
    }
  }
  exported component PlausiSensor {
    provides SensorAccess sensor
    requires LoggingService log

    double read() ← op sensor.readValue {
      double val = readSensor();
      if ( val > 100 ) {
        log.info("Sensor value unexpected big");
        return 100;
      } if
      return val;
    }
  }
}
```

```
struct Sensors_compdata_SimpleSensor {};
double Sensors_SimpleSensor_read(void* inst_data);

struct Sensors_data_PlausiSensor {
  void* port_log;
  void (*op_log_info)(char*, void*);
}
double Sensors_PlausiSensor_read(void* inst_data);
```
Sensors.h

```
#include "Sensors.h"
#include "Sensor.h"
#include "LoggingService.h"

double Sensors_SimpleSensor_read(void* inst_data) {
  return Sensor_readSensor();
}

double Sensors_PlausiSensor_read(void* inst_data) {
  double val = Sensor_readSensor();
  if (val > 100) {
    (*((struct Sensors_data_PlausiSensor*)inst_data)->op_log_info)
      ("Sensor value unexpected big",
      ((struct Sensors_data_PlausiSensor*)inst_data)->port_log);
    return 100;
  }
  return val;
}
```
Sensors.c

Figure 20.6: Two components providing the same interface. The arrow maps operations from provided ports to implementations. Indirection through function pointers allows different implementations for a single interface, enabling OO-like polymorphic invocations.

■ *State Machines* (addresses C_1, C_4, uses W_1, W_2) State machines provide a new top-level construct (the state machine itself), as well as a **trigger** statement to send events into state machines (see Fig. 20.7). State machines are transformed into a **switch/case**-based implementation in the C program. Entry, exit and transition actions may only access variables defined locally in state machines and fire out events. Out events may optionally be mapped to functions in the surrounding C program, where arbitrary behavior can be implemented. In this way state machines are semantically isolated from the rest of the code, enabling them to be model checked: if a state machine is marked as **verifiable**, we also generate a representation of the state machine in the input language of the NuSMV model checker[22], including a set of property specifications that

[22] nusmv.fbk.eu

are verified by default. Examples include dead state detection, dead transition detection, non-determinism and variable bounds checks. In addition, users can specify additional high-level properties based on the well-established catalog of temporal logic properties patterns[23]. The state machines extension also supports hierarchical states as a further means of decomposing complex behavior.

[23] M. B. Dwyer, G. S. Avrunin, and J. C. Corbett. Patterns in property specifications for finite-state verification. In *ICSE*, 1999

```
module Counter imports Sensors {
  statemachine Counter {
    in count( )
    out tick(int[0..100] val) ⇒ tickHandler
    local int[0..100] current = 0
    states ( initial = Init )
      state Init {
        on count [ ] → Counting
      }
      state Counting {
        on count [current < 100] → Counting {
          send tick(current);
          current++;
        }
        on count [current == 100] → Init
      }
  }
  void tickHandler(int8 counterVal) { ... }
  void mainLoop(Counter counter1) {
    while ( true ) {
      if ( readSensor() > 100 ) {
        trigger(counter1, count);
} } } }
```

```
#include "Counter.h"
#include "Sensor.h"
void Counter_sm_execute_Counter(struct Counter_sm_data_Counter* instance,
    Counter_sm_events_Counter event, void** arguments) {
  switch (instance->__curState) {
    case Counter__state_Init: { ... }
    case Counter__state_Counting: {
      switch (event) {
        case Counter__event_count: {
          if ( instance->current < 100 ) {
            Counter_tickHandler(instance->current);
            instance->__curState = Counter__state_Counting;
            instance->current++;
            return;
          }
          if ( instance->current == 100 ) { ... }
        }
}
void Counter_tickHandler(int8_t counterVal) { ... }
void Counter_mainLoop(struct Counter_sm_data_Counter counter1){
  while (1) {
    if ( Sensor_readSensor() > 100 ) {
      void* __args[] = {};
      Counter_sm_execute_Counter(&counter1, Counter__event_count, &__args);
}}}
```

```
typedef enum _sm_events_Counter{
  Counter__event_count
}Counter_sm_events_Counter;

typedef enum _sm_states_Counter{
  Counter__state_Init,
  Counter__state_Counting
}Counter_sm_states_Counter;

struct _sm_data_Counter {
  Counter_sm_states_Counter __curState;
  int8_t current;
};
```
Counter.h

Counter.c

Figure 20.7: A state machine is embedded in a C module as a top-level construct. It declares **in** and **out events**, as well as local variables, states and transitions. Transitions react to **in event**s, and **out event**s can be fired in actions. Through bindings (e.g., **tickHandler**), state machines interact with C code. State machines can be instantiated. They are transformed to **enums** for states and events, and a function that executes the state machine using **switch** statements. The **trigger** statement injects events into a state machine instance by calling the state machine function.

■ *Physical Units* (addresses C_3, uses W_4) Physical units are new types that specify a physical unit in addition to the data type (see Fig. 20.8). New literals support the specification of values for those types that include the physical unit. The typing rules for the existing operators (+, * or >) are overridden to perform the correct type checks for types with units. The type system also performs unit computations to deal correctly with unit computations (as in **speed = length/time**).

■ *Requirements Traces* (addresses C_5, uses W_6) Requirements traces are meta data annotations that link a program element to requirements, essentially elements in other models imported from requirements management tools[24]. Requirements traces can be attached to any program element without that element's definition having to be aware of this (see green (gray in print) highlights in Fig. 20.9 and in Fig. 20.22).

[24] We discussed traces in Chapter 17. We also briefly introduced mbeddr's approach to traces there.

```
derived unit mps = m s⁻¹ for speed
convertible unit kmh for speed
conversion kmh -> mps = val * 0.27

int8_t/mps/ calculateSpeed(int8_t/m/ length, int8_t/s/ time) {
  int8_t/mps/ s = length / time;
  if ( s > 100 mps ) { s = ⟦100 kmh → mps⟧; }
  return s;
}
```

Figure 20.8: The *units* extension ships with the SI base units. Users can define derived units (such as the **mps** in the example), as well as convertible units that require a numeric conversion for mapping back to SI units. Type checks ensure that the values associated with unit literals use the correct unit and perform unit computations (as in speed equals length divided by time). Errors are reported if incompatible units are used together (e.g., if we were to add length and time). To support this feature, the typing rules for the existing operators (such as **+** or **/**) have to be overridden.

■ *Presence Conditions* (addresses C_5 and W_6) A presence condition determines whether the program element to which it is attached is part of a product in the product line[25]. A product is configured by specifying a set of configuration flags (expressed via feature models), and the presence condition specifies a Boolean expression over these configuration switches. Like requirements traces, presence conditions can be attached to any program element[26]. Upon transformation, program elements whose presence condition evaluates to **false** for the selected product configuration are simply removed from the program (and hence will not end up in the generated binary). This program customization can also be performed by the editor, effectively supporting variant-specific editing.

[25] For details about DSLs and product lines, see Chapter 21.

[26] For example, in Fig. 20.9, the **resetted** out event and the **on start...** transition in the second state have the **resettable** presence condition, where **resettable** is a reference to a configuration flag.

■ *Safe Modules* (addresses C_2, uses W_5, W_7) Safe modules help prevent writing risky code. For example, runtime range checking is performed for arithmetic expressions and assignments. To enable this, arithmetic expressions are replaced by function calls that perform range checking and report errors if an overflow is detected. As another example, safe modules also provide the **safeheap** statement, which automatically frees dynamic variables allocated inside its body (see Fig. 20.13).

20.3.3 Addressing the Tool Integration Challenge

By building all languages (C, its extensions or any other DSLs) on top of MPS, the tool integration challenge is completely solved. All languages get an MPS-style IDE, including syntax highlighting, code completion, static error checking and annotation, quick fixes and refactorings, as well as a debugger (details see Section 15.2.5). Fig. 20.9 shows a screenshot of the tool, as we edit a module with a decision table, a state machine, requirements traces and presence conditions.

```
ADemoModule ×

module ADemoModule from cdesignpaper.screenshot imports nothing {
  enum MODE { FAIL: AUTO: MANUAL: }
  statemachine Counter {
    in start() <no binding>
       step(int[0..10] size) <no binding>  trace R2
    out started() <no binding>
        resetted() <no binding> {resettable}
        incremented(int[0..10] newVal) <no binding>
    vars int[0..10] currentVal = 0
         int[0..10] LIMIT = 10
    states (initial = start)
      state start {
        on start [ ] -> countState { send started(); }
      }                ■ start  ^inEvents (cdesignpaper.screenshot.ADemoModule)
      state           ■ step   ^inEvents (cdesignpaper.screenshot.ADemoModule)
        on step [currentVal + size > LIMIT] -> start { send resetted(); }
        on step [currentVal + size <= LIMIT] -> countState {
           Error: wrong number of arguments  + size;
           send incremented();
        }
      }
      on start [ ] -> start { send resetted(); } {resettable}
    }
  } end statemachine
  MODE nextMode(MODE mode, int8_t speed) {
    return | MODE, FAIL |             | mode == AUTO | mode == MANUAL |  trace R1;
           |            | speed < 50  | AUTO         | MANUAL         |
           |            | speed >= 50 | MANUAL       | MANUAL         |
```

20.4 Design and Implementation

This section discusses the implementation of mbeddr language extensions. We briefly discuss the structure of the C core language. The main part of this section discusses each of the ways W_m of extending C based on the extensions discussed in the previous section[27].

Figure 20.9: A somewhat overloaded example program in the mbeddr IDE (an instance of MPS). The module contains an **enum**, a decision table and a state machine. Requirements traces are attached to the table and the **step** in-event, and a presence condition is attached to an out-event and a transition.

[27] We expect you to have read the MPS examples in Part III of the book.

20.4.1 The mbeddr Core Languages

C can be partitioned into expressions, statements, functions, etc. We have factored these parts into separate language modules to make each of them reusable without pulling in all of C. The **expressions** language[28] is the most fundamental language. It depends on no other language and defines the primitive types, the corresponding literals and the basic operators. Support for pointers and user defined data types (**enum, struct, union**) is factored into the **pointers** and **udt** languages respec-

[28] The language is actually called `com.mbeddr.core.expressions`. We won't repeat the prefix in this chapter.

tively. **statements** contains the procedural part of C, and the **modules** language covers modularization. Fig. 20.10 shows an overview of some of the languages and constructs.

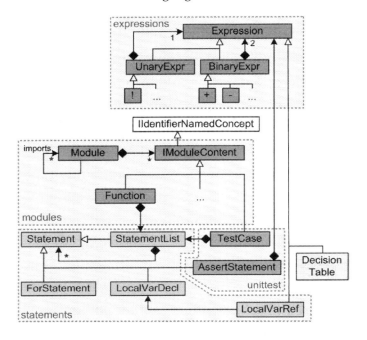

Figure 20.10: Anatomy of the mbeddr language stack: the diagram shows some of the language concepts, their relationships and the languages that contain them.

20.4.2 Addressing W_1 (Top-Level Constructs): Test Cases

In this section we illustrate the implementation of the **test case** construct, as well as of the **assert** and **fail** statements available inside test cases.

■ *Structure* **Module**s own a collection of **IModuleContent**s, an interface that defines the properties of everything that can reside directly in a module. All top-level constructs such as **Function**s implement **IModuleContent**. **IModuleContent** extends MPS' **IIdentifierNamedConcept** interface, which provides a **name** property. **IModuleContent** also defines a Boolean property **exported** that determines whether the respective module content is visible to modules that import this module[29]. Since the **IModuleContent** interface can also be implemented by concepts in other languages, new top-level constructs such as the **TestCase** in the **unittest** language can implement this interface, as long as the respective language has a dependency on the **modules** language, which defines **IModuleContent**. The class diagram in Fig. 20.10 shows some of the relevant concepts and languages.

[29] This property is queried by the scoping rules that determine which elements can be referenced.

■ *Constraints* A test case contains a **StatementList**, so any C statement can be used in a test case. **StatementList** becomes available to the unit test language through its dependency on the **statements** language. **unittest** also defines new statements: **assert** and **fail**. They extend the abstract **Statement** concept defined in the **statements** language. This makes them valid in *any* statement list, for example in a function body. This is undesirable, since the transformation of **assert**s into C depends on them being used in a **TestCase**. To enforce this, a *can be child* constraint is defined (Fig. 20.11).

```
concept constraints AssertStatement {
  can be child
    (context, scope, parentNode, link, childConcept)->boolean {
      parentNode.ancestor<TestCase>.isNotNull;
    }
}
```

Figure 20.11: This constraint restricts an **AssertStatement** to be used only inside a **TestCase** by checking that at least one of its ancestors is a **TestCase**.

■ *Transformation* The new language concepts in **unittest** are reduced to C concepts: the **TestCase** is transformed to a **void** function without arguments, and the **assert** statement is transformed into a **report** statement defined in the logging language. The **report** statement, in turn, it is transformed into a platform-specific way of reporting an error (console, serial line or error memory). Fig. 20.12 shows an example of this two-step process.

```
test case exTest {              void test_exTest {              void test_exTest {
  int x = add(2, 2);              int x = add(2, 2);              int x = add(2, 2);
  assert(0) x == 4;               report                          if (!(x == 4)) {
}                                   test.FAIL(0)                    printf("fail:0");
                                    on !(x == 4);                 }
                                }                               }
```

Figure 20.12: Two-stage transformation of **TestCase**s. The **TestCase** is transformed into a C function using the logging framework to output error messages. The **report** statement is in turn transformed into a **printf** statement *if* we generate for the Windows/Mac environment. It would be transformed to something else if we generated for the actual target device (configured by the user in the build configuration).

20.4.3 Addressing W_2 (Statements): Safeheap Statement

We have seen the basics of integrating new statements in the previous section where **assert** and **fail** extended the **Statement** concept inherited from the C core languages. In this section we focus on statements that need to handle local variable scopes and visibilities. We implement the **safeheap** statement mentioned earlier (see Fig. 20.13), which automatically frees dynamically allocated memory. The variables introduced by the **safeheap** statement must only be visible inside its body, and have to shadow variables of the same name declared in outer scopes (such as the **a** declared in the second line of the **measure** function in Fig. 20.13).

■ *Structure*   The **safeheap** statement extends **Statement**. It contains a **StatementList** as its body, as well as a list of **SafeHeapVar**s. These extend **LocalVarDecl**, so they fit with the existing mechanism for handling variable shadowing (explained below).

```
int8 measure() {
  int8 result = 0;
  int8* a = malloc(sizeof int8);
  safeheap(int8* a = malloc(10 * sizeof int8)) {
    for (int8 i = 0; i < 10; i++) { (a[i]) = readSensor(); }
    // th Error: cannot pass a safe heap var to a function  ss
    result = calcAverage(a);
  }
  return result;
}
```

Figure 20.13: A **safeheap** statement declares heap variables which can only be used inside the body of the statement. When the body is left, the memory is automatically freed. Notice also how we report an error if the variable tries to escape.

■ *Behavior*   **LocalVarRef**s are expressions that reference a **LocalVarDecl**. A scope constraint determines the set of visible variables for a given **LocalVarRef**. We implement this constraint by plugging into mbeddr's generic local variable scoping mechanism using the following approach. The constraint ascends the containment tree until it finds a node which implements **ILocalVarScopeProvider**, and calls its **getLocalVarScope** method. A **LocalVarScope** has a reference to an outer scope, which is set by finding *its* **ILocalVarScopeProvider** ancestor, effectively building a hierarchy of **LocalVarScope**s. To get at the list of the visible variables, the **LocalVarRef** scope constraint calls the **getVisibleLocalVars** method on the innermost **LocalVarScope** object. This method returns a flat list of **LocalVarDecl**s, taking into account that variables owned by a **LocalVarScope** that is *lower* in the hierarchy shadow variables of the same name from a *higher* level in the hierarchy. So, to plug the **SafeHeapStatement** into this mechanism, it has to implement **ILocalVarScopeProvider** and implement the two methods shown in Fig. 20.14.

■ *Type System*   To make the **safeheap** statement work correctly, we have to ensure that the variables declared and allocated in a **safeheap** statement do not escape from its scope. To

```
public LocalVarScope getLocalVarScope(node<> ctx, int stmtIdx) {
  LocalVarScope scope = new LocalVarScope(getContainedLocalVariables());
  node<ILocalVarScopeProvider> outer =
        this.ancestor<ILocalVarScopeProvider>;
  if (outer != null) {
    scope.setOuterScope(outer.getLocalVarScope(this, this.index));
  }
  return scope;
}
public sequence<node<LocalVariableDecl>> getContainedLocalVars() {
  this.vars;
}
```

Figure 20.14: A `safeheap` statement implements the two methods declared by the `ILocalVarScopeProvider` interface. `getContainedLocalVariables` returns the `LocalVarDecl`s that are declared between the parentheses (see Fig. 20.13). `getLocalVarScope` constructs a scope that contains these variables and then builds the hierarchy of outer scopes by relying on its ancestors that also implement `ILocalVarScopeProvider`. The index of the statement that contains the reference is passed in to make sure that only variables declared *before* the reference site can be referenced.

prevent this, an error is reported if a reference to a `safeheap` variable is passed to a function. Fig. 20.15 shows the code.

```
checking rule check_safeVarRef for concept = LocalVarRef as lvr {
  boolean isInSafeHeap =
    lvr.ancestor<SafeHeapStatement>.isNotNull;
  boolean isInFunctionCall =
    lvr.ancestor<FunctionCall>.isNotNull;
  boolean referencesSafeHeapVar =
    lvr.var.parent.isInstanceOf(SafeHeapStatement);
  if (isInSafeHeap && isInFunctionCall && referencesSafeHeapVar)
      error "cannot pass a safe heap var to a function" -> lvr;
}
```

Figure 20.15: This type system rule reports an error if a reference to a local variable declared and allocated by the `safeheap` statement is used in a function call.

20.4.4 Addressing W_3 (Expressions): Decision Tables

Fig. 20.4 showed the decision table expression. It is evaluated to the expression in a cell *c* if the column header of *c* and the row header of *c* are true[30]. If none of the condition pairs is true, then the default value, `FAIL` in the example, is used as the resulting value. A decision table also specifies the type of the value it will evaluate to, and all the expressions in content cells have to be compatible with that type. The type of the header cells has to be Boolean.

[30] Strictly speaking, it is the *first* of the cells for which the headers are true. It is optionally possible to use static verification based on an SMT solver to ensure that only one of them will be true for any given set of input values.

■ *Structure* The decision table extends the `Expression` concept defined in the `expressions` language. Decision tables contain a list of expressions for the column headers, one for the row headers and another for the result values. It also contains a child of type `Type`, to declare the type of the result expressions, as well as a default value expression. The concept defines an alias `dectab` to allow users to instantiate a decision table in the editor[31].

■ *Editor* Defining a tabular editor is straightforward: the editor definition contains a `table` cell, which delegates to a Java class that implements `ITableModel`. This is similar to

[31] Obviously, for non-textual notations such as the table, the alias will be different than the concrete syntax (in textual notations, the alias is typically made to be the same as the "leading keyword", e.g., `assert`).

the approach used by Java Swing. It provides methods such as `getValueAt( int row, int col)` or `deleteRow(int row)`, which have to be implemented for any specific table-based editor. To embed another node in a table cell (such as the expression in the decision table), the implementation of `getValueAt` simply returns the node (whose editor is then embedded in the table's editor).

■ *Type System* MPS uses unification in the type system. Language concepts specify type equations that contain type literals (such as **boolean**) as well as type variables (such as **typeof (dectab)**). The unification engine then tries to assign values to the type variables such that all applicable type equations become true. New language concepts contribute additional type equations. Fig. 20.16 shows those for decision tables[32].

```
// the type of the whole decision table expression
// is the type specified in the type field
typeof(dectab) :==: typeof(dectabc.type);
// the type of each of the column header
// expressions must be Boolean
foreach expr in dectab.colHeaders {
  typeof(expr) :==: <boolean>;
}
// ... same for row headers
foreach expr in dectabc.rowHeaders {
  typeof(expr) :==: <boolean>;
}
// the type of each of the result values must
// be the same or a subtype of the table itself
foreach expr in dectab.resultValues {
  infer typeof(expr) :<=: typeof(dcectab);
}
// ... same for the default
typeof(dc.def) :<=: typeof(dectab);
```

[32] New equations are solved along with those for existing concepts. For example, the typing rules for a `ReturnStatement` ensure that the type of the returned expression is the same or a subtype of the type of the surrounding function. If a `ReturnStatement` uses a decision table as the returned expression, the type calculated for the decision table must be compatible with the return type of the surrounding function.

Figure 20.16: The type equations for the decision table (see the comments for details).

20.4.5 Addressing W_4 (Types and Literals): Physical Units

We use physical units to illustrate the addition of new types and literals. We have already shown example code earlier in Fig. 20.8.

■ *Structure* Derived and convertible `UnitDeclaration`s are `IModuleContents`. Derived unit declarations specify a name (**mps**, **kmh**) and the corresponding SI base units (**m**, **s**), plus an exponent; a convertible unit declaration specifies a name and a conversion formula[33]. The backbone of the extension is the `UnitType`, which is a composite type that has another type (**int**, **float**) in its `valueType` slot, plus a unit (either

[33] The unit extension does not automatically support prefixes like **k**, **M** or **m**. If you need **km** or **mm** you have to define this as a convertible unit with the respective conversion formulae. This is a conscious decision driven by limited value ranges in C data types and conversion overhead.

an SI base unit or a reference to a **UnitDeclaration**). It is represented in programs as **baseType/unit/**. We also provide **LiteralWithUnit**s, which are expressions that contain a **valueLiteral** and, like the **UnitType**, a unit (so we can write, for example, **100 kmh**).

■ *Scoping*   **LiteralWithUnit**s and **UnitType**s refer to a **UnitDeclaration**, which is a module content. According to the visibility rules, valid targets for the reference are the **UnitDeclaration**s in the same module, and the *exported* ones in all imported modules. This rule applies to *any* reference to *any* module content, and is implemented generically. Fig. 20.17 shows the code for the scope of the reference to the **UnitDeclaration**. We use an interface **IVisibleNodeProvider**, (implemented by **Module**s) to find all instances of a given type. The implementation of **visibleContentsOfType** searches through the contents of the current and imported modules and collects instances of the specified concept. The result is used as the scope for the reference.

```
link {unit} search scope:
    (model, refNode, enclosingNode, operationContext)
                        ->sequence<node<UnitDeclaration>> {
    enclosingNode.ancestor<IVisibleNodeProvider>.
            visibleContentsOfType(concept/UnitDeclaration/);
}
```

Figure 20.17: The **visibleContentsOfType** operation returns all instances of the concept argument in the current module, as well as all exported instances in modules imported by the current module.

■ *Type System*   We have seen how MPS uses equations and unification to specify type system rules. However, there is special support for binary operators that makes overloading for new types easy: overloaded operations containers essentially specify 3-tuples of *(leftArgType, rightArgType, resultType)*, plus applicability conditions to match type patterns and decide on the resulting type. Typing rules for new (combinations of) types can be added by specifying additional 3-tuples. Fig. 20.18 shows the overloaded rules for C's **MultiExpression** (the language concept that implements the multiplication operator *) when applied to two **UnitType**s: the result type will be a **UnitType** as well, where the exponents of the SI units are added.

While any two units can legally be used with * and / (as long as we compute the resulting unit exponents correctly), this is not true for + and -. There, the two operand types must

```
operation concepts: MultiExpression
  left operand type: new node<UnitType>()
  right operand type: new node<UnitType>()
is applicable:
  (op, leftOpType, rightOpType)->boolean {
    node<> resultingValueType = operation type(op,
                 leftOpType.valueType , rightOpType.valueType );
    return resultingValueType != null;
  }
operation type:
  (op, leftOpType, rightOpType)->node<> {
    node<> resultingValueType = operation type(op,
                 leftOpType.valueType,  rightOpType.valueType );
    UnitType.create(resultingValueType,
                 leftOpType.unit.toSIBase().add(
                      rightOpType.unit.toSIBase(), 1 )
                 );
  }
```

Figure 20.18: This code overloads the **MultiExpression** to work for **UnitType**s. In the **is applicable** section we check whether there is a typing rule for the two value types (e.g., **int * float**). This is achieved by trying to compute the resulting value type. If none is found, the types cannot be multiplied (and consequently, the two types with unit cannot be multiplied either). In the computation of the **operation type** we create a new **UnitType** that uses the **resultingValueType** as the value type and then computes the resulting unit by adding up the exponents of component SI units of the two operand types.

be the same in terms of their representation in SI base units. We express this by using the following expression in the **is applicable** section[34]:

```
leftOpType.unit.isSameAs(rightOpType.unit)
```

In the **operation type** section we then compute the resulting unit type by adding the exponents of the components of the two unit types.

The typing rule for the **LocalVariableDeclaration** requires that the type of the **init** expression must be the same or a subtype of the **type** of the variable. To make this work correctly, we have to define a type hierarchy for **UnitType**s. We achieve this by defining the supertypes for each **UnitType**: the supertypes are those **UnitType**s whose unit is the same, and whose **valueType** is a supertype of the current **UnitType**'s value type. Fig. 20.19 shows the rule.

[34] **isSameAs** actually reduces each unit to their SI base unit (with exponents), then compares the result for structural equality.

```
subtyping rule supertypeOf_UnitType
             for concept = UnitType as ut {
  nlist<> res = new nlist<>;
  foreach st in immediateSupertypes(ut.valueType) {
    res.add(UnitType.create(st, ut.unit.copy));
  }
  return res;
}
```

Figure 20.19: This typing rule computes the direct supertypes of a **UnitType**. It iterates over all immediate supertypes of the current **UnitType**'s value type, wrapped into a **UnitType** with the same unit as the original one.

20.4.6 Addressing W_5 (Alternative Transformations): Range Checking

The **safemodules** language defines an *annotation* to mark **Modules** as safe (we will discuss annotations in the next subsection). If a module is safe, the binary operators such as + or * are replaced with calls to functions that, in addition to performing the addition or multiplication, perform a range check.

■ *Transformation*   The transformation that replaces the binary operators with function calls is triggered by the presence of this annotation on the **Module** which contains the operator. Fig. 20.20 shows the code. The **@safeAnnotation != null** checks for the presence of the annotation.

```
concept     PlusExpression
condition   (node, genContext, operationContext)->boolean {
              node.ancestor< ImplementationModule>
                              .@safeAnnotation != null;
            }
-->
module dummy imports arithmeticOps {
  void dummy() {
     <TF addWithRangeCheck($COPY_SRC$[1], $COPY_SRC$[2]) TF>;
} }
```

Figure 20.20: This reduction rule transforms instances of **PlusExpression** into a call to a library function **addWithRangeChecks**, passing in the left and right argument of the + using the two **COPY_SRC** macros. The **condition** ensures that the transformation is only executed if the containing **Module** has a **safeAnnotation** attached to it. A transformation priority defined in the properties of the transformation makes sure it runs before the C-to-text transformation.

MPS uses priorities to specify relative orderings of transformations, and MPS then calculates a global transformation order for any given model. We use a priority to express the fact that this transformation runs *before* the final transformation that maps the C tree to C text for compilation.

20.4.7   Addressing W_6 (Meta Data): Requirements Traces

Annotations are concepts whose instances can be added as children to a node N without this being specified in the definition of N's concept[35]. While structurally the annotations are children of the annotated node, the editor is defined the other way round: the annotation editor delegates to the editor of the annotated element. This allows the annotation editor to add additional syntax *around* the annotated element[36].

We illustrate the annotation mechanism based on the requirements traces. As we discussed at the end of Section 20.3.2, a requirements trace establishes a link from a program element to a requirement. It is important that this annotation can be annotated to **any** node, independent of the concept of which it is an instance. As a consequence of the projectional approach, the program can be shown with or without the annotations, controlled by a global switch. Fig. 17.5 had shown an example.

■ *Structure*   Fig. 20.21 shows the structure. Notice how it extends the MPS-predefined concept **NodeAnnotation**. It also specifies a **role**, which is the name of the property that is used to store **TraceAnnotation**s under the annotated node.

[35] We discussed annotations in Section 16.2.7.

[36] Optionally, it is possible to explicitly restrict the concepts to which a particular annotation can be attached. However, for the requirements traces discussed in this section, we do *not* want such a restriction: traces should be attachable to any program node.

```
concept TraceAnnotation extends NodeAnnotation implements <none>
  children:
    TraceKind      tracekind   1
    TraceTargetRef refs        0..n
  concept properties:
    role = trace
  concept links:
    annotated = BaseConcept
```

Figure 20.21: Annotations have to extend the MPS-predefined concept **NodeAttribute**. They can have an arbitrary child structure (**tracekind**, **refs**), but they have to specify the **role** (the name of the property that holds the annotated child under its parent), as well as the **attributed** concept. The annotations can only be attached to instances of this concept (or subconcepts).

■ *Editor* In the editor annotations look as if they *surrounded* their parent node (although they are in fact children). Fig. 20.22 shows the definition of the editor of the requirements trace annotation (an example is shown in Fig. 20.9): it puts the trace to the right of the annotated node. Since MPS is a projectional editor, there is base-language grammar that needs to be made aware of the additional syntax in the program. This is key to enabling arbitrary annotations on arbitrary program nodes.

```
editor for concept TraceAnnotation
  node cell layout:
    [> [> attributed node <] ?[> % tracekind % F(> % refs % <) <] <]
```

Annotations are typically attached to a program node via an intention. Intentions are an MPS editor mechanism: a user selects the target element, presses **Alt-Enter** and selects **Add Trace** from the popup menu. Fig. 20.23 shows the code for the intention that attaches a requirements trace.

Figure 20.22: The editor definition for the **ReqTrace** annotation (an example trace annotation is shown in Fig. 20.9). It consists of a vertical list [/ .. /] with two lines. The first line contains the reference to the requirement. The second line uses the **attributed node** construct to embed the trace into the editor of the program node to which this annotation is attached. So the annotation is always rendered over of whatever syntax the original node uses.

```
intention addTrace for BaseConcept {
  description(node)->string {
    "Add Trace";
  }
  isApplicable(node)->boolean {
    node.@trace == null;
  }
  execute(editorContext, node)->void {
    node.@trace = new node<TraceAnnotation>();
  }
}
```

20.4.8 Addressing W7 (Restriction): Preventing Use of Real Numbers

We have already seen in Section 20.4.2 how constraints can prevent the use of specific concepts in certain contexts. We use the same approach for preventing the use of real number types inside model-checkable state machines: a **can be ancestor** constraint in the state machine prevents instances of **float** in the state machine if the **verifiable** flag is set[37].

Figure 20.23: An intention definition consists of three parts. The **description** returns the string that is shown in the intentions popup menu. The **isApplicable** section determines under which conditions the intention is available in the menu – in our case, we can only add a trace if there is no trace on the target node already. Finally, the **execute** section performs the action associated with the intention. In our case we simply put an instance of **TraceAnnotation** into the **@trace** property of the target node.

[37] It is possible to define such constraints in extensions, thereby restricting existing concepts after the fact, in a modular way.

20.5 Experiences

In Section 20.5.1 we provide a brief overview of our experiences in implementing mbeddr, including the size of the project and the efforts spent. Section 20.5.2 discusses to what degree this approach leads to improvements in embedded software development.

Element	Count	LOC-Factor
Language Concepts	260	3
Property Declarations	47	1
Link Declarations	156	1
Editor Cells	841	0.25
Reference Constraints	21	2
Property Constraints	26	2
Behavior Methods	299	1
Type System Rules	148	1
Generation Rules	57	10
Statements	4,919	1.2
Intentions	47	3
Text Generators	103	2
Total LOC		**8,640**

Figure 20.24: We count various language definition elements and then use a factor to translate them into lines of code. The reasons why many factors are so low (e.g., reference constraints or behavior methods) is that the implementation of these elements is made up of statements, which are counted separately. In the case of editor cells, typically several of them are on the same line, hence the fraction. Finally, the MPS implementation language supports higher-order functions, so some statements are rather long and stretch over more than one line: this explains the 1.2 in the factor for statements.

20.5.1 Language Extension

■ *Size*   Typically, lines of code are used to describe the size of a software system. In MPS, a "line" is not necessarily meaningful. Instead we count important elements of the implementation and then estimate a corresponding number of lines of code. Fig. 20.24 shows the respective numbers for the core, i.e. C itself plus unit test support, decision tables and build/make integration (the table also shows how many LOC equivalents we assume for each language definition element, and the caption explains to some extent the rationale for these factors). According to our metric the C core is implemented with less than 10,000 lines of code.

Let us look at an incremental extension of C. The components extension (interfaces, components, pre- and post-conditions, support for mock components in testing and a generator back to plain C) is circa 3,000 LOC equivalents. The state machines extension is circa 1,000. Considering the fact that these LOC equivalents represent the language definition (including type systems and generators) and the IDE (including code completion, syntax coloring, some quick fixes and refactorings), this clearly demonstrates the efficiency of MPS for language development and extension.

■ *Effort*   In terms of effort, the core C implementation has been circa 4 person months divided between three people. This results in roughly 2,500 lines of code per person month. Extrapolated to a year, this would be 7,500 lines of code per developer. According to McConnell[38], in a project up to 10,000 LOC, a developer can typically do between 2,000 and 25,000 LOC. The fact that we are at the low end of this range can be explained by the fact that MPS provides very expressive languages for DSL development: you don't have to write a lot of code to express a lot about a DSL. Instead, MPS code is relatively dense and requires quite a bit of thought. Pair programming is very valuable in language development.

[38] www.codinghorror.com/blog/2006/07/diseconomies-of-scale-and-lines-of-code.html

Once a developer has mastered the learning curve, language extension can be very productive. The state machines and components extension have both been developed in about a month. The unit testing extension or the support for decision tables can be implemented in a few days.

■ *Language Modularity, Reuse and Growth*   Modularity and composition are central to mbeddr. Building a language extension should not require changes to the base languages. This requires that the extended languages are built with extension in mind. Just as in object-oriented programming, where only complete methods can be overridden, only specific parts of a language definition can be extended or overwritten. The implementation of the default extensions served as a test case to confirm that the C core language is in fact extensible. We found a few problems, especially in the type system, and fixed them. None of these fixes were "hacks" to enable a specific extension – they were all genuine mistakes in the design of the C core. Due to the broad spectrum covered by our extensions, we are confident that the current core language provides a high degree of extensibility.

Independently developed extensions should not interact with each other in unexpected ways. While MPS provides no automated way of ensuring this, we have not seen such interactions so far. The following steps can be taken to minimize the risk of unexpected interactions. Generated names should be qualified to make sure that no symbol name clashes occur in the generated C code. An extension should never consume "scarce resources": for example, it is a bad idea for a new `Statement` to require a particular return type of the containing function, or change that return type during transformation. Two such badly designed statements cannot be used together, because they are likely to require *different* return types[39].

Modularity should also support reuse in contexts not anticipated during the design of a language module. Just as in the case of language extension (discussed above), the languages to be reused have to be written in a suitable way so that the right parts can be reused separately. We have shown this with the state machines language. State machines can be used as top-level concepts in modules (binding out-events to C functions), and also inside components (binding out-events to component methods). Parts of the transformation of a state machine have to be different in these two cases, and these differences were successfully isolated to make them exchangeable. Also, we reuse the C expression language inside the guard conditions in a state machine's transitions. We use constraints to prevent the use of those C expression that are not allowed inside transitions (for example, references to global variables). Finally, we have successfully used physical units in components and interfaces.

Summing up, these facilities allow different user groups to develop independent extensions, growing[40] the mbeddr stack even closer towards their particular domain.

[39] Note that unintended *syntactic* integration problems between independently developed extensions (known from traditional parser-based systems) can *never* happen in MPS. This was one of the reasons to use MPS for mbeddr.

[40] "Growing" in the sense of *Growing a Language,* Guy Steele's great OOPSLA talk.

■ *Who can create Extensions?* mbeddr is built to be extended. The question is by whom. This question can be addressed in two ways: who is *able* to extend it from a skills perspective, and who *should* extend it?

Let us address the *skills* question first. We find that it takes about a month for a developer with solid object-oriented programming experience to become proficient with MPS and the structures of the mbeddr core languages[41]. Also, *designing* good languages, independent of their implementation, is a skill that requires practice and experience[42]. So, from this perspective we assume that in any given organization there should be a select group of language developers who build the extensions for the end users. Notice that such an organizational structure is common today for frameworks and other reusable artifacts.

There is also the question of who *should* create extensions.

[41] This may be reduced by better documentation, but a steep learning curve will remain.

[42] The first part of this book provides some guidance.

One could argue that, as language development becomes simpler, an uncontrolled growth in languages could occur, ultimately resulting in chaos. This concern should be addressed with governance structures that guide the development of languages. The bigger the organization is, the more important such governance becomes[43].

20.5.2 Improvements in Embedded Development

In this section we discuss preliminary results of a real-world development project. The project develops the software for a smart meter system[44]. A smart meter is an electrical meter that continuously records the consumption of electric power in a home and sends the data back to the utility for monitoring and billing. The particular software we develop will run on a 2-chip board (TI MSP-430 for metrology, another TI processor (tbd.) for the remaining application logic). Instead of the `gcc` compiler used in mbeddr by default, this project uses an IAR compiler.

The software comprises circa 30,000 lines of mbeddr code, has several time-sensitive parts that require a low-overhead implementation, and will have to be certified by an independent body. The software is derived from an existing example smart meter meter system written in traditional C, and reuses existing artifacts such as header files and libraries[45].

■ *Why mbeddr?* mbeddr was chosen to implement the smart meter for the following reasons. The project has to work with an existing code base which had no production-level quality. The code quality needed to be improved *incrementally*. So starting with the existing C code and then refactoring towards better abstractions seemed like a good idea. Also, as we will see below, the existing C extensions provided by mbeddr are a good match for what is needed in the smart meter (see below)[46]. Finally, as the goal is to have the meter certified, testing the software is very important. By using the abstraction mechanisms provided by mbeddr, and by exploiting the ability to build custom extensions, testability can be improved significantly. In particular, hardware-specifics can be isolated, which enables testing without the actual target hardware. Also, mbeddr's support for requirements traceability comes in handy for the upcoming certification.

[43] The modular nature of the mbeddr language extensions makes this problem much easier to tackle. In an large organization we assume that a few language extensions will be strategic: aligned with the needs of the whole organization, well-designed, well tested and documented, implemented by a central group, and used by many developers. In addition, small teams may decide to develop their own, smaller extensions. Their focus is much more local, and the development requires much less coordination. These could be developed by the smaller units themselves.

[44] The smart meter system is developed by itemis France. Technical contacts are Bernd Kolb (`kolb@itemis.de`) and Stephan Eberle (`eberle@itemis.de`).

[45] While the project is still going on, we can already report some experiences and draw some conclusions.

[46] In particular, the smart meter is *not* just a state-based or a data flow-based system, it contains multiple different behavioral paradigms. Using a state chart or data flow modeling tool was hence not an option.

■ *Using the Existing Extensions* The smart meter uses the following default extensions:

Components The smart meter uses components to improve the structure of the application, and to support different implementations of the same interface. This improves modularity and testability. Mocks components are used excessively for testing.

State Machines The smart meter communicates with its environment via several different protocols. So far, one of these protocols has been refactored to use a state machine. This has proven to be much more readable than the original C code. Components and state machines are combined, which allows decoupling message assembly and parsing from the application logic in the server component.

Units A major part of the smart meter application logic performs computations on physical quantities (time [s], current [A] or voltage [V]). So mbeddr's support for physical units comes in handy. The benefits of these extensions are mostly in type checking, using types with units also improves the readability and comprehensibility of the code.

Requirements Tracing The smart meter also makes use of requirements traces. During the upcoming certification process, these will be extremely useful for tracking if and how the customer requirements have been implemented. Because of their orthogonal nature, the traces can be attached to the new language concepts specifically developed for the smart meter.

■ *Custom Extensions* As part of the smart meter, so far mbeddr has been extended in the following ways:

Registers The smart meter software makes extensive use of registers (metrology: access the sensor values, UART: send and receive data). This cannot be abstracted away easily due to performance/overhead constraints. In addition, some registers are special-purpose registers: when a value is written to such a register, a hardware-implemented computation is automatically triggered based on the value supplied by the programmer. The result of this computation is then stored in the register. To run code that works with these registers on the PC for testing, developers face two problems:

first, the header files that define the addresses of the registers are not valid for the PC's processor. Second, there are no special-purpose registers on the PC, so no automatic computations or other hardware-triggered actions would be triggered. This problem was solved with a language extension that supports registers as first-class citizens and supports accessing them from mbeddr-C code (see code below).

```
exported register8 ADC10CTL0 compute as val * 1000

void calculateAndStore( int8 value ) {
  int8 result = // some calculation with value
  ADC10CTL0 = result; // actually stores result * 1000
}
```

The extension also supports specifying an expression that performs the computation. When the code is translated for the real device, the real headers are included, and access to the registers is replaced with access to the constants defined in the header. In testing, **struct**s are generated to hold the register data. Each write access to a register is replaced with a write access to the struct, and the expression that simulates the special purpose register is included in that assignment.

Interrupts Many aspects of the smart meter system are driven by interrupts. To integrate the component-based architecture used in the smart meter with interrupts, it is necessary to trigger component runnables (methods) via an interrupt. To this end, we have implemented a language extension that allows us to declare interrupts. In addition, the extension provides runnable triggers that express the fact that a runnable is triggered by an interrupt[47]. The extension also provides a concept to assign an interrupt to a runnable during component instantiation. A check makes sure that each interrupt-triggered runnable has at least one interrupt assigned[48].

Data Encoding As part of the communication protocol, data has to be encoded into messages[49]. A language extension supports the definition of data structures, and generated code deals with constructing messages. In particular, the generated code deals with packed data (where data has sizes that are not multiples of 8 bits). Also, code that processes messages can be statically checked against the message structure definition, making this code much more robust (in particular if the message definitions are changed).

[47] By default, runnables are triggered by an "incoming" invocation, upon initialization or by a timer. This new trigger connects a runnable to an interrupt.

[48] For testing purposes on the PC, special language constructs can be used to emulate the occurrence of an interrupt: the test driver simulates the triggering of interrupts based on a test-specified schedule and checks whether the system reacts correctly.

[49] The message/data format is similar to ASN.1.

■ *Conclusions* The mbeddr default extensions have proven extremely useful in the development of the smart meter. The fact that the extensions are directly integrated into C (as opposed to the classical approach of using external DSLs or separate modeling tools) reduces the hurdle of using higher-level extensions and removes any potential mismatch between DSL code and C code.

Generating code from higher-level abstractions may introduce performance and resource consumption overhead. While we have not yet performed a systematic analysis of the overhead incurred by the mbeddr extensions, it is low enough to run the smart meter system on the hardware intended for it[50].

Additional effort is required to integrate with existing legacy code. As a consequence of the projectional editor, we have to parse the C text (with an existing parser) and construct the MPS AST. mbeddr provides an importer for header files as a means of connecting to existing libraries. However, mostly as a consequence of C's preprocessor, which allows all kinds of mischief to be done to otherwise well-structured C code, this importer is not trivial. For example, we currently cannot import all alternatives expressed by **#ifdef**s. Users have to specify a specific configuration to be imported (in the future, we will support importing of all options by mapping the **#ifdef**s to mbeddr's product line variability mechanism). Also, header files often contain platform-specific keywords or macros. Since they are not supported by the mbeddr C implementation, these have to be removed before they can be imported. The header importer provides a regular expression-based facility to remove these platform specifics before the import. The smart meter project, which is heavily based on an existing code base, also drove the need for a complete source code importer (including **.c** files, not just header files), which we are currently in the process of developing[51].

We have performed scalability tests and found that mbeddr scales to at least the equivalent of 100,000 lines of C code in the developed system. These tests were based on automatically generated sample code and measured editor responsiveness and transformation times. While there are certainly systems that are substantially larger, a significant share of embedded software is below this limit and can be addressed with mbeddr[52].

---

[50] Some extensions (registers, interrupts or physical units) have no runtime overhead at all, since they have no representation in the generated C code. Others, such as the components, incur a very small overhead as a consequence of indirections from function pointers (to support polymorphism).

[51] The integration of legacy code described in this paragraph is clearly a disadvantage of projectional editing. However, because of the advantages of mbeddr and language extensibility discussed in this chapter, we feel that it is a good trade-off.

[52] The smart meter system consists of 30,000 lines of mbeddr code. Since there is a factor of about 1.5 between the mbeddr code and generated C, the smart meter system corresponds to circa 45,000 lines of C.

20.6 Discussion

■ *Why MPS?* Our choice of MPS is due to its support for all aspects of language development (structure, syntax, type systems, IDE, transformations), its support for flexible syntax as a consequence of projectional editing, and its support for advanced modularization and composition of languages. The ability to attach annotations to arbitrary program elements without a change to that element's definition is another strong advantage of MPS (we we use this for presence conditions and trace links, for example).

While the learning curve for MPS is significant (a developer who wants to become proficient in MPS language development has to invest at least a month), we found that it scales extremely well for larger and more sophisticated languages[53].

■ *Projectional Editing* Projectional editing is often considered a drawback, because the editors feel somewhat different and the programs are not stored as text, but as a tree (XML). We have already highlighted the fact that MPS does a good job regarding the editor experience, and we feel that the advantages of projectional editors regarding syntactic freedom far outweigh the drawback of requiring some initial familiarization. Our experience so far with about ten users (pilot users from industry, students) shows that after a short guided introduction of about 30 minutes, and an initial accommodation period (circa 1-2 days), users can work productively with the projectional editor. Regarding storage, the situation is not any worse than with current modeling tools that store models in a non-textual format, and MPS does provide good support for diff and merge using the projected syntax.

■ *Feasibility of Language Extension* Based on the experience with the smart meter, the effort for building extensions is reasonable. For example, the implementation of the language extensions for registers (and the simulation for testing) was done in half a day. The addition of interrupts, interrupt-triggered runnables and the way to "wire them" up was circa one day[54].

Building a language extension should not require changes to the base language. The extensions for the smart meter demonstrate this point. The registers extension discussed above has been built without changing the underlying C language[55]. Similarly, the interrupt-based runnable triggers have been hooked

[53] This is in sharp contrast to some of the other tools the authors have worked with, where implementing simple languages is quick and easy, and larger and more sophisticated languages are disproportionately more complex to build. This is illustrated by the very reasonable effort necessary for implementing mbeddr.

[54] In the context of a development project which, like the smart meter, is planned to run a few person years, these efforts can easily be absorbed. The benefits are well worth the effort in terms of the improved type safety and testability.

[55] It requires new top-level module contents (the register definition themselves), new expressions (for reading and writing into the registers), and embedding expressions into new contexts (the code that emulates the hardware computation when registers are written).

into the generic trigger facility that is part of the components language. Once a language is designed in a reasonable way, the language (or parts of it) should be reusable in contexts that have not been specifically anticipated in advance. The smart meter system contains such examples: expressions have been embedded in the register definition concept for emulating the hardware behavior, and types with units have been used in decision tables. Again, no change to the existing languages has been necessary.

One criticism that has been used against language extension is that the language will grow large and that it is hard for users to learn all its constructs. In our experience, this is not a problem in mbeddr for the following three reasons: first, the extensions provide linguistic abstractions for concepts that are well known to the users: state-based behavior, interfaces and components or test cases. Second, the additional language features are easily discoverable because of the IDE support. Third, and most important, these extensions are modularized, and any particular end user will only use those extensions that are relevant to whatever their current program addresses. This avoids overwhelming the user with too much "stuff" at a time.

21
DSLs and Product Lines

This chapter discusses the role of DSLs in Product Line Engineering (PLE). We first briefly introduce PLE and feature models and discuss how feature models can be connected to programs expressed in DSLs. We then explain the difference in expressivity between feature models and DSLs and argue why sometimes features models are not enough to express the variability in a product line, and how DSLs can help. The chapter concludes with a mapping of the concepts relevant to PLE and DSLs. This chapter is written mostly for people with a background in PLE who want to understand how DSLs fit into PLE.

21.1 Introduction

The goal of product line engineering (PLE) is to efficiently manage a range of products by factoring out commonalities such that definitions of products can be reduced to a specification of their variable aspects[1]. As a consequence of this approach, software quality can be improved and time-to-market of any single product in the product line can be reduced[2]. One way of achieving this is the expression of product configurations on a higher level of abstraction than the actual implementation[3]. An automated mapping transforms the configuration to the implementation.

[1] PLE also involves a lot product management, process and organizational aspects. We do not cover these in this book.

[2] It can also help establish a common user experience among a range of products.

[3] This higher level of abstraction is often called the problem space; the lower level is often called the solution space or implementation space.

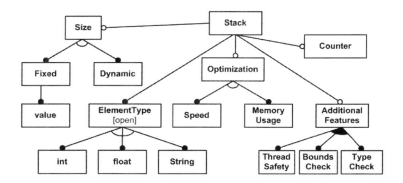

Figure 21.1: An example feature diagram for a product line of **Stack** data structures. Filled circles represent mandatory features, empty circles represent optional features. Filled arcs represent n-of-m selection and empty arcs represent 1-of-m.

21.2 Feature Models

In PLE, this higher level of abstraction is typically realized with feature models[4]. Feature models express configuration options and the constraints among them. A graphical notation, called feature diagrams, is often used to represent feature models (Fig. 21.1 shows an example). Here is why we need constraints: if a product line's variability was just expressed by a set of Boolean options, the configuration space would grow by 2^n, with n representing the number of options. With feature models, constraints are expressed regarding the combinations of features, limiting the set of valid configurations to a more manageable size. Constraints include[5]:

[4] There are other approaches, such as Orthogonal Variability Models, but they are similar in essence to feature models.

[5] Additionally, non-hierarchical constraints can be expressed as well. For example, a feature can declare **conflicts with** and a **requires also** constraints relative to arbitrary other features.

- *Mandatory* (filled circles): mandatory features have to be in each product. For example, in Fig. 21.1, each **Stack** has to have the feature **ElementType**.
- *Optional* (empty circles): optional features may or may not be in a product. **Counter** and **Optimization** are examples of optional features.
- *Or* (filled arc): a product may include zero, one or any number of the features in an **or** group. In the example, a product may include any number of features from **ThreadSafety**, **BoundsCheck** and **TypeCheck**.
- *Xor* (empty arc): a product must include exactly one of the features grouped into a **xor** group. The **ElementType** must either be **int**, **float** or **String**.

A *configuration* represents a product in the product line. It comprises a set of feature selections from a feature model that comply with the constraints expressed in the feature model.

For example, the configuration {`Optimization, Memory Use, Additional Features, Type Check, Element Type, int, Size, Dynamic`} would be valid. A configuration that includes `Speed` and `Memory Usage` would be invalid, because it violates the `xor` constraint between those two features expressed in the feature model.

Note that a feature model does not yet describe the *implementation* of a product or the product line, the feature model has to be connected to implementation artifacts in a separate step[6].

[6] While this sounds like a drawback, it is one of the main advantages of the approach: feature models support reasoning about product configurations independent of their implementation.

21.3 Connecting Feature Models to Artifacts

By definition, feature models express product line variability at a level that is more abstract than the implementation. In many systems, the implementation of variability is scattered over (parts of) many implementation artifacts. However, to result in a correct system, several variation points (VP) may need to be configured in a consistent, mutually dependent way. If each VP has to be configured separately, the overall complexity grows quickly. By identifying logical variation points and factoring them into features in a feature model, and then tying the (potentially many) implementation variation points to these logical variation points, related implementation variations can be tied together and managed as one (Fig. 21.2).

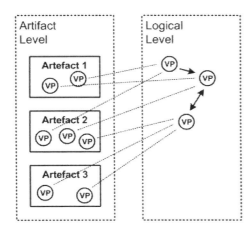

Figure 21.2: The Artifact Level represents realization artifacts such as models, code or documentation. The Logical Level is the external description of variation points and the conceptual constraints among them, typically a feature model. One or more VPs in the implementation level are associated with variation points in the logical level (n:1, n:m).

If DSLs are used to implement a software system, then the artifacts configured from the feature model are typically DSL programs, and the variation points are program elements. By using DSL models instead of low-level implementation code, the number of variation points in the artifacts will be reduced, because you use the DSL-to-code transformation to expand all the details in a consistent way. The trade-off is that you have to define this high-level domain specific language, including a way to define variants of programs written in that language. You also need to define the transformation down to the actual implementation artifacts (Fig. 21.3).

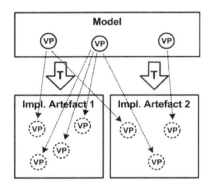

Figure 21.3: A model describes domain abstractions in a formal and concise way. Transformations map the model to (typically more than one) implementation artifact. Variability is expressed with fewer VPs in the models compared to implementation artifacts.

The configuration of models (and other artifacts) can be done in several different ways: removal, injection and parameterization.

■ *Removal* (also known as *negative variability*) In this approach, the mapping from a feature model to implementation artifacts removes parts of a comprehensive whole (Fig. 21.4). This implies marking up the various optional parts of the comprehensive whole with Boolean expressions that determine when to remove the part. These expressions are called *presence conditions*. The biggest advantage of this approach is its apparent simplicity. However, the comprehensive whole has to contain the parts for *all* variants (maybe even parts for combinations of variants), making it potentially large and complex. Also, depending on the tool support, the comprehensive whole might not even be a valid instance of the underlying language or formalism[7]. In an IDE, the respective artifact might show errors, which makes this approach annoying at times.

`ifdefs` in C and C++ are a well-known implementation of this strategy. A preprocessor removes all code regions whose `ifdef` condition evaluates to false. When calling the compiler/preprocessor, you have to provide a number of symbols

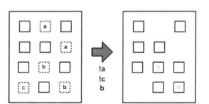

Figure 21.4: Removal represents negative variability, in that it takes optional things (small squares) away from a comprehensive whole, based on the configuration expressed over the features a, b, c. The optional parts are annotated with presence conditions referring to the configuration features.

[7] For example, a Java class may have to extend different base classes, depending on the variant, or it may contain fields with different types.

that are evaluated as part of the conditions. Conditional compilation can also be found in other languages. Preprocessors that treat the source code simply as text are available for many languages and are part of many PLE tool suites. The AUTOSAR standard, as well as other modeling formalisms, support the annotation of model elements with presence conditions. The model element (and all its children) are removed from the model if the condition evaluates to false. The same approach is available in mbeddr.

■ *Injection*   (also known as *positive variability*) In this approach, additions are defined relative to a minimal core (Fig. 21.5). The core does not know about the variability: the additions point to the place where they need to be added. The clear advantage of this approach is that the core is typically small and contains only what is common for all products. The parts specific to a variant are kept external and added to the core only when necessary. To be able to do this, however, there must be a way to refer to the location in the minimal core at which to add a variable part. This either requires the explicit definition of named hooks in the minimal core, or some way of pointing into the core from an external source. Also, interactions between the additions for various features may also be hard to manage.

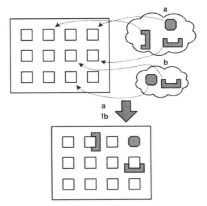

Figure 21.5: A minimal base artifact made of various parts (the small rectangles) exists. There is also variant-specific code (the strange shapes), connected to features external to the actual artifact and pointing to the parts of the artifact to which they can be attached. Implementing a variant means that the variant-specific code associated with the selected features is injected into the base artifact, attached to the parts they designate.

Aspect-oriented programming is a way of implementing this strategy. Pointcuts are a way of selecting from a set of join points in the base asset. A joint point is an addressable location in the core. Instead of explicitly defining hooks, all instances of a specific language construct are automatically addressable. Various preprocessors can also be used in this way. However, they typically require the explicit markup of hooks in the minimal core. For models, injection is especially simple, since in most formalisms model elements are addressable by default and/or the language can be extended to be able to mark up hooks. This makes it possible to point to a model element, and add additional model elements to it, as long as the result is still a valid instance of the meta model.

■ *Parameterization*   The variable artifact defines parameters. A variant is constructed by providing values for those parameters (Fig. 21.6). The parameters are usually typed to restrict the range of valid values. In most cases, the values for the parameters are relatively simple, such as strings, integers, Booleans or regular expressions. However, in principle, they can be arbi-

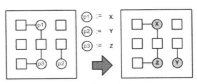

Figure 21.6: An artifact defines a number of (typed) parameters. A variant provides values for the parameters.

trarily complex[8]. The parameterized artifact needs to explicitly define the parameters, as well as a way to specify values. The artifact has to query the values of those parameters explicitly and use them for whatever it does. The approach requires the core to be explicitly aware of the variability[9].

A configuration file that is read out by the an application is a form of parameterization. The names of the parameters are predefined by the application, and when defining a variant, a set of values is supplied. The Strategy pattern is a form of parameterization, especially in combination with a factory. A variant is created by supplying an implementation of an interface defined by the configurable application. All kinds of other small, simple or domain-specific languages can be used as a form of parameterization. A macro language in an application is a form of parameterization, where the type of parameter is "valid program written in language X"[10].

[8] In the extreme case, these parameters can be complete programs in some DSL.

[9] This is not necessarily the case with the other two approaches.

[10] There is an obvious connection to DSLs – a DSL can be used here. This approach is useful when the primary product definition can be expressed with a feature model. The DSL-typed attributes can be used for those variation points for which selection is not expressive enough.

21.3.1 Example Implementation in mbeddr

In mbeddr we use a textual notation for feature models. Fig. 21.7 shows this notation for the stack feature model shown graphically above. Note how the constraint affects all children of a feature, so we had to introduce the intermediate feature **options** to separate mandatory features from optional features. Features can also have configuration attributes (of any type).

A configuration is a named set of selections from the features in a feature model. The selection has to be valid regarding the constraints defined in the feature model. Fig. 21.8 shows two example configurations. If an invalid configuration is created, errors will be shown in the configuration model.

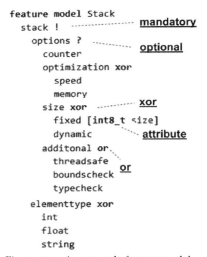

Figure 21.7: An example feature model in mbeddr. Until MPS provides support for graphical notations (planned for 2013), we use a textual notation.

Figure 21.8: Two valid configurations of the feature model.

[11] Note that the fact that you can make arbitrarily detailed program elements depend on features is not meant to imply that no further structuring of the product line is necessary, and all variability should be expressed via fine-grained presence conditions. Instead, presence conditions should be used to configure more coarse-grained entities such as the instantiation and wiring of components.

Presence conditions can be attached to any program element expressed in any language[11], without this language having to know about it, thanks to MPS' annotations (discussed in Section 16.2.7). For example the two **report** statements and the message list in the left program in Fig. 21.9 are only part of a product if the **logging** feature is selected in the product configuration. The background color of an annotated node is computed from the expression: annotated nodes using the same expression have the same color (an idea borrowed from Christian Kaestner's CIDE[12]).

It is possible to edit the program as a product line (with the annotations), undecorated (without annotations), as well as a specific product. Fig. 21.9 shows an example. During transformation, those parts of programs that are not in the product are removed from the model.

[12] C. Kaestner. Cide: Decomposing legacy applications into features. In *Software Product Lines, 11th International Conference, SPLC 2007, Kyoto, Japan, September 10-14, 2007, Proceedings. Second Volume (Workshops)*, pages 149–150. Kindai Kagaku Sha Co. Ltd., Tokyo, Japan, 2007

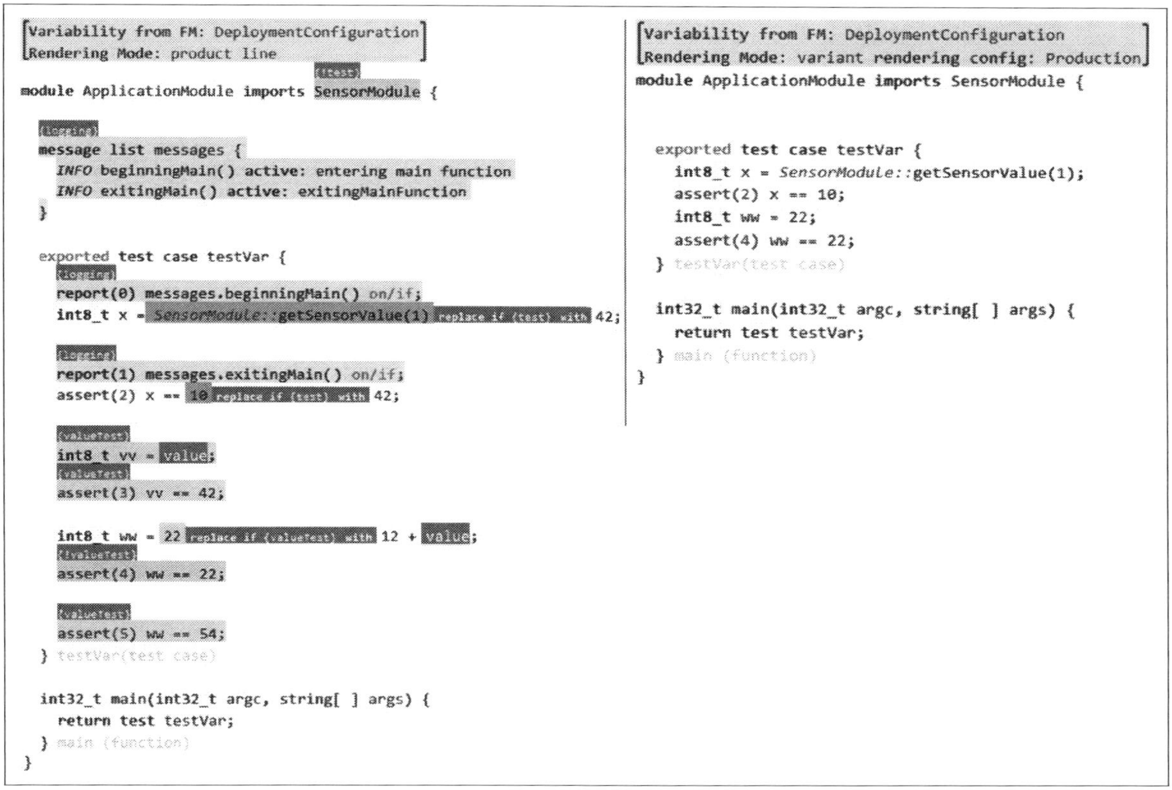

Figure 21.9: *Left:* A C program with product line annotations. *Right:* The program rendered in the **Production** variant. Note how the program is "cut down" to include only those parts that are part of the variant, even in the editor.

21.3.2 Feature Models on Language Elements

Instead of using feature models to vary programs expressed with DSLs, the opposite approach is also possible. In this case, the primary product definition is done with DSLs. However, some language concepts have a feature model associated with them for detailed configuration. When the particular language concept is instantiated, a new ("empty") feature configuration is created, and can be configured by the application engineer.

21.3.3   Variations in the Transformation or Execution

When working with DSLs, the execution of models – by transformation, code generation or interpretation – is under the control of the domain engineer. The transformations or the interpreter can also be varied based on a feature model.

■ *Negative Variability via Removal*   The transformations or the interpreter can be annotated with presence conditions; the configuration happens before the transformations or the interpreter are executed.

■ *Branching*   The interpreter or the transformations can query over a feature configuration and then branch accordingly at runtime.

■ *Positive Variability via Superimposition*   Transformations or interpreters can be composed via superposition before execution. For transformations, this is especially feasible if the transformation language is declarative, which means that the order in which the transformations are specified is irrelevant. Interpreters are usually procedural, object-oriented or functional programs, so declarativeness is hard to achieve in those.

■ *Positive Variability via Aspects*   If the transformation language or the interpreter implementation language support aspect oriented programming, then this can be used to configure the execution environment. For example, the Xpand code generation engine[13] supports AOP for code generation templates.

[13] wiki.eclipse.org/Xpand

Creating transformations with the help of other transformations, or by any of the above variability mechanisms, is also referred to as *higher-order transformations*[14]. Note that if a bootstrapped environment is used, the transformations are themselves models created with a transformation DSL. This case then reduces to just variation over models, as described in the previous subsection.

[14] J. Oldevik and O. Haugen. Higher-order transformations for product lines. In *SPLC*, pages 243–254, 2007

21.4   From Feature Models to DSLs

A feature model is a compact representation of the features of the products in a product line, as well as the constraints imposed on combinations of these features in products. Feature models are an efficient formalism for *configuration*, i.e. for select-

ing a valid combination of features from the feature model. The set of products that can be defined by feature selection is fixed and finite: each valid combination of selected features constitutes a product. This means that all valid products have to be "designed into" the feature model, encoded in the features and the constraints among them. Some typical examples of things that can be modeled with feature models are the following:

- Does the communication system support encryption?
- Should the in-car entertainment system support MP3s?
- Should the system be optimized for performance or memory footprint?
- Should messages be queued? What is the queue size?

Because of the "select from set of options" metaphor, feature model-based configuration is simple to use – product definition is basically a decision tree. This makes product configuration efficient, and potentially accessible for stakeholders other than software developers. Also, as described by Batory[15] and Czarnecki[16], one advantage of feature models is that a mapping to logic exists. Using SAT solvers, it is possible to check, for example, whether a feature model has valid configurations at all. The technique can also be used to automatically complete partial configurations.

In the rest of this section we will discuss the limitations of feature models, in particular, that they are not suited for open-ended construction of product variants. Instead of giving up on models completely and using low-level programming, we should use DSLs instead. This avoids losing the differentiation between problem space and solution space, while still supporting more expressivity in the definition of a product.

As an example, we use a product line of water fountains, as found in recreational parks[17]. Fountains can have several basins, pumps and nozzles. Software is used to program the behavior of the pumps and valves to make the sprinkling waters aesthetically pleasing. The feature model in Fig. 21.10 represents valid hardware combinations for a simple water fountain product line. Each feature corresponds to the presence of a hardware component in a particular fountain installation.

The real selling point of water fountains is their *behavior*. A fountain's behavior determines how much water each pump should pump, at which time, with what power, or how a pump

[15] D. S. Batory. Feature models, grammars, and propositional formulas. In *SPLC*, pages 7–20, 2005

[16] K. Czarnecki and A. Wasowski. Feature diagrams and logics: There and back again. In *SPLC*, pages 23–34, 2007

[17] This is an anonymized version of an actual project the author has been working on. The real domain was different, but the example languages presented in this chapter have been developed and used for that other domain.

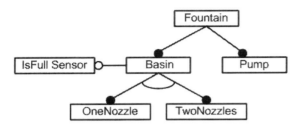

Figure 21.10: Feature model for the simple fountains product line used as the example. Fountains have basins, with one or two nozzles, and an optional full sensor. In addition, fountains have a pump.

reacts when a certain condition is met, e.g., a basin is full. Expressing the full range of such behaviors is not possible with feature models. Feature models can be used to select among a fixed number of predefined behaviors, but approximating all possible behaviors would lead to unwieldy feature models.

21.4.1 Feature Models as Grammars

To understand the limitations of feature models, we consider their relation to grammars. Feature models essentially correspond to context-free grammars without recursion[18]. For example, the feature model in Fig. 21.10 is equivalent to the following grammar[19]:

```
Fountain -> Basin PUMP
Basin    -> ISFULLSENSOR? (ONENOZZLE | TWONOZZLES)
```

This grammar represents a finite number of sentences: there are exactly four possible configurations, which correspond to the finite number of products in the product line. However, this formalism does not make sense for modeling behavior, for which there is typically an infinite range of variability. To accommodate for unbounded variability, the formalism needs to be extended. Allowing recursive grammar productions is sufficient to model unbounded configuration spaces, but for convenience, we consider also attributes and references.

Attributes express properties of features. For example, the **PUMP** could have an integer attribute `rpm`, representing the power setting of the pump[20].

```
Fountain -> Basin PUMP(rpm:int)
Basin    -> ISFULLSENSOR? (ONENOZZLE | TWONOZZLES)
```

Recursive grammars can be used to model repetition[21] and nesting. Nesting is necessary to model tree structures such as those occurring in expressions. The following grammar extends the fountain feature model with a **Behavior**, which consists of a number of **Rules**. The **Basin** can now have any number of **Nozzles**.

[18] K. Czarnecki, S. Helsen, and U. W. Eisenecker. Formalizing cardinality-based feature models and their specialization. SOPR, 10(1):7–29, 2005

[19] We use all caps to represent terminals, and camel-case identifiers as non-terminals.

[20] Some feature modeling tools support attributes on features. An example is pure::variants.

[21] Repetition is also supported by cardinality-based feature models, as described in .
K. Czarnecki, S. Helsen, and U. W. Eisenecker. Formalizing cardinality-based feature models and their specialization. SOPR, 10(1):7–29, 2005

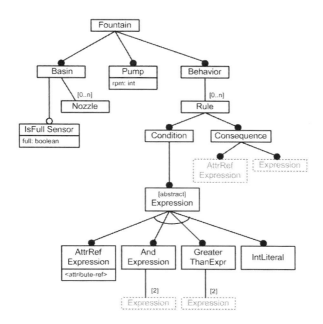

Figure 21.11: An extended feature modeling formalism is used to represent the example feature model with attributes, recursion and references (the dotted boxes).

```
Fountain  -> Basin PUMP(rpm:int) Behavior
Basin     -> ISFULLSENSOR? NOZZLE*
Behavior  -> Rule*
Rule      -> CONDITION CONSEQUENCE
```

References allow the creation of context-sensitive relations between parts of programs described by the grammar. For example, by further extending our fountain grammar we can describe a rule whose condition refers to the **full** attribute of the **ISFULLSENSOR** and whose consequence sets a **PUMP**'s **rpm** to zero.

```
Fountain                 -> Basin id:PUMP(rpm:int)? Behavior
Basin                    -> id:ISFULLSENSOR(full:boolean)? id:NOZZLE*
Behavior                 -> Rule*

Rule                     -> Condition Consequence
Condition                -> Expression
Expression               -> ATTRREFEXPRESSION | AndExpression |
                            GreaterThanExpression | INTLITERAL;

AndExpression            -> Expression Expression
GreaterThanExpression    -> Expression Expression

Consequence              -> ATTRREFEXPRESSION Expression
```

Fig. 21.11 shows a possible rendering of the grammar with an enhanced feature modeling notation. We use cardinalities, as well as references to existing features, the latter are shown as dotted boxes. A valid configuration could be the one shown in Fig. 21.12. It shows a fountain with one basin, two nozzles named **n1** and **n2**, one sensor **s** and a pump **p**. It contains a rule that expresses the condition that if the **full** attribute of **s** is set, and the **rpm** of pump **p** is greater than zero, then the **rpm** should be set to zero.

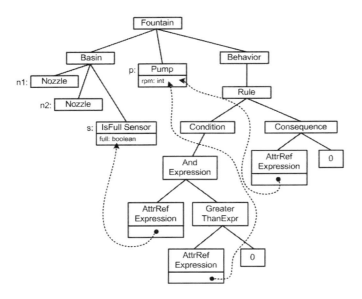

Figure 21.12: Example configuration using a tree notation. Referenceable identities are rendered as labels to the left of each box. The dotted lines represent references to variables.

21.4.2 Domain-Specific Languages

While the extended grammar formalism discussed above enables us to cover the full range of behavior variability, the use of a graphical tree notation to instantiate these grammars is not practical. Another interpretation of these grammars is as the definition of a DSL – the tree in Fig. 21.12 looks like an abstract tree (AST). To make the language readable we need to add concrete syntax definitions (keywords), as in the following extension of the fountain grammar:

```
Fountain                -> "fountain" Basin Pump Behavior
Basin                   -> "basin" IsFullSensor Nozzle*
Behavior                -> Rule*

Rule                    -> "if" Condition "then" Consequence
Condition               -> Expression
Expression              -> AttrRefExpression | AndExpression |
                           GreaterThanExpression | IntLiteral;

AndExpression           -> Expression "&&" Expression
GreaterThanExpression   -> Expression ">" Expression
AttrRefExpression       -> <attribute-ref-by-name>
IntLiteral              -> (0..9)*

Consequence             -> AttrRefExpression "=" Expression

IsFullSensor            -> "sensor" ID (full:boolean)?
Nozzle                  -> "nozzle" ID
Pump                    -> "pump" ID (rpm:int)?
```

We can now write a program that uses a convenient textual notation, which is especially useful for the expressions in the rules. We have created a DSL for configuring the composition *and* behavior of fountains[22].

```
fountain
  basin sensor s
        nozzle n1
        nozzle n2
  pump p
  if s.full && p.rpm > 0 then p.rpm = 0
```

DSLs fill the gap between feature models and programming languages. They can be more expressive than feature models, but they are not as unrestricted and low-level as programming languages. Like programming languages, DSLs support *construction*, allowing the composition of an unlimited number of programs. Construction happens by instantiating language concepts, establishing relationships, and defining values for attributes. We do not a-priori know all possible valid programs[23]. In contrast to programming languages, DSLs keep the distinction between problem space and solution space intact, since they consist of concepts and notations relevant to the problem domain. Non-programmers can continue to contribute directly to the product development process, without being exposed to implementation details.

21.4.3 Making Feature Models More Expressive

We described the limitations of the feature modeling approach above, and proposed DSLs as an alternative. However, the feature modeling community is working on alleviating some of these limitations.

For example, cardinality based feature models[24] support the multiple instantiation of feature subtrees. References between features could be established by using feature attributes typed with another feature – the value range would be the set of instances of this feature. Name references are an approximation of this approach.

Clafer[25] combines meta modeling and feature modeling. In addition to providing a unified syntax and a semantics based on sets, Clafer also provides a mapping to SAT solvers to support validation of models. The following is an example Clafer[26]:

```
abstract Person
  name : String
  firstname : String
  or Gender
    Male
    Female
```

[22] As we have discussed at length in this book, a complete language definition would also include typing rules and other constraints. However, to understand the difference in expressibility between DSLs and feature models, a grammar is sufficient.

[23] This is in contrast to *configuration*, where users select from a limited set of options. Feature models support configuration.

[24] K. Czarnecki, S. Helsen, and U. W. Eisenecker. Formalizing cardinality-based feature models and their specialization. *SOPR*, 10(1):7–29, 2005

[25] K. Bak, K. Czarnecki, and A. Wasowski. Feature and meta-models in clafer: Mixed, specialized, and coupled. In *3rd International Conference on Software Language Engineering*, 10/2010 2010

[26] adapted from Michal Antkiewicz' *Concept Modeling Using Clafer* tutorial at **gsd.uwaterloo.ca/node/310**

```
    xor MaritalStatus
        Single
        Married
        Divorced
    Address
        Street : String
        City : String
        Country : String
        PostalCode : String
        State : String ?
    abstract WaitingLine
      participants -> Person *
```

The code describes a concept **Person** with the following characteristics:

- A name and a first name of type **String** (similar to attributes).

- A gender, which is **Male** or **Female**, or both[27] (similar to **or**-groups in feature models).

- A marital status, which is either **single**, **married** or **divorced** (similar to **xor**-groups in feature models).

- An **Address** (similar composition is language definitions).

- An optional **State** attribute on the address (similar to optional features in feature modeling).

[27] Don't ask me why it's an **or** and not a **xor** constraint, so you can be two genders at once. It is in the original example :-)

The code also shows a reference: a **WaitingLine** refers to any number of **Persons**.

Note however that an important ingredient for making DSLs work in practice is the domain-specific concrete syntax. None of the approaches mentioned in this section provide customizable syntax. However, approaches like Clafer are a very interesting backend for DSLs, to support analysis, validation and automatic creation of valid programs from partial configurations.

21.5 Conceptual Mapping from PLE to DSLs

This section looks at the bigger picture of the relationship between PLE and DSLs. It contains a systematic mapping from the core concepts of PLE to the technical space of DSLs. First we briefly recap the core PLE concepts.

Core Assets designate reusable artifacts that are used in more than one product. As a consequence of their strategic relevance, they are usually high quality and maintained over time. Some of the core assets might have variation points.

A Variation Point is a well-defined location in a core asset where products differ from one another.

Kind of Variability classifies the degrees of freedom one has when binding the variation point. This ranges from setting a simple Boolean flag, through specifying a database URL or a DSL program, to a Java class hooked into a platform framework.

Binding Time denotes the point in time when the decision is made as to which alternative should be used for a variation point. Typical binding times include source time (changes to the source code are required), load time (bound when the system starts up) and runtime (the decision is made while the program is running).

The Platform is those core assets that actually form a part of the running system. Examples include libraries, frameworks or middleware.

Production Tools are core assets that are not part of the platform, but which are used during the (possibly) automated development of products.

Domain Engineering refers to activities in which the core assets are created. An important part of domain engineering is domain analysis, during which a fundamental understanding of the domain, its commonalities and variability is established.

Application Engineering is the phase in which the domain engineering artifacts are used to create products. Unless variation points use runtime binding, they are bound during this phase.

The Problem Space refers to the application domain in which the product line resides. The concepts found in the problem space are typically meaningful to non-programmers as well.

The Solution Space refers to the technical space that is used to implement the products. In the case of *software* product line engineering[28], this space is software development. The platform lives in the solution space. The production tools create or adapt artifacts in the solution space based on a specification of a product in the problem space.

[28] Product Lines often also contain non-software artifacts, often electronic hardware.

In the following sections we now elaborate on how these concepts are realized when DSLs are used.

21.5.1 Variation Points and Kinds of Variability

This represents the core of the chapter and has been discussed extensively above: DSLs provide more expressivity than feature models, while not being completely unrestricted as programming languages.

21.5.2 Domain Engineering and Application Engineering

As we develop an understanding of the domain, we classify the variability. If the variability at a particular variation point is suitable for DSLs (i.e. it cannot be expressed sensibly by pure configuration), we develop the actual languages together with the IDEs during domain engineering. The abstract syntax of the DSL constitutes a formal model of the variability found at the particular variation point[29]. The combination of several DSLs is often necessary. Different variation points may have different DSLs that must be used together to describe a complete product[30].

Application engineering involves using the DSLs to bind the respective variation points. The language definition, the constraints and the IDE guide the user along the degrees of freedom supported by the DSL.

21.5.3 Problem Space and Solution Space

DSLs can represent any domain. They can be technical, inspired by a library, framework or middleware, expected to be used by programmers and architects. DSLs can also cover application domains, inspired by the application logic for which the application is built. In this case they are expected to be used by application domain experts. In the case of application DSLs, the DSL resides in the problem space. For execution they are mapped to the solution space by the production tools. Technical DSLs can, however, also be part of the solution space. In this case, DSL programs may be *created* by the mapping of an application domain DSL to the solution space. It is also possible for technical DSLs to be used by developers as an annotation for the application domain DSLs, controlling the mapping to the solution space, or configuring some technical aspect of the solution directly.

[29] This is similar to analysis models, with the advantage that DSLs are executable. Users can immediately express example domain structures or behavior and thereby validate the DSL. This should be exploited: language definition should proceed incrementally and iteratively, with user validation after each iteration. The example models created in this way should be kept around; they constitute unit tests for the language.

[30] We discussed language composition in Section 4.6 and Chapter 16.

21.5.4 Binding Time

DSL programs can either be transformed to executable code or interpreted. This maps to the binding times introduced above in the following way:

- If we generate source code that has to be compiled, packaged and deployed, the binding time is source. We speak of static variability, or static binding.

- If the DSL programs are interpreted, and the DSL programs can be changed as the system runs, this constitutes runtime binding, and we speak of dynamic variability.

- If we transform the DSL program into another formalism that is then interpreted by the running system, we are in the middle ground. Whether the variability is load-time or runtime depends on the details of how and when the result of the transformation is (re-)loaded into the running system.

21.5.5 Core Assets, Platform and the Production Tools

DSLs constitute core assets; they are used for many, and often all, of the products in the product line. It is however not easy to answer the question of whether they are part of the platform or the production tools:

- If the DSL programs are transformed, the transformation code is a production tool; it is used in the production of the products. The DSL or the models are not part of the running system.

- In the case of interpretation, the interpreter is part of the platform. Since it directly works with the DSL program, the language definition becomes a part of the platform as well.

- If we can change the DSL programs as the system runs, even the IDE for the DSL is part of the platform.

- If the DSL programs are transformed into another formalism that is in turn interpreted by the platform, then the transformations constitute production tools, and the interpreter of the target formalism is a part of the platform.

22
DSLs for Business Users

This chapter has been written by Intentional's Mats Helander. You can reach him via `mats@intentsoft.nl`.

In this chapter we will examine using DSLs for business professionals. The example is a system in the healthcare domain – essentially a system for defining questionnaires and the business rules to process them. A secondary purpose of this chapter is to provide an impression of Intentional Software's technology for defining DSL: the example system is built with the Intentional Domain Workbench.

22.1 Intentional Software

Intentional Software was one of the first companies to create a language workbench[1], and their focus has been on business professionals and less on programmers as users for the DSLs[2]. Business professionals are often the source of domain knowledge. Today this knowledge has to be captured and explained to software engineers for it to be actionable. Agile principles help bridge this gap, but this communication gap remains the biggest obstacle in software development today. DSLs for business professionals have the potential to bridge this gap.

[1] Intentional Software was started by Charles Simonyi after he left Microsoft. There he had been one of the early employees and served as the chief architect for Excel and Word, introducing the principle of WYSIWYG. During his later years he ran the Intentional Programming research project in Microsoft Research (which is described very well in Czarnecki and Eisenecker's Generative Programming book). His company, Intentional Software, continues to work on the ideas pioneered by Intentional Programming.

K. Czarnecki and U. Eisenecker. *Generative Programming: Methods, Techniques and Applications.* Addison-Wesley, 1999

[2] This has always been a focus of DSLs. However, as we will see in this chapter, focussing on non-programmers leads to different tradeoffs in the design of the languages and the tools.

22.2 The Project Challenge

This case study describes an application in which domain knowledge is captured and maintained directly by the domain experts using DSLs, validated at the domain level, and used for code generation to create an executable application[3]. The domain is tele-health, where patients with chronic conditions or diseases like diabetes, hypertension or obesity stay at home, and are provided with daily recommendations based on observed values of various daily measurements of the patient. A medical professional has defined which values to observe for each particular patient, and the rules for the daily individual recommendations based on those values[4]. The input from the patient at home is provided through sensors, medical devices and patient interactions with the system through mobile devices, set-top boxes or web interfaces. The system needs to be flexible enough to address the requirements of multiple health care providers that will have different sets of criteria for different patients.

[3] The DSL is *complete*: no manual coding of "business logic" is required. If that were necessary, the premise of a DSL for business professionals would be infeasible.

[4] This is not an expert system. All decisions are made originally by medical doctors.

The system described in this chapter replaces a legacy system developed using a traditional approach in which domain knowledge was captured in big Excel documents that encoded the physician's rules. A typical rule looked like this:

```
if WHtR < 46 and (LDL < 100 and No LDL Meds) and (SBP < 125 and No BP Meds)
    and
(HgbA1c >= 6.5 and No Glucose Meds)
```

This Excel text should be interpreted as:

```
if the patient
   has a Weight Height ratio of less than 46
     and
   a cholesterol LDL level below 100 and does not take LDL medications
     and
   the systolic blood pressure level is less than 125
           and does not take blood pressure medication
     and
   the hemoglobin A1c test is equal or greater than 6.5
           and does not take glucose medication
then <advice according to diabetes plan>.
```

The Excel spreadsheet had hundreds of rules like this. The repetition resulting from lack of abstractions available to the rules programmer meant that for each new observable attribute the number of rules doubled[5]. Each rule was then transformed by a programmer into rules for a Drools rules engine. The patient data had a similar workflow, in which information for the patient-recorded data was captured also in Excel sheets. Once this information was confirmed with the doctor, XML documents were created for this data to feed a custom web

[5] The lack type checks, testing, refactorings, and all the other amenities we are used from an real IDE also hampered productivity and maintainability.

application application to be used by the patient to fill in the data.

The medical professional was overwhelmed with the complexity. It was clear that the doctors knew exactly what intentions they wanted to express, but the complexity to express them became a big bottleneck. Furthermore, when the doctor wanted to add or make any changes to the application, it had to go through a convoluted process, with limited traceability, to update XML documents, Drools rules, database schemas and other application-dependent logic.

22.3 The DSL-Based Solution

22.3.1 Intentional Domain Workbench

Intentional Software provides a knowledge processing platform to allow business professionals to turn their specialized expertise into software. The development environment, the Intentional Domain Workbench (IDW), is a language workbench for building DSL-oriented applications for business users. These applications can be run stand-alone, and can optionally also generate applications using various languages and runtimes (such as XML and Drools in this example).

The Intentional platform provides a number of key technologies that make the DSLs especially suited for business users. In particular, this includes a projectional editor that allows languages to be edited in multiple syntactical forms, and with multiple semantic interpretations. It can use and mix textual, tabular and graphical notations to approximate the needs of a business domain as closely as possible[6]. The projections of a language can potentially be ambiguous, but that does not cause a problem, because they are just projections of an underlying consistent representation, and a user can always switch to another projection to resolve any ambiguity. The platform also allows for combination and interaction across languages. A single projection can integrate knowledge represented in multiple disparate languages.

[6] As we will see, it also supports Word document-like headings, and more generally, looks a bit like Microsoft Office. This also helps acceptance with business users.

22.3.2 Overview of the Solution

The purpose of the custom language workbench application examined in this case study is to let business experts edit questionnaire definitions that are used as input to a web application that in turn allows end users to fill out their answers. Fig. 22.1 shows an example definition of a questionnaire.

> **Questionnaire: BMI**
> > **Category: Weight**
> > > Question: «Which units do you want to use?» «Units(ShortName)»
> > > answer: OneOf (¤ Metric (Kg, cm), ¤ Imperial (lbs, ft, in)) ✥
> > > > when answer is: Metric (Kg, cm)
> > > > > Question: «Enter your weight in Kg?» «Weight in Kg(ShortName)» answer: Quantity
> > > > > Question: «Enter your height in cm:» «Height in cm(ShortName)» answer: Quantity
> > > > when answer is: Imperial (lbs, ft, in)
> > > > > Question: «How much do you weigh (Pounds)?» «Weight in lbs(ShortName)» answer: Quantity
> > > > > Question: «Enter your height in feet:» «Height in feet(ShortName)» answer: Quantity
> > > > > Question: «Enter your height in inches:» «Height in inches(ShortName)» answer: Quantity

In addition to defining the questions, the medical professional can also define business rules that should be applied to the questionnaires, as well as tests to ensure that the business rules are working correctly. Fig. 22.2 shows an example of such rules; we will get back to testing later.

Figure 22.1: An example questionnaire, as seen and edited by the medical professional. Questionnaires are essentially trees of questions with the possible answers, as well as dependencies between questions (`when answer is...`).

22.3.3 Implementation

To implement this, we have used IDW to define a set of domain schemas[7] along with logic for validation, transformations, evaluation, code generation and projectional editors. All of these concerns are implemented with a custom language supported by IDW that extends C# with additional operators and keywords that are useful for working with tree structures[8]. The language also contains several dedicated DSLs for defining domain schemas, validators or projections[9]. The result of compiling the language definition is a custom workbench: a standalone Windows application that lets the business experts edit the defined domains in a projectional editor where all the rules for validation, projection layout and such are applied. Fig. 22.2 shows the editor for business rules with definition expressions, assessment tables, choice lists and results.

As its output the workbench in this case study generates files that are fed into a web application that executes the questionnaires and applies the business rules[10]. The web application itself is developed separately and consists of web pages with JavaScript that consumes the XML files generated by the workbench. The JavaScript then uses these XML files to produce a dynamic user interface[11]. The workbench also generates business rule files in a format that the Drools business rule engine can consume, and the web application can in turn call the Drools engine to access the running rules.

[7] A schema is the structure definition of a domain. It roughly corresponds to the abstract syntax or meta model, even though the meta meta model of the IDW is substantially different from EMF or MPS' structure definition.

[8] This approach is similar to MPS: MPS' BaseLangauage extends Java with constructs useful for working on the meta level of languages.

[9] This is similar to MPS and Spoofax, which also come with a set of DSLs specific to various aspects of language definition.

[10] The patient interacts with this web application in addition to the sensors mentioned earlier.

[11] The web application acts as an interpreter for an intermediate language whose serialization format is XML

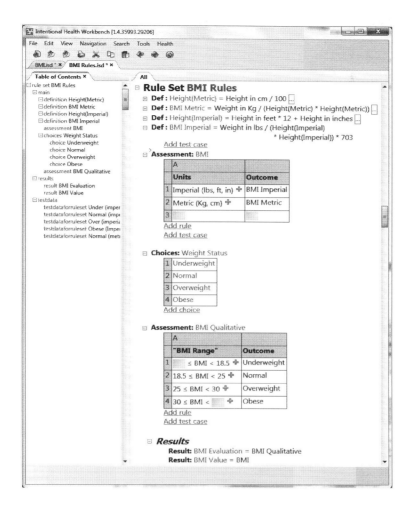

Figure 22.2: This screenshot shows how the medical professional sees and edits business rules for questionnaire questions. In this example, the body mass index is calculated.

■ *Domain Structure* The IDW is very suitable for modularizing, reusing and composing languages ("domains" in the terminology of Intentional Software). Consequently, the application consists of several domains, some of them specific to the application discussed here, others more general[12].

We use two domains that are motivated by the underlying technology: to generate the XML, we employ a reusable XHTML domain that comes with IDW. To generate the Drools rules, we have created a Drools domain (which may be reused for other applications in the future).

Similarly, the domains that are closer to the business domain are also modularized. The medical professionals in this case study have a particular subject they want to create questionnaires about, but the questionnaire domain itself is general

[12] Some are generalized because future reuse is anticipated, others are existing languages reused in this application.

and has high potential for reuse. The business rules are also general enough to be reused on their own, independent of the questionnaires. This results in two main domains: the questionnaire domain and the business rule domain. These are in turn divided into subdomains to allow selection of features to reuse. We then complement this with an adapter domain that includes the reusable questionnaire and business rule domains, and define how they should work together. Finally, we have an overarching domain for the application that we call Intentional Health Workbench (IHW), which adapts the combined questionnaire and business rule domains to the particular customer requirements. In total we end up with ten domains (Fig. 22.3 shows an overview of the relationships between them):

FitBase: The generic questionnaire domain[13]. Contains abstractions such as interviews, questions and answers.

[13] The prefix "Fit" stands for Forms, Interview, Tables.

FitRunner: In-workbench execution of the generic questionnaire domain FitBase, allowing the business expert editing the questionnaires to experiment with filling out answers inside the workbench.

FitSimple: A simplification of the generic questionnaire domain FitBase to a subset suitable for combination with the business rules domain and intuitive editing.

RulesEngine: The generic business rule domain, with table-style editing and in-workbench evaluation of business rules.

RulesChecking: Consistency validation of the rules in the generic business rule domain RulesEngine.

RulesCompiler: Generates the business rules from RulesEngine to files that the Drools business rule engine can use.

FitSimpleWithRules: Combines the simplified subset of the questionnaire domain FitSimple with the generic business rule domain RulesEngine.

Drools: Provides abstractions from the Drools business rules engine domain. Supports generation to the Drools file format.

XHTML: Provides abstractions from the XML and HTML domains. Supports generation of XHTML and XML files.

IHW: The workbench that ties all the other domains together. When compiled, this results in the workbench application that lets business users edit questionnaires and business rules, test them and generate output for the web application and the Drools business rule engine.

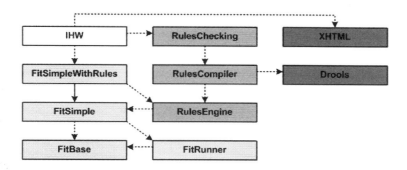

Figure 22.3: Dependencies between the ten domains that make up the system described in this chapter. The arrows represent an *includes* relationship. Like the *extends* relationship in MPS, *includes* is generic in the sense that it may be an actual include in terms of language concepts, or it represents a generic dependency. An example is the **RulesCompiler**. Its relationship with the **Drools** domain captures the fact that it generates Drools rules.

■ *Defining a Domain* The schema for each language is defined using a DSL for schema definition. Because no parser is involved, we only have to define the data structure of the tree that the user will edit. IDW provides a default projection for all domains until you create custom projections, so you can start editing and experimenting with your structures inside the editor as soon as you have defined them[14].

Defining a schema for a domain is all about deciding what types of nodes there may be in the tree structure and what types of child nodes to expect under them. To define the tree structure schema for a domain, we use the keywords **domaindef**, **def** and **fielddef**. A **domaindef** is used for defining a new domain, **def** defines a new type of node that can be used in the domain[15] and **fielddef** defines a field under a **def** where new child nodes can be added.

While **def**s and **fielddef**s are similar to **EClass**es and **EFeature**s in EMF (and consequently also quite similar to MPS' structure definition), there are a few differences. For example, a **fielddef** can be assigned more than one type. In EMF, accepting a range of types in a field would require the creation of a supertype that the field would use as its type. A **fielddef** will take a list of types that are all considered acceptable. If the same list of types is used in several places, we can package them in a reusable way using the **typedef** keyword. We can also reuse field definitions in multiple **def**s with the **includefield** keyword, potentially overriding (limiting, extending) their type[16].

As we are working with tree structures, the default relationship between a node and its child node under a field is contain-

[14] This is a very useful feature, because it allows the incremental definition of concrete syntax. Also, if a concrete syntax definition is broken (in the sense that it has a bug) or is ambiguous, the program tree can always be unambiguously rendered in this tree view like default notation (even if that notation is not necessarily as elegant as a custom projection).

[15] It is essentially what's called a *language concept* in this book.

[16] In all the other tools described in this book, fields are always owned by a language concepts. In IDW they can stand on their own and can be included in **def**s. This provides an additional level of modularization and reuse. This design also allows associating additional specifications with a field, such as constraints or projections. These can be reused along with the field.

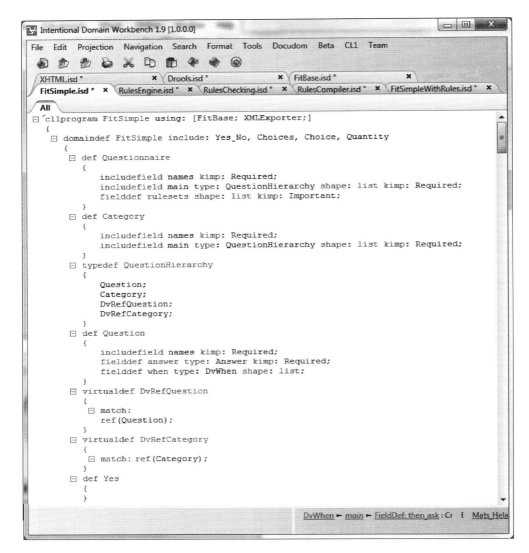

Figure 22.4: A **domaindef** defines a new domain/language. It can **include** other domains, making their contents available to the domain. A **def** defines a new language concept. **def**s contain fields. New fields are defined with **fielddef**, existing fields are included via **includefield**. Each field defines a shape (list, set, single element) and a type (one or more other **def**s). When including a field, these can be overridden. The **main** field is reused by many **def**s and has special editing support. **virtualdef**s use a **match** pattern to select existing nodes. Based on this **virtualdef**, projection rules or other aspects can be defined.

ment. The **Question** def, for example, has an **answer** fielddef with the **Answer** def as its type. Just using a **def** directly implies containment. Let us now look at references.

The **Category** def reuses the **main** field (a commonly reused fielddef that comes with IDW) and overrides its type; it expects those types listed in the **QuestionHierarchy** typedef. When we look for the definitions of the types in that list we discover that two of them are not defs, but use the **virtualdef** keyword. A **virtualdef** can use an arbitrary match pattern (not just **ref**). This allows a new virtual **def** to be assigned to any node that matches the match clause. You can then define projections or constraints for this new **virtualdef**. They will apply to all nodes that match the match clause in the `virtualdef`. In this case **DvRefQuestion** defines a type for references to **Question** nodes, and **DvRefCategory** defines a type for references to **Category** nodes, allowing questions and categories to be reused in multiple places.

■ *Constraints and Behavior*   Defining the basic shape of the tree that users should edit will usually be done in a declarative fashion using the schema DSL. However, in many cases, additional constraints are required. These are typically implemented in *validators*. Validators can enforce scoping rules (that the referenced variable is available in the scope), scan for illegal names or naming collisions, and ensure that any number of domain-specific business rules for the DSL are adhered to by users when they edit their DSL code. Fig. 22.5 shows a simple validator that ensures that the length of a name does not exceed a specified maximum.

Figure 22.5: This constraint checks for the maximum length of all kinds of names. Notice how the error message itself is represented as a **def**: it is of category **Message**. **cat** represents structural subtyping, in the sense that all the fields of **Message** are also added to **Category**

```
validator implfor: Fit
{
  def isas_must_have_names_no_more_than_length_characters_long cat: Message
  {
      fielddef isa type: ref(   );
      fielddef length type: int;
  }
  validatenode : sequence(Book) procedure Vnode(var Dmx dmx, var Node node)
  {
    code:
      assert node.StName() == null || node.StName().Length < 63 else
                        =s_must_have_names_no_more_than_=_characters_long
                            names:
                            isa:
                               Interview
                            length:
                               IntLit 60;;
        implfordef:
            Interview;;
  }
}
```

Here are some more examples of constraints: "categories should not be nested more than five levels deep", "questions may not be modified once they are published" or "negative answer options should be displayed in red".

The first constraint, about level nesting, could be implemented using the DSL for writing validators that comes with IDW[17]. A code snippet showing how such a validator could be implemented is shown below.

[17] Validators run over the tree structure as it is edited and assert conditions that go beyond what is reasonable to define in the declarative schema language, such as a recursive check to determine nesting levels. When a validator fails, an error message is produced, which is shown together with any error messages that the system generates if the user breaks the schema constraints defined in the schema DSL.

```
validator implfor: FitSimpleWithRulesets {
    def Category too deeply nested cat: Message { }
```

```
validatenode : sequence(Book) procedure Vnode(var Dmx dmx, var Node
  node) {
    code:
        var level = 0;
        var parent = node.Parent;
        while (parent != null) {
            if (parent.Isa == '(Category)) {
                level++;
            }
            parent = parent.Parent;
        }
        assert level < 5 else Category too deeply nested;
    }
}
```

The second constraint, about preventing modification to published questions, could be implemented using the DSL for *behaviors*. Behaviors are a bit like database triggers, in that they contain code that is triggered to run on events that signal changes to the tree structure, such as when nodes are inserted, modified or deleted. In this case we could use behaviors to associate code that should be run on **modify** and **delete** events for **Question** instances. The code would check if the question has been published and if so, prevent the modification or delete operation from executing. The following code snippet shows a possible implementation[18].

[18] **overproc** overrides an existing, predefined procedure. **Execres** is a type that signifies whether something is successful or not. **Error** and **Success** are subtypes. **rh** is essentially the **this** pointer.

```
def behavior implfor: Question {
    overproc: Execres procedure CanEdit() {
        if (rh->published) {
            return Error("May not modify published question!");
        }
        return Success();
    }
}
```

The third constraint, about showing negative answer options in red, could be implemented in the presentation for the **AnswerOption** nodes using IDW's DSL for defining. The code responsible for showing the **AnswerOption** node on screen would simply use the C# **if** statement to check whether the option is negative (such as the No answer option to a Yes/No question) and if so, present the node on screen using a red color. We will see examples of code using conditionals in a projection later on.

While we would use three different DSLs to define the three constraints described above, we would also mix that DSL code with standard C# code. The DSLs that come with IDW extend C#, so in addition to the DSL keywords for defining schemas, validators, behaviors and projections, it is also possible to write standard C# classes, and even to mix C# code into declarative DSLs, such as the projection DSL. Some DSLs, such as the validator and behavior DSLs, expect to be implemented using C#

and have no declarative way to be implemented. The projection for C# code uses a textual notation that looks basically like standard C#, but because it is a tree projection, albeit one that looks like text, there are a few differences from what the same code would look like in a text editor. Consider the following example code:

```
program RulesChecking using: [RulesEngine, FitBase, FitSimple, Validation,
                              Gen, DL, Core, mscorlib, System] {
  region RulesTesting {

    [SerializableAttribute()]
    public class DcsUnique : Dcs {
      static var int counter = 0;
      var int index = 0;

      public constructor DcsUnique() {
        this.index = counter++;
      }

      public override bool procedure Equals( var Object obj ) {
        var DcsUnique that = obj as DcsUnique;
        return that != null && Equals(this.index, that.index);
      }

      public override int procedure GetHashCode() {
        return this.index;
      }

      public Kselection property kselection {
        get {
          return Crown;
        }
      }
      public Kend property kend {
        get {
          return Nil;
        }
      }
    }
  }
}
```

In contrast to C#, there is the **procedure** keyword. This is shown in the projection simply to give the user something to click on if they want to select the whole procedure (or *method* as they are more commonly referred to in C#)[19]. Clicking on the **public** keyword lets the user change that keyword to for example **private**, and lets the user enter additional modifiers such as **static**. Clicking on the name lets the user change the name. But if the user wants to delete the whole method, they just click on the **procedure** keyword to select the whole method and hit the **Delete** key. In the tree structure, the name, the modifiers and the whole method body are child nodes contained by the procedure node, so deleting that node will delete all the contained child nodes as well. The **constructor** keyword is there for the same reason – something to click on to select the whole thing – as is the **var** keyword in the field definitions. When

[19] In IDW, the **procedure** keyword would be known as the *crown* of a subtree.

generated to C# source code for compilation, these additional keywords are not included in the output.

Another use case for validators is to verify the types in expressions edited by users. Depending on the DSL, the expression `1 + True` may or may not be illegal, but many languages would prevent the addition of a Boolean value to an integer. IDW includes a DSL for defining the rules for the type calculus in a mix of declarative and C# code, and uses recursive evaluation to determine the resulting type from an expression. The validator will then call the recursive IDW type calculator, and if a problem is discovered an appropriate error shows up in the error pane. In this customer case the workbench has a lot of expressions in the business rules and they are all validated for type consistency.

■ *Projection* The ability to write C# is not only useful when writing utility classes; several of the DSLs included with IDW support the ability to mix C# code into the DSL code. The projections are one example, where some projections are written in an entirely declarative manner using just the keywords from the projection DSL, while others make use of mixed in C# to produce dynamic behaviors. Before looking at examples of such mixed code we will examine a couple of purely declarative projections first.

Each **def**[20] (**Category**, **Question**, or **Answer**) comes with its own projection rules. The projection of the overall tree is then a composition of the projections of all involved nodes. The projection for each type is defined in a declarative fashion, where a template is specified that defines how nodes of that type should be presented to the user (Fig. 22.6). The parts with gray background in Fig. 22.6 constitute the template, whereas the parts with white background are either references to fields that should be projected in place or full blocks of imperative code.

Projection works by mapping domain **def**s to concepts from the Abstract Projection Language (whose concepts all have names beginning with **A** to make them easily identifiable). These concepts are then transformed further, until, at least conceptually, we arrive at the level of pixels on the screen[21]. Some of the **A** constructs are quite primitive, such as **AVert**, which only specifies that its contents should be displayed as a vertical list, or **ASeq**, which specifies that the contents should be presented in

[20] Projections can also be defined for **virtualdef**s. This allows nodes in a specific context to be projected differently.

[21] As a language developer, you don't have to care about anything below the **A** level. You just map your domain concepts to concepts from the **A** language.

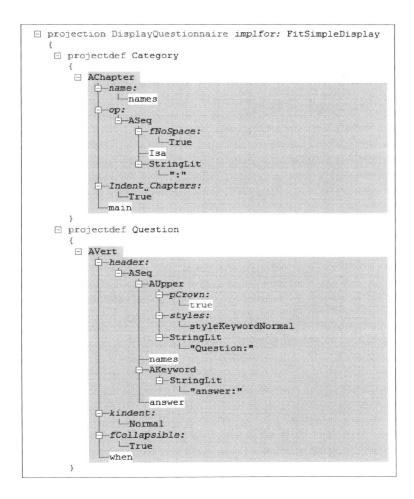

Figure 22.6: The projection rules for **Category** and **Question**. The one for **Category** creates an **AChapter** (which is rendered with large, bold font text) whose text is made up of the name of the category (cf. the **names** field under the **name**), and then a colon, with no space separating the two. In the chapter's own **main** field we put the **main** field of the **Category** (which contains all the questions in that category).

a sequence – horizontal or vertical is up to the presentation engine and depends on available screen estate. Others are more high-level, such as **AChapter**, which presents its contents in the form of a word processor-style chapter (thick text, optional chapter numbering and indentation, etc). To project something as a graph, we just have to use the **AGraph**, **AGraphNode** and **AGraphEdge** constructs. To project something as a table, we use **ATable**, **ARow** and **ACell**. **AImage** displays a bitmap image. **AButton** and **AHyperLink** make it possible to add buttons and links to the projections that execute C# code or move focus to a different place in the projection when clicked, providing an alternative to having the user type everything in with the keyboard[22].

Each A Language construct has a number of fields where values can be entered in the template. Sometimes this will be literal information that should be displayed, such as the

[22] Of course developers can define new, higher level projection concepts that are in turn transformed to **A** concepts. It is also possible to define new concepts on the abstraction level of **A** and then project them manually to the next finer level.

string literals "Question:" and "answer:" in the projection for the **Question** def. Other literals control the behavior of the projection, such as the **True** value under the **Indent_Chapters** field in the **AChapter** projection for the **Category** def. To make the child nodes of the projected type show up in the projection, we just put a reference to the relevant fielddefs in the appropriate places in the projection definition[23].

[23] These references get a white background in the definition where the rest is gray.

Templates are a good fit for a declarative DSL, because projections can often be defined in an entirely declarative way. When there is demand for dynamic behavior, the declarative context of the template can be broken out from using the **BackQuote()** function: standard C# can be entered inside it. The C# code should end by returning a new "piece of tree" that is inserted into the hosting template in the place of the **BackQuote**. A new piece of tree can be created with the **BookQuote()**[24], inside of which declarative structures can be created.

[24] A *Book* is a basically a subtree literal that can be inserted into another tree.

There are many cases in which dynamic behaviors in projections are useful. Common examples include changing the color depending on the displayed values, showing or hiding some of the values depending on editing modes or access rights, and even displaying the results from dynamic evaluation of expressions and values that the end users type in[25].

[25] This can be used nicely for hooking interpreters that execute tests based on the data entered by the user.

■ *Dynamic Schemas* Another case is when the DSLs that end users edit influence each other dynamically, such as when one DSL is the schema language for a second DSL. Consider for example an Entities DSL in which users can define entity types with attributes. A second DSL allows users to define instances of the entities, specifying values for the attributes. The schema language allows this by letting us hook in C# code to dynamically determine the fields that the schema should consider under a **def** or a **virtualdef**.

Let us look at an example. When creating a program expressed in the second DSL, a user may want to create an instance of the **Person** entity defined with the first DSL. The **Person** entity in turn contains **firstName** and **lastName** attributes. The editor should then read the definition for the **Person** entity and go on to present two fields under the new instance, label them **firstName** and **lastName**, and let the user enter the names for their new **Person** instance. This works by hooking in code into the Instances DSL that returns **fielddef**s for each attribute under the entity referenced in the **type** field[26]

[26] Here we assume that each **Instance** in the instances DSL references the **Entity** it instantiates in a field called **type**.

of the instance, and potentially from any supertypes of that entity. The IDW default projection would detect this and present **firstName** and **lastName** fields ready to be edited under a **Person** entity. In a custom projection dynamic code would be used to iterate over the appropriate fields and create projections for them.

In the case of the workbench in this case study we have a **Rule** def, which has one fielddef called **outcome** that is declaratively defined in the standard schema DSL; the rest of its fields are determined dynamically, as described above. In the projection we want to display each rule as a row in a table and each dynamic field under a rule as its own cell. The **outcome** field should also get its own cell, which is defined in the declarative way in the template, but for the dynamic fields we have to break out from the declarative template context and write some C# code. Fig. 22.7 shows the respective code.

```
projectdef Rule fOmitExtraTraits: true
{
    ARow
        ACell
            styles:
                styleTableHeader
            ASeq
                pCrown:
                    true
                BackQuote(ANumericCreate(ehi.Index + 1))
        BackQuote(
            FncRangeEx(
                foreach (current var df in ehi.GetDmx().Rgdf())
                {
                    (df.fd != `(outcome))
                    ? BookQuote(
                        ACell
                            AVert
                                BackQuote(DescendFd(df.fd))
                    )
                    : null;
                }
            )
        )
        ACell
            outcome
}
```

Figure 22.7: The projection rule for a **Rule**. The gray parts are declarative templates that are inserted "as is" into the projected screen representation of a **Rule**. The white parts, and in particular, the **BackQuote**s, use procedural C# code to dynamically project a part of the tree. Inside this procedural code, **BookQuote**s are used to escape to literal mode, where, again in gray, we construct little "pieces of tree" (called *Books*) in IDW) which are in turn inserted into the resulting projection.

The schema of the projected node can be accessed with the expression **ehi.GetDmx().Rgdf()**, where **ehi** is the input node to the projection, **GetDmx()** retrieves domain context information about it and **Rgdf()** returns the fields that are expected under the node. Normally **Rgdf()** will only return the fields we have declared in the schema DSL, but in this case it has been overridden for the **Rule** def to return a set of fields that are determined dynamically by other input to the Rule DSL. The C# code in the projection definition for the **Rule** (shown in Fig. 22.7) iterates over the fields that should go under the **Rule** def according to the schema and our overriding code, then uses the **BookQuote()** function to create a piece of tree with an **ACell** in each one[27]. A simple C# expression (**ehi.Index + 1**) is also used to display the row index in a leading cell for each row.

The ability to mix C# into projections opens up the possibility of creating very powerful dynamic projections including DSL evaluation, and even running of test cases for a DSL directly in the editor for that DSL. Projections can also be combined with transformations, such that the tree structure edited by the user undergoes a series of transformations before being projected onto the screen[28]. These transformations are two-way, so the projections built including such a transformation continue to be fully editable. They work in a similar way to projections, in that they let the developer create templates in their target language (rather than the **A** language) declaratively, but with the option of breaking out into C# code. By moving calls to things like test evaluation into a transformation that precedes the projection, code with different types of responsibilities is separated by concern and kept simple and to the point.

A testing framework was created for the case study discussed in this chapter, so that business rules can be evaluated with test data and the results verified against expected values, all directly in the workbench. The tests are run continuously, so that whenever the user modifies the business rules, the tests go red or green as the rules break or correspond to expectations. Fig. 22.8 shows an example of such a test case.

The evaluation of the business rules is implemented as an interpreter that works by evaluating each node in the tree structure according to its type in a recursive fashion. The code for this is packaged in a helper class called by a transformation that passes the test inputs to the evaluation method and decorates the transformation's output tree with the results. The projection then takes the decorated tree, presents the editable input values, expected values and calculated test results (not editable), and compares the test results with the expected values to show green, red or orange bullets as appropriate.

In this case study we see another interesting example of pro-

[27] But taking care to avoid doing so for the **outcome** fielddef, which is already projected in the declarative part of the projection rule.

[28] In fact, projections, transformations and code generation work essentially the same way in IDW. As we will see later, code generators in IDW are implemented as transformations between a source domain and a target domain. Projections are in turn just transformations that have the Abstract Projection Language as their target domain. There are two differences. First, projections are evaluated lazily, such that only the parts of the projection required for showing what is on screen will actually be executed, whereas for a code generator the whole transformation will always be executed at once. The second difference is that projections are automatically triggered as the program tree changes, whereas code generators are executed only on demand (e.g., by the user pressing a button in the Workbench.)

Test data	Normal (metric)
Height in cm	178
Weight in Kg	75
Height in feet	
Height in inches	
Weight in lbs	
Units	Metric (Kg, cm)

Tests:

#	Test Inputs	Returns	Expected
1	Under (imperial)	BMI Evaluation: ○ Underweight BMI Value: ● 18.16194076874606	BMI Evaluation: ○ Underweight BMI Value: ○ 18.16194076874606
2	Normal (imperial)	BMI Evaluation: ○ Normal BMI Value: ● 20.672127704263811	BMI Evaluation: ○ Normal BMI Value: ● 22.234234234234
3	Over (imperial)	BMI Evaluation: ○ Overweight BMI Value: ○ 28.0550304557866	BMI Evaluation: ○ Overweight BMI Value: ○ 28.0550304557866
4	Obese (Imperial)	BMI Evaluation: ○ Obese BMI Value: ○ 31.008191556395715	BMI Evaluation: ○ Obese BMI Value: ○ 31.008191556395715
5	Normal (metric)	BMI Evaluation: ● Normal BMI Value: ○ 23.671253629592222	BMI Evaluation: ● Obese BMI Value: ○ 23.671253629592222

Add test case

Figure 22.8: The testing aspect of the Health workbench lets users create test data and evaluate the business rules directly in the IDE. As mentioned earlier in this book, in-IDE-testing is an important ingredient to making a DSL accessible to non-programmers: in some sense, the tests make the DSL "come alive" and help build understanding about the semantics of the language.

jecting dynamically derived information about the user input. The projection for a questionnaire calls out to C# code that performs consistency analysis on the combined business rules and questionnaire domains. The analysis ensures that when business rules are applied to a particular questionnaire, the rules do not refer to questions absent from that questionnaire.

The tests and consistency analysis are implemented and presented in a way specific to the application, but it is also possible to use the IDW validation framework to ensure validity of user inputs. The developer then writes validators that run in the background against the tree structure as it is being edited by the user. When a rule in a validator is broken, it yields an error message, which is shown in the IDW error pane, a central place for collecting custom error messages from validators and system error messages from built-in generic validators alike.

■ *Transformation and Generation* Once the input is known to be consistent[29], the time has come to do something with the

[29] For this application this means that the structure is correct, all validators are happy, all tests are green and consistency analysis is satisfied.

```
☐ Questionnaire: BMI
    ☐ Category: Weight
        ☐ Question: «Which units do you want to use?» «Units(ShortName)» answer: OneOf (¤ Metric (Kg, cm), ¤ Imperial (lbs, ft, in))
            ☐ when answer is: Metric (Kg, cm)
                ☐ Question: «Enter your weight in Kg?» «Weight in Kg(ShortName)» answer: Quantity
                ☐ Question: «Enter your height in cm:» «Height in cm(ShortName)» answer: Quantity
            ☐ when answer is: Imperial (lbs, ft, in)
                ☐ Question: «How much do you weigh (Pounds)?» «Weight in lbs(ShortName)» answer: Quantity
                ☐ Question: «Enter your height in feet:» «Height in feet(ShortName)» answer: Quantity
                ☐ Question: «Enter your height in inches:» «Height in inches(ShortName)» answer: Quantity
    ☐ Rule Sets:
        apply rules: BMI Rules
        uses:
            • Enter your height in cm:
            • Enter your weight in Kg?
            • Enter your height in feet:
            • Enter your height in inches:
            • How much do you weigh (Pounds)?
            • Which units do you want to use?
```

information the medical professional has provided. In this case study this means invoking code generation to produce the XML files that the JavaScript in the web application will consume, and the files with business rule definitions for the Drools engine.

IDW includes a DSL for defining how to create output folders and files, and, together with the DSL for transformations, it constitutes how code generators are defined. While it is possible to take the tree that the user has edited and generate raw text files in the target format directly, it is often a better approach to use a transformation to create a tree structure in the domain of the target format from the tree structure that the user edited[30]. Such transformations that result in information being generated to files rather than being presented to the user on screen do not have to be two-way, as there is no requirement for the information to stay editable.

The workbench in this case study uses a transformation that takes the questionnaire domain as input and outputs a tree structure in the XHTML domain that is included with IDW. The resulting XHTML tree is then passed on to a second transformation that knows how to transform such trees to text. The result of this transformation is finally passed to a file generator defined with the DSL for creating files and folders, with the result that the text is saved to files on disk. To generate the Drools files a similar transformation chain is executed, but with the difference that both the Drools domain and its transformation to text had to be developed for the project.

Fig. 22.10 shows the transformation to the Drools domain. Again, parts with a gray background are declarative, whereas

Figure 22.9: The consistency analysis ensures that when a set of business rules is used together with a particular questionnaire, all questions evaluated by the rules are actually present in the selected questionnaire.

[30] As we discussed in Part II, this allows us to reuse parts of the overall transformation. For example, the Drools and XML domains are likely to be reusable in other applications.

the white background signifies imperative code. We can see the use of the **FIn()** function which determines if a given item is in a list of items. We also see the use of **BookNew()**, which creates a single node that can be inserted into a larger tree.

Figure 22.10: This is part of the transformation from the business rules domain into the Drools domain. The template-based approach is similar to projections.

```
transformation CompileToDroolsRules implfor:      xidOutput: Rules include: [RulesLogic;]
{
    transformdef Assessment fOmitExtraTraits: [true;]
    {
        Section *
           names:
              names
           rules
    }
    transformdef contains
    {
        Dot
           left
           contains
              right
    }
    transformdef DvBoolBinaryOp
    {
        BackQuote(
          valof
            {
               if (!FIn(ehi.Isa, `(Eq)))
               {
                   return base.Display();
               }
               /*transform for eq*/
               var left = ehi→main[0];
               var right = ehi→main[1];
               /*check for left/right being any/unknown, else types match*/
               if (left.Isa == `(Any) || right.Isa == `(Any))
               {
                   return BookNew(`(True));
               }
               else if (FIn(TypeForDrools(TypeOf(left)).Isa, `(ArrayList)))
               {
                   return BookNew(`(Dot), ProcessEhi(left),
                           BookNew(`(contains), ProcessEhi(right)));
               }
               else if (FIn(TypeForDrools(TypeOf(left)).Isa, `(Double)) ||
                                    (FIn(left.Isa, `(Unknown)) ||
                                    FIn(right.Isa, `(Unknown))))
               {
                   return BookQuote(
                     Eq
                        BackQuote(ProcessEhi(left))
                        BackQuote(ProcessEhi(right))
                   );
               }
               else
               {
                   return BookNew(`(Dot), ProcessEhi(left),
                           BookNew(`(equals), ProcessEhi(right)));
               }
            }
    }
}
```

22.4 Wrapping Up

With the code generators in place the whole workbench is ready for use by the medical professionals. They can now define interviews and rules that they can run and validate against tests directly in the workbench. When they are satisfied with their work, they hit the button to generate the XML and Drools rules for the web application, which can then be used immediately by end users. All the time the workbench guides them in their work with helpful validation messages, auto-completion and running tests, allowing for consistently high quality in the generated applications.

To implement the workbench we used several DSLs for schema definitions, projections, transformations and more in concert. The final product also combines several domains, with the two most prominent domains for interviews and for business rules split up into individually reusable subdomains. The projectional approach is well suited for such complex language composition and provides flexible notation, which makes it a powerful technology in scenarios that target business professionals. The ability to mix DSLs with GPLs such as C# ensures that each DSL can remain short and to the point without taking on all the burdens of a GPL as requirements grow in complexity.

Made in the USA
Lexington, KY
07 October 2013